The
American
Novel

Volume II

The American Novel

A Checklist of Twentieth Century
Criticism on Novels Written Since 1789
Volume II: Criticism Written 1960-1968

by

DONNA GERSTENBERGER

and

GEORGE HENDRICK

THE SWALLOW PRESS INC.
CHICAGO

REF.
PS
371
A1 G4 4

V. 2

Published by
The Swallow Press, Inc.
1139 S. Wabash Avenue
Chicago, Illinois 60605

LIBRARY OF CONGRESS CATALOG CARD NUMBER 61-9356

INTRODUCTION

Since *The American Novel 1789-1959: A Checklist of Twentieth-Century Criticism* was published in 1960, articles on the novel have continued to be published at a phenomenal rate. We had originally planned this volume to cover the years 1960 through 1969, but because of the number of articles and books printed within the last nine years, we decided to survey the years 1960 through 1968 only and produce a volume of more usable size. (In a few cases we discovered articles published before 1960 which were not included in our 1960 publication. These have now been listed.) As we noted in our earlier publication, our checklist is admittedly incomplete, but we have attempted to cover the standard sources and have made references to individual bibliographies, making it possible for a scholar doing intensive work to trace additional material. We suggest that the annual bibliographies published by the Modern Humanities Research Association and the Modern Language Association be consulted for additional listing.

We have kept the same general arrangement used in *The American Novel 1789-1959*. The checklist is divided into two sections: criticism of individual authors and criticism of the American novel as a genre.

In the first section we list criticism under three categories: (1) individual novels, (2) general studies, (3) bibliographies. Limitations of space have made it necessary for us to list articles dealing with more than two novels under the category *general*. We have not ordinarily attempted to list reviews. *The New York Review of Books,* therefore, was not surveyed, since it is devoted entirely to reviews. Only articles or interviews are listed from such journals as *Saturday Review, Times Literary Supplement,* or *The New York Times Book Review.* Authors studied primarily *as novelists* have received more complete treatment than authors who worked primarily in some other form. Thus, under *Melville* will be listed studies which cannot be called criticism in the strictest sense of the word but which contribute to an understanding of the canon of his novels. Under *Poe* and *Katherine Anne Porter,* on the other hand, will be listed only studies dealing with the single novel of the author—*The Narrative of A. Gordon Pym* and *Ship of Fools*. Short fiction not ordinarily classified as novels is generally excluded. For checklists of short fiction criticism, see Jarvis Thurston, O. B. Emerson, Carl Hartman, and Elizabeth V. Wright, *Short Fiction Criticism* (Swallow Press) ; Warren S. Walker, *Twentieth-Century Short Story Explication* (Shoe String Press) ; and the annual listing of short fiction criticism compiled by Elizabeth V. Wright and George Hendrick which appears in the summer issue of *Studies in Short Fiction*. We have normally not covered the individual works of short fiction listed in these checklists; we have made a few exceptions, however. Melville's *Billy Budd,* for example, is often taught in novel courses, and we have listed *Billy Budd* criticism. Faulkner's *Go Down, Moses* and a few other collections of stories are at times referred to as novels and are included.

The second major section of the checklist lists general studies of the American novel, divided, as far as possible, into centuries. Studies which span centuries are classified under the category, *general*. We also have a section listing bibliographies for these categories.

Complete bibliographic entries for individual books may be found in the master list at the end of the volume, where collections of essays by different authors are indexed by the title of the volume rather than by the name of the editor. A list of the more than 150 journals which are indexed is also appended at the end of the volume.

We have not attempted to survey material in general histories of American literature nor the headnotes and brief introductions to individual novels. Editions with introductions are listed in the checklist but are not included in the bibliography; the number of pages in the introduction is not given.

In preparation of this checklist, we wish to acknowledge the support given us by Dean Daniel Alpert and the Research Board of the University of Illinois and Dean Joseph L. McCarthy and the Graduate School Research Fund of the University of Washington; Miss Eva Benton, Mr. Richard G. Smith of the University of Illinois Library, and Mrs. Bernadette Gualtieri of the University of Washington Library were particularly helpful to us in tracing journals and books. Special assistance has been rendered by Huelene Bishop, Grace Babakhanian, Marcia Frizzell, Willene Hendrick, Jacqueline Hartwich, and Julianne Seeman.

GEORGE HENDRICK   DONNA GERSTENBERGER
University of Illinois   University of Washington
Urbana, Illinois   Seattle, Washington

ADAMIC, LOUIS

GENERAL

Christian, Henry A. "Ten Letters to Louis Adamic," *Princeton University Library* Chronicle XXVIII (Winter 1967), 76-94.

ADAMS, HENRY

DEMOCRACY

Aiken, Conrad. Introduction, *Democracy* (New York, 1961).

Blackmur, R. P. "The Novels of Henry Adams," *A Primer of Ignorance*, 201-225.

Brooks, Van Wyck. Introduction, *Democracy* (New York, 1961).

Colacurcio, Michael. "*Democracy* and *Esther:* Henry Adams' Flirtation with Pragmatism," *American Quarterly* XIX (Spring 1967), 53-70.

Hochfield, George. "Democracy," *Henry Adams: An Introduction and Interpretation*, 24-33.

Martin, Jay. *Harvests of Change. American Literature 1865-1914*, 302-304.

Milne, Gordon. *The American Political Novel*, 57-64.

Samuels, Ernest. Introduction, *Democracy and Esther* (Gloucester, Massachusetts, 1961).

Vandersee, Charles. "The Pursuit of Culture in Adams' *Democracy*," *American Quarterly* XIX (Summer 1967), 239-248.

ESTHER

Bell, Millicent. "Adams' *Esther:* The Morality of Taste," *New England Quarterly* XXXV (Jun 1962), 147-161.

Blackmur, R. P. "The Novels of Henry Adams," *A Primer of Ignorance*, 201-225.

Colacurcio, Michael. "*Democracy* and *Esther:* Henry Adams' Flirtation with Pragmatism," *American Quarterly* XIX (Spring 1967), 53-70.

Hochfield, George. "Esther," *Henry Adams: An Introduction and Interpretation*, 44-54.

Martin, Jay. *Harvests of Change. American Literature 1865-1914*, 302-304.

Paik, Nak-Chung. "On *Esther* by Henry Adams," *English Language and Literature* 17 (Nov 1965), 41-49.

Samuels, Ernest. Introduction, *Democracy and Esther* (Gloucester, Massachusetts, 1961).

ADAMS, HENRY, Continued

GENERAL

Cunliffe, Marcus. " 'What Was the Matter with Henry Adams?' " *Commentary* XXXIX (Jun 1965) , 66-71.

Edenbaum, Robert I. "The Novels of Henry Adams: Why Man Failed," *Texas Studies in Literature and Language* VIII (Summer 1966) , 245-255.

Hochfield, George. *Henry Adams: An Introduction and Interpretation.*

Hoffman, Frederick J. "Nostalgia and Christian Interpretation: Henry Adams and Faulkner," *The Imagination's New Beginning: Theology and Modern Literature,* 75-102.

Samuels, Ernest. "Henry Adams and the Gossip Mills," *Essays in American and English Literature Presented to Bruce Robert McElderry, Jr.,* 59-75.

――――. *Henry Adams: The Major Phase.*

Stevenson, Elizabeth. Introduction, *A Henry Adams Reader* (Doubleday, 1959) .

Stone, Edward. *Voices of Despair,* 171-175.

Tanner, Tony. "Henry James and Henry Adams," *Tri-Quarterly* 11 (Winter 1968) , 91-108.

――――. "The Lost America: The Despair of Henry Adams and Mark Twain," *Mark Twain: A Collection of Critical Essays,* 159-174.

Vandersee, Charles. "The Mutual Awareness of Mark Twain and Henry Adams," *English Language Notes* V (Jun 1968) , 285-292.

BIBLIOGRAPHY

Hochfield, George. *Henry Adams: An Introduction and Interpretation,* 145-147.

ADE, GEORGE

ARTIE

Farrell, James T. Introduction, *Two Novels* (Chicago, 1963) .

PINK MARSH

Farrell, James T. Introduction, *Two Novels* (Chicago, 1963) .

GENERAL

Brenner, Jack. "Howells and Ade," *American Literature* XXXVIII (May 1966) , 198-207.

Coyle, Lee. *George Ade.*

ADELER, MAX

FORTUNATE ISLAND
Foster, Edward F. *"A Connecticut Yankee* Anticipated: Max Adeler's *Fortunate Island,"* *Ball State University Forum* IX (Autumn 1968), 73-76.

AGEE, JAMES

A DEATH IN THE FAMILY
Hoffman, Frederick J. *The Art of Southern Fiction,* 75-77.

Morrisroe, Michael, Jr. "A Point of Focus in James Agee's *A Death in the Family,"* *Twentieth Century Literature* XII (Oct 1966), 149-153.

Ohlin, Peter H. *Agee,* 194-214.

Seib, Kenneth. *James Agee: Promise and Fulfillment,* 73-96.

THE MORNING WATCH
Hoffman, Frederick J. *The Art of Southern Fiction,* 77-81.

Ohlin, Peter H. *Agee,* 187-194.

Phillipson, John S. "Character, Theme, and Symbol in *The Morning Watch,"* *Western Humanities Review* XV (Autumn 1961), 359-367.

GENERAL
Burger, Nash K. "A Story to Tell: Agee, Wolfe, Faulkner," *South Atlantic Quarterly* LXIII (Winter 1964), 32-43.

Da Ponte, Durant. "James Agee: The Quest for Identity," *Tennessee Studies in Literature* VIII (1963), 25-37.

Fitzgerald, Robert. "James Agee: A Memoir," *Kenyon Review* XXX (Issue 5, 1968), 587-624.

Kramer, Victor A. "Agee in the Forties: The Struggle to Be a Writer," *Texas Quarterly* XI (Spring 1968), 9-17.

Macdonald, Dwight. "James Agee: Some Memories and Letters," *Encounter* XIX (Dec 1962), 73-84.

Matthews, T. S. "James Agee—'Strange and Wonderful,'" *Saturday Review* 49 (Apr 16, 1966), 22-23.

Ohlin, Peter H. *Agee.*

Phelps, Robert (ed.). *The Letters of James Agee to Father Flye.*

Seib, Kenneth. *James Agee: Promise and Fulfillment.*

BIBLIOGRAPHY
Fabre, Genevieve. "Bibliography of the Works of James Agee," *Bulletin of Bibliography* XXIV (May-Aug 1965), 145-148, 163-166.

Kramer, Victor A. "James Agee Papers at the University of Texas,"

ALCOTT, LOUISA MAY, Continued

Janeway, Elizabeth. "Meg, Jo, Beth, Amy and Louisa," *New York Times Book Review* 73 (Sept 29, 1968) , 42.
Meigs, Cornelia. Introduction, *Little Women* (New York, 1968) .

ALDRICH, BESS STREETER

GENERAL
Ald, Robert. Introduction, *Treasury* (New York, 1959) .

ALDRICH, THOMAS BAILEY

THE STORY OF A BAD BOY
Samuels, Charles E. *Thomas Bailey Aldrich,* 82-92.
GENERAL
Samuels, Charles E. *Thomas Bailey Aldrich.*
BIBLIOGRAPHY
Samuels, Charles E. *Thomas Bailey Aldrich,* 147-154.

ALDRICH, JOHN

THE PARTY AT CRANTON
Widmer, Kingsley. "The Academic Comedy," *Partisan Review* XXVII (Summer 1960) , 526-535.

ALGER, HORATIO, JR.

ADRIFT IN NEW YORK
Coyle, William. Introduction, *Adrift in New York* (New York, 1966) .
FRANK'S CAMPAIGN; OR, WHAT BOYS CAN DO ON THE FARM FOR THE CAMP
Tebbel, John. *From Rags to Riches: Horatio Alger, Jr., and the American Dream,* 158-167.
HELEN FORD
Tebbel, John. *From Rags to Riches: Horatio Alger, Jr., and the American Dream,* 168-184.
RAGGED DICK; OR, STREET LIFE IN NEW YORK WITH THE BOOT-BLACKS
Tebbel, John. *From Rags to Riches: Horatio Alger, Jr., and the American Dream,* 194-208.

ALGER, HORATIO, JR., Continued

STRIVE AND SUCCEED
Behrman, S. N. Introduction, *Strive and Succeed* (New York, 1967).
TIMOTHY CRUMP'S WARD
Tebbel, John. *From Rags to Riches: Horatio Alger, Jr., and the American Dream*, 184-194.
THE WORLD BEFORE HIM
Coyle, William. Introduction, *Adrift in New York*, (New York, 1966).
GENERAL
Falk, Robert. "Notes on the 'Higher Criticism' of Horatio Alger, Jr.," *Arizona Quarterly* XIX (Summer 1963), 151-167.
Gardner, Ralph D. *Horatio Alger, or The American Hero Era.*
Schroeder, Fred. "America's First Literary Realist: Horatio Alger, Junior," *Western Humanities Review* XVII (Spring 1963), 129-137.
Tebbel, John. *From Rags to Riches: Horatio Alger, Jr., and the American Dream.*
BIBLIOGRAPHY
Gardner, Ralph D. *Horatio Alger, or The American Hero Era*, 394-497.
Tebbel, John. *From Rags to Riches: Horatio Alger, Jr., and the American Dream*, 227-236.

ALGREN, NELSON

GENERAL
Donohue, H. E. F. *Conversations with Nelson Algren* (New York, 1963).
————. "Nelson Algren at Fifty-five," *Atlantic Monthly* CCXIV (Oct 1964), 79-85.
————. "Nelson Algren Interviewed: The Writer as Child, Youth and Army Privateer," *Carleton Miscellany* IV (Fall 1963), 3-36.
Eisinger, Chester E. *Fiction of the Forties*, 73-85.

ALLEN, JAMES LANE

THE ALABASTER BOX
Bottorff, William K. *James Lane Allen*, 126-134.
THE BRIDE OF THE MISTLETOE
Bottorff, William K. *James Lane Allen*, 87-102.
A KENTUCKY CARDINAL: A STORY
Bottorff, William K. *James Lane Allen*, 48-58.

ALLEN, JAMES LANE, Continued

THE METTLE OF THE PASTURE
Bottorff, William K. *James Lane Allen*, 80-86.
THE REIGN OF LAW
Bottorff, William K. *James Lane Allen*, 72-78.
GENERAL
Bottorff, William K. *James Lane Allen*.
BIBLIOGRAPHY
Bottorff, William K. *James Lane Allen*, 167-172.

ANDERSON, SHERWOOD

BEYOND DESIRE
Anderson, David D. *Sherwood Anderson: An Introduction and Interpretation*, 122-129.
Rideout, Walter. Introduction, *Beyond Desire* (New York, 1960).
DARK LAUGHTER
Anderson, David D. *Sherwood Anderson: An Introduction and Interpretation*, 87-92.
Krutch, Joseph Wood. "Vagabonds," *The Achievement of Sherwood Anderson: Essays in Criticism*, 124-126.
KIT BRANDON: A PORTRAIT
Anderson, David D. *Sherwood Anderson: An Introduction and Interpretation*, 144-149.
Burbank, Rex. *Sherwood Anderson*, 132-135.
Williams, Cratis D. *"Kit Brandon:* A Reappraisal," *Shenandoah* XIII (Spring 1962), 55-61.
MARCHING MEN
Burbank, Rex. *Sherwood Anderson*, 48-60.
————. "The Populist Temper," *The Achievement of Sherwood Anderson: Essays in Criticism*, 32-43.
Hackett, Francis. "To American Workingmen," *The Achievement of Sherwood Anderson: Essays in Criticism*, 26-29.
Weber, Brom. *Sherwood Anderson*, 17-21.
POOR WHITE
Burbank, Rex. *Sherwood Anderson*, 78-87.
Rideout, Walter. Introduction, *Poor White* (New York, 1966).
WINDY McPHERSON'S SON
Burbank, Rex. *Sherwood Anderson*, 48-60.

7

ANDERSON, SHERWOOD, Continued

————. "The Populist Temper," *The Achievement of Sherwood Anderson: Essays in Criticism*, 32-43.

Frank, Waldo. "Emerging Greatness," *The Achievement of Sherwood Anderson: Essays in Criticism*, 20-24.

Morris, Wright. Introduction, *Windy McPherson's Son* (Chicago, 1965).

Tanselle, G. Thomas. "The First Notice of Sherwood Anderson," *Notes and Queries* N.S. 9 (Aug 1962), 307-309.

Weber, Brom. *Sherwood Anderson*, 14-17.

WINESBURG, OHIO

Abcarian, Richard. "Innocence and Experience in *Winesburg, Ohio*," *University Review* XXXV (Dec 1968), 95-105.

Anderson, David D. *Sherwood Anderson: An Introduction and Interpretation*, 37-54.

————. "The Grotesque and George Willard," *Winesburg, Ohio: Text and Criticism*, 421-431.

Asselineau, Roger. "Language and Style in Sherwood Anderson's *Winesburg, Ohio*," *Winesburg, Ohio: Text and Criticism*, 345-356.

Bowden, Edwin T. *The Dungeon of the Heart: Human Isolation and the American Novel*, 114-124.

Browning, Chris. "Kate Swift: Sherwood Anderson's Creative Eros," *Tennessee Studies in Literature* XIII (1968), 141-148.

Burbank, Rex. *Sherwood Anderson*, 61-77.

Clark, Edward. "*Winesburg, Ohio*: An Interpretation," *Neueren Sprachen* (Dec 1959), 547-552.

Cowley, Malcolm. "Anderson's Lost Days of Innocence," *The Achievement of Sherwood Anderson: Essays in Criticism*, 227-230.

————. "Introduction to *Winesburg, Ohio*," *Winesburg, Ohio: Text and Criticism*, 357-368.

————. Introduction, *Winesburg, Ohio* (New York, 1965).

Frank, Waldo. "*Winesburg, Ohio* after Twenty Years," *The Achievement of Sherwood Anderson: Essays in Criticism*, 116-121.

Fussell, Edwin. "'Winesburg, Ohio': Art and Isolation," *Modern Fiction Studies* VI (Summer 1960), 106-114.

————. "*Winesburg, Ohio*: Art and Isolation," *The Achievement of Sherwood Anderson: Essays in Criticism*, 104-113.

————. "*Winesburg, Ohio*: Art and Isolation," *Winesburg, Ohio: Text and Criticism*, 383-395.

8

Howe, Irving. "The Book of the Grotesque," *The Achievement of Sherwood Anderson: Essays in Criticism*, 90-101.

———. "Sherwood Anderson: *Winesburg, Ohio*," *The American Novel from James Fenimore Cooper to William Faulkner*, 154-165.

Joselyn, Sister M. "Sherwood Anderson and the Lyric Story," *Winesburg, Ohio: Text and Criticism*, 444-454.

Laughlin, Rosemary M. "Godliness and the American Dream in *Winesburg, Ohio*," *Twentieth Century Literature* XIII (Jul 1967), 97-103.

Lorch, Thomas M. "The Choreographic Structure of *Winesburg, Ohio*," *CLA Journal* XII (Sept 1968), 56-65.

Love, Glen A. "*Winesburg, Ohio* and the Rhetoric of Silence," *American Literature* 40 (Mar 1968), 38-57.

M. A. "A Country Town," *The Achievement of Sherwood Anderson: Essays in Criticism*, 86-88.

Maresca, Carol J. "Gestures as Meaning in Sherwood Anderson's *Winesburg, Ohio*," *CLA Journal* IX (Mar 1966), 279-283.

Mellard, James M. "Narrative Forms in *Winesburg, Ohio*," *PMLA* 83 (Oct 1968), 1304-1312.

Murphy, George D. "The Theme of Sublimation in Anderson's *Winesburg, Ohio*," *Modern Fiction Studies* XIII (Summer 1967), 237-246.

Phillips, William L. "How Sherwood Anderson Wrote *Winesburg, Ohio*," *The Achievement of Sherwood Anderson: Essays in Criticism*, 62-84.

Rideout, Walter B. "The Simplicity of *Winesburg, Ohio*," *Shenandoah* XIII (Spring 1962), 20-31.

———. "The Simplicity of *Winesburg, Ohio*," *Winesburg, Ohio: Text and Criticism*, 287-300.

San Juan, Epifanio, Jr. "Vision and Reality: A Reconsideration of Sherwood Anderson's *Winesburg, Ohio*," *American Literature* XXXV (May 1963), 137-155.

———. "Vision and Reality: A Reconsideration of Sherwood Anderson's *Winesburg, Ohio*," *Winesburg, Ohio: Text and Criticism*, 468-481.

Sullivan, John H. "Winesburg Revisited," *Antioch Review* XX (Summer 1960), 213-221.

Walcutt, Charles Child. "Sherwood Anderson: Impressionism and the Buried Life," *The Achievement of Sherwood Anderson: Essays in Criticism*, 160-165.

ANDERSON, SHERWOOD, Continued

Weber, Brom. *Sherwood Anderson,* 21-26.

Winesburg, Ohio: A Critical Commentary.

GENERAL

The Achievement of Sherwood Anderson: Essays in Criticism.

Anderson, David D. "Sherwood Anderson After 20 Years," *Midwest Quarterly* III (Winter 1962), 119-132.

————. "Sherwood Anderson After 20 Years," *The Achievement of Sherwood Anderson: Essays in Criticism,* 246-256.

————. *Sherwood Anderson: An Introduction and Interpretation.*

Bridgman, Richard. *The Colloquial Style in America,* 152-164.

Burbank, Rex. *Sherwood Anderson.*

Cowley, Malcolm. "Anderson's Lost Days of Innocence," *The Achievement of Sherwood Anderson: Essays in Criticism,* 224-230.

Derleth, August. "Sherwood Anderson," *Three Literary Men,* 31-36.

Duffey, Bernard. "From *The Chicago Renaissance in American Letters,*" *The Achievement of Sherwood Anderson: Essays in Criticism,* 46-59.

Faulkner, William. "Sherwood Anderson: An Appreciation," *The Achievement of Sherwood Anderson: Essays in Criticism,* 194-199.

Feibleman, James K. "Memories of Sherwood Anderson," *Shenandoah* XIII (Spring 1962), 32-45.

Gregory, Horace. "On Sherwood Anderson," *Talks with Authors,* 12-22.

Gross, Seymour L. "Sherwood Anderson's Debt to *Huckleberry Finn,*" *Mark Twain Journal* XI (Summer 1960), 3-5, 24.

Hoffman, Frederick J. "From *Freudianism and the Literary Mind,*" *The Achievement of Sherwood Anderson: Essays in Criticism,* 174-192.

————. "The Voices of Sherwood Anderson," *Shenandoah* XIII (Spring 1962), 5-19.

————. "The Voices of Sherwood Anderson," *The Achievement of Sherwood Anderson: Essays in Criticism,* 232-244.

Joselyn, Sister M. "Sherwood Anderson and the Lyric Story," *The Twenties: Poetry and Prose,* 70-73.

Lawry, Jon S. "The Artist in America: The Case of Sherwood Anderson," *Ball State University Forum* VII (Spring 1966), 15-26.

Millgate, Michael. *American Social Fiction: James to Cozzens,* 87-93.

Morgan, H. Wayne. "Sherwood Anderson: The Search for Unity," *Writers in Transition: Seven Americans,* 82-104.

Phillips, William L. "Sherwood Anderson's Two Prize Pupils," *The Achievement of Sherwood Anderson: Essays in Criticism*, 202-210.

Poggi, Valentina. "Il Linguaggio Narrativo Di Sherwood Anderson," *Studi Americani* VIII (1962) , 93-109.

Rideout, Walter B. "Why Sherwood Anderson Employed Buck Fever," *Georgia Review* XIII (Spring 1959) , 76-85.

————. "Why Sherwood Anderson Employed Buck Fever," *The Achievement of Sherwood Anderson: Essays in Criticism*, 128-137

Schevill, James. "The Glitter of Communism," *The Achievement of Sherwood Anderson: Essays in Criticism*, 140-154.

Schorer, Mark. "Some Relationships: Gertrude Stein, Sherwood Anderson, F. Scott Fitzgerald, and Ernest Hemingway," *The World We Imagine: Selected Essays*, 299-382.

Spratling, William. "Chronicle of a Friendship: William Faulkner in New Orleans," *Texas Quarterly* IX (Spring 1966) , 34-40; "*Sherwood Anderson & Other Famous Creoles,* by William Spratling and William Faulkner—A Facsimile," 41-97; *Sherwood Anderson and other Creoles,* University of Texas Press 1967.

Sutton, William A. *Exit to Elsinore.*

————. "Sherwood Anderson's Second Wife," *Ball State University Forum* VII (Spring 1966) , 39-46.

Tanner, Tony. "Sherwood Anderson's Little Things," *The Reign of Wonder: Naivety and Reality in American Literature*, 205-227.

Tanselle, G. Thomas. "Realist or Dreamer: Letters of Sherwood Anderson and Floyd Dell," *Modern Language Review* LVIII (Oct 1963) , 532-537.

Trilling, Lionel. "Sherwood Anderson," *The Achievement of Sherwood Anderson: Essays in Criticism*, 212-221.

Walcutt, Charles Child. "Sherwood Anderson: Impressionism and the Buried Life," *The Achievement of Sherwood Anderson: Essays in Criticism*, 156-171.

Weber, Brom. *Sherwood Anderson.*

West, Thomas Reed. "Sherwood Anderson: The Machine and the Craftsman's Sensibility," *Flesh of Steel: Literature and the Machine in American Culture*, 21-34.

BIBLIOGRAPHY

The Achievement of Sherwood Anderson: Essays in Criticism, 261-263.

Anderson, David D. *Sherwood Anderson: An Introduction and Interpretation*, 174-177.

ANDERSON, SHERWOOD, Continued

Burbank, Rex. *Sherwood Anderson*, 148-152.

Sheehy, Eugene P. and Kenneth A. Lohf. *Sherwood Anderson: A Bibliography*.

Tanselle, G. Thomas. "Additional Reviews of Sherwood Anderson's Work," *Papers of the Bibliographical Society of America* 56 (Jul-Sept 1962), 358-365.

Weber, Brom. *Sherwood Anderson*, 46-48.

Winesburg, Ohio: Text and Criticism, 507-511.

ANGOFF, CHARLES

GENERAL

Liptzin, Sol. *The Jew in American Literature*, 199-209.

ARTHUR, TIMOTHY SHAY

TEN NIGHTS IN A BAR-ROOM, AND WHAT I SAW THERE

Holman, C. Hugh. Introduction, *Ten Nights in a Bar-Room* and *In His Steps* (New York, 1966).

Koch, Donald A. Introduction, *Ten Nights in a Bar-Room, and What I Saw There* (Cambridge, 1964).

ASHER, DON

DON'T THE MOON LOOK LONESOME

French, Warren. *Season of Promise*, 32-37.

ASHMEAD, JOHN

THE MOUNTAIN AND THE FEATHER

Muste, John M. "Better to Die Laughing: The War Novels of Joseph Heller and John Ashmead," *Critique* V (Fall 1962), 16-27.

ATTAWAY, WILLIAM

BLOOD ON THE FORGE

Bone, Robert. *The Negro Novel in America*, 132-140.

Margolies, Edward. "Migration: William Attaway and *Blood on the*

ATTAWAY, WILLIAM, Continued

Forge," *Native Sons: A Critical Study of Twentieth-Century Negro*
American Authors, 47-64.

AUCHINCLOSS, LOUIS

GENERAL

Adams, J. Donald. "Speaking of Books," *New York Times Book Re-*
view 68 (Sept 29, 1963) , 2.

Kane, Patricia. "Lawyers at the Top: The Fiction of Louis Auchincloss," *Critique* VII (Winter 1964-1965) , 36-46.

Milne, W. Gordon. "Auchincloss and the Novel of Manners," *Uni-*
versity of Kansas City Review XXIX (Mar 1963) , 177-185.

AUSTIN, MARY

THE FORD

Pearce, T. M. *Mary Hunter Austin,* 75-77.

NO. 26 JAYNE STREET

Pearce, T. M. *Mary Hunter Austin,* 77-80.

STARRY ADVENTURE

Pearce, T. M. *Mary Hunter Austin,* 95-101

A WOMAN OF GENIUS

Pearce, T. M. *Mary Hunter Austin,* 82-87.

GENERAL

Hahn, Emily. *Romantic Rebels: An Informal History of Bohemian-*
ism in America, 216-223.

Lyday, Jo W. *Mary Austin: The Southwest Works.*

Pearce, T. M. *Mary Hunter Austin.*

BIBLIOGRAPHY

Lyday, Jo W. *Mary Austin: The Southwest Works,* 37-40.

Pearce, T. M. *Mary Hunter Austin,* 145-152.

BAKER, ELLIOTT

A FINE MADNESS

Noland, Richard W. "Lunacy and Poetry: Elliott Baker's *A Fine*
Madness," *Critique* VIII (Spring-Summer 1966) , 71-78.

BALDWIN, JAMES

ANOTHER COUNTRY

Blount, Trevor. "A Slight Error in Continuity in James Baldwin's *Another Country*," *Notes and Queries* N.S. 13 (Mar 1966), 102-103.

Bone, Robert. *The Negro Novel in America*, 228-239.

————. "The Novels of James Baldwin," *Images of the Negro in American Literature*, 278-288.

Cox, C. B. and A. R. Jones. "After the Tranquillized Fifties: Notes on Sylvia Plath and James Baldwin," *Critical Quarterly* 6 (Summer 1964), 107-122.

Finkelstein, Sidney. *Existentialism and Alienation in American Literature*, 280-284.

Harper, Howard M., Jr. *Desperate Faith*, 151-159.

Klein, Marcus. *After Alienation: American Novels in Mid-Century*, 188-195.

Littlejohn, David. *Black on White: A Critical Survey of Writings by American Negroes*, 125-133.

Margolies, Edward. *Native Sons: A Critical Study of Twentieth-Century Negro American Authors*, 118-122.

Newman, Charles. "The Lesson of the Master: Henry James and James Baldwin," *Yale Review* LVI (Autumn 1966), 46-59.

Podhoretz, Norman. "In Defense of a Maltreated Best Seller," *On Contemporary Literature*, 232-237.

GIOVANNI'S ROOM

Bone, Robert A. "The Novels of James Baldwin," *Images of the Negro in American Literature*, 275-278.

Harper, Howard M., Jr. *Desperate Faith*, 147-151.

Klein, Marcus. *After Alienation: American Novels in Mid-Century*, 184-188.

Margolies, Edward. *Native Sons: A Critical Study of Twentieth-Century Negro American Authors*, 114-118.

GO TELL IT ON THE MOUNTAIN

Bone, Robert. *The Negro Novel in America*, 216-221, 222-225.

————. "The Novels of James Baldwin," *Images of the Negro in American Literature*, 268-275.

Graves, Wallace. "The Question of Moral Energy in James Baldwin's *Go Tell it on the Mountain*," *CLA Journal* VII (Mar 1964), 215-223.

Harper, Howard M., Jr. *Desperate Faith*, 142-147.

Klein, Marcus. *After Alienation: American Novels in Mid-Century*, 178-184.

14

BALDWIN, JAMES, Continued

Littlejohn, David. *Black on White: A Critical Survey of Writings by American Negroes,* 121-124.

Margolies, Edward. *Native Sons: A Critical Study of Twentieth-Century Negro American Authors,* 109-114.

TELL ME HOW LONG THE TRAIN'S BEEN GONE

Algren, Nelson. "Sashaying Around," *Critic* XXVII (Oct-Nov 1968), 86-87.

Hicks, Granville. "From Harlem with Hatred," *Saturday Review* 51 (Jun 1, 1968), 23-24.

Howe, Irving. "James Baldwin: At Ease in Apocalypse," *Harper's* 237 (Sept 1968), 92-100.

Long, Robert Emmet. "From Elegant to Hip," *Nation* 206 (Jun 10, 1968), 769-770.

Thompson, John. "Baldwin: The Prophet as Artist," *Commentary* 45 (June 1968), 67-69.

GENERAL

Alexander, Charlotte. "The 'Stink' of Reality: Mothers and Whores in James Baldwin's Fiction," *Literature and Psychology* XVIII (No 1, 1968), 9-26.

Baldwin, James. "As Much Truth as One Can Bear," *New York Times Book Review* 67 (Jan 14, 1962), 1, 38; see also J. Donald Adams, "Speaking of Books," *New York Times Book Review* 67 (Jan 28, 1962), 2.

Bigsby, C. W. E. "The Committed Writer: James Baldwin as Dramatist," *Twentieth Century Literature* 13 (Apr 1967), 39-48.

Bone, Robert. *The Negro Novel in America,* 215-239.

————. "The Novels of James Baldwin," *Images of the Negro in American Literature,* 265-288.

————. "The Novels of James Baldwin," *Tri-Quarterly* 1 (Winter 1965), 3-20.

Boyle, Kay. "Introducing James Baldwin," *Contemporary American Novelists,* 155-157.

Bradford, M. E. "Faulkner, James Baldwin, and the South," *Georgia Review* XX (Winter 1966), 431-443.

Breit, Harvey. "James Baldwin and Two Footnotes," *The Creative Present,* 5-26.

Charney, Maurice. "James Baldwin's Quarrel with Richard Wright," *American Quarterly* XV (Spring 1963), 65-75.

BALDWIN, JAMES, Continued

Coles, Robert. "Baldwin's Burden," *Partisan Review* XXXI (Summer 1964), 409-416.

Cook, Bruce. "Writers in Midstream," *Critic* XXI (Feb-Mar 1963), 35-40.

Eckman, Fern Marja. *The Furious Passage of James Baldwin.*

Finkelstein, Sidney. *Existentialism and Alienation in American Literature,* 276-284.

Gayle, Addison, Jr. "A Defense of James Baldwin," *CLA Journal* X (Mar 1967), 201-208.

Gross, Theodore. "The World of James Baldwin," *Critique* VII (Winter 1964-1965), 139-149.

Harper, Howard M., Jr. "James Baldwin—art or propaganda?," *Desperate Faith,* 137-161.

Jacobson, Dan. "James Baldwin as Spokesman," *Commentary* XXXII (Dec 1961), 497-502.

Kent, George E. "Baldwin and the Problem of Being," *CLA Journal* VII (Mar 1964), 202-214.

Klein, Marcus. "James Baldwin: A Question of Identity," *After Alienation: American Novels in Mid-Century,* 147-195.

Lash, John S. "Baldwin Beside Himself: A Study in Modern Phallicism," *CLA Journal* VIII (Dec 1964), 132-140.

Littlejohn, David. *Black on White: A Critical Survey of Writings by American Negroes,* 119-137.

Margolies, Edward. "The Negro Church: James Baldwin and the Christian Vision," *Native Sons: A Critical Study of Twentieth-Century Negro American Authors,* 102-126.

Noble, David W. *The Eternal Adam and the New World Garden,* 209-216.

O'Daniel, Therman B. "James Baldwin: An Interpretive Study," *CLA Journal* VII (Sept 1963), 37-47.

Sayre, Robert F. "James Baldwin's Other Country," *Contemporary American Novelists,* 158-169.

Standley, Fred L. "James Baldwin: The Critical Situation," *South Atlantic Quarterly* LXV (Summer 1966), 371-381.

VanSikle, Milton. "James Baldwin in Black and White," *Trace* 54 (Autumn 1964), 222-225.

Watson, Edward A. "The Novels and Essays of James Baldwin: Case-Book of a Lover's War with the United States," *Queen's Quarterly* LXXII (Summer 1965), 385-402.

BALDWIN, JAMES, Continued

Wüstenhagen, Heinz. "James Baldwins Essays und Romane: Versuch einer ersten Einschätzung," *Zeitschrift Für Anglistik und Amerikanistik* XIII (Heft 2, 1965), 117-157.

BIBLIOGRAPHY

Fischer, Russell G. "James Baldwin: A Bibliography, 1947-1962," *Bulletin of Bibliography* XXIV (Jan-Apr 1965), 127-130.

Kindt, Kathleen A. "James Baldwin, A Checklist: 1947-1962," *Bulletin of Bibliography* XXIV (Jan-Apr 1965), 123-126.

Standley, Fred L. "James Baldwin: A Checklist, 1963-1967," *Bulletin of Bibliography* XXV (May-Aug 1968), 135-137, 160.

BARNES, DJUNA

GENERAL

Williamson, Alan. "*The Divided Image:* The Quest for Identity in the Works of Djuna Barnes," *Critique* VII (Spring 1964), 58-74.

BIBLIOGRAPHY

Hipkiss, Robert A. "Djuna Barnes (1892-   )—A Bibliography," *Twentieth Century Literature* 14 (Oct 1968), 161-163.

BARTH, JOHN

THE END OF THE ROAD

Graff, Gerald E. "Mythotherapy and Modern Poetics," *Tri-Quarterly* 11 (Winter 1968), 76-90.

Smith, Herbert F. "Barth's Endless Road," *Critique* VI (Fall 1963), 68-76.

THE FLOATING OPERA

Schickel, Richard. "The Floating Opera," *Critique* VI (Fall 1963), 53-67.

GILES GOAT-BOY

Brooks, Peter. "John Barth," *Encounter* XXVIII (Jun 1967), 71-75.

Byrd, Scott. "*Giles Goat-Boy* Visited," Critique IX (No 1, 1966), 108-112.

Kiely, Benedict. "Ripeness Was Not All: John Barth's *Giles Goat-Boy,*" *Hollins Critic* III (Dec 1966), 1-12.

Scholes, Robert. *The Fabulators,* 135-173.

Tanner, Tony. "The Hoax that Joke Bilked," *Partisan Review* XXXIV (Winter 1967), 102-109.

BARTH, JOHN, Continued

THE SOT-WEED FACTOR

Diser, Philip E. "The Historical Ebenezer Cooke," *Critique: Studies in Modern Fiction* X (No 3, 1968) , 48-59.

Fiedler, Leslie A. "John Barth: An Eccentric Genius," *On Contemporary Literature*, 238-243.

————. *The Return of the Vanishing American*, 150-153.

Holder, Alan. " 'What Marvelous Plot . . . Was Afoot?' History in Barth's *The Sot-Weed Factor*," *American Quarterly* XX (Fall 1968) , 596-604.

Miller, Russell H. "*The Sot-Weed Factor:* A Contemporary Mock-Epic," *Critique* VIII (Winter 1965-1966) , 88-100.

Rovit, Earl. "The Novel as Parody: John Barth," *Critique* VI (Fall 1963) , 77-85.

GENERAL

Barth, John. "John Barth: An Interview," *Wisconsin Studies in Contemporary Literature* VI (Winter-Spring, 1965) , 3-14.

Binni, Francesco. "John Barth e il romanzo di società," *Studi Americani* 12 (1966) , 277-300.

Garis, Robert. "What Happened to John Barth?" *Commentary* 42 (October 1966) , 89-95.

Gross, Beverly. "The Anti-Novels of John Barth," *Chicago Review* 20 (Nov 1968) , 95-109.

Meras, Phyllis. "John Barth: A Truffle No Longer," *New York Times Book Review* 71 (Aug 7, 1966) , 22.

Noland, Richard W. "John Barth and the Novel of Comic Nihilism," *Wisconsin Studies in Contemporary Literature* 7 (Autumn 1966) , 239-257.

Scholes, Robert. "Disciple of Scheherazade," *New York Times Book Review* 71 (May 8, 1966) , 5, 22.

Stubbs, John C. "John Barth as a Novelist of Ideas: The Themes of Value and Identity," *Critique* VIII (Winter 1965-1966) , 101-116.

Trachtenberg, Alan. "Barth and Hawkes: Two Fabulists," *Critique* VI (Fall 1963) , 4-18.

BIBLIOGRAPHY

Bryer, Jackson R. "Two Bibliographies," *Critique* VI (Fall 1963) , 86-89.

BARTHELME, DONALD

SNOW WHITE
Gilman, Richard. "Barthelme's Fairy Tale," *New Republic* 156 (Jun 3, 1967), 27-30.

BAUM, LYMAN FRANK

THE WONDERFUL WIZARD OF OZ
Littlefield, Henry M. "The Wizard of Oz: Parable on Populism," *American Quarterly* XVI (Spring 1964), 47-58.

GENERAL
Baum, Harry Neal. "How My Father Wrote the Oz Books," *American Book Collector* XIII (Dec 1962), 17.

Brotman, Jordan. "A Late Wanderer in Oz," *Chicago Review* XVIII (No 2, 1965), 63-73.

Erisman, Fred. "L. Frank Baum and the Progressive Dilemma," *American Quarterly* XX (Fall 1968), 616-623.

Gardner, Martin. "Why Librarians Dislike Oz," *American Book Collector* XIII (Dec 1962), 14-16.

MacFall, Russell P. "L. Frank Baum—Shadow and Substance," *American Book Collector* XIII (Dec 1962), 9-11.

Sackett, S. J. "The Utopia of Oz," *Georgia Review* XIV (Fall 1960), 275-291.

Wagenknecht, Edward. " 'Utopia Americana' a Generation Afterwards," *American Book Collector* XIII (Dec 1962), 12-13.

BIBLIOGRAPHY
"L (yman) Frank Baum: A Chronological Checklist of his Published Writings," *American Book Collector* XIII (Dec 1962), 28-31.

Martin, Dick. "The First Edition of the Wonderful Wizard," *American Book Collector* XIII (Dec 1962), 26-27.

BEAGLE, PETER S.

GENERAL
Kiely, Benedict. "American Wandering Minstrel: Peter S. Beagle and *The Last Unicorn,*" *Hollins Critic* V (Apr 1968), 1-9, 12.

BELLAMY, EDWARD

LOOKING BACKWARD

Bleich, David. "Eros and Bellamy," *American Quarterly* XVI (Fall 1964), 445-459.

Boggs, W. Arthur. "*Looking Backward* at the Utopian Novel, 1888-1900," *Bulletin of the New York Public Library* LXIV (Jun 1960), 329-336.

Cooperman, Stanley. "Utopian Realism: The Futurist Novels of Bellamy and Howells," *College English* XXIV (Mar 1963), 464-467.

Elliott, Robert C. Introduction, *Looking Backward* (Boston, 1966).

Fromm, Erich. Foreword, *Looking Backward* (New York, 1960).

Martin, Jay. *Harvests of Change. American Literature 1865-1914*, 220-223.

Thomas, John L. Introduction, *Looking Backward* (Cambridge, 1967).

GENERAL

Bowman, Sylvia E. *Edward Bellamy Abroad.*

Martin, Jay. *Harvests of Change. American Literature 1865-1914*, 220-226.

BIBLIOGRAPHY

Bowman, Sylvia E. *Edward Bellamy Abroad,* 479-528.

————. "Edward Bellamy (1850-1898)," *American Literary Realism* 1 (Fall 1967), 7-12.

BELLOW, SAUL

THE ADVENTURES OF AUGIE MARCH

Allen, Michael. "Idiomatic Language in Two Novels by Saul Bellow," *Journal of American Studies* I (Oct 1967), 275-280.

Crozier, Robert D., S. J. "Theme in *Augie March,*" *Critique* VII (Spring-Summer 1965), 18-32.

Eisinger, Chester E. *Fiction of the Forties,* 354-362.

Galloway, David D. *The Absurd Hero in American Fiction,* 94-104.

Gibson, Walker. *Tough, Sweet and Stuffy: An Essay on Modern American Prose Styles,* 59-63.

Goldberg, Gerald Jay. "Life's Customer, Augie March," *Critique* III (Summer 1960), 15-27.

Guerard, Albert J. "Saul Bellow and the Activitists: On *The Adventures of Augie March,*" *Southern Review* III (Summer 1967), 582-596.

BELLOW, SAUL, Continued

Hall, James. *The Lunatic Giant in the Drawing Room,* 149-159.

Harper, Howard M., Jr. *Desperate Faith,* 23-32.

Hassan, Ihab. *Radical Innocence: Studies in the Contemporary American Novel,* 304-311.

Klein, Marcus. *After Alienation: American Novels in Mid-Century,* 37-39, 53-54, 59-60.

Opdahl, Keith Michael. "Life Among the Machiavellians," *The Novels of Saul Bellow: An Introduction,* 70-95

Overbeck, Pat Trefzger. "The Women in *Augie March,*" *Texas Studies in Literature and Language* X (Fall 1968) , 471-484.

Tanner, Tony. *Saul Bellow,* 41-56.

Trilling, Lionel. Introduction, *The Adventures of Augie March* (New York, 1965) .

Way, Brian. "Character and Society in *The Adventures of Augie March,*" *British Association For American Studies Bulletin* 8 (Jun 1964) , 36-44.

DANGLING MAN

Galloway, David D. *The Absurd Hero in American Fiction,* 82-89.

Harper, Howard M., Jr. *Desperate Faith,* 8-16.

Opdahl, Keith Michael. "The Generalized Man," *The Novels of Saul Bellow: An Introduction,* 28-49.

Tanner, Tony. *Saul Bellow,* 18-25.

HENDERSON THE RAIN KING

Allen, Michael. "Idiomatic Language in Two Novels by Saul Bellow," *Journal of American Studies* I (Oct 1967) , 275-280.

Arnavon, Cyrille. "Le Roman Africain De Saul Bellow: Henderson, The Rain King," *Études Anglaises* XIV (Jan-Mars 1961) , 25-35.

Chase, Richard. "The Adventures of Saul Bellow: Progress of a Novelist," *Saul Bellow and his Critics,* 33-38.

Clayton, John J. *Saul Bellow: In Defense of Man,* 166-185.

Detweiler, Robert. "Patterns of Rebirth in *Henderson the Rain King,*" *Modern Fiction Studies* XII (Winter 1966-67) , 405-414.

Galloway, David D. *The Absurd Hero in American Fiction,* 110-123.

Guttmann, Allen. "Bellow's *Henderson,*" *Critique* VII (Spring-Summer 1965) , 33-42.

Harper, Howard M., Jr. *Desperate Faith,* 39-50.

Hassan, Ihab. "Quest and Affirmation in *Henderson the Rain King,*" *The Modern Novel: Essays in Criticism,* 223-229.

Rovit, Earl. "Bellow in Occupancy," *Saul Bellow and his Critics,* 177-183.

Rubin, Louis D., Jr. "The Experience of Difference," *The Curious Death of the Novel: Essays in American Literature,* 271-275.

Tanner, Tony. *Saul Bellow,* 87-102.

Uphaus, Suzanne Henning. "From Innocence to Experience: A Study of Herzog," *Dalhousie Review* 46 (Spring 1966) , 67-78.

Young, James Dean. "Bellow's View of the Heart," *Critique* VII (Spring-Summer 1965) , 5-17.

SEIZE THE DAY

Handy, William J. "Saul Bellow and the Naturalistic Hero," *Texas Studies in Literature and Language* V (Winter 1964) , 538-545.

Harper, Howard M., Jr. *Desperate Faith,* 32-39.

Hassan, Ihab. *Radical Innocence: Studies in the Contemporary American Novel,* 311-316.

Klein, Marcus. *After Alienation: American Novels in Mid-Century,* 39-42, 48.

Mathis, James C. "The Theme of *Seize the Day,*" *Critique* VII (Spring-Summer 1965) , 43-45.

Opdahl, Keith Michael. "Come Then, Sorrow," *The Novels of Saul Bellow: An Introduction,* 96-117.

Tanner, Tony. *Saul Bellow,* 58-70.

Trowbridge, Clinton. "Water Imagery in Seize the Day," *Critique* IX No 3, 1967) , 62-73.

Weiss, Daniel. "Caliban on Prospero: A Psychoanalytic Study on the Novel *Seize the Day,* by Saul Bellow, *American Imago* XIX (Fall 1962) , 277-306.

————. "Caliban on Prospero: A Psychoanalytic Study on the Novel *Seize the Day,* by Saul Bellow," *Saul Bellow and his Critics,* 114-139.

————. "Caliban on Prospero: A Psychoanalytic Study on the Novel *Seize the Day,*" *Psychoanalysis and American Fiction,* 279-307.

THE VICTIM

Baumbach, Jonathan. "The Double Vision: *The Victim* by Saul Bellow," *The Landscape of Nightmare: Studies in the Contemporary American Novel,* 35-54.

Bradbury, Malcolm. "Saul Bellow's *The Victim,*" *Critical Quarterly* 5 (Summer 1963) , 119-128.

Clayton, John J. *Saul Bellow: In Defense of Man,* 139-165.

Galloway, David D. *The Absurd Hero in American Fiction,* 89-94.

Hall, James. *The Lunatic Giant in the Drawing Room,* 138-149.

Harper, Howard M., Jr. *Desperate Faith,* 16-23.

Opdahl, Keith Michael. "The Ifrit and the Fellahin," *The Novels of Saul Bellow: An Introduction,* 50-69.

Tanner, Tony. *Saul Bellow,* 26-37.

GENERAL

Baker, Sheridan. "Saul Bellow's Bout with Chivalry," *Criticism* IX (Spring 1967) , 109-122.

Bellow, Saul. "Facts that Put Fancy to Flight," *New York Times Book Review* 67 (Feb 11, 1962) , 1, 28.

————. "Saul Bellow: An Interview," *Wisconsin Studies in Contemporary Literature* VI (Summer 1965) , 156-160.

Chapman, Abraham. "The Image of Man as Portrayed by Saul Bellow," *CLA Journal* X (Jun 1967) 285-298.

Clayton, John J. *Saul Bellow: In Defense of Man.*

Davis, Robert Gorham. "The American Individualist Tradition: Bellow and Styron," *The Creative Present,* 111-130, 139-141.

Dickstein, Morris. "For Art's Sake," *Partisan Review* XXXIII (Fall 1966) , 617-621.

Fiedler, Leslie A. "Saul Bellow," *On Contemporary Literature,* 286-295.

Finkelstein, Sidney. *Existentialism and Alienation in American Literature,* 262-268.

Fossum, Robert H. "The Devil and Saul Bellow," *Comparative Literature Studies* III (No 2, 1966) , 197-206.

Freedman, Ralph. "Saul Bellow: The Illusion of Environment," *Wisconsin Studies in Contemporary Literature* 1 (Winter 1960) , 50-65.

Frohock, W. M. "Saul Bellow and His Penitent Picaro," *Southwest Review* LIII (Winter 1968) , 36-44.

Galloway, David D. "The Absurd Man as Picaro," *The Absurd Hero in American Fiction,* 82-139.

————. "The Absurd Man as Picaro: The Novels of Saul Bellow," *Texas Studies in Literature and Language* VI (Summer 1964) , 226-254.

————. "Moses-Bloom-Herzog: Bellow's Everyman," *Southern Review* II (Jan 1966) , 61-76.

Gutwillig, Robert. "Talk With Saul Bellow," *New York Times Book Review* 69 (Sept 20, 1964) , 40-41.

BELLOW, SAUL, Continued

Harper, Gordon Lloyd. "An Interview with Saul Bellow: The Art of Fiction XXXVII," *Paris Review* IX (Winter 1966), 48-73.

Harper, Howard M., Jr. "Saul Bellow—the Heart's Ultimate Need," *Desperate Faith,* 7-64.

Hassan, Ihab H. "Saul Bellow: Five Faces of a Hero," *Critique* III (Summer 1960), 28-36.

Hoffman, Frederick J. "The Fool of Experience: Saul Bellow's Fiction," *Contemporary American Novelists,* 80-94.

Kazin, Alfred. "My Friend Saul Bellow," *Atlantic Monthly* CCXV (Jan 1965), 51-54.

Klein, Marcus. "Saul Bellow: A Discipline of Nobility," *After Alienation: American Novels in Mid-Century,* 33-70.

Levenson, J. C. "Bellow's Dangling Men," *Critique* III (Summer 1960), 3-14.

Lombardo, Agostino. "La Narrativa Di Saul Bellow," *Studi Americani* XI (1965), 309-344.

Ludwig, Jack. "Postscript, 1962," *On Contemporary Literature,* 296-299.

Morrow, Patrick. "Threat and Accommodation: The Novels of Saul Bellow," *Midwest Quarterly* VIII (Summer 1967), 389-411.

Noble, David W. *The Eternal Adam and the New World Garden,* 216-223.

Opdahl, Keith Michael. *The Novels of Saul Bellow. An Introduction.*

Rovit, Earl. *Saul Bellow.*

Saul Bellow and his Critics.

Shulman, Robert. "The Style of Bellow's Comedy," *PMLA* 83 (Mar 1968), 109-117.

Stock, Irvin. "The Novels of Saul Bellow," *Southern Review* III (Winter 1967), 13-42.

Symons, Julian. "Bellow Before *Herzog,*" *Critical Occasions,* 112-118.

Tanner, Tony. *Saul Bellow.*

————. "Saul Bellow: The Flight from Monologue," *Encounter* XXIV (Feb 1965), 58-70.

Trachtenberg, Stanley. "Saul Bellow's *Luftmenschen:* The Compromise with Reality," *Critique* IX (No 3, 1967), 37-61.

Weber, Ronald. "Bellow's Thinkers," *Western Humanities Review* XXII (Autumn 1968), 305-313.

BIBLIOGRAPHY

Clayton, John J. *Saul Bellow: In Defense of Man,* 255-257.

BELLOW, SAUL, Continued

Galloway, David D. *The Absurd Hero in American Fiction,* 210-226.

Opdahl, Keith Michael. *The Novels of Saul Bellow: An Introduction,* 181-193.

Rovit, Earl. *Saul Bellow,* 44-46.

Schneider, Harold W. "Two Bibliographies: Saul Bellow-William Styron," *Critique* III (Summer 1960) , 71-91.

Tanner, Tony. *Saul Bellow,* 118-120.

BENEFIELD, BARRY

GENERAL

Hatley, Donald W. "Folklore in the Fiction of Barry Benefield," *Mississippi Quarterly* XXI (Winter 1967-68) , 63-70.

BERGER, THOMAS

LITTLE BIG MAN

Fiedler, Leslie A. *The Return of the Vanishing American,* 160-164.

Lee, L. L. "American, Western, Picaresque: Thomas Berger's *Little Big Man*," *South Dakota Review* 4 (Summer 1964) , 35-42.

GENERAL

Hassan, Ihab. "Conscience and Incongruity: The Fiction of Thomas Berger," *Critique* V (Fall 1962) , 4-15.

BIRD, ROBERT MONTGOMERY

CALAVAR

Dahl, Curtis. *Robert Montgomery Bird,* 73-79.

THE HAWKS OF HAWK HOLLOW

Dahl, Curtis. *Robert Montgomery Bird,* 86-91.

THE INFIDEL

Dahl, Curtis. *Robert Montgomery Bird,* 79-84.

NICK OF THE WOODS

Bryant, James C. "The Fallen World in *Nick of the Woods*," *American Literature* XXXVIII (Nov 1966) , 352-364.

Dahl, Curtis. *Robert Montgomery Bird,* 91-102.

Hall, Joan Joffe. "*Nick of the Woods:* An Interpretation of the American Wilderness," *American Literature* XXXV (May 1963) , 173-182.

BIRD, ROBERT MONTGOMERY, Continued

GENERAL
Dahl, Curtis. *Robert Montgomery Bird.*
BIBLIOGRAPHY
Dahl, Curtis. *Robert Montgomery Bird,* 132-140.

BISHOP, JOHN PEALE

GENERAL
Elby, Cecil D., Jr. "The Fiction of John Peale Bishop," *Twentieth Century Literature* VII (Apr 1961) , 3-9.
Fiedler, Leslie A. "John Peale Bishop and the Other Thirties," *Commentary* XLIII (Apr 1967) , 74-82.
Moore, S. C. "The Criticism of John Peale Bishop," *Twentieth Century Literature* XII (Jul 1966) , 66-77.

BISSELL, RICHARD

GENERAL
Anderson, Frank J. "The View from the River: Richard Bissell's Satirical Humor," *Midwest Quarterly* V (Summer 1964) , 311-322.

BORLAND, HAL

WHEN THE LEGENDS DIE
Adkins, Carl A. "A Novel for High School Seniors: Hal Borland's *When the Legends Die,*" *English Journal* 57 (Jan 1968) , 30-33.

BOURJAILY, VANCE

THE END OF MY LIFE
Bourjaily, Vance. "Vance Bourjaily," *Talks With Authors,* 201-214.
GENERAL
Dienstfrey, Harris. "The Novels of Vance Bourjaily," *Commentary* XXXI (Apr 1961) , 360-363.

BOWLES, PAUL

GENERAL
Evans, Oliver. "Paul Bowles and The 'Natural' Man," *Critique* III (Spring-Fall 1959) , 43-59.

BOYD, THOMAS

GENERAL
Robbins, J. Albert. "Fitzgerald and the Simple, Inarticulate Farmer,"
Modern Fiction Studies VII (Winter 1961-62) , 365-369.

BOYESEN, H. H.

GENERAL
Ratner, Marc L. "Howells and Boyesen: Two Views of Realism," *New England Quarterly* XXXV (Sept 1962) , 376-390.
————. "The Iron Madonna: H. H. Boyesen's American Girl,"
Jahrbuch Für Amerikastudien 9 (1964) , 166-172.

BOYLE, KAY

THE BRIDEGROOM'S BODY
Carpenter, Richard C. "Kay Boyle: The Figure in the Carpet," *Critique*
VII (Winter 1964-1965) , 65-78.
THE CRAZY HUNTER
Carpenter, Richard C. "Kay Boyle: The Figure in the Carpet," *Critique*
VII (Winter 1964-1965) , 65-78.
PLAGUED BY THE NIGHTINGALE
Moore, Harry. Introduction, *Plagued by the Nightingale* (Carbondale, Illinois, 1966) .
GENERAL
Boyle, Kay. "Kay Boyle," *Talks With Authors,* 215-236.

BRACE, GERALD WARNER

THE GARRETSON CHRONICLE
Holman, C. H. Introduction, *The Garretson Chronicle* (New York, 1964) .

BRACKENRIDGE, HUGH HENRY

MODERN CHIVALRY
Hemenway, Robert. "Fiction in the Age of Jefferson: The Early American Novel as Intellectual Document," *Midcontinent American Studies Journal* IX (Spring 1968) , 91-102.

BRACKENRIDGE, HUGH HENRY, Continued

Leary, Lewis. Introduction, *Modern Chivalry* (New Haven, Connecticut, 1966).

Marder, Daniel. *Hugh Henry Brackenridge,* 83-98.

Nance, William L. "Satiric Elements in Brackenridge's *Modern Chivalry," Texas Studies in Literature and Language* IX (Autumn 1967), 381-389.

GENERAL

Marder, Daniel. *Hugh Henry Brackenridge.*

BIBLIOGRAPHY

C., E.E., "Brackenridge's *Modern Chivalry," Princeton University Library Chronicle* XXVII (Autumn 1965), 60.

Marder, Daniel. *Hugh Henry Brackenridge,* 151-155.

BRADBURY, RAY

GENERAL

Pagetti, Carlo. "Ray Bradbury E La Fantascienza Americana," *Studi Americani* XI (1965), 409-429.

BREWER, LUCY

THE FEMALE MARINE

Medlicott, Alexander, Jr. "The Legend of Lucy Brewer: An Early American Novel," *New England Quarterly* XXXIX (Dec 1966), 461-473.

BROMFIELD, LOUIS

EARLY AUTUMN

Anderson, David D. *Louis Bromfield,* 40-46.

THE FARM

Anderson, David D. *Louis Bromfield,* 78-89.

A GOOD WOMAN

Anderson, David D. *Louis Bromfield,* 46-52.

THE GREEN BAY TREE

Anderson, David D. *Louis Bromfield,* 27-34.

MRS. PARKINGTON

Anderson, David D. *Louis Bromfield,* 129-136.

POSSESSION

Anderson, David D. *Louis Bromfield,* 34-40.

THE RAINS CAME

Anderson, David D. *Louis Bromfield,* 99-111.

THE STRANGE CASE OF MISS ANNIE SPRAGG

Anderson, David D. *Louis Bromfield,* 56-62.

TWENTY-FOUR HOURS

Anderson, David D. *Louis Bromfield,* 64-70.

GENERAL

Anderson, David D. *Louis Bromfield.*

DeJong, David Cornel. "Louis Bromfield and a Malabar Farm Weekend," *Carleton Miscellany* VII (Winter 1966), 14-27.

Geld, Ellen Bromfield. *The Heritage: A Daughter's Memories of Louis Bromfield.*

BIBLIOGRAPHY

Anderson, David D. *Louis Bromfield,* 183-186.

BROWN, CHARLES BROCKDEN

ARTHUR MERVYN

Bernard, Kenneth. "*Arthur Mervyn:* The Ordeal of Innocence," *Texas Studies in Literature and Language* VI (Winter 1965), 441-459.

Berthoff, Walter. Introduction, *Arthur Mervyn, or Memoirs of the Year* (New York, 1962).

Kimball, Arthur. *Rational Fictions: A Study of Charles Brockden Brown,* 154-157, 171-185.

Ringe, Donald A. *Charles Brockden Brown,* 65-85.

CLARA HOWARD

Ringe, Donald A. *Charles Blockden Brown,* 65-85.

EDGAR HUNTLEY

Fiedler, Leslie A. *Love and Death in the American Novel,* 143-147.

Kimball, Arthur. *Rational Fictions: A Study of Charles Brockden Brown,* 103-114.

Ringe, Donald A. *Charles Brockden Brown,* 86-107.

JANE TALBOT

Ringe, Donald A. *Charles Brockden Brown,* 120-128.

ORMOND

Davies, Rosemary Reeves. "Charles Brockden Brown's *Ormond:* A

Possible Influence Upon Shelly's Conduct," *Philological Quarterly* XLIII (Jan 1964) , 133-137.

Fiedler, Leslie A. *Love and Death in the American Novel,* 136-137.

Kimball, Arthur. *Rational Fictions: A Study of Charles Brockden Brown,* 115-124.

Ringe, Donald A. *Charles Brockden Brown,* 49-64.

STEPHEN CALVERT

Ringe, Donald A. *Charles Brockden Brown,* 108-113.

WIELAND

Fiedler, Leslie A. *Love and Death in the American Novel,* 134-136.

Garrow, Scott. "Character Transformation in *Wieland," Southern Quarterly* IV (Apr 1966) , 308-318.

Kimball, Arthur. "A Closet Shut from Light," *Rational Fictions: A Study of Charles Brockden Brown,* 44-74.

Kirkham, E. Bruce. "A Note on *Wieland," American Notes & Queries* V (Feb 1967) , 86-87.

Manly, William M. "The Importance of Point of View in Brockden Brown's *Wieland," American Literature* XXXV (Nov 1963) , 311-321.

Ringe, Donald A. *Charles Brockden Brown,* 25-48.

Ziff, Larzer. "A Reading of *Wieland," PMLA* LXXVII (Mar 1962) , 51-57.

GENERAL

Bernard, Kenneth. "Charles Brockden Brown and the Sublime," *Personalist* XLV (Spring 1964) , 235-249.

Bulgheroni, Marisa. "Charles Brockden Brown Tra Il Romanzo E La Storia," *Studi Americani* X (1964) , 57-69.

Fiedler, Leslie A. *Love and Death in the American Novel,* 73-80, 106-148.

Hemenway, Robert. "Brockden Brown's Twice Told Insanity Tale," *American Literature* 40 (May 1968) , 211-215.

————. "Fiction in the Age of Jefferson: The Early American Novel as Intellectual Document," *Micontinent American Studies Journal* IX (Spring 1968) , 91-102.

Hirsch, David H. "Charles Brockden Brown as a Novelist of Ideas," *Books at Brown* XX (1965) , 165-184.

Kimball, Arthur. *Rational Fictions: A Study of Charles Brockden Brown.*

BROWN, CHARLES BROCKDEN, Continued

————. "Savages and Savagism: Brockden Brown's Dramatic Irony," *Studies in Romanticism* VI (Summer 1967), 214-225.

Ringe, Donald A. *Charles Brockden Brown.*

Strozier, Robert. "*Wieland* and Other Romances: Horror in Parentheses," *Emerson Society Quarterly* 50 (I Quarter 1968), 24-29.

Wager, Willis. *American Literature: A World View,* 53-56.

Weber, Alfred. "Essays und Rezensionen von Charles Brockden Brown," *Jahrbuch Für Amerikastudien* 6 (1961), 168-330.

BIBLIOGRAPHY

Green, David Bonnell. "Charles Brockden Brown, America's First Important Novelist: A Check List of Biography and Criticism," *Papers of the Bibliographical Society of America* LX (Jul-Sept 1966), 349-363.

Kimball, Arthur. *Rational Fictions: A Study of Charles Brockden Brown,* 229-238.

Ringe, Donald A. *Charles Brockden Brown,* 151-155.

BROWN, WILLIAM HILL

THE POWER OF SYMPATHY

Brown, Herbert. Introduction, *The Power of Sympathy* (Chester, Pennsylvania, 1961).

BUCK, PEARL

THE GOOD EARTH

Doyle, Paul A. *Pearl S. Buck,* 36-48.

A HOUSE DIVIDED

Doyle, Paul A. *Pearl S. Buck,* 64-70.

THE MOTHER

Doyle, Paul A. *Pearl S. Buck,* 70-75.

SONS

Doyle, Paul A. *Pearl S. Buck,* 57-64.

GENERAL

Doyle, Paul A. *Pearl S. Buck.*

Thompson, Dody Weston. "Pearl Buck," *American Winners of the Nobel Literary Prize,* 85-110.

BIBLIOGRAPHY

Doyle, Paul A. *Pearl S. Buck,* 169-170.

BUECHNER, FREDERICK

A LONG DAY'S DYING
Hassan, Ihab. *Radical Innocence: Studies in the Contemporary American Novel,* 153-161.
THE RETURN OF ANSEL GIBBS
Blotner, Joseph. *The Modern American Political Novel,* 330-334.

BURDICK, EUGENE

THE NINTH WAVE
Milne, Gordon. *The American Political Novel,* 116-118.

BURDICK, EUGENE and WILLIAM J. LEDERER

THE UGLY AMERICAN
Beerman, Hans. *"The Ugly American:* Two Views; European Reflections," *Midwest Quarterly* I (Winter 1960) , 194-198.
Page, Alex. "Pakistan's Hemingway," *Antioch Review* XXIII (Summer 1963) , 203-211.
Swisher, Earl. *"The Ugly American:* Two Views, in the Far East," *Midwest Quarterly* I (Winter 1960) , 184-193.

BURGESS, GELETT

GENERAL
Backus, Joseph M. "Gelett Burgess and Names for Characters," *Names* 9 (Jun 1961) , 95-107.
————. " 'I Never Done a Burgess!': Three Unpublished Letters from Booth Tarkington Touched off by His Use of a Name," *Names* 12 (Sept-Dec 1964) , 137-153.

BURROUGHS, EDGAR RICE

JOHN CARTER TRILOGY
Flautz, John T. "An American Demagogue in Barsoom," *Journal of Popular Culture* I (Winter 1967) , 263-275.
GENERAL
Maloff, Saul. "Tarzan's First Love," *New York Times Book Review* 73 (Dec 22, 1968) , 2, 14.

NAKED LUNCH

Kostelanetz, Richard. "From Nightmare to Serendipity: A Retrospective Look at William Burroughs," *Twentieth Century Literature* XI (Oct 1965) , 123-130.

Mailer, Norman, Allen Ginsberg and others. "The Boston Trial of 'Naked Lunch,' " *Evergreen Review* 36 (Jun 1965) , 40-49, 87-88.

McCarthy, Mary. "Burroughs' *Naked Lunch*," *Encounter* XX (Apr 1963) , 92-98.

McConnell, Frank D. "William Burroughs and the Literature of Addiction," *Massachusetts Review* VIII (Autumn 1967) , 665-680.

Peterson, R. G. "A Picture is a Fact: Wittgenstein and *The Naked Lunch*," *Twentieth Century Literature* XII (Jul 1966) , 78-86.

NOVA EXPRESS

Lodge, David. "Objections to William Burroughs," *Critical Quarterly* 8 (Autumn 1966) , 203-212.

THE TICKET THAT EXPLODED

Solotaroff, Theodore. "The Algebra of Need," *New Republic* 157 (Aug 5, 1967) , 29-34.

GENERAL

Burroughs, W. S. "The Literary Techniques of Lady Sutton-Smith," *Times Literary Supplement* 63 (Aug 6, 1964) , 682.

Hassan, Ihab. "The Subtracting Machine: The Work of William Burroughs," *Critique* VI (Spring 1963) , 4-23. ·

Knickerbocker, Conrad. "An Interview with William Burroughs: The Art of Fiction XXXVI," *Paris Review* IX No. 31 (Fall 1965) , 13-49.

Manganotti, Donatella. "William Burroughs," *Studi Americani* VIII (1962) , 245-287.

McLuhan, Marshall. "Notes on Burroughs," *Nation* 199 (Dec. 28, 1964) , 517-519.

Michelson, Peter. "Beardsley, Burroughs, Decadence, and the Poetics of Obscenity," *Tri-Quarterly* 12 (Spring 1968) , 139-155.

Phillips, William. "The New Immoralists," *Commentary* XXXIX (Apr 1965) , 66-69.

Tanner, Tony. "The New Demonology," *Partisan Review* XXXIII (Fall 1966) , 547-572.

CABELL, JAMES BRANCH

CHIVALRY

Davis, Joe Lee. *James Branch Cabell,* 79-83.

Tarrant, Desmond. *James Branch Cabell: The Dream and the Reality,* 113-129.

THE CREAM OF THE JEST

Davis, Joe Lee. *James Branch Cabell,* 121-127.

Tarrant, Desmond. *James Branch Cabell: The Dream and the Reality,* 192-199.

Wells, Arvin R. *Jesting Moses: A Study in Cabellian Comedy,* 94-104.

THE EAGLE'S SHADOW

Davis, Joe Lee. *James Branch Cabell,* 121-127.

FIGURES OF EARTH

Davis, Joe Lee. *James Branch Cabell,* 66-72.

Tarrant, Desmond. *James Branch Cabell: The Dream and the Reality,* 77-101.

Wells, Arvin R. *Jesting Moses: A Study in Cabellian Comedy,* 109-118.

THE FIRST GENTLEMAN OF AMERICA

Davis, Joe Lee. *James Branch Cabell,* 135-141.

Tarrant, Desmond. *James Branch Cabell: The Dream and the Reality,* 28-29, 262-268.

HAMLET HAD AN UNCLE

Davis, Joe Lee. *James Branch Cabell,* 135-141.

Tarrant, Desmond. *James Branch Cabell. The Dream and the Reality,* 256-263.

THE HIGH PLACE

Tarrant, Desmond. *James Branch Cabell: The Dream and the Reality,* 151-159.

JURGEN

Davis, Joe Lee. *James Branch Cabell,* 88-94.

Tarrant, Desmond. *James Branch Cabell: The Dream and the Reality,* 26-29, 86-89, 129-145.

Wells, Arvin R. *Jesting Moses: A Study in Cabellian Comedy,* 109-118.

MUSIC FROM BEHIND THE MOON

Tarrant, Desmond. *James Branch Cabell: The Dream and the Reality,* 107-113.

THE SILVER STALLION

Rubin, Louis D., Jr. "Two in Richmond: Ellen Glasgow and James Branch Cabell," *The Curious Death of the Novel: Essays in American Literature,* 172-176.

Tarrant, Desmond. *James Branch Cabell: The Dream and the Reality*, 95-101.

GENERAL

Canary, Robert H. "Cabell's Dark Comedies," *Mississippi Quarterly* XXI (Spring 1968) , 83-92.

————. "James Branch Cabell and the Comedy of Skeptical Conservatism," *Midcontinent American Studies Journal* VI (Spring 1965) , 52-60.

Colum, Padraic and Margaret Freeman Cabell, editors. *Between Friends: Letters of James Branch Cabell and Others.*

Davis, Joe Lee. *James Branch Cabell.*

Durham, Frank. "The Author Who Died Twice: James Branch Cabell," *Georgia Review* XVI (Summer 1962) , 162-168.

Godshalk, William Leigh. "James Branch Cabell at William and Mary: The Education of a Novelist," *William and Mary Review* V (Spring 1967) , 1-10.

McCollum, Nancy Minter. "Glasgow's and Cabell's Comedies of Virginia," *Georgia Review* XVIII (Summer 1964) , 236-241.

Parks, Edd Winfield. "James Branch Cabell," *Mississippi Quarterly* XX (Spring 1967) , 97-102.

Rubin, Louis D., Jr. "Two in Richmond: Ellen Glasgow and James Branch Cabell," *The Curious Death of the Novel: Essays in American Literature*, 168-180.

Schlegel, Dorothy B. "Cabell and His Critics," Richard K. Meeker, ed., *The Dilemma of the Southern Writer*, 119-142.

————. "James Branch Cabell and Southern Romanticism," *Southern Writers: Appraisals in Our Time*, 124-141.

Tarrant, Desmond. *James Branch Cabell: The Dream and the Reality.*

Wells, Arvin R. *Jesting Moses: A Study in Cabellian Comedy.*

BIBLIOGRAPHY

Davis, Joe Lee. *James Branch Cabell*, 162-166.

CABLE, GEORGE WASHINGTON

DR. 3EVIER

Butcher, Philip. *George W. Cable*, 65-66, 68-77.

Turner, Arlin. "*Dr. Sevier*," *George W. Cable: A Biography*, 160-170.

CABLE, GEORGE WASHINGTON, Continued

THE GRANDISSIMES

Butcher, Philip. "Cable to Boyesen on *The Grandissimes*," *American Literature* 40 (Nov 1968), 391-394.

————. *George W. Cable*, 45-56.

Martin, Jay. *Harvests of Change. American Literature 1865-1914*, 100-105.

Mehta, R. N. "*The Grandissimes:* 'A Minor Masterpiece,'" *Literary Criterion* VI (Summer 1964), 16-22.

Turner, Arlin. "*The Grandissimes*," *George W. Cable: A Biography*, 89-104.

JOHN MARCH, SOUTHERNER

Butcher, Philip. *George W. Cable*, 114-127.

Rubin, Louis D., Jr. "The Road To Yoknapatawpha: George W. Cable and *John March, Southerner*," *The Faraway Country: Writers of the Modern South*, 21-42.

GENERAL

Butcher, Philip. *George W. Cable*.

Edstrom, Kjell. *George Washington Cable: A Study of His Early Life and Work*.

Pugh, Griffith T. "George Washington Cable," *Mississippi Quarterly* XX (Spring 1967), 69-76.

Turner, Arlin. *George W. Cable: A Biography*.

————. *Mark Twain and George W. Cable: The Record of a Literary Friendship*.

BIBLIOGRAPHY

Butcher, Philip. *George W. Cable*, 178-181.

————. "George Washington Cable (1844-1925)," *American Literary Realism* 1 (Fall 1967), 20-25.

Turner, Arlin. *George W. Cable: A Biography*, 358-372.

CAHAN, ABRAHAM

YEKL; A TALE OF THE NEW YORK GHETTO

Marovitz, Sanford. "The Lonely New Americans of Abraham Cahan," *American Quarterly* XX (Summer 1968), 196-210.

CAIN, JAMES M.

THE POSTMAN ALWAYS RINGS TWICE

Oates, Joyce Carol. "Man Under Sentence of Death: The Novels of James M. Cain," *Tough Guy Writers of the Thirties,* 118-124.

GENERAL

Madden, David. "James Cain and the 'Pure' Novel," *University Review* XXX (Dec 1963) , 143-148.

————. "James M. Cain and the Tough Guy Novelists of the 30s," *The Thirties: Fiction, Poetry, Drama,* 63-71.

————. "James M. Cain: Twenty-Minute Egg of the Hard Boiled School," *Journal of Popular Culture* I (Winter 1967) , 178-192.

————. "The 'Pure' Novel and James Cain," *University Review* XXX (Mar 1964) , 235-239.

Oates, Joyce Carol. "Man Under Sentence of Death: The Novels of James M. Cain," *Tough Guy Writers of the Thirties,* 110-128.

Van Nostrand, Albert. *The Denatured Novel,* 125-132.

BIBLIOGRAPHY

Hagemann, E. R. and Philip C. Durham, "James M. Cain, 1922-1958: A Selected Checklist," *Bulletin of Bibliography* XXIII (Sept-Dec 1960) , 57-60.

CALDWELL, ERSKINE

GENERAL

Benedict, Stewart H. "Gallic Light on Erskine Caldwell," *South Atlantic Quarterly* LX (Summer 1961) , 390-397.

Burke, Kenneth. "Caldwell: Maker of Grotesques," *Psychoanalysis and American Fiction,* 245-253.

Caldwell, Erskine. "The Art, Craft, and Personality of Writing," *Texas Quarterly* VII (Spring 1964) , 37-43.

Gossett, Louise Y. *Violence in Recent Southern Fiction,* 16-29.

Hazel, Robert. "Notes on Erskine Caldwell," *South: Modern Southern Literature in Its Cultural Setting,* 323-332.

Van Nostrand, Albert. *The Denatured Novel,* 148-154.

CALDWELL, TAYLOR

THE DEVIL'S ADVOCATE

Blotner, Joseph. *The Modern American Political Novel,* 157-159.

CALISHER, HORTENSE

GENERAL

Calisher, Hortense. "The Writer: Being and Doing Or: Five Monday Nights from a Journal," *American Scholar* XXXVI (Winter 1966-67), 121-124.

Hahn, Emily. "In Appreciation of Hortense Calisher," *Wisconsin Studies in Contemporary Literature* VI (Summer 1965), 243-249.

CANTWELL, ROBERT

LAND OF PLENTY

Conroy, Jack. "Robert Cantwell's *Land of Plenty*," *Proletarian Writers of the Thirties,* 74-84.

CAPOTE, TRUMAN

BREAKFAST AT TIFFANY'S

Hassan, Ihab H. "Birth of a Heroine," *Prairie Schooner* XXXIV (Spring 1960), 78-83.

————. *Radical Innocence: Studies in the Contemporary American Novel,* 250-255.

THE GRASS HARP

Garcia Castro, Ramon. *Truman Capote: de la captura a la libertad,* 103-112.

Hassan, Ihab. *Radical Innocence: Studies in the Contemporary American Novel,* 245-250.

Hoffman, Frederick J. *The Art of Southern Fiction,* 123-124.

IN COLD BLOOD

Editors. "A Machine and Sympathy," *Times Literary Supplement* 65 (Mar 17, 1966), 223.

Editors. "Is That a Fact?" *Times Literary Supplement* 64 (Nov 25, 1965), 1061-1062.

Garrett, George. "Crime and Punishment in Kansas: Truman Capote's *In Cold Blood*," *Hollins Critic* III (Feb 1966), 1-12.

Kauffmann, Stanley. "Capote in Kansas," *New Republic* 154 (Jan 22, 1966), 19-23.

Wiegand, William. "The 'Non-fiction' Novel," *New Mexico Quarterly* XXXVII (Autumn 1967), 243-250.

Yurick, Sol. "Sob-Sister Gothic," *Nation* 202 (Feb 7, 1966), 158-160.

CAPOTE, TRUMAN, Continued

OTHER VOICES, OTHER ROOMS

Garcia Castro, Ramon. *Truman Capote: de la captura a la libertad,* 13-29.

Hassan, Ihab. *Radical Innocence: Studies in the Contemporary American Novel,* 239-245.

Hoffman, Frederick J. *The Art of Southern Fiction,* 118-122.

Malin, Irving. *New American Gothic,* 15-16, 50-52, 80-81, 107-109, 127-129.

Mengeling, Marvin E. "*Other Voices, Other Rooms:* Oedipus Between the Covers," *American Imago* XIX (Winter 1962), 361-374.

GENERAL

Eisinger, Chester E. *Fiction of the Forties,* 237-243.

Garcia Castro, Ramon. *Truman Capote: de la captura a la libertad.*

Gossett, Louise Y. "Violence in a Private World," *Violence in Recent Southern Fiction,* 145-158.

Hassan, Ihab. "The Daydream and Nightmare of Narcissus," *Wisconsin Studies in Contemporary Literature* 1 (Spring-Summer 1960), 5-21.

Moravia, Alberto. "Two American Writers," *Sewanee Review* LXVIII (Summer 1960), 477-481.

Plimpton, George, interviewer. "The Story Behind a Nonfiction Novel," *New York Times Book Review* 71 (Jan 16, 1966), 2-3, 38-43.

Rubin, Louis D., Jr. "The Curious Death of the Novel," *The Curious Death of the Novel: Essays in American Literature,* 14-18.

Schorer, Mark. "Carson McCullers and Truman Capote," *The World We Imagine: Selected Essays,* 285-296.

————. "McCullers and Capote: Basic Patterns," *The Creative Present,* 94-107.

BIBLIOGRAPHY

Garcia Castro, Ramon. *Truman Capote: de la captura a la libertad,* 125-126.

Wall, Richard J. and Carl L. Craycraft. "A Checklist of Works about Truman Capote," *Bulletin of the New York Public Library* LXXI (Mar 1967), 165-172.

ALEXANDER'S BRIDGE

Giannone, Richard. "Alexander's Bridge," *Music in Willa Cather's Fiction*, 59-67.

Randall, John H., III. *The Landscape and the Looking Glass: Willa Cather's Search for Value*, 38-42, 62-63.

DEATH COMES FOR THE ARCHBISHOP

Bloom, Edward A. and Lillian D. "On the Composition of a Novel," *Willa Cather and her Critics*, 323-355.

————. *Willa Cather's Gift of Sympathy*, 19-21, 197-236.

Charles, Sister Peter Damian, O. P. "*Death Comes For The Archbishop*: A Novel of Love and Death," *New Mexico Quarterly* XXXVI (Winter 1966-67), 389-403.

Gale, Robert L. "Cather's *Death Comes For the Archbishop*," *Explicator* XXI (May 1963), No. 75.

Giannone, Richard. "Death Comes for the Archbishop," *Music in Willa Cather's Fiction*, 185-200.

————. "The Southwest's Eternal Echo: Music in *Death Comes For The Archbishop*," *Arizona Quarterly* XXII (Spring 1966), 6-18.

Keeler, Clinton. "Narrative Without Accent: Willa Cather and Puvis de Chavannes," *American Quarterly* XVII (Spring 1965), 119-126.

Randall, John H., III. *The Landscape and the Looking Glass: Willa Cather's Search for Value*, 257-310.

Robinson, Cecil. *With the Ears of Strangers: The Mexican in American Literature*, 237-238, 265-267.

Stewart, D. H. "Cather's Mortal Comedy," *Queen's Quarterly* LXXIII (Summer 1966), 244-259.

A LOST LADY

Bloom, Edward A. and Lillian D. *Willa Cather's Gift of Sympathy*, 67-74.

Giannone, Richard. "A Lost Lady," *Music in Willa Cather's Fiction*, 141-149.

Priestley, J. B. Introduction, *A Lost Lady* (London, 1961).

Randall, John H., III. *The Landscape and the Looking Glass: Willa Cather's Search for Value*, 174-202.

LUCY GAYHEART

Giannone, Richard. *Music in Willa Cather's Fiction*, 214-231.

MY ÁNTONIA

Bloom, Edward A. and Lillian D. *Willa Cather's Gift of Sympathy*, 30-31, 60-62, 66-67.

Bowden, Edwin T. *The Dungeon of the Heart: Human Isolation and the American Novel,* 43-54.

Charles, Sister Peter Damian, O.P. *"My Ántonia:* A Dark Dimension," *Western American Literature II* (Summer 1967), 91-108.

Giannone, Richard. "My Ántonia," *Music in Willa Cather's Fiction,* 107-123.

Miller, James E. "My Ántonia: A Frontier Drama of Time," *Quests Surd and Absurd: Essays in American Literature,* 66-75.

Randall, John H., III. "Interpretation of *My Ántonia," Willa Cather and her Critics,* 272-322.

————. *The Landscape and the Looking Glass: Willa Cather's Search for Value,* 105-149.

Scholes, Robert E. "Hope and Memory in *My Ántonia," Shenandoah* XIV (Autumn 1962), 24-29.

Stegner, Wallace. "Willa Cather: *My Ántonia," The American Novel From James Fenimore Cooper to William Faulkner,* 144-153.

MY MORTAL ENEMY

Giannone, Richard. "My Mortal Enemy," *Music in Willa Cather's Fiction,* 169-183.

————. "Willa Cather's *My Mortal Enemy* and Bellini's *Norma," Neueren Sprachen* (Sept 1965), 401-411.

Randall, John H., III. *The Landscape and the Looking Glass: Willa Cather's Search for Value,* 234-240.

O PIONEERS!

Charles, Sister Peter Damian, O.P. "Love and Death in Willa Cather's *O Pioneers!," CLA Journal* IX (Dec 1965), 140-150.

Giannone, Richard. "O Pioneers!," *Music in Willa Cather's Fiction,* 69-81.

Lee, Robert Edson. *From West to East,* 131-134.

Randall, John H., III. *The Landscape and the Looking Glass: Willa Cather's Search for Value,* 64-105.

Schneider, Sister Lucy, C.S.J. *"O Pioneers!* in the Light of Willa Cather's 'Land Philosophy,' " *Colby Library Quarterly* VIII (Jun 1968), 55-70.

ONE OF OURS

Cooperman, Stanley. "Willa Cather and the Bright Face of Death," *Literature and Psychology* XIII (Summer 1963), 81-87.

————. *World War I and the American Novel,* 29-33, 51-53, 129-137.

Giannone, Richard. "One of Ours," *Music in Willa Cather's Fiction*, 125-140.

―――. *"One of Ours:* Willa Cather's Suppressed, Bitter Melody," *South Atlantic Quarterly* LXIV (Winter 1965), 72-86.

Randall, John H., III. *The Landscape and the Looking Glass: Willa Cather's Search for Value*, 160-174.

THE PROFESSOR'S HOUSE

Charles, Sister Peter Damian, O.P. *"The Professor's House:* An Abode of Love and Death," *Colby Library Quarterly* VIII (Jun 1968), 70-82.

Edel, Leon. "Willa Cather and the Professor's House," *Psychoanalysis and American Fiction*, 199-221.

Fox, Maynard. "Two Primitives: Huck Finn and Tom Outland," *Western American Literature* 1 (Spring 1966), 26-33.

Giannone, Richard. "Music in *The Professor's House*," *College English* XXVI (Mar 1965), 464-469.

―――. *"The Professor's House:* A Novel In Sonata-Form," *Colby Library Quarterly* VII (Jun 1965), 53-60.

―――. "The Professor's House," *Music in Willa Cather's Fiction*, 151-168.

Jobes, Lavon Mattes. "Willa Cather's *The Professor's House*," *University Review* XXXIV (Dec 1967), 154-160.

Priestley, J. B. Introduction, *The Professor's House* (London, 1961).

Randall, John H., III. *The Landscape and the Looking Glass: Willa Cather's Search for Value*, 203-234.

Schroeter, James. "Willa Cather and *The Professor's House*," *Willa Cather and her Critics*, 363-381.

―――. "Willa Cather and *The Professor's House*," Yale *Review* LIV (Summer 1965), 494-512.

SAPPHIRA AND THE SLAVE GIRL

Jobes, Lavon Mattes. "Willa Cather's Last Novel," *University Review* XXXIV (Oct 1967), 77-80.

Randall, John H., III. *The Landscape and the Looking Glass: Willa Cather's Search for Value*, 357-367.

SHADOWS ON THE ROCK

Giannone, Richard. "The Shadow on the Rock," *Music in Willa Cather's Fiction*, 201-212.

Murphy, John J. *"Shadows on the Rock:* Cather's Medieval Refuge," *Renascence* XV (Winter 1963), 76-78.

CATHER, WILLA, Continued

Randall, John H., III. *The Landscape and the Looking Glass: Willa Cather's Search for Value,* 310-341.

THE SONG OF THE LARK

Giannone, Richard. *Music in Willa Cather's Fiction,* 85-99.

Randall, John H., III. *The Landscape and the Looking Glass: Willa Cather's Search for Value,* 42-51.

GENERAL

Auchincloss, Louis. "Willa Cather," *Pioneers & Caretakers,* 92-122.

Baker, Bruce, II. "Nebraska Regionalism in Selected Works of Willa Cather," *Western American Literature* III (Spring 1968), 19-35.

Bennett, Mildred R. "How Willa Cather Chose Her Names," *Names* 10 (Mar 1962), 29-37.

Berthoff, Warner. *The Ferment of Realism: American Literature, 1884-1919,* 255-263.

Bloom, Edward A. and Lillian D. *Willa Cather's Gift of Sympathy.*

Curtin, William M. "Willa Cather: Individualism and Style," *Colby Library Quarterly* VIII (Jun 1968), 37-55.

Edel, Leon. *Willa Cather: The Paradox of Success.*

———. "Willa Cather: The Paradox of Success," *Willa Cather and her Critics,* 249-271.

Forman, Henry James. "Willa Cather: A Voice from the Prairie," *Southwest Review* XLVII (Summer 1962), 248-258.

Grant, Douglas. *Purpose and Place,* 142-147.

Helmick, Evelyn Thomas. "Myth in the Works of Willa Cather," *Midcontinent American Studies Journal* IX (Fall 1968), 63-69.

Jacks, L. V. "The Classics and Willa Cather," *Prairie Schooner* XXXV (Winter 1961-62), 289-296.

Lee, Robert Edson. *From West to East,* 112-135.

Miller, James E., Jr. "The Nebraska Encounter: Willa Cather and Wright Morris," *Prairie Schooner* XLI (Summer 1967), 165-167.

———. "Wharton and Cather: The Quest for Culture," *Quests Surd and Absurd: Essays in American Literature,* 76-83, 86-92.

Morgan, H. Wayne. "Willa Cather: The Artist's Quest," *Writers in Transition: Seven Americans,* 60-81.

Randall, John H., III. *The Landscape and the Looking Glass: Willa Cather's Search for Value.*

———. "Willa Cather and the Decline of Greatness," *The Twenties: Poetry and Prose,* 78-81.

CATHER, WILLA, Continued

————. "Willa Cather: The Middle West Revisited," *New Mexico Quarterly* XXXI (Spring 1961) , 25-36.

Schneider, Sister Lucy, C.S.J. "Artistry and Intuition: Willa Cather's 'Land-Philosophy,' " *South Dakota Review* 6 (Winter 1968-69) , 53-64.

Slote, Bernice. "Part One: First Principles," *The Kingdom of Art: Willa Cather's First Principles and Critical Statements.*

Thorberg, Raymond. "Willa Cather: From *Alexander's Bridge* to *My Antonia,*" *Twentieth Century Literature* VII (Jan 1962) , 147-158.

Thorp, Willard. *American Writing in the Twentieth Century,* 54-62.

Toler, Sister Colette, S. C. "Willa Cather's Vision of the Artist," *Personalist* XLV (Autumn 1964) , 503-523.

Van Ghent, Dorothy. *Willa Cather.*

Walker, Don D. "The Western Humanism of Willa Cather," *Western American Literature* I (Summer 1966) , 75-90.

Whipple, T. K. "Willa Cather," *Willa Cather and her Critics,* 35-51.

Willa Cather and Her Critics.

BIBLIOGRAPHY

Cary, Richard. "A Willa Cather Collection," *Colby Library Quarterly* VIII (Jun 1968) , 82-95.

Randall, John H., III. *The Landscape and the Looking Glass: Willa Cather's Search for Value,* 413-415.

Van Ghent, Dorothy. *Willa Cather,* 45-46.

Willa Cather and her Critics, 383-387.

CHANDLER, RAYMOND

THE BIG SLEEP

Durham, Philip. *Down These Mean Streets a Man Must Go: Raymond Chandler's Knight,* 32-35, 125-128.

PLAYBACK

Orel, Harold. "Raymond Chandler's Last Novel: Some Observations on the 'Private Eye,' " *Midcontinent American Studies Journal* II (Spring 1961) , 59-63.

GENERAL

Durham, Philip. *Down These Mean Streets a Man Must Go: Raymond Chandler's Knight.*

Elliott, George P. "Country Full of Blondes," *Nation* 190 (Apr 23, 1960) , 354-360.

CHANDLER, RAYMOND, Continued

Powell, Lawrence Clark. "Speaking of Books," *New York Times Book Review* 68 (Dec 22, 1963), 2.

Ruhm, Herbert. "Raymond Chandler: From Bloomsbury to the Jungle—and Beyond," *Tough Guy Writers of the Thirties*, 170-185.

Schickel, Richard. "Raymond Chandler, Private Eye," *Commentary* XXXV (Feb 1963), 158-161.

BIBLIOGRAPHY

Bruccoli, M. J. *Raymond Chandler: A Checklist.*

Durham, Philip. *Down These Mean Streets a Man Must Go: Raymond Chandler's Knight*, 148-168.

CHASE, MARY ELLEN

MARY PETERS

Westbrook, Perry D. *Mary Ellen Chase*, 71-79.

SILAS CROCKETT

Westbrook, Perry D. *Mary Ellen Chase*, 79-89.

WINDSWEPT

Westbrook, Perry D. *Mary Ellen Chase*, 100-108.

GENERAL

Chase, Mary Ellen. "My Novels about Maine," *Colby Library Quarterly* VI (Mar 1962), 14-20.

Duckett, Eleanor Shipley. "A Portrait: 1962," *Colby Library Quarterly* VI (Mar 1962), 1-4.

Iorio, John J. "Mary Ellen Chase and the Novel of Regional Crisis," *Colby Library Quarterly* VI (Mar 1962), 21-34.

Milbank, Helen Kirkpatrick. "Mary Ellen Chase: Teacher, Writer, Lecturer," *Colby Library Quarterly* VI (Mar 1962), 5-13.

Westbrook, Perry D. *Mary Ellen Chase.*

BIBLIOGRAPHY

Cary, Richard. "A Bibliography of the Published Writings of Mary Ellen Chase," *Colby Library Quarterly* VI (Mar 1962), 34-45.

Westbrook, Perry D. *Mary Ellen Chase*, 166-171.

CHEEVER, JOHN

THE WAPSHOT CHRONICLE

Hassan, Ihab. *Radical Innocence: Studies in the Contemporary American Novel*, 188-194.

CHEEVER, JOHN, Continued

THE WAPSHOT SCANDAL
Garrett, George. "John Cheever and the Charms of Innocence: The Craft of *The Wapshot Scandal*," *Hollins Critic* I⃰ (Apr 1964) , 1-12.

GENERAL
Bracher, Frederick. "John Cheever: A Vision of the World," *Claremont Quarterly* XI (Winter 1964) , 47-57.

————. "John Cheever and Comedy," *Critique* VI (Spring 1963) , 66-77.

Nichols, Lewis. "A Visit with John Cheever," *New York Times Book Review* 69 (Jan 5, 1964) , 28.

CHESNUTT, CHARLES WADDELL

GENERAL
Mason, Julian D., Jr. "Charles W. Chesnutt as Southern Author," *Mississippi Quarterly* XX (Spring 1967) , 77-89.

Render, Sylvia Lyons. "Tar Heelia in Chesnutt," *CLA Journal* IX (Sept 1965) , 39-50.

BIBLIOGRAPHY
Keller, Dean H. "Charles Waddell Chesnutt (1858-1932) ," *American Literary Realism* 3 (Summer 1968) , 1-4.

CHILD, LYDIA M.

GENERAL
Baer, Helene G. *The Heart is Like Heaven: The Life of Lydia Maria Child.*

Meltzer, Milton. *Tongue of Flame: The Life of Lydia Maria Child.*

BIBLIOGRAPHY
Baer, Helene G. *The Heart is Like Heaven: The Life of Lydia Maria Child*, 317-333.

Meltzer, Milton. *Tongue of Flame: The Life of Lydia Maria Child,* 197-202.

CHOPIN, KATE

AT FAULT
Leary, Lewis. "Kate Chopin's Other Novel," *Southern Literary Journal* I (Autumn 1968) , 60-74.

CHOPIN, KATE, Continued

THE AWAKENING

Arms, George. "Kate Chopin's *The Awakening* in the Perspective of Her Literary Career," *Essays on American Literature in Honor of Jay Hubbell,* 215-228.

Eble, Kenneth. Introduction, *The Awakening* (New York, 1964).

GENERAL

Ziff, Larzer. *The American 1890s: Life and Times of a Lost Generation,* 296-305.

CHURCHILL, WINSTON

CONISTON

Milne, Gordon. *The American Political Novel,* 87-95.

Titus, Warren I. "The Progressivism of the Muckrakers: A Myth Re-examined through Fiction," *Midcontinent American Studies Journal* I (Spring 1960), 10-16.

————. *Winston Churchill,* 68-76.

THE CRISIS

Titus, Warren I. *Winston Churchill,* 46-52.

THE CROSSING

Titus, Warren I. *Winston Churchill,* 53-59.

THE DWELLING-PLACE OF LIGHT

Titus, Warren I. *Winston Churchill,* 121-129.

THE INSIDE OF THE CUP

Titus, Warren I. *Winston Churchill,* 99-107.

MR. CREWE'S CAREER

Milne, Gordon. *The American Political Novel,* 87-95.

Titus, Warren I. "The Progressivism of the Muckrakers: A Myth Re-examined through Fiction," *Midcontinent American Studies Journal* I (Spring 1960), 10-16.

————. *Winston Churchill,* 77-83.

A MODERN CHRONICLE

Titus, Warren I. *Winston Churchill,* 86-94.

RICHARD CARVEL

Titus, Warren I. *Winston Churchill,* 36-44.

GENERAL

Schneider, Robert W. "Two Novelists and Progressivism: II—Novelist to a Generation: The American Winston Churchill," *Midwest Quarterly* III (Winter 1962), 163-179.

CHURCHILL, WINSTON, Continued

Titus, Warren I. *Winston Churchill.*
BIBLIOGRAPHY
Titus, Warren I. "Winston Churchill (1871-1947)," *American Literary Realism* 1 (Fall 1967), 26-31.
———. *Winston Churchill,* 163-168.

CLARK, WALTER VAN TILBURG

THE OX-BOW INCIDENT
Bates, Barclay W. "Clark's Man For All Seasons: The Achievement of Wholeness in *The Ox-Bow Incident*," *Western American Literature* III (Spring 1968), 37-49.
Westbrook, Max. "The Archetypal Ethic of *The Ox-Bow Incident*," *Western American Literature* 1 (Summer 1966), 105-118.
GENERAL
Clark, W. V. T. "The Western Novel—A Symposium," *South Dakota Review* 2 (Autumn 1964), 17-19.
Eisinger, Chester E. *Fiction of the Forties,* 310-324.
Herrmann, John. "The Death of the Artist as Hero," *South Dakota Review* 4 (Summer 1964), 51-55.
Lee, L. L. "Walter Van Tilburg Clark's Ambiguous American Dream," *College English* XXVI (Feb 1965), 382-387.
Milton, John R. "The Western Attitude: Walter Van Tilburg Clark," *Critique* II (Winter 1959), 57-73.
BIBLIOGRAPHY
Etulain, Richard. "Walter Van Tilburg Clark: A Bibliography," *South Dakota Review* 3 (Autumn 1965), 73-77.

COFFIN, ROBERT P. TRISTRAM

GENERAL
MacKay, Colin E. "The Novels of Robert P. Tristram Coffin," *Colby Library Quarterly* VII (Dec 1965), 151-161.
BIBLIOGRAPHY
Cary, Richard. "A Bibliography of Robert P. Tristram Coffin: Part I," *Colby Library Quarterly* VII (Dec 1965), 170-191; "Part II," (Jun 1966), 270-299; "Part III," (Dec 1966), 355-382.

CONNELL, EVAN S., JR.

GENERAL
Blaisdell, Gus. "After Ground Zero: The Writings of Evan S. Connell, Jr." *New Mexico Quarterly* XXXVI (Summer 1966), 181-207.

CONROY, JACK

THE DISINHERITED
Aaron, Daniel. Introduction, *The Disinherited* (New York, 1963).
Larsen, Erling. "Jack Conroy's *The Disinherited* or, The Way it Was," *Proleterian Writers of the Thirities,* 85-95.

COOKE, ROSE TERRY

GENERAL
Martin, Jay. *Harvests of Change. American Literature 1865-1914,* 139-142.

COOPER, JAMES FENIMORE

AFLOAT AND ASHORE
Dekker, George. *James Fenimore Cooper: The American Scott,* 204-212.
Philbrick, Thomas. *James Fenimore Cooper and the Development of American Sea Fiction,* 131-165.

THE BRAVO
Dekker, George. *James Fenimore Cooper: The American Scott,* 127-134.
Ringe, Donald A. Introduction, *The Bravo* (New York, 1963).

THE CRATER
Philbrick, Thomas. Introduction, *The Crater* (Cambridge, 1962).

THE DEERSLAYER
Anderson, Quentin. Introduction, *The Deerslayer* (Tarrytown, New York, 1962).
Beard, James Franklin. Introduction, *The Deerslayer* (New York, 1960).
Bowden, Edwin T. *The Dungeon of the Heart: Human Isolation and the American Novel,* 20-30.
Dekker, George. *James Fenimore Cooper: The American Scott,* 170-191.

COOPER, JAMES FENIMORE, Continued

House, Kay Seymour. *Cooper's Americans,* 315-326.

Krause, Sydney J. "Cooper's Literary Offences: Mark Twain in Wonderland," *New England Quarterly* XXXVIII (Sept 1965), 291-311.

Mizener, Arthur. "James Fenimore Cooper: *The Deerslayer,*" *Twelve Great American Novels,* 1-8.

Ringe, Donald A. *James Fenimore Cooper,* 84-90.

Walker, Warren S. *James Fenimore Cooper: An Introduction and Interpretation,* 32-36, 49-53.

Winterick, John T. Introduction, *The Deerslayer* (New York, 1961).

HOME AS FOUND

Dekker, George. *James Fenimore Cooper: The American Scott,* 153-160.

Gates, W. B. "A Neglected Satire on James Fenimore Cooper's *Home As Found,*" *American Literature* XXXV (Mar 1963), 13-21.

Leary, Lewis. Introduction, *Home as Found* (New York, 1961).

HOMEWARD BOUND

Ross, Morton L. "Captain Truck and Captain Boomer," *American Literature* XXXVII (Nov 1965), 316.

JACK TIER

Philbrick, Thomas. *James Fenimore Cooper and the Development of American Sea Fiction,* 203-209.

THE LAST OF THE MOHICANS

Brooks, Van Wyck. Introduction, *The Last of the Mohicans* (Tarrytown, New York, 1967).

Darnell, Donald. "Uncas as Hero: The *Ubi Sunt* Formula in *The Last of the Mohicans,*" *American Literature* XXXVII (Nov 1965), 259-266.

Fiedler, Leslie A. *Love and Death in the American Novel,* 197-206.

French, David P. "James Fenimore Cooper and Fort William Henry," *American Literature* XXXII (Mar 1960), 28-38.

Heller, Louis G. "Two Pequot Names in American Literature," *American Speech* XXXVI (Feb 1961), 54-57.

House, Kay Seymour. *Cooper's Americans,* 277-293.

Philbrick, Thomas. "The Sources of Cooper's Knowledge of Fort William Henry," *American Literature* XXXVI (May 1964), 209-214.

MILES WALLINGFORD

House, Kay Seymour. *Cooper's Americans,* 219-232.

THE OAK OPENINGS

House, Kay Seymour. *Cooper's Americans,* 249-260.

COOPER, JAMES FENIMORE, Continued

THE PATHFINDER

Berger, Thomas. Afterword, *The Pathfinder* (New York, 1961) .

Bush, Sargent, Jr. "Charles Cap of *The Pathfinder:* A Foil to Cooper's Views on the American Character in the 1840's," *Nineteenth-Century Fiction* XX (Dec 1965) , 267-273.

Dekker, George. *James Fenimore Cooper: The American Scott,* 161-169.

————. "*The Pathfinder:* Leatherstocking in Love," *British Association for American Studies Bulletin* 10 (Jun 1965) , 40-47.

House, Kay Seymour. *Cooper's Americans,* 306-315.

THE PILOT

Philbrick, Thomas. *James Fenimore Cooper and the Development of American Sea Fiction,* 52-54, 81-83, 127-128.

THE PIONEERS

Bercovitch, Sacvan. "Huckleberry Bumppo: A Comparison of '*Tom Sawyer*' and '*The Pioneers,*'" *Mark Twain Journal* XIV (Summer 1968) , 1-4.

Dekker, George. *James Fenimore Cooper: The American Scott,* 43-63.

House, Kay Seymour. *Cooper's Americans,* 263-277, 303-307.

————. "James Fenimore Cooper: *The Pioneers,*" *The American Novel from James Fenimore Cooper to William Faulkner,* 1-12.

Philbrick, Thomas. "Cooper's *The Pioneers:* Origins and Structure," *PMLA* LXXIX (Dec 1964) , 579-593.

Ringe, Donald A. *James Fenimore Cooper,* 32-37.

Robinson, E. Arthur. "Conservation in Cooper's *The Pioneers,*" *PMLA* LXXXII (Dec 1967) , 564-578.

THE PRAIRIE

Bier, Jesse. "Lapsarians on *The Prairie:* Cooper's Novel," *Texas Studies in Literature and Language* IV (Spring 1962) , 49-57.

Dekker, George. *James Fenimore Cooper: The American Scott,* 89-103, 169-174.

Fackler, Herbert V. "Cooper's Pawnees," *American Notes & Queries* VI (Oct 1967) , 21-22.

House, Kay Seymour. *Cooper's Americans,* 293-305.

Ringe, Donald A. "Man and Nature in Cooper's *The Prairie,*" *Nineteenth-Century Fiction* XV (Mar 1961) , 313-323.

Wasserstrom, William. "Cooper, Freud and the Origins of Culture," *American Imago* XVII (Winter 1960) , 423-437.

COOPER, JAMES FENIMORE, Continued

————. "Cooper, Freud and the Origins of Culture," *Leatherstocking and the Critics*, 104-113.

————. "The Origins of Culture: Cooper and Freud," *Psychoanalysis and American Fiction*, 47-60.

THE RED ROVER

House, Kay Seymour. *Cooper's Americans*, 192-200.

Philbrick, Thomas. *James Fenimore Cooper and the Development of American Sea Fiction*, 51-75.

Walker, Warren. Introduction, *The Red Rover* (Lincoln, Nebraska, 1963).

SATANSTOE

Bier, Jesse. "The Bisection of Cooper: *Satanstoe* as Prime Example," *Texas Studies in Literature and Language* IX (Winter 1968), 511-521.

Dekker, George. *James Fenimore Cooper: The American Scott*, 218-227.

Hough, Robert L. Introduction, *Satanstoe* (Lincoln, Nebraska, 1962).

Pickering, James H. "*Satanstoe*: Cooper's Debt to William Dunlap," *American Literature* XXXVIII (Jan 1967), 468-477.

THE SEA LIONS

Philbrick, Thomas. *James Fenimore Cooper and the Development of American Sea Fiction*, 209-259.

Walker, Warren. Introduction, *The Sea Lions* (Lincoln, Nebraska, 1965).

THE SPY

House, Kay Seymour. *Cooper's Americans*, 206-216.

Hubbell, Jay B. *Southern Life in Fiction*, 47-48.

Marpurgo, J. E. Introduction, *The Spy* (New York, 1968).

Walker, Warren. Introduction, *The Spy* (New York, 1960).

————. *James Fenimore Cooper: An Introduction and Interpretation*, 12-13, 22-29.

THE WATER-WITCH

Dekker, George. *James Fenimore Cooper: The American Scott*, 116-126.

House, Kay Seymour. *Cooper's Americans*, 94-103.

Philbrick, Thomas. *James Fenimore Cooper and the Development of American Sea Fiction*, 70-77, 81-83.

THE WEPT OF WISH-TON-WISH

Dekker, George. *James Fenimore Cooper: The American Scott*, 76-83.

COOPER, JAMES FENIMORE, Continued

House, Kay Seymour. *Cooper's Americans,* 120-130.

GENERAL

Abcarian, Richard. "Cooper's Critics and the Realistic Novel," *Texas Studies in Literature and Language* VIII (Spring 1966), 33-41.

Beard, James Franklin, (ed.). *The Letters and Journals of James Fenimore Cooper.*

Clavel, Marcel. "Le 'Cooper Revival' Aux États-Unis," *Études Anglaises* XV (Jan-Mar 1962), 36-45.

Collins, Frank M. "Cooper and the American Dream," *PMLA* LXXXI (Mar 1966), 79-94.

Dekker, George. *James Fenimore Cooper: The American Scott.*

Fiedler, Leslie A. "James Fenimore Cooper and the Historical Romance," *Leatherstocking and the Critics,* 97-103.

————. *Love and Death in the American Novel,* 149-212.

Folsom, James K. "James Fenimore Cooper: The Materials of a Western Story," *The American Western Novel,* 36-59.

Fussell, Edwin. "The Leatherstocking Tales of James Fenimore Cooper," *Frontier: American Literature and the American West,* 27-68.

Grant, Douglas. *Purpose and Place,* 14-20.

House, Kay Seymour. *Cooper's Americans.*

Howard, David. "James Fenimore Cooper's *Leatherstocking Tales:* 'without a cross,'" *Tradition and Tolerance in Nineteenth Century Fiction: Critical Essays on Some English and American Novels,* 9-54.

Jones, Howard Mumford. *Belief and Disbelief in American Literature,* 39-47.

Kaul, A. N. "James Fenimore Cooper: The History and Myth of American Civilization," *The American Vision: Actual and Ideal Society in Nineteenth Century Fiction,* 84-138.

————. "Washington and Natty Bumppo," *Leatherstocking and the Critics,* 134-137.

Kurtz, Kenneth. "Emerson and Cooper: American Versions of the Heroic," *Emerson Society Quarterly* 42 (I Quarter 1966), 1-8.

Lanzinger, Klaus. *Die Epik in Amerikanischen Roman: Eine Studie zu James F. Cooper, Herman Melville, Frank Norris und Thomas Wolfe,* Studen zur Sprache und Literatur Amerikas, no. 1.

————. "James Fenimore Coopers progressive Haltung zur Westexpansion," *Neueren Sprachen* (Oct 1966), 456-470.

Leatherstocking and the Critics.

COOPER, JAMES FENIMORE, Continued

Maxwell, D. E. S. "Politics and Pastoral in Cooper," *American Fiction: The Intellectual Background,* 97-140.

McAleer, John J. "Biblical Analogy in the Leatherstocking Tales," *Leatherstocking and the Critics,* 123-134.

Milne, Gordon. *The American Political Novel,* 12-18.

Noble, David W. "Cooper, Leatherstocking and the Death of the American Adam," *American Quarterly* XVI (Fall 1964), 419-431.

————. *The Eternal Adam and the New World Garden,* 8-24.

O'Donnell, Charles. "Progress and Property: The Later Cooper," *American Quarterly* XIII (Fall 1961), 402-409.

Price, Lawrence Marsden. *The Reception of United States Literature in Germany,* 85-97.

Ringe, Donald A. "Chiaroscuro as an Artistic Device in Cooper's Fiction," *PMLA* LXVIII (Sept 1963), 349-357.

————. "Cooper's Last Novels, 1847-1850," *PMLA* (Dec 1960), 583-590.

————. "Cooper's Littlepage Novels: Change and Stability in American Society," *American Literature* XXXII (Nov 1960), 280-290.

————. *James Fenimore Cooper.*

Spiller, Robert E. "James Fenimore Cooper," *Six American Novelists of the Nineteenth Century,* 10-44.

————. *James Fenimore Cooper.*

Tuttleton, James W. "The New England Character in Cooper's Social Novels," *Bulletin of the New York Public Library* LXX (May 1966), 305-317.

Wager, Willis. *American Literature: A World View,* 62-67.

Walker, Warren S. "The Frontiersman as Recluse and Redeemer," *Leatherstocking and the Critics,* 113-122.

————. *James Fenimore Cooper: An Introduction and Interpretation.*

Woodress, James. "The Fortunes of Cooper in Italy," *Studi Americani* XI (1965), 53-76.

Wright, Nathalia. "The Fruits of Civilization: Cooper," *American Novelists in Italy: The Discoverers: Allston to James,* 115-137.

Zoellner, Robert H. "Conceptual Ambivalence in Cooper's Leatherstocking," *American Literature* XXXI (Jan 1960), 397-420.

————. "Fenimore Cooper: Alienated American," *American Quarterly* XIII (Spring 1961), 55-66.

COOPER, JAMES FENIMORE, Continued

BIBLIOGRAPHY

Barnes, Warner. "American First Editions At TxU XIII. James Fenimore Cooper (1789-1851)," *Library Chronicle of the University of Texas* VII (Summer 1962), 15-18.

House, Kay Seymour. *Cooper's Americans*, 331-340.

Leatherstocking and the Critics, 145-149.

Price, Lawrence Marsden. *The Reception of United States Literature in Germany*, 206-207.

Ringe, Donald A. *James Fenimore Cooper*, 165-171.

Six American Novelists of the Nineteenth Century, 229-231.

Spiller, Robert E. *James Fenimore Cooper*, 45-48.

Walker, Warren S. *James Fenimore Cooper: An Introduction and Interpretation*, 127-133.

COZZENS, JAMES GOULD

ASK ME TOMORROW

Maxwell, D. E. S. *Cozzens*, 27-34.

Mooney, Harry John, Jr. "*Ask Me Tomorrow*," *James Gould Cozzens: Novelist of Intellect*, 63-73.

BY LOVE POSSESSED

Mooney, Harry John, Jr. "*By Love Possessed*," *James Gould Cozzens: Novelist of Intellect*, 125-156.

Straumann, Heinrich. "The Quarrel About Cozzens or The Vagaries of Book Reviewing," *English Studies* XL (Aug 1959), 251-265.

Thompson, John. "Return of the Repressed," *Commentary* 46 (Sept 1968), 86-89.

Walcutt, Charles Child. *Man's Changing Mask: Modes and Methods of Characterization in Fiction*, 281-286.

CASTAWAY

Fowler, Alastair. "Isolation and Its Discontents," *Twentieth Century Literature* VI (Jul 1960), 51-64.

Mooney, Harry John, Jr. *James Gould Cozzens: Novelist of Intellect*, 17-26.

A CURE OF FLESH

Maxwell, D. E. S. *Cozzens*, 49-57.

GUARD OF HONOR

Maxwell, D. E. S. *Cozzens*, 92-102.

COZZENS, JAMES GOULD, Continued

Mizener, Arthur. "James Gould Cozzens: *Guard of Honor,*" *Twelve Great American Novels,* 160-176.

Mooney, Harry John, Jr. *"Guard of Honor,"* James Gould Cozzens: *Novelist of Intellect,* 99-124.

Stuckey, W. J. *The Pulitzer Prize Novels: A Critical Backward Look,* 143-151.

THE JUST AND THE UNJUST

Hicks, Granville. *James Gould Cozzens,* 23-28.

Maxwell, D. E. S. *Cozzens,* 81-92.

Mooney, Harry John, Jr. *"The Just and the Unjust,"* James Gould Cozzens: *Novelist of Intellect,* 75-97.

THE LAST ADAM

Lewis, R. B. "The Conflicts of Reality: Cozzens' *The Last Adam,"* *Seven Contemporary Authors,* 3-22.

Mooney, Harry John, Jr. *"The Last Adam,"* James Gould Cozzens: *Novelist of Intellect,* 27-46.

Ober, William B., M.D. "Compare and Contrast Sinclair Lewis's *Arrowsmith* with James Gould Cozzen's *The Last Adam,"* *Carleton Miscellany* IV (Fall 1963) , 101-110.

MEN AND BRETHREN

Maxwell, D. E. S. *Cozzens,* 61-69.

Mooney, Harry John, Jr. *"Men and Brethren,"* James Gould Cozzens: *Novelist of Intellect,* 47-61.

S.S. SAN PEDRO

Maxwell, D. E. S. *Cozzens,* 38-43.

Mooney, Harry John, Jr. *James Gould Cozzens: Novelist of Intellect,* 5-17.

GENERAL

Bracher, Frederick. "James Gould Cozzens: Humanist," *Claremont Quarterly* VII (Autumn 1959) , 5-21.

Eisinger, Chester E. *Fiction of the Forties,* 150-171.

Frohock, W. M. "Cozzens and His Critics: A Problem in Perspective," *Strangers To This Ground: Cultural Diversity in Contemporary American Writing,* 63-83.

Hamblen, Abigail Ann. "The Paradox of James Gould Cozzens," *Western Humanities Review* XIX (Autumn 1965) , 355-361.

Hicks, Granville. *James Gould Cozzens.*

Long, Richard A. "The Image of Man in James Gould Cozzens," *CLA Journal* X (Jun 1967) , 299-307.

COZZENS, JAMES GOULD, Continued

Maxwell, D. E. S. *Cozzens.*

Millgate, Michael. *American Social Fiction: James to Cozzens,* 181-194.

Mooney, Harry John, Jr. *James Gould Cozzens: Novelist of Intellect.*

Nobles, David W. *The Eternal Adam and the New World Garden,* 186-193.

Parrish, James A., Jr. "James Gould Cozzens Fights a War," *Arizona Quarterly* XVIII (Winter 1962), 335-340.

Scholes, Robert E. "The Commitment of James Gould Cozzens," *Arizona Quarterly* XVI (Summer 1960), 129-144.

BIBLIOGRAPHY

Hicks, Granville. *James Gould Cozzens,* 46-47.

Maxwell, D. E. S. *Cozzens,* 118-119.

Meriwether, James B. "The English Editions of James Gould Cozzens," *Studies in Bibliography* XV (1962), 207-217.

CRADDOCK, CHARLES EGBERT
(Mary Noailles Murfree)

WHERE THE BATTLE WAS FOUGHT

Shuman, R. Baird. "Mary Murfree's Battle," *Tennessee Studies in Literature* VI (1961), 33-37.

CRANE, STEPHEN

GEORGE'S MOTHER

Bassan, Maurice. "An Early Draft of *George's Mother,*" *American Literature* XXXVI (Jan 1965), 518-522.

Brennan, Joseph X. "The Imagery and Art of *George's Mother,*" *CLA Journal* IV (Dec 1960), 106-115.

Gibson, Donald B. *The Fiction of Stephen Crane,* 40-52.

Gullason, Thomas A. Introduction, *The Complete Novels of Stephen Crane* (New York, 1967), 77-82.

Solomon, Eric. *Stephen Crane: From Parody to Realism,* 47-67.

Stallman, R. W. *Stephen Crane: A Biography,* 204-217.

MAGGIE: A GIRL OF THE STREETS

Brennan, Joseph X. "Ironic and Symbolic Structure in Crane's *Maggie,*" *Nineteenth-Century Fiction* XVI (Mar 1962), 303-315.

Cady, Edwin H. *Stephen Crane,* 104-111.

Fitelson, David. "Stephen Crane's *Maggie* and Darwinism," *American Quarterly* XVI (Summer 1964) , 182-194.

Gibson, Donald B. *The Fiction of Stephen Crane,* 26-39.

Gullason, Thomas A. Introduction, *The Complete Novels of Stephen Crane* (New York, 1967) , 55-65.

————. "The First Known Review of Stephen Crane's 1893 *Maggie,"* *English Language Notes* V (Jun 1968) , 300-302.

Katz, Joseph. Introduction, *Maggie: A Girl of the Streets* (Gainesville, Florida, 1966) .

————. "The *Maggie* Nobody Knows," *Modern Fiction Studies* XII (Summer 1966) , 200-212.

Martin, Jay. *Harvests of Change. American Literature 1865-1914,* 57-59.

Overmyer, Janet. "The Structure of Crane's *Maggie,"* *University of Kansas City Review* XXIX (Oct 1962) , 71-72.

Pizer, Donald. Introduction, *Maggie* (San Francisco, 1968) .

————. "Stephen Crane's 'Maggie' and American Naturalism," *Criticism* VII (Spring 1965) , 168-175.

————. "Stephen Crane's *Maggie* and American Naturalism," *Realism and Naturalism in Nineteenth-Century American Literature,* 121-131.

————. "Stephen Crane's *Maggie* and American Naturalism," *Stephen Crane: A Collection of Critical Essays,* 110-117.

Sansom, William. Introduction, *Maggie: A Girl of the Streets* (London, 1966) .

Solomon, Eric. *Stephen Crane: From Parody to Realism,* 23-44.

Stallman, R. W. *The Houses That James Built,* 63-81.

————. *Stephen Crane: A Biography,* 66-86.

Stephen Crane's Maggie: Text and Context.

Ziff, Larzer. "Outstripping the Event: Crane's *Maggie,"* *Stephen Crane: A Collection of Critical Essays,* 106-109.

THE RED BADGE OF COURAGE

Albrecht, Robert C. "Content and Style in *The Red Badge of Courage,"* *College English* XXVII (Mar 1966) , 487-492.

Anderson, Warren D. "Homer and Stephen Crane," *Nineteenth-Century Fiction* XIX (Jun 1964) , 77-86.

————. "Homer and Stephen Crane," *Stephen Crane: A Collection of Critical Essays,* 146-149.

Bache, William B. *"The Red Badge of Courage* and 'The Short Happy

CRANE, STEPHEN, Continued

Life of Francis Macomber,'" *Western Humanities Review* XV (Winter 1961) , 83-84.

Berryman, John "Stephen Crane: *The Red Badge of Courage,"* *The American Novel From James Fenimore Cooper to William Faulkner,* 86-96.

Cady, Edwin H. *Stephen Crane,* 115-144.

Chase, Richard. Introduction, *The Red Badge of Courage and Other Writings* (Boston, 1960) .

Dillingham, William B. "Insensibility in *The Red Badge of Courage,"* *College English* XXV (Dec 1963) , 194-198.

Eby, Cecil D., Jr. "General Philip Kearny's 'Red Badge of Courage,' " *The Red Badge of Courage: An Annotated Text; Backgrounds and Sources; Essays in Criticism,* 184-186.

————. "Stephen Crane's 'Fierce Red Wafer,' " *English Language Notes* I (Dec 1963) , 128-130.

————. "The Source of Crane's Metaphor, 'Red Badge of Courage,' " *American Literature* XXXII (May 1960) , 204-207.

Fadiman, Clifton. Afterword, *The Red Badge of Courage* (New York, 1962) .

Fraser, John. "Crime and Forgiveness: *The Red Badge* in Time of War," *Criticism* IX (Summer 1967) , 243-256.

Fryckstedt, Olov W. "Cosmic Pessimism in *The Red Badge of Courage,"* *Stephen Crane: A Collection of Critical Essays,* 141-145.

Gibson, Donald B. "Crane's *The Red Badge of Courage,"* *Explicator* XXIV (Feb 1966) , No. 49.

————. *The Fiction of Stephen Crane,* 60-89.

Gullason, Thomas A. Introduction, *The Complete Novels of Stephen Crane* (New York, 1967) , 65-77.

Howarth, William L. *"The Red Badge of Courage* Manuscript: New Evidence for a Critical Edition," *Studies in Bibliography* XVIII (1965) , 229-247.

Hungerford, Harold R. " 'That Was at Chancellorsville': The Factual Framework of *The Red Badge of Courage,"* *American Literature* XXXIV (Jan 1963) , 520-531.

Johnson, George W. "Stephen Crane's Metaphor of Decorum," *PMLA* LXXVIII (June 1963) , 250-256.

Katz, Joseph. Introduction, *The Red Badge of Courage* (Gainesville, Florida, 1967) .

Klotz, Marvin. "Romance or Realism?: Plot, Theme, and Character in *The Red Badge of Courage*," *CLA Journal* VI (Dec 1962), 98-106.

LaFrance, Marston. "A Few Facts about Stephen Crane and 'Holland,'" *American Literature* XXXVII (May 1965), 195-202.

—————. "Stephen Crane's Private Fleming: His Various Battles," *Patterns of Commitment in American Literature*, 113-133.

Lavers, Norman. "Order in *The Red Badge of Courage*," *University Review* XXXII (Jun 1966), 287-295.

Lorch, Thomas M. "The Cyclical Structure of *The Red Badge of Courage*," *CLA Journal* X (Mar 1967), 229-238.

Lynn, Kenneth. Introduction, *The Red Badge of Courage* (Boston, Massachusetts, 1964).

Marcus, Mordecai. "The Unity of *The Red Badge of Courage*," *The Red Badge of Courage: Text and Criticism* (New York, 1960), 189-195.

Martin, Jay. *Harvests of Change. American Literature 1865-1914*, 62-65.

McDermott, John J. "Symbolism and Psychological Realism in *The Red Badge of Courage*," *Nineteenth-Century Fiction* XXIII (Dec 1968), 324-331.

Osborn, Neal J. "William Ellery Channing and *The Red Badge of Courage*," *Bulletin of the New York Public Library* LXIX (Mar 1965), 182-196.

Pelletier, Gaston. "*Red Badge* Revisited," *English Journal* 57 (Jan 1968), 24-25, 99.

Pizer, Donald. *Realism and Naturalism in Nineteenth-Century American Literature*, 24-30.

Pritchett, V. S. Introduction, *The Red Badge of Courage* (New York, 1960).

Rosch, William. Introduction, *The Red Badge of Courage* (New York, 1964).

Solomon, Eric. *Stephen Crane: From Parody to Realism*, 68-98.

—————. "Yet Another Source for *The Red Badge of Courage*," *English Language Notes* II (Mar 1965), 215-217.

Stallman, R. W. *The Houses That James Built*, 81-103.

—————. "Notes toward an Analysis of *The Red Badge of Courage*," *Stephen Crane: A Collection of Critical Essays*, 128-140.

—————. *Stephen Crane: A Biography*, 168-188.

Stone, Edward. "Introducing Private Smithers," *Georgia Review* XVI (Winter 1962), 442-445.

CRANE, STEPHEN, Continued

————. *Voices of Despair,* 55-57.

Tuttleton, James W. "The Imagery of *The Red Badge of Courage,"* *Modern Fiction Studies* VIII (Winter 1962-63) , 410-415.

Vanderbilt, Kermit and Daniel Weiss. "From Rifleman to Flagbearer: Henry Fleming's Separate Peace in *The Red Badge of Courage," Modern Fiction Studies* XI (Winter 1965-1966) , 371-380.

Weeks, Robert P. "The Power of the Tacit in Crane and Hemingway," *Modern Fiction Studies* VIII (Winter 1962-63) , 415-418.

Weiss, Daniel. "The Red Badge of Courage," *Psychoanalytic Review* 52 (Summer 1965) , 32-52; Part II (Fall 1965) , 130-154.

Westbrook, Max. "Stephen Crane and the Personal Universal," *Modern Fiction Studies* VIII (Winter 1962-63) , 351-360.

Wogan, Claudia C. "Crane's Use of Color in 'The Red Badge of Courage,' " *Modern Fiction Studies* VI (Summer 1960) , 168-172.

GENERAL

Berthoff, Warner. *The Ferment of Realism: American Literature, 1884-1919,* 227-235.

Cady, Edwin Harrison. "Stephen Crane and the Strenuous Life," *ELH* 28 (Dec 1961) , 376-382.

Cady, Edwin H. *Stephen Crane.*

Colvert, James B. "Stephen Crane's Magic Mountain," *Stephen Crane: A Collection of Critical Essays,* 95-105.

Denny, Neville. "Imagination and Experience in Stephen Crane," *English Studies in Africa* 9 (Mar 1966) , 28-42.

Gibson, Donald B. *The Fiction of Stephen Crane.*

Gilkes, Lillian. *Cora Crane: A Biography of Mrs. Stephen Crane.*

Grant, Douglas. *Purpose and Place,* 136-141.

Gullason, Thomas A. Introduction, *The Complete Novels of Stephen Crane* (New York, 1967) .

————. "The Jamesian Motif in Stephen Crane's Last Novels," *Personalist* XLII (Winter 1961) , 77-84.

————. "Thematic Patterns in Stephen Crane's Early Novels," *Nineteenth Century Fiction* XVI (Jun 1961) , 59-67.

Hagemann, E. R. "Stephen Crane Faces the Storms of Life," *Journal of Popular Culture* II (Winter 1968) , 347-360.

Hahn, Emily. *Romantic Rebels: An Informal History of Bohemianism in America,* 99-108.

Hicks, Granville. "The Short Story Was His Medium," *Saturday Review* 50 (July 22, 1967) , 31-32.

CRANE, STEPHEN, Continued

Hoffman, Daniel G. "Stephen Crane's Last Novel," *Bulletin of the New York Library* LXIV (Jun 1960), 337-343.

Johnson, George W. "Stephen Crane's Metaphor of Decorum," *Stephen Crane: A Collection of Critical Essays,* 67-79.

Katz, Joseph. "Stephen Crane, 'Samuel Carlton,' and a Recovered Letter," *Nineteenth-Century Fiction* XXIII (Sept 1968), 220-225.

Leaver, Florence. "Isolation in the Work of Stephen Crane," *South Atlantic Quarterly* LXI (Autumn 1962), 521-532.

Liebling, A. J. "The Dollars Damned Him," *Stephen Crane: A Collec-lection of Critical Essays,* 18-26.

Martin, Jay. *Harvests of Change. American Literature 1865-1914,* 55-70.

Milne, W. Gordon. "Stephen Crane: Pioneer in Technique," *Neueren Sprachen* (Jul 1959), 297-303.

Morgan, H. Wayne. "Stephen Crane: The Ironic Hero," *Writers in Transition: Seven Americans,* 1-22.

Noble, David W. *The Eternal Adam and the New World Garden,* 115-123.

Osborn, Neal J. "The Riddle in 'The Clan': A Key to Crane's Major Fiction?" *Bulletin of the New York Public Library* LXIX (Apr 1965), 247-258.

Perosa, Sergio. "Naturalism and Impressionism in Stephen Crane's Fiction," *Stephen Crane: A Collection of Critical Essays,* 80-94.

Pizer, Donald. "The Garland-Crane Relationship," *Huntington Library Quarterly* XXIV (Nov 1960), 75-82.

―――. *Realism and Naturalism in Nineteenth-Century American Literature,* 94-98, 114-120.

Randel, William. "From Slate to Emerald Green: More Light on Crane's Jacksonville Visit," *Nineteenth-Century Fiction* XIX (Mar 1965), 357-368.

―――. "Stephen Crane's Jacksonville," *South Atlantic Quarterly* LXII (Spring 1963), 268-274.

Schneider, Robert W. "The Promethean Protest," *Five Novelists of the Progressive Era,* 60-111.

―――. "Stephen Crane and the Drama of Transition," *Midcontinent American Studies Journal* II (Spring 1961), 1-16.

Solomon, Eric. *Stephen Crane: From Parody to Realism.*

―――. *Stephen Crane in England: A Portrait of the Artist.*

―――. "Stephen Crane's War Stories," *Texas Studies in Literature and Language* III (Spring 1961), 67-80.

Stallman, R. W. Introduction, *Stephen Crane: Letters* (New York, 1960).

―――. *Stephen Crane: A Biography.*

Stone, Edward. "Crane and Zola," *English Language Notes* I (Sept 1963), 46-47.

Stronks, James B. "Stephen Crane's English Years: The Legend Corrected," *Papers of the Bibliographical Society of America* 57 (Jul-Sept 1963), 340-349.

Weimer, David R. *The City as Metaphor,* 52-64.

Wertheim, Stanley. "Stephen Crane and the Wrath of Jehova," *Literary Review* VII (Summer 1964), 499-508.

West, Ray B., Jr. "Stephen Crane: Author in Transition," *American Literature* XXXIV (May 1962), 215-228.

―――. "Stephen Crane: Author in Transition," *Critical Approaches to American Literature: Volume II, Walt Whitman to William Faulkner,* 166-178.

―――. "Stephen Crane: Author in Transition," *The Writer in the Room: Selected Essays,* 102-117.

Westbrook, Max. "Stephen Crane's Social Ethic," *American Quarterly* XIV (Winter 1962), 587-596.

Ziff, Larzer. "Outstripping the Event: Stephen Crane," *The American 1890s: Life and Times of a Lost Generation,* 185-205.

BIBLIOGRAPHY

Cady, Edwin H. *Stephen Crane,* 169-180.

Critical Approaches to American Literature: Volume II, Walt Whitman to William Faulkner, 336-337.

The Red Badge of Courage: An Annotated Text; Backgrounds and Sources; Essays in Criticism, 342-344.

Solomon, Eric. *Stephen Crane in England: A Portrait of the Artist,* 121-129.

Stallman, R. W. *Stephen Crane: A Biography,* 625-641.

Stephen Crane: A Collection of Critical Essays, 181-184.

CRAWFORD, FRANCIS MARION

GENERAL

Gale, Robert L. "Four Letters to Francis Marion Crawford from Theodore Roosevelt, Clyde Fitch, Julia Ward Howe, Henry James," *Literary Review* III (Spring 1960), 438-443.

CRAWFORD, FRANCIS MARION, Continued

Pilkington, John, Jr. *Francis Marion Crawford.*

CUMMINGS, *e.e.*

THE ENORMOUS ROOM

Friedman, Norman. *e.e. Cummings,* 22-35.

Smith, David E. *"The Enormous Room* and *The Pilgrim's Progress,"* *Twentieth Century Literature* XI (Jul 1965), 67-75.

CURTIS, GEORGE WILLIAM

TRUMPS

Milne, Gordon. *The American Political Novel,* 19-22.

DAHLBERG, EDWARD

BOTTOM DOGS

Chametzky, Jules. "Edward Dahlberg, Early and Late," *Proletarian Writers of the Thirties,* 65-69.

Dahlberg, Edward. "Preface to *Bottom Dogs,* 1961," *Edward Dahlberg: American Ishmael of Letters,* 51-53.

THE FLEA OF SODOM

Williams, William Carlos. *"The Flea of Sodom,"* *Edward Dahlberg: American Ishmael of Letters,* 55-62.

GENERAL

Billings, Harold. "Introduction: Cabalist in the Wrong Season," *Edward Dahlberg: American Ishmael of Letters,* 15-25.

Boyle, Kay. "A Man in the Wilderness," *Edward Dahlberg: American Ishmael of Letters,* 159-162.

Carroll, Paul. "An Introduction to Edward Dahlberg," *Edward Dahlberg: American Ishmael of Letters,* 149-158.

─────. Introduction, *The Edward Dahlberg Reader* (New York, 1967).

Chametzky, Jules. "Edward Dahlberg, Early and Late," *Proletarian Writers of the Thirties,* 64-73.

Dahlberg, Edward. "The Expatriates: A Memoir," *Texas Quarterly* VI (Summer 1963), 50-55.

Hassan, Ihab. "The Sorrows of Edward Dahlberg," *Massachusetts Review* V (Spring 1964), 457-461.

DAHLBERG, EDWARD, Continued

Herbst, Josephine. "Edward Dahlberg's *Because I Was Flesh*," *Edward Dahlberg: American Ishmael of Letters,* 95-109.

————. "Edward Dahlberg's *Because I Was Flesh*," *Southern Review* I (Apr 1965), 337-351.

Kazin, Alfred. "The Eloquence of Failure," *Edward Dahlberg: American Ishmael of Letters,* 111-115.

Kindrick, Robert. "The Benevolent Scourge: Edward Dahlberg and Modern American Letters," *Edward Dahlberg: American Ishmael of Letters,* 135-147.

Moramarco, Fred. "An Interview with Edward Dahlberg," *Western Humanities Review* XX (Summer 1966), 249-253.

Unali, Lina Garegnani. "Introduzione A Edward Dahlberg," *Studi Americani* XI (1965), 271-308.

Williams, Jonathan. "Edward Dahlberg's Book of Lazarus," *Edward Dahlberg: American Ishmael of Letters,* 27-42.

————. "Edward Dahlberg's Book of Lazarus," *Texas Quarterly* VI (Summer 1963), 34-49.

BIBLIOGRAPHY

Edward Dahlberg: American Ishmael of Letters, 163-167.

DANA, RICHARD H.

TWO YEARS BEFORE THE MAST

Kemble, John H. Introduction, *Two Years Before the Mast* (Los Angeles, California, 1964).

Lucid, Robert F. "*Two Years Before the Mast* as Propaganda," *American Quarterly* XII (Fall 1960), 392-403.

McFee, William. Introduction, *Two Years Before the Mast* (New York, 1966).

Shapiro, Samuel. "The History of a Book," *Richard Henry Dana, Jr.,* 187-198.

DAVIS, H. L.

HONEY IN THE HORN

Brunvand, Jan Harold. "*Honey in the Horn* and 'Acres of Clams': The Regional Fiction of H. L. Davis," *Western American Literature* II (Summer 1967), 135-145.

DAVIS, H. L., Continued

Lauber, John. "A Western Classic: H. L. Davis' *Honey in the Horn*," *Western Humanities Review* XVI (Winter 1962) , 85-86.
GENERAL
Bryant, Paul T. "H. L. Davis: Viable Uses for the Past," *Western American Literature* III (Spring 1968) , 3-18.
Jones, Philip L. "The West of H. L. Davis," *South Dakota Review* 6 (Winter 1968-69) , 72-84.

DAVIS, REBECCA HARDING

GENERAL
Austin, James C. "Success and Failure of Rebecca Harding Davis," *Midcontinent American Studies Journal* III (Spring 1962) , 44-49.

DAVIS, RICHARD HARDING

GENERAL
Osborn, Scott C. "Richard Harding Davis: Critical Battleground," *American Quarterly* XII (Spring 1960) , 84-92.
Ziff, Larzer. "The Poles of Violence: Ambrose Bierce and Richard Harding Davis," *The American 1890s: Life and Times of a Lost Generation,* 173 184.
BIBLIOGRAPHY
Elliott, Fannie Mae and others. *The Barrett Library: Richard Harding Davis: A Checklist of Printed and Manuscript Works.*

DEAL, BORDEN

GENERAL
Deal, Borden. "Storytelling as Symbolism," *Southwest Review* LIII (Summer 1968) , 293-298.

DE FOREST, JOHN WILLIAM

HONEST JOHN VANE
Levy, Leo B. "Naturalism in the Making: De Forest's *Honest John Vane*," *New England Quarterly* XXXVII (Mar 1964) , 89-98.
Light, James F. *John William De Forest,* 138-144.
Milne, Gordon. *The American Political Novel,* 45-52.

DE FOREST, JOHN WILLIAM, Continued

Rubin, Joseph Jay. Introduction, *Honest John Vane* (State College, Pennsylvania, 1960) .

KATE BEAUMONT

Light, James F. *John William De Forest,* 121-129.

Rubin, Joseph J. Introduction, *Kate Beaumont* (State College, Pennsylvania, 1963) .

MISS RAVENEL'S CONVERSION FROM SECESSION TO LOYALTY

Light, James F. *John William De Forest,* 87-97.

Simpson, Claude M., Jr. "John W. De Forest: *Miss Ravenel's Conversion," The American Novel From James Fenimore Cooper to William Faulkner,* 35-46.

PLAYING THE MISCHIEF

Light, James F. *John William De Forest,* 144-153.

Milne, Gordon. *The American Political Novel,* 52-57.

Rubin, Joseph J. Introduction, *Playing the Mischief* (State College, Pennsylvania, 1961) .

WETHEREL AFFAIR

Light, James F. *John William De Forest,* 129-138.

WITCHING TIMES

Light, James F. *John William De Forest,* 47-53.

GENERAL

Bergmann, Frank. "Mark Twain and the Literary Misfortunes of John William De Forest," *Jahrbuch für Amerikastudien* 13 (1968) , 249-252.

Falk, Robert. "The Panoramic Novel of Realism," *The Victorian Mode in American Fiction: 1865-1885,* 32-43.

Light, James F. *John William DeForest.*

Mariani, Umberto. "Il Realismo Di John W. De Forest," *Studi Americani* VII (1961) , 77-103.

Martin, Jay. *Harvests of Change: American Literature, 1865-1914,* 29-35.

BIBLIOGRAPHY

Bergmann, Frank. "De Forest in Germany," *American Literary Realism* 4 (Fall 1968) , 80-81.

Editors. "John William De Forest (1826-1906) : A Critical Bibliography of Secondary Comment," *American Literary Realism* 4 (Fall 1968) , 1-56.

DE FOREST, JOHN WILLIAM, Continued

Gargano, James W. "John W. DeForest and the Critics," *American Literary Realism* 4 (Fall 1968), 57-64.

Hagemann, E. R. "A Checklist of Critical Comments in *The Nation* on John William De Forest, 1866-1879," *American Literary Realism* 4 (Fall 1968), 76-79.

—————. "John William DeForest Faces *The Nation*," *American Literary Realism* 4 (Fall 1968), 65-75.

Light, James F. "John William DeForest (1826-1906)," *American Literary Realism* 1 (Fall 1967), 32-35.

—————. *John William De Forest,* 184-188.

Robillard, Douglas. "De Forest Literary Manuscripts in the Yale Library," *American Literary Realism* 4 (Fall 1968), 81-83.

DELL, FLOYD

MOON-CALF

Tanselle, G. Thomas. "Sinclair Lewis and Floyd Dell: Two Views of the Midwest," *Twentieth Century Literature* IX (Jan 1964), 175-184.

GENERAL

Butler, Francelia and Richard H. W. Dillard. "Parnassus in the 1920's: Floyd Dell Contemplates His Own Period," *Tennessee Studies in Literature* XII (1967), 131-148.

Hahn, Emily. *Romantic Rebels: An Informal History of Bohemianism in America,* 176-185.

Tanselle, G. Thomas. "Realist or Dreamer: Letters of Sherwood Anderson and Floyd Dell," *Modern Language Review* LVIII (Oct 1963), 532-537.

DEMBY, WILLIAM

BEETLECREEK

Margolies, Edward. *Native Sons: A Critical Study of Twentieth-Century Negro American Authors,* 175-179.

THE CATACOMBS

Margolies, Edward. *Native Sons: A Critical Study of Twentieth-Century Negro American Authors,* 179-189.

GENERAL

Bone, Robert. *The Negro Novel in America,* 191-196.

DEMBY, WILLIAM, Continued

Margolies, Edward. "The Expatriate as Novelist: William Demby," *Native Sons: A Critical Study of Twentieth-Century Negro American Authors,* 173-189.

DeVOTO, BERNARD

GENERAL

Sawey, Orlan. "Bernard DeVoto's Western Novels," *Western American Literature* II (Fall 1967), 171-182.

DI DONATO, PIETRO

CHRIST IN CONCRETE

French, Warren. *The Social Novel at the End of an Era,* 180-184.

DIXON, THOMAS, JR.

THE LEOPARD'S SPOTS

Bloomfield, Maxwell. "Dixon's *The Leopard's Spots:* A Study in Popular Racism," *American Quarterly* XVI (Fall 1964), 389-401.

DONLEAVY, J. P.

A SINGULAR MAN

Moore, John Rees. "Hard Times and The Noble Savage: J. P. Donleavy's *A Singular Man,*" *Hollins Critic* I (Feb 1964), 1-4, 6-11.

THE BEASTLY BEATITUDES OF BALTHAZAR B.

Scholes, Robert. "Of Life and Laughter, Death and Loneliness," *Saturday Review* 51 (Nov 23, 1968), 64-65.

THE GINGER MAN

Corrigan, Robert A. "The Artist as Censor: J. P. Donleavy and *The Ginger Man,*" *Midcontinent American Studies Journal* 8 (Spring 1967), 60-72.

Hassan, Ihab. *Radical Innocence: Studies in the Contemporary American Novel,* 194-200.

GENERAL

Sherman, William David. "J. P. Donleavy: Anarchic Man as Dying Dionysian," *Twentieth Century Literature* 13 (Jan 1968), 216-228.

Weales, Gerald. "No Face and No Exit: The Fiction of James Purdy and J. P. Donleavy," *Contemporary American Novelists,* 149-154.

DONNELLY, IGNATIUS

CAESAR'S COLUMN: A STORY OF THE TWENTIETH CENTURY

Saxton, Alexander. *"Caesar's Column:* The Dialogue of Utopia and Catastrophe," *American Quarterly* XIX (Summer 1967), 224-238.

DOS PASSOS, JOHN

ADVENTURES OF A YOUNG MAN

Blotner, Joseph. *The Modern American Political Novel,* 312-315.
Brantley, John D. *The Fiction of John Dos Passos,* 79-85.
Milne, Gordon. *The American Political Novel,* 137-138.

THE BIG MONEY

Brantley, John D. *The Fiction of John Dos Passos,* 74-75.
Mizener, Arthur. "John Dos Passos: *The Big Money,*" *Twelve Great American Novels,* 87-103.

CHOSEN COUNTRY

Brantley, John D. *The Fiction of John Dos Passos,* 102-108.

THE 42ND PARALLEL

Brantley, John D. *The Fiction of John Dos Passos,* 72-73.

THE GRAND DESIGN

Blotner, Joseph. *The Modern American Political Novel,* 312-315.
Brantley, John D. *The Fiction of John Dos Passos,* 89-98.

THE GREAT DAYS

Brantley, John D. *The Fiction of John Dos Passos,* 114-122.

MANHATTAN TRANSFER

Brantley, John D. *The Fiction of John Dos Passos,* 45-54.
Lowry, E. D. *"Manhattan Transfer: Dos Passos' Wasteland,"* *University Review* XXX (Oct 1963), 47-52.
Ruoff, Gene W. "Social Mobility and the Artist in *Manhattan Transfer* and *The Music of Time,*" *Wisconsin Studies in Contemporary Literature* 5 (Winter-Spring 1964), 64-76.
Wrenn, John H. *John Dos Passos,* 121-132.

MIDCENTURY

Brantley, John D. *The Fiction of John Dos Passos,* 122-126.
Dos Passos, John. "John Dos Passos," *Talks With Authors,* 6-9.

MOST LIKELY TO SUCCEED

Brantley, John D. *The Fiction of John Dos Passos,* 108-111.

1919

Cooperman, Stanley. *World War I and the American Novel,* 141-145.

DOS PASSOS, JOHN, Continued

NUMBER ONE

Brantley, John D. *The Fiction of John Dos Passos,* 85-89.

Rubin, Louis D., Jr. "All the King's Meanings," *The Curious Death of the Novel: Essays in American Literature,* 227-231.

ONE MAN'S INITIATION-1917

Brantley, John D. *The Fiction of John Dos Passos,* 1-21.

Holditch, Kenneth. *"One Man's Initiation:* The Origin of Technique in the Novels of John Dos Passos," *Explorations of Literature,* 115-123.

STREETS OF NIGHT

Brantley, John D. *The Fiction of John Dos Passos,* 38-45.

Wrenn, John H. *John Dos Passos,* 116-121.

THE THEME IS FREEDOM

Brantley, John D. *The Fiction of John Dos Passos,* 111-114.

THREE SOLDIERS

Brantley, John D. *The Fiction of John Dos Passos,* 21-36.

Cooperman, Stanley. *World War I and the American Novel,* 121-122, 152-155, 175-181.

West, Thomas Reed. *Flesh of Steel: Literature and the Machine in American Culture,* 59-62.

Wrenn, John H. *John Dos Passos,* 108-117.

U.S.A.

Brantley, John D. *The Fiction of John Dos Passos,* 55-78.

Chametzky, Jules. "Reflections on *U.S.A.* as Novel and Play," *Massachusetts Review* I (Winter 1960) , 391-399.

Gurko, Leo. "John Dos Passos' *U.S.A.:* A 1930's Spectacular," *Proletarian Writers of the Thirities,* 46-63.

Hoffman, Arnold R. "An Element of Structure in *U.S.A.,*" *CEA Critic* XXXI (Oct 1968) , 12-13.

Knox, George. "Voice in the *U.S.A.* Biographies," *Texas Studies in Literature and Language* IV (Spring 1962) , 109-116.

Lydenberg, John. "Dos Passos's U.S.A.: The Words of the Hollow Men," *Essays on Determinism in American Literature,* 97-107.

Thorp, Williard. *American Writing in the Twentieth Century,* 139-142.

West, Thomas Reed. *Flesh of Steel: Literature and the Machine in American Culture,* 66-68.

Widmer, Eleanor. "The Lost Girls of *U.S.A.:* Dos Passos' 30s Movie," *The Thirities: Fiction, Poetry, Drama,* 11-19.

DOS PASSOS, JOHN, Continued

Wrenn, John H. *John Dos Passos,* 153-166.
GENERAL
Aaron, Daniel. "The Riddle of John Dos Passos," *Harper's* CCXXIV (Mar 1962), 55-60.
Brantley, John D. "Some Conclusions," *The Fiction of John Dos Passos,* 127-131.
Chase, Richard. "The Chronicles of Dos Passos," *Commentary* XXXI (May 1961), 395-400.
Davis, Robert G. *John Dos Passos.*
Diggins, John P. "Dos Passos and Veblen's Villains," *Antioch Review* XXIII (Winter 1963), 485-500.
Dos Passos, John. "Contemporary Chronicles," *Carleton Miscellany* II (Spring 1961), 25-29.
————. "John Dos Passos," *Talks With Authors,* 3-11.
Eisinger, Chester E. *Fiction of the Forties,* 119-125.
Feied, Frederick. *No Pie in the Sky: The Hobo as American Cultural Hero in the works of Jack London, John Dos Passos, and Jack Kerouac,* 41-56.
Finkelstein, Sidney. *Existentialism and Alienation in American Literature,* 198-203.
Gelfant, Blanche H. "The Search for Identity in the Novels of John Dos Passos," *PMLA* LXXVI (Mar 1961), 133-149.
Irwin, William R. "Dos Passos and Fitzgerald as Reviewers of the American Social Scene," *Neueren Sprachen* (Sept 1960), 417-428.
Knox, George. "Dos Passos and Painting," *Texas Studies in Literature and Language* VI (Spring 1964), 22-38.
Landsberg, Melvin. "John R. Dos Passos: His Influence on the Novelist's Early Political Development," *American Quarterly* XVI (Fall 1964), 473-485.
Lynn, Kenneth S. "Dos Passos' Chosen Country," *New Republic* 155 (Oct 15, 1966), 15-20.
————. Introduction, *World in a Glass: A View of our Century Selected from the Novels of John Dos Passos* (Boston, 1966).
Millgate, Michael. *American Social Fiction: James to Cozzens,* 128-141.
Sanders, David. "The 'Anarchism' of John Dos Passos," *South Atlantic Quarterly* LX (Winter 1961), 44-55.
————. "Interview with John Dos Passos," *Claremont Quarterly* XI (Spring 1964), 89-100.
————. " 'Lies' and the System: Enduring Themes from Dos Passos'

73

Early Novels," *South Atlantic Quarterly* LXV (Spring 1966), 215-228.

Stoltzfus, Ben. "John Dos Passos and the French," *Comparative Literature* XV (Spring 1963), 146-163.

Thorp, Willard. *American Writing in the Twentieth Century*, 136-142.

Ward, John William. "Lindbergh, Dos Passos and History," *Carleton Miscellany* VI (Summer 1965), 20-41.

West, Thomas Reed. "John Dos Passos: The Libertarian Cause," *Flesh of Steel: Literature and the Machine in American Culture*, 54-70.

BIBLIOGRAPHY

Brantley, John D. *The Fiction of John Dos Passos*, 132-134.

Davis, Robert G. *John Dos Passos*, 46-47.

Price, Lawrence Marsden. *The Reception of United States Literature in Germany*, 216.

Reinhart, Virginia. "John Dos Passos 1950-1966 Bibliography," *Twentieth Century Literature* XIII (Oct 1967), 167-178.

Wrenn, John H. *John Dos Passos*, 198-205.

DREISER, THEODORE

AN AMERICAN TRAGEDY

Coursen, Herbert R., Jr. "Clyde Griffiths and the American Dream," *New Republic* 145 (Sept 4, 1961), 21-22.

Flanagan, John T. "Dreiser's Style in *An American Tragedy*," *Texas Studies in Literature and Language* VII (Autumn 1965), 285-294.

Gerber, Philip L. *Theodore Dreiser*, 127-153.

Grebstein, Sheldon Norman. "*An American Tragedy:* Theme and Structure," *The Twenties: Poetry and Prose*, 62-66.

Hoffman, Frederick J. "The Scene of Violence: Dostoevsky and Dreiser," *Modern Fiction Studies* VI (Summer 1960), 91-105.

Lane, Lauriat, Jr. "The Double in *An American Tragedy*," *Modern Fiction Studies* XII (Summer 1966), 213-220.

Lehan, Richard. "Dreiser's *An American Tragedy:* A Critical Study," *College English* XXV (Dec 1963), 187-193.

————. "Dreiser's *An American Tragedy:* A Critical Study," *The Modern American Novel: Essays in Criticism*, 21-32.

DREISER, THEODORE, Continued

Markels, Julian. "Dreiser and the Plotting of Inarticulate Experience," *Massachusetts Review* II (Spring 1961), 431-448.

McAleer, John J. *Theodore Dreiser: An Introduction and Interpretation,* 127-146.

Morgan, W. Wayne. "Theodore Dreiser: The Naturalist as Humanist," *American Writers in Rebellion,* 175-180.

Purdy, Strother B. *"An American Tragedy* and L'Étranger," *Comparative Literature* XIX (Summer 1967), 252-268.

Samuels, Charles Thomas. "Letters and Comment: Mr. Trilling, Mr. Warren and *An American Tragedy,"* *Yale Review* LIII (Summer 1964), 629-640.

Shapiro, Charles. "An American Tragedy: The Dream, the Failure, and the Hope," *Theodore Dreiser,* 81-113.

Warren, Robert Penn. "An American Tragedy," *Yale Review* LII (Autumn 1962), 1-15.

————. Introduction, *An American Tragedy* (New York, 1962).

THE BULWARK

Chang, Wang-Rok. *"The Bulwark:* Dreiser's Last Stand," *English Language and Literature* 8 (Jun 1960), 36-42.

Gerber, Philip L. *Theodore Dreiser,* 154-171.

McAleer, John J. *Theodore Dreiser: An Introduction and Interpretation,* 147-161.

Richman, Sidney. "Theodore Dreiser's *The Bulwark:* A Final Resolution," *American Literature* XXXIV (May 1962), 229-245.

Shapiro, Charles. "The Bulwark: American Religion and the American Dream," *Theodore Dreiser,* 65-80.

THE FINANCIER

Gerber, Philip L. *Theodore Dreiser,* 87-110.

Rosenthal, T. B. Introduction, *The Financier* (London, 1968).

Shapiro, Charles. *Theodore Dreiser,* 25-42.

THE 'GENIUS'

Gerber, Philip L. *Theodore Dreiser,* 111-126.

McAleer, John J. *Theodore Dreiser: An Introduction and Interpretation,* 120-126.

Morgan, W. Wayne. "Theodore Dreiser: The Naturalist as Humanist," *American Writers in Rebellion,* 171-174.

Shapiro, Charles. "The Genius: The American Artist and the American Dream," *Theodore Dreiser,* 45-64.

DREISER, THEODORE, Continued

JENNIE GERHARDT

Gerber, Philip L. *Theodore Dreiser,* 71-86.

McAleer, John J. *Theodore Dreiser: An Introduction and Interpretation,* 93-102.

Morgan, W. Wayne. "Theodore Dreiser: The Naturalist as Humanist," *American Writers in Rebellion,* 163-166.

Shapiro, Charles. *Theodore Dreiser,* 14-24.

SISTER CARRIE

Freedman, William A. "A Look at Dreiser as Artist: The Motif of Circularity in *Sister Carrie,*" *Modern Fiction Studies* VIII (Winter 1962-63), 384-392.

Gerber, Philip L. *Theodore Dreiser,* 51-70.

Grebstein, Sheldon Norman. "Dreiser's Victorian Vamp," *Midcontinent American Studies Journal* IV (Spring 1963), 3-12.

Hakutani, Yoshinobu. "*Sister Carrie* and the Problem of Literary Naturalism," *Twentieth Century Literature* 13 (Apr 1967), 3-17.

Long, Robert E. "*Sister Carrie* and the Rhythm of Failure in Fitzgerald," *Fitzgerald Newsletter* 25 (Spring 1964), 2-4.

Markels, Julian. "Dreiser and the Plotting of Inarticulate Experience," *Massachusetts Review* II (Spring 1961), 431-448.

Martin, Jay. *Harvests of Change. American Literature 1865-1914,* 252-253, 256-258.

McAleer, John J. *Theodore Dreiser: An Introduction and Interpretation,* 76-92.

Millgate, Michael. Introduction, *Sister Carrie* (New York, 1965).

Moers, Ellen. "The Finesse of Dreiser," *American Scholar* XXXIII (Winter 1963-64), 109-114.

Morgan, W. Wayne. "Theodore Dreiser: The Naturalist as Humanist," *American Writers in Rebellion,* 156-162.

Pizer, Donald. *Realism and Naturalism in Nineteenth-Century American Literature,* 19-24.

Poirier, Richard. *A World Elsewhere,* 235-252.

Shapiro, Charles. *Theodore Dreiser,* 1-14.

Simpson, Claude M., Jr. "Theodore Dreiser: *Sister Carrie,*" *The American Novel from James Fenimore Cooper to William Faulkner,* 106-116.

Thorp, Willard. *American Writing in the Twentieth Century,* 166-168.

Tippetts, Sally L. "The Theatre in Dreiser's *Sister Carrie,*" *Notes and Queries* N.S. 13 (Mar 1966), 99-100.

DREISER, THEODORE, Continued

Walcutt, Charles Child. *"Sister Carrie:* Naturalism or Novel of Manners?" *Genre* I (Jan 1968) , 76-85.

Williams, Philip. "The Chapter Titles of *Sister Carrie,"* *American Literature* XXXVI (Nov 1964) , 359-365.

THE STOIC

Gerber, Philip L. *Theodore Dreiser,* 87-110.

McAleer, John J. *Theodore Dreiser: An Introduction and Interpretation,* 113-119.

THE TITAN

Gerber, Philip L. *Theodore Dreiser,* 87-110.

Rosenthal, T. G. Introduction, *The Titan* (London, 1968) .

GENERAL

Anzilotti, Rolando. "Il viaggio di Dreiser in Italia (in appendice, pagine inedite di *A Traveler at Forty) ,"* *Studi Americani* 12 (1966) , 323-398.

Bernard, Kenneth. "The Flight of Theodore Dreiser," *University of Kansas City Review* XXVI (Jun 1960) , 251-259.

Binni, Francesco. "Dreiser Oltre Il Naturalismo," *Studi Americani* XI (1965) , 251-269.

Blackstock, Walter. "Dreiser's Dramatizations of Art, the Artist, and the Beautiful in American Life," *Southern Quarterly* I (Oct 1962) , 63-86.

Conroy, Jack. "Theodore Dreiser," *American Book Collector* XV (Feb 1965) , 11-16; reprinted from *Inland:* The Magazine of the Middle West.

Fiedler, Leslie A. *Love and Death in the American Novel,* 241-248.

Gerber, Philip L. *Theodore Dreiser.*

Hakutani, Yoshinobu. "Dreiser and French Realism," *Texas Studies in Literature and Language* VI (Summer 1964) , 200-212.

Houston, Dustin. "Theodore Dreiser: Naturalist or Theist?" *Brigham Young University Studies* III (Winter 1961) , 41-49.

Howe, Irving. "The Stature of Theodore Dreiser," *New Republic* 151 (July 25, 1964) , 19-21; Part II, "Dreiser and Tragedy," (Aug 22, 1964) , 25-28.

Liptzin, Sol. *The Jew in American Literature,* 159-166.

Martin, Jay. *Harvests of Change. American Literature 1865-1914,* 252-263.

McAleer, John J. *Theodore Dreiser: An Introduction and Interpretation.*

Millgate, Michael. *American Social Fiction: James to Cozzens,* 67-86.

————. "Theodore Dreiser and the American Financier," *Studi Americani* VII (1961) , 133-145.

Morgan, W. Wayne. "Theodore Dreiser: The Naturalist as Humanist," *American Writers in Rebellion,* 146-189.

Noble, David W. *The Eternal Adam and the New World Garden,* 124-132.

Phillips, William L. "The Imagery of Dreiser's Novels," *PMLA* LXXVIII (Dec 1963) , 572-585.

Price, Lawrence Marsden. *The Reception of United States Literature in Germany,* 141-144.

Putzel, Max. "Dreiser, Reedy, and 'De Maupassant, Junior,' " *American Literature* XXXIII (Jan 1962) , 466-484.

Schneider, Robert W. "The Cry of Despair," *Five Novelists of the Progressive Era,* 153-204.

Springer, Anne M. *The American Novel in Germany: A Study of the Critical Reception of Eight American Novelists Between The Two World Wars,* 60-74.

Swanberg, W. A. *Dreiser.*

Thorp, Willard. *American Writing in the Twentieth Century,* 164-168.

Tjader, Marguerite. *Theodore Dreiser: A New Dimension.*

Wagner, Vern. "The Maligned Style of Theodore Dreiser," *Western Humanities Review* XIX (Spring 1965) , 175-184.

Weimer, David R. *The City as Metaphor,* 65-77.

Wilson, William Edward. "The Titan and the Gentleman," *Antioch Review* XXIII (Spring 1963) , 25-34.

Ziff, Larzer. "A Decade's Delay," *The American 1890s: Life and Times of a Lost Generation,* 334-348.

BIBLIOGRAPHY

Critical Approaches to American Literature: Volume II, Walt Whitman to William Faulkner, 337-338.

Gerber, Philip L. *Theodore Dreiser,* 201-211.

McAleer, John J. *Theodore Dreiser: An Introduction and Interpretation,* 162-170.

Morgan, W. Wayne. *American Writers in Rebellion,* 206.

Price, Lawrence Marsden. *The Reception of United States Literature in Germany,* 216-217.

DRURY, ALLEN

ADVISE AND CONSENT
Milne, Gordon. *The American Political Novel,* 171-179.
Stuckey, W. J. *The Pulitzer Prize Novels: A Critical Backward Look,* 187-193.

DU BOIS, WILLIAM E.

GENERAL
Margolies, Edward. *Native Sons: A Critical Study of Twentieth-Century Negro American Authors,* 21-23.

EASTLAKE, WILLIAM

GENERAL
Phelps, Donald. "The Land of Grace and Isolation," *Nation* 199 (Oct 12, 1964), 225-227.
Wylder, Delbert E. "The Novels of William Eastlake," *New Mexico Quarterly* XXXIV (Summer 1964), 188-203.
BIBLIOGRAPHY
Angell, Richard C. "Eastlake: At Home and Abroad," *New Mexico Quarterly* XXXIV (Summer 1964), 204-209.

EDMONDS, WALTER D.

CHAD HANNA
Wyld, Lionel D. "Fiction, Fact, and Folklore: The World of *Chad Hanna,*" *English Journal* LVI (May 1967), 716-719.

EGGLESTON, EDWARD

THE CIRCUIT RIDER, A TALE OF THE HEROIC AGE
Randel, William. Introduction, *The Circuit Rider, a Tale of the Heroic Age* (New Haven, Connecticut, 1966).
————. *Edward Eggleston,* 104-107.
THE END OF THE WORLD
Randel, William. *Edward Eggleston,* 97-99.
THE FAITH DOCTOR
Randel, William. *Edward Eggleston,* 119-122.

EGGLESTON, EDWARD, Continued

THE GRAYSONS
Randel, William. *Edward Eggleston,* 117-119.
HOOSIER SCHOOL-BOY
Randel, William. *Edward Eggleston,* 91-97.
THE HOOSIER SCHOOL-MASTER
Quintus, John A. *"The Hoosier School-Master:* A Correction," *Notes and Queries* N.S. 15 (Nov 1968) , 423.
THE MYSTERY OF METROPOLISVILLE
Randel, William. *Edward Eggleston,* 99-104.
ROXY
Randel, William. *Edward Eggleston,* 111-115.
GENERAL
Martin, Jay. *Harvests of Change. American Literature 1865-1914,* 111-116.
Randel, William. *Edward Eggleston.*
Stone, Edward. "Eggleston," *Voices of Despair,* 137-178.
BIBILOGRAPHY
Randel, William. "Edward Eggleston (1837-1902) ," *American Literary Realism* 1 (Fall 1967) , 36-38.
————. *Edward Eggleston,* 172-187.

ELLIOTT, GEORGE P.

GENERAL
Gelfant, Blanche H. "Beyond Nihilism: The Fiction of George P. Elliott," *Hollins Critic* V (Dec 1968) , 1-12.

ELLIS, EDWARD S.

SETH JONES
Durham, Philip. Introduction, *Seth Jones* and *Deadwood Dick on Deck* (New York, 1966) .

ELLISON, RALPH WALDO

INVISIBLE MAN
Baumbach, Jonathan. "Nightmare of a Native Son: *Invisible Man* by Ralph Ellison," *The Landscape of Nightmare: Studies in the Contemporary American Novel,* 68-86.

ELLISON, RALPH WALDO, Continued

————. "Nightmare of a Native Son: Ralph Ellison's *Invisible Man*," *Critique* VI (Spring 1963), 48-65.

Bloch, Alice. "Sight Imagery in *Invisible Man*," *English Journal* LV (Nov 1966), 1019-1021, 1024.

Bone, Robert. *The Negro Novel in America*, 196-212.

Fraiberg, Selma. "Two Modern Incest Heroes," *Partisan Review* XXVIII (5-6, 1961), 646-661.

Hassan, Ihab. *Radical Innocence: Studies in the Contemporary American Novel*, 168-179.

Horowitz, Ellin. "The Rebirth of the Artist," *On Contemporary Literature*, 330-346.

Horowitz, Floyd Ross. "The Enigma of Ellison's Intellectual Man," *CLA Journal* VII (Dec 1963), 126-132.

————. "Ralph Ellison's Modern Version of Brer Bear and Brer Rabbit in *Invisible Man*," *Midcontinent American Studies Journal* IV (Fall 1963), 21-27.

Klein, Marcus. *After Alienation: American Novels in Mid-Century*, 82-85, 107-146.

————. "Ralph Ellison's *Invisible Man*," *Images of the Negro in American Literature*, 249-264.

Kostelanetz, Richard. "The Politics of Ellison's Booker: *Invisible Man* as Symbolic History," *Chicago Review* XIX (No 2, 1967), 5-26.

Littlejohn, David. *Black on White, A Critical Survey of Writings by American Negroes*, 110-119.

Margolies, Edward. "History as Blues: Ralph Ellison's *Invisible Man*," *Native Sons: A Critical Study of Twentieth-Century Negro American Authors*, 127-148.

O'Daniel, Therman B. "The Image of Man as Portrayed by Ralph Ellison," *CLA Journal* X (Jun 1967), 277-284.

Olderman, Raymond M. "Ralph Ellison's Blues and *Invisible Man*," *Wisconsin Studies in Contemporary Literature* 7 (Summer 1966), 142-159.

Rovit, Earl H. "Ralph Ellison and the American Comic Tradition," *Wisconsin Studies in Contemporary Literature* 1 (Fall 1960), 34-42.

Schafer, William J. "Ralph Ellison and the Birth of the Anti-Hero," *Critique* X (No 2, 1968), 81-93.

Singleton, M. K. "Leadership Mirages as Antagonists in *Invisible Man*," *Arizona Quarterly* XXII (Summer 1966), 157-171.

ELLISON, RALPH WALDO, Continued

GENERAL

Bone, Robert. "Ralph Ellison and the Uses of the Imagination," *Anger and Beyond,* 86-111.

————. "Ralph Ellison and the Uses of Imagination," *Tri-Quarterly* 6 (1966), 39-54.

Ellison, Ralph. "On Becoming a Writer," *Commentary* XXXVIII (Oct 1964), 57-60.

Howe, Irving. "Black Boys and Native Sons," *A World More Attractive: A View of Modern Literature and Politics,* 100-122.

Klein, Marcus. "Ralph Ellison," *After Alienation: American Novels in Mid-Century,* 71-146.

Thompson, James, Lennox Raphael and Steve Cannon. "'A Very Stern Discipline,'" *Harper's* CCXXXIV (Mar 1967), 76-95.

BIBLIOGRAPHY

Lillard, R. S. "A Ralph Waldo Ellison Bibliography (1914-1967)," *American Book Collector* XIX (Nov 1968) 18-22.

EVANS, MAX

GENERAL

Milton, John R., interviewer. "Interview: Max Evans," *South Dakota Review* 5 (Summer 1967), 77-87.

FARRELL, JAMES T.

BERNARD CARR

Kligerman, Jack. "The Quest for Self: James T. Farrell's Character Bernard Carr," *University of Kansas City Review* XXIX (Oct 1962), 9-16.

STUDS LONIGAN

Berry, Newton. "A Preface to the Death Fantasy Sequence of 'Judgment Day,'" *Tri-Quarterly* 1 (Winter 1965), 124-126.

Branch, Edgar M. "Destiny, Culture, and Technique: *Studs Lonigan,*" *University of Kansas City Review* XXXIX (Dec 1962), 103-113.

————. "Freedom and Determinism in James T. Farrell's Fiction," *Essays on Determinism in American Literature,* 83-88.

————. "James T. Farrell's 'Studs Lonigan,'" *American Book Collector* XI (Summer 1961), 9-19.

FARRELL, JAMES T., Continued

Farrell, James T. "C'est Droll," *American Book Collector* XI (Summer 1961), 33.

———. "Fragments from the Unpublished Death Fantasy Sequence of 'Judgment Day,'" *Tri-Quarterly* 1 (Winter 1965), 127-138.

———. "James T. Farrell," *Talks With Authors,* 90-98.

———. "Farrell's Introduction to Chilean Edition of *Young Lonigan*," *American Book Collector* XVII (May 1967) 7-8.

Halperin, Irving. "Studs Lonigan Revisited," *American Book Collector* XIX (Dec 1968), 10-12.

Mitchell, Richard. "*Studs Lonigan:* Research in Morality," *Centennial Review* VI (Spring 1962), 202-214.

GENERAL

Alexis, Gerhard T. "Farrell Since Our Days of Anger," *College English* XXVII (Dec 1965), 221-226.

Branch, Edgar M. "American Writer in the Twenties: James T. Farrell and The University of Chicago," *American Book Collector* XI (Summer 1961), 25-32.

———. "Freedom and Determinism in James T. Farrell's Fiction," *Essays on Determinism in American Literature,* 79-96.

———. *James T. Farrell.*

Clecak, Peter. "James T. Farrell: An Impossible Comeback," *Nation* 206 (Jun 3, 1968), 733-734.

Douglas, Wallace. "The Case of James T. Farrell," *Tri-Quarterly* 1 (Winter 1965), 105-123.

Farrell, James T. "James T. Farrell," *Talks With Authors,* 89-102.

———. "A Note on Future Plans," *Tri-Quarterly* 1 (Winter 1965), 139-140.

Thorp, Willard. *American Writing in the Twentieth Century,* 123-126, 170-173.

BIBLIOGRAPHY

Branch, Edgar M. "A Supplement to the Bibliography of James T. Farrell's Writings," *American Book Collector* XI (Summer 1961), 42-48.

———. "Bibliography of James T. Farrell: A Supplement," *American Book Collector* XVII (May 1967), 9-19.

———. *James T. Farrell.*

Farrell, James T. "Introduction," *American Book Collector* XVII (May 1967), 5.

Westlake, Neda M. "The James T. Farrell Collection at the University of Pennsylvania," *American Book Collector* XI (Summer 1961), 21-23.

FAST, HOWARD

FREEDOM'S ROAD
DuBois, W. E. B. Introduction, *Freedom's Road* (New York, 1964).
GENERAL
Adams, J. Donald. "Speaking of Books," *New York Times Book Review* 66 (May 14, 1961), 2.

FAULKNER, WILLIAM

ABSALOM, ABSALOM!
Adams, Richard P. "Work: Absalom, Absalom!" *Faulkner: Myth and Motion,* 172-214.

Aguilar, Esperanza. *Yoknapatawpha, Propiedad de William Faulkner,* 66-73.

Aswell, Duncan. "The Puzzling Design of Absalom, Absalom!" *Kenyon Review* XXX (Issue 1, 1968), 67-84.

Backman, Melvin. "Sutpen and the South: A Study of *Absalom, Absalom!" PMLA* LXXX (Dec 1965), 596-604.

Baldanza, Frank. "Faulkner and Stein: A Study in Stylistic Intransigence," *Georgia Review* XIII (Fall 1959), 274-286.

Björk, Lennart. "Ancient Myths and the Moral Framework of Faulkner's *Absalom, Absalom!" American Literature* XXXV (May 1963), 196-204.

Brooks, Cleanth. "History, Tragedy, and the Imagination in *Absalom, Absalom!" Yale Review* LII (Spring 1963), 340-351.

————. *William Faulkner: The Yoknapatawpha County,* 295-324.

Brumm, Ursula. "Geschichte als Geschehen und Erfahrung: Eine Analyse von William Faulkners *Absalom, Absalom!" Archiv für das Studium der Neueren Sprachen und Literaturen* 204:1 (1967), 26-50.

Brylowski, Walter. *Faulkner's Olympian Laugh: Myth in the Novels,* 17-42; 120-21.

Clark, William G. "Is King David a Racist?" *University Review* XXXIV (Dec 1967), 121-126.

Connolly, Thomas E. "A Skeletal Outline of *Absalom, Absalom!*" *College English* XXV (Nov 1963) , 110-114.

———. "Fate and 'the Agony of Will': Determinism in Some Works of William Faulkner," *Essays on Determinism in American Literature,* 45-47.

Fiedler, Leslie A. *Love and Death in the American Novel,* 394-398.

Guetti, James. *The Limits of Metaphor: A Study of Melville, Conrad, and Faulkner,* 69-108.

Hagan, John. "*Déjà Vu* and the Effect of Timelessness in Faulkner's *Absalom, Absalom!*" *Bucknell Review* XI (Mar 1963) , 31-52.

———. "Fact and Fancy in *Absalom, Absalom!*" *College English* XXIV (Dec 1962) , 215-218.

Hartt, Julian N. *The Lost Image of Man,* 39-41.

Hawkins, E. O. "Faulkner's 'Duke John of Lorraine,'" *American Notes & Queries* IV (Oct 1965) , 22.

Hoffman, Frederick J. *William Faulkner,* 74-79.

Holmes, Edward M. *Faulkner's Twice Told Tales; His Re-Use of His Material,* 83-87.

Howell, Elmo. "Faulkner's *Wash Jones* and the Southern Poor White," *Ball State University Forum* 8 (Winter 1967) , 8-12.

Hunt, John W. *William Faulkner: Art in Theological Tension,* 101-136.

Justus, James H. "The Epic Design of *Absalom, Absalom!*" *Texas Studies in Literature and Language* IV (Summer 1962) , 157-176.

Kartiganer, Donald M. "Faulkner's *Absalom, Absalom!:* The Discovery of Values," *American Literature* XXXVII (Nov 1965) , 291-306.

———. "The Role of Myth in *Absalom, Absalom!*" *Modern Fiction Studies* IX (Winter 1963-64) , 357-369.

Levin, David. "*Absalom, Absalom!:* The Problem of Re-creating History," *In Defense of Historical Literature,* 118-139.

Lorch, Thomas M. "Thomas Sutpen and the Female Principle," *Mississippi Quarterly* XX (Winter 1966-1967) , 38-42.

Loughrey, Thomas F. "Aborted Sacrament in *Absalom! Absalom!*" *Four Quarters* XIV (Nov 1964) , 13-21.

Mathews, James. "The Civil War of 1936: *Gone With The Wind* and *Absalom! Absalom!*" *Georgia Review* XXI (Winter 1967) , 462-469.

Miller, James E. "William Faulkner: Descent into the Vortex," *Quests Surd and Absurd: Essays in American Literature,* 52-53, 55, 58-59, 61-62.

Millgate, Michael. *The Achievement of William Faulkner*, 150-164.

Narain, S. K. *"Absalom, Absalom!* By William Faulkner: An Interpretation," *Literary Criterion* VI (Summer 1964), 116-122.

Nilon, Charles H. *Faulkner and the Negro*, 93-96.

Richardson, Kenneth E. *Force and Faith in the Novels of William Faulkner*, Studies in American Literature, Volume VII, 29-35.

Seiden, Melvin. "Faulkner's Ambiguous Negro," *Massachusetts Review* IV (Summer 1963), 675-690.

Singleton, Marvin K. "Personae at Law and in Equity: The Unity of Faulkner's *Absalom, Absalom!" Papers on Language and Literature* III (Summer 1967), 354-370.

Slabey, Robert M. "Faulkner's 'Waste Land' Vision in *Absalom, Absalom!" Mississippi Quarterly* XIV (Summer 1961), 153-161.

Slatoff, Walter J. *Quest for Failure: A Study of William Faulkner*, 198-203.

Sowder, William J. "Colonel Thomas Sutpen as Existentialist Hero," *American Literature* XXXIII (Jan 1962), 485-499.

Steinberg, Aaron. *"Absalom, Absalom!:* The Irretrievable Bon," *CLA Journal* IX (Sept 1965), 61-67.

Stewart, David H. *"Absalom* Reconsidered," *University of Toronto Quarterly* XXX (Oct 1960), 31-44.

Swiggart, Peter. "A Puritan Tragedy: *Absalom, Absalom!" The Art of Faulkner's Novels*, 149-170.

Thompson, Lawrance. *William Faulkner*, 53-65.

Tuck, Dorothy. *Crowell's Handbook of Faulkner*, 56-66.

Tuso, Joseph F. "Faulkner's Wash," *Explicator* XXVII (Nov 1968), No. 17.

Van Nostrand, A. D. *Everyman His Own Poet*, 184-189.

Watkins, Floyd C. "What Happens in *Absalom, Absalom!?" Modern Fiction Studies* XIII (Spring 1967), 79-87.

Yu, Beong-Cheon. "Quentin's Troubled Vision," *English Language and Literature* 18 (Summer 1966), 112-119.

AS I LAY DYING

Adams, Richard P. *Faulkner: Myth and Motion*, 71-84.

Aguilar, Esperanza. *Yoknapatawpha, Propiedad de William Faulkner*, 47-53.

Backman, Melvin. *Faulkner: The Major Years: A Critical Study*, 50-66.

Bedient, Calvin. "Pride and Nakedness: *As I Lay Dying," Modern Language Quarterly* XXIX (Mar 1968), 61-76.

FAULKNER, WILLIAM, Continued

Beidler, P. G. "Faulkner's Techniques of Characterization: Jewel in *As I Lay Dying,*" *Études Anglaises* XXI (Jul-Sept 1968), 236-242.

Bridgman, Richard. "As Hester Prynne Lay Dying," *English Language Notes* II (Jun 1965), 294-296.

Brooks, Cleanth. *William Faulkner: The Yoknapatawpha County,* 141-166.

Brylowski, Walter. *Faulkner's Olympian Laugh: Myth in the Novels,* 86-96.

Cross, Barbara M. "Apocalypse and Comedy in *As I Lay Dying,*" *Texas Studies in Literature and Language* III (Summer 1961), 251-258.

Dickerson, Mary Jane. "*As I Lay Dying* and 'The Waste Land'—Some Relationships," *Mississippi Quarterly* XVII (Summer 1964), 129-135.

————. "Some Sources of Faulkner's Myth in *As I Lay Dying,*" *Mississippi Quarterly* XIX (Summer 1966), 132-142.

Franklin, R. W. "Narrative Management in *As I Lay Dying,*" *Modern Fiction Studies* XIII (Spring 1967), 57-65.

Franklin, Rosemary. "Animal Magnetism in *As I Lay Dying,*" *American Quarterly* XVIII (Spring 1966), 24-34.

Hoffman, Frederick J. *William Faulkner,* 60-65.

Howell, Elmo. "Faulkner's Jumblies: The Nonsense World of *As I Lay Dying,*" *Arizona Quarterly* XVI (Spring 1960), 70-78.

Kerr, Elizabeth M. "*As I Lay Dying* as Ironic Quest," *Wisconsin Studies in Contemporary Literature* 3 (Winter 1962), 5-19.

Kirk, Robert W. "Faulkner's Anse Bundren," *Georgia Review* XIX (Winter 1965), 446-452.

Mellard, James M. "Faulkner's Philosophical Novel: Ontological Themes in *As I Lay Dying,*" *Personalist* XLVIII (Autumn 1967), 509-523.

Miller, James E. "William Faulkner: Descent into the Vortex," *Quests Surd and Absurd: Essays in American Literature,* 49, 54, 57-60.

Millgate, Michael. *The Achievement of William Faulkner,* 104-112.

Roberts, J. L. "The Individual and the Family: Faulkner's *As I Lay Dying,*" *Arizona Quarterly* XVI (Spring 1960), 26-38.

Rossky, William. "*As I Lay Dying:* The Insane World," *Texas Studies in Literature and Language* IV (Spring 1962), 87-95.

Sadler, David F. "The Second Mrs. Bundren: Another Look at the

FAULKNER, WILLIAM, Continued

Ending of *As I Lay Dying*," *American Literature* XXXVII (Mar 1965) , 65-69.

Simon, John K. "The Scene and the Imagery of Metamorphosis in *As I Lay Dying*," *Criticism* VII (Winter 1965) , 1-22.

————. "What Are You Laughing At, Darl? Madness and Humor in *As I Lay Dying*," *College English* XXV (Nov 1963) , 104-110.

Slabey, Robert M. "*As I Lay Dying* as an Existential Novel," *Bucknell Review* XI (Dec 1963) , 12-23.

Slatoff, Walter J. *Quest for Failure: A Study of William Faulkner,* 158-173.

Stallman, R. W. *The Houses That James Built,* 200-211.

Sutherland, Ronald. "*As I Lay Dying:* A Faulkner Microcosm," *Queen's Quarterly* LXXIII (Winter 1966) , 541-549.

Swiggart, Peter. "A Modern Mock-Epic: *As I Lay Dying*," *The Art of Faulkner's Novels,* 108-130.

Tuck, Dorothy. *Crowell's Handbook of Faulkner,* 34-39.

Watkins, Floyd C. and William B. Dillingham. "The Mind of Vardaman Bundren," *Philological Quarterly* XXXIX (Apr 1960) , 247-251.

Weber, Robert W. "Raskol'nikov, Addie Bundren, Meursault: Sur la continuité d'un mythe," *Archiv für das Studium der Neueren Sprachen und Literaturen* 202:2 (1966) , 81-92.

THE BEAR

Backman, Melvin. "The Wilderness and the Negro in Faulkner's 'The Bear,' " *PMLA* LXXVI (Dec. 1961) , 595-600.

Baumharten, Murray. "The Language of Faulkner's *The Bear*," *Western Humanities Review* XV (Spring 1961) , 180-182.

Bell, H. H., Jr. "A Footnote to Faulkner's 'The Bear,' " *College English* XXIV (Dec 1962) , 179-183.

Carpenter, Thomas P. "A Gun for Faulkner's Old Ben," *American Notes & Queries* V (May 1967) , 133-134.

Harrison, Robert. "Faulkner's 'The Bear': Some Notes on Form," *Georgia Review* XX (Fall 1966) , 318-327.

Jensen, Eric G., S. J. "The Play Element in Faulkner's 'The Bear,' " *Texas Studies in Literature and Language* VI (Summer 1964) , 170-187.

Lehan, Richard. "Faulkner's Poetic Prose: Style and Meaning in *The Bear*," *College English* XXVII (Dec 1965) , 243-247.

FAULKNER, WILLIAM, Continued

Nestrick, William V. "The Function of Form in *The Bear*, Section IV," *Twentieth Century Literature* XII (Oct 1966), 131-137.

Stone, Emily Whitehurst. "How a Writer Finds His Material," *Harper's* CCXXXI (Nov 1965), 157-161.

A FABLE

Adams, Richard P. *Faulkner: Myth and Motion*, 161-169.

Aguilar, Esperanza. *Yoknapatawpha, Propiedad de William Faulkner*, 128-139.

Connolly, Thomas E. "The Three Plots of *A Fable*," *Twentieth Century Literature* VI (Jul 1960), 70-75.

Dillistone, F. W. "The Friend Lays Down His Life," *The Novelist and the Passion Story*, 92-118.

Gold, Joseph. "A Fable: You'll Put Your Own Ideas in His Mouth," *William Faulkner: A Study in Humanism; From Metaphor to Discourse*, 111-147.

————. "Delusion and Redemption in Faulkner's *A Fable*," *Modern Fiction Studies* VII (Summer 1961), 145-156.

Hoffman, Frederick J. *William Faulkner*, 111-115.

Holmes, Edward M. *Faulkner's Twice Told Tales; His Re-Use of His Material*, 88-94.

Howe, Irving. *William Faulkner: A Critical Study*, 268-281.

Millgate, Michael. *The Achievement of William Faulkner*, 227-234.

Richardson, Kenneth E. *Force and Faith in the Novels of William Faulkner*, Studies in American Literature, Volume VII, 156-162.

Slatoff, Walter J. *Quest for Failure: A Study of William Faulkner*, 221-238.

Smith, Julian. "A Source for Faulkner's *A Fable*," *American Literature* 40 (Nov 1968), 394-397.

Sowder, William J. "Faulkner and Existentialism: A Note on the Generalissimo," *Wisconsin Studies in Contemporary Literature* 4 (Spring-Summer 1963), 163-171.

Tuck, Dorothy. *Crowell's Handbook of Faulkner*, 143-156.

Turaj, Frank. "The Dialectic in Faulkner's *A Fable*," *Texas Studies in Literature and Language* VIII (Spring 1966), 93-102.

GO DOWN, MOSES

Aguilar, Esperanza. *Yoknapatawpha, Propiedad de William Faulkner*, 96-104.

Brooks, Cleanth. *William Faulkner: The Yoknapatawpha County*, 244-278.

Collins, Carvel. "On William Faulkner," *Talks With Authors*, 40-46, 48-49.

Hogan, Patrick G., Jr., Dale A. Myers and John E. Turner. "Muste's 'Failure of Love' in Faulkner's *Go Down, Moses*," *Modern Fiction Studies* XII (Summer 1966), 267-270.

Mellard, James M. "The Biblical Rhythm Of *Go Down, Moses*," *Mississippi Quarterly* XX (Summer 1967), 135-147.

Millgate, Jane. "Short Story into Novel: Faulkner's Reworking of 'Gold is not Always,'" *English Studies* XLV (Aug 1964), 310-317.

Millgate, Michael. *The Achievement of William Faulkner*, 201-214.

Muste, John M. "The Failure of Love in *Go Down, Moses*," *Modern Fiction Studies* X (Winter 1964-65), 366-378.

Stewart, David H. "The Purpose of Faulkner's Ike," *Criticism* III (Fall 1961), 333-342.

Taylor, Walter. "The Freedman in *Go Down, Moses*: Historical Fact and Imaginative Failure," *Ball State University Forum* VIII (Winter 1967), 3-7.

Thompson, Lawrance. *William Faulkner*, 81-98.

Tick, Stanley. "The Unity of *Go Down, Moses*," *Twentieth Century Literature* VIII (Jul 1962), 67-73.

THE HAMLET

Adams, Richard P. *Faulkner: Myth and Motion*, 115-129.

Aguilar, Esperanza. *Yoknapatawpha, Propiedad de William Faulkner*, 87-95.

Backman, Melvin. *Faulkner: The Major Years: A Critical Study*, 139-159.

Beck, Warren. *Man in Motion: Faulkner's Trilogy*.

Brooks, Cleanth. "Faulkner's Savage Arcadia: Frenchman's Bend," *Virginia Quarterly Review* XXXIX (Autumn 1963), 598-611.

————. *William Faulkner: The Yoknapatawpha County*, 167-191.

Brylowski, Walter. *Faulkner's Olympian Laugh: Myth in the Novels*, 139-149.

Cross, Richard K. "The Humor of *The Hamlet*," *Twentieth Century Literature* XII (Jan 1967), 203-215.

Eby, Cecil D., Jr. "Ichabod Crane in Yoknapatawpha," *Georgia Review* XVI (Winter 1962), 465-469.

French, Warren. *The Social Novel at the End of an Era*, 18-41, 157-170.

Gold, Joseph. "The 'Normality' of Snopesism: Universal Themes in

FAULKNER, WILLIAM, Continued

Faulkner's *The Hamlet," Wisconsin Studies in Contemporary Literature* 3 (Winter 1962), 25-34.

Greiner, Donald J. "Universal Snopesism: The Significance of 'Spotted Horses,'" *English Journal* LVII (Nov 1968), 1133-1137.

Hall, James. *The Lunatic Giant in the Drawing Room,* 65-74.

Heald, William F. "Morality In 'Spotted Horses,'" *Mississippi Quarterly* XV (Spring 1962), 85-91.

Hoffman, Frederick J. *William Faulkner,* 85-92.

Holmes, Edward M. *Faulkner's Twice Told Tales; His Re-Use of His Material,* 19-45; 87-88.

Millgate, Michael. *The Achievement of William Faulkner,* 180-200.

Nathan, Monique. "Un Sartoris Chez Les Snopes," *Critique* XVI (Mar 1960), 222-227.

Richardson, Kenneth E. *Force and Faith in the Novels of William Faulkner,* Studies in American Literature, Volume VII, 118-125.

Slatoff, Walter J. *Quest for Failure: A Study of William Faulkner,* 203-205.

Thompson, Lawrance. *William Faulkner,* 133-147.

Thonon, Robert. "William Faulkner: From *The Hamlet* to *The Town," English Studies in Africa* 2 (Sept 1959), 190-202.

Tuck, Dorothy. *Crowell's Handbook of Faulkner,* 74-80.

Wall, Carey. "Drama and Technique in Faulkner's *The Hamlet," Twentieth Century Literature* 14 (Apr 1968), 17-23.

INTRUDER IN THE DUST

Aguilar, Esperanza. *Yoknapatawpha, Propiedad de William Faulkner,* 104-111.

Brooks, Cleanth. *William Faulkner: The Yoknapatawpha County,* 279-294.

Brylowski, Walter. *Faulkner's Olympian Laugh: Myth in the Novels,* 168-173.

Connolly, Thomas E. "Fate and 'the Agony of Will': Determinism in Some Works of William Faulkner," *Essays on Determinism in American Literature,* 49-52.

Gerstenberger, Donna. "Meaning and Form in Intruder in the Dust," *College English* XXIII (Dec 1961), 223-225.

Gold, Joseph. "*Intruder in the Dust:* There is Always Somewhere Someone," *William Faulkner: A Study in Humanism; from Metaphor to Discourse,* 76-93.

Hoffman, Frederick J. *William Faulkner,* 99-101.

Millgate, Michael. *The Achievement of William Faulkner*, 215-220.

Nilon, Charles H. *Faulkner and the Negro*, 6-42.

Slatoff, Walter J. *Quest for Failure: A Study of William Faulkner*, 215-220.

Sowder, William J. "Lucas Beauchamp as Existential Hero," *College English* XXV (Nov 1963), 115-127.

Steinberg, Aaron. *"Intruder in the Dust:* Faulkner as Psychologist of the Southern Psyche," *Literature and Psychology* XV (Spring 1965), 120-124.

Tuck, Dorothy. *Crowell's Handbook of Faulkner*, 107-111.

Van Nostrand, A. D. *Everyman His Own Poet*, 177-181.

LIGHT IN AUGUST

Adams, Richard P. *Faulkner: Myth and Motion*, 84-95.

Asals, Frederick. "Faulkner's *Light in August,"* *Explicator* XXVI (May 1968), No. 74.

Backman, Melvin. *Faulkner: The Major Years: A Critical Study*, 67-87.

Baldanza, Frank. "The Structure of *Light in August,"* *Modern Fiction Studies* XIII (Spring 1967), 67-78.

Berland, Alwyn. *"Light in August:* The Calvinism of William Faulkner," *Modern Fiction Studies* VIII (Summer 1962), 159-170.

Bowden, Edwin T. *The Dungeon of the Heart: Human Isolation and the American Novel*, 124-138.

Brooks, Cleanth. *The Hidden God*, 36-40.

————. *William Faulkner: The Yoknapatawpha County*, 47-74.

Brylowski, Walter. *Faulkner's Olympian Laugh: Myth in the Novels*, 102-117.

Clark, William G. "Faulkner's *Light in August,"* *Explicator* XXVI (Mar 1968), No. 54.

Connolly, Thomas E. "Fate and 'the Agony of Will': Determinism in Some Works of William Faulkner," *Essays on Determinism in American Literature*, 41-45.

Dunn, Richard J. "Faulkner's *Light in August,* Chapter 5," *Explicator* XXV (Oct 1966), No. 11.

Gold, Joseph. "The Two Worlds of *Light In August,"* *Mississippi Quarterly* XVI (Summer 1963), 160-167.

Hartt, Julian N. *The Lost Image of Man*, 42-48.

Hoffman, Frederick J. *William Faulkner*, 69-74.

Howell, Elmo. "A Note on Faulkner's Presbyterian Novel," *Papers on Language and Literature* II (Spring 1966), 182-187.

FAULKNER, WILLIAM, Continued

————. "Reverend Hightower and the Uses of Southern Adversity," *College English* XXIV (Dec 1962) , 183-187.

Kimmey, John L. "The Good Earth in *Light In August,*" *Mississippi Quarterly* XVII (Winter 1963-64) , 1-8.

Kirk, Robert W. "Faulkner's Lena Grove," *Georgia Review* XXI (Spring 1967) , 57-64.

Langston, Beach. "The Meaning of Lena Grove and Gail Hightower in *Light in August,*" *Boston University Studies in English* V (Spring 1961) , 46-63.

Longley, John Lewis, Jr. "Faulkner's Byron Bunch," *Georgia Review* XV (Summer 1961) , 197-208.

Loughrey, Thomas F. *"Light In August:* Religion and the Agape of Nature," *Four Quarters* XII (May 1963) , 14-25.

Miller, James E. "William Faulkner: Descent into the Vortex," *Quests Surd and Absurd: Essays in American Literature,* 50-52, 58-59, 61-64.

Millgate, Michael. *The Achievement of William Faulkner,* 124-137.

Morrison, Sister Kristin, IHM. "Faulkner's Joe Christmas: Character Through Voice," *Texas Studies in Literature and Language* II (Winter 1961) , 419-443.

Nilon, Charles H. *Faulkner and the Negro,* 73-93.

Pearce, Richard. "Faulkner's One Ring Circus," *Wisconsin Studies in Contemporary Literature* 7 (Autumn 1966) , 270-283.

Pommer, Henry F. *"Light in August:* A Letter by Faulkner," *English Language Notes* IV (Sept 1966) , 47-48.

Roberts, James L. "The Individual and the Community: Faulkner's *Light in August,*" *Studies in American Literature,* 132-153.

Rubin, Louis D., Jr. "Notes on a Rear-Guard Action," *The Curious Death of the Novel: Essays in American Literature,* 139-144, 149-150.

Slabey, Robert M. "Faulkner's Geography and Hightower's House," *American Notes and Queries* III (Feb 1965) , 85-86.

————. "Myth and Ritual in *Light in August,*" *Texas Studies in Literature and Language* II (Autumn 1960) , 328-349.

Slatoff, Walter J. *Quest for Failure: A Study of William Faulkner,* 173-198.

Sowder, William J. "Christmas as Existentialist Hero," *University Review* XXX (Jun 1964) , 279-284.

Swiggart, Peter. "The Puritan Sinner: *Light in August,*" *The Art of Faulkner's Novels,* 131-148.

Thompson, Lawrance. *William Faulkner,* 66-80.

Tuck, Dorothy. *Crowell's Handbook of Faulkner*, 46-55.

―――. "The Inwardness of the Understanding," *Approaches to the Twentieth-Century Novel*, 79-107.

West, Ray B., Jr. "Faulkner's *Light in August:* A View of Tragedy," *Wisconsin Studies in Contemporary Literature* 1 (Winter 1960), 5-12.

―――. "Faulkner's *Light in August:* A View of Tragedy," *The Writer in the Room: Selected Essays*, 175-184.

Williams, John S. " 'The Final Copper Light of Afternoon': Hightower's Redemption," *Twentieth Century Literature* 13 (Jan 1968), 205-215.

THE MANSION

Beck, Warren. "Faulkner in 'The Mansion,' " *Virginia Quarterly Review* XXXVI (Spring 1960), 272-292.

―――. *Man in Motion: Faulkner's Trilogy.*

Brooks, Cleanth. *William Faulkner: The Yoknapatawpha County*, 219-243.

Brylowski, Walter. *Faulkner's Olympian Laugh: Myth in the Novels*, 206-214.

Gold, Joseph. "*The Mansion:* To Trust in God without Depending on Him," *William Faulkner: A Study in Humanism; from Metaphor to Discourse*, 162-173.

Greene, Theodore M. "The Philosophy of Life Implicit in Faulkner's *The Mansion*," *Texas Studies in Literature and Language* II (Winter 1961), 401-418.

Holmes, Edward M. *Faulkner's Twice Told Tales; His Re-Use of His Material*, 19-45.

Howe, Irving. *William Faulkner: A Critical Study*, 282-294.

Millgate, Michael. *The Achievement of William Faulkner*, 245-252.

Richardson, Kenneth E. *Force and Faith in the Novels of William Faulkner*, Studies in American Literature, Volume VII, 163-171.

Rossky, William. "Faulkner: The Image of the Child in *The Mansion*," *Mississippi Quarterly* XV (Winter 1961-62), 17-20.

Tuck, Dorothy. *Crowell's Handbook of Faulkner*, 86-94.

MOSQUITOES

Adams, Richard P. *Faulkner: Myth and Motion*, 40-49.

Brylowski, Walter. *Faulkner's Olympian Laugh: Myth in the Novels*, 48-51.

Hughes, Richard. Introduction, *Mosquitoes* (London, 1964).

FAULKNER, WILLIAM, Continued

Millgate, Michael. *The Achievement of William Faulkner,* 68-75.

Richardson, H. Edward. "Faulkner, Anderson, and Their Tall Tale," *American Literature* XXXIV (May 1962) , 287-291.

Rideout, Walter B. and James B. Meriwether. "On the Collaboration of Faulkner and Anderson," *American Literature* XXXV (Mar 1963) , 85-87.

Smart, George K. *Religious Elements in Faulkner's Early Novels: A Selective Concordance.*

Tuck, Dorothy. *Crowell's Handbook of Faulkner,* 129-131.

Warren, Joyce W. "Faulkner's 'Portrait of the Artist,'" *Mississippi Quarterly* XIX (Summer 1966) , 121-131.

OLD MAN

Tuck, Dorothy. *Crowell's Handbook of Faulkner,* 137-142.

PYLON

Adams, Richard P. *Faulkner: Myth and Motion,* 95-102.

Brylowski, Walter. *Faulkner's Olympian Laugh: Myth in the Novels,* 117-120.

Millgate, Michael. *The Achievement of William Faulkner,* 138-149.

Price, Reynolds. "*Pylon:* The Posture of Worship," *Shenandoah* XIX (Spring 1968) , 49-61.

Slatoff, Walter J. *Quest for Failure: A Study of William Faulkner,* 211-215.

Tuck, Dorothy. *Crowell's Handbook of Faulkner,* 132-135.

THE REIVERS

Brooks, Cleanth. *William Faulkner: The Yoknapatawpha County,* 349-368.

Brylowski, Walter. *Faulkner's Olympian Laugh: Myth in the Novels,* 215-219.

Bungert, Hans. "William Faulkners letzter Roman," *Neueren Sprachen* (Nov 1963) , 498-506.

Gold, Joseph. "*The Reivers:* A Gentleman Accepts the Responsibility," *William Faulkner: A Study in Humanism; from Metaphor to Discourse,* 174-187.

Kerr, Elizabeth M. "*The Reivers:* The Golden Book of Yoknapatawpha County," *Modern Fiction Studies* XIII (Spring 1967) , 95-113.

Mellard, J. M. "Faulkner's 'Golden Book': *The Reivers* as Romantic Comedy," *Bucknell Review* XIII (Dec 1965) , 19-31.

Millgate, Michael. *The Achievement of William Faulkner,* 253-258.

Rossky, William. *"The Reivers* and *Huckleberry Finn:* Faulkner and Twain," *Huntington Library Quarterly* XXVIII (Aug 1965), 373-387.

————. *"The Reivers:* Faulkner's 'Tempest,' " *Mississippi Quarterly* XVIII (Spring 1965), 82-93.

Southern, Terry. "Tom Sawyer in the Brothel," *Nation* 194 (Jun 9, 1962), 519-521.

Swiggart, Peter. "A Note on *The Reivers,*" *The Art of Faulkner's Novels,* 207-214.

Tuck, Dorothy. *Crowell's Handbook of Faulkner,* 121-124.

Vickery, Olga W. *The Novels of William Faulkner: A Critical Interpretation,* revised edition, 228-239.

REQUIEM FOR A NUN

Aguilar, Esperanza. *Yoknapatawpha, Propiedad de William Faulkner,* 116-128.

Brooks, Cleanth. *William Faulkner: The Yoknapatawpha County,* 114-140.

Brylowski, Walter. *Faulkner's Olympian Laugh: Myth in the Novels,* 173-183.

Gold, Joseph. *"Requiem for a Nun:* The Tragic Life of a Prostitute," *William Faulkner: A Study in Humanism; from Metaphor to Discourse,* 94-110.

Graham, Philip. "Patterns in Faulkner's *Sanctuary* and *Requiem for A Nun,*" *Tennessee Studies in Literature* VIII (1963), 39-46.

Hamblen, Abigail Ann. "Faulkner's Pillar of Endurance: *Sanctuary* and *Requiem for a Nun,*" *Midwest Quarterly* VI (Summer 1965), 369-375.

Holmes, Edward M. *Faulkner's Twice Told Tales; His Re-Use of His Material,* 65-66.

McHaney, Thomas L. "Faulkner Borrows from the Mississippi Guide," *Mississippi Quarterly* XIX (Summer 1966), 116-120.

Millgate, Michael. *The Achievement of William Faulkner,* 221-226.

Slatoff, Walter J. *Quest for Failure: A Study of William Faulkner,* 208-210.

Thompson, Lawrance. *William Faulkner,* 117-132.

Tuck, Dorothy. *Crowell's Handbook of Faulkner,* 115-120.

SANCTUARY

Adams, Richard P. *Faulkner: Myth and Motion,* 59-71.

Backman, Melvin, *Faulkner: The Major Years: A Critical Study,* 41-49.

FAULKNER, WILLIAM, Continued

Brooks, Cleanth. "Faulkner's *Sanctuary:* The Discovery of Evil," *Sewanee Review* LXXI (Winter 1963), 1-24.

————. *The Hidden God,* 25-28.

————. *William Faulkner: The Yoknapatawpha County,* 116-140.

Brylowski, Walter. *Faulkner's Olympian Laugh: Myth in the Novels,* 97-102.

Cole, Douglas. "Faulkner's *Sanctuary:* Retreat from Responsibility," *Western Humanities Review* XIV (Summer 1960), 291-298.

Cypher, James R. "The Tangled Sexuality of Temple Drake," *American Imago* XIX (Fall 1962), 243-252.

Gold, Joseph. "No Refuge: Faulkner's *Sanctuary,*" *University Review* XXXIII (Dec 1966), 129-135.

Graham, Philip. "Patterns in Faulkner's *Sanctuary* and *Requiem for A Nun,*" *Tennessee Studies in Literature* VIII (1963), 39-46.

Hamblen, Abigail Ann. "Faulkner's Pillar of Endurance: *Sanctuary* and *Requiem for a Nun,*" *Midwest Quarterly* VI (Summer 1965), 369-375.

Mason, Robert L. "A Defense of Faulkner's *Sanctuary,*" *Georgia Review* XXI (Winter 1967), 430-438.

Meriwether, James B. "Some Notes on the Text of Faulkner's *Sanctuary,*" *Papers of the Bibliographical Society of America* 55 (Jul Sept 1961), 192-206.

Miller, James E. "William Faulkner: Descent into the Vortex," *Quests Surd and Absurd: Essays in American Literature,* 58-61, 63.

Millgate, Michael. *The Achievement of William Faulkner,* 113-123.

Slabey, Robert M. "Faulkner's *Sanctuary,*" *Explicator* (Jan 1963), No. 45.

Slatoff, Walter J. *Quest for Failure: A Study of William Faulkner,* 210-211.

Tate, Allen. "Faulkner's *Sanctuary* and the Southern Myth," *Virginia Quarterly* 44 (Summer 1968), 418-427.

Thompson, Lawrance. *William Faulkner,* 99-116.

SARTORIS

Adams, Richard P. *Faulkner: Myth and Motion,* 49-56.

Backman, Melvin. *Faulkner: The Major Years: A Critical Study,* 3-12.

Brooks, Cleanth. *William Faulkner: The Yoknapatawpha County,* 100-115.

Bruccoli, Matthew. "A Source for *Sartoris?*" *Mississippi Quarterly* XX (Summer 1967), 163.

FAULKNER, WILLIAM, Continued

Brylowski, Walter. *Faulkner's Olympian Laugh: Myth in the Novels*, 51-58.

Connolly, Thomas E. "Fate and 'the Agony of Will': Determinism in Some Works of William Faulkner," *Essays on Determinism in American Literature*, 37-39.

Millgate, Michael. *The Achievement of William Faulkner*, 76-85.

Nilon, Charles H. *Faulkner and the Negro*, 70-73.

Page, Ralph. "John Sartoris: Friend or Foe," *Arizona Quarterly* XXIII (Spring 1967), 27-33.

Richardson, Kenneth E. *Force and Faith in the Novels of William Faulkner*, Studies in American Literature, Volume VII, 20-25.

Scholes, Robert. "Myth and Manners in *Sartoris*," *Georgia Review* XVI (Summer 1962), 195-201.

Smart, George K. *Religious Elements in Faulkner's Early Novels: A Selective Concordance.*

Tuck, Dorothy. *Crowell's Handbook of Faulkner*, 16-21.

SOLDIERS' PAY

Adams, Richard P. *Faulkner: Myth and Motion*, 34-40.

Bross, Addison. "*Soldiers' Pay* and the Art of Aubrey Beardsley," *American Quarterly* XIX (Spring 1967), 3-23.

Brylowski, Walter. *Faulkner's Olympian Laugh: Myth in the Novels*, 43-51.

Cooperman, Stanley. *World War I and the American Novel*, 159-162.

Frederick, John T. "Anticipation and Achievement in Faulkner's *Soldiers' Pay*," *Arizona Quarterly* XXIII (Autumn 1967), 243-249.

Materassi, Mario. "Le Immagini in 'Soldiers' Pay,'" *Studi Americani* IX (1964), 353-370.

Millgate, Michael. *The Achievement of William Faulkner*, 61-67.

Nilon, Charles H. *Faulkner and the Negro*, 67-70.

Richardson, H. E. "The Decadence in Faulkner's First Novel: The Faun, the Worm and the Tower," *Études Anglaises* XXI (Jul-Sept 1968), 225-235.

Smart, George K. *Religious Elements in Faulkner's Early Novels: A Selective Concordance.*

Tuck, Dorothy. *Crowell's Handbook of Faulkner*, 125-128.

THE SOUND AND THE FURY

Adams, Richard P. "Work: The Sound and the Fury," *Faulkner: Myth and Motion*, 215-248.

FAULKNER, WILLIAM, Continued

Aguilar, Esperanza. *Yoknapatawpha, Propiedad de William Faulkner,* 36-42.

Aswell, Duncan. "The Recollection and the Blood: Jason's Role in *The Sound and the Fury,*" *Mississippi Quarterly* XXI (Summer 1968), 211-218.

Backman, Melvin. *Faulkner: The Major Years: A Critical Study,* 13-40.

Bassan, Maurice. "Benjy at the Monument," *English Language Notes* II (Sept 1964), 46-50.

Baum, Cathcrine B. " 'The Beautiful One': Caddy Compson as Heroine of *The Sound and the Fury,*" *Modern Fiction Studies* XIII (Spring 1967), 33-44.

Bowling, Lawrence Edward. "Faulkner and the Theme of Isolation," *Georgia Review* XVIII (Spring 1964), 50-66.

―――. "Faulkner: The Theme of Pride in *The Sound and the Fury,*" *Modern Fiction Studies* XI (Summer 1965), 129-139.

Broderick, John C. "Faulkner's *The Sound and the Fury,*" *Explicator* XIX (Nov 1960) No. 12.

Brooks, Cleanth. *The Hidden God,* 40-43.

―――. "Man, Time, and Eternity," *Twentieth Century Interpretations of The Sound and the Fury,* 63-70.

―――. *William Faulkner: The Yoknapatawpha County,* 325-348.

Brylowski, Walter. *Faulkner's Olympian Laugh: Myth in the Novels,* 58-85.

Clerc, Charles. "Faulkner's *The Sound and the Fury,*" *Explicator* XXIV (Nov 1965), No. 29.

Coffee, Jessie. "Faulkner's *The Sound and the Fury,*" *Explicator* XXIV (Oct 1965), No. 21.

Coindreau, Maurice. "Preface to *Le Bruit et la fureur,*" *Twentieth Century Interpretations of The Sound and the Fury,* 30-32.

―――. "Preface to *The Sound and the Fury,*" *Mississippi Quarterly* XIX (Summer 1966), 107-115.

Collins, Carvel. "The Interior Monologues of *The Sound and the Fury,*" *Psychoanalysis and American Fiction,* 223-243.

―――. "Miss Quentin's Paternity Again," *Texas Studies in Literature and Language* II (Autumn 1960), 253-260.

―――. "William Faulkner: *The Sound and the Fury,*" *The American Novel from James Fenimore Cooper to William Faulkner,* 219-228.

Connolly, Thomas E. "Fate and 'the Agony of Will': Determinism in Some Works of William Faulkner," *Essays on Determinism in American Literature*, 39-41.

Cowan, Michael H. Introduction, *Twentieth Century Interpretations of "The Sound and the Fury,"* 1-13.

Cross, Barbara M. *"The Sound and the Fury:* The Pattern of Sacrifice," *Arizona Quarterly* XVI (Spring 1960), 5-16.

Dauner, Louise. "Quentin and the Walking Shadow: The Dilemma of Nature and Culture," *Arizona Quarterly* XXI (Summer 1965), 159-171.

————. "Quentin and the Walking Shadow," *Twentieth Century Interpretations of The Sound and the Fury,* 75-80.

Edel, Leon. "How to Read *The Sound and the Fury, Varieties of Literary Experience: Eighteen Essays in World Literature.*

England, Martha Winburn. "Quentin's Story: Chronology and Explication," *College English* XXII (Jan 1961), 228-235.

Fasel, Ida. "A 'Conversation' Between Faulkner and Eliot," *Mississippi Quarterly* XX (Fall 1967), 195-206.

Fredrickson, Michael A. "A Note on 'The Idiot Boy' as a Probable Source for *The Sound and the Fury,"* *Minnesota Review* VI (No 4, 1966), 368-370.

Freedman, William A. "The Technique of Isolation in *The Sound and the Fury,"* *Mississippi Quarterly* XV (Winter 1961-62), 21-26.

Garmon, Gerald. "Faulkner's *The Sound and the Fury,"* *Explicator* XXV (Sept 1966), No. 2.

Gibbons, Kathryn Gibbs. "Quentin's Shadow," *Literature and Psychology* XII (Winter 1962), 16-24.

Gibson, William M. "Faulkner's *The Sound and the Fury,"* *Explicator* XXII (Jan 1964), No. 33.

Gold, Joseph. "Faulkner's *The Sound and the Fury,"* *Explicator* XIX (Feb 1961), No. 29.

Graves, T. W., Jr. "A Portrait of Benjy," *William and Mary Review* II (Winter 1964), 53-57.

Gresset, Michel. "Psychological Aspects of Evil in *The Sound and the Fury,"* *Mississippi Quarterly* XIX (Summer 1966), 143-153.

Gross, Beverly. "Form and Fulfillment in *The Sound and the Fury,"* *Modern Language Quarterly* XXIX (Dec 1968), 439-449.

Guetti, James. *The Limits of Metaphor: A Study of Melville, Conrad, and Faulkner,* 148-153.

Hagopian, John V. "Nihilism in Faulkner's *The Sound and the Fury,*" *Modern Fiction Studies* XIII (Spring 1967), 45-55.

Harris, Wendell V. "Faulkner's *The Sound and the Fury,*" *Explicator* XXI (Mar 1963), No. 54.

Hoffman, Frederick J. *William Faulkner,* 49-60.

Hornback, Vernon T., Jr. "The Uses of Time in Faulkner's *The Sound and the Fury,*" *Papers on English Language and Literature* I (Winter 1965), 50-58.

Howell, John M. "Hemingway and Fitzgerald in Sound and Fury," *Papers on Language and Literature* II (Summer 1966), 234-242.

Hunt, John W. "The Locus and Status of Meaning," *Twentieth Century Interpretations of The Sound and the Fury,* 83-92.

————. *William Faulkner: Art in Theological Tension,* 35-99.

Izsak, Emily K. "The Manuscript of *The Sound and the Fury:* The Revisions in the First Section," *Studies in Bibliography* XX (1967), 189-202.

Kermenli, Leyla. "William Faulkner's *The Sound and the Fury,*" *Litera* VIII (1965), 99-115.

Marshall, Lenore. "The Power of Words," *Saturday Review* 45 (Jul 28, 1962), 16-17.

Mellard, James M. "Faulkner's Jason and the Tradition of Oral Narrative," *Journal of Popular Culture* II (Fall 1968), 195-210.

Meriwether, James B. "Notes on the Textual History of *The Sound and the Fury,*" *Papers of the Bibliographical Society of America* 56 (Jul-Sept 1962), 285-316.

Miller, James E. "William Faulkner: Descent into the Vortex," *Quests Surd and Absurd: Essays in American Literature,* 53-54, 56-57, 59-60, 63.

Millgate, Michael. *The Achievement of William Faulkner,* 86-103.

————. "*The Sound and the Fury,*" *Faulkner: A Collection of Critical Essays,* 94-108.

————. "William Faulkner: The Problem of Point of View," *Patterns of Commitment in American Literature,* 182-186.

Mizener, Arthur. "William Faulkner: *The Sound and the Fury,*" *Twelve Great American Novels,* 142-159.

Morillo, Marvin. "Faulkner's *The Sound and the Fury,*" *Explicator* XXIV (Feb 1966), No. 50.

Nilon, Charles H. *Faulkner and the Negro,* 101-103.

FAULKNER, WILLIAM, Continued

Peavy, Charles D. "An Early Casting of Benjy: Faulkner's 'The Kingdom of God,'" *Studies in Short Fiction* III (Spring 1966), 347-348.

————. "Faulkner's Use of Folklore in *The Sound and the Fury,*" *Journal of American Folklore* 79 (Jul-Sept 1966), 437-447.

————. "A Note on the 'Suicide Pact' in *The Sound and the Fury,*" *English Language Notes* V (Mar 1968), 207-209.

Pratt, J. Norwood. "Faulkner's *The Sound and the Fury,*" *Explicator* XXIII (Jan 1965), No. 37.

Richardson, Kenneth E. *Force and Faith in the Novels of William Faulkner,* Studies in American Literature, Volume VII, 24-29, 70-73, 100-103.

Rodrigues, Eusebio L. "Time and Technique in *The Sound and the Fury,*" *Literary Criterion* VII (Summer 1965), 61-67.

Simpson, Hassell A. "Faulkner's *The Sound and the Fury,* Appendix," *Explicator* XXI (Dec 1962), No. 27.

Slabey, Robert M. "Quentin as Romantic," *Twentieth Century Interpretations of The Sound and the Fury,* 81-82.

————. "The 'Romanticism' Of *The Sound and the Fury,*" *Mississippi Quarterly* XVI (Summer 1963), 146-159.

Slatoff, Walter J. *Quest for Failure: A Study of William Faulkner,* 149-158.

Swiggart, Peter. "Faulkner's *The Sound and the Fury,*" *Explicator* XXII (Dec 1963), No. 31.

————. "Rage against Time: *The Sound and The Fury,*" *The Art of Faulkner's Novels,* 87-107.

Thompson, Lawrance. *William Faulkner,* 29-52.

Tuck, Dorothy. *Crowell's Handbook of Faulkner,* 22-33.

Underwood, Henry J., Jr. "Sartre on *The Sound and the Fury:* Some Errors," *Modern Fiction Studies* XII (Winter 1966-67), 477-479.

Van Nostrand, A. D. *Everyman His Own Poet,* 181-184.

Volpe, Edmond L. "Appendix: Chronology and Scene Shifts in Benjy's and Quentin's Sections," *Twentieth Century Interpretations of The Sound and the Fury,* 103-108.

Walters, Paul S. "Theory and Practice in Faulkner's *The Sound and the Fury,*" *English Studies in Africa* 10 (Mar 1967), 22-39.

Weisgerber, Jean. "Faulkner Et Dostoievski: *The Sound and the Fury,*" *Revue de Littérature Comparée* 39 (Jul-Sept 1965), 406-421.

Young, James Dean. "Quentin's Maundy Thursday," *Tulane Studies in English* X (1960), 143-151.

FAULKNER, WILLIAM, Continued

THE TOWN

Beck, Warren. *Man in Motion: Faulkner's Trilogy.*

Brooks, Cleanth. *William Faulkner: The Yoknapatawpha County,* 192-218.

Brylowski, Walter. *Faulkner's Olympian Laugh: Myth in the Novels,* 201-216.

Gold, Joseph. *"The Town:* All People Learn a Little More," *William Faulkner: A Study in Humanism; from Metaphor to Discourse,* 148-161.

————. "Truth or Consequences: Faulkner's *The Town,*" *Mississippi Quarterly* XIII (Summer 1960) , 112-116.

Holmes, Edward M. *Faulkner's Twice Told Tales; His Re-Use of His Material,* 19-45.

Howe, Irving. *William Faulkner: A Critical Study,* 282-294.

Millgate, Michael. *The Achievement of William Faulkner,* 235-244.

Mooney, Stephen L. "Faulkner's 'The Town': A Question of Voices," *Mississippi Quarterly* XIII (Summer 1960) , 117-122.

Slatoff, Walter J. *Quest for Failure: A Study of William Faulkner,* 203-205.

Thompson, Lawrance. *William Faulkner,* 148-158.

Thonon, Robert. "William Faulkner: From *The Hamlet* to *The Town,*" *English Studies in Africa* 2 (Sept 1959) , 190-202.

Tuck, Dorothy. *Crowell's Handbook of Faulkner,* 81-85.

THE UNVANQUISHED

Backman, Melvin. *Faulkner; The Major Years: A Critical Study,* 113-126.

————. "Faulkner's 'An Odor of Verbena': Dissent from the South," *College English* XXII (Jan 1961) , 253-256.

Bianchi, Ruggero. "Faulkner E *The Unvanquished,*" *Studi Americani* VIII (1962) , 129-150.

Brooks, Cleanth. *The Hidden God,* 30-34.

————. *William Faulkner: The Yoknapatawpha County,* 75-99.

Brylowski, Walter. *Faulkner's Olympian Laugh: Myth in the Novels,* 121-126.

Collins, Carvel. Introduction, *The Unvanquished* (New York, 1959) .

Holmes, Edward M. *Faulkner's Twice Told Tales; His Re-Use of His Material,* 46-57.

Meriwether, James B. "A Source in Balzac for *The Unvanquished,*" *Mississippi Quarterly* XX (Summer 1967) , 165-166.

Millgate, Michael. *The Achievement of William Faulkner,* 165-170.

Nilon, Charles H. *Faulkner and the Negro,* 59-66.

Tuck, Dorothy. *Crowell's Handbook of Faulkner,* 67-71.

Walker, William E. *"The Unvanquished:* The Restoration of Tradition," *Reality and Myth: Essays in American Literature in Memory of Richmond Croom Beatty,* 275-297.

THE WILD PALMS

Adams, Richard P. *Faulkner: Myth and Motion,* 111-114.

Backman, Melvin. *Faulkner: The Major Years: A Critical Study,* 127-138.

————. "Faulkner's *The Wild Palms,"* *University of Kansas City Review* XXVIII (Mar 1962) , 199-204.

Brylowski, Walter. *Faulkner's Olympian Laugh: Myth in the Novels,* 127-139.

Feaster, John. "Faulkner's *Old Man:* A Psychoanalytic Approach," *Modern Fiction Studies* XIII (Spring 1967) , 89-93.

Jewkes, W. T. "Counterpoint in Faulkner's *The Wild Palms,"* *Wisconsin Studies in Contemporary Literature* 2 (Winter 1961) , 39-53.

Millgate, Michael. *The Achievement of William Faulkner,* 171-179.

Moldenhauer, Joseph J. "Unity of Theme and Structure in *The Wild Palms,"* *William Faulkner: Three Decades of Criticism,* 305-322.

Reeves, Carolyn H. *"The Wild Palms:* Faulkner's Chaotic Cosmos," *Mississippi Quarterly* XX (Summer 1967) , 148-157.

Richardson, Kenneth E. *Force and Faith in the Novels of William Faulkner,* Studies in American Literature, Volume VII, 67-70, 96-99, 117-118.

Slatoff, Walter J. *Quest for Failure: A Study of William Faulkner,* 205-208.

Stone, Edward. *Voices of Despair,* 69-72.

Taylor, Nancy Dew. "The River of Faulkner and Mark Twain," *Mississippi Quarterly* XVI (Fall 1963) , 191-199.

Vickery, Olga W. *The Novels of William Faulkner: A Critical Interpretation,* revised edition, 156-166.

GENERAL

Adams, Percy G. "The Franco-American Faulkner," *Tennessee Studies in Literature* V (1960) , 1-13.

————. "Humor as Structure and Theme in Faulkner's Trilogy," *Wisconsin Studies in Contemporary Literature* 5 (Autumn 1964) , 205-212.

Adams, Richard P. "The Apprenticeship of William Faulkner," *Tulane Studies in English* XII (1962) , 113-156.

————. "Faulkner and the Myth of the South," *Mississippi Quarterly* XIV (Summer 1961) , 131-137.

————. *Faulkner: Myth and Motion.*

————. "Some Key Words in Faulkner," *Tulane Studies in English* XVI (1968), 135-148.

Aguilar, Esperanza. *Yoknapatawpha, Propiedad de William Faulkner.*

Allen, Charles A. "William Faulkner: Comedy and the Purpose of Humor," *Arizona Quarterly* XVI (Spring 1960) , 59-69.

Allen, Gay Wilson. "With Faulkner in Japan," *American Scholar* XXXI (Autumn 1962) , 566-571.

Antrim, Harry T. "Faulkner's Suspended Style," *University Review* XXXII (Dec 1965) , 122-128.

Backman, Melvin. *Faulkner: The Major Years; A Critical Study,* 185-186.

Baker, Carlos. "William Faulkner: The Doomed and the Damned," *The Young Rebel and American Literature,* 145-169.

Baldanza, Frank. "Faulkner's 1699-1945: The Compsons," *Explicator* XIX (May 1961) , No. 59.

Basso, Hamilton. "William Faulkner: Man and Writer," *Saturday Review* 45 (Jul 28, 1962) , 11-14.

Beck, Warren. *Man in Motion: Faulkner's Trilogy.*

————. "1941: Faulkner's Point of View," *College English* XXII (Nov 1960) , 86-93.

Beja, Morris. "A Flash, A Glare: Faulkner and Time," *Renascence* XVI (Spring 1964) , 133-141,145.

Beringause, A. F. "Faulkner's Yoknapatawpha Register," *Bucknell Review* XI (May 1963) , 71-82.

Bigelow, Gordon E. "Faulkner's Snopes Saga," *English Journal* XLIX (Dec 1960) , 595-605.

Blotner, Joseph. "William Faulkner's Name Was in the Books He Loved Best," *New York Times Book Review* 68 (Dec 8, 1963) 4-5, 45.

Bowling, Lawrence Edward. "William Faulkner: The Importance of Love," *Dalhousie Review* XLIII (Winter 1963-64) , 474-482.

Bradford, M. E. "Faulkner, James Baldwin, and the South," *Georgia Review* XX (Winter 1966) , 431-443.

_____. "Faulkner's 'Tall Men,'" *South Atlantic Quarterly* LXI (Winter 1962), 29-39.

_____. "On the Importance of Discovering God: Faulkner and Hemingway's *The Old Man and the Sea*," *Mississippi Quarterly* XX (Summer 1967), 158-162.

Brasil, Assis. *Faulkner e a Téchnica do romance: Ensaio.*

Brennan, Joseph X. and Seymour L. Gross. "The Problem of Moral Values in Conrad and Faulkner," *Personalist* XLI (Winter 1960), 60-70.

Brocki, Sister Mary Damascene. "Faulkner and Hemingway Values in a Modern World," *Mark Twain Journal* XI (Summer 1962), 5-9, 15.

Brooks, Cleanth. "The American 'Innocence': in James, Fitzgerald, and Faulkner," *Shenandoah* XVI (Autumn 1964), 21-37.

_____. "Faulkner's Vision of Good and Evil," *Massachusetts Review* III (Summer, 1962), 692-712.

_____. *The Hidden God*, 22-43.

_____. *William Faulkner: The Yoknapatawpha County.*

Brown, Calvin S. "Faulkner's Geography and Topography," *PMLA* LXXVII (Dec 1962), 652-659.

_____. "Faulkner's Manhunts: Fact into Fiction," *Georgia Review* XX (Winter 1966), 388-395.

_____. "Faulkner's Use of the Oral Tradition," *Georgia Review* XXII (Summer 1968), 160-169.

Brown, William R. "Faulkner's Paradox in Pathology and Salvation: *Sanctuary, Light in August, Requiem for a Nun*," *Texas Studies in Literature and Language*," IX (Autumn 1967), 429-449.

Brylowski, Walter. *Faulkner's Olympian Laugh, Myth in the Novels.*

Buckley, G. T. "Is Oxford the Original of Jefferson in William Faulkner's Novels?" *PMLA* LXXVI (Sept 1961), 447-454.

Bungert, Hans. "William Faulkner on 'Moby-Dick' An Early Letter," *Studi Americani* IX (1964), 371-375.

Burger, Nash K. "A Story to Tell: Agee, Wolfe, Faulkner," *South Atlantic Quarterly* LXIII (Winter 1964), 32-43.

Burrows, Robert N. "Institutional Christianity as Reflected in the Works of William Faulkner," *Mississippi Quarterly* XIV (Summer 1961), 138-147.

Cambon, Glauco. "Stile E Percezione Del Numinoso In Un Racconto Di Faulkner," *Studi Americani* VII (1961), 147-162.

Campbell, Harry M. "William Faulkner: A New Look," *Mississippi Quarterly* XIV (Summer 1961) , 115-116.

Capps, Lt. Col. Jack L. "West Point's William Faulkner Room," *Georgia Review* XX (Spring 1966) , 3-8.

Carey, Glenn O. "William Faulkner as a Critic of Society," *Arizona Quarterly* XXI (Summer 1965) , 101-108.

Christadler, Martin. "Natur und Geschichte im Werk von William Faulkner," Beihefte zum *Jahrbuch für Amerikastudien* 8 (1963) , 1-200.

Coffee, Jessie A. "Empty Steeples: Theme, Symbol, and Irony in Faulkner's Novels," *Arizona Quarterly* XXIII (Autumn 1967) , 197-206.

Coindreau, Maurice Edgar. "The Faulkner I Knew," *Shenandoah* XVI (Winter 1965) , 27-35.

Collins, Carvel. "On William Faulkner," *Talks With Authors,* 39-55.

Cowley, Malcolm. *The Faulkner-Cowley File: Letters and Memories, 1944-1962.*

―――. "A Fresh Look at Faulkner," *Saturday Review* 49 (June 11, 1966) , 22-26.

―――. "The Solitude of William Faulkner," *Atlantic Monthly* CCXVII (Jun 1966) , 97-115.

Day, Douglas. "The War Stories of William Faulkner," *Georgia Review* XV (Winter 1961) , 385-394.

Donnelly, Doris and William. "William Faulkner: In Search of Peace," *Personalist* XLIV (Autumn 1963) , 490-498.

Doyle, Charles. "The Moral World of Faulkner," *Renascence* XVIII (Fall 1966) , 3-12.

Eisinger, Chester E. *Fiction of the Forties,* 178-186.

Ellison, Ralph. "Twentieth-Century Fiction and the Black Mask of Humanity," *Images of the Negro in American Literature,* 129-131.

Emerson, O. B. "Prophet Next Door," *Reality and Myth: Essays in American Literature in Memory of Richmond Croom Beatty,* 237-274.

Falkner, Murry C. "The Falkners of Oxford: The Enchanted Years," *Southern Review* III (Spring 1967) , 357-386.

Fant, Joseph L, III, and Robert Ashley. *Faulkner at West Point.*

Farner, Norman, Jr. "The Love Theme: A Principal Source of Thematic Unity in Faulkner's Snopes Trilogy," *Twentieth Century Literature* VIII (Oct 1962-Jan 1963) , 111-123.

FAULKNER, WILLIAM, Continued

Farnham, James F. "Faulkner's Unsung Hero: Gavin Stevens," *Arizona Quarterly* XXI (Summer 1965), 115-132.

Fiedler, Leslie A. "The Blackness of Darkness: The Negro and the Development of American Gothic," *Images of the Negro in American Literature*, 101-105.

————. *Love and Death in the American Novel*, 309-315, 443-449.

————. *Waiting for the End*, 10-12, 18-19.

Finkelstein, Sidney. *Existentialism and Alienation in American Literature*, 184-197.

Fisher, Richard E. "The Wilderness, the Commissary, and the Bedroom: Faulkner's Ike McCaslin as Hero in a Vacuum," *English Studies* XLIV (Feb 1963), 19-28.

Flanagan, John T. "Faulkner's Favorite Word," *Georgia Review* XVII (Winter 1963), 429-434.

Ford, Margaret Patricia and Suzanne Kincaid. *Who's Who in Faulkner.*

Foster, Ruel E. "Social Order and Disorder in Faulkner's Fiction," *Approach* 54 (Winter 1965), 20-28.

French, Warren G. "The Background of Snopesism in Mississippi," *Midcontinent American Studies Journal* V (Fall 1964), 3-17.

————. "William Faulkner and the Art of the Detective Story," *The Thirties: Fiction, Poetry, Drama*, 55-62.

Frohock, W. M. "Faulkner and the 'Roman Nouveau': An Interim Report," *Bucknell Review* X (Mar 1962), 186-193.

Garrett, George. "The Influence of William Faulkner," *Georgia Review* XVIII (Winter 1964), 419-427.

Giannitrapani, Angela. "Il Procedimento Dello Stupore In Faulkner," *Studi Americani* VI (1960), 275-305.

Gold, Joseph. "Early Works: The Furious Motion of Being Alive," *William Faulkner: A Study in Humanism; from Metaphor to Discourse*, 21-48.

————. "William Faulkner's 'One Compact Thing,'" *Twentieth Century Literature* VIII (Apr 1962), 3-9.

Gorman, Thomas R. "Faulkner's Ethical Point of View," *CEA Critic* XXVIII (Jun 1966), 4-5, 6.

Gossett, Louise Y. *Violence in Recent Southern Fiction*, 29-47.

Grant, Douglas. *Purpose and Place*, 183-188.

Green, Martin. "Faulkner: The Triumph of Rhetoric," *Re-Appraisals: Some Commonsense Readings of American Literature*, 167-195.

Guetti, James. *The Limits of Metaphor: A Study of Melville, Conrad, and Faulkner.*

Guttmann, Allen. "Collisions and Confrontations," *Arizona Quarterly* XVI (Spring 1960), 46-52.

Hagopian, John V. "The Adyt and the Maze: Ten Years of Faulkner Studies in America," *Jahrbuch Für Amerikastudien* 6 (1961), 134-151.

Hall, James. *The Lunatic Giant in the Drawing Room,* 56-74.

Hardy, John Edward. "William Faulkner: The Legend Behind the Legend," *Man in the Modern Novel,* 137-158.

Harkness, Bruce. "Faulkner and Scott," *Mississippi Quarterly* XX (Summer 1967), 164.

Hawkins, E. O., Jr. "Jane Cook and Cecilia Farmer," *Mississippi Quarterly* XVIII (Fall 1965), 248-251.

Hoffman, Frederick J. "Nostalgia and Christian Interpretation: Henry Adams and Faulkner," *The Imagination's New Beginning: Theology and Modern Literature,* 75-102.

————. *William Faulkner.*

————. "William Faulkner," *American Winners of the Nobel Literary Prize,* 138-157.

————. "William Faulkner: A Review of Recent Criticism," *Renascence* XIII (Autumn 1960), 3-9, 32.

Holman, C. Hugh. *Three Modes of Modern Southern Fiction,* 27-47.

Holmes, Edward M. *Faulkner's Twice Told Tales; His Re-use of His Material.*

Hovde, Carl F. "Faulkner's Democratic Rhetoric," *South Atlantic Quarterly* LXIII (Autumn 1964), 530-541.

Howe, Irving. "Faulkner and the Negroes," *Images of the Negro in American Literature,* 204-220.

————. "Yoknapatawpha County Was a World that Was Complete in Itself," *New York Times Book Review* 67 (Jul 22, 1962), 7, 24.

Howell, Elmo. "Mark Twain, William Faulkner and the First Families of Virginia," *Mark Twain Journal* XIII (Summer 1966), 1-3, 19.

————. "Mink Snopes and Faulkner's Moral Conclusions," *South Atlantic Quarterly* LXVII (Winter 1968), 13-22.

————. "A Name for Faulkner's City," *Names* XVI (Dec 1968), 415-421.

————. "William Faulkner and the New Deal," *Midwest Quarterly* V (Summer 1964), 323-332.

————. "William Faulkner's Southern Baptists," *Arizona Quarterly* XXIII (Autumn 1967), 220-226.

Hughes, Richard. "Faulkner and Bennett," *Encounter* XXI (Sept 1963), 59-61.

Hunt, John W. *William Faulkner: Art in Theological Tension.*

Inge, M. Thomas, (ed.). "Donald Davidson on Faulkner: An Early Recognition," *Georgia Review* XX (Winter 1966), 454-462.

————. "William Faulkner and George Washington Harris: In the Tradition of Southwestern Humor," *Tennessee Studies in Literature* VII (1962), 47-59.

Jackson, Naomi. "Faulkner's Woman: 'Demon-Nun and Angel-Witch,'" *Ball State University Forum* VIII (Winter 1967), 12-20.

Jacobs, Robert D. "William Faulkner: The Passion and the Penance," *South: Modern Southern Literature in its Cultural Setting,* 142-176.

Jordan, Robert M. "The Limits of Illusion: Faulkner, Fielding, and Chaucer," *Criticism* II (Summer 1960), 278-305.

Kay, Wallace G. "Faulkner's Mississippi: The Myth and the Microcosm," *Southern Quarterly* VI (Oct 1967), 13-24.

Kerr, Elizabeth M. "Snopes," *Wisconsin Studies in Contemporary Literature* 1 (Spring-Summer 1960), 66-84.

————. "William Faulkner and the Southern Concept of Woman," *Mississippi Quarterly* XV (Winter 1961-1962), 1-16.

Kirk, Robert W. *Faulkner's People : A Complete Guide and Index to Characters in the Fiction of William Faulkner.*

Klotz, Marvin. "The Triumph Over Time: Narrative Form in William Faulkner and William Styron," *Mississippi Quarterly* XVII (Winter 1963-64), 9-20.

Kunkel, Francis L. "Christ Symbolism in Faulkner: Prevalence of the Human," *Renascence* XVII (Spring 1965), 148-156.

Larsen, Eric. "The Barrier of Language: The Irony of Language in Faulkner," *Modern Fiction Studies* XIII (Spring 1967), 19-31.

Lawson, Lewis A. "The Grotesque-Comic in the Snopes Trilogy," *Literature and Psychology* XV (Spring 1965), 107-119.

Leibowitz, Herbert A. "The Snopes Dilemma and the South," *University of Kansas City Review* XXVIII (Jun 1962), 273-284.

Lion in the Garden: Interviews with William Faulkner.

Longley, John Lewis, Jr. *The Tragic Mask: A Study of Faulkner's Heroes.*

FAULKNER, WILLIAM, Continued

Marković, Vida. "Interview with Faulkner," *Texas Studies in Literature and Language* V (Winter 1964), 463-466.

Materassi, Mario. "Faulkner E La Presentazione Del Personaggio," *Studi Americani* VII (1961), 163-193.

Meriwether, James B. "Early Notices of Faulkner by Phil Stone and Louis Cochran," *Mississippi Quarterly* XVII (Summer 1964), 136-164.

————, (ed.). *Essays, Speeches and Public Letters by William Faulkner.*

————. "Faulkner and the New Criticism," *Books Abroad* XXXVII (Summer 1963), 265-268; see also "Remarks" by Wolfgang Bernard Fleishmann, 268-270.

————. "Faulkner and the South," *Southern Writers: Appraisals in Our Time,* 142-161.

————. *The Literary Career of William Faulkner: A Bibliographical Study.*

————. "The Text of Faulkner's Books: An Introduction and Some Notes," *Modern Fiction Studies* IX (Summer 1963), 159-170.

Miller, David M. "Faulkner's Women," *Modern Fiction Studies* XIII (Spring 1967), 3-17.

Miller, Douglas T. "Faulkner and the Civil War: Myth and Reality," *American Quarterly* XV (Summer 1963), 200-209.

Miller, James E. "William Faulkner: Descent into the Vortex," *Quests Surd and Absurd: Essays in American Literature,* 41-65.

Millgate, Michael. *The Achievement of William Faulkner.*

————. "Faulkner in Toronto: A Further Note," *University of Toronto Quarterly* XXXVII (Jan 1968), 197-202.

————. "William Faulkner," *British Association for American Studies Bulletin* 5 (Dec 1962), 43-46.

————. "William Faulkner, Cadet," *University of Toronto Quarterly* XXXV (Jan 1966), 117-132.

————. "William Faulkner: The Problem of Point of View," *Patterns of Commitment in American Literature,* 181-192.

Mizener, Arthur. "The American Hero as Gentleman: Gavin Stevens," *The Sense of Life in the Modern Novel,* 161-181.

Moses, W. R. "The Limits of Yoknapatawpha County," *Georgia Review* XVI (Fall 1962), 297-305.

Nathan, Monique. *Faulkner par luimeme.*

Nilon, Charles H. *Faulkner and the Negro.*

FAULKNER, WILLIAM, Continued

Noble, David W. *The Eternal Adam and the New World Garden,* 163-177.

O'Brien, Frances Blazer. "Faulkner and Wright, Alias S.S. Van Dine," *Mississippi Quarterly* XIV (Spring 1961), 101-107.

O'Connor, William Van. "Faulkner, Hemingway, and the 1920's," *The Twenties: Poetry and Prose,* 95-98.

––––––. "Faulkner's One-Sided 'Dialogue' With Hemingway," *College English* XXIV (Dec 1962), 208-215.

––––––. *The Grotesque: An American Genre and Other Essays,* 59-77.

––––––. *William Faulkner.*

––––––. "William Faulkner," *Seven Modern American Novelists: An Introduction,* 118-152.

O'Dea, Richard J. "Faulkner's Vestigial Christianity," *Renascence* XXI (Autumn 1968), 44-54.

Otten, Terry. "Faulkner's Use of the Past: A Comment," *Renascence* XX (Summer 1968), 198-207, 214.

Palmer, William J. "The Mechanistic World of *Snopes,*" *Mississippi Quarterly* XX (Fall 1967), 185-194.

Paterson, John. "Hardy, Faulkner, and the Prosaics of Tragedy," *Centennial Review* V (Spring 1961), 156-175.

Peavy, Charles D. "Faulkner and the Howe Interview," *CLA Journal* XI (Dec 1967), 117-123.

Price, Lawrence Marsden. *The Reception of United States Literature in Germany,* 152-157.

Price-Stephens, Gordon. "The British Reception of William Faulkner—1929-1962," *Mississippi Quarterly* XVIII (Summer 1965), 119-185.

––––––. "Faulkner and the Royal Air Force," *Mississippi Quarterly* XVII (Summer 1964), 123-128.

Richardson, H. Edward. "Anderson and Faulkner," *American Literature* XXXVI (Nov 1964), 298-314.

––––––. "The Ways that Faulkner Walked: A Pilgrimage," *Arizona Quarterly* XXI (Summer 1965), 133-145.

Richardson, Kenneth E. *Force and Faith in the Novels of William Faulkner,* Studies in American Literature, Volume VII.

Riese, Utz. "Das Dilemma eines dritten Weges: William Faulkners widerspruchlicher Humanismus [1. Teil]," *Zeitschrift für Anglistik und Amerikanistik* 16 (1968), 138-155; "[Part II]," 257-273.

Rinaldi, Nicholas M. "Game Imagery and Game-Consciousness in

Faulkner's Fiction," *Twentieth Century Literature* X (Oct 1964), 108-118.

Roberts, James L. "Snopeslore," *University of Kansas City Review* XXVIII (Oct 1961), 65-71.

Rubin, Louis D., Jr. "Chronicles of Yoknapatawha: The Dynasties of William Faulkner," *The Faraway Country: Writers of the Modern South*, 43-72.

―――――. "The Difficulties of Being a Southern Writer Today: Or, Getting Out from Under Faulkner," *The Curious Death of the Novel: Essays in American Literature*, 282-293.

Runyan, Harry. *A Faulkner Glossary*.

Shaw, Joe C. "Sociological Aspects of Faulkner's Writing," *Mississippi Quarterly* XIV (Summer 1961), 148-152.

Sidney, George. "An Addition to the Faulkner Canon: The Hollywood Writings," *Twentieth Century Literature* VI (Jan 1961), 172-174.

―――――. "William Faulkner and Hollywood," *Colorado Quarterly* IX (Spring 1961), 367-377.

Simon, John K. "Faulkner and Sartre: Metamorphosis and the Obscene," *Comparative Literature* XV (Summer 1963), 216-225.

Slabey, Robert M. "Quentin Compson's 'Lost Childhood,'" *Studies in Short Fiction* I (Spring 1964), 173-183.

Slatoff, Walter J. *Quest for Failure. A Study of William Faulkner.*

Solomon, Eric. "Joseph Conrad, William Faulkner, and the Nobel Prize Speech," *Notes and Queries* N.S. 14 (Jul 1967), 247-248.

Spratling, William. "Chronicle of a Friendship: William Faulkner in New Orleans," *Texas Quarterly* IX (Spring 1966), 34-40; "*Sherwood Anderson & Other Famous Creoles*, by William Spratling and William Faulkner—A Facsimile," 41-97; *Sherwood Anderson and other Creoles*, Austin: University of Texas Press, 1967.

Stern, Richard G. "Faulkner, at Home Abroad," *Books Abroad* XXXIX (Autumn 1965), 408-411.

Stewart, Randall. "Hawthorne and Faulkner," *Regionalism and Beyond: Essays of Randall Stewart*, 126-135.

―――――. "1956: Hawthorne and Faulkner," *College English* XXII (Nov 1960), 128-132.

―――――. "The Old Cost of Human Redemption," *Regionalism and Beyond: Essays of Randall Stewart*, 204-211.

Stone, Emily Whitehurst. "Faulkner Gets Started," *Texas Quarterly* VIII (Winter 1965), 142-148.

Strandberg, Victor. "Faulkner's Poor Parson and the Technique of Inversion," *Sewanee Review* LXXIII (Spring 1965), 182-190.

Sultan, Stanley. "Call Me Ishmael: The Hagiography of Isaac McCaslin," *Texas Studies in Literature and Language* III (Spring 1961), 50-66.

Swiggart, Peter. *The Art of Faulkner's Novels.*

—————. "The Snopes Trilogy," *Modern American Fiction: Essays in Criticism,* 194-200.

Tate, Allen. "The State of Letters: William Faulkner 1897-1962," *Sewanee Review* LXXI (Winter 1963), 160-164; reprinted from the *New Statesman* (London).

Thompson, Lawrance. *William Faulkner.*

Thorp, Willard. *American Writing in the Twentieth Century,* 263-274.

Tuck, Dorothy. *Crowell's Handbook of Faulkner,* 1-15.

Turner, Arlin. "William Faulkner, Southern Novelist," *Mississippi Quarterly* XIV (Summer 1961), 117-130.

Van Nostrand, A. D. "The Poetic Dialogues of William Faulkner," *Everyman His Own Poet,* 175-196.

Vickery, Olga W. *The Novels of William Faulkner: A Critical Interpretation,* revised edition.

—————. "William Faulkner and the Figure in the Carpet," *Critical Approaches to American Literature: Volume II, Walt Whitman to William Faulkner,* 304-319.

—————. "William Faulkner and the Figure in the Carpet," *South Atlantic Quarterly* LXIII (Summer 1964), 318-335.

Wager, Willis. *American Literature: A World View,* 235-238.

Warren, Robert Penn. "Faulkner: The South and the Negro," *Southern Review* I (Jul 1965), 501-529.

—————. "Faulkner: The South, the Negro, and Time," *Faulkner: A Collection of Critical Essays,* 251-271.

Watkins, Floyd C. "Faulkner and his Critics," *Texas Studies in Literature and Language* X (Summer 1968), 317-329.

—————. "The Gentle Reader and Mr. Faulkner's Morals," *Georgia Review* XIII (Spring 1959), 68-75.

—————. "William Faulkner, the Individual, and the World," *Georgia Review* XIV (Fall 1960), 238-247.

Way, Brian. "William Faulkner," *Critical Quarterly* 3 (Spring 1961), 42-53.

FAULKNER, WILLIAM, Continued

Weatherby, H. L. "Sutpen's Garden," *Georgia Review* XXI (Fall 1967) , 354-369.

Webb, James W. and A. Wigfall Green. *William Faulkner of Oxford.*

Weber, Robert. "Aspekte der Faulkner-Kritik in Frankreich," *Jahrbuch für Amerikastudien,* 6 (1961) , 152-167.

Weisgerber, Jean. "Faulkner's Monomaniacs: Their Indebtedness to Raskolnikov," *Comparative Literature Studies* V (Jun 1968) , 181-193.

Wertenbaker, Thomas J., Jr. "Faulkner's Point of View and the Chronicle of Ike McCaslin," *College English* XXIV (Dec 1962) , 169-178.

Wheeler, Otis B. "Some Uses of Folk Humor by Faulkner," *Mississippi Quarterly* XVII (Spring 1964) , 107-122.

White, William. "Unpublished Faulkner: Reply to a Nathanael West Questionnaire," *American Book Collector* XVII (Sept 1966) , 27.

Woodworth, Stanley D. *William Faulkner en France (1931-1952).*

Wynne, Carolyn. "Aspects of Space: John Marin and William Faulkner," *American Quarterly* XVI (Spring 1964) , 59-71.

BIBLIOGRAPHY

Backman, Melvin. *Faulkner: The Major Years: A Critical Study,* 187-199.

Beebe, Maurice. "Criticism of William Faulkner: A Selected Checklist," *Modern Fiction Studies* XIII (Spring 1967) , 115-161.

Blotner, Joseph. *William Faulkner's Library—A Catologue.*

Brylowski, Walter. *Faulkner's Olympian Laugh: Myth in the Novels,* 230-232.

Critical Approaches to American Literature: Volume II, Walt Whitman to William Faulkner, 343-344.

Faulkner: A Collection of Critical Essays, 310-311.

Hoffman, Frederick J. *William Faulkner,* 126-128.

Holmes, Edward M. *Faulkner's Twice Told Tales; His Re-Use of His Material,* 116-118.

Meriwether, James B. *The Literary Career of William Faulkner.*

————. "The Literary Career of William Faulkner: Catalogue of an Exhibition in the Princeton University Library," *Princeton University Library Chronicle* XXI (Spring 1960) , 111-164.

————. "Sartoris and Snopes: An Early Notice," *Library Chronicle of the University of Texas* VII (Summer 1962) , 36-39.

O'Connor, William Van. *William Faulkner,* 45-47.

FAULKNER, WILLIAM, Continued

Price, Lawrence Marsden. *The Reception of United States Literature in Germany*, 217-218.

Price-Stephens, Gordon. Appendix to "The British Reception of William Faulkner—1929-1962," *Mississippi Quarterly* XVIII (Summer 1965) , 186-200.

Richardson, Kenneth E. *Force and Faith in the Novels of William Faulkner,* Studies in American Literature, Volume VII, 176-184.

Slatoff, Walter J. *Quest for Failure: A Study of William Faulkner*, 266-269.

Sleeth, Irene Lynn. *William Faulkner: A Bibliography of Criticism.*

————. "William Faulkner: A Bibliography of Criticism," *Twentieth Century Literature* VIII (Apr 1962) , 18-43.

Thompson, Lawrance. *William Faulkner*, 177-179.

Tuck, Dorothy. *Crowell's Handbook of Faulkner*, 247-250.

FAWCETT, EDGAR

GENERAL

Harrison, Stanley R. "Through a Nineteenth-Century Looking Glass: The Letters of Edgar Fawcett," *Tulane Studies in English* XV (1967) , 107-157.

FEIKEMA, FEIKE

(*see* MANFRED, FREDERICK)

FERBER, EDNA

SHOW BOAT

Plante, Patricia R. "Mark Twain, Ferber and the Mississippi," *Mark Twain Journal* XIII (Summer 1966) , 8-10.

FERGUSSON, HARVEY

THE CONQUEST OF DON PEDRO

Robinson, Cecil. *With the Ears of Strangers: The Mexican in American Literature*, 87-94.

FERGUSSON, HARVEY, Continued

FOLLOWERS OF THE SUN
Robinson, Cecil. *With the Ears of Strangers: The Mexican in American Literature,* 75-77, 82-84, 156-159.

GENERAL
Pilkington, William T. "The Southwestern Novels of Harvey Fergusson," *New Mexico Quarterly* XXXV (Winter 1965-66), 330-343.

FIEDLER, LESLIE A.

GENERAL
Davis, Robert Gorham. "Leslie Fiedler's Fictions," *Commentary* XLIII (Jan 1967), 73-77.

Schulz, Max F. "Leslie A. Fiedler and the Hieroglyphs of Life," *Twentieth Century Literature* 14 (Apr 1968), 24-34.

FISHER, VARDIS

APRIL
Flora, Joseph M. *Vardis Fisher,* 109-113.

CHILDREN OF GOD
Flora, Joseph M. *Vardis Fisher,* 131-138.

CITY OF ILLUSION
Flora, Joseph M. *Vardis Fisher,* 129-131.

DARK BRIDWELL
Flora, Joseph M. *Vardis Fisher,* 21-22, 106-109.

THE DARKNESS AND THE DEEP
Flora, Joseph M. *Vardis Fisher,* 74-78.

THE DIVINE PASSION
Flora, Joseph M. *Vardis Fisher,* 85-87.

THE GOLDEN ROOMS
Flora, Joseph M. *Vardis Fisher,* 78-82.

THE INHERITORS
Duncan, Kirby L. "William Golding and Vardis Fisher," *College English* XXVII (Dec 1965), 232-235.

INTIMATIONS OF EVE
Flora, Joseph M. *Vardis Fisher,* 82-84.

THE ISLAND OF THE INNOCENT
Flora, Joseph M. *Vardis Fisher,* 89-91.

Holmes, Opal Laurel. "Once in a Wifetime," *American Book Collector* XIV (Sept 1963) , 13-14.

Margarick, P. "Vardis Fisher and His Testament of Man," *American Book Collector* XIV (Sept 1963) , 20-24.

Taber, Ronald W. "Vardis Fisher: New Directions for the Historical Novel," *Western American Literature* 1 (Winter 1967) , 285-296.

BIBLIOGRAPHY

Flora, Joseph M. *Vardis Fisher,* 149-152.

Kellog, George. *Vardis Fisher: A Bibliography.*

————. "Vardis Fisher: A Bibliography," *American Book Collector* XIV (Sept 1963) , 37-39.

FITZGERALD, F. SCOTT

THE BEAUTIFUL AND DAMNED

Astro, Richard. *"Vandover and the Brute* and *The Beautiful and Damned:* A Search for Thematic and Stylistic Reinterpretations," *Modern Fiction Studies* XIV (Winter 1968-1969) , 397-413.

Bruccoli, Matthew. "Bibliographical Notes on F. Scott Fitzgerald's *The Beautiful and Damned,"* *Studies in Bibliography* XIII (1960) , 258-261.

Eble, Kenneth. *F. Scott Fitzgerald,* 68-75.

Goldhurst, William *F. Scott Fitzgerald and His Contemporaries,* 91-104, 184-186.

Gross, Barry. "The Dark Side of Twenty-Five: Fitzgerald and *The Beautiful and Damned,"* *Bucknell Review* XVI (Dec 1968) , 40-52.

Hindus, Milton. *F. Scott Fitzgerald,* 27-34.

Katz, Joseph. "Gloria Patch's Tomatoes," *Fitzgerald Newsletter* 37 (Spring 1967) , 3-4.

Lehan, Richard D. *F. Scott Fitzgerald and the Craft of Fiction,* 78-90.

Miller, James E., Jr. *F. Scott Fitzgerald: His Art and His Technique,* 59-77.

Perosa, Sergio. *The Art of F. Scott Fitzgerald,* 36-51.

Piper, Henry Dan. *F. Scott Fitzgerald,* 82-99.

Sklar, Robert. *F. Scott Fitzgerald: The Last Laocoon,* 92-107.

Turnbull, Andrew. *Scott Fitzgerald,* 122-125.

THE GREAT GATSBY

Anderson, Hilton. "The Rich Bunch in *The Great Gatsby,"* *Southern Quarterly* VI (Jan 1968) , 163-173.

Arnold, Aerol. "Picture, Scene, and Social Comment: *The Great Gatsby*," *University Review* XXX (Dec 1963), 111-117.

Babb, Howard S. "*The Great Gatsby* and the Grotesque," *Criticism* V (Fall 1963), 336-348.

Bettina, Sister M., SSND. "The Artifact in Imagery: Fitzgerald's *The Great Gatsby*," *Twentieth Century Literature* IX (Oct 1963), 140-142.

Bruccoli, Matthew J. "A Further Note on the First Printing of *The Great Gatsby*," *Studies in Bibliography* XVI (1963), 244.

———. "Gatsby's Car," *Fitzgerald Newsletter* 20 (Winter 1963), 4-5.

———. "The *Orgastic-Orgiastic* Case Reopened," *Fitzgerald Newsletter* 30 (Summer 1965), 4.

Burleson, Richard A. "Color Imagery in *Great Gatsby*," *Fitzgerald Newsletter* 39 (Fall 1967), 13-14.

Carlisle, E. Fred. "The Triple Vision of Nick Carraway," *Modern Fiction Studies* XI (Winter 1965-1966), 351-360.

Carpenter, Richard C. "Fitzgerald's *The Great Gatsby*," *Explicator* XIX (Jun 1961), No. 63.

D'Avanzo, Mario L. "Gatsby and Holden Caulfield," *Fitzgerald Newsletter* 38 (Summer 1967), 4-6.

Doyno, Victor A. "Patterns in *The Great Gatsby*," *Modern Fiction Studies* XII (Winter 1966-67), 415-426.

Dyson, A. E. "*The Great Gatsby:* Thirty-Six Years After," *F. Scott Fitzgerald: A Collection of Critical Essays*, 112-124.

———. "*The Great Gatsby:* Thirty-Six Years After," *Modern Fiction Studies* VII (Spring 1961), 37-48.

Eble, Kenneth. "The Craft of Revision: *The Great Gatsby*," *American Literature*, XXXVI (Nov 1964), 315-326.

———. *F. Scott Fitzgerald*, 86-103.

Fiedler, Leslie A. *Love and Death in the American Novel*, 300-304.

Fraser, John. "Dust and Dreams and *The Great Gatsby*," *ELH* XXXII (Dec 1965), 554-564.

Goldhurst, William. *F. Scott Fitzgerald and His Contemporaries*, 36-41, 79-81, 138-140, 145-147, 150-154, 182-184.

Gross, Barry Edward. "Fitzgerald's 'Anti-Semitism': A Reply to William Goldhurst," *Fitzgerald Newsletter* 21 (Spring 1963), 3-5; William Goldhurst, "An Answer to Barry Edward Gross," *Fitzgerald Newsletter* 22 (Summer 1963), 1-2.

FITZGERALD, F. SCOTT, Continued

————. "Jay Gatsby and Myrtle Wilson: A Kinship," *Tennessee Studies in Literature,* VIII (1963) , 57-60.

————. "A Note on Fitzgerald's Use of the House," *Fitzgerald Newsletter* 23 (Fall 1963) , 2-4.

Guerin, Wilfred Louis. "Christian Myth and Naturalistic Deity: *The Great Gatsby,*" *Renascence* XIV (Winter 1962) , 80-89.

Hakac, John. "*The Great Gatsby:* 'moving her hands like Frisco,' " *Fitzgerald Newsletter* 36 (Winter 1967) , 4-6.

Hardy, John Edward. "*The Great Gatsby:* One in Two," *Man in the Modern Novel,* 82-95.

Hill, John S. "Henry James: Fitzgerald's Literary Ancestor," *Fitzgerald Newsletter* 40 (Winter 1968) , 6-10.

Hindus, Milton. *F. Scott Fitzgerald,* 35-49.

Hoffman, Frederick J. *The Great Gatsby: A Study.*

Joseph, Gerhard. "The American Triumph of the Egg: Anderson's 'The Egg' and Fitzgerald's *The Great Gatsby,*" *Criticism* VII (Spring 1965) , 131-140.

Lauter, Paul. "Plato's Stepchildren, Gatsby and Cohn," *Modern Fiction Studies* IX (Winter 1963-64) , 338-346.

Lehan, Richard D. *F. Scott Fitzgerald and the Craft of Fiction,* 91-122.

Le Vot, A. E. "*Our Mutual Friend* and *The Great Gatsby,*" *Fitzgerald Newsletter* 20 (Winter 1963) , 1-4.

Lisca, Peter. "Nick Carraway and the Imagery of Disorder," *Twentieth Century Literature* 13 (Apr 1967) , 18-28.

Lockridge, Ernest H. Introduction, *Twentieth Century Interpretations of "The Great Gatsby,"* 1-18.

Long, Robert Emmet. "*The Great Gatsby* and the Tradition of Joseph Conrad: Part ·I," *Texas Studies in Literature and Language* VIII (Summer 1966) , 257-276; "Part II," VIII (Fall 1966) , 407-422.

————. "A Note on Color Symbolism in *The Great Gatsby,*" *Fitzgerald Newsletter* 17 (Spring 1962) , 1-3.

Marx, Leo. *The Machine in the Garden: Technology and the Pastoral Ideal in America,* 356-365.

McDonnell, Robert F. "Eggs and Eyes in *The Great Gatsby,*" *Modern Fiction Studies* VII (Spring 1961) , 32-36.

Mellard, James M. "Counterpoint as Technique in *The Great Gatsby,*" *English Journal* LV (Oct 1966) , 853-859.

Miller, James E., Jr. "Boats Against the Current," *Twentieth Century Interpretations of "The Great Gatsby,"* 19-36.

————. *F. Scott Fitzgerald: His Art and His Technique,* 98-126, 159-160.

Millgate, Michael. "Scott Fitzgerald as Social Novelist: Statement and Technique in 'The Great Gatsby,' " *Modern Language Review* LVII (Jul 1962) , 335-339.

Minter, David L. "Dream, Design and Interpretation," *Twentieth Century Interpretations of "The Great Gatsby,"* 82-89.

Mizener, Arthur. "F. Scott Fitzgerald: *The Great Gatsby,"* *The American Novel from James Fenimore Cooper to William Faulkner,* 180-191.

————. "Gatsby, 35 Years Later," *New York Times Book Review* 65 (Apr 24, 1960) , 4, 46.

Natterstad, J. H. "Fitzgerald's *The Great Gatsby,"* *Explicator* XXVI (Apr 1968) , No. 68.

Perosa, Sergio. *The Art of F. Scott Fitzgerald,* 60-82.

Piper, Henry Dan. *F. Scott Fitzgerald,* 100-154.

Raleigh, John Henry. "Fitzgerald's Great Gatsby," *Time, Place, and Idea: Essays on the Novel,* 56-74.

Randall, Dale B. J. "The 'Seer' and 'Seen' Themes in *Gatsby* and Some of Their Parallels in Eliot and Wright," *Twentieth Century Literature* X (Jul 1964) , 51-63.

Randall, John H., III. "Jay Gatsby's Hidden Source of Wealth," *Modern Fiction Studies* XIII (Summer 1967) , 247-257.

Richards, Robert and Chris. "Feeling in *The Great Gatsby,"* *Western Humanities Review* XXI (Summer 1967) , 257-265.

Rodda, Peter. *"The Great Gatsby,"* *English Studies in Africa* 11 (Sept 1968) , 95-126.

Samuels, Charles Thomas. "The Greatness of Gatsby," *Massachusetts Review* VII (Autumn 1966) , 783-794.

Satterwhite, Joseph N. "The Midsummer Fires in East Egg: A Note on Technique in *The Great Gatsby,"* *Ball State Teachers College Forum* I (Spring 1960) , 43-48.

Sawyer, Paul. "The Schedule in *Great Gatsby,"* *Fitzgerald Newsletter* 39 (Fall 1967) , 4-8.

Schneider, Daniel J. "Color-Symbolism in *The Great Gatsby,"* *University Review* XXXI (Oct 1964) , 13-18.

Scrimgeour, Gary J. "Against *The Great Gatsby,"* *Criticism* VIII (Winter 1966) , 75-86.

Shroeder, John. " 'Some Unfortunate Idyllic Love Affair': The Legends of Taji and Jay Gatsby," *Books at Brown* XXII (1968), 143-153.

Sklar, Robert. *F. Scott Fitzgerald: The Last Laocoon,* 163-196.

Slattery, Sister Margaret Patrice. "The Function of Time in *Great Gatsby* and 'Babylon,' " *Fitzgerald Newsletter* 39 (Fall 1967), 1-4.

Slevin, James F. "Water Images in *Great Gatsby," Fitzgerald Newsletter* 39 (Fall 1967), 12-13.

Stallman, R. W. *The Houses That James Built,* 131-158.

Stein, William Bysshe. "Gatsby's Morgan Le Fay," *Fitzgerald Newsletter* 15 (Fall 1961), 1.

Tamke, Alexander R. "The 'Gat' in Gatsby: Neglected Aspect of a Novel," *Modern Fiction Studies* XIV (Winter 1968-1969), 443-445.

Tanner, Bernard. "The Gospel of Gatsby," *English Journal* LIV (Sept 1965), 467-474.

Tanselle, G. Thomas and Jackson R. Bryer. "*The Great Gatsby:* A Study in Literary Reputation," *New Mexico Quarterly* XXXIII (Winter 1963-64), 409-425.

Trask, David F. "A Note on Fitzgerald's *The Great Gatsby," University Review* XXXIII (Mar 1967), 197-202.

Turnbull, Andrew. *Scott Fitzgerald,* 138-142, 218-220, 267-269.

Twentieth Century Interpretations of the Great Gatsby: A Collection of Critical Essays.

Vanderbilt, Kermit. "James, Fitzgerald, and the American Self Image," *Massachusetts Review* VI (Winter-Spring 1965), 289-304.

Westbrook, J. S. "Nature and Optics in *The Great Gatsby," American Literature* XXXII (Mar 1960), 78-84.

Young, Philip. "Scott Fitzgerald's Waste Land," *Literary Criterion* V (Winter 1961), 75-83.

THE LAST TYCOON

Goldhurst, William. *F. Scott Fitzgerald and His Contemporaries,* 65-68, 186-187, 223-227.

Hart, John E. "Fitzgerald's *The Last Tycoon:* A Search for Identity," *Modern Fiction Studies* VII (Spring 1961), 63-70.

Hindus, Milton. *F. Scott Fitzgerald,* 70-86.

Lehan, Richard D. *F. Scott Fitzgerald and the Craft of Fiction,* 153-163.

Miller, James E., Jr. *F. Scott Fitzgerald: His Art and His Technique,* 148-158, 161-162.

Millgate, Michael. "Scott Fitzgerald as Social Novelist: Statement and

Technique in *The Last Tycoon,*" *English Studies* XLIII (Feb 1962), 29-34.

Mizener, Arthur. "The American Hero as Entrepreneur: Monroe Stahr," *The Sense of Life in the Modern Novel,* 183-204.

Perosa, Sergio. "The Wise and Tragic Sense of Life," *The Art of F. Scott Fitzgerald,* 152-178.

Piper, Henry Dan. *F. Scott Fitzgerald,* 258-286.

Sklar, Robert. *F. Scott Fitzgerald: The Last Laocoon,* 329-342.

Turnbull, Andrew. *Scott Fitzgerald,* 185-6, 272-3, 283-4.

TENDER IS THE NIGHT

Bruccoli, Matthew J. *The Composition of Tender is the Night: A Study of the Manuscripts.*

―――. "Inscribed *Tender is the Night,*" *Fitzgerald Newsletter* 31 (Fall 1965), 4.

―――. "Material for a Centenary Edition of *Tender is the Night,*" *Studies in Bibliography* XVII (1964), 177-193.

―――. "*Tender Is the Night* and the Reviewers," *Modern Fiction Studies* VII (Spring 1961), 49-54.

Bryer, Jackson R. "A Psychiatrist Reviews *Tender is the Night,*" *Literature and Psychology* XVI 3, 4 (1966), 198-199.

Doherty, William E. "*Tender is the Night* and the 'Ode to a Nightingale,' " *Explorations of Literature,* 100-114.

Eble, Kenneth. *F. Scott Fitzgerald,* 133-140.

Ellis, James. "Fitzgerald's Fragmented Hero: Dick Diver," *University Review* XXXII (Oct 1965), 43-49.

Goldhurst, William. *F. Scott Fitzgerald and His Contemporaries,* 63-65, 115-119, 168-169, 200-203, 206-208, 210-215.

Grube, John. "*Tender is the Night:* Keats and Scott Fitzgerald," *Dalhousie Review* XLIV (Winter 1964-65), 433-441.

Hindus, Milton. *F. Scott Fitzgerald,* 50-69.

Lehan, Richard D. *F. Scott Fitzgerald and the Craft of Fiction,* 123-148.

Long, Robert Emmet. "Dreiser and Frederic: The Upstate New York Exile of Dick Diver," *Fitzgerald Newsletter* 37 (Spring 1967), 1-2.

Lucas, John. "In Praise of Scott Fitzgerald," *Critical Quarterly* 5 (Summer 1963), 132-147.

Miller, James E., Jr. *F. Scott Fitzgerald: His Art and His Technique,* 132-139, 140-148.

Mizener, Arthur. "F. Scott Fitzgerald: *Tender is the Night,*" *Twelve Great American Novels,* 104-119.

FITZGERALD, F. SCOTT, Continued

————. "On F. Scott Fitzgerald," *Talks With Authors*, 26-38.

Perosa, Sergio. "Intricate Destiny," *The Art of F. Scott Fitzgerald*, 102-130.

Phillips, Robert S. "Fitzgerald and *The Day of the Locust*," *Fitzgerald Newsletter* 15 (Fall 1961), 2-3.

Piper, Henry Dan. *F. Scott Fitzgerald*, 205-228.

Sklar, Robert. *F. Scott Fitzgerald: The Last Laocoon*, 249-292.

Stallman, R. W. *The Houses That James Built*, 158-172.

Stevens, A. Wilber. "Fitzgerald's *Tender is the Night:* The Idea as Morality," *Brigham Young University Studies* III (Spring-Summer 1961), 95-104.

Turnbull, Andrew. *Scott Fitzgerald*, 158-9, 218-224, 269-70.

White, Eugene. "The 'Intricate Destiny' of Dick Diver," *Modern Fiction Studies* VII (Spring 1961), 55-62.

Whitehead, Lee M. "*Tender is the Night* and George Herbert Mead: An 'Actor's' Tragedy," *Literature and Psychology* XV (Summer 1965), 180-191.

THIS SIDE OF PARADISE

Brown, Paul Allan. "Fitzgerald and Petting," *Fitzgerald Newsletter* 26 (Summer 1964), 4.

Eble, Kenneth. *F. Scott Fitzgerald*, 40-51.

————. "Gloria Gilbert's Age," *Fitzgerald Newsletter* 22 (Summer 1963), 1.

Hamblen, Abigail Ann. "The Fitzgeralds' Coming of Age," *University Review* XXXV (Dec 1968), 157-160.

Hindus, Milton. *F. Scott Fitzgerald*, 17-26.

Kahn, Sy. "*This Side of Paradise:* The Pageantry of Disillusion," *Midwest Quarterly* VII (Winter 1966), 177-194.

Lehan, Richard D. *F. Scott Fitzgerald and the Craft of Fiction*, 63-77.

Miller, James E., Jr. *F. Scott Fitzgerald: His Art and His Technique*, 16-44.

Perosa, Sergio. *The Art of F. Scott Fitzgerald*, 15-29.

Piper, Henry Dan. *F. Scott Fitzgerald*, 37-63.

Shain, Charles E. "This Side of Paradise," *F. Scott Fitzgerald: A Collection of Critical Essays*, 77-79.

Sklar, Robert. *F. Scott Fitzgerald: The Last Laocoon*, 31-58.

Turnbull, Andrew. *Scott Fitzgerald*, 47-48, 54-56, 69-70, 111-114, 118-119, 123-4, 301-02.

Tuttleton, James W. "The Presence of Poe in *This Side of Paradise,*" *English Language Notes* III (Jun 1966) , 284-289.

Yates, Donald A. "The Road to 'Paradise': Fitzgerald's Literary Apprenticeship," *Modern Fiction Studies* VII (Spring 1961) , 19-31.

GENERAL

Bachelor, R. E. "The Weft of Experience in F. Scott Fitzgerald," *Trace* 40 (Jan-Mar 1961) , 2-5.

Bedingfield, Dolores. "Fitzgerald's Corruptible Dream," *Dalhousie Review* XLI (Winter 1961-62) , 513-521.

Bezanson, Walter. "Scott Fitzgerald: Bedevilled Prince Charming," *The Young Rebel in American Literature,* 79-96.

Brooks, Cleanth. "The American 'Innocence': In James, Fitzgerald, and Faulkner," *Shenandoah* XVI (Autumn 1964) , 21-37.

Brown, Paul Allan. "Fitzgerald and Charles G. Norris," *Fitzgerald Newsletter* 26 (Summer 1964) , 3-4.

Bruccoli, M. J. "Fitzgerald, Brooks, Hemingway and James: A New Fitzgerald Letter," *Fitzgerald Newsletter* 29 (Spring 1965) , 1-3.

Bryer, Jackson R. "F. Scott Fitzgerald: A Review of Research and Scholarship," *Texas Studies in Literature and Language* V (Spring 1963) , 147-163.

————. "F. Scott Fitzgerald and the State of American Letters in 1921," *Modern Fiction Studies* XII (Summer 1966) , 265-267.

Callaghan, Morley. *That Summer in Paris.*

Cappon, Alexander P. "Idealism in F. Scott Fitzgerald," *University Review* XXX (Dec 1963) , 159-160.

Cardwell, Guy A. "The Lyric World of Scott Fitzgerald," *Virginia Quarterly Review* XXXVIII (Spring 1962) , 299-323.

Cross, K.G.W. *Scott Fitzgerald.*

Eble, Kenneth. *F. Scott Fitzgerald.*

Finkelstein, Sidney. *Existentialism and Alienation in American Literature,* 169-173.

Fitzgerald, F. Scott. "An Interview with F. Scott Fitzgerald," *Saturday Review* 43 (Nov 5, 1960) , 26, 56.

————. "Scott Fitzgerald's 'Thoughtbook,' with an Introduction by John Kuehl," *Princeton University Library Chronicle* XXVI (Winter 1965) , 102-108.

Foster, Richard. "Mailer and the Fitzgerald Tradition," *Novel* I (Winter 1968) , 219-230.

FITZGERALD, F. SCOTT, Continued

Friedrich, Otto. "F. Scott Fitzgerald: Money, Money, Money," *American Scholar* XXIX (Summer 1960), 392-405.

Frohock, W. M. "F. Scott Fitzgerald: Manners and Morals," *Strangers to This Ground: Cultural Diversity in Contemporary American Writing,* 36-62.

Goldhurst, William. *F. Scott Fitzgerald and His Contemporaries.*

Graham, Sheilah. *College of One.*

Grendhal, Jay S. "Gorgeous: Fitzgerald's Epithet for the Jazz Age," *Fitzgerald Newsletter* 30 (Summer 1965), 2-3.

Gross, Theodore L. "F. Scott Fitzgerald: The Hero in Retrospect," *South Atlantic Quarterly* LXVII (Winter 1968), 64-77.

Hindus, Milton. *F. Scott Fitzgerald.*

Hobsbaum, Philip. "Scott Fitzgerald and His Critics: The Appreciation of Minor Art," *British Association For American Studies Bulletin* 6 (Jun 1963), 31-41.

Hoffman, Frederick J. "The 'Irresistible Lothario': F. Scott Fitzgerald's Romantic Hero," *The Twenties: Poetry and Prose,* 59-61.

Howell, John M. "Hemingway and Fitzgerald in Sound and Fury," *Papers on Language and Literature* II (Summer 1966), 234-242.

Irwin, William R. "Dos Passos and Fitzgerald as Reviewers of the American Social Scene," *Neueren Sprachen* (Sept 1960), 417-428.

Jacobson, Dan. "F. Scott Fitzgerald," *Encounter* XIV (Jun 1960), 71-77.

Kreuter, Kent and Gretchen. "The Moralism of the Later Fitzgerald," *Modern Fiction Studies* VII (Spring 1961), 71-81.

Kuehl, John. Introduction, *The Apprentice Fiction of F. Scott Fitzgerald* (New Brunswick, New Jersey, 1965).

————. "The Ordeal of Scott Fitzgerald," *Georgia Review* XVII (Fall 1963), 306-311.

————. "Scott Fitzgerald's Critical Opinions," *Modern Fiction Studies* VII (Spring 1961), 3-18.

————. "Scott Fitzgerald's Reading," *Princeton University Library Chronicle* XXII (Winter 1961), 58-89.

Lehan, Richard D. *F. Scott Fitzgerald and the Craft of Fiction.*

Light, James F. "Political Conscience in the Novels of F. Scott Fitzgerald," *Ball State Teachers College Forum* IV (Spring 1963), 13-25.

Long, Robert E. "*Sister Carrie* and the Rhythm of Failure in Fitzgerald," *Fitzgerald Newsletter* 25 (Spring 1964), 2-4.

Millard, G. C. "F. Scott Fitzgerald: *The Great Gatsby, Tender is the*

Night, The Last Tycoon," English Studies in Africa 8 (Mar 1965), 5-30.

Miller, James E., Jr. *F. Scott Fitzgerald: His Art and His Technique.*

Millgate, Michael. *American Social Fiction: James to Cozzens,* 107-127.

Mizener, Arthur. Introduction, *The Fitzgerald Reader* (New York, 1963).

————. "The Maturity of Scott Fitzgerald," *Sewanee Review* LXVII (Autumn 1959), 658-675.

————. "On F. Scott Fitzgerald," *Talks With Authors,* 23-26, 32-33.

————. "Scott Fitzgerald and the 1920's," *Minnesota Review* I (Winter 1961), 161-174.

————. "Scott Fitzgerald and the Top Girl," *Atlantic Monthly* CCVII (Mar 1961), 55-60.

Morrill, Thomas. "F. Scott Fitzgerald Under the Figlinden Leaf," *Trace* 53 (Summer 1964), 97-104, 185-202.

Myers, Alonzo F. "Lieutenant F. Scott Fitzgerald, United States Army," *Papers on English Language and Literature* I (Spring 1965), 167-176.

Noble, David W. *The Eternal Adam and the New World Garden,* 152-160.

Perosa, Sergio. *The Art of F. Scott Fitzgerald.*

Piper, Henry Dan. *F. Scott Fitzgerald: A Critical Portrait.*

Riddel, Joseph N. "F. Scott Fitzgerald, the Jamesian Inheritance, and the Morality of Fiction," *Modern Fiction Studies* XI (Winter 1965-1966), 331-350.

Robbins, J. Albert. "Fitzgerald and the Simple, Inarticulate Farmer," *Modern Fiction Studies* VII (Winter 1961-62), 365-369.

Rougé, R. "F. Scott Fitzgerald: La Femme et al Mort," *Études Anglaises* XXI (Apr-Jun 1968), 160-167.

Schorer, Mark. "Some Relationships: Gertrude Stein, Sherwood Anderson, F. Scott Fitzgerald, and Ernest Hemingway," *The World We Imagine; Selected Essays,* 299-382.

Shain, Charles E. *F. Scott Fitzgerald.*

————. "F. Scott Fitzgerald," *Seven Modern American Novelists: An Introduction,* 81-117.

Sklar, Robert. *F. Scott Fitzgerald: The Last Laocoon.*

Spatz, Jonas. "Fitzgerald, Hollywood, and the Myth of Success," *The Thirties: Fiction, Poetry, Drama,* 31-37.

FITZGERALD, F. SCOTT, Continued

Spencer, Benjamin T. "Fitzgerald and the American Ambivalence," *South Atlantic Quarterly* LXVI (Summer 1967), 367-381.

Stallman, R. W. "Two New Scott Fitzgerald Letters," *Modern Fiction Studies* XI (Summer 1965), 189-191.

Stephens, Robert O. and James Ellis. "Hemingway, Fitzgerald and the Riddle of 'Henry's Bicycle,'" *English Language Notes* V (Sept 1967), 46-49.

Sugawara, Seiji. "Fitzgerald's Reputation in Japan," *Fitzgerald Newsletter* 15 (Fall 1961), 5-6.

Turnbull, Andrew, (ed.). *The Letters of F. Scott Fitzgerald.*

————. *Scott Fitzgerald.*

————, (ed.). *Scott Fitzgerald: Letters to his Daughter.*

Weimer, David R. *The City as Metaphor,* 88-103.

Wycherley, H. Alan. "Fitzgerald Revisited," *Texas Studies in Literature and Language* VIII (Summer 1966), 277-283.

Young, Philip. "Scott Fitzgerald on his Thirtieth Birthday Sends a Small Gift to Ernest Hemingway," *Modern Fiction Studies* XIV (Summer 1968), 229-230.

BIBLIOGRAPHY

Beebe, Maurice and Jackson R. Bryer. "Criticism of F. Scott Fitzgerald: A Selected Checklist," *Modern Fiction Studies* VII (Spring 1961), 82-94.

Bryer, Jackson R. *The Critical Reputation of F. Scott Fitzgerald. A Bibliographical Study.*

————. "F. Scott Fitzgerald and His Critics: A Bibliographical Record," *Bulletin of Bibliography* XXIII (Jan-Apr 1962), 155-158; (May-Aug), 180-183; (Sept-Dec), 201-208.

Critical Approaches to American Literature: Volume II, Walt Whitman to William Faulkner, 341-342.

Eble, Kenneth. *F. Scott Fitzgerald,* 165-170.

Goldhurst, William. *F. Scott Fitzgerald and His Contemporaries,* 237-242.

Hindus, Milton. *F. Scott Fitzgerald,* 117-119.

Lehan, Richard D. *F. Scott Fitzgerald and the Craft of Fiction,* 196-198.

Miller, James E., Jr. *F. Scott Fitzgerald: His Art and His Technique,* 163-165.

Perosa, Sergio. *The Art of F. Scott Fitzgerald,* 227-235.

Porter, Bernard H. "The First Publications of F. Scott Fitzgerald," *Twentieth Century Literature* V (Jan 1960), 176-182.

FITZGERALD, F. SCOTT, Continued

Price, Lawrence Marsden. *The Reception of United States Literature in Germany*, 218.

FLINT, TIMOTHY

FRANCIS BERRIAN
Folsom, James K. *Timothy Flint*, 33-34, 107-118, 124-125, 127-128, 161-162.
GEORGE MASON
Folsom, James K. *Timothy Flint*, 27-28, 36-38, 131-133.
THE LIFE AND ADVENTURES OF ARTHUR CLENNING
Folsom, James K. *Timothy Flint*, 33-34, 118-130, 161-162.
THE LOST CHILD
Folsom, James K. *Timothy Flint*, 133-136.
SHOSHONEE VALLEY
Folsom, James K. *Timothy Flint*, 136-145, 169-170.
GENERAL
Folsom, James K. *Timothy Flint*.
Lee, Robert Edson. *From West to East*, 37-54.
Lombard, C. M. "Timothy Flint: Early American Disciple of French Romanticism," *Revue de Littérature Comparée* 36 (Apr-Jun 1962), 276-282.
BIBLIOGRAPHY
Folsom, James K. *Timothy Flint*, 180-186.

FORBES, ESTHER

GENERAL
Bertram, Martin. "The Private Lives of Esther Forbes," *University of Kansas City Review* XXVI (Jun 1960), 295-301.

FORD, JESSE HILL

THE LIBERATION OF LORD BYRON JONES
McGill, Ralph. "The Clearest Truth is in Fiction: Jesse Hill Ford's Novel of the South," *Atlantic Monthly* CCXVI (Aug 1965), 92-93.

FOX, JOHN, JR.

BIBLIOGRAPHY
Titus, Warren I. "John Fox, Jr. (1862-1919)," *American Literary Realism* 3 (Summer 1968), 5-8.

FRANK, WALDO

THE BRIDEGROOM COMETH
Carter, Paul J. *Waldo Frank,* 118-124.
CHALK FACE
Carter, Paul J. *Waldo Frank,* 62-67.
CITY BLOCK
Carter, Paul J. *Waldo Frank,* 49-54.
THE DEATH AND BIRTH OF DAVID MARKAND
Carter, Paul J. *Waldo Frank,* 103-113.
ISLAND IN THE ATLANTIC
Carter, Paul J. *Waldo Frank,* 137-143.
NOT HEAVEN
Carter, Paul J. *Waldo Frank,* 150-157.
GENERAL
Carter, Paul J. *Waldo Frank.*
West, Thomas Reed. "Waldo Frank: The Machine in Cultural Ferment," *Flesh of Steel: Literature and the Machine in American Culture,* 35-53.
BIBLIOGRAPHY
Carter, Paul J. *Waldo Frank,* 184-186.

FREDENBURGH, THEODORE

SOLDIERS MARCH!
Cooperman, Stanley. *World War I and the American Novel,* 137-141.

FREDERICK, HAROLD

THE DAMNATION OF THERON WARE
Carter, Everett. Introduction, *The Damnation of Theron Ware* (Cambridge, Massachusetts, 1960).
Johnson, George W. "Harold Frederic's Young Goodman Ware: The Ambiguities of a Realistic Romance," *Modern Fiction Studies* VIII (Winter 1962-63), 361-374.

FREDERICK, HAROLD, Continued

O'Donnell, Thomas F. and Hoyt C. Franchere. *Harold Frederic*, 108-117.

Raleigh, John Henry. *"The Damnation of Theron Ware," Time, Place, and Idea: Essays on the Novel*, 75-95.

————. Introduction, *The Damnation of Theron Ware* (New York, 1960).

Vanderbeets, Richard. "The Ending of *The Damnation of Theron Ware," American Literature* XXXVI (Nov 1964), 358-359.

Woodward, Robert H. "Some Sources for Harold Frederic's *The Damnation of Theron Ware," American Literature* XXXIII (Mar 1961), 46-51.

GLORIA MUNDI

O'Donnell, Thomas F. and Hoyt C. Franchere. *Harold Frederic*, 120-130.

IN THE VALLEY

O'Donnell, Thomas F. and Hoyt C. Franchere. *Harold Frederic*, 82-89.

THE LAWTON GIRL

O'Donnell, Thomas F. and Hoyt C. Franchere. *Harold Frederic*, 89-96.

Wüstenhagen, Heinz. "Harold Frederics *The Lawton Girl," Zeitschrift Für Anglistik und Amerikanistik* XII (Heft 1, 1964), 32-53.

THE MARKET-PLACE

Eichelberger, Clayton L. "Philanthropy in Frederic's *The Market-Place," American Quarterly* XX (Spring 1968), 111-116.

O'Donnell, Thomas F. and Hoyt C. Franchere. *Harold Frederic*, 130-140.

THE RETURN OF THE O'MAHONY

O'Donnell, Thomas F. and Hoyt C. Franchere. *Harold Frederic*, 96-103.

SETH'S BROTHER'S WIFE

O'Donnell, Thomas F. and Hoyt C. Franchere. *Harold Frederic*, 73-82.

Towers, Tom H. "The Problem of Determinism in Frederic's First Novel," *College English* XXVI (Feb 1965), 361-366.

GENERAL

Garner, Stanton. "The Publishing History of Harold Frederic: A Correction," *Books at Brown* XXII (1968), 95-101.

O'Donnell, Thomas F. and Hoyt C. Franchere. *Harold Frederic*.

Ziff, Larzer. *The American 1890s: Life and Times of a Lost Generation*, 206-219.

FREDERICK, HAROLD, Continued

BIBLIOGRAPHY

Editors. "Harold Frederic (1856-1898): A Critical Bibliography of Secondary Comment," *American Literary Realism* 2 (Spring 1968), 1-70.

Garner, Stanton B. "A Harold Frederic First," *Studies in Bibliography* XV (1962), 268-269.

O'Donnell, Thomas F. "Harold Frederic (1856-1898)," *American Literary Realism* 1 (Fall 1967), 39-44.

O'Donnell, Thomas F. and Hoyt C. Franchere. *Harold Frederic*, 176-179.

Woodward, Robert H. "Frederic's Collection of Reviews: Supplement to the Checklist of Contemporary Reviews of Frederic's Writings," *American Literary Realism* 2 (Spring 1968), 84-89.

————. "Harold Frederic: A Bibliography," *Studies in Bibliography* XIII (1960), 247-257.

FREDERICK, JACKSON

THE EFFINGHAMS, OR HOME AS I FOUND IT

Gates, W. B. "A Neglected Satire on James Fenimore Cooper's *Home As Found*," *American Literature* XXXV (Mar 1963), 13-21.

FREEMAN, MARY WILKINS

GILES COREY, YEOMAN

Hamblen, Abigail Ann. *The New England Art of Mary E. Wilkins Freeman*, 48-54.

Westbrook, Perry D. *Mary Wilkins Freeman*, 134-139.

JEROME, A POOR MAN

Westbrook, Perry D. *Mary Wilkins Freeman*, 118-125.

MADELON

Westbrook, Perry D. *Mary Wilkins Freeman*, 105-110.

PEMBROKE

Hamblen, Abigail Ann. *The New England Art of Mary E. Wilkins Freeman*, 34-47.

Westbrook, Perry D. *Mary Wilkins Freeman*, 91-105.

PORTION OF LABOR

Westbrook, Perry D. *Mary Wilkins Freeman*, 126-131.

FREEMAN, MARY WILKINS, Continued

GENERAL

Hamblen, Abigail Ann. *The New England Art of Mary E. Wilkins Freeman.*

Martin, Jay. *Harvests of Change. American Literature 1865-1914,* 148-152.

Warren, Austin. "Mary E. Wilkins," *The New England Conscience,* 157-169.

Westbrook, Perry D. *Mary Wilkins Freeman.*

BIBLIOGRAPHY

Hamblen, Abigail Ann. *The New England Art of Mary E. Wilkins Freeman,* 67-70.

Westbrook, Perry D. *Mary Wilkins Freeman,* 182-186.

FRIEDMAN, BRUCE JAY

GENERAL

Algren, Nelson. "The Radical Innocent," *Nation* 199 (Sept 21, 1964), 142-143.

Friedman, Bruce Jay. "What's In It for Me," *Harper's* CCXXXI (Nov 1965), 168-169.

Schulz, M. F. "Wallant and Friedman: The Glory and the Agony of Love," *Critique: Studies in Modern Fiction* X (No 3, 1968), 31-47.

FUCHS, DANIEL

GENERAL

Howe, Irving. "Daniel Fuchs' Williamsburg Trilogy: A Cigarette and a Window," *Proletarian Writers of the Thirties,* 96-105.

FULLER, HENRY BLAKE

WITH THE PROCESSION

Harris, Mark. Introduction, *With the Procession* (Chicago, 1965).

GENERAL

Ziff, Larzer. "Crushed Yet Complacent: Hamlin Garland and Henry Blake Fuller," *The American 1890s: Life and Times of a Lost Generation,* 106-119.

BIBLIOGRAPHY

Williams, Kenny Jackson. "Henry Blake Fuller (1857-1929)," *American Literary Realism* 3 (Summer 1968), 9-13.

GADDIS, WILLIAM

THE RECOGNITIONS

Benstock, Bernard. "On William Gaddis: In Recognition of James Joyce," *Wisconsin Studies in Contemporary Literature* VI (Summer 1965), 177-189.

GALE, ZONA

BIRTH

Simonson, Harold P. *Zona Gale,* 73-78.

MISS LULU BETT

Simonson, Harold P. *Zona Gale,* 78-84.

PREFACE TO A LIFE

Simonson, Harold P. *Zona Gale,* 101-106.

GENERAL

Simonson, Harold P. *Zona Gale.*

BIBLIOGRAPHY

Simonson, Harold P. *Zona Gale,* 147-150.

————. "Zona Gale (1874-1938)," *American Literary Realism* 3 (Summer 1968), 14-17.

GARDNER, EARL STANLEY

GENERAL

Morton, Charles W. "The World of Earl Stanley Gardner," *Atlantic Monthly* CCXIX (Jan 1967), 79-91.

GARLAND, HAMLIN

ROSE OF DUTCHER'S COOLLY

Daly, J. P. "Hamlin Garland's *Rose of Dutcher's Coolly,*" *English Language and Literature* 11 (Jun 1962), 51-65.

Holloway, Jean. *Hamlin Garland: A Biography,* 117-124.

Morgan, W. Wayne. "Hamlin Garland: The Rebel as Escapist," *American Writers in Rebellion,* 96-98.

GENERAL

Holloway, Jean. *Hamlin Garland: A Biography.*

Martin, Jay. *Harvests of Change. American Literature 1865-1914,* 124-132.

Meyer, Roy W. "Hamlin Garland and the American Indian," *Western American Literature* II (Summer 1967), 109-125.

Miller, Charles T. "Hamlin Garland's Retreat from Realism," *Western American Literature* 1 (Summer 1966), 119-129.

Morgan, W. Wayne. "Hamlin Garland: The Rebel as Escapist," *American Writers in Rebellion,* 76-103.

Pizer, Donald. "The Garland-Crane Relationship," *Huntington Library Quarterly* XXIV (Nov 1960), 75-82.

————. *Hamlin Garland's Diaries.*

————. *Realism and Naturalism in Nineteenth-Century American Literature,* 88-94, 114-120.

Reamer, Owen J. "Garland and the Indians," *New Mexico Quarterly* XXXIV (Autumn 1964), 257-280.

Stronks, James B. "A Realist Experiments with Impressionism: Hamlin Garland's 'Chicago Studies,'" *American Literature* XXXVI (Mar 1964), 38-52.

Whitford, Kathryn. "Crusader Without a Cause: An Examination of Hamlin Garland's Middle Border," *Midcontinent American Studies Journal* VI (Spring 1965), 61-72.

Ziff, Larzer. "Crushed Yet Complacent: Hamlin Garland and Henry Blake Fuller," *The American 1890s: Life and Times of a Lost Generation,* 93-106.

BIBLIOGRAPHY

Holloway, Jean. *Hamlin Garland: A Biography,* 313-334.

Morgan, W. Wayne. *American Writers in Rebellion,* 205.

Pizer, Donald. "Hamlin Garland (1860-1940)," *American Literary Realism* 1 (Fall 1967), 45-51.

University of Southern California Library. *Hamlin Garland: A Bibliography.*

GIPSON, FRED

HOUND DOG MAN

Gipson, Tommie. "Helpless in Hollywood Or, How Much Is That Hound Dog?" *Southwest Review* XLV (Summer 1960), 259-265.

GLASGOW, ELLEN

BARREN GROUND

Marshall, George O., Jr. "Hardy's *Tess* and Ellen Glasgow's *Barren Ground,*" *Texas Studies in Literature and Language* I (Winter 1960), 517-521.

GLASGOW, ELLEN, Continued

McDowell, Frederick P. W. *Ellen Glasgow and the Ironic Art of Fiction,* 146-160.

Rouse, Blair. *Ellen Glasgow,* 86-97.

Santas, Joan Foster. *Ellen Glasgow's American Dream,* 138-163.

Welsh, John R. "Egdon Heath Revisited: Ellen Glasgow's *Barren Ground,*" *Reality and Myth: Essays in American Literature in Memory of Richmond Croom Beatty,* 71-79.

THE BATTLE-GROUND

McDowell, Frederick P. W. *Ellen Glasgow and the Ironic Art of Fiction,* 62-68.

Santas, Joan Foster. *Ellen Glasgow's American Dream,* 48-66.

BEYOND DEFEAT

Gore, Luther Y. Introduction, *Beyond Defeat* (Charlottesville, Virginia, 1966) .

THE DELIVERANCE

McDowell, Frederick P. W. *Ellen Glasgow and the Ironic Art of Fiction,* 69-81.

Rouse, Blair. *Ellen Glasgow,* 56-62.

Santas, Joan Foster. *Ellen Glasgow's American Dream,* 64-74.

THE DESCENDANT

McDowell, Frederick P. W. *Ellen Glasgow and the Ironic Art of Fiction,* 40-48.

IN THIS OUR LIFE

McDowell, Frederick P. W. *Ellen Glasgow and the Ironic Art of Fiction,* 215-228.

Santas, Joan Foster. *Ellen Glasgow's American Dream,* 212-222.

LIFE AND GABRIELLA

McDowell, Frederick P. W. *Ellen Glasgow and the Ironic Art of Fiction,* 127-134.

Santas, Joan Foster. *Ellen Glasgow's American Dream,* 99-111.

THE MILLER OF OLD CHURCH

McDowell, Frederick P. W. *Ellen Glasgow and the Ironic Art of Fiction,* 96-110.

Steele, Oliver L. "Early Impressions of Ellen Glasgow's *The Miller of Old Church,* 1911," *Library* XVI (Mar 1961) , 50-52.

THE ROMANCE OF A PLAIN MAN

McDowell, Frederick P. W. *Ellen Glasgow and the Ironic Art of Fiction,* 89-95.

Rouse, Blair. *Ellen Glasgow,* 64-70.

THE ROMANTIC COMEDIANS

McDowell, Frederick P. W. *Ellen Glasgow and the Ironic Art of Fiction,* 161-171.

Santas, Joan Foster. *Ellen Glasgow's American Dream,* 164-173.

THE SHELTERED LIFE

McDowell, Frederick P. W. *Ellen Glasgow and the Ironic Art of Fiction,* 185-201.

————. "Theme and Artistry in Ellen Glasgow's *The Sheltered Life," Texas Studies in Literature and Language* I (Winter 1960), 502-516.

Rouse, Blair. *Ellen Glasgow,* 108-115.

Santas, Joan Foster. *Ellen Glasgow's American Dream,* 185-197.

THEY STOOPED TO FOLLY

McDowell, Frederick P. W. *Ellen Glasgow and the Ironic Art of Fiction,* 171-184.

Rouse, Blair. *Ellen Glasgow,* 102-109.

Santas, Joan Foster. *Ellen Glasgow's American Dream,* 173-185.

VEIN OF IRON

McDowell, Frederick P. W. *Ellen Glasgow and the Ironic Art of Fiction,* 202-214.

Rouse, Blair. *Ellen Glasgow,* 115-122.

Santas, Joan Foster. *Ellen Glasgow's American Dream,* 197-212.

VIRGINIA

McDowell, Frederick P. W. *Ellen Glasgow and the Ironic Art of Fiction,* 111-126.

Santas, Joan Foster. *Ellen Glasgow's American Dream,* 82-96.

THE VOICE OF THE PEOPLE

McDowell, Frederick P. W. *Ellen Glasgow and the Ironic Art of Fiction,* 55-62.

GENERAL

Adams, J. Donald. "Speaking of Books," *New York Times Book Review* 68 (Jun 16, 1963), 2.

Auchincloss, Louis. *Ellen Glasgow.*

————. "Ellen Glasgow," *Pioneers & Caretakers,* 56-91.

Colvert, James B. "Agent and Author: Ellen Glasgow's Letters to Paul Revere Reynolds," *Studies in Bibliography* XIV (1961), 177-196.

Curlee, Joan. "Ellen Glasgow's South," *Ball State Teachers College Forum* II (Winter 1961-62), 53-59.

Day, Douglas. "Ellen Glasgow's Letters to the Saxtons," *American Literature* XXXV (May 1963), 230-236.

GLASGOW, ELLEN, Continued

Gore, Luther Y., (ed.). " 'Literary Realism or Nominalism' by Ellen Glasgow: An Unpublished Essay," *American Literature* XXXIV (Mar 1962) , 72-79.

Heald, William F. "Ellen Glasgow and the Grotesque," *Mississippi Quarterly* XVIII (Winter 1964-1965) , 7-11.

Holman, C. Hugh. "Ellen Glasgow and the Southern Literary Tradition," *Southern Writers: Appraisals in Our Time,* 103-123.

————. *Three Modes of Modern Southern Fiction,* 11-25.

Hubbell, Jay B. "Ellen Glasgow: Artist and Social Historian," *South and Southwest: Literary Essays and Reminiscences,* 90-99.

————. *Southern Life in Fiction,* 57-59.

McCollum, Nancy Minter. "Glasgow's and Cabell's Comedies of Virginia," *Georgia Review* XVIII (Summer 1964) , 236-241.

McDowell, Frederick P. W. *Ellen Glasgow and the Ironic Art of Fiction.*

Morgan, H. Wayne. "Ellen Glasgow: The Qualities of Endurance," *Writers in Transition: Seven Americans,* 42-59.

Parent, Monique. *Ellen Glasgow: Romancière.*

Rouse, Blair. *Ellen Glasgow.*

Rubin, Louis D., Jr. "Two in Richmond: Ellen Glasgow and James Branch Cabell," *The Curious Death of the Novel: Essays in American Literature,* 155-168.

Santas, Joan Foster. *Ellen Glasgow's American Dream.*

Steele, Oliver L. "Ellen Glasgow, Social History, and the 'Virginia Edition,' " *Modern Fiction Studies* VII (Summer 1961) , 173-176.

BIBLIOGRAPHY

Auchincloss, Louis. *Ellen Glasgow,* 47-48.

Kelly, W. W. *Ellen Glasgow: A Bibliography.*

McDowell, Frederick P. W. *Ellen Glasgow and the Ironic Art of Fiction,* 264-280.

Parent, Monique. *Ellen Glasgow: Romancière,* 527-542.

Rouse, Blair. *Ellen Glasgow,* 148-155.

Santas, Joan Foster. *Ellen Glasgow's American Dream,* 239-244.

Steele, Oliver L. "Evidence of Plate Damage as Applied to the First Impressions of Ellen Glasgow's *The Wheel of Life* (1906) ," *Studies in Bibliography* XVI (1963) , 223-231.

GOLD, HERBERT

THE OPTIMIST
Hassan, Ihab. *Radical Innocence: Studies in the Contemporary American Novel,* 180-187.
GENERAL
Hicks, Granville. "Generations of the Fifties: Malamud, Gold, and Updike," *The Creative Present,* 224-232.

Moore, Harry T. "The Fiction of Herbert Gold," *Contemporary American Novelists,* 170-181.

GOLD, MICHAEL

JEWS WITHOUT MONEY
Folsom, Michael Brewster. "The Book of Poverty," *Nation* 202 (Feb 28, 1966), 242-245.

————. "The Education of Michael Gold," *Proletarian Writers of the Thirties,* 236-242.
GENERAL
Folsom, Michael Brewster. "The Education of Michael Gold," *Proletarian Writers of the Thirties,* 222-251.

GOLDMAN, WILLIAM

THE THING OF IT IS . . .
French, Warren. *Season of Promise,* 26-32.

GOODMAN, PAUL

THE EMPIRE CITY
Paul, Sherman. "Paul Goodman's Mourning Labor: *The Empire City,*" *Southern Review* IV (Autumn 1968), 894-926.

GORDON, CAROLINE

THE DRAGON'S TEETH
Brown, Ashley. "A Note on *'The Dragon's Teeth,'*" *Shenandoah* XIII (Autumn 1961), 20-21.
THE STRANGE CHILDREN
Rocks, James E. "The Christian Myth as Salvation: Caroline Gordon's *The Strange Children,*" *Tulane Studies in English* XVI (1968), 149-160.

GORDON, CAROLINE, Continued

GENERAL

Brown, Ashley. "The Achievement of Caroline Gardon," *Southern Humanities Review* II (Summer 1968) , 279-289.

————. "The Novel as Christian Comedy," *Reality and Myth: Essays in American Literature in Memory of Richmond Croom Beatty,* 161-178.

Cheney, Brainard. "Caroline Gordon's Ontological Quest," *Renascence* XVI (Fall 1963) , 3-12.

Eisinger, Chester E. *Fiction of the Forties,* 186-193.

Fletcher, Marie. "The Fate of Women in a Changing South: A Persistent Theme in the Fiction of Caroline Gordon," *Mississippi Quarterly* XXI (Winter 1967-68) , 17-28.

Hoffman, Frederick J. *The Art of Southern Fiction,* 36-39.

McDowell, Frederick P. W. *Caroline Gordon.*

O'Connor, William Van. "Art and Miss Gordon," *South: Modern Southern Literature in Its Cultural Setting,* 314-322.

————. *The Grotesque: An American Genre and Other Essays,* 168-176.

Rocks, James E. "The Mind and Art of Caroline Gordon," *Mississippi Quarterly* XXI (Winter 1967-68) , 1-16.

BIBLIOGRAPHY

McDowell, Frederick P. W. *Caroline Gordon,* 46-48.

GOYEN, WILLIAM

THE HOUSE OF BREATH

Hoffman, Frederick J. *The Art of Southern Fiction,* 124-127.

IN A FARTHER COUNTRY

Hoffman, Frederick J. *The Art of Southern Fiction,* 127-129.

GENERAL

Gossett, Louise Y. "The Voices of Distance," *Violence in Recent Southern Fiction,* 131-144.

Sühnel, Rudolf. "Die Wiederentdeckung des Wunderbaren: William Goyen zum Gruss anlässlich seines Deutschlandbesuches," *Neueren Sprachen* (Jun 1962) , 249-255.

GRANT, ROBERT

THE CHIPPENDALES
Hamblen, Abigail Ann. "Judge Grant and the Forgotten Chippendales," *University Review* XXXIII (Mar 1967), 175-179.

GRAU, SHIRLEY ANN

GENERAL
Berland, Alwyn. "The Fiction of Shirley Ann Grau," *Critique* VI (Spring 1963), 78-84.
Gossett, Louise Y. "Primitives and Violence," *Violence in Recent Southern Fiction*, 177-195.
Hoffman, Frederick J. *The Art of Southern Fiction*, 106-109.

GRESHAM, WILLIAM LINDSAY

NIGHTMARE ALLEY
Shapiro, Charles. "*Nightmare Alley*: Geeks, Cons, Tips, and Marks," *Tough Guy Writers of the Thirties*, 218-224.

GRIFFIN, JOHN HOWARD

GENERAL
Geismar, Maxwell. Introduction, *John Howard Griffin Reader* (Boston, 1968).
BIBLIOGRAPHY
Daniel, Bradford. *John Howard Griffin Reader* (Boston, 1968), 585-588.

GROSECLOSE, ELGIN

ARARAT
French, Warren. *The Social Novel at the End of an Era*, 142-156.

GUTHRIE, A. B., JR.

THE BIG SKY
Ford, Thomas W. *A. B. Guthrie, Jr.*, 10-18.
Stegner, Wallace. Introduction, *The Big Sky* (Boston, 1965).
THESE THOUSAND HILLS
Ford, Thomas W. *A. B. Guthrie, Jr.*, 27-33.

GUTHRIE, A. B. JR., Continued

THE WAY WEST
Ford, Thomas W. *A. B. Guthrie, Jr.,* 18-26.
GENERAL
Ford, Thomas W. *A. B. Guthrie, Jr.*
BIBLIOGRAPHY
Ford, Thomas W. *A. B. Guthrie, Jr.,* 43-44.

HALL, JAMES NORMAN

GENERAL
Briand, Paul L., Jr. *In Search of Paradise: The Nordhoff-Hall Story.*
BIBLIOGRAPHY
Briand, Paul L., Jr. *In Search of Paradise: The Nordhoff-Hall Story,*
377-384.

HALL, SAMUEL STONE

GENERAL
Dykes, J. C. "Buckskin Sam, Ranger and Writer; or, The Life and
Sub-Literary Labors of Samuel Stone Hall," *American Book Collector* X (Mar 1960) , 9-14.
BIBLIOGRAPHY
Dykes, J. C. "A Bibliographical Check List of the Writings of Samuel
Stone Hall," *American Book Collector* X (Mar 1960) , 15-18.

HALLAS, RICHARD

YOU PLAY THE BLACK AND THE RED COMES UP
Hagemann, E. R. "Focus on *You Play the Black and the Red Comes
Up:* 'No bet,'" *Tough Guy Writers of the Thirties,* 163-170.

HALLET, RICHARD MATTHEWS

GENERAL
Cary, Richard. "Richard Matthews Hallet: Architect of the Dream,"
Colby Library Quarterly VII (Jun 1967) , 417-452.
BIBLIOGRAPHY
Cary, Richard. "A Bibliography of Richard Matthews Hallet," *Colby
Library Quarterly* VII (Jun 1967) , 453-463.

HALPER, ALBERT

GENERAL

Hart, John E. "Albert Halper's World of the Thirties," *Twentieth Century Literature* IX (Jan 1964), 185-195.

HAMMETT, DASHIELL

THE DAIN CURSE

Edenbaum, Robert I. "The Poetics of the Private-Eye: The Novels of Dashiell Hammett," *Tough Guy Writers of the Thirties*, 95-99.

THE MALTESE FALCON

Edenbaum, Robert I. "The Poetics of the Private-Eye: The Novels of Dashiell Hammett," *Tough Guy Writers of the Thirties*, 80-89.

Malin, Irving. "Focus on *The Maltese Falcon:* The Metaphysical Falcon," *Tough Guy Writers of the Thirties*, 104-109.

RED HARVEST

Edenbaum, Robert I. "The Poetics of the Private-Eye: The Novels of Dashiell Hammett," *Tough Guy Writers of the Thirties*, 89-94.

GENERAL

Blair, Walter. "Dashiell Hammett, Themes and Techniques," *Essays on American Literature in Honor of Jay Hubbell*, 295-306.

Edenbaum, Robert I. "The Poetics of the Private-Eye: The Novels of Dashiell Hammett," *Tough Guy Writers of the Thirties*, 80-103.

Stoddard, Roger E. "Some Uncollected Authors XXXI: Dashiell Hammett, 1894-1961," *Book Collector* XI (Spring 1962), 71-78.

HARBEN, WILL N.

GENERAL

Bush, Robert. "Will N. Harben's North Georgia Fiction," *Mississippi Quarterly* XX (Spring 1967), 103-117.

HARRIS, JOEL CHANDLER

GENERAL

Turner, Darwin T. "Daddy Joel Harris and His Old-Time Darkies," *Southern Literary Journal* I (Autumn 1968), 20-41.

HARRIS, MARK

GENERAL
Harris, Mark. "Mark Harris: An Interview," *Wisconsin Studies in Contemporary Literature* VI (Winter-Spring 1965), 15-26.

HARTE, BRET

GABRIEL CONROY
O'Connor, Richard. *Bret Harte: A Biography*, 169-174.
GENERAL
Duckett, Margaret. *Mark Twain and Bret Harte*.
Hahn, Emily. *Romantic Rebels: An Informal History of Bohemianism in America*, 46-52.
O'Connor, Richard. *Bret Harte: A Biography*.
BIBLIOGRAPHY
Duckett, Margaret. *Mark Twain and Bret Harte*, 345-353.

HAWKES, JOHN

THE CANNIBAL
Guerard, Albert J. Introduction, *The Cannibal* (New York, 1962).
Malin, Irving. "The Gothic Family," *Psychoanalysis and American Fiction*, 272-274.
Reutlinger, D. P. "*The Cannibal*: 'The Reality of Victim,'" *Critique* (Fall 1963), 30-37.
CHARIVARI
Scholes, Robert. *The Fabulators*, 74-79.
THE LIME TWIG
Edenbaum, Robert I. "John Hawkes: *The Lime Twig* and Other Tenuous Horrors," *Massachusetts Review* VII (Summer 1966), 462-475.
Fiedler, Leslie A. Introduction, *The Lime Twig* (New York, 1961).
Scholes, Robert. *The Fabulators*, 79-94.
Schott, Webster. "Vision of a Nightmare," *Nation* 193 (Sept 2, 1961), 122-123.
GENERAL
Brooks, Peter. "John Hawkes," *Encounter* XXVI (Jun 1966), 68-72.
Frohock, W. M. "John Hawkes's Vision of Violence," *Southwest Review* L (Winter 1965), 69-79.

HAWKES, JOHN, Continued

Graham, John, interviewer. "John Hawkes on His Novels," *Massachusetts Review* VII (Summer 1966) , 449-461.

Guerard, Albert J. "The Prose Style of John Hawkes," *Critique* VI (Fall 1963) , 19-29.

Hawkes, John. "John Hawkes: An Interview," *Wisconsin Studies in Contemporary Literature* VI (Summer 1965) , 141-155.

Malin, Irving. *New American Gothic,* 38-44, 71-75, 99-103, 124-126.

Matthews, Charles. "The Destructive Vision of John Hawkes," *Critique* VI (Fall 1963) , 38-52.

Oberbeck, S. K. "John Hawkes: The Smile Slashed by a Razor," *Contemporary American Novelists,* 193-204.

Ratner, Marc. "The Constructed Vision: The Fiction of John Hawkes," *Studi Americani* XI (1965) , 345-357.

Rovit, Earl. "The Fiction of John Hawkes: An Introductory View," *Modern Fiction Studies* X (Summer 1964) , 150-162.

Scholes, Robert. *The Fabulators,* 59-60, 66-94.

Schott, Webster. "John Hawkes, American Original," *New York Times Book Review* 71 (May 29, 1966) , 4, 24-25.

Trachtenberg, Alan. "Barth and Hawkes: Two Fabulists," *Critique* VI (Fall 1963) , 4-18.

BIBLIOGRAPHY

Bryer, Jackson R. "Two Bibliographies," *Critique* VI (Fall 1963) , 86-94.

HAWLEY, CAMERON

GENERAL

Hamblen, Abigail Ann. "Novelist of the Business World," *Trace* 56 (Spring 1965) , 9-12.

HAWTHORNE, JULIAN

BIBLIOGRAPHY

Bassan, Maurice. "The Literary Career of Julian Hawthorne: A Selected Check List," *Bulletin of Bibliography* XXIV (May-Aug 1965) , 157-162.

Monteiro, George. "Additions to the Bibliography of Julian Hawthorne," *Bulletin of Bibliography* XXV (May-Aug 1967) , 64.

HAWTHORNE, NATHANIEL

THE BLITHEDALE ROMANCE

Baym, Nina. *"The Blithedale Romance:* A Radical Reading," *Journal of English and Germanic Philology* LXVII (Oct 1968), 545-569.

Bell, Millicent. *Hawthorne's View of the Artist,* 151-159.

The Centenary Edition of the Works of Nathaniel Hawthorne, vol III (Columbus, Ohio, 1964).

Crews, Frederick C. *The Sins of the Fathers: Hawthorne's Psychological Themes,* 194-212.

"Editor's Notes & Reading," *American Notes & Queries* I (Mar 1963), 105.

Folsom, James K. *Man's Accidents and God's Purposes: Multiplicity in Hawthorne's Fiction,* 139-141, 147-151.

Gordon, Joseph T. "Nathaniel Hawthorne and Brook Farm," *Emerson Society Quarterly* 33 (IV Quarter 1963), 51-61.

Griffith, Kelley, Jr. "Form in *The Blithedale Romance,*" *American Literature* 40 (Mar 1968), 15-26.

Hedges, William L. "Hawthorne's *Blithedale:* The Function of the Narrator," *Nineteenth-Century Fiction* XIV (Mar 1960), 303-316.

Hoffman, Daniel G. *Form and Fable in American Fiction,* 202-218.

Howard, David. *"The Blithedale Romance* and a Sense of Revolution," *Tradition and Tolerance in Nineteenth Century Fiction: Critical Essays on Some English and American Novels,* 55-97.

Kaul, A. N. *"The Blithedale Romance," A Collection of Critical Essays,* 153-163.

Lefcowitz, Allan and Barbara. "Some Rents in the Veil: New Light on Priscilla and Zenobia in *The Blithedale Romance,*" *Nineteenth-Century Fiction* XXI (Dec 1966), 263-275.

Levy, Leo. *"The Blithedale Romance:* Hawthorne's 'Voyage Through Chaos,'" *Studies in Romanticism* VIII (Autumn 1968), 1-15.

Long, Robert Emmet. "The Society and the Masks: *The Blithedale Romance* and *The Bostonians,*" *Nineteenth-Century Fiction* XIX (Sept 1964), 105-122.

Marenco, Franco. "Nathaniel Hawthorne E *Il Blithedale Romance,*" *Studi Americani* VI (1960), 135-182.

Martin, Terence. *Nathaniel Hawthorne,* 145-159.

Murray, Peter B. "Mythopoesis in *The Blithedale Romance,*" *PMLA* LXXV (Dec 1960), 591-596.

Poirier, Richard. *A World Elsewhere,* 93-143.

Ragan, James F. "The Irony in Hawthorne's Blithedale," *New England Quarterly* XXXV (Jun 1962), 239-246.

Shroeder, John. "Miles Coverdale as Actaeon, as Faunus, and as October: With Some Consequences," *Papers on Language and Literature* II (Spring 1966), 126-139.

Smith, Julian. "Why Does Zenobia Kill Herself?" *English Language Notes* VI (Sept 1968), 37-39.

Stanton, Robert. "The Trial of Nature: An Analysis of *The Blithedale Romance*," *PMLA* LXXVI (Dec 1961), 528-538.

Tharpe, Jac. *Nathaniel Hawthorne: Identity and Knowledge*, 40-46, 125-133.

Waggoner, Hyatt H. *Hawthorne: A Critical Study*, 175-194.

––––––. "Nathaniel Hawthorne," *Six American Novelists of the Nineteenth Century*, 75-78.

FANSHAWE

The Centenary Edition of the Works of Nathaniel Hawthorne, vol III (Columbus, Ohio, 1964).

Gross, Robert Eugene. "Hawthorne's First Novel: The Future of a Style," *PMLA* LXXVIII (Mar 1963), 60-68.

Male, Roy R. "Hawthorne's Allegory of Guilt and Redemption," *Emerson Society Quarterly* 25 (IV Quarter 1961), 16-18.

THE HOUSE OF THE SEVEN GABLES

Battaglia, Francis Joseph. "*The House of the Seven Gables:* New Light on Old Problems," *PMLA* LXXXII (Dec 1967), 579-590.

Bell, Millicent. *Hawthorne's View of the Artist*, 159-167.

Carpenter, Richard C. "Hawthorne's Scarlet Bean Flower," *University Review* XXX (Oct 1963), 64-71.

The Centenary Edition of the Works of Nathaniel Hawthorne, vol II (Columbus, Ohio, 1965).

Crews, Frederick C. *The Sins of the Fathers: Hawthorne's Psychological Themes*, 171-194.

Farmer, Norman, Jr. "Maule's Curse and the Rev. Nicholas Noyes: A Note on Hawthorne's Source," *Notes and Queries* N. S. 11 (Jun 1964), 224-225.

Fogle, Richard Harter. Introduction, *The House of the Seven Gables* (New York, 1962).

Gerber, John C. "A Critical Exercise in the Teaching of *The House of the Seven Gables*," *Emerson Society Quarterly* 25 (IV Quarter 1961), 8-11.

Hawthorne, Manning. *"The House of the Seven Gables* and Hawthorne's Family History," *Literary Half-Yearly* VII (Jan 1966), 61-66.

Hoffman, Daniel G. *Form and Fable in American Fiction,* 187-201.

Junkins, Donald. "Hawthorne's *The House of the Seven Gables:* A Prototype of the Human Mind," *Literature and Psychology* XVII, (No. 4, 1967), 193-209.

Lenhart, C. S. Introduction, *The House of the Seven Gables* (New York, 1966).

Levy, Alfred J. *"The House of the Seven Gables:* The Religion of Love," *Nineteenth-Century Fiction* XVI (Dec 1961), 189-203.

————. "Picturesque Style in *The House of the Seven Gables,"* *New England Quarterly* XXXIX (Jun 1966), 147-160.

Lewis, R. W. B. *Trials of the Word,* 85-96.

Marks, Alfred H. "Hawthorne's Daguerreotypist: Scientist, Artist, Reformer," *Ball State Teachers Forum* III (Spring 1962), 61-74.

Martin, Terence. *Nathaniel Hawthorne,* 128-144.

Miller, James E. "Hawthorne and Melville: No! in Thunder," *Quests Surd and Absurd: Essays in American Literature,* 201-204.

Monteiro, George. "Maule's Curse and Julian Hawthorne," *Notes and Queries* N.S. 14 (Feb 1967), 62-63.

Rees, John O., Jr. "Elizabeth Peabody and 'The Very A B C': A Note on *The House of The Seven Gables,"* *American Literature* XXXVIII (Jan 1967), 537-540.

Sampson, Edward C. Afterword, *The House of the Seven Gables* (New York, 1961).

Smith, Henry Nash. "The Morals of Power, Business Enterprise as a Theme of Mid-Nineteenth Century Fiction," *Essays on American Literature in Honor of Jay Hubbell,* 92-98.

Stewart, Randall. "Recurrent Themes in Hawthorne's Fiction," *Regionalism and Beyond: Essays of Randall Stewart,* 60-68.

Tharpe, Jac. *Nathaniel Hawthorne: Identity and Knowledge,* 110-124.

Waggoner, Hyatt H. *Hawthorne: A Critical Study,* 151-175.

————. Introduction, *The House of the Seven Gables* (New York, 1964).

THE MARBLE FAUN

Barnett, Gene A. "Hawthorne's Italian Calendar," *Emerson Society Quarterly* 43 (II Quarter 1966), 68-70.

————. "Hawthorne's Italian Towers," *Studies in Romanticism* III (Summer 1964) , 252-256.

Beidler, Peter G. "Theme of the Fortunate Fall in *The Marble Faun,"* *Emerson Society Quarterly* 47 (II Quarter 1967) , 56-62.

Bercovitch, Sacvan. "Of Wise and Foolish Virgins: Hilda Versus Miriam in Hawthorne's *Marble Faun,"* *New England Quarterly* XLI (Jun 1968) , 281-286.

————. "The Frontier Fable of Hawthorne's *Marble Faun,"* *South Dakota Review* 4 (Summer 1964) , 44-50.

Brodtkorb, Paul, Jr. "Art Allegory in *The Marble Faun,"* *PMLA* LXXVII (Jun 1962) , 254-267.

The Centenary Edition of the Works of Nathaniel Hawthorne, vol IV (Columbus, Ohio, 1968) .

Crews, Frederick C. *The Sins of the Fathers: Hawthorne's Psychological Themes,* 213-239.

Flanagan, John T. "Point of View in *The Marble Faun,"* *Neueren Sprachen* (May 1962) , 218-224.

Gale, Robert L. *"The Marble Faun* and *The Sacred Fount:* A Resemblance," *Studi Americani* VIII (1962) , 21-33.

Guilds, John C. "Miriam of *The Marble Faun:* Hawthorne's Subtle Sinner," *Cairo Studies in English* (1960) , 61-68.

Gullace, Giovanni. "Péché et Pécheurs Dans La Lettre Écarlate et La Faune De Marbre," *Etudes Anglaises* XV (Avril-Juin 1962) , 113-121.

Hart, James D. "Hawthorne's Italian Diary," *American Literature* XXXIV (Jan 1963) , 562-567.

Hoeltje, Hubert H. *Inward Sky: The Mind and Heart of Nathaniel Hawthorne,* 508-515.

Krieger, Murray. Afterword, *The Marble Faun* (New York, 1961) .

Liebman, Sheldon W. "The Design of *The Marble Faun,"* *New England Quarterly* XL (Mar 1967) , 61-78.

Martin, Terence. *Nathaniel Hawthorne,* 160-176.

Moss, Sidney P. "The Problem of Theme in *The Marble Faun,"* *Nineteenth-Century Fiction* XVIII (Mar 1964) , 393-399.

————. "The Symbolism of the Italian Background in *The Marble Faun,"* *Nineteenth-Century Fiction* XXIII (Dec 1968) , 332-336.

Pattison, Joseph C. "The Guilt of the Innocent Donatello," *Emerson Society Quarterly* 31 (II Quarter 1963) , 66-68.

Schwartz, Joseph. "Myth and Ritual in *The Marble Faun,"* *Emerson Society Quarterly* 25 (IV Quarter 1961) , 26-29.

Scrimgeour, Gary J. *"The Marble Faun:* Hawthorne's Faery Land," *American Literature* XXXVI (Nov 1964) , 271-287.

Waggoner, Hyatt H. *Hawthorne: A Critical Study,* 195-222.

THE SCARLET LETTER

Arden, Eugene. "Hawthorne's 'Case of Arthur D.' " *American Imago* XVIII (Spring 1961) , 45-55.

Arthos, John. *"The Scarlet Letter* Once More," *Ball State Teachers College Forum* V (Winter 1964) , 31-38.

Austin, Allen. "Hester Prynne's Plan of Escape," *University of Kansas City Review* XXVIII (Jun 1962) , 317-318.

————. "Satire and Theme in *The Scarlet Letter,"* *Philological Quarterly* XLI (Apr 1962) , 508-511.

Baskett, Sam S. *"The* (Complete) *Scarlet Letter,"* *College English* XXII (Feb 1961) , 321-328.

Baughman, Ernest W. "Public Confession and *The Scarlet Letter,"* *New England Quarterly* XL (Dec 1967) , 532-550.

Boewe, Charles and Murray G. Murphey. "Hester Prynne in History," *American Literature* XXXII (May 1960) , 202-204.

————. "Hester Prynne in History," *The Scarlet Letter: An Annotated Text; Backgrounds and Sources; Essays in Criticism,* 219-221.

Bowden, Edwin T. *The Dungeon of the Heart: Human Isolation and the American Novel,* 73-89.

Bridgman, Richard. "As Hester Prynne Lay Dying," *English Language Notes* II (Jun 1965) , 294-296.

Bruccoli, Matthew J. "Notes on the Destruction of *The Scarlet Letter* Manuscript," *Studies in Bibliography* XX (1967) , 257-259.

Canaday, Nicholas, Jr. " 'Some Sweet Moral Blossom': A Note on Hawthorne's Rose," *Papers on Language and Literature* III (Spring 1967) , 186-187.

Cecil, L. Moffitt. *"The Scarlet Letter:* A Puritan Love Story," *Reality and Myth: Essays in American Literature in Memory of Richmond Croom Beatty,* 52-59.

The Centenary Edition of the Works of Nathaniel Hawthorne, vol 1 (Columbus, Ohio, 1962) .

Chari, V. K. *"The Scarlet Letter* Without Allegory," *Literary Criterion* VI (Summer 1964) , 23-25.

Charvat, William. Introduction, *The Scarlet Letter* (Boston, 1963) .

Coanda, Richard. "Hawthorne's Scarlet Alphabet," *Renascence* XIX (Spring 1967) , 161-166.

Crews, Frederick C. "The Ruined Wall," *Twentieth Century Interpretations of The Scarlet Letter,* 93-104.

————. "The Ruined Wall: Unconscious Motivation in *The Scarlet Letter,*" *New England Quarterly* XXXVIII (Sept 1965) , 312-330.

————. *The Sins of the Fathers: Hawthorne's Psychological Themes,* 135-154.

Davidson, Edward H. "Dimmesdale's Fall," *New England Quarterly* XXXVI (Sept 1963) , 358-370.

————. "Dimmesdale's Fall," *Twentieth Century Interpretations of The Scarlet Letter,* 82-92.

————. "The Question of History in *The Scarlet Letter,*" *Emerson Society Quarterly* 25 (IV Quarter 1961) , 2-3.

Donovan, Alan B. Introduction, *The Scarlet Letter* (Cambridge, 1968) .

Feidelson, Charles, Jr. *"The Scarlet Letter," Critical Approaches to American Literature: Volume I, Roger Williams to Herman Melville,* 178-200.

Fiedler, Leslie A. "From 'Achievement and Frustration,' " *Twentieth Century Interpretations of The Scarlet Letter,* 113-114.

————. *Love and Death in the American Novel,* 222-225, 485-519.

Folsom, James K. *Man's Accidents and God's Purposes: Multiplicity in Hawthorne's Fiction,* 59-62, 95-98.

Fussell, Edwin. "Nathaniel Hawthorne," *Frontier: American Literature and the American West,* 91-114.

George, A. G. Introduction, *The Scarlet Letter* and *Hawthorne* by Henry James (Calcutta and New York, 1964) .

Gibson, William M. "The Art of Nathaniel Hawthorne: An Examination of *The Scarlet Letter,*" *The American Renaissance, the History of an Era: Essays and Interpretations,* 97-106.

Granger, Bruce Ingham. "Arthur Dimmesdale as Tragic Hero," *Nineteenth-Century Fiction* XIX (Sept 1964) , 197-203.

Grant, Douglas. Introduction, *The Scarlet Letter* (New York, 1965) .

Green, Martin. *Re-Appraisals: Some Commonsense Readings in American Literature,* 76-83.

Grewal, O. P. "Hawthorne's Criticism of the Puritan Society in *The Scarlet Letter,*" *Literary Criterion* VI (Summer 1964) , 26-30.

Gross, Seymour L. "Solitude, and Love, and Anguish: The Tragic Design of *The Scarlet Letter,*" *CLA Journal* III (Mar 1960) , 154-165.

————. "Solitude, and Love, and Anguish: The Tragic Design of *The*

Scarlet Letter," The Scarlet Letter: An Annotated Text; Backgrounds and Sources; Essays in Criticism, 359-367.

Hagopian, John V. and Martin Dolch. *Insight I: Analyses of American Literature,* 82-91.

Hawthorne, Manning. *"The Scarlet Letter," Literary Half-Yearly* VII (Jul 1966), 37-39.

Hoeltje, Hubert H. *Inward Sky: The Mind and Heart of Nathaniel Hawthorne,* 284-296, 311-316.

Hoffman, Daniel G. *Form and Fable in American Fiction,* 169-186.

————. "Hester's Double Providence: The Scarlet Letter and the Green," *The Scarlet Letter: An Annotated Text; Backgrounds and Sources; Essays in Criticism,* 367-373.

Katz, Seymour. " 'Character,' 'Nature,' and Allegory in *The Scarlet Letter," Nineteenth-Century Fiction* XXIII (Jun 1968), 3-17.

Kaul, A. N. "Character and Motive in *The Scarlet Letter," Critical Quarterly* 10 (Winter 1968), 373-384.

Kearns, Francis E. "Margaret Fuller as a Model for Hester Prynne," *Jahrbuch Für Amerikastudien* 10 (1965), 191-197.

Kim, Ku-San. "Transformation of *The Scarlet Letter," English Language and Literature* 25 (Spring 1968), 43-53.

Kim, Yong-chol. "Hawthorne's Treatment of the 'Fortunate Fall' in *The Scarlet Letter," English Language and Literature* 16 (Jun 1964-Jun 1965), 80-104.

Lane, Lauriat, Jr. "Allegory and Character and *The Scarlet Letter," Emerson Society Quarterly* 25 (IV Quarter 1961), 13-16.

Lasser, Michael L. "Mirror Imagery in *The Scarlet Letter," English Journal* LVI (Feb 1967), 274-277.

Ledger, Marshall A. "George Eliot and Nathaniel Hawthorne," *Notes and Queries* N.S. 11 (Jun 1964), 225-226.

Levin, David. "Nathaniel Hawthorne: *The Scarlet Letter," The American Novel from James Fenimore Cooper to William Faulkner,* 13-24.

Levin, Harry. Introduction, *The Scarlet Letter* (Boston, 1960).

Lewis, R. W. B. *Trials of the Word,* 79-84.

Lucke, Jessie Ryon. "Hawthorne's Madonna Image in *The Scarlet Letter," New England Quarterly* XXXVIII (Sept 1965), 391-392.

Maes-Jelinek, Hena. "Roger Chillingworth: An Example of the Creative Process in *The Scarlet Letter," English Studies* XLIX (Aug 1968), 341-348.

Marcus, Fred H. "*The Scarlet Letter:* The Power of Ambiguity," *English Journal* LI (Oct 1962) , 449-458.

Martin, Terence. "Adam Blair and Arthur Dimmesdale: A Lesson from the Master," *American Literature* XXXIV (May 1962) , 274-279.

————. Introduction, *The Scarlet Letter* (Cleveland, 1967) .

————. *Nathaniel Hawthorne,* 108-127.

Marx, Leo. Introduction, *The Scarlet Letter* (New York, 1959) .

McCall, Dan. "The Design of Hawthorne's 'Custom-House,' " *Nineteenth-Century Fiction* XXI (Mar 1967) , 349-358.

Mizener, Arthur. "Nathaniel Hawthorne: *The Scarlet Letter,*" *Twelve Great American Novels,* 9-18.

Nolte, William H. "Hawthorne's Dimmesdale: A Small Man Gone Wrong," *New England Quarterly* XXXVIII (Jun 1965) , 168-186.

O'Donnell, Charles R. "Hawthorne and Dimmesdale: The Search for the Realm of Quiet," *Nineteenth-Century Fiction* XIV (Mar 1960) , 317-332.

Parcher, Adrian, OSB. "Hawthorne's *The Scarlet Letter,*" *Explicator* XXI (Feb 1963) , No. 48.

Putzel, Max. "The Way Out of the Minister's Maze: Some Hints for Teachers of *The Scarlet Letter,*" *Neueren Sprachen* (Mar 1960) , 127-131.

Ramaswamy, S. "A Note On Hawthorne's Scaffold," *Literary Half-Yearly* IX (Jan 1968) , 49-52.

Rovit, Earl. "Ambiguity in Hawthorne's *Scarlet Letter,*" *Archiv für das Studium der Neueren Sprachen und Literaturen* 198:2 (1962) , 76-88.

Sandeen, Ernest. "*The Scarlet Letter* as a Love Story," *PMLA* LXXVII (Sept 1962) , 425-435.

————. "*The Scarlet Letter* as a Love Story," *Twentieth Century Interpretations of The Scarlet Letter,* 111-112.

Scanlon, Lawrence E. "The Heart of *The Scarlet Letter,*" *Texas Studies in Literature and Language* IV (Summer 1962) , 198-213.

Schwarz, Peter. "Zwei mögliche 'Faust'—Quellen Für Hawthornes Roman *The Scarlet Letter,*" *Jahrbuch Für Amerikastudien* 10 (1965) , 198-205.

Seib, Kenneth. "A Note on Hawthorne's Pearl," *Emerson Society Quarterly* 39 (II Quarter 1965) , 20-21.

Steele, Oliver L. "On the Imposition of the First Edition of Hawthorne's *The Scarlet Letter*," *Library* XVII (Sept 1962), 250-255.

Stubbs, John C. "Hawthorne's *The Scarlet Letter*: The Theory of the Romance and the Use of the New England Situation," *PMLA* 83 (Oct 1968), 1439-1447.

————. "A Note on the Source of Hawthorne's Heraldic Device in *The Scarlet Letter*," *Notes and Queries* N.S. 15 (May 1968), 175-176.

Tanner, Bernard R. "Tone as an Approach to *The Scarlet Letter*," *English Journal* LIII (Oct 1964), 528-530.

Tharpe, Jac. *Nathaniel Hawthorne: Identity and Knowledge*, 95-110.

Thorp, Willard. Introduction, *The Scarlet Letter* (New York, 1962).

Van Dusen, Marshall. "Narrative Tone in 'The Custom House' and *The Scarlet Letter*," *Nineteenth-Century Fiction* XXI (Jun 1966), 61-71.

Van Nostrand, Albert. *The Denatured Novel*, 35-40.

Vogel, Dan. "Roger Chillingworth: The Satanic Paradox in *The Scarlet Letter*," *Criticism* V (Summer 1963), 272-280.

Waggoner, Hyatt H. *Hawthorne: A Critical Study*, 118-150.

Waggoner, Hyatt H. and George Monteiro. Introduction, *The Scarlet Letter* (San Francisco, 1968).

Walsh, Thomas F. "Dimmesdale's Election Sermon," *Emerson Society Quarterly* 44 (III Quarter 1966), 64-66.

Warfel, Harry R. "Metaphysical Ideas in *The Scarlet Letter*," *College English* XXIV (Mar 1963), 421-425.

Warren, Austin. "*The Scarlet Letter*: A Literary Exercise in Moral Theology," *Southern Review* I (Jan 1965), 22-45.

Wells, Arvin R. *Insight I*, 82-91.

Ziff, Larzer. Introduction, *The Scarlet Letter* (New York, 1963).

SEPTIMIUS FELTON

Fussell, Edwin. "Indian Summer of the Literary West," *Frontier: American Literature and the American West*, 360-374.

Stewart, Randall. "Recurrent Themes in Hawthorne's Fiction," *Regionalism and Beyond: Essays of Randall Stewart*, 73-76.

GENERAL

Adams, John F. "Hawthorne's Symbolic Gardens," *Texas Studies in Literature and Language* V (Summer 1963), 242-254.

Arvin, Newton. "The Relevance of Hawthorne," *The American Pantheon*, 60-69.

Askew, Melvin W. "Hawthorne, the Fall, and the Psychology of Maturity," *American Literature* XXXIV (Nov 1962), 335-343.

Baym, Nina. "The Head, The Heart, and The Unpardonable Sin," *New England Quarterly* XL (Mar 1967), 31-47.

Bell, Millicent. *Hawthorne's View of the Artist.*

Birdsall, Virginia Ogden. "Hawthorne's Fair-Haired Maidens: The Fading Light," *PMLA* LXXV (Jun 1960), 250-256.

Cameron, Kenneth Walter. *Hawthorne Among his Contemporaries: A Harvest of Estimates, Insights, and Anecdotes from the Victorian Literary World and an Index.*

————. *Hawthorne Index to Themes, Motifs, Topics.*

————. "New Light on Hawthorne's Removal from the Customs House," *Emerson Society Quarterly* 23 (II Quarter 1961), 2-5.

A Casebook on the Hawthorne Question.

Cecil, L. Moffitt. "Hawthorne's Optical Device," *American Quarterly* XV (Spring 1963), 76-84.

Charney, Maurice. "Hawthorne and the Gothic Style," *New England Quarterly* XXXIV (Mar 1961), 36-49.

Clark, Harry Hayden. "Hawthorne: Tradition versus Innovation," *Patterns of Commitment in American Literature,* 19-37.

Clark, Marden J. "The Wages of Sin in Hawthorne," *Brigham Young University Studies* I (Winter 1959), 21-36.

Clough, Wilson O. *The Necessary Earth: Nature and Solitude in American Literature,* 116-125.

Cracroft, Richard H. "Liverpool, 1856: Nathaniel Hawthorne Meets Orson Pratt," *Brigham Young University Studies* VIII (Spring 1968), 270-272.

Crews, Frederick C. *The Sins of the Fathers: Hawthorne's Psychological Themes.*

Emerson, Everett H. "Hawthorne in General Education," *CEA Critic* XXV (Jun 1963), 1, 6.

Erlich, Gloria Chasson. "Deadly Innocence: Hawthorne's Dark Women," *New England Quarterly* XLI (Jun 1968), 163-179.

Fairbanks, Henry George. *The Lasting Loneliness of Nathaniel Hawthorne.*

Fiedler, Leslie A. *Love and Death in the American Novel,* 222-232, 282-284, 419-429.

Flint, Allen. "Hawthorne and the Slavery Crisis," *New England Quarterly* XLI (Sept 1968), 393-408.

Fogle, Richard Harter. *Hawthorne's Fiction: The Light & the Dark,* revised edition.

Folsom, James K. *Man's Accidents and God's Purposes: Multiplicity in Hawthorne's Fiction.*

Franklin, H. Bruce. "Hawthorne and Science Fiction," *Centennial Review* X (Winter 1966), 112-130.

Frederick, John T. "Hawthorne and the Workhouse Baby," *Arizona Quarterly* 24 (Summer 1968), 169-173.

Fussell, Edwin. "Nathaniel Hawthorne," *Frontier: American Literature and the American West,* 69-131.

Grant, Douglas. *Purpose and Place,* 21-33.

Green, Martin. *Re-Appraisals: Some Commonsense Readings in American Literature,* 61-85.

Griffith, Albert J. "Heart Images in Hawthorne's Names," *Emerson Society Quarterly* 43 (II Quarter 1966), 78-79.

Gross, Seymour L. "Hawthorne's Moral Realism," *Emerson Society Quarterly* 25 (IV Quarter 1961), 11-13.

Gross, Theodore L. "Nathaniel Hawthorne: The Absurdity of Heroism," *Yale Review* LVII (Winter 1968), 182-195.

Gupta, R. K. "Hawthorne's Theory of Art," *American Literature* 40 (Nov 1968), 309-324.

Hawthorne's Centenary Essays.

Holmes, Edward M. "Hawthorne and Romanticism," *New England Quarterly* XXXIII (Dec 1960), 476-488.

Hull, Raymona E. "Hawthorne's Efforts to Help Thoreau," *Emerson Society Quarterly* 33 (IV Quarter 1963), 24-28.

Jacobson, Richard J. *Hawthorne's Conception of the Creative Process.*

Joseph, Sister M. Evelyn, I.H.M. "Substance as Suggestion: Ambiguity in Hawthorne," *Renascence* XVII (Summer 1965), 216-220.

Josipovici, G. D. "Hawthorne's Modernity," *Critical Quarterly* 8 (Winter 1966), 351-360.

Kaul, A. N. "Nathaniel Hawthorne: Heir and Critic of the Puritan Tradition," *The American Vision: Actual and Ideal Society in Nineteenth Century Fiction,* 139-213.

Kazin, Alfred. "Hawthorne: The Artist of New England," *Atlantic Monthly* CCXVIII (Dec 1966), 109-113.

Kesterson, David B. "Hawthorne and Nature: Thoreauvian Influence?" *English Language Notes* IV (Mar 1967), 200-206.

Kimmey, John L. "Pierre and Robin: Melville's Debt to Hawthorne," *Emerson Society Quarterly* 38 (I Quarter 1965), 90-92.

Kuhlmann, Susan. "The Window of Fiction," *CEA Critic* XXX (Nov 1967), 15-16.

Lang, H. J. "How Ambiguous is Hawthorne?," *Geist einer freien Gesellschaft: Festschrift zu Ehren von Senator James William Fulbright aus Anlass des zehnjahrigen Bestehens des deutschen Fulbright-Programms,* 195-220.

Levin, David. "Hawthorne's Romances: The Value of Puritan History," *In Defense of Historical Literature,* 98-117.

Levy, Leo B. "Hawthorne and the Sublime," *American Literature* XXXVII (Jan 1966), 391-402.

Lohmann, Christoph. "The Burden on the Past in Hawthorne's American Romances," *South Atlantic Quarterly* LXVI (Winter 1967), 92-104.

Manley, Seon. *Nathaniel Hawthorne: Captain of the Imagination.*

Marks, Barry A. "The Origin of Original Sin in Hawthorne's Fiction," *Nineteenth-Century Fiction* XIV (Mar 1960), 359-362.

Martin, Terence. *Nathaniel Hawthorne.*

Marx, Leo. *The Machine in the Garden: Technology and the Pastoral Ideal in America,* 11-19, 27-33, 265-277.

Mathews, James W. "The Heroines of Hawthorne and Howells," *Tennessee Studies in Literature* VII (1962), 37-46.

Maxwell, D. E. S. "The Tragic Phase: Melville and Hawthorne," *American Fiction: The Intellectual Background,* 179-191.

McCall, Dan. "Hawthorne's 'Familiar Kind of Preface,'" *ELH* XXXV (Sept 1968), 422-439.

————. "Robert Lowell's 'Hawthorne,'" *New England Quarterly* XXXIX (Jun 1966), 237-239.

McCullen, Joseph T. and John C. Guilds. "The Unpardonable Sin in Hawthorne: a Re-Examination," *Nineteenth-Century Fiction* XV (Dec 1960), 221-237.

Metzger, Charles R. "Effictio and Notatio: Hawthorne's Technique of Characterization," *Western Humanities Review* XIV (Spring 1960), 224-226.

Michel, Pierre. "Hawthorne Rehabilitated," *English Studies* XLV (Feb 1964), 44-48.

Miller, James E. "Hawthorne and Melville: No! in Thunder," *Quests Surd and Absurd: Essays in American Literature,* 186-208.

————. "Hawthorne and Melville: The Unpardonable Sin," *Quests Surd and Absurd: Essays in American Literature,* 209-227.

Monteiro, George. "Hawthorne, James, and the Destructive Self," *Texas Studies in Literature and Language* IV (Spring 1962), 58-71.

More, Paul Elmer. "Hawthorne: Looking Before and After," *Paul Elmer More's Shelburne Essays on American Literature,* 126-135.

————. "The Origins of Hawthorne and Poe," *Paul Elmer More's Shelburne Essays on American Literature,* 86-98.

————. "The Solitude of Nathaniel Hawthorne," *Paul Elmer More's Shelburne Essays on American Literature,* 107-125.

Murphy, John J. "The Function of Sin in Hawthorne's Novels," *Emerson Society Quarterly* 50 (I Quarter 1968), 65-71.

Nevius, Blake R. "The Hawthorne Centenary," *Nineteenth-Century Fiction* XIX (Sept 1964), 103-104.

Noble, David W. *The Eternal Adam and the New World Garden,* 24-34.

Normand, Jean. *Nathaniel Hawthorne: Esquisse d'une Analyse de la Creation Artistique.*

O'Connor, Evangeline M. J. *An Analytical Index to the Works of Nathaniel Hawthorne with a Sketch of his Life.*

O'Connor, William Van. *The Grotesque: An American Genre and Other Essays,* 59-77.

Pattison, Joseph C. "Point of View in Hawthorne," *PMLA* LXXXII (Oct 1967), 363-369.

Perkins, George. "Howells and Hawthorne," *Nineteenth-Century Fiction* XV (Dec 1960), 259-262.

Pochmann, Henry A. "Hawthorne at Wisconsin," *Emerson Society Quarterly* 25 (IV Quarter 1961), 18-20.

Price, Lawrence Marsden. *The Reception of United States Literature in Germany,* 97-98.

Ragan, James F. "Hawthorne's Bulky Puritans," *PMLA* LXXV (Jun 1960), 420-423.

Rubin, Joseph Jay. "Hawthorne's Theology: The Wide Plank," *Emerson Society Quarterly* 25 (IV Quarter 1961), 20-24.

Schwartz, Joseph. "Three Aspects of Hawthorne's Puritanism," *New England Quarterly* XXXVI (Jun 1963), 192-208.

————. "Three Aspects of Hawtorne's Puritanism," *Twentieth Century Interpretations of The Scarlet Letter,* 34-47.

Shulman, Robert. "Hawthorne's Quiet Conflict," *Philological Quarterly* XLVII (April 1968), 216-236.

Stavrou, C. N. "Hawthorne on Don Juan," *Georgia Review* XVI (Summer 1962), 210-221.

————. "Hawthorne's Quarrel with Man," *Personalist* XLII (Summer 1961), 352-360.

Stewart, Randall. "The Development of Character Types in Hawthorne's Fiction," *Regionalism and Beyond: Essays of Randall Stewart,* 9-46.

————. "Editing the American Notebooks," *Regionalism and Beyond: Essays of Randall Stewart,* 3-8.

————. "Editing Hawthorne," *Mississippi Quarterly* XV (Summer 1962), 97-99.

————. "The Golden Age of Hawthorne Criticism," *Regionalism and Beyond: Essays of Randall Stewart,* 136-140.

————. "Hawthorne and the Civil War," *Regionalism and Beyond: Essays of Randall Stewart,* 94-112.

————. "Hawthorne and *The Faerie Queene,*" *Regionalism and Beyond: Essays of Randall Stewart,* 80-93.

————. "Hawthorne and Faulkner," *Regionalism and Beyond: Essays of Randall Stewart,* 126-135.

————. "Melville and Hawthorne," *Regionalism and Beyond: Essays of Randall Stewart,* 113-125.

————. "1956: Hawthorne and Faulkner," *College English* XXII (Nov 1960), 128-132.

————. "Recurrent Themes in Hawthorne's Fiction," *Regionalism and Beyond: Essays of Randall Stewart,* 47-79.

Stone, Edward. "Two More Glimpses of Hawthorne," *English Language Notes* III (Sept 1965), 52-55.

Strauch, Carl F. "The Problem of Time and the Romantic Mode in Hawthorne, Melville and Emerson," *Emerson Society Quarterly* 35 (II Quarter 1964), 50-60.

Suh, In-Jae. "Hawthorne's Attitude Toward New England Religious Doctrine," *English Language and Literature* 14 (Jun 1963-Oct 1963), 78-105.

Taylor, J. Golden. *Hawthorne's Ambivalence Toward Puritanism.*

Tharpe, Jac. *Nathaniel Hawthorne: Identity and Knowledge.*

Thornslev, Peter L., Jr. "Hawthorne's Determinism: An Analysis," *Nineteenth-Century Fiction* XIX (Sept 1964), 141-157.

Trilling, Lionel. "Our Hawthorne," *Partisan Review* XXXI (Summer 1964), 329-351.

Turner, Arlin. "Nathaniel Hawthorne in American Studies," *College English* XXVI (Nov 1964), 133-139.

————. *Nathaniel Hawthorne: An Introduction and Interpretation.*

Wagenknecht, Edward C. *Nathaniel Hawthorne: Man and Writer.*

Wager, Willis. *American Literature: A World View*, 93-97.

Waggoner, Hyatt H. "From 'Art and Belief,' " *Twentieth Century Interpretations of The Scarlet Letter*, 67-68.

————. *Hawthorne: A Critical Study*, Rev. Ed.

————. "Nathaniel Hawthorne," *Six American Novelists of the Nineteenth Century*, 45-81.

Warren, Austin. "Nathaniel Hawthorne," *The New England Conscience*, 132-142.

Wheeler, Otis B. "Hawthorne and the Fiction of Sensibility," *Nineteenth-Century Fiction* XIX (Sept 1964), 159-170.

Wright, Nathalia. "The Language of Art: Hawthorne," *American Novelists in Italy: The Discoverers: Allston to James,* 138-167.

Young, Philip. "Hawthorne and 100 Years: A Report From the Academy," *Kenyon Review* XXVII (Spring 1965), 215-232.

BIBLIOGRAPHY

Adkins, Nelson F. "Notes on the Hawthorne Canon," *Papers of the Bibliographical Society of America* LX (Jul-Sept 1966), 364-367.

Bruccoli, Matthew J. "Concealed Printings in Hawthorne," *Papers of the Bibliographical Society of America* 57 (Jan-Mar 1963), 42-49.

Cameron, Kenneth W. "Inventory of Hawthorne's Manuscripts Part One," *Emerson Society Quarterly* 29 (IV Quarter 1962), 5-20.

————. "Notes on Hawthorne's Manuscripts," *Emerson Society Quarterly* 25 (IV Quarter 1961), 35-36.

Folsom, James K. *Man's Accidents and God's Purposes: Multiplicity in Hawthorne's Fiction,* 172-176.

Harwell, R. B. *Hawthorne and Longfellow: A Guide to an Exhibit.*

Hoeltje, Hubert H. *Inward Sky: The Mind and Heart of Nathaniel Hawthorne,* 563-571.

Jones, Buford A. A *Checklist of Hawthorne Criticism, 1951-1966.*

————. "A Checklist of Hawthorne Criticism: 1951-1966 with a Detailed Index," *Emerson Society Quarterly* 52 Supplement in Two Parts (III Quarter 1968), 1-91.

Martin, Terence. *Nathaniel Hawthorne,* 185-201.

Mathews, J. Chesley. "Bibliographical Supplement: A Selective Check-list, 1955-1962," *Eight American Authors: A Review of Research and Criticism*, 428-434.

Phillips, Robert S. *"The Scarlet Letter:* A Selected Checklist of Criticism," *Bulletin of Bibliography* XXIII (Sept-Dec 1962), 213-216.

Price, Lawrence Marsden. *The Reception of United States Literature in Germany*, 208.

The Scarlet Letter: An Annotated Text; Backgrounds and Sources; Essays in Criticism, 374-375.

Six American Novelists of the Nineteenth Century, 231-234.

Tharpe, Jac. *Nathaniel Hawthorne: Identity and Knowledge*, 161-172.

Turner, Arlin. *Nathaniel Hawthorne: An Introduction and Interpretation*, 141-144.

Waggoner, Hyatt H. and George Monteiro. *The Scarlet Letter*, liv-lviii.

Zauli-Naldi, Camilla. "La Fortuna Di Hawthorne In Italia," *Studi Americani* VI (1960), 183-201.

HAYCOX, ERNEST

GENERAL

Etulain, Richard. "Ernest Haycox: The Historical Western, 1937-43," *South Dakota Review* 5 (Spring 1967), 35-54.

HEARN, LAFCADIO

CHITA

Yu, Beongcheon. *An Ape of Gods: The Art and Thought of Lafcadio Hearn*, 66-71.

GENERAL

Hahn, Emily. *Romantic Rebels: An Informal History of Bohemianism in America*, 73-83.

Kennard, Nina H. *Lafcadio Hearn.*

Leary, Lewis. "Lafcadio Hearn, One of Our Southern Writers: A Footnote to Southern Literary History," *Essays on American Literature in Honor of Jay Hubbell*, 202-214.

Stevenson, Elizabeth. *Lafcadio Hearn.*

Yu, Beongcheon. *An Ape of Gods: The Art and Thought of Lafcadio Hearn.*

HEARN, LAFCADIO, Continued

BIBLIOGRAPHY

Stevenson, Elizabeth. *Lafcadio Hearn*, 337-346.

Yu, Beongcheon. *An Ape of Gods: The Art and Thought of Lafcadio Hearn*, 327-333.

————. "Lafcadio Hearn (or Koizumi Yakumo) (1850-1904)," *American Literary Realism* 1 (Fall 1967), 52-55.

IIECIIT, BEN

ERIC DORN

Algren, Nelson. Introduction, *Eric Dorn, a Novel* (Chicago, 1963).

GENERAL

Lieberman, H. *The Man and His Perfidy*.

Ravitz, Abe C. "Ballyhoo, Gargoyles, & Firecrackers: Ben Hecht's Aesthetic Calliope," *Journal of Popular Culture* I (Summer 1967), 37-51.

HELLER, JOSEPH

CATCH-22

Algren, Nelson. "The Catch," *Nation* 193 (Nov 4, 1961), 357-358.

Doskow, Minna. "The Night Journey in *Catch-22*," *Twentieth Century Literature* XII (Jan 1967), 186-193.

Gordon, Caroline and Jeanne Richardson. "Flies in Their Eyes? A Note on Joseph Heller's *Catch-22*," *Southern Review* III (Winter 1967), 96-105.

Greenfield, Josh. "22 Was Funnier than 14," *New York Times Book Review* 73 (Mar 3, 1968), 1, 49-53.

Ishag, Saada. "The American Romance-Parody: A Study of Purdy's *Malcolm* and Heller's *Catch-22*," *The American Novel: Two Studies*, 42-47, 52-59.

Karl, Frederick R. "Joseph Heller's *Catch-22*: Only Fools Walk in Darkness," *Contemporary American Novelists*, 134-142.

Lehan, Richard and Jerry Patch. "*Catch-22*: The Making of a Novel," *Minnesota Review* VII (Number 3 1967), 238-244.

McDonald, James L. "I See Everything Twice! The Structure of Joseph Heller's *Catch-22*," *University Review* XXXIV (Mar 1968), 175-180.

Mellard, James M. "*Catch-22*: Deja vu and the Labyrinth of Memory," *Bucknell Review* XVI (May 1968), 29-44.

Muste, John M. "Better to Die Laughing: The War Novels of Joseph Heller and John Ashmead," *Critique* V (Fall, 1962), 16-27.

Pinsker, Sanford. "Heller's *Catch-22:* The Protest of a *Puer Eternis,*" *Critique* VII (Winter 1964-1965), 150-162.

Ramsey, Vance. "From Here to Absurdity: Heller's *Catch 22,*" *Seven Contemporary Authors,* 99-118.

Solomon, Jan. "The Structure of Joseph Heller's *Catch-22,*" *Critique* IX (No 2, 1966), 46-57.

Stern, J. P. "War and the Comic Muse: *The Good Soldier Schweik* and *Catch-22,*" *Comparative Literature* XX (Summer 1968), 193-216.

Waldmeir, Joseph J. "Two Novelists of the Absurd: Heller and Kesey," *Wisconsin Studies in Contemporary Literature* 5 (Autumn 1964), 192-204.

Way, Brian. "Formal Experiment and Social Discontent: Joseph Heller's *Catch-22,*" *Journal of American Studies* II (Oct 1968), 253-270.

Wincelberg, Shimon. "A Deadly Serious Lunacy," *On Contemporary Literature,* 388-391.

HEMINGWAY, ERNEST

ACROSS THE RIVER AND INTO THE TREES

Gurko, Leo. *Ernest Hemingway and the Pursuit of Heroism,* 152-158.

Hovey, Richard B. *Hemingway: The Inward Terrain,* 177-190.

Lewis, Robert W., Jr. *Hemingway on Love,* 182-196.

Lisca, Peter. "The Structure of Hemingway's *Across the River and into the Trees,*" *Modern Fiction Studies* XII (Summer 1966), 232-250.

Sanderson, Stewart. *Ernest Hemingway,* 103-111.

A FAREWELL TO ARMS

Anderson, Charles R. "Hemingway's Other Style," *Ernest Hemingway: Critiques of Four Major Novels,* 41-46.

Baker, Carlos. "Ernest Hemingway: *A Farewell to Arms,*" *The American Novel from James Fenimore Cooper to William Faulkner,* 192-205.

————. "On Ernest Hemingway," *Talks With Authors,* 73-88.

————. "Two Rivers: Mark Twain and Hemingway," *Mark Twain Journal* XI (Summer 1962), 2.

Baker, Sheridan. *Ernest Hemingway: An Introduction and Interpretation,* 56-73.

Cooperman, Stanley. *World War I and the American Novel,* 181-190.

HEMINGWAY, ERNEST, Continued

————. "Death and *Cojones*: Hemingway's *A Farewell to Arms*," *South Atlantic Quarterly* LXIII (Winter 1964), 85-92.

Gelfant, Blanche. "Language as a Moral Code in *A Farewell to Arms*," *Modern Fiction Studies* IX (Summer 1963), 173-176.

Gerstenberger, Donna. "The Waste Land in *A Farewell to Arms*," *Modern Language Notes* LXXV (Jan 1961), 24-25.

Gibson, Walker. "Tough Talk: The Rhetoric of Frederic Henry," *Tough, Sweet and Stuffy: An Essay on Modern American Prose Styles*, 28-42.

Glasser, William A. "*A Farewell to Arms*," *Sewanee Review* LXXIV (Spring 1966), 453-469.

————. "Hemingway's *A Farewell to Arms*," *Explicator* XX (Oct 1961), No. 18.

Gurko, Leo. *Ernest Hemingway and the Pursuit of Heroism*, 81-109.

Hardy, John Edward. "*A Farewell to Arms*: The Death of Tragedy," *Man in the Modern Novel*, 123-136.

Hemingway, Ernest. "The Original Conclusion to *A Farewell to Arms*," *Ernest Hemingway: Critiques of Four Major Novels*, 75.

Hovey, Richard B. "*A Farewell to Arms*: Hemingway's Liebestod," *University Review* XXXIII (Dec 1966), 93-100; XXXIII (Mar 1967), 163-168.

————. *Hemingway: The Inward Terrain*, 73-91.

Lewis, Robert W., Jr. *Hemingway on Love*, 40-54.

Liedloff, Helmut. "Two War Novels: A Critical Comparison," *Revue de Littérature Comparée* 42 (Jul-Sept 1968), 390-406.

Light, James F. "The Religion of Death in *A Farewell to Arms*," *Ernest Hemingway: Critiques of Four Major Novels*, 37-40.

————. "The Religion of Death in *A Farwell to Arms*," *Modern Fiction Studies* VII (Summer 1961), 169-173.

Marcus, Fred H. "*A Farewell to Arms*: The Impact of Irony and the Irrational," *English Journal* LI (Nov 1962), 527-535.

McAleer, John J. "*A Farewell to Arms*: Frederic Henry's Rejected Passion," *Renascence* XIV (Winter 1962), 72-79, 89.

Meriwether, James B. "The Dashes in Hemingway's *A Farewell to Arms*," *Papers of the Bibliographical Society of America* 58 (Oct-Dec 1964), 449-457.

Naik, M. K. "Thematic Structure in *A Farewell to Arms*," *Indian Journal of English Studies* VIII (1967), 79-82.

Rovit, Earl. *Ernest Hemingway*, 98-106.

Sanderson, Stewart. *Ernest Hemingway,* 51-61.

Schneider, Daniel J. "Hemingway's *A Farewell to Arms:* The Novel as Pure Poetry," *Modern Fiction Studies* XIV (Autumn 1968) , 283-296.

Schweitzer, John. Introduction, *A Farewell to Arms* (New York, 1967) .

Slattery, Sister Margaret Patrice. "Hemingway's *A Farewell To Arms,*" *Explicator* XXVII (Oct 1968) , No. 8.

West, Ray B., Jr. *"A Farewell to Arms,"* The Writer in the Room: Selected Essays, 158-174.

FOR WHOM THE BELL TOLLS

Adler, Jack. "Theme and Character in Hemingway: *For Whom the Bell Tolls,*" *University Review* XXX (Jun 1964) , 293-299.

Baker, Sheridan. *Ernest Hemingway: An Introduction and Interpretation,* 107-118.

Cooperman, Stanley. "Hemingway's Blue-eyed Boy: Robert Jordan and 'Purging Ecstacy,' " *Criticism* VIII (Winter 1966) , 87-96.

Eby, Cecil D. "The Real Robert Jordan," *American Literature* XXXVIII (Nov 1966) , 380-386.

French, Warren. *The Social Novel at the End of an Era,* 87-125, 157-170.

Gurko, Leo. *Ernest Hemingway and the Pursuit of Heroism,* 110-136.

Guttmann, Allen. "Mechanized Doom: Ernest Hemingway and the American View of the Spanish Civil War," *Ernest Hemingway: Critiques of Four Major Novels,* 95-107.

————. "Mechanized Doom: Ernest Hemingway and the Spanish Civil War," *Massachusetts Review* I (May 1960) , 541-561.

Hovey, Richard B. *Hemingway: The Inward Terrain,* 151-172.

Lewis, Robert W., Jr. *Hemingway on Love,* 144-178.

Parsons, Thornton H. "Hemingway's Tyrannous Plot," *University of Kansas City Review* XXVII (Jun 1961) , 261-266.

Ramsey, Paul. "Hemingway as Moral Thinker: A Look at Two Novels," *The Twenties: Poetry and Prose,* 92-94.

Rovit, Earl. *Ernest Hemingway,* 136-146.

Sanderson, Stewart. *Ernest Hemingway,* 92-102.

Weeks, Robert P. "The Power of the Tacit in Crane and Hemingway," *Modern Fiction Studies* VIII (Winter 1962-63) , 415-418.

West, Ray B., Jr. "Ernest Hemingway: The Failure of Sensibility," *The Writer in the Room: Selected Essays,* 144-156.

THE OLD MAN AND THE SEA

Baker, Sheridan. *Ernest Hemingway: An Introduction and Interpretation,* 126-134.

Bradford, M. E. "On the Importance of Discovering God: Faulkner and Hemingway's *The Old Man and the Sea,*" *Mississippi Quarterly* XX (Summer 1967) , 158-162.

Broadus, Robert N. "The New Record Set by Hemingway's Old Man," *Notes and Queries* N.S. 10 (April 1963) , 152-153.

Burhans, Clinton S., Jr. *"The Old Man and The Sea:* Hemingway's Tragic Vision of Man," *American Literature* XXXI (Jan 1960) , 446-455.

————. *"The Old Man and the Sea:* Hemingway's Tragic Vision of Man," *Ernest Hemingway: Critiques of Four Major Novels,* 150-155.

————.*"The Old Man and the Sea:* Hemingway's Tragic Vision of Man," *Hemingway and his Critics: An International Anthology,* 259-268.

————. *"The Old Man and the Sea:* Hemingway's Tragic Vision of Man," *The Modern American Novel: Essays in Criticism,* 118-130.

Cotter, Janet M. *"The Old Man and the Sea:* An Open Literary Experience," *English Journal* LI (Oct 1962) , 459-463.

Gurko, Leo. *Ernest Hemingway and the Pursuit of Heroism,* 159-174.

Hagopian, John V. and Martin Dolch. *Insight I: Analyses of American Literature,* 111-122.

Halverson, John. "Christian Resonance in *The Old Man and the Sea,*" *English Language Notes* II (Sept 1964) , 50-54.

Handy, William J. "A New Dimension for a Hero: Santiago of *The Old Man and the Sea,*" *Six Contemporary Novels: Six Introductory Essays in Modern Fiction,* 58-75.

Harada, Keiichi. "The Marlin and the Shark: A Note on *The Old Man and the Sea,*" *Hemingway and his Critics: An International Anthology,* 269-276.

Hofling, Charles K. "Hemingway's *The Old Man and The Sea* and The Male Reader," *American Imago* XX (Summer 1963) , 161-173.

Hovey, Richard B. *Hemingway: The Inward Terrain,* 191-203.

Kallapur, S. T. *"The Old Man and the Sea:* Three Parallels," *Journal of the Karnatak University* IX (1965) , 108-117.

Kim, Byung-Chol. "Hemingway's Dualism," *English Language and Literature* 14 (Jun 1963-Oct 1963) , 56-77, (In Korean) .

Lewis, Robert W., Jr. *Hemingway on Love,* 200-213.

Rovit, Earl. *Ernest Hemingway,* 85-94.

Scoville, Samuel. "The *Weltanschauung* of Steinbeck and Hemingway: An Analysis of Themes," *English Journal* LVI (Jan 1967) , 60-63, 66.

Stephens, Robert O. "Hemingway's Old Man and the Iceberg," *Modern Fiction Studies* VII (Winter 1961-62) , 295-304.

Sylvester, Bickford. "Hemingway's Extended Vision: *The Old Man and The Sea,*" *PMLA* LXXXI (Mar 1966) , 130-138.

————. " 'They Went Through This Fiction Every Day': Informed Illusion in *The Old Man and the Sea,*" *Modern Fiction Studies* XII (Winter 1966-67) , 473-477.

Twentieth Century Interpretations of The Old Man and the Sea.

Ueno, Naozo. "An Oriental View of *The Old Man and the Sea,*" *East-West Review* II (Spring-Summer 1965) , 67-76.

Weeks, Robert P. "Fakery in *The Old Man and the Sea,*" *College English* XXIV (Dec 1962) , 188-192.

Wells, Arvin R. "A Ritual of Transfiguration: *The Old Man and the Sea,*" *University Review* XXX (Dec 1963) , 95-101.

THE SUN ALSO RISES

Baker, Sheridan. *Ernest Hemingway: An Introduction and Interpretation,* 40-55.

Cochran, Robert W. "Circularity in *The Sun Also Rises,*" *Modern Fiction Studies* XIV (Autumn 1968) , 297-305.

Ganzel, Dewey. "Cabestro and Vaquilla: The Symbolic Structure of *The Sun Also Rises,*" *Sewanee Review* LXXVI (Winter 1968) , 26-48.

Gurko, Leo. *Ernest Hemingway and the Pursuit of Heroism,* 55-80.

Hovey, Richard B. *Hemingway: The Inward Terrain,* 60-73.

Kobler, J. F. "Confused Chronology in *The Sun Also Rises,*" *Modern Fiction Studies* XIII (Winter 1967-68) , 517-520.

Lauter, Paul. "Plato's Stepchildren, Gatsby and Cohn," *Modern Fiction Studies* IX (Winter 1963-64) , 338-346.

Lewis, Robert W., Jr. *Hemingway on Love,* 19-35.

————. "Tristan or Jacob: The Choice of *The Sun Also Rises,*" *The Modern American Novel: Essays in Criticism,* 93-113.

Mizener, Arthur. "Ernest Hemingway: *The Sun Also Rises,*" *Twelve Great American Novels,* 120-141.

Newman, Paul B. "Hemingway's Grail Quest," *University of Kansas City Review* XXVIII (Jun 1962) , 295-303.

HEMINGWAY, ERNEST, Continued

Ramsey, Paul. "Hemingway as Moral Thinker: A Look at Two Novels," *The Twenties: Poetry and Prose*, 92-94.

Rouch, John S. "Jake Barnes as Narrator," *Modern Fiction Studies* XI (Winter 1965-1966) , 361-370.

Rovit, Earl. *Ernest Hemingway*, 147-162.

Sanderson, Stewart. *Ernest Hemingway*, 40-50.

Schroeter, James. "Hemingway's *The Sun Also Rises*," *Explicator* XX (Nov 1961) , No. 28.

Stallman, R. W. *The Houses That James Built*, 173-193.

Vance, William L. "Implications of Form in *The Sun Also Rises*," *The Twenties: Poetry and Prose*, 87-91.

Wertheim, Stanley. "The Conclusion of Hemingway's *The Sun Also Rises*," *Literature and Psychology* XVII (No 1, 1967) , 55-56.

TO HAVE AND HAVE NOT

Grebstein, Sheldon Norman. "The Tough Hemingway and His Hard-Boiled Children," *Tough Guy Writers of the Thirties*, 36-41.

Gurko, Leo. *Ernest Hemingway and the Pursuit of Heroism*, 143-152.

Hovey, Richard B. *Hemingway: The Inward Terrain*, 131-144.

Lewis, Robert W., Jr. *Hemingway on Love*, 114-140.

Ryan, William James. "Uses of Irony in *To Have and Have Not*," *Modern Fiction Studies* XIV (Autumn 1968) , 329-336.

Sanderson, Stewart. *Ernest Hemingway*, 79-88.

Young, Phillip. "Focus on *To Have and Have Not*: Tough Luck," *Tough Guy Writers of the Thirties*, 42-50.

THE TORRENTS OF SPRING

Hovey, Richard B. *Hemingway: The Inward Terrain*, 55-60.

————. "*The Torrents of Spring*: Prefigurations in the Early Hemingway," *College English* XXVI (Mar 1965) , 460-464.

White, Ray Lewis. "Hemingway's Private Explanation of *The Torrents of Spring*," *Modern Fiction Studies* XIII (Summer 1967) , 261-263.

Wylder, Delbert E. "*The Torrents of Spring*," *South Dakota Review* 5 (Winter 1967-68) , 23-35.

GENERAL

Aldridge, John W. "Hemingway and Europe," *Shenandoah* XII (Spring 1961) , 11-24.

Algren, Nelson. "Hemingway: The Dye that Did Not Run," *Nation* 193 (Nov 18, 1961) , 387-390.

Anderson, David D. "Ernest Hemingway, the Voice of an Era," *Personalist* XLVII (Spring 1966), 234-247.

Arnold, Lloyd R. *High on the Wild with Hemingway.*

Aronowitz, Ernest. *Hemingway: The Life and Death of a Man.*

Astre, Georges-Albert. *Ernest Hemingway in Selbstzeugnissen und Bilddokumenten.*

Baden, Hans Jurgen. "Ernest Hemingway," *Literatur und Selbstmord,* 147-213.

Baker, Carlos. "Hemingway," *Saturday Review* XLIV (Jul 29, 1961), 11-13.

————. "Hemingway's Italia," *New York Times Book Review* 71 (Jan 23, 1966), 2.

————. "A Search for the Man as He Really Was," *New York Times Book Review* 69 (Jul 26, 1964), 4, 14.

Barnes, Robert J. "Two Modes of Fiction: Hemingway and Greene," *Renascence* XIV (Summer 1962), 193-198.

Benson, Frederick R. *Writers in Arms: The Literary Impact of the Spanish Civil War,* 60-63, 123-129, 292-296.

Betsky, Seymour. "A Last Visit," *Saturday Review* XLIV (Jul 29, 1961), 22-24.

Bridgman, Richard. "Ernest Hemingway," *The Colloquial Style in America,* 195-230.

Brocki, Sister Mary Damascene. "Faulkner and Hemingway: Values in a Modern World," *Mark Twain Journal* XI (Summer 1962), 5-9, 15.

Brooks, Cleanth. "Ernest Hemingway, Man on his Moral Uppers," *The Hidden God,* 6-21.

Broussard, Louis. "Hemingway as a Literary Critic," *Arizona Quarterly* XX (Autumn 1964), 197-204.

Brown, John. *Hemingway.*

Bryan, James E. "Hemingway as Vivisector," *University Review* XXX (Oct 1963), 3-12.

Callaghan, Morley. *That Summer in Paris.*

Ciardi, John. "The Language of an Age," *Saturday Review* XLIV (Jul 29, 1961), 32.

Clendenning, John. "Hemingway's Gods, Dead and Alive," *Texas Studies in Literature and Language* III (Winter 1962), 489-502.

Cooperman, Stanley. "Hemingway and Old Age," *College English* XXVII (Dec 1965), 215-220.

D'Agostino, Nemi. "The Later Hemingway," *Hemingway: A Collection of Critical Essays*, 152-160.

―――. "The Later Hemingway," *Sewanee Review* LXVIII (Summer 1960), 482-493.

de Madriaga, Salvador and Frank Moraes, Carlo Levi, Ilya Ehrenburg, Alan Pryce-Jones, Edward Seidensticker. "The World Weighs a Writer's Influence," *Saturday Review* XLIV (Jul 29, 1961), 18-22.

Drinnon, Richard. "In the American Heartland: Hemingway and Death," *Psychoanalytic Review* 52 (Summer 1965), 5-31.

Egri, Péter. *Hemingway*.

Ellison, Ralph. "Twentieth-Century Fiction and the Black Mask of Humanity," *Images of the Negro in American Literature*, 123-129.

"Ernest Hemingway Memorial Number," *Mark Twain Journal* XI (Summer 1962). Brief notes by: John F. Kennedy, Mary Hemingway, Carlos Baker, Edward A. Dieckmann, Jr., Sister Mary Damascene Brocki, CSSF., Ernest Hemingway, Andre Maurois, William White, Frank Swinnerton, Lowell Thomas, Thomas Caldecot Chubb, August Derleth, Upton Sinclair, Homer Croy, Robert Graves, Marguerite Steen, Phyllis Bottome, Neil Bell, Fraser Drew and Langston Hughes.

Evans, Robert. "Hemingway and the Pale Cast of Thought," *American Literature* XXXVIII (May 1966), 161-176.

Farquhar, Robin H. "Dramatic Structure in the Novels of Ernest Hemingway," *Modern Fiction Studies* XIV (Autumn 1968), 271-282.

Fiedler, Leslie. "An Almost Imaginary Interview: Hemingway in Ketchum," *Partisan Review* XXIX (Summer 1962), 395-405.

―――. *Love and Death in the American Novel*, 304-309.

―――. "Men Without Women," *Hemingway: A Collection of Critical Essays*, 86-92.

―――. *The Return of the Vanishing American*, 144-147.

―――. *Waiting for the End*, 12-18.

Floor, Richard. "Fate and Life: Determinism in Ernest Hemingway," *Renascence* XV (Fall 1962), 23-27.

Fuchs, Daniel. "Ernest Hemingway, Literary Critic," *American Literature* XXXVI (Jan 1965), 431-451.

Galligan, Edward L. "Hemingway's Staying Power," *Massachusetts Review* VIII (Summer 1967), 431-439.

Geismar, Maxwell. "Was 'Papa' a Truly Great Writer?" *New York Times Book Review* 67 (Jul 1, 1962), 1, 16.

Gifford, William. "Ernest Hemingway: The Monsters and the Critics," *Modern Fiction Studies* XIV (Autumn 1968), 255-270.

Gordon, David. "The Son and the Father: Patterns of Response to Conflict in Hemingway's Fiction," *Literature and Psychology* XVI (Nos 3 & 4, 1966), 122-138.

Graham, John. "Ernest Hemingway: The Meaning of Style," *Ernest Hemingway: Critiques of Four Major Novels,* 183-192.

————. "Ernest Hemingway: The Meaning of Style," *Modern Fiction Studies* VI (Winter 1960-61), 298-313.

Grant, Douglas. *Purpose and Place,* 169-182.

Gray, James. "Hemingway in Pigott," *Approach* 48 (Summer 1963), 30-32.

Grebstein, Sheldon Norman. "The Tough Hemingway and His Hard-Boiled Children," *Tough Guy Writers of the Thirties,* 18-41.

Gurko, Leo. *Ernest Hemingway and the Pursuit of Heroism,* 1-54.

Hale, Nancy. "Hemingway and the Courage to Be," *Virginia Quarterly Review* XXXVIII (Autumn 1962), 620-639.

Hass, Rudolf. "Zum Todesmotiv im Werk Hemingways," *Neueren Sprachen* (Oct 1959), 455-465.

Hayes, Curtis W. "A Study in Prose Styles: Edward Gibbon and Ernest Hemingway," *Texas Studies in Literature and Language* VII (Winter 1966), 371-386.

Hemingway: Collection Génies et Réalités.

Hertzel, Leo J. "The Look of Religion: Hemingway and Catholicism," *Renascence* XVII (Winter 1964), 77-81.

Hicks, Granville. "A Feeling about Life," *Saturday Review* XLIV (Jul 29, 1961), 30, 38.

Holder, Alan. "The Other Hemingway," *Twentieth Century Literature* IX (Oct 1963), 153-157.

Holman, C. Hugh. "Ernest Hemingway: A Tribute," *Books Abroad* XXXVI (Winter 1962), 5-8.

Hotchner, A. E. *Papa Hemingway: A Personal Memoir.*

Hovey, Richard B. *Hemingway: The Inward Terrain.*

Howe, Irving. "Hemingway: The Conquest of Panic," *New Republic* 145 (Jul 24, 1961), 19-20.

Howell, John M. "Hemingway and Fitzgerald in Sound and Fury," *Papers on Language and Literature* II (Summer 1966), 234-242.

Isabelle, Julanne. *Hemingway's Religious Experience.*

Jones, John A. "Hemingway: The Critics and the Public Legend," *Western Humanities Review* XIII (Autumn 1959), 387-400.

Joost, Nicholas. *Ernest Hemingway and the Little Magazines: The Paris Years.*

Kazin, Alfred. "Hemingway as his own Fable," *Atlantic Monthly* CCXIII (Jun 1964), 54-57.

Kiley, Jed. *Hemingway: An Old Friend Remembers.*

Kim, Byung-chull. "Hemingway's Nihilism," *English Language and Literature* 17 (Nov 1965), 102-137, (In Korean).

Kim, Suk-Choo. "Stoicism in Hemingway," *English Language and Literature* 10 (Sept 1961), 292-306, (In Korean).

Krauss, William A. "Footnote from Hemingway's Paris, 1964," *Harper's* CCXXXI (Aug 1965), 91-95.

Krzyzanowski, Jerzy R. *Ernest Hemingway.*

Lair, Robert L. "Hemingway and Cézanne: An Indebtedness," *Modern Fiction Studies* VI (Summer 1960), 165-168.

Lehan, Richard. "Camus and Hemingway," *Wisconsin Studies in Contemporary Literature* 1 (Spring-Summer 1960), 37-48.

Lid, R. W. "Hemingway and the Need for Speech," *Modern Fiction Studies* VIII (Winter 1962-63), 401-407.

The Literary Reputation of Hemingway in Europe.

Loeb, Harold. "The Young Writer in Paris and Pamplona," *Saturday Review* XLIV (Jul 29, 1961), 25-26.

Lupan, Radu. "The Old Man and the World: Some Final Thoughts on Ernest Hemingway," *Literary Review* X (Winter 1966-67), 159-165.

Lyons, Leonard. "Trade Winds," *Saturday Review* XLIV (Jul 29, 1961), 6, 8.

Macdonald, Dwight. "Ernest Hemingway," *Encounter* XVIII (Jan 1962), 115-121.

Machlin, Milton. *The Private Hell of Hemingway.*

Marin, Dave. "Seven Hours with Papa," *Southwest Review* LIII (Spring 1968), 167-177.

Miglior, Giorgio. "L'Idillio In Hemingway," *Studi Americani* VII (1961), 195-214.

Mizener, Arthur. "The American Hero as Leatherstocking: Nick Adams," *The Sense of Life in the Modern Novel*, 205-226.

————. "The Two Hemingways," *The Great Experiment in American Literature,* 135-151.

Montgomery, Constance Cappel. *Hemingway in Michigan.*

Moritz, Ken. "Ernest Hemingway," *American Winners of the Nobel Literary Prize,* 158-192.

Morris, Wright. "One Law for the Lion," *Partisan Review* XXVIII (5-6, 1961), 541-551.

Moses, W. R. "Victory in Defeat: 'Ad Astra' and 'A Farewell To Arms,'" *Mississippi Quarterly* XIX (Spring 1966), 85-89.

Motola, Gabriel. "Hemingway's Code: Literature and Life," *Modern Fiction Studies* X (Winter 1964-65), 319-329.

Noble, David W. *The Eternal Adam and the New World Garden,* 144-152.

O'Connor, William Van. "Faulkner, Hemingway, and the 1920's," *The Twenties: Poetry and Prose,* 95-98.

————. "Faulkner's One-Sided 'Dialogue' With Hemingway," *College English* XXIV (Dec 1962), 208-215.

Oldsey, Bern. "The Snows of Ernest Hemingway," *Wisconsin Studies in Contemporary Literature* 4 (Spring-Summer 1963), 172-198.

Page, Alex. "Pakistan's Hemingway," *Antioch Review* XXIII (Summer 1963), 203-211.

Parker, Stephen Jan. "Hemingway's Revival in the Soviet Union: 1955-1962," *American Literature* XXXV (Jan 1964), 485-501.

Poor, Charles. Preface, *The Hemingway Reader* (New York, 1965).

Portz, John. "Allusion and Structure in Hemingway's 'A Natural History of the Dead,'" *Tennessee Studies in Literature* X (1965), 27-41.

Price, Lawrence Marsden. *The Reception of United States Literature in Germany,* 147-150.

Reardon, John. "Hemingway's Esthetic and Ethical Sportsmen," *University Review* XXXIV (Oct 1967), 13-23.

Ross, Lillian. *Portrait of Hemingway.*

Rovit, Earl. *Ernest Hemingway.*

Sanders, David. "Ernest Hemingway's Spanish Civil War Experience," *American Quarterly* XII (Summer 1960), 133-143.

Sanderson, Stewart. *Ernest Hemingway.*

Sanford, Marcelline Hemingway. *At the Hemingways.*

————. "At the Hemingways: Ernest Returns from War," *Atlantic Monthly* CCIX (Feb 1962), 60-66.

————. "At the Hemingways: My Doctor Father," *Atlantic Monthly* CCIX (Jan 1962), 32-37.

————. "At the Hemingways: Walloon Lake," *Atlantic Monthly* CCVIII (Dec 1961), 31-39.

Schorer, Mark. "Some Relationships: Gertrude Stein, Sherwood Anderson, F. Scott Fitzgerald, and Ernest Hemingway," *The World We Imagine: Selected Essays*, 299-382.

Scott, Nathan A. *Ernest Hemingway: A Critical Essay.*

Singer, Kurt. *Hemingway: Life and Death of a Giant.*

Smetana, Josette. *La Philosophie de l'Action Chez Hemingway et Saint-Exupery.*

Spivey, Ted R. *Religious Themes in Two Modern Novelists,* 1-11.

Stephens, Robert O. "Ernest Hemingway and the Rhetoric of Escape," *The Twenties: Poetry and Prose,* 82-86.

Stephens, Robert O. and James Ellis. "Hemingway, Fitzgerald and the Riddle of 'Henry's Bicycle,'" *English Language Notes* V (Sept 1967), 46-49.

Stone, Edward. *Voices of Despair,* 72-77.

Stresau, Hermann. *Ernest Hemingway.*

Tanner, Tony. "Ernest Hemingway's Unhurried Sensations," *The Reign of Wonder: Naivety and Reality in American Literature,* 228-260.

Thorp, Willard. *American Writing in the Twentieth Century,* 185-195.

Walcutt, Charles Child. "Hemingway's Naked Eyeballs," *Man's Changing Mask: Modes and Methods of Characterization in Fiction,* 305-313.

Webster, Harvey Curtis. "Ernest Hemingway: The Pursuit of Death," *Texas Observer* VII (Summer 1964), 149-159.

Wegelin, Christof. "Hemingway and the Decline of International Fiction," *Sewanee Review* LXXIII (Spring 1965), 285-298.

West, Ray B., Jr. "Ernest Hemingway: The Failure of Sensibility," *The Writer in the Room: Selected Essays,* 142-157.

White, William. "Ernest Hemingway and Nathanael West: How Well Known Is Your Collector's 'Item?'" *American Book Collector* XIV (May 1964), 29.

Wiegand, William. "The 'Non-fiction' Novel," *New Mexico Quarterly* XXXVII (Autumn 1967), 251-257.

Wyatt, Bryant N. "*Huckleberry Finn* and the Art of Ernest Hemingway," *Mark Twain Journal* XIII (Summer 1967), 1-8.

HEMINGWAY, ERNEST, Continued

Young, Philip. *Ernest Hemingway: a Reconsideration.*

————. "Ernest Hemingway," *Seven Modern American Novelists: An Introduction,* 153-188.

————. "Hemingway and Me: A Rather Long Story," *Kenyon Review* XXVIII (Jan 1966), 15-37.

————. "In the Vault With Hemingway," *New York Times Book Review* 73 (Sept 29, 1968), 2, 28.

————. "On Dismembering Hemingway," *Atlantic Monthly* CCXVIII (Aug 1966), 45-49.

————. "Our Hemingway Man," *Kenyon Review* XXVI (Autumn 1964), 676-707.

————. "Scott Fitzgerald on his Thirtieth Birthday Sends a Small Gift to Ernest Hemingway," *Modern Fiction Studies* XIV (Summer 1968), 229-230.

Yunck, John A. "The Natural History of a Dead Quarrel: Hemingway and the Humanists," *South Atlantic Quarterly* LXII (Winter 1963), 29-42.

BIBLIOGRAPHY

Baker, Carlos. "Letters from Hemingway," *Princeton University Library Chronicle* XXIV (Winter 1963), 101-107.

Baker, Sheridan. *Ernest Hemingway: An Introduction and Interpretation,* 137-142.

Beebe, Maurice and John Feaster. "Criticism of Ernest Hemingway: A Selected Checklist," *Modern Fiction Studies* XIV (Autumn 1968), 337-369.

Bentz, Hans W. *Ernest Hemingway in Ubersetzungen.*

Brown, John. *Hemingway,* 281-292.

Hanneman, Audre. *Ernest Hemingway: A Comprehensive Bibliography.*

Hemingway: A Collection of Critical Essays, 179-180.

Hemingway and his Critics: An International Anthology, 279-298.

Hovey, Richard B. *Hemingway: The Inward Terrain,* 239-241.

Lewis, Robert W., Jr. *Hemingway on Love,* 229-235.

Meriwether, James B. "The Text of Ernest Hemingway," *Papers of the Bibliographical Society of America* 57 (Oct-Dec 1963), 403-421.

Pandolfi, Anna. "La Fortuna Di Ernest Hemingway in Italia," *Studi Americani* VIII (1962), 151-199.

Price, Lawrence Marsden. *The Reception of United States Literature in Germany,* 218-220.

Rovit, Earl. *Ernest Hemingway,* 184-188.

Stephens, Robert O. "Some Additions to the Hemingway Checklist," *American Book Collector* XVII (Apr 1967), 9-11.

Twentieth Century Interpretations of The Old Man and the Sea, 119-120.

Westbrook, Max. "Necessary Performance: The Hemingway Collection at Texas," *Library Chronicle of the University of Texas* VII (Spring 1964), 26-31.

White, William. "Hemingway Hunting in Scandinavia," *American Book Collector* XVI (Jan 1966), 22-24.

————. "Hemingway in Korea," *Papers of the Bibliographical Society of America* LIX (Apr-Jun 1965), 190-192.

————. "Hemingway-iana: Annotated," *Mark Twain Journal* XI (Summer 1962), 11-13.

————. "'The Old Man and the Sea' as a German Textbook," *Papers of the Bibliographical Society of America* 60 (Jan-Mar 1966), 89-90; see also White's "Addendum to Hanneman: Hemingway's 'The Old Man and the Sea,'" *Papers of the Bibliographical Society of America* 62 (Oct-Dec 1968), 613-614.

————. "Why Collect Ernest Hemingway—or Anyone?" *Prairie Schooner* XL (Fall 1966), 232-246.

HERGESHEIMER, JOSEPH

BALISAND
Martin, Ronald E. *The Fiction of Joseph Hergesheimer,* 199-228.
CYTHEREA
Martin, Ronald E. *The Fiction of Joseph Hergesheimer,* 111-139.
JAVA HEAD
Martin, Ronald E. *The Fiction of Joseph Hergesheimer,* 86-110.
THE LIMESTONE TREE
Martin, Ronald E. *The Fiction of Joseph Hergesheimer,* 140-168.
TAMPICO
Martin, Ronald E. *The Fiction of Joseph Hergesheimer,* 169-198.
THE THREE BLACK PENNYS
Martin, Ronald E. *The Fiction of Joseph Hergesheimer,* 51-85.
GENERAL
Angoff, Charles. "Recollections of Elinor Wylie, Thomas Mann,

Joseph Hergesheimer, James Stevens, Logan Clendening," *Literary Review* X (Winter 1966-67), 169-179.

Langford, Gerald, (ed.). *Ingenue among the Lions: The Letters of Emily Clark to Joseph Hergesheimer.*

Martin, Ronald E. *The Fiction of Joseph Hergesheimer.*

Napier, James J. "Letters of Sinclair Lewis to Joseph Hergesheimer, 1915-1922," *American Literature* XXXVIII (May 1966), 236-246.

BIBLIOGRAPHY

Martin, Ronald E. *The Fiction of Joseph Hergesheimer*, 272-283.

Napier, James J. "Joseph Hergesheimer: A Selected Bibliography, 1913-1945," *Bulletin of Bibliography* XXIV (Sept-Dec 1963), 46-48; (Jan-Apr 1964), 52, 69-70.

Slate, Joseph Evans. "The Joseph Hergesheimer Collection," *Library Chronicle of the University of Texas* VII (Fall 1961), 24-31.

HERRICK, ROBERT

THE HEALER

Nevius, Blake. *Robert Herrick: The Development of a Novelist,* 214-220.

A LIFE FOR A LIFE

Nevius, Blake. *Robert Herrick: The Development of a Novelist,* 204-213.

THE MEMOIRS OF AN AMERICAN CITIZEN

Nevius, Blake. *Robert Herrick: The Development of a Novelist,* 121-137.

ONE WOMAN'S LIFE

Nevius, Blake. *Robert Herrick: The Development of a Novelist,* 234-240.

THE REAL WORLD

Nevius, Blake. *Robert Herrick: The Development of a Novelist,* 112-122.

TOGETHER

Nevius, Blake. *Robert Herrick: The Development of a Novelist,* 166-189.

THE WEB OF LIFE

Nevius, Blake. *Robert Herrick: The Development of a Novelist,* 94-102.

HERRICK, ROBERT, Continued

WASTE
Robinson, Cecil. *With the Ears of Strangers: The Mexican in American Literature,* 184, 206, 218-220.
GENERAL
Jackson, Kenny A. "Robert Herrick's Use of Chicago," *Midcontinent American Studies Journal* V (Spring 1964), 24-32.
Nevius, Blake. *Robert Herrick: The Development of a Novelist.*
Towers, Tom H. "Self and Society in the Novels of Robert Herrick," *Journal of Popular Culture* I (Fall 1967), 141-157.
BIBLIOGRAPHY
Carlson, Douglas O. "Robert Herrick: An Addendum," *American Literary Realism* 3 (Summer 1968), 67-68.
Genthe, Charles V. "Robert Herrick (1868-1938)," *American Literary Realism* 1 (Fall 1967), 56-60.
Nevius, Blake. *Robert Herrick: The Development of a Novelist,* 352-357.

HERSEY, JOHN

A BELL FOR ADANO
Sanders, David. *John Hersey,* 31-37.
THE CHILD BUYER
Halsey, Margaret and B. F. Skinner, Carl F. Hansen, William Jay Smith, Robert Gorham Davis. "What Shall We Do with the Gifted Child?" *New Republic* 143 (Oct 10, 1960), 21-26.
Sanders, David. *John Hersey,* 108-121.
THE MARMOT DRIVE
Sanders, David. *John Hersey,* 75-82.
THE WALL
Sanders, David. *John Hersey,* 56-73.
THE WAR LOVER
Sanders, David. *John Hersey,* 95-107.
WHITE LOTUS
Sanders, David. *John Hersey,* 122-135.
GENERAL
Sanders, David. *John Hersey.*
BIBLIOGRAPHY
Sanders, David. *John Hersey,* 150-156.

HEYWARD, DUBOSE

GENERAL
Durham, Frank M. *DuBose Heyward's Use of Folklore in His Negro Fiction.*

HIMES, CHESTER

THE PRIMITIVE
Margolies, Edward. *Native Sons: A Critical Study of Twentieth-Century Negro American Authors,* 93-99.
GENERAL
Margolies, Edward. "Race and Sex: The Novels of Chester Himes," *Native Sons: A Critical Study of Twentieth-Century Negro American Authors,* 87-101.

HOLMES, OLIVER WENDELL

ELSIE VENNER
Hamblen, Abigail Ann. "*The Bad Seed:* A Modern *Elsie Venner,*" *Western Humanities Review* XVII (Autumn 1963), 361-363.
GENERAL
Small, Miriam Rossiter. *Oliver Wendall Holmes.*
BIBLIOGRAPHY
Small, Miriam Rossiter. *Oliver Wendall Holmes,* 166-172.
Virginia University Library. *The Barrett Library: Oliver Wendell Holmes.*

HOUGH, EMERSON

HEART'S DESIRE
Wylder, D. E. "Emerson Hough's *Heart's Desire:* Revisit to Eden," *Western American Literature* 1 (Spring 1966), 44-54.

HOWE, EDGAR WATSON

THE STORY OF A COUNTRY TOWN
Martin, Jay. *Harvests of Change. American Literature 1865-1914,* 116-120.
Powers, Richard Grid. "Tradition in E. W. Howe's *The Story of A*

HOWE, EDGAR WATSON, Continued

Country Town," *Midcontinent American Studies Journal* IX (Fall
1968), 51-62.
Simpson, Claude M. Introduction, *The Story of a Country Town*
(Cambridge, 1961).
Weber, Brom. Introduction, *The Story of a Country Town* (New
York, 1964).

HOWELLS, WILLIAM DEAN

THE ALTRURIAN ROMANCES
Kirk, Clara and Rudolf. Introduction, *A Selected Edition of W. D.
Howells* v. 20. (Bloomington, 1968).
ANNIE KILBURN
Budd, Louis J. *"Annie Kilburn,"* American Literary Realism 4 (Fall
1968), 84-87.
McMurray, William. *The Literary Realism of William Dean Howells,*
55-66.
A FOREGONE CONCLUSION
Giannone, Richard. "Howells' *A Foregone Conclusion:* Theme and
Structure," *CLA Journal* VI (Mar 1963), 216-220.
McMurray, William. *The Literary Realism of William Dean Howells,*
3-15.
A HAZARD OF NEW FORTUNES
Behrens, Ralph. "Howells' *A Hazard of New Fortunes,"* Explicator
XVIII (Jun 1960), No. 52.
Bennett, George N. *William Dean Howells: The Development of a
Novelist,* 185-199.
Carrington, George C., Jr. *The Immense Complex Drama: The World
and Art of the Howells Novel,* 82-100, 206-211.
Martin, Jay. *Harvests of Change. American Literature 1865-1914,* 42-45.
McMurray, William. *The Literary Realism of William Dean Howells,*
67-75.
Morgan, W. Wayne. "William Dean Howells: The Realist as Per-
former," *American Writers in Rebellion,* 64-67.
Tanner, Tony. Introduction, *A Hazard of New Fortunes* (New York,
1967).
Vanderbilt, Kermit. *The Achievement of William Dean Howells: A
Reinterpretation,* 144-191.

AN IMPERATIVE DUTY

Cady, Edwin H. Introduction, *The Shadow of a Dream* and *An Imperative Duty* (New York, 1962) .

Ford, Thomas W. "Howells and the American Negro," *Texas Studies in Literature and Language* V (Winter 1964) , 530-537.

THE LADY OF THE AROOSTOOK

McMurray, William. *The Literary Realism of William Dean Howells,* 16-26.

THE LANDLORD AT LION'S HEAD

McMurray, William. *The Literary Realism of William Dean Howells,* 90-100.

————. "Point of View in Howell's *The Landlord at Lion's Head,"* *American Literature* XXXIV (May 1962) , 207-214.

Sullivan, Sister Mary Petrus, R.S.M. "The Function of Setting in Howell's *The Landlord at Lion's Head,"* *American Literature* XXXV (Mar 1963) , 38-52.

THE LEATHERWOOD GOD

McMurray, William. *The Literary Realism of William Dean Howells,* 111-121.

A MODERN INSTANCE

Anthony, Mother Mary. "Howells' *A Modern Instance,"* *Explicator* XX (Nov 1961) , No. 20.

Bennett, George N. *William Dean Howells: The Development of a Novelist,* 113-123.

Carrington, George C., Jr. *The Immense Complex Drama: The World and Art of the Howells Novel,* 69-77.

Duffy, Myrtle M. "Twain in Howells' *A Modern Instance,"* *American Quarterly* XVI (Winter 1964) , 612-614.

Fertig, Walter L. "Maurice Thompson and *A Modern Instance,"* *American Literature* XXXVIII (Mar 1966) , 103-111.

Gargano, James W. "*A Modern Instance:* The Twin Evils of Society," *Texas Studies in Literature and Language* IV (Autumn 1962) , 399-407.

Gibson, Walker. *Tough, Sweet and Stuffy: An Essay on Modern American Prose Styles,* 29-37.

McMurray, William. *The Literary Realism of William Dean Howells,* 35-42.

Stronks, James. "*A Modern Instance,"* *American Literary Realism* 4 (Fall 1968) , 87-89.

HOWELLS, WILLIAM DEAN, Continued

Vanderbilt, Kermit. *The Achievement of William Dean Howells: A Reinterpretation*, 49-95.

―――――. "Marcia Gaylord's Electra Complex: A Footnote to Sex in Howells," *American Literature* XXXIV (Nov 1962), 365-374.

Walsh, Thomas F. "Howells' *A Modern Instance*," *Explicator* XXIII (Apr 1965), No. 59.

THE QUALITY OF MERCY

McMurray, William. *The Literary Realism of William Dean Howells*, 76-89.

THE RISE OF SILAS LAPHAM

Bennett, George N. *William Dean Howells: The Development of a Novelist*, 150-160.

Bowden, Edwin T. *The Dungeon of the Heart: Human Isolation and the American Novel*, 103-114.

Bryan, James E. "The Chronology of *Silas Lapham*," *American Notes & Queries* IV (Dec 1965), 56.

Cecioni, Cesare G. Introduction, *Le Fortune di Silas Lapham* (Rome, 1962).

Coanda, Richard. "Howells' *The Rise of Silas Lapham*," *Explicator* XXII (Nov 1963), No. 16.

Conti, Giuseppi Gadda. "Le Due Ascese di *Silas Lapham*," *Studi Americani* 12 (1966), 137-167.

Hart, John E. "The Commonplace as Heroic in *The Rise of Silas Lapham*," *Modern Fiction Studies* VIII (Winter 1962-63), 375-383.

Hough, Robert Lee. "William Dean Howells: *The Rise of Silas Lapham*," *The American Novel from James Fenimore Cooper to William Faulkner*, 73-86.

Kirk, Clara Marburg and Rudolph. Introduction, *The Rise of Silas Lapham* (New York, 1962).

McMurray, William. *The Literary Realism of William Dean Howells*, 43-54.

Mead, C. David. Introduction, *The Rise of Silas Lapham* (New York, 1964).

Morgan, W. Wayne. "William Dean Howells: The Realist as Performer," *American Writers in Rebellion*, 59-61.

Pizer, Donald. "The Ethical Unity of *The Rise of Silas Lapham*," *American Literature* XXXII (Nov 1960), 322-327.

―――――. "The Ethical Unity of *The Rise of Silas Lapham*," *Realism and Naturalism in Nineteenth-Century American Literature,* 108-113.

Solomon, Eric. "Howells, Houses, and Realism," *American Literary Realism* 4 (Fall 1968) , 89-93.

Tanselle, G. Thomas. "The Architecture of *The Rise of Silas Lapham,*" *American Literature* XXXVII (Jan 1966) , 430-457.

Vanderbilt, Kermit. *The Achievement of William Dean Howells: A Reinterpretation,* 96-143.

————. "Howells among the Brahmins: Why 'The Bottom Dropped Out' During *The Rise of Silas Lapham,*" *New England Quarterly* XXXV (Sept 1962) , 291-317.

Wasserstrom, William. "Howells' Mansion and Thoreau's Cabin," *College English* XXVI (Feb 1965) , 366-372.

THE SHADOW OF A DREAM

Cady, Edwin H. Introduction, *The Shadow of a Dream* and *An Imperative Duty* (New York, 1962) .

Hedges, Elaine. "Howells on a Hawthornesque Theme," *Texas Studies in Literature and Language* III (Spring 1961) , 129-143.

THE SON OF ROYAL LANGBRITH

Burrows, David J. "Manuscript and Typescript Material Relating to Howells's *The Son of Royal Langbrith,*" *Journal of the Rutgers University Library* XXIX (Jun 1966) , 56-58.

McMurray, William. *The Literary Realism of William Dean Howells,* 101-110.

THEIR WEDDING JOURNEY

Martin, Jay. *Harvests of Change. American Literature 1865-1914,* 37-40.

Reeves, John K. "The Limited Realism of Howells' *Their Wedding Journey,*" *PMLA* LXXVII (Dec 1962) , 617-628.

————. (ed.) . *Their Wedding Journey* (Bloomington, 1968) .

A TRAVELER FROM ALTRURIA

Carrington, George C., Jr. *The Immense Complex Drama: The World and Art of the Howells Novel,* 103-112.

Cooperman, Stanley. "Utopian Realism: The Futurist Novels of Bellamy and Howells," *College English* XXIV (Mar 1963) , 464-467.

THE UNDISCOVERED COUNTRY

Bennett, George N. *William Dean Howells: The Development of a Novelist,* 97-105.

McMurray, William. *The Literary Realism of William Dean Howells,* 27-34.

HOWELLS, WILLIAM DEAN, Continued

Vanderbilt, Kermit. *The Achievement of William Dean Howells: A Reinterpretation,* 11-48.

————. *"The Undiscovered Country:* Howells' Version of American Pastoral," *American Quarterly* XVII (Winter 1965), 634-655.

THE VACATION OF THE KELWYNS

McMurray, William. *The Literary Realism of William Dean Howells,* 122-130.

GENERAL

Anderson, Frederick, William M. Gibson, and Henry Nash Smith, (eds.). *Selected Mark Twain-Howells Letters.*

Arvin, Newton. "The Usableness of Howells," *The American Pantheon,* 128-134.

Baxter, Annette K. "Caste and Class: Howells' Boston and Wharton's New York," *Midwest Quarterly* IV (Summer 1963), 353-361.

Bennett, George N. *William Dean Howells: The Development of a Novelist.*

Berthoff, Warner. *The Ferment of Realism: American Literature, 1884-1919,* 50-61.

Bridgman, Richard. *The Colloquial Style in America,* 73-77.

Cady, Edwin H. "Howells and Twain: The World in Midwestern Eyes," *Ball State Teachers College Forum* III (Winter 1962-63), 3-8.

Cary, Richard. "William Dean Howells to Thomas Sergeant Perry," *Colby Library Quarterly* VIII (Dec 1968), 157-216.

Cecil, L. Moffitt. "William Dean Howells and the South," *Mississippi Quarterly* XX (Winter 1966-1967), 13-24.

Commager, Henry Steele. "For Fifty Years a Literary Dynamo," *Howells: A Century of Criticism,* 231-235.

Coyle, Leo. P. "Restoration of a Howells Letter," *Mark Twain Journal* XI (Summer 1960), 12, 15.

Discovery of a Genius: William Dean Howells and Henry James.

Dowling, Joseph A. "W. D. Howells' Literary Reputation in England, 1882-1897," *Dalhousie Review* XLV (Autumn 1965), 277-288.

Duchet, M. "Cinq Lettres Inédites de Juan Valera a W. Dean Howells," *Revue de Littérature Comparée* 42 (Jan-Mar 1968), 76-102.

Ellis, James. "William Dean Howells and the Family Home," *CLA Journal* VIII (Mar 1965), 240-245.

Falk, Robert. *The Victorian Mode in American Fiction: 1865-1885,* 43-53, 121-137.

Gibson, William M. *William D. Howells.*

―――. "William D. Howells," *Six American Novelists of the Nineteenth Century,* 155-190.

Goldfarb, Clare R. "From Complicity to Altruria," *University Review* XXXII (Jun 1966) , 311-317.

Grant, Douglas. *Purpose and Place,* 118-126.

Hirsch, David H. "William Dean Howells and *Daisy Miller,*" *English Language Notes* I (Dec 1963) , 123-128.

Hough, Robert L. *The Quiet Rebel: William Dean Howells as Social Commentator.*

Inge, M. Thomas. "William Dean Howells on Southern Literature," *Mississippi Quarterly* XXI (Fall 1968) , 291-304.

Kirk, Clara Marburg. " 'The Brighter Side' of Fiction: According to Howells and James," *College English* XXIV (Mar 1963) , 463-464.

―――. *W. D. Howells and Art in his Time.*

―――. *W. D. Howells, Traveler from Altruria, 1889-1894.*

―――. "Toward a Theory of Art: A Dialogue Between W. D. Howells and C. E. Norton," *New England Quarterly* XXXVI (Sept 1963) , 291-319.

Kirk, Clara M. and Rudolph, (eds.) *Letters from an Altrurian Traveler.*

―――. *William Dean Howells.*

Martin, Jay. *Harvests of Change. American Literature 1865-1914,* 35-50; 226-231.

Mathews, James W. "Howells and the Shakers," *Personalist* XLIV (Spring 1963) , 212-219.

―――. "The Heroines of Hawthorne and Howells," *Tennessee Studies in Literature* VII (1962) , 37-46.

McMurray, William. "The Concept of Complicity in Howells' Fiction," *New England Quarterly* XXXV (Dec 1962) , 489-496.

Millgate, Michael. *American Social Fiction: James to Cozzens,* 18-37.

Mitchell, Robert Earl. "Aesthetic Values as Depicted in the Fiction of William Dean Howells," *Essays and Studies in Language and Literature.*

Monteiro, George. "William Dean Howells: Two Mistaken Attributions," *Papers of the Bibliographical Society of America* 56 (Apr-Jun 1962) , 254-257.

Morgan, H. Wayne. "William Dean Howells: The Realist as Performer," *American Writers in Rebellion,* 37-75.

Noble, David W. *The Eternal Adam and the New World Garden*, 67-79.

―――――. "Two Novelists and Progressivism: I―William Dean Howells: The Discovery of Society," *Midwest Quarterly* III (Winter 1962), 149-162.

Payne, Alma J. "The Family in the Utopia of William Dean Howells," *Georgia Review* XV (Summer 1961), 217-229.

Perkins, George. "Howells and Hawthorne," *Nineteenth-Century Fiction* XV (Dec 1960), 259-262.

Pizer, Donald. "The Evolutionary Foundation of W. D. Howells's *Criticism and Fiction*," *Philological Quarterly* XL (Jan 1961) 91-103.

―――――. "Evolutionary Literary Criticism and the Defense of Howellsian Realism," *Journal of English and Germanic Philology* LXI (Apr 1962), 296-304.

Ratner, Marc L. "Howells and Boyesen: Two Views of Realism," *New England Quarterly* XXXV (Sept 1962), 376-390.

Salomon, Roger B. "Realism as Disinheritance: Twain, Howells and James," *American Quarterly* XVI (Winter 1964), 531-544.

Schneider, Robert W. "The Mugwump Rebellion," *Five Novelists of the Progressive Era*, 19-59.

Smith, Henry Nash and William M. Gibson, (eds.). *Mark Twain-Howells Letters*

Stronks, James B. "An Early Autobiographical Letter by William Dean Howells," *New England Quarterly* XXXIII (Jun 1960), 240-242.

Timpe, Eugene F. "Howells and his German Critics," *Jahrbuch Für Amerikastudien* 11 (1966), 256-259.

Turaj, Frank. "The Social Gospel in Howells' Novels," *South Atlantic Quarterly* LXVI (Summer 1967), 449-464.

Vanderbilt, Kermit. "Howells and Norton: Some Frustrations of the Biographer," *New England Quarterly* XXXVII (Mar 1964), 84-89.

Wager, Willis. *American Literature: A World View*, 139-145.

Woodress, James. "The Dean's Comeback: Four Decades of Howells Scholarship," *Howells: A Century of Criticism*, 236-247.

―――――. "The Dean's Comeback: Four Decades of Howells Scholarship," *Texas Studies in Literature and Language* II (Spring 1960), 115-123.

―――――. "The Dean's Comeback: Four Decades of Howells Scholarship," *The War of the Critics over William Dean Howells*, 232-240.

HUMPHREY, WILLIAM, Continued
GENERAL
Lee, James W. *William Humphrey.*
BIBLIOGRAPHY
Lee, James W. *William Humphrey,* 44.

HUNEKER, JAMES GIBBONS

PAINTED VEILS
Schwab, Arnold T. *James Gibbons Huneker: Critic of the Seven Arts,*
259-273.
GENERAL
Schwab, Arnold T. *James Gibbons Huneker: Critic of the Seven Arts.*
BIBLIOGRAPHY
Schwab, Arnold T. *James Gibbons Huneker: Critic of the Seven Arts,*
367-376.

JACKSON, SHIRLEY

WE HAVE ALWAYS LIVED IN THE CASTLE
Woodruff, Stuart C. "The Real Horror Elsewhere: Shirley Jackson's
Last Novel," *Southwest Review* LII (Spring 1967), 152-162.
GENERAL
Hyman, Stanley Edgar (ed.) *Come Along with Me; Part of a Novel,*
Sixteen Stories, and Three Lectures (New York, 1968).
BIBLIOGRAPHY
Phillips, Robert S. "Shirley Jackson: A Checklist," *Papers of the Bibli-
ographical Society of America* 56 (Jan-Mar 1962), 110-113.
————. "Shirley Jackson: A Chronology and a Supplementary Check-
list," *Papers of the Bibliographical Society of America* LX (Apr-
Jun 1966), 203-213.

JAMES, HENRY

THE AMBASSADORS
Busch, Frieder. *Erzähler-, Figuren- und Leserperspektive in Henry
James Roman The Ambassadors.*
Cargill, Oscar. "*The Ambassadors:* A New View," *PMLA* LXXV (Jun
1960), 439-452.
————. *The Novels of Henry James,* 303-337.

JAMES, HENRY, Continued

Cecil, L. Moffitt. " 'Virtuous Attachment' in James' *The Ambassadors*," *American Quarterly* XIX (Winter 1967), 719-724.

Coursen, Herbert R., Jr. "The Mirror of Allusion: *The Ambassadors*," *New England Quarterly* XXXIV (Sept 1961), 382-384.

Dooley, D. J. "The Hourglass Pattern in *The Ambassadors*," *New England Quarterly* XLI (Jun 1968), 273-281.

Dupee, F. W. Introduction, *The Ambassadors* (New York, 1960).

Edel, Leon. Introduction, *The Ambassadors* (Boston, 1960).

―――. "The Text of *The Ambassadors*," *Harvard Library Bulletin* XIV (Autumn 1960), 453-560.

Fiedler, Leslie A. *Love and Death in the American Novel*, 337-339.

Garis, Robert E. "The Two Lambert Strethers: A New Reading of *The Ambassadors*," *Modern Fiction Studies* VII (Winter 1961-62), 305-316.

Geismar, Maxwell. "*The Ambassadors:* A New View," *Studi Americani* VII (1961), 105-132.

―――. *Henry James and the Jacobites*, 271-290.

Hartsock, Mildred E. "The Dizzying Crest: Strethers as Moral Man," *Modern Language Quarterly* XXVI (Sept 1965), 414-425.

Holland, Laurence Bedwell. *The Expense of Vision: Essays on the Craft of Henry James*, 229-282.

Hudspeth, Robert N. "The Definition of Innocence: James's *The Ambassadors*," *Texas Studies in Literature and Language* VI (Autumn 1964), 354-360.

Jefferson, D. W. *Henry James and the Modern Reader*, 188-201.

Knoepflmacher, U. C. " 'O rare for Strether!': *Anthony and Cleopatra* and *The Ambassadors*," *Nineteenth-Century Fiction* XIX (Mar 1965), 333-344.

Leavis, F. R. "The Meaning of Paris in *The Ambassadors:* A Disagreement," *The Ambassadors: An Authoritative Text; the Author on the Novel; Criticism*, 438-439.

Lebowitz, Naomi. *The Imagination of Loving: Henry James's Legacy to the Novel*, 131-137.

Leyburn, Ellen Douglass. *The Strange Alloy: The Relation of Comedy to Tragedy in the Fiction of Henry James*, 130-135, 137-148.

Marks, Robert. *James's Later Novels: An Interpretation*, 57-110.

Martin, Jay. *Harvests of Change. American Literature 1865-1914*, 350-352.

McElderry, Bruce E., Jr. *Henry James*, 129-135.

McLean, Robert C. "The Completed Vision: A Study of *Madame de Mauves* and *The Ambassadors,*" *Modern Language Quarterly* XXVIII (Dec 1967), 446-461.

Mizener, Arthur. "Henry James: *The Ambassadors,*" *Twelve Great American Novels,* 49-67.

Murray, Donald M. "The Balcony, the Pond and the Literary Traveler," *Antioch Review* XXV (Summer 1965), 333-336.

O'Grady, Walter. "On Plot in Modern Fiction: Hardy, James, and Conrad," *Modern Fiction Studies* XI (Summer 1965), 107-115.

Paterson, John. "The Language of 'Adventure' in Henry James," *The Ambassadors: An Authoritative Text; The Author on the Novel; Criticism,* 458-465.

Putt, S. Gorley. *Henry James: A Reader's Guide,* 343-359.

Reed, John Q. "*The Ambassadors:* Henry James' Method," *Midwest Quarterly* IV (Autumn 1962), 55-67.

Rosenbaum, S. P. "The Editions of *The Ambassadors,*" *Library* XXI (Sept 1966), 248-250. A reply to Brian Birch's "Henry James: Some Bibliographical and Textual Matters," *Library* XX (Jun 1965), 108-123; Mr. Birch's reply, *Library* XXI (Sept 1966), 250-252.

Ryan, Marjorie. "Forster, James and Flaubert: A Parallel," *Notes and Queries* N.S. 8 (Mar 1961), 102-103.

San Juan, Epifanio, Jr. "James' *The Ambassadors:* The Trajectory of the Climax," *Midwest Quarterly* V (Summer 1964), 295-310.

Schneider, Daniel J. "The Ironic Imagery and Symbolism of James's *The Ambassadors,*" *Criticism* IX (Spring 1967), 174-196.

Sears, Sallie. "The Ambassadors," *The Negative Imagination: Form and Perspective in the Novels of Henry James,* 101-151.

Sharp, Sister M. Corona, O.S.U. *The Confidante in Henry James: Evolution and Moral Value of a Fictive Character,* 150-180.

Stallman, R. W. *The Houses That James Built,* 34-53.

Stone, Edward. *The Battle and the Books: Some Aspects of Henry James,* 117-120, 127-136, 167-170.

Swinnerton, Frank. Introduction, *The Ambassadors* (New York, 1963).

Tanner, Tony. "The Watcher from the Balcony: Henry James's *The Ambassadors,*" *Critical Quarterly* 8 (Spring 1966), 35-52.

Terrie, Henry L., Jr. "The Image of Chester in 'The Ambassadors,' " *English Studies* XLVI (Feb 1965), 46-50.

Ward, J. A. *The Imagination of Disaster: Evil in the Fiction of Henry James,* 110-126.

Warren, Austin. "The New England Conscience, Henry James, and Ambassador Strether," *Minnesota Review* II (Winter 1962), 149-161.

————. *The New England Conscience,* 149-156.

Watt, Ian. "The First Paragraph of *The Ambassadors:* An Explication," *The Ambassadors: An Authoritative Text; The Author on the Novel; Criticism,* 465-484.

Weimer, David R. *The City as Metaphor,* 46-51.

West, Ray B., Jr. "Henry James: *The Ambassadors,*" *The Writer in the Room: Selected Essays,* 74-82.

Williamson, Marilyn L. "'Almost Wholly In French': The Crisis in *The Ambassadors,*" *Notes and Queries* N.S. 9 (Mar 1962), 106-107.

Wright, Walter F. *The Madness of Art: A Study of Henry James,* 232-242.

THE AMERICAN

Bernard, F. V. "James's Florabella and the 'Land of the Pink Sky,'" *Notes and Queries* N.S. 13 (Feb 1966), 70.

Blackmur, R. P. Introduction, *The American* (New York, 1960).

Cargill, Oscar. *The Novels of Henry James,* 41-61.

Cook, George A. "Names in *The American,*" *CEA Critic* XXVIII (Apr 1966), 5, 14.

Creeth, Edmund. "Moonshine and Bloodshed: A Note on *The American,*" *Notes and Queries* N.S. 9 (Mar 1962), 105-106.

Horowitz, Floyd R. "The Christian Time Sequence in Henry James's *The American,*" *CLA Journal* IX (Mar 1966), 234-245.

Knox, George. "Romance and Fable in James's *The American,*" *Anglia* 83 (No 3, 1965), 308-323.

Maseychik, William J. "Points of Departure from *The American,*" *Henry James: Modern Judgements,* 116-127.

Parker, Hershel. "An Error in the Text of James's *The American,*" *American Literature* XXXVII (Nov 1965), 316-318.

Pearce, Roy Harvey. Introduction, *The American* (Boston, 1962).

Poirier, Richard. *The Comic Sense of Henry James: A Study of the Early Novels,* 44-94.

Stafford, William T. "The Ending of James's *The American:* A Defense of the Early Version," *Nineteenth-Century Fiction* XVIII (Jun 1963), 86-89.

Stone, Edward. *The Battle and the Books: Some Aspects of Henry James,* 157-162.

Taylor, Marion A. "Henry James' *American* and American Millionaires," *Litera* 9 (1968), 78-85.

VanDerBeets, Richard. "A Note on Henry James' 'Western Barbarian,'" *Western Humanities Review* XII (Spring 1963), 175-178.

Vanderbilt, Kermit. "James, Fitzgerald, and the American Self-Image," *Massachusetts Review* VI (Winter-Spring 1965), 289-304.

Weimer, David R. *The City as Metaphor,* 38-42.

West, Ray B., Jr. "Henry James: *The American,*" *The Writer in the Room: Selected Essays,* 60-73.

Willett, Maurita. "Henry James's Indebtedness to Balzac," *Revue de Littérature Comparée* 41 (Apr-June 1967), 204-227.

Zietlow, Edward R. "A Flaw in *The American,*" *CLA Journal* IX (Mar 1966), 246-254.

THE ASPERN PAPERS

Hartsock, Mildred. "Unweeded Garden: A View of *The Aspern Papers,*" *Studies in Short Fiction* V (Fall 1967), 60-68.

Holland, Laurence Bedwell. *The Expense of Vision: Essays on the Craft of Henry James,* 139-154.

McLean, Robert C. " 'Poetic Justice' in James's *Aspern Papers,*" *Papers on Language and Literature* III (Summer 1967), 260-266.

Mellard, James M. "Modal Counterpoint in James's *The Aspern Papers,*" *Papers on Language and Literature* IV (Summer 1968), 299-307.

THE AWKWARD AGE

Bass, Eben. "Dramatic Scene and *The Awkward Age,*" *PMLA* LXXIX (Mar 1964), 148-157.

Cargill, Oscar. *The Novels of Henry James,* 263-279.

Colognesi, Silvana. " 'Apparenza E Realta' in *The Awkward Age,*" *Studi Americani* IX (1964), 227-248.

Gargano, James W. "The Theme of 'Salvation' in *The Awkward Age,*" *Texas Studies in Literature and Language* IX (Summer 1967), 273-287.

Hall, William F. "James's Conception of Society in *The Awkward Age,*" *Nineteenth-Century Fiction* XXIII (Jun 1968), 28-48.

Hartsock, Mildred. "The Exposed Mind: A View of *The Awkward Age,*" *Critical Quarterly* 9 (Spring 1967), 49-59.

Hill, Hamlin L., Jr. " 'The Revolt of the Daughters': A Suggested

Source for *The Awkward Age,*" *Notes & Queries* N.S. 8 (Sept 1961), 347-349.

Isle, Walter. "The Awkward Age," *Experiments in Form: Henry James's Novels, 1896-1901,* 165-204.

Jefferson, D. W. *Henry James and the Modern Reader,* 164-176.

Krook, Dorothea. *The Ordeal of Consciousness in Henry James,* 135-166.

Levin, Gerald. "Why Does Vanderbank Not Propose?" *University of Kansas City Review* XXVII (Jun 1961), 314-318.

Leyburn, Ellen Douglass. *The Strange Alloy: The Relation of Comedy to Tragedy in the Fiction of Henry James,* 110-121.

Marks, Robert. *James's Later Novels: An Interpretation,* 15-43.

Martin, Jay. *Harvests of Change. American Literature 1865-1914,* 346-348.

Rao, N. Krishna. "The Idea of Refinement in Henry James's *The Awkward Age,*" *Literary Criterion* VII (Summer 1965), 56-60.

Ward, J. A. *The Imagination of Disaster: Evil in the Fiction of Henry James,* 90-101.

Wiesenfarth, Joseph, F.S.C. *Henry James and the Dramatic Analogy: A Study of the Major Novels of the Middle Period,* 76-95.

THE BOSTONIANS

Cargill, Oscar. *The Novels of Henry James,* 123-145.

Geismar, Maxwell. *Henry James and the Jacobites,* 60-66.

Green, David Bonnell. "Witch and Bewitchment in *The Bostonians,*" *Papers on Language and Literature* III (Summer 1967), 267-269.

Hamblen, Abigail Ann. "Henry James and the Freedom Fighters of the Seventies," *Georgia Review* XX (Spring 1966), 35-44.

Kimmey, John L. *"The Bostonians* and *The Princess Casamassima,*" *Texas Studies in Literature and Language* IX (Winter 1968), 537-546.

Long, Robert Emmet. "A Source for Dr. Mary Prance in *The Bostonians,*" *Nineteenth-Century Fiction* XIX (Jun 1964), 87-88.

————. "The Society and the Masks: *The Blithedale Romance* and *The Bostonians,*" *Nineteenth-Century Fiction* XIX (Sept 1964), 105-122.

McElderry, Bruce E., Jr. *Henry James,* 63-68.

McMurray, William. "Pragmatic Realism in *The Bostonians,*" *Nineteenth Century Fiction* XVI (Mar 1962), 339-344.

JAMES, HENRY, Continued

————. "Pragmatic Realism in *The Bostonians*," *Henry James: Modern Judgements*, 160-183.

Putt, S. Gorley. "The Private Life and The Public Life: *The Princess Casamassima* and *The Bostonians*," *Scholars of the Heart: Essays in Criticism*, 174-203.

————. *Henry James: A Reader's Guide*, 178-194.

Selig, Robert L. "The Red Haired Lady Orator: Parallel Passages in *The Bostonians* and *Adam Bede*," *Nineteenth-Century Fiction* XVI (Sept 1961), 164-169.

Walcutt, Charles Child. "Discourse on Feminism: *The Bostonians*," *Man's Changing Mask: Modes and Methods of Characterization in Fiction*, 182-193.

CONFIDENCE

Cargill, Oscar. *The Novels of Henry James*, 73-77.

Poirier, Richard. *The Comic Sense of Henry James: A Study of the Early Novels*, 145-164.

Ruhm, Herbert. Introduction, *Confidence* (New York, 1962).

DAISY MILLER

Fiedler, Leslie A. *Love and Death in the American Novel*, 298-300.

Gargano, James W. "*Daisy Miller:* An Abortive Quest for Innocence," *South Atlantic Quarterly* LIX (Winter 1960), 114-120.

Hagopian, John V. *Insight I*, 132-139.

Hirsch, David H. "William Dean Howells and *Daisy Miller*," *English Language Notes* I (Dec 1963), 123-128.

James's Daisy Miller: The Story, The Play, The Critics.

Monteiro, George. " 'Girlhood on the American Plan': A Contemporary Defense of *Daisy Miller*," *Books At Brown* XIX (May 1963), 89-93.

Ohmann, Carol. "*Daisy Miller:* A Study of Changing Intentions," *American Literature* XXXVI (Mar 1964), 1-11.

Randall, John H., III. "The Genteel Reader and *Daisy Miller*," XVII (Fall 1965), 568-581.

Stone, Edward. *The Battle and the Books: Some Aspects of Henry James*, 88-93, 120-122.

THE EUROPEANS

Bass, Eben. "James' *The Europeans*," *Explicator* XXIII (Sept 1964), No. 9.

Buitenhuis, Peter. "Comic Pastoral: Henry James's *The Europeans*," *University of Toronto Quarterly* XXXI (Jan 1962), 152-163.

Cargill, Oscar. *The Novels of Henry James,* 62-72.

Jefferson, D. W. *Henry James and the Modern Reader,* 25-37.

Poirier, Richard. *The Comic Sense of Henry James: A Study of the Early Novels,* 95-144.

Ward, J. A. *"The Europeans* and the Structure of Comedy," *Henry James: Modern Judgements,* 128-142.

————. "James's *The Europeans* and the Structure of Comedy," *Nnieteenth-Century Fiction* XIX (Jun 1964), 1-16.

————. *The Search for Form: Studies in the Structure of James's Fiction,* 95-113.

THE GOLDEN BOWL

Bayley, John. "Love and Knowledge: *The Golden Bowl," The Characters of Love: A Study in the Literature of Personality,* 203-262.

————. "Love and Knowledge: *The Golden Bowl," Discussions of Henry James,* 80-88.

Cargill, Oscar. *The Novels of Henry James,* 383-440.

Clair, John A. *The Ironic Dimension in the Fiction of Henry James,* 79-102.

Gale, Robert L. "James' *The Golden Bowl," Explicator* XIX (Oct 1960), No. 5.

Geismar, Maxwell. *Henry James and the Jacobites,* 297-334, 305-334.

Holland, Laurence Bedwell. *The Expense of Vision: Essays on the Craft of Henry James,* 331-407.

Jefferson, D. W. *Henry James and the Modern Reader,* 216-225.

Krook, Dorothea. *The Ordeal of Consciousness in Henry James,* 232-324.

Lebowitz, Naomi. *The Imagination of Loving: Henry James's Legacy to the Novel,* 71-85, 99-103, 121-127.

————. "Magic and Metamorphosis in *The Golden Bowl," Sewanee Review* LXXIII (Winter 1965), 58-73.

————. "Magic and Metamorphosis in *The Golden Bowl," Henry James: Modern Judgements,* 327-339.

Leyburn, Ellen Douglass. *The Strange Alloy: The Relation of Comedy to Tragedy in the Fiction of Henry James,* 64-73.

Marks, Robert. *James's Later Novels: An Interpretation,* 111-130.

Martin, Jay. *Harvests of Change. American Literature 1865-1914,* 355-359.

Naik, M. K. "The Draught from the 'Golden Bowl,'" *Journal of the Karnatak University* VII (1963), 199-217.

Putt, S. Gorley. *Henry James: A Reader's Guide*, 363-386.

Rose, Alan. "The Spatial Form of *The Golden Bowl*," *Modern Fiction Studies* XII (Spring 1966), 103-116.

Sears, Sallie. "The Golden Bowl," *The Negative Imagination: Form and Perspective in the Novels of Henry James*, 155-222.

Sharp, Sister M. Corona, O.S.U. *The Confidante in Henry James: Evolution and Moral Value of a Fictive Character*, 214-246.

Todasco, Ruth Taylor. "Theme and Imagery in *The Golden Bowl*," *Texas Studies in Literature and Language* IV (Summer 1962), 228-240.

Walcutt, Charles Child. "Convulsions in the Major Phase," *Man's Changing Mask: Modes and Methods of Characterization in Fiction*, 203-208.

Ward, J. A. "Evil in *The Golden Bowl*," *Western Humanities Review* XIV (Winter 1960), 47-59.

————. *The Imagination of Disaster: Evil in the Fiction of Henry James*, 139-156.

————. *The Search for Form: Studies in the Structure of James's Fiction*, 199-221.

Wright, Walter F. *The Madness of Art: A Study of Henry James*, 242-254.

THE IVORY TOWER

Buitenhuis, Peter. " 'The Fresh Start and the Broken Link': Henry James's *The Ivory Tower*," *University of Toronto Quarterly* XXXIII (Jul 1964), 355-368.

Cargill, Oscar. *The Novels of Henry James*, 462-478.

Marks, Robert. *James's Later Novels: An Interpretation*, 131-157.

Putt, S. Gorley. *Henry James: A Reader's Guide*, 403-410.

————. "Henry James: An Unfinished Masterpiece," *English* XVI (Summer 1966), 45-48.

THE OTHER HOUSE

Cargill, Oscar. *The Novels of Henry James*, 205-217.

Isle, Walter. "*The Other House*," *Experiments in Form: Henry James's Novels, 1896-1901*, 39-76.

THE OUTCRY

Cargill, Oscar. *The Novels of Henry James*, 443-452.

THE PORTRAIT OF A LADY

Anderson, Charles R. Introduction, *The Portrait of a Lady* (New York, 1962).

JAMES, HENRY, Continued

————. "Person, Place, and Thing in James' *Portrait of a Lady*," *Essays on American Literature in Honor of Jay Hubbell,* 164-182.

Blackmur, R. P. Introduction, *The Portrait of a Lady* (New York, 1961).

Blehl, Vincent F., S.J. "Freedom and Commitment in James's 'Portrait of a Lady,' " *Personalist* XLII (Summer 1961), 368-381.

Bowden, Edwin T. *The Dungeon of the Heart: Human Isolation and the American Novel,* 89-102.

Bridgman, Richard. *The Colloquial Style in America,* 95-100.

Chauhan, P. S. "*The Portrait of a Lady:* Its Moral Design," *Literary Criterion* VI (Summer 1964), 56-70.

Dove, John Roland. "Tragic Consciousness in Isabel Archer," *Studies in American Literature,* 78-94.

Edel, Leon. Introduction, *The Portrait of a Lady* (London, 1968).

————. "Who Was Gilbert Osmond?" *Modern Fiction Studies* VI (Summer 1960), 164.

Friend, Joseph H. "The Structure of *The Portrait of a Lady,*" *Nineteenth-Century Fiction* XX (Jun 1965), 85-95.

Gale, Robert L. "A Possible Source for Elements in *The Portrait of a Lady,*" *Studi Americani* XI (1965), 137-141.

Galloway, David. *Henry James: The Portrait of a Lady.*

Geismar, Maxwell. "Nostalgic Poison," *Twentieth Century Interpretations of The Portrait of a Lady: A Collection of Critical Essays,* 45-50.

Grenander, M. E., Beverly J. Rahn and Francine Valvo. "The Time-Scheme in *The Portrait of a Lady,*" *American Literature* XXXII (May 1960), 127-135.

Holland, Laurence Bedwell. *The Expense of Vision: Essays on the Craft of Henry James,* 3-54.

Jefferson, D. W. *Henry James and the Modern Reader,* 108-113.

Kelley, Cornelia Pulsifer. *The Early Development of Henry James,* revised edition, 284-300.

Krook, Dorothea. *The Ordeal of Consciousness in Henry James,* 26-61, 357-369.

————. "Two Problems in *The Portrait of a Lady,*" *Twentieth Century Interpretations of The Portrait of a Lady: A Collection of Critical Essays,* 97-106.

Lebowitz, Naomi. *The Imagination of Loving: Henry James's Legacy to the Novel,* 64-86.

Leyburn, Ellen Douglass. *The Strange Alloy: The Relation of Comedy to Tragedy in the Fiction of Henry James,* 30-49.

Mackenzie, Manfred. "Ironic Melodrama in *The Portrait of A Lady,*" *Modern Fiction Studies* XII (Spring 1966) , 7-23.

————. "Ironic Melodrama in *The Portrait of a Lady,*" *Twentieth Century Interpretations of The Portrait of a Lady: A Collection of Critical Essays,* 83-96.

McElderry, Bruce R., Jr. *Henry James,* 58-63.

Marcell, David W. "High Ideals and Catchpenny Realities in Henry James's *The Portrait of a Lady,*" *Essays in Modern American Literature,* 26-34.

Martin, Jay. *Harvests of Change. American Literature 1865-1914,* 330-334.

Monteiro, George. "John Hay's Review of *The Portrait of a Lady,*" *Books At Brown* XIX (May 1963) , 95-104.

Montgomery, Marion. "The Flaw in the Portrait," *University of Kansas City Review* XXVI (Mar 1960) , 215-220.

————. "The Flaw in the Portrait," *Twentieth Century Interpretations of The Portrait of a Lady: A Collection of Critical Essays,* 60-66.

Moss, Leonard Jerome. "Transitional Devices in Henry James," *CEA Critic* XXII (Feb 1960) , 1, 6, 12.

Patterson, Rebecca. "Two Portraits of a Lady," *Midwest Quarterly* 1 (Summer 1960) , 343-361.

Perspectives on James's The Portrait of a Lady: A Collection of Critical Essays.

Poirier, Richard. *The Comic Sense of Henry James: A Study of the Early Novels,* 183-246.

————. "Drama in *The Portrait of a Lady,*" *Twentieth Century Interpretations of The Portrait of a Lady: A Collection of Critical Essays,* 29-36.

————. "Henry James: *The Portrait of a Lady,*" *The American Novel from James Fenimore Cooper to William Faulkner,* 47-60.

Putt, S. Gorley. *Henry James: A Reader's Guide,* 137-160.

Reid, Stephen. "Moral Passion in *The Portrait of A Lady* and *The Spoils of Poynton,*" *Modern Fiction Studies* XII (Spring 1966) , 24-43.

Rodenbeck, John. "The Bolted Door in James's *Portrait of a Lady,*" *Modern Fiction Studies* X (Winter 1964-65) , 330-340.

Schneider, Sister Lucy, C.S.J. "Osculation and Integration: Isabel Archer in the One-Kiss Novel," *CLA Journal* X (Dec 1966), 149-161.

Sharp, Sister M. Corona, O.S.U. *The Confindante in Henry James: Evolution and Moral Value of a Fictive Character,* 67-96.

Smith, Thomas F. "Balance in Henry James's *The Portrait of a Lady,*" *Four Quarters* XIII (May 1964), 11-16.

Stallman, R. W. *The Houses That James Built,* 3-33.

—————. Introduction, *The Portrait of a Lady* (New York, 1967).

Stein, William Bysshe. "*The Portrait of a Lady:* Vis Inertiae," *Western Humanities Review* XIII (Spring 1959), 177-190.

Strandberg, Victor H. "Isabel Archer's Identity Crisis: The Two Portraits of a Lady," *University Review* XXXIV (Jun 1968), 283-290.

Tanner, Tony. "The Fearful Self: Henry James's *The Portrait of a Lady,*" *Critical Quarterly* 7 (Autumn 1965), 205-219.

—————. "The Fearful Self: Henry James's *The Portrait of a Lady,*" *Henry James: Modern Judgements,* 143-159.

—————. "The Fearful Self," *Twentieth Century Interpretations of the Portrait of a Lady: A Collection of Critical Essays,* 67-82.

Tribble, Joseph L. "Cherbuliez's *Le Roman d'une Honnête Femme:* Another Source of James's *The Portrait of a Lady,*" *American Literature* 40 (Nov 1968), 280-293.

of a Lady," *Man's Changing Mask: Modes and Methods of Characterization in Fiction,* 194-202.

Walcutt, Charles Child. "Launching the American Girl: *The Portrait*

Wallace, Jack E. "Henry James and Gestation: Isabel and the Ironies," *College English* XXI (May 1960), 497. See also, Broderick, John C. " 'Henry James and Gestation': A Reply," *College English* (May 1960), 497-499; Key, Howard C. "Author's Comment," *College English* (May 1960), 499-500.

Ward, J. A. *The Imagination of Disaster: Evil in the Fiction of Henry James,* 44-55.

Weimer, David R. *The City as Metaphor,* 43-46.

Williams, Paul O. "James' *The Portrait of a Lady,*" *Explicator* XXII (Mar 1964), No. 50.

THE PRINCESS CASAMASSIMA

Cargill, Oscar. *The Novels of Henry James,* 146-173.

Dubler, Walter. "*The Princess Casamassima:* Its Place in the James Canon," *Modern Fiction Studies* XII (Spring 1966), 44-60.

JAMES, HENRY, Continued

Geismar, Maxwell. *Henry James and the Jacobites,* 66-76.

Grenander, M. E. "Henry James's Capricciosa: Cristina Light in *Roderick Hudson* and *The Princess Casamassima,*" *PMLA* LXXV (Jun 1960), 309-319.

Halliburton, D. G. "Self and Secularization in *The Princess Casamassima,*" *Modern Fiction Studies* XI (Summer 1965), 116-128.

Hamilton, Eunice C. "Henry James's *The Princess Casamassima* and Ivan Turgenev's *Virgin Soil,*" *South Atlantic Quarterly* LXI (Summer 1962), 354-364.

Kimmey, John L. "*The Bostonians* and *The Princess Casamassima,*" *Texas Studies in Literature and Language* IX (Winter 1968), 537-546.

Leyburn, Ellen Douglass. *The Strange Alloy: The Relation of Comedy to Tragedy in the fiction of Henry James,* 96-103, 121-130.

Luecke, Sister Jane Marie, O.S.B. "*The Princess Casamassima:* Hyacinth's Fallible Consciousness," *Modern Philology* LX (May 1963), 274-280.

————. "*The Princess Casamassima:* Hyacinth's Fallible Consciousness," *Henry James: Modern Judgements,* 184-193.

Monteiro, George. "The Campaign of Henry James's Disinherited Princess," *English Studies* XLV (Dec 1964), 442-454.

Oliver, Clinton F. Introduction, *The Princess Casamassima* (New York, 1060).

Putt, S. Gorley. *Henry James: A Reader's Guide,* 163-179.

————. "The Private Life and The Public Life: *The Princess Casamassima* and *The Bostonians,*" *Scholars of the Heart: Essays in Criticism,* 174-203.

Tilley, W. H. *The Background of The Princess Casamassima.*

Ward, J. A. *The Search for Form: Studies in the Structure of James's Fiction,* 114-140.

THE REVERBERATOR

Cargill, Oscar. *The Novels of Henry James,* 174-181.

Durkin, Sister Mary Brian. "Henry James's Revisions of the Style of *The Reverberator,*" *American Literature* XXXIII (Nov 1961), 330-349.

Jefferson, D. W. *Henry James and the Modern Reader,* 96-102.

Leyburn, Ellen Douglass. *The Strange Alloy: The Relation of Comedy to Tragedy in the Fiction of Henry James,* 56-64.

RODERICK HUDSON

Cargill, Oscar. *The Novels of Henry James,* 19-40.

Edel, Leon. Introduction, *Roderick Hudson* (New York, 1961).

Engelberg, Edward. "James and Arnold: Conscience and Consciousness in a Victorian 'Künstlerroman,'" *Criticism* X (Spring 1968), 93-114.

Gale, Robert L. "*Roderick Hudson* and Thomas Crawford," *American Quarterly* XIII (Winter 1961), 495-504.

Grenander, M. E. "Henry James's Capricciosa: Cristina Light in *Roderick Hudson* and *The Princess Casamassima,*" PMLA LXXV (Jun 1960), 309-319.

Kelley, Cornelia Pulsifer. *The Early Development of Henry James,* revised edition, 182-194.

Leyburn, Ellen Douglass. *The Strange Alloy: The Relation of Comedy to Tragedy in the Fiction of Henry James,* 11-20.

Martin, Jay. *Harvests of Change. American Literature 1865-1914,* 324-326.

Poirier, Richard. *The Comic Sense of Henry James: A Study of the Early Novels,* 11-43.

Putt, S. Gorley. *Henry James: A Reader's Guide,* 94-99, 322-323.

Snow, Lotus. "The Prose and the Modesty of the Matter": James's Imagery for the Artist in *Roderick Hudson* and *The Tragic Muse,*" *Modern Fiction Studies* XII (Spring 1966), 61-82.

Weimer, David R. *The City as Metaphor,* 35-38.

THE SACRED FOUNT

Blackall, Jean Frantz. *Jamesian Ambiguity and The Sacred Fount.*

————. "*The Sacred Fount* as a Comedy of the Limited Observer," *PMLA* LXXVIII (Sept 1963), 384-393.

Burns, Landon C., Jr. "Henry James's Mysterious Fount," *Texas Studies in Literature and Language* II (Winter 1961), 520-528.

Cargill, Oscar. *The Novels of Henry James,* 280-300.

Finkelstein, Sidney. "The 'Mystery' of Henry James's *The Sacred Fount,*" *Massachusetts Review* III (Summer 1962), 753-776.

Folsom, James K. "Archimago's Well: An Interpretation of *The Sacred Fount,*" *Modern Fiction Studies* VII (Summer 1961), 136-144.

Gale, Robert L. "*The Marble Faun* and *The Sacred Fount:* A Resemblance," *Studi Americani* VIII (1962), 21-33.

Geismar, Maxwell. *Henry James and the Jacobites,* 197-218.

JAMES, HENRY, Continued

Hinchliffe, Arnold P. "Henry James's *The Sacred Fount,*" *Texas Studies in Literature and Language* 11 (Spring 1960), 88-94.

Holland, Laurence Bedwell. *The Expense of Vision: Essays on the Craft of Henry James*, 183-226.

Isle, Walter. "The Sacred Fount," *Experiments in Form: Henry James's Novels, 1896-1901*, 205-233.

Jefferson, D. W. *Henry James and the Modern Reader*, 176-187.

Krook, Dorothea. *The Ordeal of Consciousness in Henry James*, 167-194.

Lebowitz, Naomi. *The Imagination of Loving: Henry James's Legacy to the Novel*, 119-129.

————. "*The Sacred Fount:* An Author in Search of his Characters," *Criticism* IV (Summer 1962), 148-159.

Melchiori, Georgio. "Cups of Gold for *The Sacred Fount:* Aspects of James's Symbolism," *Critical Quarterly* 7 (Winter 1965), 301-316.

Ozick, Cynthia. "The Jamesian Parable: *The Sacred Fount,*" *Bucknell Review* XI (May 1963), 55-70.

Paik, Nak-chung. "Henry James' *The Sacred Fount* as a Work of Art and as the Portrait of a Consciousness," *English Language and Literature* 16 (Jun 1964-Jun 1965), 105-136.

Perlongo, Robert A. "*The Sacred Fount:* Labyrinth or Parable?" *Kenyon Review* XXII (Autumn 1960), 635-647.

Phillips, Norma. "*The Sacred Fount:* The Narrator and the Vampires," *PMLA* LXXVI (Sept 1961), 407-412.

Ranald, Ralph A. "*The Sacred Fount:* James's Portrait of the Artist Manqué," *Nineteenth Century Fiction* XV (Dec 1960) 239-248.

Reaney, James. "The Condition of Light: Henry James's *The Sacred Fount,*" *University of Toronto Quarterly* XXXI (Jan 1962), 136-151.

Samuels, Charles Thomas. "At The Bottom of the *Fount,*" *Novel* 2 (Fall 1968), 46-54.

Tanner, Tony. *The Reign of Wonder: Naivety and Reality in American Literature*, 319-331.

Tyler, Parker. "*The Sacred Fount:* 'The Actuality Pretentious and Vain' vs. 'The Case Rich and Edifying,'" *Modern Fiction Studies* IX (Summer 1963), 127-138.

Wiesenfarth, Joseph, F.S.C. *Henry James and the Dramatic Analogy: A Study of the Major Novels of the Middle Period*, 96-111.

Wilson, Edmund. "The Ambiguity of Henry James," *Psychoanalysis and American Fiction,* 151-155.

THE SENSE OF THE PAST

Beams, David W. "Consciousness in James's *The Sense of the Past,*" *Criticism* V (Spring 1963) , 148-172.

Cargill, Oscar. *The Novels of Henry James,* 479-492.

Geismar, Maxwell. *Henry James and the Jacobites,* 422-438.

Perosa, Sergio. "Tema e tecnica in *The Sense of the Past,*" *Studi Americani* 12 (1966) , 169-199.

Stone, Edward. *The Battle and the Books: Some Aspects of Henry James,* 183-205.

THE SPOILS OF POYNTON

Cargill, Oscar. *The Novels of Henry James,* 218-243.

Clair, John A. *The Ironic Dimension in the Fiction of Henry James,* 59-78.

Gargano, James W. "*The Spoils of Poynton:* Action and Responsibility," *Sewanee Review* LXIX (Autumn 1961) , 650-660.

Goldsmith, Arnold. "The Maltese Cross as Sign in *The spoils of Poynton,*" *Renascence* XVI (Winter 1964) , 73-77.

Greene, Philip L. "Point of View in *The Spoils of Poynton,*" *Nineteenth-Century Fiction* XXI (Mar 1967) , 359-368.

Holland, Laurence Bedwell. *The Expense of Vision: Essays on the Craft of Henry James,* 57-113.

Isle, Walter. "*The Spoils of Poynton,*" *Experiments in Form: Henry James's Novels, 1896-1901,* 77-119.

Izsak, Emily K. "The Composition of *The Spoils of Poynton,*" *Texas Studies in Literature and Language* VI (Winter 1965) , 460-471.

Leyburn, Ellen Douglass. *The Strange Alloy: The Relation of Comedy to Tragedy in the Fiction of Henry James,* 75-81.

McLean, Robert C. "The Subjective Adventure of Fleda Vetch," *American Literature* XXXVI (Mar 1964) , 12-30.

————. "The Subjective Adventure of Fleda Vetch," *Henry James: Modern Judgements,* 204-221.

Reid, Stephen. "Moral Passion in *The Portrait of a Lady* and *The Spoils of Poynton,*" *Modern Fiction Studies* XII (Spring 1966) , 24-43.

Roper, Alan H. "The Moral and Metaphorical Meaning of *The Spoils of Poynton,*" *American Literature* XXXII (May 1960) , 182-196.

Rosenbaum, S. P. "Henry James and Creativity: 'The Logic of the Particular Case,'" *Criticism* VIII (Winter 1966), 44-52.

————. "*The Spoils of Poynton:* Revisions and Editions," *Studies in Bibliography* XIX (1966), 161-174.

Sharp, Sister M. Corona, O.S.U. *The Confidante in Henry James: Evolution and Moral Value of a Fictive Character,* 97-126.

Stein, William Bysshe. "The Method at the Heart of Madness: *The Spoils of Poynton*," *Modern Fiction Studies* XIV (Summer 1968), 187-202.

Ward, J. A. *The Imagination of Disaster: Evil in the Fiction of Henry James,* 57-63.

Wiesenfarth, Joseph, F.S.C. *Henry James and the Dramatic Analogy: A Study of the Major Novels of the Middle Period,* 44-56.

Willey, Frederick. "The Free Spirit and the Clever Agent in Henry James," *Southern Review* II (Apr 1966), 315-328.

THE TRAGIC MUSE

Blackmur, R. P. Introduction, *The Tragic Muse* (New York, 1961).

Cargill, Oscar. *The Novels of Henry James,* 182-202.

Edel, Leon. Introduction, *The Tragic Muse* (New York, 1960).

Geismar, Maxwell. *Henry James and the Jacobites,* 102-110.

Hall, William F. "Gabriel Nash: 'Famous Centre' of *The Tragic Muse*," *Nineteenth-Century Fiction* XXI (Sept 1966), 167-184.

Krook, Dorothea. *The Ordeal of Consciousness in Henry James,* 62-105.

Lockridge, Ernest H. "A Vision of Art: Henry James's *The Tragic Muse*," *Modern Fiction Studies* XII (Spring 1966), 83-92.

Monteiro, George. "The Manuscript of *The Tragic Muse*," *American Notes & Queries* I (Jan 1963), 68.

Putt, S. Gorley. *Henry James: A Reader's Guide,* 204-214.

Snow, Lotus. " 'The Prose and the Modesty of the Matter': James's Imagery for the Artist in *Roderick Hudson* and *The Tragic Muse*," *Modern Fiction Studies* XII (Spring 1966), 61-82.

Stone, Edward. *The Battle and the Books: Some Aspects of Henry James,* 93-112.

THE TURN OF THE SCREW

Aldrich, C. Knight. "Another Twist to *The Turn of the Screw*," *Modern Fiction Studies* XIII (Summer 1967), 167-178.

Allott, Miriam. "Mrs. Gaskell's 'The Old Nurse's Story': A Link Between *Wuthering Heights* and *The Turn of the Screw*," *Notes and Queries* N.S. 8 (Mar 1961), 101-102.

Aswell, E. Duncan. "Reflections of a Governess: Image and Distortion in *The Turn of the Screw,*" *Nineteenth-Century Fiction* XXIII (Jun 1968) , 49-63.

Cargill, Oscar. "*The Turn of the Screw* and Alice James," *PMLA* LXXVIII (June 1963) , 238-249.

Cranfill, Thomas Mabry and Robert Lanier Clark, Jr. *An Anatomy of The Turn of the Screw.*

————. "Caste in James's *The Turn of the Screw,*" *Texas Studies in Literature and Language* V (Summer 1963) , 189-198.

————. "James's Revisions of *The Turn of the Screw,*" *Nineteenth-Century Fiction* XIX (Mar 1965) , 394-398.

Domaniecki, Hildegard. "Complementary Terms in *The Turn of the Screw:* The Straight Turning," *Jahrbuch Für Amerikastudien* 10 (1965) , 206-214.

Fraser, John. "*The Turn of the Screw* Again," *Midwest Quarterly* VII (Summer 1966) , 327-336.

Gargano, James W. "The Turn of the Screw," *Western Humanities Review* XV (Spring 1961) , 173-179.

Heilman, Robert B. "The Lure of the Demonic: James and Dürrenmatt," *Comparative Literature* XIII (Fall 1961) , 346-357.

Ives, C. B. "James's Ghosts in *The Turn of the Screw,*" *Nineteenth-Century Fiction* XVIII (Sept 1963) , 183-189.

Lang, Hans-Joachim. "The Turns in *The Turn of the Screw,*" *Jahrbuch Für Amerikastudien* 9 (1964) , 110-128.

Rubin, Louis D., Jr. "One More Turn of the Screw," *Modern Fiction Studies* IX (Winter 1963-64) , 314-328.

————. "One More Turn of the Screw," *The Curious Death of the Novel: Essays in American Literature,* 67-87.

Samuels, Charles Thomas. "Reappraisals, II: Giovanni and the Governess," *American Scholar* 37 (Autumn 1968) , 655-678.

Siegel, Paul N. " 'Miss Jessel': Mirror Image of the Governess," *Literature and Psychology* XVIII (No 1, 1968) , 30-38.

Slabey, Robert M. " 'The Holy Innocents' and *The Turn of the Screw,*" *Neueren Sprachen* (Apr 1963) , 170-173.

————. " 'The Turn of the Screw': Grammar and Optics," *CLA Journal* IX (Sept 1965) , 68-72.

Solomon, Eric. "The Return of the Screw," *University Review* XXX (Mar 1964) , 205-211.

JAMES, HENRY, Continued

Spilka, Mark. "Turning the Freudian Screw: How Not to Do It," *Literature and Psychology* XIII (Fall 1963), 105-111.

Trachtenberg, Stanley. "The Return of the Screw," *Modern Fiction Studies* XI (Summer 1965), 180-182.

West, Muriel. "The Death of Miles in *The Turn of the Screw*," *PMLA* LXXIX (Jun 1964), 283-288.

WASHINGTON SQUARE

Poirier, Richard. *The Comic Sense of Henry James: A Study of the Early Novels,* 165-182.

WATCH AND WARD

Cargill, Oscar. *The Novels of Henry James,* 3-18.

Edel, Leon. Introduction, *Watch and Ward* (New York, 1960).

Levy, Leo B. "The Comedy of *Watch and Ward*," *Arlington Quarterly* I (Summer 1968), 86-98.

Putt, S. Gorly. *Henry James: A Reader's Guide,* 27-33.

Stone, Edward. *The Battle and the Books: Some Aspects of Henry James,* 64-67, 71-76.

Ward, J. A. "The Double Structure of *Watch and Ward*," *Texas Studies in Literature and Language* IV (Winter 1963), 613-624.

————. *The Search for Form: Studies in the Structure of James's Fiction,* 60-76.

WHAT MAISIE KNEW

Cambon, Glauco. "What Maisie and Huck Knew," *Studi Americani* VI (1960), 203-220.

Cargill, Oscar. *The Novels of Henry James,* 244-262.

Gargano, James W. "*What Maisie Knew*: the Evolution of a 'Moral Sense,'" *Nineteenth-Century Fiction* XVI (Jun 1961), 33-46.

————. "*What Maisie Knew*: The Evolution of a 'Moral Sense,'" *Henry James: Modern Judgements,* 222-235.

Geismar, Maxwell. *Henry James and the Jacobites,* 146-155.

Hamblen, Abigail Ann. "Henry James and the Power of Eros: *What Maisie Knew*," *Midwest Quarterly* IX (Jul 1968), 391-399.

Hynes, Joseph A. "The Middle Way of Miss Farange: A Study of James's *Maisie*," *ELH* XXXII (Dec 1965), 528-553.

Isle, Walter. "*What Maisie Knew*," *Experiments in Form: Henry James's Novels, 1896-1901,* 120-164.

Martin, Jay. *Harvests of Change. American Literature 1865-1914,* 344-346.

McCloskey, John C. "What Maisie Knows: A Study of Childhood and Adolescence," *American Literature* XXXVI (Jan 1965), 485-513.

Sears, Sallie. *The Negative Imagination: Form and Perspective in the Novels of Henry James,* 20-34.

Sharp, Sister M. Corona, O.S.U. *The Confidante in Henry James: Evolution and Moral Value of a Fictive Character,* 127-149.

Wasiolek, Edward. "Maisie: Pure or Corrupt?" *College English* XXII (Dec 1960), 167-172.

Wiesenfarth, Joseph, F. S. C. *Henry James and the Dramatic Analogy: A Study of the Major Novels of the Middle Period,* 57-75.

Wolf, H. R. *"What Maisie Knew:* The Rankian Hero," *American Imago* XXIII (Fall 1966), 227-234.

Wright, Walter F. *The Madness of Art: A Study of Henry James,* 162-168.

THE WINGS OF THE DOVE

Bersani, Leo. "The Narrator as Center in 'The Wings of the Dove,'" *Modern Fiction Studies* VI (Summer 1960), 131-144.

Cargill, Oscar. *The Novels of Henry James,* 338-382.

Cromphout, Gustaaf Van. *"The Wings of the Dove:* Intention and Achievement," *Minnesota Review* VI (No 2, 1966), 149-154.

Geismar, Maxwell. *Henry James and the Jacobites,* 226-243.

————. *"The Wings of the Dove:* or, False Gold," *Atlantic Monthly* CCXII (Aug 1963), 93-98.

Hagan, John. "A Note on a Symbolic Pattern in *The Wings of The Dove,*" *CLA Journal* X (Mar 1967), 256-262.

Holland, Laurence Bedwell. *The Expense of Vision: Essays on the Craft of Henry James,* 285-327.

Jefferson, D. W. *Henry James and the Modern Reader,* 201-216.

Koch, Stephen. "Transcendence in *The Wings of the Dove,*" *Modern Fiction Studies* XII (Spring 1966), 93-102.

Kraft, Quentin G. "Life Against Death in Venice," *Criticism* VII (Summer 1965), 217-223.

Krook, Dorothea. *The Ordeal of Consciousness in Henry James,* 195-231.

Lebowitz, Naomi. *The Imagination of Loving: Henry James's Legacy to the Novel,* 73-78.

Lewis, R. W. B. *Trials of the Word,* 120-128.

Leyburn, Ellen Douglass. *The Strange Alloy: The Relation of Comedy to Tragedy in the Fiction of Henry James,* 92-96, 148-155, 174-175.

JAMES, HENRY, Continued

Marks, Robert. *James's Later Novels: An Interpretation,* 44-56.
Martin, Jay. *Harvests of Change. American Literature 1865-1914,* 352-356.
Putt, S. Gorley. *Henry James: A Reader's Guide,* 309-339.
————. "*The Wings of the Dove:* A Study in Construction," *Scholars of the Heart: Essays in Criticism,* 204-235.
Sears, Sallie. "The Wings of the Dove," *The Negative Imagination: Form and Perspective in the Novels of Henry James,* 61-98.
Sharp, Sister M. Corona, O.S.U. *The Confidante in Henry James: Evolution and Moral Value of a Fictive Character,* 181-213.
Ward, J. A. *The Imagination of Disaster: Evil in the Fiction of Henry James,* 127-139.
————. *The Search for Form: Studies in the Structure of James's Fiction,* 164-198.
————. "Social Disintegration in *The Wings of the Dove*," *Criticism* II (Spring 1960), 190-203.
Wright, Walter F. *The Madness of Art: A Study of Henry James,* 219-232.

GENERAL

Abel, Robert H. "Gide and Henry James: Suffering Death and Responsibility," *Midwest Quarterly* IX (Jul 1968), 403-415.
Adams, Percy G. "Young Henry James and the Lesson of his Master Balzac," *Revue de Littérature Comparée* 35 (Jul Sept 1961), 458-467.
Auchincloss, Louis. "A Strategy for James Readers," *Nation* 190 (Apr 23, 1960), 364-367.
Banta, Martha. "Henry James and 'The Others,'" *New England Quarterly* XXXVII (Jun 1964), 171-184.
————. "The House of the Seven Ushers and How They Grew: A Look at Jamesian Gothicism," *Yale Review* LVII (Autumn 1967), 56-65.
Beattie, Munro. "Henry James, Novelist," *Dalhousie Review* XXXIX (Winter 1960), 455-463.
————. "The Many Marriages of Henry James," *Patterns of Commitment in American Literature,* 93-112.
Bell, Millicent. *Edith Wharton and Henry James: The Story of Their Friendship.*
Berland, Alwyn. "Henry James and the Aesthetic Tradition," *Journal of the History of Ideas* XXIII (Jul-Sept 1962), 407-419.

Berthoff, Warner. *The Ferment of Realism: American Literature, 1884-1919,* 103-126.

Birch, Brian. "Henry James: Some Bibliographical and Textual Matters," *Library* XX (Jun 1965), 108-123.

Borklund, Elmer. "Howard Sturgis, Henry James, and *Belchamber,*" *Modern Philology* 58 (May 1961), 255-269.

Bridgman, Richard. "Henry James and Mark Twain," *The Colloquial Style in America,* 78-130.

Brooks, Cleanth. "The American 'Innocence': in James, Fitzgerald, and Faulkner," *Shenandoah* XVI (Autumn 1964), 21-37.

Bruccoli, M. J. "Fitzgerald, Brooks, Hemingway, and James: A New Fitzgerald Letter," *Fitzgerald Newsletter* 29 (Spring 1965), 1-3.

Bruneau, Jean. "Une Lettre Inédite De Henry James à Gustave Flaubert Autour De Monckton Milnes, Lord Houghton," *Revue de Littérature Comparée* 41 (Oct-Dec 1968), 520-533.

Burgess, C. F. "The Seeds of Art: Henry James's *Donnée,*" *Literature and Psychology* XIII (Summer 1963), 67-73.

Calisher, Hortense. "A Short Note on a Long Subject: Henry James," *Texas Quarterly* X (Summer 1967), 57-59.

Cambon, Glauco. "The Negative Gesture in Henry James," *Nineteenth-Century Fiction* XV (Mar 1961), 335-343.

Cawelti, John G. "Form as Cultural Criticism in the Work of Henry James," *Literature and Society,* 202-212.

Clair, John A. *The Ironic Dimension in the Fiction of Henry James. The Critical Heritage.*

Deakin, Motley F. "The Real and Fictive Quest of Henry James," *Bucknell Review* XIV (May 1966), 82-97.

Discovery of a Genius: William Dean Howells and Henry James.

Dove, John Roland. "The Tragic Sense in Henry James," *Texas Studies in Literature and Language* II (Autumn 1960), 303-314.

Dupee, F. W. *Henry James.*

Edel, Leon. *Henry James,* Volumes 1, 2, and 3.

————. "Henry James: The Americano-European Legend," *University of Toronto Quarterly* XXXVI (Jul 1967), 321-334.

————. "Henry James," *Six American Novelists of the Nineteenth Century,* 191-225.

————. "To the Poet of Prose," *Modern Fiction Studies* XII (Spring 1966), 3-6. Reprinted from *Book Week,* February 27, 1966.

Emerson, Donald. "Henry James and Limitations of Realism," *College English* XXII (Dec 1960), 161-166.

Fabris, Alberta. "La Francia Di Henry James," *Studi Americani* IX (1964), 173-226.

Falk, Robert. *The Victorian Mode in American Fiction: 1865-1885,* 54-91, 138-156.

Feinstein, Herbert. "Two Pair of Gloves: Mark Twain and Henry James," *American Imago* XVII (Winter 1960), 349-387.

Felstiner, John. "Max Beerbohm and the Wings of Henry James," *Kenyon Review* XXIX (Sept 1967), 449-471.

Fiedler, Leslie A. *Love and Death in the American Novel,* 288-295.

Gale, Robert L. *The Caught Image: Figurative Language in the Fiction of Henry James.*

———. "Names in James," *Names* 14 (Jun 1966), 83-108.

———. *Plots and Characters in the Fiction of Henry James.*

Geismar, Maxwell. "Henry James and the Jacobites," *American Scholar* XXXI (Summer 1962), 373-381.

———. *Henry James and the Jacobites.*

Gerber, Richard. "Die Magie Der Namen Bei Henry James," *Anglia* 81 (Heft 1-2, 1963), 175-197.

Goode, John. "The Art of Fiction: Walter Besant and Henry James," *Tradition and Tolerance in Nineteenth Century Fiction: Critical Essays on Some English and American Novels,* 243-281.

Grant, Douglas. *Purpose and Place,* 127-135.

Green, Martin. "Henry James and the Great Tradition," *Re-Appraisals: Some Commonsense Readings in American Literature,* 145-166.

Grover, P. R. "Merimee's Influence on Henry James," *Modern Language Review* LXIII (Oct 1968), 810-817.

Gullason, Thomas Arthur. "The Jamesian Motif in Stephen Crane's Last Novels," *Personalist* XLII (Winter 1961), 77-84.

Halpern, Martin. "Henry B. Brewster (1850-1908): An Introduction," *American Quarterly* XIV (Fall 1962), 464-482.

Hamblen, Abigail Ann. "Henry James and Disease," *Dalhousie Review* XLIV (Spring 1964), 57-63.

Hartsock, Mildred. "Henry James and the Cities of the Plain," *Modern Language Quarterly* XXIX (Sept 1968), 297-311.

Hasler, Jorg. *Switzerland in the Life and Work of Henry James.*

Heimer, Jackson W. *The Lesson of New England: Henry James and His Native Region.*

Hill, John S. "Henry James: Fitzgerald's Literary Ancestor," *Fitzgerald Newsletter* 40 (Winter 1968), 6-10.

Holder, Alan. "The Lesson of the Master: Ezra Pound and Henry James," *American Literature* XXXV (Mar 1963), 71-79.

—————. *Three Voyagers in Search of Europe: A Study of Henry James, Ezra Pound, and T. S. Eliot.*

—————. "T. S. Eliot on Henry James," *PMLA* LXXIX (Sept 1964), 490-497.

Holder, Alex. "On the Structure of Henry James's Metaphors," *English Studies* XLI (Oct 1960), 289-297.

Holder-Barell, Alexander. *The Development of Imagery and Its Functional Significance in Henry James's Novels.*

Hopkins, Viola. "Gloriani and the Tides of Taste," *Nineteenth-Century Fiction* XVIII (Jun 1963), 65-71.

—————. "Visual Art Devices and Parallels in the Fiction of Henry James," *PMLA* LXXVI (Dec 1961), 561-574.

—————. "Visual Art Devices and Parallels in the Fiction of Henry James," *Henry James: Modern Judgements,* 89-115.

Howe, Irving. "Henry James' Return to America," *New Republic* 157 (Sept 30, 1967), 23-26.

Hyde, H. Montgomery. "The Lamb House Library of Henry James," *Book Collector* XVI (Winter 1967), 477-480.

Jefferson, D. W. *Henry James.*

—————. *Henry James and the Modern Reader.*

Kelley, Cornelia Pulsifer. *The Early Development of Henry James,* revised edition.

Keynes, Geoffrey. *Henry James in Cambridge.*

Kirk, Clara M. " 'The Brighter Side' of Fiction: According to Howells and James," *College English* XXIV (Mar 1963), 463-464.

Kraft, James. "An Unpublished Review by Henry James," *Studies in Bibliography* XX (1967), 267-273.

Kraft, Quentin G. "The Question of Freedom in James's Fiction," *College English* XXVI (Feb 1965), 372-381.

Krook, Dorothea. *The Ordeal of Consciousness in Henry James.*

Kubal, David L. "Henry James and the Supreme Value," *Arizona Quarterly* XXII (Summer 1966), 101-114.

Lebowitz, Naomi. *The Imagination of Loving: Henry James's Legacy to the Novel.*

JAMES, HENRY, Continued

Lee, B. C. "A Felicity Forever Gone: Henry James's Last Visit to America," *British Association for American Studies Bulletin* 5 (Dec 1962), 31-42.

Lee, Brian. "Henry James's 'Divine Consensus': *The Ambassadors, The Wings of the Dove, The Golden Bowl,*" *Renaissance and Modern Studies* VI (1962), 5-24.

Lewis, R. W. B. *Trials of the Word,* 77-96.

Leyburn, Ellen Douglass. *Strange Alloy: The Relation of Comedy to Tragedy in the Fiction of Henry James.*

Lowery, Bruce. *Marcel Proust et Henry James: Une confrontation.*

Lucas, John. "Manliest of Cities: The Image of Rome in Henry James," *Studi Americani* XI (1965), 117-136.

Mackenzie, Manfred. "Henry James: Serialist Early and Late," *Philological Quarterly* XLI (Apr 1962), 492-499.

Mariani, Umberto. "L'Esperienza Italiana Di Henry James," *Studi Americani* VI (1960), 221-253.

————. "The Italian Experience of Henry James," *Nineteenth-Century Fiction* XIX (Dec 1964), 237-254.

Marks, Robert. *James's Later Novels: An Interpretation,* 9-14, 148-176.

Martin, Jay. "Henry James: The Wings of the Artist," *Harvests of Change. American Literature 1865-1914,* 310-364.

McClary, Ben Harris. "'In Abject Terror of Rising': An Unpublished Henry James Letter," *English Language Notes* III (Mar 1966), 208-211.

McElderry, Bruce R., Jr. *Henry James.*

Melchiori, Giorgio. "Il 'Déjeuner Sur L'Herbe' Di Henry James," *Studi Americani* X (1964), 201-228.

Millgate, Michael. *American Social Fiction: James to Cozzens,* 1-17.

Monteiro, George. "Hawthorne, James, and the Destructive Self," *Texas Studies in Literature and Language* IV (Spring 1962), 58-71.

————. "Henry James and the American Academy of Arts and Letters," *New England Quarterly* XXXVI (Mar 1963), 82-84.

————. "Henry James and John Hay," *Books at Brown* XIX (May 1963), 69-88.

————. *Henry James and John Hay: The Record of a Friendship.*

————. "Letters to a 'Countryman,' " *Books at Brown* XIX (May 1963), 105-112.

————. "The New York *Tribune* on Henry James, 1881-1882," *Bulletin of the New York Public Library* LXVII (Feb 1963), 71-81.

————. "Some Unpublished Letters of Henry James to John Hay," *Texas Studies in Literature and Language* IV (Supplement 1963), 641-695.

Morrison, Sister Kristin. "James's and Lubbock's Differing Points of View," *Nineteenth-Century Fiction* XVI (Dec 1961), 245-255.

Murray, Donald M. "Henry James in the Advanced Composition Course," *College English* XXV (Oct 1963), 26-30.

Newman, Charles. "The Lesson of the Master: Henry James and James Baldwin," *Yale Review* LVI (Autumn 1966), 46-59.

Noble, David W. *The Eternal Adam and the New World Garden,* 79-98.

Paterson, John. "The Language of 'Adventure' in Henry James," *American Literature* XXXII (Nov 1960), 291-301.

Phillips, LeRoy. Introduction, *Views and Reviews* (New York, 1968).

Poirier, Richard. *A World Elsewhere,* 93-143.

Powers, Lyall H. "Henry James's Antinomies," *University of Toronto Quarterly* XXXI (Jan 1962), 125-135.

————. "Henry James and Zola's Roman Experimental," *University of Toronto Quarterly* XXX (Oct 1960), 16-30.

Putt, S. Gorley. "'Cher Maitre' and 'Mon Bon': Henry James, Man and Legend," *Scholars of the Heart: Essays in Criticism,* 141-151.

————. *Henry James: A Reader's Guide,* 7-15.

Raleigh, John Henry. "Henry James: The Poetics of Empiricism," *Time, Place, and Idea, Essays on the Novel,* 3-24.

Raskin, Jonah. "Henry James and the French Revolution," *American Quarterly* XVII (Winter 1965), 724-733.

Roberts, James L. "An Approach to Evil in Henry James," *Arizona Quarterly* XVII (Spring 1961), 5-16.

Rovit, Earl. "James and Emerson: The Lesson of the Master," *American Scholar* XXXIII (Summer 1964), 434-440.

Salomon, Roger B. "Realism as Disinheritance: Twain, Howells and James," *American Quarterly* XVI (Winter 1964), 531-544.

Samuel, Irene. "Henry James on Imagination and the Will to Power," *Bulletin of the New York Public Library* LXIX (Feb 1965), 117-130.

Sanford, Charles L. *The Quest for Paradise: Europe and the American Moral Imagination.*

Sears, Sallie. "Perspective and Form," *The Negative Imagination: Form and Perspective in the Novels of Henry James.*

Sharp, Sister M. Corona, O.S.U. *The Confidante in Henry James: Evolution and Moral Value of a Fictive Character.*

————. "Fatherhood in Henry James," *University of Toronto Quarterly* XXXV (Apr 1966), 279-292.

Shulman, Robert. "Henry James and the Modern Comedy of Knowledge," *Criticism* X (Winter 1968), 41-53.

Silverstein, Henry. "The Utopia of Henry James," *New England Quarterly* XXXV (Dec 1962), 458-468.

Smith, J. Oates. "Henry James and Virginia Woolf: The Art of Relationships," *Twentieth Century Literature* X (Oct 1964), 119-129.

Snow, Lotus. "Some Stray Fragrance of an Ideal: Henry James's Imagery for Youth's Discovery of Evil," *Harvard Library Bulletin* XIV (Winter 1960), 107-125.

Stafford, William T. "Literary Allusions in James's Prefaces," *American Literature* XXXV (Mar 1963), 60-70.

————. "William James as Critic of His Brother Henry," *Personalist* XL (Autumn 1959), 341-353.

Stallman, Robert W. *The Houses that James Built and Other Literary Studies.*

Steen, James T. "The Vision of Henry James," *Lectures on Modern Novelists,* 55-65.

Stone, Edward. *The Battle and the Books: Some Aspects of Henry James.*

Tanner, Tony. "Henry James and Henry Adams," *Tri-Quarterly* 11 (Winter 1968), 91-108.

————. "The Literary Children of James and Clemens," *Nineteenth-Century Fiction* XVI (Dec 1961), 205-218.

————. *The Reign of Wonder: Naivety and Reality in American Literature,* 261-335.

Terrie, Henry L., Jr. "Henry James and the 'Explosive Principle,'" *Nineteenth-Century Fiction* XV (Mar 1961), 283-299.

Tuttleton, James W. "Fiction as the House of Fame," *Midcontinent American Studies Journal* 7 (Spring 1966), 25-36.

Van Nostrand, A. D. "The Dense Totality of Henry James," *Everyman His Own Poet,* 149-174.

Wager, Willis. *American Literature: A World View,* 145-156.

Wagner, Linda Welshimer. "The Dominance of Heredity in the Characterizations of Henry James," *South Dakota Review* 2 (Spring 1965), 69-77.

Walker, Don D. "The Gun and Lasso of Henry James," *Western Humanities Review* XVII (Spring 1963), 178-180.

Ward, J. A. "Henry James's America: Versions of Oppression," *Mississippi Quarterly* XIII (Winter 1959-60), 30-44.

————. "Henry James and the Nature of Evil," *Twentieth Century Literature* VI (Jul 1960), 65-69.

————. "Henry James and the Nature of Evil," *Critical Approaches to American Literature: Volume II, Walt Whitman to William Faulkner,* 119-125.

————. *The Imagination of Disaster: Evil in the Fiction of Henry James.*

————. "The Ineffectual Heroes of James's Middle Period," *Texas Studies in Literature and Language* II (Autumn 1960), 315-327.

————. "James's Idea of Structure," *PMLA* LXXX (Sept 1965), 419-426.

————. *The Search for Form: Studies in the Structure of James's Fiction.*

Warren, Austin. "Henry James," *The New England Conscience,* 143-156.

Wasiolek, Edward. "Tolstoy's 'The Death of Ivan Ilyich' and Jamesian Fictional Imperatives," *Modern Fiction Studies* VI (Winter 1960-61), 314-324.

Watanabe, Hisayoshi. "Past Perfect Retrospection in the Style of Henry James," *American Literature* XXXIV (May 1962), 165-181.

Weber, Carl J. "Hardy and James," *Harvard Library Bulletin* XVI (Jan 1968), 18-25.

Wegelin, Christof. "Jamesian Biography," *Nineteenth-Century Fiction* XVIII (Dec 1963), 283-287.

Weimer, David R. *The City as Metaphor,* 34-51.

Wiesenfarth, Joseph, F.S.C. "The Dramatic Novel: Its Qualities and Elements," *Henry James and the Dramatic Analogy: A Study of the Major Novels of the Middle Years,* 1-43.

————. "Henry James: Action and the Art of Life," *Four Quarters* XV (Jan 1966), 18-26.

Wilson, Edmund. "The Ambiguity of Henry James," *Psychoanalysis and American Fiction,* 143-186.

Wilson, Richard. "Henry James and 'The Note Absolute,'" *English Studies* XLVII (Feb 1966), 31-35.

Wright, Nathalia. "The Moral Field: James," *American Novelists in Italy: The Discoverers: Allston to James,* 198-248.

Wright, Walter F. *The Madness of Art: A Study of Henry James.*

Ziff, Larzer. "Literary Absenteeism," *The American 1890s: Life and Times of a Lost Generation,* 50-66.

BIBLIOGRAPHY

The Ambassadors: An Authoritative Text; The Author on the Novel; Criticism, 485-486.

Beebe, Maurice and William T. Stafford. "Criticism of Henry James: A Selected Checklist," *Modern Fiction Studies* XII (Spring 1966), 117-177.

Blackall, Jean Frantz. *Jamesian Ambiguity and The Sacred Fount,* 176-188.

Bowden, Edwin T. "In Defense of a Henry James Collection," *Library Chronicle of the University of Texas* VI (Winter 1960), 7-12.

Clair, John A. *The Ironic Dimension in the Fiction of Henry James,* 129-140.

Edel, Leon. *Henry James,* 42-47.

Hagemann, E. R. "*Life* Buffets (and Comforts) Henry James, 1883-1916: An Introduction and an Annotated Checklist," *Papers of the Bibliographical Society of America* LXII (Apr-Jun 1968), 207-225.
Henry James: Modern Judgements, 341-343.

Holder-Barell, Alexander. *The Development of Imagery and Its Functional Significance in Henry James's Novels,* 212-215.

Jefferson, D. W. *Henry James,* 114-120.

————. *Henry James and the Modern Reader,* 229-236.

Kelley, Cornelia Pulsifer. *The Early Development of Henry James,* revised edition, 301-314.

Lowery, Bruce. *Marcel Proust et Henry James: Une confrontation,* 381-397.

Mathews, J. Chesley. "Bibliographical Supplement: A Selective Checklist, 1955-1962," *Eight American Authors: A Review of Research and Criticism,* 458-466.

McElderry, Bruce E., Jr. *Henry James,* 179-186.

Moore, Rayburn S. "The Full Light of a Higher Criticism: Edel's Biography and Other Recent Studies of Henry James," *South Atlantic Quarterly* LXIII (Winter 1964), 104-114.

JAMES, HENRY, Continued

Six American Novelists of the Nineteenth Century, 243-247.

Stafford, William T., (ed.) . *Perspectives on James's Portrait of a Lady: A Collection of Critical Essays,* 297-303.

Twentieth Century Interpretations of The Portrait of a Lady: A Collection of Critical Essays, 121-122.

Wiesenfarth, Joseph, F.S.C. *Henry James and the Dramatic Analogy: A Study of the Major Novels of the Middle Years,* 135-139.

Wright, Walter F. *The Madness of Art: A Study of Henry James,* 255-266.

JEWETT, SARAH ORNE

A COUNTRY DOCTOR

Biron, Archile H., translator. "Madame Blanc's 'Le Roman De La Femme-Médecin,' " *Colby Library Quarterly* VII (Sept 1967) , 488-503.

THE COUNTRY OF THE POINTED FIRS

Cary, Richard. *Sarah Orne Jewett,* 144-152.

Fike, Francis. "An Interpretation of *Pointed Firs,*" *New England Quarterly* XXXIV (Dec 1961) , 478-491.

Magowan, Robin. "Pastoral and the Art of Landscape in *The Country of the Pointed Firs,*" *New England Quarterly* XXXVI (Jun 1963) , 229-240.

DEEPHAVEN

Cary, Richard. *Sarah Orne Jewett,* 132-138.

GENERAL

Auchincloss, Louis. "Sarah Orne Jewett," *Pioneers & Caretakers,* 6-19.

Boggio-Sola, Jean. "The Poetic Realism of Sarah Orne Jewett," *Colby Library Quarterly* VII (Jun 1965) , 74-81.

Cary, Richard. "In Memoriam: Sarah Orne Jewett," *Colby Library Quarterly* V (Sept 1959) , 37-38.

————. "Jewett and the Gilman Women," *Colby Library Quarterly* V (Mar 1960) , 94-111.

————. "Jewett's Cousins Charles and Charlie," *Colby Library Quarterly* V (Sept 1959) , 48-59.

————. "Jewett's Literary Canons," *Colby Library Quarterly* VII (Jun 1965) , 82-87.

————. "Miss Jewett and Madame Blanc," *Colby Library Quarterly* VII (Sept 1967) , 467-488.

JEWETT, SARAH ORNE, Continued

————. *Sarah Orne Jewett.*

Chase, Mary Ellen. "Sarah Orne Jewett as a Social Historian," *Prairie Schooner* XXXVI (Fall 1962) , 231-237.

Eakin, Paul John. "Sarah Orne Jewett and the Meaning of Country Life," *American Literature* XXXVIII (Jan 1967) , 508-531.

Frost, John Eldridge. "The Letters of Sarah Orne Jewett," *Colby Library Quarterly* V (Sept 1959) , 38-45.

Hollis, C. Carroll. "Letters of Sarah Orne Jewett to Anna Laurens Dawes," *Colby Library Quarterly* VIII (Sept 1968) , 97-138.

Martin, Jay. *Harvests of Change. American Literature 1865-1914*, 142-148.

Nye, George P. "Jewett and the Juvenile Critics," *Colby Library Quarterly* V (Sept 1959) , 45-48.

Pool, Eugene Hillhouse. "The Child in Sarah Orne Jewett," *Colby Library Quarterly* VII (Sept 1967) , 503-509.

Ziff, Larzer. *The American 1890s: Life and Times of a Lost Generation*, 286-292.

BIBLIOGRAPHY

Cary, Richard. "Sarah Orne Jewett (1849-1909) ," *American Literary Realism* 1 (Fall 1967) , 61-66.

————. "Some Bibliographic Ghosts of Sarah Orne Jewett," *Colby Library Quarterly* VIII (Sept 1968) , 139-145.

————. *Sarah Orne Jewett*, 165-171.

Frost, John Eldridge, "Sarah Orne Jewett Bibliography: 1949-1963," *Colby Library Quarterly* VI (Jun 1964) , 405-417.

JOHNSON, JAMES WELDON

GENERAL

Margolies, Edward. *Native Sons: A Critical Study of Twentieth-Century Negro American Authors*, 25-27.

JOHNSTON, MARY

GENERAL

Nelson, Lawrence G. "Mary Johnston and the Historic Imagination," *The Dilemma of the Southern Writer*, 61-94.

————. "Mary Johnston and the Historic Imagination," *Southern Writers: Appraisals in Our Time*, 71-102.

JOHNSTON, RICHARD MALCOLM

GENERAL
Bush, Robert. "Richard Malcolm Johnston's Marriage Group," *Georgia Review* XVIII (Winter 1964) , 429-436.

JONES, JAMES

GENERAL
Aldrich, Nelson W., Jr. "An Interview with James Jones: The Art of Fiction XXIII," *Paris Review* V, No. 20, (Autumn-Winter 1958-59) , 34-55.

Sheed, Wilfrid. "The Jones Boy Forever," *Atlantic Monthly* CCXIX (Jun 1967) , 68-72.

Stevenson, David. "James Jones and Jack Kerouac: Novelists of Disjunction," *The Creative Present,* 194-206, 211-212.

Volpe, Edmond L. "James Jones—Norman Mailer," *Contemporary American Novelists,* 106-112.

JONES, MADISON

A BURIED LAND
Rubin, Louis D., Jr. "The Difficulties of Being a Southern Writer Today: Or, Getting out from under Faulkner," *The Curious Death of the Novel: Essays in American Literature,* 287-292.

KANTOR, MacKINLAY

ANDERSONVILLE
Stuckey, W. J. *The Pulitzer Prize Novels: A Critical Backward Look,* 175-180.

KENNEDY, JOHN PENDLETON

HORSE-SHOE ROBINSON
Bohner, Charles H. *John Pendleton Kennedy,* 91-100.

Leisy, Ernest E. Introduction, *Horse-Shoe Robinson* (New York, 1962) .

Ridgely, J. V. *John Pendleton Kennedy,* 65-91.

QUODLIBET
Bohner, Charles H. *John Pendleton Kennedy,* 131-139.

KENNEDY, JOHN PENDLETON, Continued

————. "J. P. Kennedy's *Quodlibet:* Whig Counterattack," *American Quarterly* XIII (Spring 1961), 84-92.

Ridgely, J. V. *John Pendleton Kennedy,* 114-127.

ROB OF THE BOWL

Bohner, Charles H. *John Pendleton Kennedy,* 100-111.

Ridgely, J. V. *John Pendleton Kennedy,* 92-113.

SWALLOW BARN

Bohner, Charles H. *John Pendleton Kennedy,* 72-88.

Osborne, William S. Introduction, *Swallow Barn, or A Sojourn in the Old Dominion* (New York, 1962).

Ridgely, J. V. *John Pendleton Kennedy,* 36-64.

GENERAL

Bohner, Charles H. *John Pendleton Kennedy.*

Ridgely, J. V. *John Pendleton Kennedy.*

BIBLIOGRAPHY

Ridgely, J. V. *John Pendleton Kennedy,* 149-152.

KEROUAC, JACK

DESOLATION ANGELS

Krim, Seymour. Introduction, *Desolation Angels* (New York, 1965).

ON THE ROAD

Askew, Melvin W. "Quests, Cars, and Kerouac," *University of Kansas City Review* XXVIII (Mar 1962), 231-240.

GENERAL

Allen, Eliot D. "That Was No Lady—That Was Jack Kerouac's Girl," *Essays in Modern American Literature,* 97-102.

Berrigan, Ted, interviewer. "The Art of Fiction XLI: Jack Kerouac," *Paris Review* 11 No. 43 (Summer 1968), 61-105.

Feied, Frederick. *No Pie in the Sky: The Hobo as American Cultural Hero in the Works of Jack London, John Dos Passos, and Jack Kerouac,* 57-80.

Frohock, W. M. "Jack Kerouac and the Beats," *Strangers to this Ground: Cutural Diversity in Contemporary American Writing,* 132-147.

Holmes, John Clellon. *Nothing More to Declare,* 68-86.

Jones, Granville H. "Jack Kerouac and the American Conscience," *Lectures on Modern Novelists,* 25-39.

Stevenson, David. "James Jones and Jack Kerouac: Novelists of Disjunction," *The Creative Present,* 195-200, 206-212.

Tallman, Warren. "Kerouac's Sound," *Evergreen Review* IV (Jan-Feb 1960), 153-169.

Wakefield, Dan. "Jack Kerouac Comes Home," *Atlantic Monthly* CCXVI (Jul 1965), 69-72.

Webb, Howard W., Jr. "The Singular Worlds of Jack Kerouac," *Contemporary American Novelists,* 120-133.

BIBLIOGRAPHY

Charters, Ann. *A Bibliography of Works of Jack Kerouac* (*Jean Louis Lebris de Kerouac*), 1939-1967.

KESEY, KEN

ONE FLEW OVER THE CUCKOO'S NEST

Fiedler, Leslie A. *The Return of the Vanishing American,* 178-185.

Waldmeir, Joseph J. "Two Novelists of the Absurd: Heller and Kesey," *Wisconsin Studies in Contemporary Literature* 5 (Autumn 1964), 192-204.

GENERAL

Wolfe, Tom. "The Author's Story," *New York Times Book Review* 73 (Aug 18, 1968), 2, 40-41.

KING, CHARLES

GENERAL

Peterson, Clell T. "Charles King: Soldier and Novelist," *American Book Collector* XVI (Sept 1965), 9-12.

Sackett, S. J. "Captain Charles King, U.S.A.," *Midwest Quarterly* III (Autumn 1961), 69-80.

BIBLIOGRAPHY

Dornbush, C. E. *Charles King: American Army Novelist,* vi, 19.

KIRKLAND, CAROLINE

GENERAL

Stronks, James B. "Author Rejects Publisher: Caroline Kirkland and *The Gift,*" *Bulletin of the New York Public Library* LXIV (Oct 1960), 548-550.

KIRKLAND, JOSEPH

THE McVEYS
Henson, Clyde E. *Joseph Kirkland,* 118-124.
A NEW HOME—WHO'LL FOLLOW?
Osborne, William S. Introduction, *A New Home—Who'll Follow?* (New Haven, 1966).
ZURY: THE MEANEST MAN IN SPRING COUNTY
Henson, Clyde E. *Joseph Kirkland,* 93-117.
GENERAL
Henson, Clyde E. *Joseph Kirkland.*
BIBLIOGRAPHY
Henson, Clyde E. "Joseph Kirkland (1830-1894)," *American Literary Realism* 1 (Fall 1967), 67-70.
————. *Joseph Kirkland,* 150-156.

KNOWLES, JOHN

A SEPARATE PEACE
Ely, Sister M. Amanda, O. P. "The Adult Image in Three Novels of Adolescent Life," *English Journal* LVI (Nov 1967), 1127-1131.
Greiling, Franziska Lynne. "The Theme of Freedom in *A Separate Peace,*" *English Journal* LVI (Dec 1962), 1269-1272.
Mellard, James M. "Counterpoint and 'Double Vision' In *A Separate Peace,*" *Studies in Short Fiction* IV (Winter 1967), 127-134.
GENERAL
Halio, Jay L. "John Knowles' Short Novels," *Studies in Short Fiction* I (Winter 1964), 107-112.
Knowles, John. "Where Does the Young Writer Find His Real Friends?" *New York Times Book Review* 67 (Apr 8, 1962), 6, 36.
McDonald, James L. "The Novels of John Knowles," *Arizona Quarterly* XXIII (Winter 1967), 335-342.

KRAUSE, HERBERT

THE THRESHER
Janssen, Judith M. " 'Black Frost in Summer': Central Themes in the Novels of Herbert Krause," *South Dakota Review* 5 (Spring 1967), 55-65.

KRAUSE, HERBERT, Continued

THE WIND WITHOUT RAIN
Janssen, Judith M. " 'Black Frost in Summer': Central Themes in the Novels of Herbert Krause," *South Dakota Review* 5 (Spring 1967), 55-65.

LANGLEY, ADRIA LOCKE

A LION IS IN THE STREETS
Rubin, Louis D., Jr. "All the King's Meanings," *The Curious Death of the Novel: Essays in American Literature,* 222-227.

LANIER, CLIFFORD ANDERSON

GENERAL
Jones, David. "Clifford Anderson Lanier," *Georgia Review* XIV (Summer 1960), 205-214.

LANIER, SIDNEY

TIGER-LILIES
Mayfield, John S. "Lanier in the Florae or, What Would You Have Done?" *American Book Collector* X (Feb 1960), 7-11.
Mayfield, John S. "Sidney Lanier's *Tiger-Lilies: A Bibliographical Mystery*," *Papers of the Bibliographical Society of America* 54 (Oct-Dec 1960), 265-272.

LEDERER, WILLIAM J.
(*see* BURDICK, EUGENE)

LEE, HARPER

TO KILL A MOCKINGBIRD
Schuster, Edgar H. "Discovering Theme and Structure in the Novel," *English Journal* LII (Oct 1963), 506-511.

LEWIS, ALFRED HENRY

THE BOSS: A ROMANCE OF AMERICAN POLITICS
Blother, Joseph. *The Modern American Political Novel,* 65-68.

LEWIS, JAMES FRANKLIN

STRANGE SPECIES

Lund, Mary Graham. " (A Preview of *Strange Species*) from the Jungle Floor," *Trace* 41 (Apr-Jun 1961) , 65-69.

LEWIS, JANET

GENERAL

Davie, Donald. "The Historical Narratives of Janet Lewis," *Southern Review* II (Jan 1966) , 40-60.

Inglis, Fred. "The Novels of Janet Lewis," *Critique* VII (Winter 1964-1965) , 47-64.

LEWIS, SINCLAIR

ARROWSMITH

Dooley, D. J. "Arrowsmith," *Twentieth Century Interpretations of Arrowsmith,* 61-67.

————. *The Art of Sinclair Lewis,* 99-103, 105-117.

Duffy, Charles. "A Sinclair Lewis Letter," *American Notes & Queries* V (Apr 1967) , 118-119.

Grebstein, Sheldon N. "The Best of the Great Decade," *Twentieth Century Interpretations of Arrowsmith,* 68-76.

————. *Sinclair Lewis,* 85-96.

Helleberg, Marilyn Morgan. "The Paper-Doll Characters of Sinclair Lewis' *Arrowsmith*," *Mark Twain Journal* XIV (Summer 1968) , 17-21.

Ober, William B. "Arrowsmith and the Last Adam," *Twentieth Century Interpretations of Arrowsmith,* 57-60.

————. "Compare and Contrast Sinclair Lewis's *Arrowsmith* with James Gould Cozzens's *The Last Adam*," *Carleton Miscellany* IV (Fall 1963) , 101-110.

Rosenberg, Charles E. "Martin Arrowsmith: The Scientist as Hero," *American Quarterly* XV (Fall 1963) , 447-458.

————. "Martin Arrowsmith: The Scientist as Hero," *Twentieth Century Interpretations of Arrowsmith,* 47-56.

Schorer, Mark. "On Arrowsmith," *Twentieth Century Interpretations of Arrowsmith,* 40-46.

————. *Sinclair Lewis: An American Life,* 414-420.

LEWIS, SINCLAIR, Continued

MAIN STREET

Aaron, Daniel. "Sinclair Lewis: *Main Street*," *The American Novel from James Fenimore Cooper to William Faulkner,* 166-179.

Dooley, D. J. *The Art of Sinclair Lewis,* 57-76.

Grebstein, Sheldon Norman. *Sinclair Lewis,* 61-73.

McCarthy, John F. "A New Look at an Old Street," *English Journal* LVII (Oct 1968), 985-987.

Schier, Donald. "*Main Street* by Sinclair Lewis," *Carleton Miscellany* IV (Fall 1963), 95-101.

Schorer, Mark. Afterword, *Main Street* (New York, 1961).

Tanselle, G. Thomas. "Sinclair Lewis and Floyd Dell: Two Views of the Midwest," *Twentieth Century Literature* IX (Jan 1964), 175-184.

THE MAN WHO KNEW COOLIDGE

Dooley, D. J. *The Art of Sinclair Lewis,* 141-148.

OUR MR. WRENN

Dooley, D. J. *The Art of Sinclair Lewis,* 16-28.

THE TRAIL OF THE HAWK

Dooley, D. J. *The Art of Sinclair Lewis,* 28-35.

GENERAL

Angoff, Charles. *The Tone of the Twenties and Other Essays,* 69-73.

Babcock, C. Merton. "Americanisms in the Novels of Sinclair Lewis," *American Speech* XXXV (May 1960), 110-116.

Brand, Peter. "A Letter from Sauk Centre," *Carleton Miscellany* I (Spring 1960), 103-110.

Brown, Daniel R. "Lewis's Satire: A Negative Emphasis," *Renascence* XVIII (Winter 1966), 63-72.

Coard, Robert L. "Names in the Fiction of Sinclair Lewis," *Georgia Review* XVI (Fall 1962), 318-329.

Conti, Giuseppe Gadda. "Sinclair Lewis," *Studi Americani* IX (1964), 249-286.

Couch, William, Jr. "Sinclair Lewis: Crisis in the American Dream," *CLA Journal* VII (Mar 1964), 224-234.

Derleth, August. "Sinclair Lewis," *Three Literary Men,* 9-27.

Dooley, D. J. *The Art of Sinclair Lewis.*

Edener, Wilfried. *Die Religionskritik in den Romanen von Sinclair Lewis.*

————. "Die Religionskritik in den Romanen von Sinclair Lewis," Beihefte zum *Jahrbuch für Amerikastudien* 10 (1963), 1-240.

Fife, Jim L. "Two Views of the American West," *Western American Literature* 1 (Spring 1966), 34-43.

Geismar, Maxwell. "Sinclair Lewis: Forgotten Hero," *Saturday Review* 43 (Jun 18, 1960), 29-30.

Grant, Douglas. *Purpose and Place*, 163-168.

Grebstein, Sheldon Norman. *Sinclair Lewis*.

Griffin, Robert J. "Sinclair Lewis," *American Winners of the Nobel Literary Prize*, 16-53.

Hendricks, King and Irving Shepard, (eds.). *Letters from Jack London to Sinclair Lewis*.

Kramer, Maurice. "Sinclair Lewis and the Hollow Center," *The Twenties: Poetry and Prose*, 67-69.

Light, Martin. "A Further Word on Sinclair Lewis' Prize-Consciousness," *Western Humanities Review* XV (Autumn 1961), 368-371.

————. "Lewis' Finicky Girls and Faithful Workers," *University Review* XXX (Dec 1963), 151-159.

Lockerbie, D. Bruce. "Sinclair Lewis and William Ridgway," *American Literature* XXXVI (Mar 1964), 68-72.

Millgate, Michael. *American Social Fiction: James to Cozzens*, 93-106.

————. "Sinclair Lewis and the Obscure Hero," *Studi Americani* VIII (1962), 112-127.

Moore, Geoffrey. "Sinclair Lewis: A Lost Romantic," *Sinclair Lewis: A Collection of Critical Essays*, 151-165.

————. "Sinclair Lewis: A Lost Romantic," *The Young Rebel in American Literature*, 51-78.

Napier, James J. "Letters of Sinclair Lewis to Joseph Hergesheimer, 1915-1922," *American Literature* XXXVIII (May 1966), 236-246.

Price, Lawrence Marsden. *The Reception of United States Literature in Germany*, 135-141.

Schorer, Mark. Introduction, *Lewis at Zenith: A Three Novel Omnibus* (New York, 1961).

————. *Sinclair Lewis*.

————. *Sinclair Lewis: An American Life*.

————. "Sinclair Lewis and his Critics," *The World We Imagine: Selected Essays*, 182-194.

————. "Sinclair Lewis and the Nobel Prize," *Atlantic Monthly* CCVIII (Oct 1961), 83-88.

————. "Sinclair Lewis," *Seven Modern American Novelists: An Introduction*, 46-80.

LEWIS, SINCLAIR, Continued

————. "Two Houses, Two Ways: The Florentine Villas of Lewis and Lawrence," *The World We Imagine: Selected Essays,* 195-218.

Sheean, Vincent. *Dorothy and Red.*

Springer, Anne M. *The American Novel in Germany: A Study of the Critical Reception of Eight American Novelists Between the Two World Wars,* 46-59.

Thompson, Dorothy. "The Boy and Man from Sauk Centre," *Atlantic Monthly* CCVI (Nov 1960), 40-48.

Thorp, Willard. *American Writing in the Twentieth Century,* 119-123.

Van Nostrand, Albert. *The Denatured Novel,* 95-98.

West, Thomas Reed. "Sinclair Lewis: In Affirmation of Main Street," *Flesh of Steel: Literature and the Machine in American Culture,* 116-131.

BIBLIOGRAPHY

Dooley, D. J. *The Art of Sinclair Lewis,* 269-277.

Grebstein, Sheldon Norman. *Sinclair Lewis,* 180-188.

Price, Lawrence Marsden. *The Reception of United States Literature in Germany,* 220-221.

Schorer, Mark. *Sinclair Lewis: An American Life,* 815-826.

————. *Sinclair Lewis,* 45-47.

Sinclair Lewis: A Collection of Critical Essays, 173-174.

LIPPARD, GEORGE

GENERAL

Fiedler, Leslie A. *Love and Death in the American Novel,* 235-239.

LOCKE, DAVID ROSS

GENERAL

Austin, James C. *Petroleum V. Nasby (David Ross Locke),* 127-138.

BIBLIOGRAPHY

Austin, James C. *Petroleum V. Nasby (David Ross Locke),* 148-154.

LOCKRIDGE, ROSS

RAINTREE COUNTY

Litzinger, Boyd. "Mythmaking in America: 'The Great Stone Face' and *Raintree County,*" *Tennessee Studies in Literature* VIII (1963), 81-84.

LONDON, JACK

THE CALL OF THE WILD

Benoit, Raymond. "Jack London's *The Call of the Wild,*" *American Quarterly* XX (Summer 1968), 246-248.

Labor, Earle. "Jack London's *Mondo Cane: The Call of the Wild* and *White Fang,*" *Jack London Newsletter* 1 (Jul-Dec 1967), 2-13.

O'Connor, Richard. *Jack London: A Biography,* 171-177.

Poor, Henry Varnum. Introduction, *The Call of the Wild* (New York, 1960).

Walker, Franklin. Foreword, *The Call of the Wild and Selected Stories* (New York, 1960).

Warner, Richard H. "A Contemporary Sketch of Jack London," *American Literature* XXXVIII (Nov 1966), 376-380.

THE CRUISE OF THE DAZZLER

Evans, I. O. Introduction, *The Cruise of the Dazzler* (New York, 1963).

THE IRON HEEL

Blotner, Joseph. *The Modern American Political Novel,* 151-153.

Walker, Franklin. "Ideas and Action in Jack London's Fiction," *Essays on American Literature in Honor of Jay Hubbell,* 262-266.

MARTIN EDEN

Fuller, Frank A. "*Martin Eden* and Critical Realism," *American Book Collector* XVII (Nov 1966), 19-21.

Walcutt, Charles Child. *Jack London,* 34-41.

Walker, Franklin. "Jack London: *Martin Eden,*" *The American Novel from James Fenimore Cooper to William Faulkner,* 133-143.

THE SCARLET PLAGUE

Walker, Franklin. "Ideas and Action in Jack London's Fiction," *Essays on American Literature in Honor of Jay Hubbell,* 270-272.

THE SEA WOLF

Ellis, James. "A New Reading of *The Sea Wolf,*" *Western American Literature* II (Summer 1967), 127-134.

O'Connor, Richard. *Jack London: A Biography,* 191-200.

THE SON OF THE WOLF

Vanderbeets, Richard. "Nietzsche of the North: Heredity and Race in London's *The Son of the Wolf,*" *Western American Literature* II (Fall 1967), 229-233.

THE VALLEY OF THE MOON

Walker, Franklin. "Ideas and Action in Jack London's Fiction," *Essays on American Literature in Honor of Jay Hubbell,* 266-270.

LONDON, JACK, Continued

WHITE FANG

Labor, Earle. "Jack London's *Mondo Cane: The Call of the Wild* and *White Fang,*" *Jack London Newsletter* 1 (Jul-Dec 1967), 2-13.

GENERAL

Allatt, Edward. "Jack London and Upton Sinclair," *Jack London Newsletter* 1 (Jan-Jun 1968), 22-27.

Bykov, Vil. "Traditions of Jack London," *Jack London Newsletter* I (Jul-Dec 1968), 62-66.

Calder-Marshall, Arthur. *Lone Wolf: The Story of Jack London.*

Carroll, Lavon B. "Jack London and the American Image," *American Book Collector* XIII (Jan 1963), 23-27.

Feied, Frederick. *No Pie in the Sky: The Hobo as American Cultural Hero in the Works of Jack London, John Dos Passos, and Jack Kerouac,* 23-40.

Foner, Philip S. *Jack London: American Rebel.*

———. "Jack London: An Appreciation," *American Book Collector* XVII (Nov 1966), 9-10.

Gurian, Jay. "The Romantic Necessity in Literary Naturalism: Jack London," *American Literature* XXXVIII (Mar 1966), 112-120.

Hahn, Emily. *Romantic Rebels: An Informal History of Bohemianism in America,* 108-118.

Hendricks, King and Irving Shepard, (eds.). *Letters from Jack London to Sinclair Lewis.*

Martin, Jay. *Harvests of Change. American Literature 1865-1914,* 234-239.

O'Connor, Richard. *Jack London: A Biography.*

Price, Lawrence Marsden. *The Reception of United States Literature in Germany,* 130-132.

Shivers, Samuel A. "The Demoniacs in Jack London," *American Book Collector* XII (Sept 1961), 11-14.

———. "Jack London: Author in Search of a Biographer," *American Book Collector* XII (Mar 1962), 25-27.

Shivers, Alfred S. "Jack London's Mate-Women," *American Book Collector* XV (Oct 1964), 17-21.

Springer, Anne M. *The American Novel in Germany: A Study of the Critical Reception of Eight American Novelists Between the Two World Wars,* 31-39.

Thorp, Willard. *American Writing in the Twentieth Century,* 161-164.

Walcutt, Charles Child. *Jack London.*

Walker, Franklin. "Ideas and Action in Jack London's Fiction," *Essays on American Literature in Honor of Jay Hubbell,* 259-272.

————. *Jack London and the Klondike: The Genesis of an American Writer.*

BIBLIOGRAPHY

Foner, Philip S. *Jack London: American Rebel,* 154-155.

Haydock, James. "Jack London: A Bibliography of Criticism," *Bulletin of Bibliography* XXIII (May-Aug 1960) , 42-46.

Labor, Earle. "Jack London: An Addendum," *American Literary Realism* 2 (Spring 1968) , 91-93.

McMillan, Marilyn. "Unrecorded Contemporary Reviews of London's Novels," *Jack London Newsletter* 1 (Jul-Dec 1967) , 14-19.

O'Connor, Richard. *Jack London: A Biography,* 411-414.

Price, Lawrence Marsden. *The Reception of United States Literature in Germany,* 221.

Walcutt, Charles Child. *Jack London,* 45-48.

Walker, Dale L. "Jack London (1876-1916) ," *American Literary Realism* 1 (Fall 1967) , 71-78.

Walker, Franklin. *Jack London and the Klondike: The Genesis of an American Writer,* 266-275.

Woodbridge, Hensley C. "Jack London: A Bibliography; A Supplement," *American Book Collector* XVII (Nov 1966) , 32-35.

————, John London and George Tweney. *Jack London: A Bibliography.*

————. "More References Concerning Jack London," *Jack London Newsletter* 1 (Jan-Jun 1968) , 34-40.

LONGFELLOW, HENRY WADSWORTH

HYPERION

Arvin, Newton. *Longfellow: His Life and Work,* 115-124.

Williams, Cecil B. *Henry Wadsworth Longfellow,* 114-120.

KAVANAGH

Arvin, Newton. *Longfellow: His Life and Work,* 124-131.

Williams, Cecil B. *Henry Wadsworth Longfellow,* 120-125.

LUTHER, MARK LEE

THE HENCHMAN

Milne, Gordon. *The American Political Novel,* 83-86.

LYTLE, ANDREW

A NAME FOR EVIL
De Bellis, Jack. "Andrew Lytle's *A Name for Evil:* A Transformation of *The Turn of the Screw*," *Critique* VIII (Spring-Summer 1966), 26-40.

THE VELVET HORN
Trowbridge, Clinton. "The Word Made Flesh: Andrew Lytle's *The Velvet Horn*," *Critique* X (No 2, 1968), 53-68.

GENERAL
Hoffman, Frederick J. *The Art of Southern Fiction*, 99-102.

MacDONALD, JOHN D.

THE DAMNED
Hoyt, Charles Alva. "*The Damned:* Good Intentions: The Tough Guy as Hero and Villain," *Tough Guy Writers of the Thirties*, 224-230.

MAILER, NORMAN

AN AMERICAN DREAM
Bersani, Leo. "The Interpretation of Dreams," *Partisan Review* XXXII (Fall 1965), 603-608.

Corrington, John William. "An American Dreamer," *Chicago Review* XVIII (No 1, 1965), 58-66

Harper, Howard M., Jr. *Desperate Faith*, 120-124.

Wagenheim, Allan J. "Square's Progress: *An American Dream*," *Critique: Studies in Modern Fiction* X (No 1, 1968), 45-68.

Weber, Brom. "A Fear of Dying: Norman Mailer's *An American Dream*," *Hollins Critic* II (Jun 1965), 1-6, 8-11.

Wood, Margery. "Norman Mailer and Nathalie Sarraute: A Comparison of Existential Novels," *Minnesota Review* VI (No 1, 1966), 67-72.

BARBARY SHORE
Blotner, Joseph. *The Modern American Political Novel*, 320-322.

Harper, Howard M., Jr. *Desperate Faith*, 103-109.

THE DEER PARK
Fiedler, Leslie A. *Waiting for the End*, 97-98, 100-102.

Harper, Howard M., Jr. *Desperate Faith*, 109-119.

MAILER, NORMAN, Continued

THE NAKED AND THE DEAD

Finkelstein, Sidney. *Existentialism and Alienation in American Literature,* 270-272.

Harper, Howard M., Jr. *Desperate Faith,* 96-103.

Hassan, Ihab. *Radical Innocence: Studies in the Contemporary American Novel,* 140-151.

Thorp, Willard. *American Writing in the Twentieth Century,* 144-147.

WHY ARE WE IN VIETNAM?

Hicks, Granville. "Lark in Race for Presidency," *Saturday Review* 50 (Sept 16, 1962) , 39-40.

Samuels, Charles T. "The Novel, USA: Mailerrhea," *Nation* 205 (Oct 23, 1967) , 405-406.

GENERAL

Cook, Bruce A. "Norman Mailer: The Temptation to Power," *Renascence* XIV (Summer 1962) , 206-215, 222.

Corona, Mario. "Norman Mailer," *Studi Americani* XI (1965) , 359-407.

DeMott, Benjamin. "An Unprofessional Eye: Docket No. 15883," *American Scholar* XXX (Spring 1961) , 232-237.

Dienstfrey, Harris. "The Fiction of Norman Mailer," *On Contemporary Fiction,* 422-436.

Dupee, F. W. "The American Norman Mailer," *Commentary* XIX (Feb 1960) , 128-132.

Finkelstein, Sidney. *Existentialism and Alienation in American Literature,* 269-275.

Foster, Richard. "Mailer and the Fitzgerald Tradition," *Novel* I (Winter 1968) , 219-230.

————. *Norman Mailer.*

Glicksberg, Charles I. "Norman Mailer: The Angry Young Novelist in America," *Wisconsin Studies in Contemporary Literature* 1 (Winter 1960) , 25-34.

Harper, Howard M., Jr. "Norman Mailer—a Revolution in the Consciousness of our Time," *Desperate Faith,* 96-136.

Hoffman, Frederick J. "Norman Mailer and the Revolt of the Ego: Some Observations on Recent American Literature," *Wisconsin Studies in Contemporary Literature* 1 (Fall 1960) , 5-12.

Howe, Irving. "A Quest for Peril: Norman Mailer," *A World More Attractive: A View of Modern Literature and Politics,* 123-129.

MAILER, NORMAN, Continued

Hux, Samuel. "Mailer's Dream of Violence," *Minnesota Review* VIII (No 2, 1968), 152-157.

Langbaum, Robert. "Mailer's New Style," *Novel* 2 (Fall 1968), 69-78.

Mailer, Norman. "The First Day's Interview," *Paris Review* VII (No 26, 1962), 140-153.

————. "Mr. Mailer Interviews Himself," *New York Times Book Review* 72 (Sept 17, 1967), 4, 40.

Marcus, Steve. "An Interview with Norman Mailer: The Art of Fiction XXXII," *Paris Review* VIII No. 31 (Winter-Spring 1964), 28-58.

Martien, Norman. "Norman Mailer at Graduate School or: One Man's Effort," *New American Review* 1 (1967), 233-241.

Mudrick, Marvin. "Mailer and Styron: Guests of the Establishment," *Hudson Review* XVII (Autumn 1964), 346-366.

Noble, David W. *The Eternal Adam and the New World Garden,* 198-208.

Podhoretz, Norman. "Norman Mailer: The Embattled Vision," *Partisan Review* XXVI (Summer 1959), 371-391.

Richler, Mordecai. "Norman Mailer," *Encounter* XXV (Jul 1965), 61-64.

Schrader, George Alfred. "Norman Mailer and the Despair of Defiance," *Yale Review* LI (Winter 1962), 267-280.

Schulz, Max F. "Mailer's Divine Comedy," *Contemporary Literature* IX (Winter 1968), 36-57.

Solotaroff, Robert. "Down Mailer's Way," *Chicago Review* XIX No. 3 (Jun 1967), 11-25.

Toback, James. "Norman Mailer Today," *Commentary* XLIV (Oct 1967), 68-76.

Trilling, Diana. "Norman Mailer," *Encounter* XIX (Nov 1962), 45-56.

————. "The Radical Moralism of Norman Mailer," *The Creative Present,* 145-171.

Vidal, Gore. "The Norman Mailer Syndrome," *Nation* 190 (Jan 2, 1960), 13-16.

Volpe, Edmond L. "James Jones—Norman Mailer," *Contemporary American Novelists,* 112-119.

Wüstenhagen, Heinz. "Instinkt kontra Venunft: Norman Mailers ideologische und ästhetische Konfusion," *Zeitschrift für Anglistik und Amerikanistik* 16 (1968), 362-389.

BIBLIOGRAPHY

Foster, Richard. *Norman Mailer*, 44-46.

MALAMUD, BERNARD

THE ASSISTANT

Alley, Alvin D. and Hugh Agee. "Existential Heroes: Frank Alpine and Rabbit Angstrom," *Ball State University Forum* IX (Winter 1968), 3-5.

Baumbach, Jonathan. "All Men are Jews: *The Assistant* by Bernard Malamud," *The Landscape of Nightmare: Studies in the Contemporary American Novel*, 101-122.

Hassan, Ihab. *Radical Innocence: Studies in the Contemporary American Novel*, 162-168.

Klein, Marcus. *After Alienation: American Novels in Mid-Century*, 267-276.

Mandel, Ruth B. "Bernard Malamud's *The Assistant* and *A New Life*: Ironic Affirmation," *Critique* VII (Winter 1964-1965), 110-122.

Mellard, James M. "Malamud's *The Assistant:* The City Novel as Pastoral," *Studies in Short Fiction* V (Fall 1967), 1-11.

Richman, Sidney. *Bernard Malamud*, 50-76.

Shear, Walter. "Culture Conflict in *The Assistant*," *Midwest Quarterly* VII (Summer 1966), 367-380.

THE FIXER

Fanger, Donald. "The Fixer in Another Country," *Nation* 203 (Oct 17, 1966), 389-390.

THE NATURAL

Edelstein, J. M. "Binding Variants in Malamud's *The Natural*," *American Notes & Queries* I (May 1963), 133-134.

Freese, Peter. "Parzival als Baseballstar: Bernard Malamuds *The Natural*," *Jahrbuch für Ameriksstudien* 13 (1968), 143-157.

Klein, Marcus. *After Alienation: American Novels in Mid-Century*, 255-263.

Richman, Sidney. *Bernard Malamud*, 27-49.

Turner, Frederick W., III. "Myth Inside and Out: Malamud's *The Natural*," *Novel* I (Winter 1968), 133-139.

Wasserman, Earl R. "*The Natural:* Malamud's World Ceres," *Centennial Review* IX (Fall 1965), 438-460.

MALAMUD, BERNARD, Continued

A NEW LIFE

Klein, Marcus. *After Alienation: American Novels in Mid-Century,* 280-293.

Maloff, Saul. "Between the Real and the Absurd," *Nation* 193 (Nov 18, 1961), 407-408.

Mandel, Ruth B. "Bernard Malamud's *The Assistant* and *A New Life:* Ironic Affirmation," *Critique* VII (Winter 1964-1965), 110-122.

Richman, Sidney. *Bernard Malamud,* 78-97.

GENERAL

Alter, Robert. "Malamud as Jewish Writer," *Commentary* XLII (Sept 1966), 71-76.

Baumbach, Jonathan. "The Economy of Love: The Novels of Bernard Malamud," *Kenyon Review* XXV (Summer 1963), 438-457.

Bellman, Samuel Irving. "Women, Children, and Idiots First: The Transformation Psychology of Bernard Malamud," *Critique* VII (Winter 1964-1965), 123-138.

Eigner, Edwin M. "Malamud's Use of the Quest Romance," *Genre* I (January 1968), 55-75.

Featherstone, Joseph. "Bernard Malamud," *Atlantic Monthly* CCXIX (Mar 1967), 95-98.

Fiedler, Leslie A. *Waiting For The End,* 92-93.

Friedman, Alan Warren. "Bernard Malamud: The Hero as Schnook," *Southern Review* IV (Autumn 1968), 927-944.

Goldman, Mark. "Bernard Malamud's Comic Vision and the Theme of Identity," *Critique* VII (Winter 1964-1965), 92-109.

Hicks, Granville. "Generations of the Fifties: Malamud, Gold, and Updike," *The Creative Present,* 218-224.

Hoyt, Charles Alva. "Bernard Malamud and the New Romanticism," *Contemporary American Novelists,* 65-79.

Kazin, Alfred. "The Magic and the Dread," *On Contemporary Fiction,* 437-441.

Klein, Marcus. "Bernard Malamud: The Sadness of Goodness," *After Alienation: American Novels in Mid-Century,* 247-293.

Mellard, James M. "Malamud's Novels: Four Versions of Pastoral," *Critique* IX (No 2, 1966), 5-19.

Miller, Letizia Ciotti. "L'Arte Di Bernard Malamud," *Studi Americani* VII (1961), 261-297.

Ratner, Marc L. "Style and Humanity in Malamud's Fiction," *Massachusetts Review* V (Summer 1964), 663-683.

MALAMUD, BERNARD, Continued

Richman, Sidney. *Bernard Malamud.*

Rovit, Earl H. "Bernard Malamud and the Jewish Literary Tradition," *Critique* III (Winter-Spring 1960), 3-10.

Solotaroff, Theodore. "Bernard Malamud's Fiction: The Old Life and the New," *Commentary* XXXIII (Mar 1962), 197-204.

Tanner, Tony. "Bernard Malamud and the New Life," *Critical Quarterly* 10 (Spring-Summer 1968), 151-168.

BIBLIOGRAPHY

Richman, Sidney. *Bernard Malamud,* 150-153.

MANFRED, FREDERICK

LORD GRIZZLY

Austin, James C. "Legend, Myth, and Symbol in Frederick Manfred's *Lord Grizzly,*" *Critique* VI (Winter 1963-1964), 122-130.

Milton, John R. "*Lord Grizzly:* Rhythm, Form and Meaning in the Western Novel," *Western American Literature* 1 (Spring 1966), 6-14.

GENERAL

Editors. "West of the Mississippi: An Interview with Frederick Manfred," *Critique* II (Winter, 1959), 35-56.

Manfred, F. "The Western Novel: A Symposium," *South Dakota Review* 2 (Autumn 1964), 7-9.

BIBLIOGRAPHY

Kellogg, George. "Frederick Manfred: A Bibliography," *Twentieth Century Literature* XI (Apr 1965), 30-35.

MARCH, WILLIAM

THE BAD SEED

Hamblen, Abigail Ann. "*The Bad Seed:* A Modern *Elsie Venner,*" *Western Humanities Review* XVII (Autumn 1963), 361-363.

MARQUAND, JOHN P.

B. F.'S DAUGHTER

Gross, John J. *John P. Marquand,* 101-110.

H. M. PULHAM, ESQUIRE

Gross, John J. *John P. Marquand,* 64-83.

MARQUAND, JOHN P., Continued

THE LATE GEORGE APLEY
Goodwin, George, Jr. "The Last Hurrahs: George Apley and Frank Skeffington," *Massachusetts Review* I (Spring 1960), 461-471.
Gross, John J. *John P. Marquand,* 31-50.
Warren, Austin. *The New England Conscience,* 195-201.
MELVILLE GOODWIN
Gross, John J. *John P. Marquand,* 127-139.
POINT OF NO RETURN
Gross, John J. *John P. Marquand,* 111-126.
Van Nostrand, Albert. *The Denatured Novel,* 161-166.
SINCERELY, WILLIS WAYDE
Gross, John J. *John P. Marquand,* 141-152.
SO LITTLE TIME
Gross, John P. *John P. Marquand,* 84-96.
WARNING HILL
Hetzel, Frederick A. "Fitzgerald and Marquand," *Fitzgerald Newsletter* 28 (Winter 1965), 8-9.
WICKFORD POINT
Gross, John P. *John P. Marquand,* 51-63.
WOMEN AND THOMAS HARROW
Gross, John J. *John P. Marquand,* 158-175.
GENERAL
Adams, J. Donald. "Speaking of Books," *New York Times Book Review* 65 (Jul 31, 1960), 2.
Auchincloss, Louis. "Marquand and O'Hara: The Novel of Manners," *Nation* 191 (Nov 19, 1960), 383-388.
Benedict, Stewart H. "The Pattern of Determinism in J. P. Marquand's Novels," *Ball State Teachers College Forum* II (Winter 1961-62), 60-64.
Brown, John Mason. "John P. Marquand: The Man," *Saturday Review* 43 (Aug 13, 1960), 14-15.
Driver, Josephine P. "The Young John Marquand," *Atlantic Monthly* CCXVI (Aug 1965), 69-72.
Geismar, Maxwell. "John P. Marquand: The Writer," *Saturday Review* 43 (Aug 13, 1960), 15, 39.
Greene, George. "A Tunnel From Persepolis: The Legacy of John Marquand," *Queen's Quarterly* LXXIII (Autumn 1966), 345-356.
Gross, John J. *John P. Marquand.*

MARQUAND, JOHN P., Continued

Weeks, Edward. "John P. Marquand," *Atlantic Monthly* CCVI (Oct 1960) , 74-76.
BIBLIOGRAPHY
Gross, John J. *John P. Marquand,* 181-185.
White, William. "A Treasury Cavalcade of the Best of Marquand," *American Book Collector* XIV (Dec 1963) , 17-18.

MASTERS, EDGAR LEE

GENERAL
Derleth, August. "Edgar Lee Masters," *Three Literary Men,* 39-56.

McCARTHY, MARY

A CHARMED LIFE
McKenzie, Barbara. *Mary McCarthy,* 121-135.
Stock, Irvin. *Mary McCarthy,* 29-35.
THE COMPANY SHE KEEPS
Stock, Irvin. *Mary McCarthy,* 14-20.
THE GROUP
McCarthy, Mary. "Letter to a Translator: About 'The Group,' " *Encounter* XXIII (Nov 1964) , 69-76.
McKenzie, Barbara. *Mary McCarthy,* 134-154.
Stock, Irvin. *Mary McCarthy,* 35-43.
THE GROVES OF ACADEME
McKenzie, Barbara. *Mary McCarthy,* 112-122.
GENERAL
Auchincloss, Louis. "Mary McCarthy," *Pioneers & Caretakers,* 170-186.
Chamberlain, John. "The Novels of Mary McCarthy," *The Creative Present,* 242-255.
Eisinger, Chester E. *Fiction of the Forties,* 128-135.
Grumbach, Doris. *The Company She Kept.*
Hardwick, Elizabeth. "Mary McCarthy," *A View of My Own: Essays in Literature and Society,* 33-40.
McKenzie, Barbara. *Mary McCarthy.*
Niebuhr, Elisabeth. "An Interview with Mary McCarthy: The Art of Fiction XXVII," *Paris Review* VII No. 27 (Winter-Spring 1962) , 58-94.

McCARTHY, MARY, Continued

Poli, Sara. "La Narrativa Di Mary McCarthy," *Studi Americani* VII (1961), 215-259.

Schlueter, Paul. "The Dissections of Mary McCarthy," *Contemporary American Novelists,* 54-64.

Stock, Irvin. *Mary McCarthy.*

Symons, Julian. "That Elegant Miss McCarthy," *Critical Occasions,* 90-98.

BIBLIOGRAPHY

Goldman, Sherli E. *Mary Mc Carthy: A Bibliography.*

McKenzie, Barbara. *Mary McCarthy,* 187-188.

Stock, Irvin. *Mary McCarthy,* 46-47.

McCOY, HORACE

THEY SHOOT HORSES, DON'T THEY?

Coates, Robert M. Afterword, *They Shoot Horses, Don't They?* (New York, 1966).

Sturak, Thomas. "Horace McCoy's Objective Lyricism," *Tough Guy Writers of the Thirties,* 145-162.

GENERAL

Sturak, Thomas. "Horace McCoy's Objective Lyricism," *Tough Guy Writers of the Thirties,* 137-162.

McCULLERS, CARSON

THE BALLAD OF THE SAD CAFÉ

Evans, Oliver. *The Ballad of Carson McCullers: A Biography,* 126-143.

Griffith, Albert J. "Carson McCullers' Myth of the Sad Café," *Georgia Review* XXI (Spring 1967), 46-56.

Hoffman, Frederick J. *The Art of Southern Fiction,* 68-71.

Phillips, Robert S. "Dinesen's 'Monkey' and McCullers' 'Ballad': A Study in Literary Affinity," *Studies in Short Fiction* I (Spring 1964), 184-190.

―――――. "Painful Love: Carson McCullers' Parable," *Southwest Review* LI (Winter 1966), 80-86.

CLOCK WITHOUT HANDS

Emerson, Donald. "The Ambiguities of *Clock Without Hands,*" *Wisconsin Studies in Contemporary Literature* 3 (Fall 1962), 15-28.

Evans, Oliver. *The Ballad of Carson McCullers: A Biography,* 170-187.

McCULLERS, CARSON, Continued

THE HEART IS A LONELY HUNTER

Evans, Oliver. *The Ballad of Carson McCullers: A Biography,* 36-58, 195-215.

————. "The Case of the Silent Singer: A Revaluation of *The Heart Is a Lonely Hunter,*" *Georgia Review* XIX (Summer 1965) , 188-203.

Madden, David. "The Paradox of the Need for Privacy and the Need for Understanding in Carson McCullers' *The Heart is a Lonely Hunter,*" *Literature and Psychology* XVII (Nos 2 & 3, 1967) , 128-140.

Moore, Jack B. "Carson McCullers: The Heart is a Timeless Hunter," *Twentieth Century Literature* XI (Jul 1965) , 76-81.

Taylor, Horace. "*The Heart is a Lonley Hunter:* A Southern Wasteland," *Studies in American Literature,* 154-160.

THE MEMBER OF THE WEDDING

Evans, Oliver. *The Ballad of Carson McCullers: A Biography,* 97-125.

Phillips, Robert S. "The Gothic Architecture of *The Member of the Wedding,*" *Renascence* XVI (Winter 1964) , 59-72.

REFLECTIONS IN A GOLDEN EYE

Evans, Oliver. *The Ballad of Carson McCullers: A Biography,* 60-81.

GENERAL

Auchincloss, Louis. "Carson McCullers," *Pioneers & Caretakers,* 161-169.

Dodd, Wayne D. "The Development of Theme through Symbol in the Novels of Carson McCullers," *Georgia Review* XVII (Summer 1963) , 206-213.

Eisinger, Chester E. *Fiction of the Forties,* 243-258.

Evans, Oliver. "The Achievement of Carson McCullers," *English Journal* LI (May 1962) , 301-308.

————. *The Ballad of Carson McCullers: A Biography.*

————. "The Case of Carson McCullers," *Georgia Review* XVIII (Spring 1964) , 40-45.

————. "The Theme of Spiritual Isolation in Carson McCullers," *South: Modern Southern Literature in Its Cultural Setting,* 333-348.

Felheim, Marvin. "Eudora Welty and Carson McCullers," *Contemporary American Novelists,* 48-53.

Folk, Barbara Nauer. "The Sad Sweet Music of Carson McCullers," *Georgia Review* XVI (Summer 1962) , 202-209.

Gossett, Louise Y. "Dispossessed Love," *Violence in Recent Southern Fiction,* 159-177.

McCULLERS, CARSON, Continued

Hassan, Ihab. *Radical Innocence: Studies in the Contemporary American Novel,* 205-229.

Hendrick, George. " 'Almost Everyone Wants to Be the Lover': The Fiction of Carson McCullers," *Books Abroad* 42 (Summer 1968), 389-391.

Hoffman, Frederick J. *The Art of Southern Fiction,* 65-73.

Lubbers, Klaus. "The Necessary Order: A Study of Theme and Structure in Carson McCullers' Fiction," *Jahrbuch für Amerikastudien* 8 (1963), 187-204.

Malin, Irving. "The Gothic Family," *Psychoanalysis and American Fiction,* 255-277.

————. *New American Gothic,* 19-26, 54-59, 83-86, 111-117, 133-139.

Micha, René. "Carson MacCullers Ou La Cabane De L'Enfance," *Critique* XVIII (Aug-Sept 1962), 696-707.

Robinson, W. R. "The Life of Carson McCullers' Imagination," *Southern Humanities Review* II (Summer 1968), 291-302.

Rechnitz, Robert M. "The Failure of Love: The Grotesque in Two Novels by Carson McCullers," *Georgia Review* XXII (Winter 1968), 454-463.

Schorer, Mark. "Carson McCullers and Truman Capote," *The World We Imagine: Selected Essays,* 274-285.

————. "McCullers and Capote: Basic Patterns," *The Creative Present,* 84-94.

Symons, Julian. "The Lonely Heart," *Critical Occasions,* 106-111.

Vickery, John B. "Carson McCullers: A Map of Love," *Wisconsin Studies in Contemporary Literature* I (Winter 1960), 13-24.

BIBLIOGRAPHY

Phillips, Robert S. "Carson McCullers: 1956-1964: A Selected Checklist," *Bulletin of Bibliography* XXIV (Sept-Dec 1964), 113-116.

McMURTRY, LARRY

THE LAST PICTURE SHOW

Peavy, Charles D. "Larry McMurtry and Black Humor: A Note on *The Last Picture Show,*" *Western American Literature* II (Fall 1967), 223-227.

BIBLIOGRAPHY

Peavy, Charles D. "A Larry McMurtry Bibliography," *Western American Literature* III (Fall 1968), 235-248.

BILLY BUDD

Barnet, Sylvan. "The Execution in *Billy Budd*," *American Literature* XXXIII (Jan 1962), 517-519.

Bernstein, John. *Pacifism and Rebellion in the Writings of Herman Melville,* 202-213.

Berthoff, Werner. " 'Certain Phenomenal Men': The Example of *Billy Budd*," *ELH* 27 (Dec 1960) 334-351.

————. *The Example of Melville,* 182-203.

Bowen, Merlin. *The Long Encounter: Self and Experience in the Writings of Herman Melville,* 216-233.

————. "On *Billy Budd*," *Critical Approaches to American Literature: Volume I, Roger Williams to Herman Melville,* 326-339.

Brodtkorb, Paul, Jr. "The Definitive *Billy Budd:* 'But Aren't It All Sham?,' " *PMLA* LXXXII (Dec 1967), 602-612.

Callan, Richard J. "The Burden of Innocence in Melville and Twain," *Renascence* XVII (Summer 1965), 191-194.

Chandler, Alice. "Captain Vere and the 'Tragedies of the Palace,' " *Modern Fiction Studies* XIII (Summer 1967), 259-261.

Dillistone, F. W. "The Angel Must Hang," *The Novelist and the Passion Story,* 45-68.

Doubleday, Neal F. "Jack Easy and *Billy Budd*," *English Language Notes* II (Sept 1964), 39-42.

Dryden, Edgar A. *Melville's Thematics of Form,* 209-216.

Duerksen, Roland A. "Caleb Williams, Political Justice, and *Billy Budd*," *American Literature* XXXVIII (Nov 1966), 372-376.

————. "The Deep Quandry in *Billy Budd*," *New England Quarterly* XLI (Mar 1968), 51-66.

Ellen, Sister Mary, I.H.M. "Parallels in Contrast: A Study of Melville's Imagery in *Moby Dick* and *Billy Budd*," *Studies in Short Fiction* II (Spring 1965), 284-290.

Ensslen, Klaus. "Melvilles Erzählungen," Beihefte zum *Jahrbuch für Amerikastudien* 14 (1966), 144-173.

Fite, Olive L. "Billy Budd, Claggart, and Schopenhauer," *Nineteenth-Century Fiction* XXIII (Dec 1968), 336-343.

Fogle, Richard Harter. "*Billy Budd:* The Order of the Fall," *Nineteenth-Century Fiction* XV (Dec 1960), 189-205.

Frank, Max. *Die Farb—und Lichtsymbolik im Prosawerk Herman Melvilles,* 137-143.

MELVILLE, HERMAN, Continued

Franklin, H. Bruce. *The Wake of the Gods: Melville's Mythology*, 188-202.

Gaskins, Avery F. "Symbolic Nature of Claggart's Name," *American Notes & Queries* VI (Dec 1967) , 56.

Geismar, Maxwell. Introduction, *Billy Budd and Typee* (New York, 1962) .

Hagopian, John V. and Martin Dolch. *Insight I: Analyses of American Literature*, 155-165.

Hall, Joan Joffe. "The Historical Chapters in *Billy Budd*," *University Review* XXX (Oct 1963) , 35-40.

Harford, Harrison and Merton M. Sealtz, Jr. Introduction, *Billy Budd, Sailor (An Inside Narrative: Reading Text and Genetic Text* (Chicago, 1962) .

Hillway, Tyrus. *Herman Melville*, 138-144.

Howard, Leon. "Herman Melville," *Six American Novelists of the Nineteenth Century*, 115-117.

Ives, C. B. "*Billy Budd* and the Articles of War," *American Literature* XXXIV (Mar 1962) , 31-39.

Kallapur, S. T. "*Billy Budd:* A Study in Ambivalence," *Journal of the Karnatak University* X (1966) , 53-60.

Kilbourne, W. G., Jr. "Montaigne and Captain Vere," *American Literature* XXXIII (Jan 1962) , 514-517.

Ledbetter, Kenneth. "The Ambiguity of *Billy Budd*," *Texas Studies in Literature and Language* IV (Spring 1962) , 130-134.

Lemon, Lee T. "*Billy Budd:* The Plot Against the Story," *Studies in Short Fiction* II (Fall 1964) , 32-43.

London, Philip W. "The Military Necessity; *Billy Budd* and Vigny," *Comparative Literature* XIV (Spring 1962) , 174-186.

Malbone, Raymond G. "How Shall We Teach the New Billy Budd, Sailor?" *College English* XXVII (Mar 1966) , 499-500.

Mansfield, Luther Stearns. "Some Patterns from Melville's 'Loom of Time,' " *Essays on Determinism in American Literature*, 30-35.

Maxwell, D. E. S. *Herman Melville*, 88-96.

McNamara, Anne. "Melville's *Billy Budd*," *Explicator* XXI (Oct 1962) , No. 11.

Miller, James E., Jr. "*Billy Budd:* The Catastrophe of Innocence," *A Reader's Guide to Herman Melville*, 218-228.

Millgate, Michael. "Melville and Marvell: A Note on *Billy Budd*," *English Studies* XLIX (Feb 1968) , 47-50.

Montale, Eugenio. "An Introduction to *Billy Budd*," *Sewanee Review* LXVIII (Summer 1960), 419-422.

Monteiro, George. "Melville and Keats," *Emerson Society Quarterly* 31 (II Quarter 1963), 55.

Nathanson, Leonard. "Melville's *Billy Budd*," *Explicator* XXII (May 1964), No. 75.

Rathbun, John W. "*Billy Budd* and the Limits of Perception," *Nineteenth-Century Fiction* XX (Jun 1965), 19-34.

Reich, Charles A. "The Tragedy of Justice in *Billy Budd*," *Yale Review* LVI (Spring 1967), 368-389.

Reid, B. L. "Old Melville's Fable," *Massachusetts Review* IX (Summer 1968), 529-546.

Renvoisé, J. P. "Billy Budd: Opéra de Benjamin Britten." *Études Anglaises* XVIII (Oct-Dec 1965), 367-382.

Rogers, Robert. "The 'Ineludible Gripe' of *Billy Budd*," *Literature and Psychology* XIV (Winter 1964), 9-22.

Rosenberry, Edward H. "The Problem of *Billy Budd*," *PMLA* LXXX (Dec 1965), 489-498.

Shattuck, Robert. "Two Inside Narratives: *Billy Budd* and *L'Etranger*," *Texas Studies in Literature and Language* IV (Autumn 1962), 314-320.

Sherwood, John C. "Vere as Collingwood: A Key to *Billy Budd*," *American Literature* XXXV (Jan 1964), 476-484.

Shulman, Robert. "Melville's 'Timoleon': From Plutarch to the Early Stages of *Billy Budd*," *Comparative Literature* XIX (Fall 1967), 351-361.

————. "Montaigne and the Techniques and Tragedy of Melville's *Billy Budd*," *Comparative Literature* XVI (Fall 1964), 322-330.

Stafford, William T. "The New *Billy Budd* and the Novelistic Fallacy: An Essay-Review," *Modern Fiction Studies* VIII (Autumn 1962), 306-311.

Stein, William Bysshe. "*Billy Budd:* The Nightmare of History," *Criticism* III (Summer 1961), 237-250.

————. "The Motif of the Wise Old Man in *Billy Budd*," *Western Humanities Review* XIV (Winter 1960), 99-101.

Stokes, Gary. "The Dansker, Melville's Manifesto on Survival," *English Journal* LVII (Oct 1968), 980-981.

Suits, Bernard. "*Billy Budd* and Historical Evidence: A Rejoinder," *Nineteenth-Century Fiction* XVIII (Dec 1963), 288-291.

Sutton, Walter. "Melville and the Great God Budd," *Prairie Schooner* XXXIV (Summer 1960), 128-133.

Thorp, Willard. Afterword, *Billy Budd and Other Tales* (New York, 1961).

West, Ray B., Jr. "The Unity of *Billy Budd*," *The Writer in the Room: Selected Essays*, 48-59.

Widmer, Kingsley. "The Perplexed Myths of Melville: *Billy Budd*," *Novel* 2 (Fall 1968), 25-35.

Willett, Ralph W. "Nelson and Vere: Hero and Victim in *Billy Budd, Sailor*," *PMLA* LXXXII (Oct 1967), 370-376.

Wilson, G. R., Jr. "*Billy Budd* and Melville's Use of Dramatic Technique," *Studies in Short Fiction* IV (Winter 1967), 105-111.

Yang, Byung-Taik. "Billy Budd," *English Language and Literature* 26 (Summer 1968), 36-57. (In Korean).

THE CONFIDENCE MAN

Anderson, David D. "Melville and Mark Twain in Rebellion," *Mark Twain Journal* XI (Fall 1961), 8-9.

Drew, Philip. "Appearance and Reality in Melville's *The Confidence-Man*," *ELH* XXXI (Dec 1964), 418-442.

Dubler, Walter. "Theme and Structure in Melville's *The Confidence Man*," *American Literature* XXXIII (Nov 1961), 307-319.

Grauman, Lawrence, Jr. "Suggestions on the Future of *The Confidence-Man*," *Papers on English Language and Literature* I (Summer 1965), 241-249.

Hoffman, Daniel G. *Form and Fable in American Fiction*, 279-313.

Bernstein, John. *Pacifism and Rebellion in the Writings of Herman Melville*, 146-164.

Cohen, Hennig. Introduction, *The Confidence Man* (New York, 1964).

Dryden, Edgar E. *Melville's Thematics of Form*, 149-195.

Franklin, H. Bruce. Introduction, *Confidence Man: His Masquerade* (New York, 1967).

————. *The Wake of the Gods: Melville's Mythology*, 153-187.

Fussell, Edwin. "Herman Melville," *Frontier: American Literature and the American West*, 303-326.

Hoffman, Daniel G. "The Confidence-Man: His Masquerade," *Melville: A Collection of Critical Essays*, 125-143.

Humphreys, A. R. *Melville*, 102-110.

Ishag, Saada. "Herman Melville as Existentialist: An Analysis of

Typee, Mardi, Moby Dick, and *The Confidence Man," The American Novel: Two Studies,* 32-41.

Karcher, Carolyn Lury. "The Story of Charlemont: A Dramatization of Melville's Concepts of Fiction in *The Confidence-Man: His Masquerade," Nineteenth-Century Fiction* XXI (Jun 1966), 73-84.

Lang, Hans-Joachim. "Ein Ärgerteufel bei Hawthorne und Melville: Quellenuntersuchung zu *The Confidence-Man," Jahrbuch für Amerikastudien* 12 (1967), 246-251.

Lewis, R. W. B. *Trials of the Word,* 61-76.

Magaw, Malcolm O. "*The Confidence-Man* and Christian Deity: Melville's Imagery of Ambiguity," *Explorations of Literature,* 81-99.

Maxwell, D. E. S. *Herman Melville,* 68-87.

McCarthy, Paul. "The 'Soldier of Fortune' in Melville's *The Confidence Man," Emerson Society Quarterly* 33 (IV Quarter 1963), 21-24.

Miller, James E., Jr. "*The Confidence Man:* A Comic Masquerade," *A Reader's Guide to Herman Melville,* 170-192.

Mitchell, Edward. "From Action to Essence: Some Notes on the Structure of Melville's *The Confidence-Man," American Literature* 40 (Mar 1968), 27-37.

Orth, Ralph H. "An Early Review of *The Confidence-Man," Emerson Society Quarterly* 43 (II Quarter 1966), 48.

Parker, Hershel. "The Metaphysics of Indian-Hating," *Nineteenth-Century Fiction* XVIII (Sept 1963), 165-173.

Seelye, John. Introduction, *The Confidence-Man* (San Francisco, 1968).

―――――. "Timothy Flint's 'Wicked River' and *The Confidence-Man," PMLA* LXXVIII (Mar 1963), 75-79.

Seltzer, Leon F. "Camus's Absurd and the World of Melville's *Confidence-Man," PMLA* LXXXII (Mar 1967), 14-27.

Smith, Paul. "*The Confidence-Man* and the Literary World of New York," *Nineteenth-Century Fiction* XVI (Mar 1962), 329-337.

Swanson, Donald R. "The Structure of *The Confidence Man," CEA Critic* XXX (May 1968), 6-7.

Travis, Mildred K. "Spenserian Analogues in *Mardi* and *The Confidence Man," Emerson Society Quarterly* 50 (I Quarter 1968), 55-58.

Tuveson, Ernest. "The Creed of *The Confidence-Man," ELH* XXXIII (Jun 1966), 247-270.

Weissbuch, Ted N. "A Note on the Confidence-Man's Counterfeit Detector," *Emerson Society Quarterly* 19 (II Quarter 1960) , 16-18.

ISRAEL POTTER

Bernstein, John. *Pacifism and Rebellion in the Writings of Herman Melville,* 146-164.

Cecchi, Emilia. "Two Notes on Melville," *Sewanee Review* LXVIII (Summer 1960) , 400-406.

Dryden, Edgar E. *Melville's Thematics of Form,* 115-148.

Farnsworth, Robert M. "*Israel Potter:* Pathetic Comedy," *Bulletin of the New York Public Library* LXV (Feb 1961) , 125-132.

Fussell, Edwin. "Herman Melville," *Frontier: American Literature and the American West,* 294-299.

Hull, Raymona. "London and Melville's *Israel Potter,*" *Emerson Society Quarterly* 47 (II Quarter 1967) , 78-81.

Jackson, Kenny. "Israel Potter: Melville's 'Fourth of July Story,' " *CLA Journal* VI (Mar 1963) , 194-204.

Kriegel, Leonard. Introduction, *Life and Remarkable Adventures of Israel Potter* (New York, 1962) .

Miller, James E., Jr. "*Israel Potter:* Survival in the Desert," *A Reader's Guide to Herman Melville,* 140-151.

Russell, Jack. "*Israel Potter* and 'Song of Myself,' " *American Literature* 40 (Mar 1968) , 72-77.

MARDI

Bernstein, John. *Pacifism and Rebellion in the Writings of Herman Melville,* 31-56.

Blansett, Barbara Niewig. " 'From Dark to Dark': *Mardi:* A Foreshadowing of *Pierre,*" *Southern Quarterly* I (Apr 1963) , 213-227.

Bowen, Merlin. *The Long Encounter: Self and Experience in the Writings of Herman Melville,* 140-143, 204-209.

Davison, Richard Allan. "Melville's *Mardi* and John Skelton," *Emerson Society Quarterly* 43 (II Quarter 1966) , 86-87.

Dryden, Edgar A. *Melville's Thematics of Form,* 46-58.

Fiedler, Leslie A. *Love and Death in the American Novel,* 295-298.

Finkelstein, Dorothee M. *Melville's Orienda,* 189-223.

Franklin, H. Bruce. *The Wake of the Gods: Melville's Mythology,* 17-52.

Fussell, Edwin. "Herman Melville," *Frontier: American Literature and the American West,* 240-248.

MELVILLE, HERMAN, Continued

Guido, John F. "Melville's *Mardi;* Bentley's Blunder?" *Papers of the Bibliographical Society of America* LXII (Jul-Sept 1968), 361-371.

Hillway, Tyrus. *Herman Melville,* 78-83.

Howard, Leon. "Herman Melville," *Six American Novelists of the Nineteenth Century,* 88-90.

Ishag, Saada. "Herman Melville as Existentialist: An Analysis of *Typee, Mardi, Moby Dick,* and *The Confidence Man,*" *The American Novel: Two Studies,* 13-18.

Kaplan, Sidney. "Herman Melville and the American National Sin," *Images of the Negro in American Literature,* 138-141.

Lanzinger, Klaus. "Melvilles Beschreibung des Meeres in *Mardi* im Hinblick auf *Moby-Dick,*" *Neueren Sprachen* (Jan 1960), 1-15.

Levine, Stuart. "Melville's 'Voyage Thither,'" *Midwest Quarterly* III (Summer 1962), 341-353.

Mayoux, Jean-Jacques. *Melville,* 49-55.

Miller, James E., Jr. *"Mardi:* The Search for Innocence," *A Reader's Guide to Herman Melville,* 36-53.

Shroeder, John. "'Some Unfortunate Idyllic Love Affair': The Legends of Taji and Jay Gatsby," *Books At Brown* XXII (1968), 143-153.

Travis, Mildred K. *"Mardi:* Melville's Allegory of Love," *Emerson Society Quarterly* 43 (II Quarter 1966), 88-94.

————. "Melville's Furies: Technique in *Mardi* and *Moby-Dick,*" *Emerson Society Quarterly* 47 (II Quarter 1967), 71-73.

————. "Spenserian Analogues in *Mardi* and *The Confidence Man,*" *Emerson Society Quarterly* 50 (I Quarter 1968), 55-58.

MOBY-DICK

Anderson, Quentin. Introduction, *Moby Dick* (New York, 1962).

Aspiz, Harold. "Phrenologizing the Whale," *Nineteenth-Century Fiction* XXIII (Jun 1968), 18-27.

Austin, Allen. "The Three-Stranded Allegory of Moby-Dick," *College English* XXVI (Feb 1965), 344-349.

Bell, Millicent. "The Irreducible *Moby-Dick,*" *Emerson Society Quarterly* 28 (III Quarter 1962), 4-6.

Bernstein, John. *Pacifism and Rebellion in the Writings of Herman Melville,* 82-125.

Berthoff, Warner. *The Example of Melville,* 78-98, 159-170, 175-182.

————. "Characterization in *Moby Dick,*" *Moby Dick: An Authorita-*

tive Text; Reviews and Letters by Melville; Analogues and Sources; Criticism, 702-708.

Boies, J. J. "The Whale Without Epilogue," *Modern Language Quarterly* XXIV (Jun 1963), 172-176.

Bowden, Edwin T. *The Dungeon of the Heart: Human Isolation and the American Novel,* 156-172.

Bowen, Merlin. *The Long Encounter: Self and Experience in the Writings of Herman Melville,* 143-157, 240-252.

Brashers, H. C. "Ishmael's Tattoos," *Sewanee Review* LXX (Winter 1962), 137-154.

Braswell, William. "The Main Theme of *Moby-Dick,*" *Emerson Society Quarterly* 28 (III Quarter 1962), 15-17.

Braude, William G. "Melville's *Moby Dick,*" *Explicator* XXI (Nov 1962), No. 23.

Bridgman, Richard. *The Colloquial Style in America,* 69-72.

Brodtkorb, Paul, Jr. *Ishmael's White World: A Phenomenological Reading of Moby Dick.*

Burgert, Hans. "William Faulkner on '*Moby-Dick*': An Early Letter," *Studi Americani* IX (1964), 371-375.

Cambon, Glauco. "La Caccia Ermeneutica A *Moby-Dick,*" *Studi Americani* VIII (1962), 9-19.

Cameron, Kenneth Walter. "A Note on the Corpusants in *Moby Dick,*" *Emerson Society Quarterly* 19 (II Quarter 1960), 22-24.

——————. "Etymological Significance of Melville's *Pequod,*" *Emerson Society Quarterly* 29 (IV Quarter 1962), 3-4.

Cecchi, Emilio. "Two Notes on Melville," *Sewanee Review* LXVIII (Summer 1960), 398-400.

Clark, Harry Hayden. "American Literary History and American Literature," *Reinterpretations of American Literature,* 207-212.

Cleopatra, Sr. "*Moby-Dick:* An Interpretation," *Literary Half-Yearly* VI (Jul 1965), 49-54.

Clough, Wilson O. *The Necessary Earth: Nature and Solitude in American Literature,* 125-131.

Clubb, Merrel D. "The Second Personal Pronoun in *Moby-Dick,*" *American Speech* XXXV (Dec 1960), 252-260.

Cowan, S. A. "In Praise of Self-Reliance: The Role of Bulkington in *Moby-Dick,*" *American Literature* XXXVIII (Jan 1967), 547-556.

Dahlberg, Edward. "Moby-Dick: An Hamitic Dream," *Literary Review* IV (Autumn 1960), 87-118.

————. "Moby Dick: An Hamitic Dream," *Varieties of Literary Experience: Eighteen Essays in World Literature,* 183-213.

D'Avanzo, Mario L. " 'The Cassock' and Carlyle's 'Church-Clothes,' " *Emerson Society Quarterly* 50 (I Quarter 1968) , 74-76.

Dillingham, William B. "The Narrator of *Moby-Dick,*" *English Studies* XLIX (Feb 1968) 20-29.

Discussions of Moby Dick.

Dryden, Edgar E. *Melville's Thematics of Form,* 81-113.

Eby, Cecil D., Jr. "Another Breaching of 'Mocha Dick,' " *English Language Notes* IV (Jun 1967) , 277-279.

————. "William Starbuck Mayo and Herman Melville," *New England Quarterly* XXXV (Dec 1962) , 515-523.

Ellen, Sister Mary, I.H.M. "Duplicate Imagery in *Moby-Dick,*" *Modern Fiction Studies* VIII (Autumn 1962) , 252-275.

————. "Parallels in Contrast: A Study of Melville's Imagery in *Moby Dick* and *Billy Budd,*" *Studies in Short Fiction* II (Spring 1965) , 284-290.

Farnsworth, Robert M. "Ishmael to the Royal Masthead," *University of Kansas City Review* XXVIII (Mar 1962) , 183-190.

Feidelson, Charles. Introduction, *Moby Dick* (Indianapolis, Indiana, 1964) .

Fiedler, Leslie A. *Love and Death in the American Novel,* 520-552.

Finkelstein, Dorothee M. *Melville's Orienda,* 223-239.

Foster, Charles H. "Something in Emblems: A Reinterpretation of Moby-Dick," *New England Quarterly* XXXIV (Mar 1961) , 3-35.

Frank, Max. *Die Farb—und Lichtsymbolik im Prosawerk Herman Melvilles,* 93-115.

Franklin, H. Bruce. *The Wake of the Gods: Melville's Mythology,* 53-98.

Fussell, Edwin. "Herman Melville," *Frontier: American Literature and the American West,* 256-280.

Gale, Robert L. "Melville's *Moby Dick,* Chapters 91-93," *Explicator* XXII (Jan 1964) , No. 32.

Gibson, William M. Introduction, *Moby Dick* (New York, 1959) .

Gleason, Philip. "*Moby-Dick:* Meditation for Democracy," *Personalist* XLIV (Oct 1963) , 499-517.

Goldfarb, Russell and Clare. "The Doubloon in *Moby Dick,*" *Midwest Quarterly* II (Spring 1961) , 251-258.

MELVILLE, HERMAN, Continued

Green, Martin. *Re-Appraisals: Some Commonsense Readings in American Literature,* 87-108.

Guetti, James. *The Limits of Metaphor: A Study of Melville, Conrad, and Faulkner,* 12-45.

Halverson, John. "The Shadow in *Moby-Dick,*" *American Quarterly* XV (Fall 1963) , 436-446.

Heimert, Alan. "*Moby-Dick* and American Politicial Symbolism," *American Quarterly* XV (Winter 1963) , 498-534.

Heller, Louis G. "Two Pequot Names in American Literature," *American Speech* XXXVI (Feb 1961) , 54-57.

Hillway, Tyrus. *Herman Melville,* 83-106.

Hirsch, David H. "The Dilemma of the Liberal Intellectual: Melville's Ishmael," *Texas Studies in Literature and Language* V (Summer 1963) , 169-188.

———. "Melville's Ishmaelite," *American Notes & Queries* V (Apr 1967) , 115-116.

Hoffman, Daniel G. *Form and Fable in American Fiction,* 221-278.

———. "*Moby-Dick:* Jonah's Whale or Job's?" *Sewanee Review* LXIX (Spring 1961) , 205-224.

Horsford, Howard C. "The Design of the Argument in *Moby-Dick,*" *Modern Fiction Studies* VIII (Autumn 1962) , 233-251.

Howard, Leon. "Herman Melville: *Moby Dick,*" *The American Novel from James Fenimore Cooper to William Faulkner,* 25-34.

———. "Herman Melville," *Six American Novelists of the Nineteenth Century,* 94-101.

Humphreys, A. R. *Melville,* 41-82.

Isani, Mukhtar Ali. "Melville and the 'Bloody Battle in Affghanistan,'" *American Quarterly* XX (Fall 1968) , 645-649.

———. "The Naming of Fedallah in *Moby-Dick,*" *American Literature* 40 (Nov 1968) , 380-385.

Ishag, Saada. "Herman Melville as Existentialist: An Analysis of *Typee, Mardi, Moby Dick,* and *The Confidence Man,*" *The American Novel: Two Studies,* 19-31.

Jaffé, David. "The Captain Who Sat for the Portrait of Ahab," *Boston University Studies in English* IV (Spring 1960) , 1-22.

Kallapur, S. T. "*The Old Man and the Sea:* Three Parallels," *Journal of the Karnatak University* IX (1965) , 108-117.

Kaplan, Charles. "Jack Burden: Modern Ishmael," *College English* XXII (Oct 1960) , 19-24.

Kaplan, Sidney. "Herman Melville and the American National Sin," *Images of the Negro in American Literature,* 146-150.

Kim, Suk-Ju. "A Study of Melville's Counter-Point Symbol," *English Language and Literature* 8 (Jun 1960), 91-106. (In Korean).

Kim, Yong-Kwon. "Landscape Imagery in *Moby-Dick,*" *English Language and Literature* 20 (Winter 1966), 110-113.

Kosok, Heinz. "Ishmael's Audience in 'The Town-Ho's Story,' " *Notes and Queries* N.S. 14 (Feb 1967), 54-56.

Lanzinger, Klaus. "Melvilles Beschreibung des Meeres in *Mardi* im Hinblick auf *Moby-Dick,*" *Neueren Sprachen* (Jan 1960), 1-15.

La Violette, Wesley. "*Moby-Dick:* A Study in Symphonic Prose," *Literary Criterion* IV (Summer 1960), 19-23.

Lefcowitz, Allan and Barbara. "Ahab's Other Leg: Notes on Melville's Symbolic Method," *Emerson Society Quarterly* 47 (II Quarter 1967), 23-28.

Liebman, Sheldon W. "The 'Body and Soul' Metaphor in *Moby-Dick,*" *Emerson Society Quarterly* 50 (I Quarter 1968), 29-34.

Mansfield, Luther Stearns. "Some Patterns from Melville's 'Loom of Time,' " *Essays on Determinism in American Literature,* 20, 24-25, 29-30.

―――――. "Symbolism and Biblical Allusion in *Moby-Dick,*" *Emerson Society Quarterly* 28 (III Quarter 1962), 20-23.

Markels, Julian. "*King Lear* and *Moby-Dick:* The Cultural Connection," *Massachusetts Review* IX (Winter 1968), 169-176.

Marx, Leo. *The Machine in the Garden: Technology and the Pastoral Ideal in America,* 277-319.

Maxwell, D. E. S. *Herman Melville,* 32-53.

Maxwell, J. C. "Three Notes on *Moby Dick,*" *Notes and Queries* N. S. 14 (Feb 1967), 53.

Mayoux, Jean-Jacques. *Melville,* 59-94.

McAleer, John J. "Poe and Gothic Elements in *Moby-Dick,*" *Emerson Society Quarterly* 27 (II Quarter 1962), 34.

McCarthy, Paul. "A Note on Teaching *Moby Dick,*" *Emerson Society Quarterly* 35 (II Quarter 1964), 73-79.

McClary, Ben Harris. "Melville's *Moby Dick,*" *Explicator* XXI (Sept 1962), No. 9.

Mengeling, Marvin E. "Moby-Dick: The Fundamental Principles," *Emerson Society Quarterly* 38 (I Quarter 1965), 74-87.

MELVILLE, HERMAN, Continued

Miller, James E. "Hawthorne and Melville: No! in Thunder," *Quests Surd and Absurd: Essays in American Literature*, 196-198, 206-207.

————. "Hawthorne and Melville: The Unpardonable Sin," *Quests Surd and Absurd: Essays in American Literature*, 227-238.

————. "*Moby Dick:* The Grand Hooded Phantom," *A Reader's Guide to Herman Melville*, 75-117.

Mizener, Arthur. "Herman Melville: *Moby Dick*," *Twelve Great American Novels*, 19-33.

Moore, Jack B. "*Ahab* and *Bartleby:* Energy and Indolence," *Studies in Short Fiction* I (Summer 1964), 291-294.

Oliver, Egbert S. "To Light the Gay Bridals: One Aspect of Moby-Dick," *Emerson Society Quarterly* 35 (II Quarter 1964), 30-34.

————. "To Light the Gay Bridals: One Aspect of Moby-Dick," *Studies in American Literature: Whitman, Emerson, Melville, and Others*, 78-85.

Pagnini, Marcello. "Struttura Ideologica E Struttura Stilistica in *Moby-Dick*," *Studi Americani* VI (1960), 87-134.

Pavese, Cesare. "The Literary Whaler," *Sewanee Review* LXVIII (Summer 1960), 407-418.

Pilkington, William T. " 'Benito Cereno' and the 'Valor-Ruined Man' of *Moby-Dick*," *Texas Studies in Literature and Language* VII (Summer 1965), 201-207.

Powers, William. "Bulkington as Henry Chatillon," *Western American Literature* III (Summer 1968), 153-155.

Reid, John T. *Indian Influences in American Literature and Thought,* 52-55.

Roper, Gordon. "On Teaching *Moby-Dick*," *Emerson Society Quarterly* 28 (III Quarter 1962), 2-4.

Rosenfeld, William. "Uncertain Faith: Queequeg's Coffin and Melville's Use of the Bible," *Texas Studies in Literature and Language* VII (Winter 1966), 317-327.

Ross, Morton L. "Captain Truck and Captain Boomer," *American Literature* XXXVII (Nov 1965), 316.

Rust, R. Dilworth. "Vision in *Moby Dick*," *Emerson Society Quarterly* 33 (IV Quarter 1963), 73-75.

Schless, Howard H. "*Moby Dick* and Dante," *Bulletin of the New York Public Library* LXV (May 1961), 289-312.

Schroeder, Fred E. H. "Enter Ahab, Then All: Theatrical Elements in Melville's Fiction," *Dalhousie Review* 46 (Summer 1966), 223-232.

Seelye, John D. "The Golden Navel: The Cabalism of Ahab's Doubloon," *Nineteenth-Century Fiction* XIV (Mar 1960), 350-355.

Senescu, Betty Cobey. "Melville's *Moby Dick*," *Explicator* XXV (May 1967), No. 78.

Sewall, Richard B. "Moby Dick as Tragedy," *Moby Dick: An Authoritative Text; Reviews and Letters by Melville; Analogues and Sources; Criticism,* 692-702.

Shulman, Robert. "Melville's Thomas Fuller: An Outline for Starbuck and an Instance of the Creator as Critic," *Modern Language Quarterly* XXIII (Dec 1962), 337-352.

————. "The Serious Functions of Melville's Phallic Jokes," *American Literature* XXXIII (May 1961), 179-194.

Stanonik, Janez. *Moby Dick, the Myth and Symbol: A Study in Folklore and Literature.*

Stavrou, C. N. "Ahab and Dick Again," *Texas Studies in Literature and Language* III (Autumn 1961), 309-320.

Stern, Milton R. "Melville's Tragic Imagination: The Hero Without a Home," *Patterns of Commitment in American Literature,* 42-50.

Stone, Edward. *Voices of Despair,* 93-102.

Sullivan, Sister Mary Petrus. "*Moby-Dick:* Chapter CXXIX, 'The Cabin,' " *Nineteenth-Century Fiction* XX (Sept 1965), 188-190.

Sutcliffe, Denham. Afterword, *Moby Dick* (New York, 1961).

Tanselle, G. Thomas. "A Further Note on 'Whiteness' in Melville and Others," *PMLA* LXXXI (Dec 1966), 604.

Travis, Mildred K. "Melville's Furies: Technique in *Mardi* and *Moby-Dick*," *Emerson Society Quarterly* 47 (II Quarter 1967), 71-73.

Tucker, Harry, Jr. "A Glance at 'Whiteness' in Melville and Camus," *PMLA* LXXX (Dec 1965), 605.

Van Nostrand, A. D. "The Linked Analogies of *Moby Dick*," *Everyman His Own Poet,* 113-140.

Vargish, Thomas. "Gnostic Mythos in *Moby-Dick*," *PMLA* LXXXI (Jun 1966), 272-277.

Walcutt, Charles Child. "Quest for the Antagonist: Herman Melville's *Moby Dick*," *Man's Changing Mask: Modes and Methods of Characterization in Fiction,* 104-123.

————. "The Soundings of *Moby Dick*," *Arizona Quarterly* 24 (Summer 1968), 101-116.

Weathers, Willie T. "*Moby-Dick* and the Nineteenth-Century Scene," *Texas Studies in Literature and Language* I (Winter 1960), 477-501.

Weissbuch, Ted N. and Bruce Stillians. "Ishmael the Ironist: The Anti-Salvation Theme in Moby-Dick," *Emerson Society Quarterly* 31 (II Quarter 1963), 71-75.

West, Ray B., Jr. "Primitivism in Melville," *The Writer in the Room: Selected Essays,* 35-44.

Williams, David Park. "Hook and Ahab: Barrie's Strange Satire on Melville," *PMLA* LXXX (Dec 1965), 483-488.

Woodruff, Stuart C. "Stubb's Supper," *Emerson Society Quarterly* 43 (II Quarter 1966), 46-48.

Woodson, Thomas. "Ahab's Greatness: Prometheus as Narcissus," *ELH* (Sept 1966), 351-369.

Wright, Nathalia. "*Moby Dick:* Jonah's or Job's Whale?" *American Literature* XXXVII (May 1965), 190-195.

Yu, Beongcheon. "Ishmael's Equal Eye: The Source of Balance in *Moby-Dick,*" *ELH* XXXII (Mar 1965), 110-125.

OMOO

Brooks, Van Wyck. Introduction, *Omoo* (New York, 1967).

Bernstein, John. *Pacifism and Rebellion in the Writings of Herman Melville,* 15-30.

Eigner, Edwin M. "The Romantic Unity of Melville's *Omoo,*" *Philological Quarterly* XLVI (Jan 1967), 95-108.

Miller, James E., Jr. "*Typee* and *Omoo:* The Quest for the Garden," *A Reader's Guide to Herman Melville,* 18-37.

The Writings of Herman Melville, vol. II. Northwestern-Newberry Edition (Evanston and Chicago, Illinois, 1968).

PIERRE

Bernstein, John. *Pacifism and Rebellion in the Writings of Herman Melville,* 126-145.

Berthoff, Warner. *The Example of Melville,* 47-54.

Blansett, Barbara Niewig. "'From Dark to Dark': *Mardi,* a Foreshadowing of *Pierre,*" *Southern Quarterly* I (Apr 1963), 213-227.

Bush, C. W. "This Stupendous Fabric: the Metaphysics of Order in Melville's *Pierre* and Nathanael West's *Miss Lonelyhearts,*" *Journal of American Studies* I (Oct 1967), 269-274.

Davison, Richard Allan. "Redburn, Pierre and Robin: Melville's Debt to Hawthorne?" *Emerson Society Quarterly* 47 (II Quarter 1967), 32-34.

Dryden, Edgar E. *Melville's Thematics of Form,* 115-148.

Fiedler, Leslie A. *Love and Death in the American Novel,* 403-408.

Frank, Max. *Die Farb—und Lichtsymbolik im Prosawerk Herman Melvilles,* 116-127.

Franklin, H. Bruce. *The Wake of the Gods: Melville's Mythology,* 99-125.

Fussell, Edwin. "Herman Melville," *Frontier: American Literature and the American West,* 280-294.

Gupta, R. K. "Melville's Use of Non-Novelistic Conventions in *Pierre,"* Emerson Society Quarterly 48 (III Quarter 1967), 141-145.

Hillway, Tyrus. *Herman Melville,* 106-112.

Howard, Leon. "Herman Melville," *Six American Novelists of the Nineteenth Century,* 101-105.

Humphreys, A. R. *Melville,* 83-92.

Kimmey, John L. "Pierre and Robin: Melville's Debt to Hawthorne," *Emerson Society Quarterly* 38 (I Quarter 1965), 90-92.

Maxwell, J. C. "Melville and Milton," *Notes and Queries* N.S. 12 (Feb 1965), 60.

Mayoux, Jean-Jacques. *Melville,* 100-111.

Miller, James E., Jr. *"Pierre:* The Flowing River in the Cave of Man," *A Reader's Guide to Herman Melville,* 118-139.

Mogan, Joseph J., Jr. *"Pierre* and *Manfred:* Melville's Study of the Byronic Hero," *Papers on English Language and Literature* I (Summer 1965), 230-240.

Poggi, Valentina. *"Pierre:* Il 'Kraken' Di Melville," *Studi Americani* X (1964), 71-100.

Schless, Howard H. "Flaxman, Dante, and Melville's *Pierre,"* Bulletin of the New York Public Library LXIV (Feb 1960), 65-82.

Travis, Mildred K. "The Idea of Poe in *Pierre,"* Emerson Society Quarterly 50 (I Quarter 1968), 59-62.

Watkins, Floyd C. "Melville's Plotinus Plinlimmon and Pierre," *Reality and Myth: Essays in American Literature in Memory of Richmond Croom Beatty,* 39-51.

Wright, Nathalia. *"Pierre:* Herman Melville's *Inferno,"* American Literature XXXII (May 1960), 167-181.

REDBURN

Bernstein, John. *Pacifism and Rebellion in the Writings of Herman Melville,* 57-67.

Berthoff, Warner. *The Example of Melville,* 30-36.

Davison, Richard Allan. "Redburn, Pierre and Robin: Melville's Debt

MELVILLE, HERMAN, Continued

to Hawthorne?" *Emerson Society Quarterly* 47 (II Quarter 1967), 32-34.

Dryden, Edgar A. *Melville's Thematics of Form*, 58-67.

Fiess, Edward. "Byron's Dark Blue Ocean and Melville's Rolling Sea," *English Language Notes* III (Jun 1966), 274-278.

Franklin, H. Bruce. "Redburn's Wicked Eye," *Nineteenth-Century Fiction* XX (Sept 1965), 190-194.

Gozzi, Raymond D. "Melville's *Redburn: Civilization and Its Discontents*," *Literature and Psychology* XIII (Fall 1963), 104.

Humphreys, A. R. *Melville*, 28-40.

Kosok, Heinz. " 'A Sadder and a wiser boy': Herman Melvilles *Redburn* als novel of initiation," *Jahrbuch Für Amerikastudien* 10 (1965), 126-152.

——. "Redburn's Image of Childhood," *Emerson Society Quarterly* 39 (II Quarter 1965), 40-42.

Lish, Terrence G. "Melville's *Redburn:* A Study in Dualism," *English Language Notes* V (Dec 1967), 113-120.

Maxwell, J. C. "Melville Allusion to Pope," *American Notes and Queries* III (Sept 1964), 7.

Miller, James E., Jr. "*Redburn* and *White Jacket:* Initiation and Baptism," *A Reader's Guide to Herman Melville*, 54-74.

TYPEE

Bernstein, John. *Pacifism and Rebellion in the Writings of Herman Melville*, 15-30.

Dryden, Edgar A. *Melville's Thematics of Form*, 37-46.

Geismar, Maxwell. Introduction, *Billy Budd and Typee* (New York, 1962).

Houghton, Donald E. "The Incredible Ending of Melville's *Typee*," *Emerson Society Quarterly* 22 (I Quarter 1961), 28-31.

Ishag, Saada. "Herman Melville as Existentialist: An Analysis of *Typee, Mardi, Moby Dick*, and *The Confidence Man*," *The American Novel: Two Studies*, 7-13.

Mayoux, Jean-Jacques. *Melville*, 36-42.

Miller, James E., Jr. "*Typee* and *Omoo:* The Quest for the Garden," *A Reader's Guide to Herman Melville*, 18-37.

Ruland, Richard. "Melville and the Fortunate Fall: Typee as Eden," *Nineteenth-Century Fiction* XXIII (Dec 1968), 312-323.

Tanselle, G. Thomas. "The First Review of *Typee*," *American Literature* XXXIV (Jan 1963), 567-571.

————. " 'Typee' and de Voto Once More," *Papers of the Biblio-graphical Society of America* 62 (Oct-Dec 1968), 601-604.

Walser, Richard. "Another Early Review of *Typee*," *American Literature* XXXVI (Jan 1965), 515-516.

Weathers, Winston. "Melville and the Comedy of Communications," *ETC.* XX (Dec 1963), 411-420.

The Writings of Herman Melville, vol I. Northwestern-Newberry Edition (Evanston and Chicago, Illinois, 1968).

WHITE-JACKET

Bernstein, John. *Pacifism and Rebellion in the Writings of Herman Melville,* 68-81.

Dryden, Edgar A. *Melville's Thematics of Form,* 67-79.

Humphreys, A. R. Introduction, *White Jacket, or The World in a Man of War* (London, 1966).

————. *Melville,* 28-40.

Kaplan, Sidney. "Herman Melville and the American National Sin," *Images of the Negro in American Literature,* 142-146.

McCarthy, Paul. "Symbolic Elements in *White Jacket*," *Midwest Quarterly* VII (Summer 1966), 309-325.

————. "The Use of Tom Brown in Melville's *White Jacket*," *Emerson Society Quarterly* 47 (II Quarter 1967), 14-15.

Miller, James E., Jr. "*Redburn* and *White Jacket:* Initiation and Baptism," *A Reader's Guide to Herman Melville,* 54-74.

Philbrick, Thomas. "Melville's 'Best Authorities,' " *Nineteenth Century Fiction* 15 (Sept 1960), 171-179.

Regan, Charles L. "Melville's Horned Woman," *English Language Notes* V (Sept 1967), 34-39.

Seelye, John D. " 'Spontaneous Impress of Truth': Melville's Jack Chase: A Source, an Analogue, a Conjecture," *Nineteenth-Century Fiction* XX (Mar 1966), 367-376.

Zirker, Priscilla Allen. "Evidence of the Slavery Dilemma in *White-Jacket*," *American Quarterly* XVIII (Fall 1966), 477-492.

GENERAL

Anderson, David D. "Melville Criticism . . . Past and Present," *Midwest Quarterly* II (Winter 1961), 169-184.

André, Robert. "Melville et Shakespeare," *Critique* XX (Aug-Sept 1964), 705-715.

Bercovitch, Sacvan. "Melville's Search for National Identity: Son and

MELVILLE, HERMAN, Continued

Father in *Redburn, Pierre* and *Billy Budd*," *CLA Journal* X (Mar 1967), 217-228.

Bernstein, John. *Pacifism and Rebellion in the Writings of Herman Melville.*

Berthoff, Warner. "Words, Sentences, Paragraphs, Chapters," *The Recognition of Herman Melville: Selected Criticism Since 1846,* 313-333.

Beum, Robert. "Melville's Course," *Dalhousie Review* XLV (Spring 1965), 17-33.

Bezanson, Walter E. "The Context of Melville's Fiction," *Emerson Society Quarterly* 28 (III Quarter 1962), 9-12.

Boies, Jack Jay. "Melville's Quarrel with Anglicanism," *Emerson Society Quarterly* 33 (IV Quarter 1963), 75-79.

Bowen, Merlin. *The Long Encounter: Self and Experience in the Writings of Herman Melville.*

Chase, Richard. "An Approach to Melville," *Psychoanalysis and American Fiction,* 111-120.

Cohen, Hennig. "Wordplay on Personal Names in the Writings of Herman Melville," *Tennessee Studies in Literature* VIII (1963), 85-97.

Cowen, Walker. "Melville's 'Discoveries': A Dialogue of the Mind with Itself," *The Recognition of Herman Melville: Selected Criticism Since 1846,* 333-347.

Creeger, George R. "The Symbolism of Whiteness in Melville's Prose Fiction," *Jahrbuch Für Amerikastudien* 5 (1960), 147-163.

Davis, Merrell R. and William H. Gilman. *The Letters of Herman Melville.*

Donow, Herbert S. "Melville and the Craft of Fiction," *Modern Language Quarterly* XXV (Jun 1964), 181-186.

Dryden, Edgar A. *Melville's Thematics of Form.*

Farnsworth, Robert M. "From Voyage to Quest in Melville," *Emerson Society Quarterly* 28 (III Quarter 1962), 17-20.

Fiedler, Leslie A. *Love and Death in the American Novel,* 429-437.

Flanagan, John T. "*The Spirit of the Times* Reviews Melville," *Journal of English and Germanic Philology* LXIV (Jan 1965), 57-64.

Fletcher, Richard M. "Melville's Use of Marquesan," *American Speech* XXXIX (May 1964), 135-138.

Frank, Max. *Die Farb—und Lichtsymbolik im Prosawerk Herman Melvilles.*

Franklin, H. Bruce. "The Island Worlds of Darwin and Melville," *Centennial Review* XI (Summer 1967), 353-370.

————. *The Wake of the Gods: Melville's Mythology.*

Fussell, Edwin. "Herman Melville," *Frontier: American Literature and the American West,* 232-326.

Grant, Douglas. *Purpose and Place,* 34-39.

Green, Jesse D. "Diabolism, Pessimism, and Democracy: Notes on Melville and Conrad," *Modern Fiction Studies* VII (Autumn 1962), 287-305.

Green, Martin. "Melville and the American Romance," *Re-Appraisals: Some Commonsense Readings in American Literature,* 87-112.

Gross, John J. "The Face of Plinlimmon and the 'Failures' of the Fifties," *Emerson Society Quarterly* 28 (III Quarter 1962), 6-9.

Gross, Theodore. "Herman Melville: The Nature of Authority," *Colorado Quarterly* XVI (Spring 1968), 397-412.

Guetti, James. *The Limits of Metaphor: A Study of Melville, Conrad, and Faulkner.*

Guttmann, Allen. "From *Typee* to *Moby-Dick:* Melville's Allusive Art," *Modern Language Quarterly* XXIV (Sept 1963), 237-244.

Hagopian, John V. "Melville's L'Homme Révolté," *English Studies* XLVI (Oct 1965), 390-402.

Hall, Joan Joffe. "Melville's Use of Interpolations," *University Review* XXXIII (Oct 1966), 51-59.

Hayman, Allen. "The Real and the Original: Herman Melville's Theory of Prose Fiction," *Modern Fiction Studies* VIII (Autumn 1962), 211-232.

Hillway, Tyrus. *Herman Melville.*

————. "Two Books in Young Melville's Library," *Bulletin of the New York Public Library* LXXI (Sept 1967), 474-476.

Howard, Leon. "The Case of the Missing Whaler," *Manuscripts* XII (Fall 1960), 3-9.

————. "Herman Melville," *Six American Novelists of the Nineteenth Century,* 82-117.

Kaplan, Sidney. "Herman Melville and the American National Sin," *Images of the Negro in American Literature,* 135-162.

Kaul, A. N. "Herman Melville: The New-World Voyageur," *The American Vision: Actual and Ideal Society in Nineteenth Century Fiction,* 214-279.

Kosok, Heinz. *Die Bedeutung der Gothic Novel für das Erzahlwerk Herman Melvilles.*

Lanzinger, Klaus. *Die Epik im Amerikanischen Roman: Eine Studie zu James F. Cooper, Herman Melville, Frank Norris und Thomas Wolfe.*

———. *Primitivismus und Naturalismus im Prosaschaffen Herman Melvilles.*

Lease, Benjamin. "The Chemistry of Genius: Herman Melville and Anton Bruckner," *Personalist* XLVIII (Spring 1967), 224-241.

Lewis, R. W. B. Introduction, *Herman Melville: Stories, Poems, Letters* (New York, 1962).

Mansfield, Luther Stearns. "Some Patterns from Melville's 'Loom of Time,'" *Essays on Determinism in American Literature*, 19-35.

Marx, Leo. *The Machine in the Garden: Technology and the Pastoral Ideal in America*, 277-319.

Maxwell, D. E. S. "The Tragic Phase: Melville and Hawthorne," *American Fiction: The Intellectual Background*, 141-179.

Mayoux, Jean-Jacques. "La Langue et Le Style De Melville," *Études Anglaises* XIII (Jul-Sept 1960), 337-345.

———. *Melville.*

McEniry, W. Hugh. "Some Contrapuntal Themes in Herman Melville," *Essays in Modern American Literature*, 14-25.

Miller, James E., Jr. "The Complex Figure in Melville's Carpet," *A Reader's Guide to Herman Melville*, 3-17.

———. "Hawthorne and Melville: No! in Thunder," *Quests Surd and Absurd: Essays in American Literature*, 186-208.

———. "Melville's Quest in Art and Life," *Quests Surd and Absurd: Essays in American Literature*, 161-185.

Mitchell, Charles. "Melville and the Spurious Truth of Legalism," *Centennial Review* XII (Winter 1968), 110-126.

Moss, Sidney P. "'Cock-A-Doodle-Doo!' and Some Legends in Melville Scholarship," *American Literature* 40 (May 1968), 192-210.

Mumford, Lewis. *Herman Melville: A Study of His Life and Vision*, revised edition.

Myers, Margaret. "Mark Twain and Melville," *Mark Twain Journal* XIV (Summer 1968), 5-8.

Noble, David W. *The Eternal Adam and the New World Garden*, 34-47.

Oates, J. C. "Melville and the Manichean Illusion," *Texas Studies in Literature and Language* IV (Spring 1962) , 117-129.

O'Daniel, Therman B. "Herman Melville as a Writer of Journals," *CLA Journal* IV (Dec 1960) , 94-105.

Oliver, Egbert S. "Herman Melville's Lightning-Rod Man," *Studies in American Literature: Whitman, Emerson, Melville and Others*, 71-77.

Price, Lawrence Marsden. *The Reception of United States Literature in Germany*, 127-130.

The Recognition of Herman Melville: Selected Criticism Since 1846.

Rees, Robert A. "Melville's Alma and *The Book of Mormon*," *Emerson Society Quarterly* 43 (II Quarter 1966) , 41-46.

Rose, E. J. "Melville, Emerson, and the Sphinx," *New England Quarterly* XXXVI (Jun 1963) , 249-258.

Rosenberry, Edward H. "Melville's Ship of Fools," *PMLA* LXXV (Dec 1960) , 604-608.

Sealts, Mertin M., Jr. "Approaching Melville Through 'Hawthorne and His Mosses,' " *Emerson Society Quarterly* 28 (III Quarter 1962) , 12-15.

————. "Melville's Geniality," *Essays in American and English Literature Presented to Bruce Robert McElderry, Jr.*, 3-23.

Seelye, John D. "The Ironic Diagram," *The Recognition of Herman Melville: Selected Criticism Since 1846*, 347-364.

Stein, William Bysshe. "Melville's Cock and the Bell of Saint Paul," *Emerson Society Quarterly* 27 (II Quarter 1962) , 5-10.

————. "Melville's Eros," *Texas Studies in Literature and Language* III (Summer 1961) , 297-308.

Stern, Milton R. "Melville's Tragic Imagination: The Hero Without a Home," *Patterns of Commitment in American Literature*, 39-52.

Stewart, Randall. "Melville and Hawthorne," *Regionalism and Beyond: Essays of Randall Stewart*, 113-125.

Strandberg, Victor H. "God and the Critics of Melville," *Texas Studies in Literature and Language* VI (Autumn 1964) , 322-333.

Strauch, Carl F. "The Problem of Time and the Romantic Mode in Hawthorne, Melville and Emerson," *Emerson Society Quarterly* 35 (II Quarter 1964) , 50-60.

Wager, Willis. *American Literature: A World View*, 110-115.

Ward, Joseph A., Jr. "Melville and Failure," *Emerson Society Quarterly* 33 (IV Quarter 1963) , 43-46.

Ward, Robert S. "Longfellow and Melville: The Ship and the Whale," *Emerson Society Quarterly* 22 (I Quarter 1961), 57-63.

West, Ray B., Jr. "Primitivism in Melville," *The Writer in the Room: Selected Essays*, 31-47.

Wright, Nathalia. "An Approach to Melville Through His Themes and Literary Genres," *Emerson Society Quarterly* 28, (III Quarter 1962), 25-27.

BIBLIOGRAPHY

Beebe, Maurice, Harrison Hayford and Gordon Roper. "Criticism of Herman Melville: A Selected Checklist," *Modern Fiction Studies* VIII (Autumn 1962), 312-346.

Bernstein, John. *Pacifism and Rebellion in the Writings of Herman Melville*, 222-230.

Bibliographical Committee of the Melville Society. *Melville Bibliography, 1952-1957*.

Cohen, Hennig. "Melville's Copy of Broughton's 'Popular Poetry of the Hindoos,'" *Papers of the Bibliographical Society of America* LXI (Jul-Sept 1967), 266-267.

Finkelstein, Dorothee M. *Melville's Orienda*, 283-302.

Frank, Max. *Die Farb—und Lichtsymbolik im Prosawerk Herman Melvilles*, 153-157.

Hillway, Tyrus. *Herman Melville*, 162-170.

Humphreys, A. R. *Melville*, 115-120.

Ives, Sidney. "A Melville Ghost," *Papers of the Bibliographical Society of America* LIX (Jul-Sept 1965), 318.

Mathews, J. Chesley. "Bibliographical Supplement: A Selective Checklist, 1955-1962," *Eight American Authors: A Review of Research and Criticism*, 438-445.

Maxwell, D. E. S. *Herman Melville*, 97-101.

Miller, James E., Jr. "Selected Bibliography," *A Reader's Guide to Herman Melville*, 253-258.

Price, Lawrence Marsden. *The Reception of United States Literature in Germany*, 222.

Six American Novelists of the Nineteenth Century, 234-237.

Zimmerman, Michael. "Herman Melville in the 1920's: An Annotated Bibliography," *Bulletin of Bibliography* XXIV (Sept-Dec 1964), 117-120, 106; (Jan-Apr 1965), 139-144.

MICHENER, JAMES A.

THE BRIDGES AT TOKO-RI
Day, A. Grove. *James A. Michener,* 76-81.
THE FIRES OF SPRING
Day, A. Grove. *James A. Michener,* 56-65.
HAWAII
Day, A. Grove. *James A. Michener,* 111-130.
TALES OF THE SOUTH PACIFIC
Day, A. Grove. *James A. Michener,* 36-54.
Stuckey, W. J. *The Pulitzer Prize Novels: A Critical Backward Look,* 138-143.
GENERAL
Day, A. Grove. *James A. Michener.*
BIBLIOGRAPHY
Day, A. Grove. *James A. Michener,* 157-167.

MILLER, ARTHUR

FOCUS
Moss, Leonard. *Arthur Miller,* 33-37.

MILLER, HENRY

BLACK SPRING
Hassan, Ihab. *The Literature of Silence: Henry Miller and Samuel Beckett,* 67-72.
Widmer, Kingsley. *Henry Miller,* 41-51.
SEXUS
Widmer, Kingsley. *Henry Miller,* 79-88.
TROPIC OF CANCER
"About A Book Named 'Tropic': Boston Courtroom Scene," *Evergreen Review* 28 (Jan-Feb 1963), 81-84.
Bess, Donovan. "Miller's 'Tropic' on Trial," *Evergreen Review* 23 (Mar-Apr 1962), 12-37.
Chester, Alfred. "Thoughts of an Unserious Reader of Erotica," *Partisan Review* XXIX (Fall 1962), 617-625.
Foster, Steven. "A Critical Appraisal of Henry Miller's *Tropic of Cancer,*" *Twentieth Century Literature* IX 196-208.
Hassan, Ihab. *The Literature of Silence: Henry Miller and Samuel Beckett,* 59-67.

266

Kauffmann, Stanley. "An Old Shocker Comes Home," *Henry Miller and the Critics,* 154-160.

————. "An Old Shocker Comes Home," *New Republic* 145 (Jul 10, 1961), 17-19.

Lewis, Anthony. "The Most Recent Troubles of 'Tropic': A Chapter in Censorship," *New York Times Book Review* 67 (Jan 21, 1962), 4-5, 16, 18.

Lowenfels, Walter. "A Note on *Tropic of Cancer:* Paris, 1931," *Henry Miller and the Critics,* 16-19.

————. "Unpublished Preface to *Tropic of Cancer,*" *Massachusetts Review* V (Spring 1964), 481-491.

Norris, Hoke. " 'Cancer' in Chicago," *Evergreen Review* 25 (Jul-Aug 1962), 40-66.

Rexroth, Kenneth. "The Empty Zone," *Nation* 193 (Jul 1, 1961), 15-16.

Shapiro, Karl. Introduction, *The Tropic of Cancer* (New York, 1961).

Solotaroff, Theodore. " 'All That Cellar-Deep Jazz': Henry Miller and Seymour Krim," *Commentary* XXXII (Oct 1961), 317-324.

Widmer, Kingsley. *Henry Miller,* 17-40.

TROPIC OF CAPRICORN

Hassan, Ihab. *The Literature of Silence: Henry Miller and Samuel Beckett,* 72-81.

Widmer, Kingsley. *Henry Miller,* 99-110.

GENERAL

Armitage, Merle. "The Man Behind the Smile: Doing Business with Henry Miller," *Texas Quarterly* IV (Winter 1961), 154-161.

Baxter, Annette Kar. *Henry Miller: Expatriate.*

Bode, Elroy. "The World on Its Own Terms: A Brief for Steinbeck, Miller and Simenon," *Southwest Review* LIII (Autumn 1968), 406-416.

Childs, J. Rives. "What Miller Means to Me," *International Henry Miller Letter* 3 (Aug 1962), 11-14.

Denat, Antoine. "Henry Miller: Baroque Clown and Prophet Triumphant," *International Henry Miller Letter* 3 (Aug 1962), 16-22; 4 (Dec 1962), 4-11.

Dick, Kenneth C. *Henry Miller: Colossus of One.*

Fiedler, Leslie A. *Waiting for the End,* 37-45.

Finkelstein, Sidney. *Existentialism and Alienation in American Literature,* 203-210.

Friedman, Alan. "The Pitching of Love's Mansion in the Tropics of Henry Miller," *Seven Contemporary Authors,* 25-48.

Gordon, William A. *The Mind and Art of Henry Miller.*

————. *Writer and Critic: A Correspondence with Henry Miller.*

Haan, Jacques den. *Milleriana.*

Hassan, Ihab. *The Literature of Silence: Henry Miller and Samuel Beckett,* 33-109.

Henry Miller—Between Heaven and Hell: A Symposium.

Henry Miller on Writing.

Hoffman, Frederick J. "Henry Miller, Defender of the Marginal Life," *The Thirties: Fiction, Poetry, Drama,* 73-80.

Kermode, Frank. "Henry Miller and John Betjeman," *Encounter* XVI (Mar 1961) , 69-75.

Littlejohn, David. "The Tropics of Miller," *New Republic* 146 (Mar 5, 1962) , 31-35.

May, James Boyer. "Henry Miller (An Individualist as Social Thinker) ," *Trace* 40 (Jan-Mar 1961) , 24-31.

Mitchell, Edward B. "Artists and Artists: The 'Aesthetics' of Henry Miller," *Texas Studies in Literature and Language* VIII (Spring 1966) , 103-115.

Moravia, Alberto. "Two American Writers," *Sewanee Review* LXVIII (Summer 1960) , 473-477.

Omarr, Sydney. *Henry Miller: His World of Urania.*

Perles, Alfred. *My Friend Henry Miller.*

Porter, Bernard H. *What Henry Miller Said and Why It Is Important.*

Schmiele, Walter. *Henry Miller in Selbstzeugnissen und Bilddokumenten.*

Smithline, Arnold. "Henry Miller and the Transcendental Spirit," *Emerson Society Quarterly* 43 (II Quarter 1966) , 50-56.

Southern, Terry. "Miller: Only the Beginning," *Nation* 193 (Nov 18, 1961) , 399-401.

Symons, Julian. "Goodby Henry Miller," *Critical Observations,* 126-133.

Traschen, Isadore. "Henry Miller: The Ego and I," *South Atlantic Quarterly* LXV (Summer 1966) , 345-354.

Wickes, George, (ed.) . "An Exchange of Letters between Henry Miller and Lawrence Durrell," *Paris Review* VIII (No 29, 1964) , 132-159.

————. *Henry Miller.*

MILLER, HENRY, Continued

―――――. "Henry Miller at Seventy," *Claremont Quarterly* IX (Winter 1962) , 5-20.

―――――. "An Interview with Henry Miller: The Art of Fiction XXVIII," *Paris Review* VII No. 28 (Summer-Fall 1962) , 128-159.

―――――. *Lawrence Durrell and Henry Miller: A Private Correspondence.*

Widmer, Kingsley. *Henry Miller.*

Williams, John. "Henry Miller: The Success of Failure," *Virginia Quarterly Review* 44 (Spring 1968) , 226-245.

Wood, Richard C. *Collector's Quest: The Correspondence of Henry Miller and J. Rives Childs, 1947-1965.*

BIBLIOGRAPHY

Baxter, Annette Kar. *Henry Miller: Expatriate,* 191-201.

Hassan, Ihab. *The Literature of Silence: Henry Miller and Samuel Beckett,* 221-222.

Moore, Thomas H. *Bibliography of Henry Miller.*

Renken, Maxine. *A Bibliography of Henry Miller.*

―――――. "Bibliography of Henry Miller: 1945-1961," *Twentieth Century Literature* VII (Jan 1962) , 180-190.

Riley, Esta Lou. *Henry Miller: An Informal Bibliography: 1924-1960.*

Schmiele, Walter. *Henry Miller in Selbstzeugnissen und Bilddokumenten,* 170-173.

Wickes, George. *Henry Miller,* 44-46.

Widmer, Kingsley. *Henry Miller,* 186-188.

MILLER, MERLE

THE SURE THING

Blotner, Joseph. *The Modern American Political Novel,* 290-294.

MITCHELL, MARGARET

GONE WITH THE WIND

Commager, Henry Steele. Introduction, *Gone with the Wind* (New York, 1968) .

Farr, Finis. *Margaret Mitchell of Atlanta.*

Gutwillig, Robert. "In History There's Never Been Anything Like It," *New York Times Book Review* 66 (Jun 25, 1961) , 6, 22.

MITCHELL, MARGARET, Continued

Mathews, James. "The Civil War of 1936: *Gone With The Wind* and *Absalom! Absalom!" Georgia Review* XXI (Winter 1967), 462-469.

Stuckey, W. J. *The Pulitzer Prize Novels: A Critical Backward Look*, 107-112.

Van Nostrand, Albert. *The Denatured Novel*, 32-40.

GENERAL

Cole, Lois Dwight. "The Story Begins at a Luncheon Bridge in Atlanta," *New York Times Book Review* 66 (Jun 25, 1961), 7, 22.

MORLEY, CHRISTOPHER

BIBLIOGRAPHY

Bracker, Jon. "The Christopher Morley Collection," *Library Chronicle of the University of Texas* VII (Summer 1962), 19-35.

MORRIS, WRIGHT

A BILL OF RIGHTS, A BILL OF WRONGS, A BILL OF GOODS

Hicks, Granville. "Sounds of an Uneasy Artist," *Saturday Review* 51 (Mar 16, 1968), 29-30.

CAUSE FOR WONDER

Klein, Marcus. *After Alienation: American Novels in Mid-Century*, 242-246.

CEREMONY IN LONE TREE

Baumbach, Jonathan. "Wake Before Bomb: *Ceremony in Lone Tree*," *Critique* IV (Winter 1961-1962), 56-71.

―――. "Wake before Bomb: *Ceremony in Lone Tree* by Wright Morris," *The Landscape of Nightmare: Studies in the Contemporary American Novel*, 152-169.

Klein, Marcus. *After Alienation: American Novels in Mid-Century*, 238-242.

THE DEEP SLEEP

Klein, Marcus. *After Alienation: American Novels in Mid-Century*, 220-226.

Madden, David. *Wright Morris*, 92-101.

FIELD OF VISION

Klein, Marcus. *After Alienation: American Novels in Mid-Century*, 238-242.

MORRIS, WRIGHT, Continued

THE HUGE SEASON

Klein, Marcus. *After Alienation: American Novels in Mid-Century,* 226-229.

IN ORBIT

Garrett, George. "Morris The Magician: A Look at *In Orbit,*" *Hollins Critic* IV (Jun 1967), 1-12.

Madden, David. "Wright Morris' *In Orbit:* An Unbroken Series of Poetic Gestures," *Critique* X (No 2, 1968), 102-119.

LOVE AMONG THE CANNIBALS

Klein, Marcus. *After Alienation: American Novels in Mid-Century,* 229-234.

Madden, David. *Wright Morris,* 112-130.

MAN AND BOY

Klein, Marcus. *After Alienation: American Novels in Mid-Century,* 211-214.

Madden, David, *Wright Morris,* 83-91.

THE MAN WHO WAS THERE

Madden, David. *Wright Morris,* 32-34, 41-48.

MY UNCLE DUDLEY

Klein, Marcus. *After Alienation: American Novels in Mid-Century,* 198-201.

Madden, David. *Wright Morris,* 32 41.

WHAT A WAY TO GO

Klein, Marcus. *After Alienation: American Novels in Mid-Century,* 234-238.

Madden, David. *Wright Morris,* 112-130.

THE WORKS OF LOVE

Klein, Marcus. *After Alienation: American Novels in Mid-Century,* 214-220.

Madden, David. *Wright Morris,* 64-75.

THE WORLD IN THE ATTIC

Klein, Marcus. *After Alienation: American Novels in Mid-Century,* 206, 209-211.

Madden, David. *Wright Morris,* 57-63.

GENERAL

Eisinger, Chester E. *Fiction of the Forties,* 328-341.

Guettinger, Roger J. "The Problem with Jigsaw Puzzles: Form in the Fiction of Wright Morris," *Texas Quarterly* XI (Spring 1968), 209-220.

Howard, Leon. *Wright Morris.*

Hunt, John W., Jr. "The Journey Back: The Early Novels of Wright Morris," *Critique* V (Spring-Summer, 1962) , 41-60.

Klein, Marcus. "Wright Morris: The American Territory," *After Alienation: American Novels in Mid-century,* 196-246.

Madden, David. "The Great Plains in the Novels of Wright Morris," *Critique* IV (Winter 1961-1962) , 5-23.

————. "The Hero and the Witness in Wright Morris' Field of Vision," *Prairie Schooner* XXXIV (Fall 1960) , 263-278.

————. *Wright Morris.*

Miller, James E., Jr. "The Nebraska Encounter: Willa Cather and Wright Morris," *Prairie Schooner* XLI (Summer 1967) , 165-167.

Trachtenberg, Alan. "The Craft of Vision," *Critique* IV (Winter 1961-1962) , 41-55.

Waterman, Arthur E. "The Novels of Wright Morris: An Escape from Nostalgia," *Critique* IV (Winter 1961-62) , 24-40.

BIBLIOGRAPHY

Howard, Leon. *Wright Morris,* 44-48.

Linden, Stanton J. and David Madden. "A Wright Morris Bibliography," *Critique* IV (Winter 1961-1962) , 77-87.

Madden, David. *Wright Morris,* 177-184.

MOTLEY, WILLARD

GENERAL

Weissgärber, Alfred. "Willard Motley and the Sociological Novel," *Studi Americani* VII (1961) , 299-309.

MURFREE, MARY NOAILLES

FAIR MISSISSIPPIAN
Cary, Richard. *Mary N. Murfree,* 153-160.

IN THE CLOUDS
Cary, Richard. *Mary N. Murfree,* 88-94.

THE PROPHET OF THE GREAT SMOKY MOUNTAINS
Cary, Richard. *Mary N. Murfree,* 80-88.

WHERE THE BATTLE WAS FOUGHT
Cary, Richard. *Mary N. Murfree,* 115-123.

MURFREE, MARY NOAILLES, Continued

GENERAL
Cary, Richard. *Mary N. Murfree.*
BIBLIOGRAPHY
Cary, Richard. *Mary N. Murfree,* 181-185.
―――. "Mary Noailles Murfree (1850-1922)," *American Literary Realism* 1 (Fall 1967), 79-83.

NABOKOV, VLADIMIR

BEND SINISTER
Field, Andrew. *Nabokov: His Life in Art,* 198-203.
Lee, L. L. *"Bend Sinister:* Nabokov's Political Dream," *Nabokov: The Man and his Work,* 95-105.
―――. *"Bend Sinister:* Nabokov's Political Dream," *Wisconsin Studies in Contemporary Literature* 8 (Spring 1967), 193-203.
Nabokov, Vladimir. "Introduction to *Bend Sinister," Nabokov's Congeries,* 239-246.
Stegner, Page. *Escape into Aesthetics: The Art of Vladimir Nabokov,* 76-89.
DESPAIR
Anderson, Quentin. "Nabokov in Time," *New Republic* 154 (Jun 4, 1966), 23-28.
Rosenfield, Clair. *"Despair* and the Lust for Immortality," *Nabokov: The Man and his Work,* 66-84.
―――. *"Despair* and the Lust for Immortality," *Wisconsin Studies in Contemporary Literature* 8 (Spring 1967), 174-192.
LOLITA
Aldridge, A. Owen. *"Lolita* and *Les Liaisons Dangereuses," Wisconsin Studies in Contemporary Literature* 2 (Fall 1961), 20-26.
Appel, Alfred, Jr. *"Lolita:* The Springboard of Parody," *Nabokov: The Man and his Work,* 106-143.
―――. *"Lolita:* The Springboard of Parody," *Wisconsin Studies in Contemporary Literature* 8 (Spring 1967), 204-241.
DuBois, Arthur E. "Poe and *Lolita," CEA Critic* XXVI (Mar 1964), 1, 7.
Fiedler, Leslie A. *Love and Death in the American Novel,* 326-328.
Field, Andrew. *Nabokov: His Life in Art,* 323-350.
Girodias, Maurice. "Lolita, Nabokov, and I," *Evergreen Review* 37 (Sept 1965), 44-47, 89-91.

Gold, Joseph. "The Morality of *'Lolita,'* " *British Association for American Studies Bulletin* 1 (Sept 1960), 50-54.

Green, Martin. "The Morality of *Lolita,*" *Kenyon Review* XXVIII (Jun 1966), 352-377.

Hinchliffe, Arnold P. "Belinda in American," *Studi Americani* VI (1960), 339-347.

Hollander, John. "The Perilous Magic of Nymphets," *On Contemporary Literature,* 477-480.

Hughes, Daniel J. "Reality and the Hero: 'Lolita' and 'Henderson the Rain King,' " *Modern Fiction Studies* VI (Winter 1960-61), 345-364.

————. "Reality and the Hero: *Lolita* and *Henderson the Rain King,*" *Saul Bellow and his Critics,* 69-80, 87-90.

Josipovici, G. D. "*Lolita:* Parody and the Pursuit of Beauty," *Critical Quarterly* 6 (Spring 1964), 35-48.

Mitchell, Charles. "Mythic Seriousness in *Lolita,*" *Texas Studies in Literature and Language* V (Autumn 1963), 329-343.

Nabokov, Vladimir. "Lolita and Mr. Girodias," *Evergreen Review* 45 (Feb 1967), 37-41.

————. "On a Book Entitled *Lolita,*" *Nabokov's Congeries,* 231-238.

Phillips, Elizabeth. "The Hocus-Pocus of *Lolita,*" *Literature and Psychology* X (Autumn 1960), 97-101.

Proffer, Carl R. *Keys to Lolita.*

Rubinstein, E. "Approaching Lolita," *Minnesota Review* VI (No 4, 1966), 361-367.

Stegner, Page. *Escape into Aesthetics: The Art of Vladimir Nabokov,* 102-115.

Teirlinck, Herman, translated by Elisabeth Eybers. "Marginal Notes on Nabokov's *Lolita,*" *Literary Review* VII (Spring 1964), 439-442.

Uphaus, Robett W. "Nabokov's Kunstlerroman: Portrait of the Artist as a Dying Man," *Twentieth Century Literature* XIII (Jul 1967), 104-110.

THE LUZHIN DEFENSE

Field, Andrew. "The Defenseless Luzhin," *On Contemporary Literature,* 473-476.

PALE FIRE

Field, Andrew. *Nabokov: His Life in Art,* 291-322.

————. "*Pale Fire:* The Labyrinth of a Great Novel," *Tri-Quarterly* 8 (Winter 1967), 13-36.

NABOKOV, VLADIMIR, Continued

Kostelanetz, Richard. "Nabokov's Obtuse Fool," *On Contemporary Literature,* 481-485.

Lyons, John O. *"Pale Fire* and the Fine Art of Annotation," *Nabokov: The Man and his Work,* 157-164.

————. *"Pale Fire* and the Fine Art of Annotation," *Wisconsin Studies in Contemporary Literature* 8 (Spring 1967), 242-249.

Maloff, Saul. "The World of Rococo," *Nation* 194 (Jun 16, 1962), 541-542.

McCarthy, Mary. "A Bolt from the Blue," *New Republic* 146 (Jun 4, 1962), 21-27.

————. "Vladimir Nabokov's *Pale Fire,*" *Encounter* XIX (Oct 1962), 71-84.

Stegner, Page. *Escape into Aesthetics: The Art of Vladimir Nabokov,* 116-132.

Williams, Carol T. " 'Web of Sense': *Pale Fire* in the Nabokov Canon," *Critique* VI (Winter 1963-1964), 29-45.

PNIN

Field, Andrew. *Nabokov: His Life in Art,* 129-140.

Gordon, Ambrose, Jr. "The Double Pnin," *Nabokov: The Man and his Work,* 144-156.

Stegner, Page. *Escape into Aesthetics: The Art of Vladimir Nabokov,* 90-101.

————, Introduction, *Nabokov's Congeries* (New York, 1968).

THE REAL LIFE OF SEBASTIAN KNIGHT

Field, Andrew. *Nabokov: His Life in Art,* 26-32.

Fromberg, Susan. "The Unwritten Chapters in *The Real Life of Sebastian Knight,*" *Modern Fiction Studies* XIII (Winter 1967-68), 427-442.

Johnson, W. R. *"The Real Life of Sebastian Knight* by Vladimir Nabokov," *Carleton Miscellany* IV (Fall 1963), 111-114.

Nicol, Charles. "The Mirrors of Sebastian Knight," *Nabokov: The Man and his Work,* 85-94.

Stegner, Page. *Escape into Aesthetics: The Art of Vladimir Nabokov,* 63-75.

————. "The Immortality of Art: Vladimir Nabokov's *The Real Life of Sebastian Knight,*" *Southern Review* II (Apr 1966), 286-296.

Stuart, Dabney. *"The Real Life of Sebastian Knight:* Angles of Perception," *Modern Language Quarterly* XXIX (Sept 1968), 312-328.

GENERAL

Appel, Alfred, Jr., interviewer. "An Interview with Vladimir Nabokov," *Wisconsin Studies in Contemporary Literature* 8 (Spring 1967), 127-152.

————. "An Interview with Vladimir Nabokov," *Nabokov: The Man and his Work,* 19-44.

Brick, Allan. "The Madman in his Cell: Joyce, Beckett, Nabokov and the Stereotypes," *Massachusetts Review* I (Fall 1959), 40-55.

Brown, Clarence. "Nabokov's Pushkin and Nabokov's Nabokov," *Nabokov: The Man and his Work,* 195-208.

Dembo, L. S. "Vladimir Nabokov: An Introduction," *Nabokov: The Man and his Work,* 3-18.

————. "Vladimir Nabokov: An Introduction," *Wisconsin Studies in Contemporary Literature* 8 (Spring 1967), 111-126.

Dillard, R. H. W. "Not Text, But Texture: The Novels of Vladimir Nabokov," *Hollins Critic* III (Jun 1966), 1-12.

Editors. "Nabokov on Nabokov and Things," *New York Times Book Review* 73 (May 12, 1968), 4, 50-51.

Field, Andrew. "The Artist as Failure in Nabokov's Early Prose," *Nabokov: The Man and his Work,* 57-65.

————. "The Artist as Failure in Nabokov's Early Prose," *Wisconsin Studies in Contemporary Literature* 8 (Spring 1967), 165-173.

————. *Nabokov: His Life in Art.*

Gold, Herbert. "An Interview with Vladimir Nabokov: The Art of Fiction XL," *Paris Review* XI No. 41 (Summer-Fall 1967), 92-111.

Green, Martin. *Re-Appraisals: Some Commonsense Readings of American Literature,* 211-229.

Grosshans, Henry. "Vladimir Nabokov and the Dream of Old Russia," *Texas Studies in Literature and Language* VII (Winter 1966), 401-409.

Janeway, Elizabeth. "Nabokov the Magician," *Atlantic Monthly* 220 (July 1967), 66-71.

Lee, L. L. "Vladimir Nabokov's Great Spiral of Being," *Western Humanities Review* XVIII (Summer 1964), 225-236.

Merivale, Patricia. "The Flaunting of Artifice in Vladimir Nabokov and Jorge Luis Borges," *Nabokov: The Man and his Work,* 209-224.

Moynahan, Julian. "A Russian Preface for Nabokov's Beheading," *Novel* I (Fall 1967), 12-18.

NABOKOV, VLADIMIR, Continued

————. "Vladimir Nabokov," *New York Times Book Review* 71 (Apr 3, 1966) , 2, 14.

Pryce-Jones, Alan. "The Fabulist's Worlds: Vladimir Nabokov," *The Creative Present,* 66-78.

Purdy, Strother B. "Solus Rex: Nabokov and the Chess Novel," *Modern Fiction Studies* XIV (Winter 1968-1969) , 379-395.

Stegner, Page. *Escape into Aesthetics: The Art of Vladimir Nabokov.*

————. Introduction, *Nabokov's Congeries* (New York, 1968) .

Struve, Gleb. "Notes on Nabokov as a Russian Writer," *Nabokov: The Man and his Work,* 45-56.

Williams, Carol T. "Nabokov's Dialectical Structure," *Nabokov: The Man and his Work,* 165-182.

————. "Nabokov's Dialectical Structure," *Wisconsin Studies in Contemporary Literature* 8 (Spring 1967) , 250-267.

BIBLIOGRAPHY

Bryer, Jackson R. "Vladimir Nabokov's Critical Reputation in English: A Note and a Checklist," *Wisconsin Studies in Contemporary Literature* 8 (Spring 1967) , 312-315.

Bryer, Jackson R. and Thomas J. Bergin, Jr. "Vladimir Nabokov's Critical Reputation in English: A Note and a Checklist," *Nabokov: The Man and his Work,* 225-276.

————. "A Checklist of Nabokov Criticism in English," *Wisconsin Studies in Contemporary Literature* 8 (Spring 1967) , 316-364.

Field, Andrew. *Nabokov: His Life in Art,* 352-380.

Nabokov: The Man and his Work, 277-278.

Stegner, Page. *Escape into Aesthetics: The Art of Vladimir Nabokov,* 137-141.

————. *Nabokov's Congeries,* xxxiii-xxxvi.

Zimmer, Dieter. "Selected Bibliography of Nabokov's Work," *Wisconsin Studies in Contemporary Literature* 8 (Spring 1967) , 310-311.

————. *Vladimir Nabokov, Bibliographie des Gesamtwerks.*

NATHAN, ROBERT

GENERAL

Feis, Herbert. "Robert Nathan: Storyteller," *New York Times Book Review* 70 (Dec 19, 1965) , 2.

BIBLIOGRAPHY

Lawrence, Don H. *Robert Nathan, A Bibliography.*

NEAL, JOHN

RANDOLPH
Fabris, Alberta. "Il 'Randolph' di John Neal," *Studi Americani* XII (1966), 15-44.
BIBLIOGRAPHY
Richards, Irving T. "John Neal: A Bibliography," *Jahrbuch für Amerikastudien* 7 (1962), 296-319.

NEMEROV, HOWARD

THE HOMECOMING GAME
White, Robert L. "The Trying-out of *The Homecoming Game*," *Colorado Quarterly* X (Summer 1961), 84-96.

NEWMAN, FRANCES

GENERAL
Drake, Robert Y., Jr. "Frances Newman: Fabulist of Decadence," *Georgia Review* XIV (Winter 1960), 389-398.

NIN, ANAÏS

GENERAL
Evans, Oliver. *Anaïs Nin.*
————. "Anaïs Nin and the Discovery of Inner Space," *Prairie Schooner* XXXVI (Fall 1962), 217-230.
Zinnes, Harriet. "Anais Nin's Works Reissued," *Books Abroad* XXXVII (Summer 1963), 283-286.

NORDHOFF, CHARLES BERNARD

GENERAL
Briand, Paul L., Jr. *In Search of Paradise: The Nordhoff-Hall Story.*
BIBLIOGRAPHY
Briand, Paul L., Jr. *In Search of Paradise: The Nordhoff-Hall Story,* 377-384.

NORRIS, CHARLES G.

BRASS: A NOVEL OF MARRIAGE
Brown, Paul Allan. "Fitzgerald and Charles G. Norris," *Fitzgerald Newsletter* 26 (Summer 1964) , 3-4.

GENERAL
Goldsmith, Arnold L. "Charles and Frank Norris," *Western American Literature* II (Spring 1967) , 30-49.

NORRIS, FRANK

BLIX
French, Warren. *Frank Norris,* 78-84.

Morgan, W. Wayne. "Frank Norris: The Romantic as Naturalist," *American Writers in Rebellion,* 129-131.

Pizer, Donald. *The Novels of Frank Norris,* 96-102.

A MAN'S WOMAN
Katz, Joseph and John J. Manning. "Notes on Frank Norris's Revision of Two Novels: *A Man's Woman,*" *Papers of the Bibliographical Society of America* LXII (Apr-Jun 1968) , 257-259.

Pizer, Donald. *The Novels of Frank Norris,* 102-110.

McTEAGUE
Childs, James. "The First Draft of *McTeague:* 1893," *American Notes and Queries* III (Nov 1964) , 37-38.

Collins, Carvel. "Frank Norris: *McTeague: A Story of San Francisco,*" *The American Novel from James Fenimore Cooper to William Faulkner,* 97-105.

Dillingham, William B. "The Old Folks of *McTeague,*" *Nineteenth-Century Fiction* XVI (Sept 1961) , 169-173.

French, Warren. *Frank Norris,* 62-75.

Frohock, W. M. *Frank Norris,* 9-16.

Hill, John S. "Trina Sieppe," *University of Kansas City Review* XXIX (Oct 1962) 77-80.

Johnson, George W. "The Frontier Behind Frank Norris' *McTeague,*" *Huntington Library Quarterly* XXVI (Nov 1962) , 91-104.

Katz, Joseph and John J. Manning. "Notes on Frank Norris's Revision of Two Novels: *McTeague,*" *Papers of the Bibliographical Society of America* LXII (Apr-Jun 1968) , 256-257.

Martin, Jay. *Harvests of Change. American Literature 1865-1914,* 249-252.

Geismar, Maxwell. "Frank Norris, A Gulf Without Bottom," *Psycho-analysis and American Fiction,* 187-198.

Morgan, W. Wayne. "Frank Norris: The Romantic as Naturalist," *American Writers in Rebellion,* 111-114.

Pizer, Donald. *The Novels of Frank Norris,* 31-52.

GENERAL

Davison, Richard Allan. "Frank Norris's Thirteen Uncollected News-letters," *Notes and Queries* N. S. 11 (Feb 1964), 71-73.

Dillingham, William B. "Frank Norris and the Genteel Tradition," *Tennessee Studies in Literature* V (1960), 15-24.

French, Warren. *Frank Norris.*

Frohock, W. M. *Frank Norris.*

Goldsmith, Arnold L. "Charles and Frank Norris," *Western American Literature* II (Spring 1967), 30-49.

Hill, John S. "The Writing and Publication of the Novels of Frank Norris," *American Notes and Queries* II (Jun 1964), 151.

Johnson, George W. "Frank Norris and Romance," *American Literature* XXXIII (Mar 1961), 52-63.

Kwiat, Joseph J. "Frank Norris: The Novelist as Social Critic and Literary Theorist," *Arizona Quarterly* XVIII (Winter 1962), 319-328.

Lanzinger, Klaus. "Das episch Grundkonzept in Frank Norris' Weizen-trilogie," *Neueren Sprachen* (Oct 1963), 437-451.

――――. *Die Epik in Amerikanischen Roman: Eine Studie zu James F. Cooper, Herman Melville, Frank Norris und Thomas Wolfe.*

The Literary Criticism of Frank Norris.

Martin, Jay. *Harvests of Change. American Literature 1865-1941,* 70-77.

Millgate, Michael. *American Social Fiction: James to Cozzens,* 38-53.

Morgan, W. Wayne. "Frank Norris: The Romantic as Naturalist," *American Writers in Rebellion,* 104-145.

Noble, David W. *The Eternal Adam and the New World Garden,* 105-115.

Pizer, Donald. "Evolutionary Ethical Dualism in Frank Norris' *Vandover and the Brute* and *McTeague*," *PMLA* LXXVI (Dec 1961), 552-560.

――――. "Frank Norris' Definition of Naturalism" *Modern Fiction Studies* VIII (Winter 1962-63), 408-410.

――――. "The Masculine-Feminine Ethic in Frank Norris' Popular

Novels," *Texas Studies in Literature and Language* VI (Spring 1964), 84-91.

————. "The Significance of Frank Norris's Literary Criticism," *Realism and Naturalism in Nineteenth-Century American Literature,* 99-107.

Schneider, Robert W. "Frank Norris: The Naturalist as Victorian," *Midcontinent American Studies Journal* III (Spring 1962), 13-27.

————. "The Romantic Rebel," *Five Novelists of the Progressive Era,* 112-152.

Thorp, Willard. *American Writing in the Twentieth Century,* 158-161.

Walker, Don D. "The Western Naturalism of Frank Norris," *Western American Literature* II (Spring 1967), 14-29.

Ziff, Larzer. "Life Without Style," *The American 1890s: Life and Times of a Lost Generation,* 250-274.

BIBLIOGRAPHY

Davison, Richard Allan. "The Remaining Seven of Frank Norris' 'Weekly Letters,'" *American Literary Realism* 3 (Summer 1968), 47-65.

French, Warren. *Frank Norris,* 148-154.

————. "Frank Norris (1870-1902)," *American Literary Realism* 1 (Fall 1967), 84-89.

Frohock, W. M. *Frank Norris,* 46-47.

Morgan, W. Wayne. *American Writers in Rebellion,* 205-206.

Pizer, Donald. *The Novels of Frank Norris,* 198-204.

O'CONNOR, EDWIN

THE EDGE OF SADNESS

Rank, Hugh. "O'Connor's Image of the Priest," *New England Quarterly* XLI (Mar 1968), 3-29.

THE LAST HURRAH

Blotner, Joseph. *The Modern American Political Novel,* 82-85.

Goodwin, George, Jr. "The Last Hurrahs: George Apley and Frank Skeffington," *Massachusetts Review* I (Spring 1960), 461-471.

Milne, Gordon. *The American Political Novel,* 163-171.

O'Connor, Edwin. "James Michael Curley and *The Last Hurrah,*" *Atlantic Monthly* CCVIII (Sept 1961), 48-50.

O'CONNOR, EDWIN, Continued

GENERAL

Jones, Howard Mumford. "Politics, Mr. O'Connor, and the Family Novel," *Atlantic Monthly* CCXVIII (Oct 1966), 117-120.

Kelleher, John V. "Edwin O'Connor and the Irish-American Process," *Atlantic Monthly* 222 (Jul 1968), 48-52.

O'Connor, Edwin. "For Whom the Novelist Writes," *Critic* XXI (Apr-May 1963), 13-17.

O'CONNOR, FLANNERY

THE VIOLENT BEAR IT AWAY

Burns, Stuart L. "Flannery O'Connor's *The Violent Bear It Away:* Apotheosis in Failure," *Sewanee Review* LXXVI (Spring 1968), 319-336.

Drake, Robert. *Flannery O'Connor: A Critical Essay,* 33-37.

Ferris, Sumner J. "The Outside and the Inside: Flannery O'Connor's *The Violent Bear It Away,*" *Critique* III (Winter-Spring 1960), 11-19.

Hoffman, Frederick J. *The Art of Southern Fiction,* 90-94.

Hyman, Stanley Edgar. *Flannery O'Connor,* 19-25.

Jeremy, Sister, C.S.J. "*The Violent Bear It Away:* A Linguistic Education," *Renascence* XVII (Fall 1964), 11-16.

Martin, Carter W. *The True Country: Themes in the Fiction of Flannery O'Connor,* 55-61, 77-82, 125-129.

Rubin, Louis D., Jr. "Flannery O'Connor and the Bible Belt," *The Curious Death of the Novel: Essays in American Literature,* 248-259.

Trowbridge, Clinton W. "The Symbolic Vision of Flannery O'Connor: Patterns of Imagery in *The Violent Bear It Away,*" *Sewanee Review* LXXVI (Spring 1968), 298-318.

WISE BLOOD

Baumbach, Jonathan. "The Acid of God's Grace: *Wise Blood* by Flannery O'Connor," *The Landscape of Nightmare: Studies in the Contemporary American Novel,* 87-100.

Drake, Robert. *Flannery O'Connor: A Critical Essay,* 18-23.

Hoffman, Frederick J. *The Art of Southern Fiction,* 85-89.

Hyman, Stanley Edgar. *Flannery O'Connor,* 9-16.

Lawson, Lewis A. "Flannery O'Connor and the Grotesque: *Wise Blood,*" *Renascence* XVII (Spring 1965), 137-147, 156.

Martin, Carter W. *The True Country: Themes in the Fiction of Flannery O'Connor,* 47-55, 66-71, 117-125.

Rechnitz, Robert M. "Passionate Pilgrim: Flannery O'Connor's *Wise Blood,*" *Georgia Review* XIX (Fall 1965), 310-316.

Rubin, Louis D., Jr. "Flannery O'Connor and the Bible Belt," *The Curious Death of the Novel: Essays in American Literature,* 245-248.

GENERAL

Alice, Sister Rose, S.S.J. "Flannery O'Connor: Poet to the Outcast," *Renascence* XVI (Spring 1964), 126-132.

Bassan, Maurice. "Flannery O'Connor's Way: Shock, with Moral Intent," *Renascence* XV (Summer 1963), 195-199, 211.

Baumbach, Jonathan. "The Creed of God's Grace: The Fiction of Flannery O'Connor," *Georgia Review* XVII (Fall 1963), 334-346.

Brittain, Joan. "The Fictional Family of Flannery O'Connor," *Renascence* XIX (Fall 1966), 48-52.

Burns, Stuart L. " 'Torn by the Lord's Eye': Flannery O'Connor's Use of Sun Imagery," *Twentieth Century Literature* XIII (Oct 1967), 154-166.

Cheney, Brainard. "Flannery O'Connor's Campaign for her Country," *Sewanee Review* LXXII (Autumn 1964), 555-558.

Coffey, Warren. "Flannery O'Connor," *Commentary* 40 (Nov 1965), 93-99.

Detweiler, Robert. "The Curse of Christ in Flannery O'Connor's Fiction," *Comparative Literature Studies* III (No 2, 1966), 335-345.

Dowell, Bob. "The Moment of Grace in the Fiction of Flannery O'Connor," *College English* XXVII (Dec 1965), 235-239.

Drake, Robert. " 'The Bleeding Stinking Mad Shadow of Jesus' in the Fiction of Flannery O'Connor," *Comparative Literature Studies* III (No 2, 1966), 183-196.

————. *Flannery O'Connor: A Critical Essay.*

Driskell, Leon. " 'Parker's Back' vs. 'The Partridge Festival': Flannery O'Connor's Critical Choice," *Georgia Review* XXI (Winter 1967), 476-490.

Duhamel, P. Albert. "The Novelist as Prophet," *The Added Dimension: The Art and Mind of Flannery O'Connor,* 88-107.

Fitzgerald, Robert. "The Countryside and the True Country," *Sewanee Review* LXX (Summer 1962), 380-394.

Friedman, Melvin J. "Flannery O'Connor: Another Legend in Southern Fiction," *English Journal* LI (Apr 1962), 233-243.

O'CONNOR, FLANNERY, Continued

————. "Flannery O'Connor's Sacred Objects," *The Added Dimension: The Art and Mind of Flannery O'Connor*, 196-208.

Gardiner, Harold C., S.J. "Flannery O'Connor's Clarity of Vision," *The Added Dimension: The Art and Mind of Flannery O'Connor*, 184-195.

Gordon, Caroline. "An American Girl," *The Added Dimension: The Art and Mind of Flannery O'Connor*, 123-137.

————. "Heresy in Dixie," *Sewanee Review* LXXVI (Spring 1968), 263-297.

Gossett, Louise Y. "The Test by Fire," *Violence in Recent Southern Fiction*, 75-97.

Hawkes, John. "Flannery O'Connor's Devil," *Sewanee Review* LXX (Summer 1962), 395-407.

Hoffman, Frederick J. *The Art of Southern Fiction*, 81-95.

————. "The Search for Redemption: Flannery O'Connor's Fiction," *The Added Dimension: The Art and Mind of Flannery O'Connor*, 32-48.

Holman, C. Hugh. "Her Rue with a Difference: Flannery O'Connor and the Southern Literary Tradition," *The Added Dimension: The Art and Mind of Flannery O'Connor*, 73-87.

Hyman, Stanley Edgar. *Flannery O'Connor*.

Lawson, Lewis A. "Flannery O'Connor in Her Own Words: A Collection of Statements," *The Added Dimension: The Art and Mind of Flannery O'Connor*, 226-263.

Lensing, George. "De Chardin's Ideas In Flannery O'Connor," *Renascence* XVIII (Spring 1966), 171-175.

Lorch, Thomas. "Flannery O'Connor: Christian Allegorist," *Critique* X (No 2, 1968), 69-80.

Malin, Irving. "Flannery O'Connor and the Grotesque," *The Added Dimension: The Art and Mind of Flannery O'Connor*, 108-122.

————. "The Gothic Family," *Psychoanalysis and American Fiction*, 266-271.

————. *New American Gothic*, 32-35, 67-71, 90-99, 143-151.

Martin, Carter W. *The True Country: Themes in the Fiction of Flannery O'Connor*.

McCarthy, John F. "Human Intelligence Versus Divine Truth: The Intellectual in Flannery O'Connor's Works," *English Journal* IV (Dec 1966), 1143-1148.

Meaders, Margaret Inman. "Flannery O'Connor: 'Literary Witch,' " *Colorado Quarterly* X (Spring 1962), 377-386.

Montgomery, Marion. "Flannery O'Connor and the Natural Man," *Mississippi Quarterly* XXI (Fall 1968), 235-242.

————. "Miss O'Connor and the Christ-Haunted," *Southern Review* IV (Summer 1968), 665-672.

Murray, James G. "Southland a la Russe," *Critic* XXI (Jun-Jul 1963), 26-28.

Quinn, Sister M. Bernetta, O.S.F. "Flannery O'Connor, a Realist of Distances," *The Added Dimension: The Art and Mind of Flannery O'Connor,* 157-183.

Rubin, Louis D., Jr. "Flannery O'Connor and the Bible Belt," *The Added Dimension: The Art and Mind of Flannery O'Connor,* 49-72.

————. "Flannery O'Connor and the Bible Belt," *The Curious Death of the Novel: Essays in American Literature,* 239-261.

Scott, Nathan A., Jr. "Flannery O'Connor's Testimony: The Pressure of Glory," *The Added Dimension: The Art and Mind of Flannery O'Connor,* 138-156.

Sessions, William. "Flannery O'Connor in Her own Words: A Correspondence," *The Added Dimension: The Art and Mind of Flannery O'Connor,* 209-225.

Shear, Walter. "Flannery O'Connor: Character and Characterization," *Renascence* XX (Spring 1968), 140-146.

Sherry, Gerard. "An Interview with Flannery O'Connor," *Critic* XXI (Jun-Jul 1963), 29-31.

Shinn, Thelma J. "Flannery O'Connor and the Violence of Grace," *Contemporary Literature* IX (Winter 1968), 58-73.

Snow, Ollye Tine. "The Functional Gothic of Flannery O'Connor," *Southwest Review* L (Summer 1965), 286-299.

Spivey, Ted R. "Flannery O'Connor's View of God and Man," *Studies in Short Fiction* I (Spring 1964), 200-206.

Stephens, Martha. "Flannery O'Connor and the Sanctified-Sinner Tradition," *Arizona Quarterly* 24 (Autumn 1968), 223-238.

Stern, Richard. "Flannery O'Connor: A Remembrance and Some Letters," *Shenandoah* XVI (Winter 1965), 5-10.

Sullivan, Walter. "The Achievement of Flannery O'Connor," *Southern Humanities Review* II (Summer 1968), 303-308.

Taylor, Henry. "The Halt Shall Be Gathered Together: Physical De-

O'CONNOR, FLANNERY, Continued

formity in the Fiction of Flannery O'Connor," *Western Humanities Review* XXII (Autumn 1968), 325-338.

Vande Kieft, Ruth M. "Judgment in the Fiction of Flannery O'Connor," *Sewanee Review* LXXVI (Spring 1968), 337-356.

BIBLIOGRAPHY

Brittain, Joan T. "Flannery O'Connor: A Bibliography," *Bulletin of Bibliography* XXV (Sept-Dec 1967), 98-100; (Jan-Apr 1968), 123-124.

————. "Flannery O'Connor: Addenda," *Bulletin of Bibliography* XXV (May-Aug 1968), 142.

Drake, Robert. *Flannery O'Connor: A Critical Essay*, 44-48.

Hyman, Stanley Edgar. *Flannery O'Connor*, 47-48.

Lawson, Lewis A. "Bibliography," *The Added Dimension: The Art and Mind of Flannery O'Connor*, 281-302.

Martin, Carter W. *The True Country: Themes in the Fiction of Flannery O'Connor*, 243-247.

O'HARA, JOHN

APPOINTMENT IN SAMARRA

Bier, Jesse. "O'Hara's *Appointment in Samarra*: His First and Only Real Novel," *College English* XXV (Nov 1963), 135-141.

Bruccoli, Matthew J. "Focus on *Appointment in Samarra*: The Importance of Knowing What You Are Talking About," *Tough Guy Writers of the Thirties*, 129-136.

Carson, Edward Russell. *The Fiction of John O'Hara*, 9-14.

Donaldson, Scott. "Appointment with the Dentist: O'Hara's Naturalistic Novel," *Modern Fiction Studies* XIV (Winter 1968-1969), 435-442.

Grebstein, Sheldon Norman. *John O'Hara*, 34-45.

Hierth, Harrison E. "The Class Novel," *CEA Critic* XXVII (Dec 1964) 1, 3-4.

ELIZABETH APPLETON

Grebstein, Sheldon Norman. *John O'Hara*, 75-82.

FROM THE TERRACE

Carson, Edward Russell. *The Fiction of John O'Hara*, 29-40.

A RAGE TO LIVE

Carson, Edward Russell. *The Fiction of John O'Hara*, 14-21.

Grebstein, Sheldon Norman. *John O'Hara*, 45-54.

O'HARA, JOHN, Continued

TEN NORTH FREDERICK
Carson, Edward Russell. *The Fiction of John O'Hara,* 21-29.
Grebstein, Sheldon Norman. *John O'Hara,* 54-63.
GENERAL
Auchincloss, Louis. "Marquand and O'Hara: the Novel of Manners," *Nation* 191 (Nov 19, 1960), 383-388.
Grebstein, Sheldon Norman. *John O'Hara.*
Van Nostrand, Albert. *The Denatured Novel,* 211-214.
BIBLIOGRAPHY
Carson, Edward Russell. *The Fiction of John O'Hara,* 73.
Clark, Alexander P. "Belles Letters: The John O'Hara Manuscripts at Penn State," *Manuscripts* XX (Fall 1968), 47-49.
Grebstein, Sheldon Norman. *John O'Hara,* 161-171.

OWEN, GUY

THE BALLAD OF THE FLIM-FLAM MAN
Owen, Guy. "My Successful Novel: Two Sides (of the story)," *Trace* 68 (1968), 217-221.

PAGE, THOMAS NELSON

GORDON KEITH
Gross, Theodore L. *Thomas Nelson Page,* 119-126.
King, Kimball. "Satirical Portraits by Thomas Nelson Page," *Mississippi Quarterly* XVIII (Spring 1965), 74-81.
JOHN MARVEL, ASSISTANT
Gross, Theodore L. *Thomas Nelson Page,* 129-139.
King, Kimball. "Satirical Portraits by Thomas Nelson Page," *Mississippi Quarterly* XVIII (Spring 1965), 74-81.
RED ROCK
Gross, Theodore L. *Thomas Nelson Page,* 78-95.
GENERAL
Gross, Theodore L. *Thomas Nelson Page.*
————. "Thomas Nelson Page: Creator of a Virginia Classic," *Georgia Review* XX (Fall 1966), 338-351.
Sowder, William J. "Gerald W. Johnson, Thomas Nelson Page, and the South," *Mississippi Quarterly* XIV (Fall 1961), 197-203.

PAGE, THOMAS NELSON, Continued

BIBLIOGRAPHY

Gross, Theodore L. *Thomas Nelson Page,* 165-172.

―――. "Thomas Nelson Page (1853-1922)," *American Literary Realism* 1 (Fall 1967), 90-92.

PARKMAN, FRANCIS

VASSALL MORTON

Doughty, Howard. *Francis Parkman,* 216-220.

PATCHEN, KENNETH

BIBLIOGRAPHY

See, Carolyn. "Kenneth Patchen, 1934-1958: A Partial Bibliography," *Bulletin of Bibliography* XXIII (Jan-Apr 1961), 81-84.

PAUL, ELLIOT

IMPROMPTU

Cooperman, Stanley. *World War I and the American Novel,* 148-152.

PAULDING, JAMES KIRKE

GENERAL

Aderman, Ralph M. "James Kirke Paulding as Social Critic," *Papers on English Language and Literature* I (Summer 1965), 217-229.

―――. "James Kirke Paulding's Literary Income," *Bulletin of the New York Public Library* LXIV (Mar 1960), 117-129.

――― (ed.). *The Letters of James Kirke Paulding.*

Herold, Amos L. "Paulding's Literary Theories," *Bulletin of the New York Public Library* LXVI (Apr 1962), 236-243.

BIBLIOGRAPHY

Aderman, Ralph M. "James Kirke Paulding's Contributions to American Magazines," *Studies in Bibliography* XVII (1964), 141-151.

―――. "Publication Dates of Three Early Works by James Kirke Paulding," *Papers of the Bibliographical Society of America* LIX (Jan-Mar 1965), 49-50.

PERCY, WALKER

THE LAST GENTLEMAN
Hoffman, Frederick J. *The Art of Southern Fiction,* 133-137.
THE MOVIEGOER
Hoffman, Frederick J. *The Art of Southern Fiction,* 129-133.
Thale, Mary. "The Moviegoer of the 1950's," *Twentieth Century Literature* 14 (Jul 1968), 84-89.
GENERAL
Brown, Ashley. "An Interview With Walker Percy," *Shenandoah* XVIII (Spring 1967), 3-10.
Cremeens, Carlton. "Walker Percy, the Man and the Novelist: An Interview," *Southern Review* IV (Spring 1968), 271-290.
Lehan, Richard. "The Way Back: Redemption in the Novels of Walker Percy," *Southern Review* IV (Spring 1968), 306-319.
Maxwell, Robert. "Walker Percy's Fancy," *Minnesota Review* VII (No 3, 1967), 231-237.

PHILLIPS, DAVID GRAHAM

THE DELUGE
Ravitz, Abe C. *David Graham Phillips,* 76-81.
THE HUNGRY HEART
Ravitz, Abe C. *David Graham Phillips,* 116-122.
SUSAN LENOX: HER FALL AND RISE
Ravitz, Abe C. *David Graham Phillips,* 141-160.
GENERAL
Blotner, Joseph. *The Modern American Political Novel,* 33-37.
Milne, Gordon. *The American Political Novel,* 95-103.
Ravitz, Abe C. *David Graham Phillips.*
BIBLIOGRAPHY
Ravitz, Abe C. *David Graham Phillips,* 180-184.
————. "David Graham Phillips (1867-1911)," *American Literary Realism* 3 (Summer 1968), 24-29.

PIERCE, OVID WILLIAMS

GENERAL
Betts, Doris. "The House by the River: Ovid Williams Pierce," *South Atlantic Quarterly* LXIV (Summer 1965), 283-295.

POE, EDGAR ALLAN

THE NARRATIVE OF ARTHUR GORDON PYM

Ashmore, Basil. Introduction, *The Mystery of Arthur Gordon Pym and Jules Verne* (Westport, Connecticut, 1961).

Bezanson, Walter E. "The Troubled Sleep of Arthur Gordon Pym," *Essays in Literary History*, 149-176.

Cecil, L. Moffitt. "The Two Narratives of Arthur Gordon Pym," *Texas Studies in Literature and Language* V (Summer 1963), 232-241.

Covici, Pascal, Jr. "Toward a Reading of Poe's *Narrative of A. Gordon Pym,*" *Mississippi Quarterly* XXI (Spring 1968), 111-118.

Fiedler, Leslie A. "The Blackness of Darkness: The Negro and the Development of American Gothic," *Images of the Negro in American Literature*, 84-89.

————. *Love and Death in the American Novel*, 370-382.

Fussell, Edwin. "Edgar Allan Poe," *Frontier: American Literature and the American West*, 149-155.

Kaplan, Sydney. "An Introduction to *Pym,*" *Poe: A Collection of Critical Essays*, 145-163.

Lee, Helen. "Possibilities of *Pym,*" *English Journal* LV (Dec 1966), 1149-1154.

Maxwell, D. E. S. "Poe and the Romantic Experiment," *American Fiction: The Intellectual Background*, 84-94.

Moss, Sydney P. "*Arthur Gordon Pym,* or The Fallacy of Thematic Interpretation," *University Review* XXXIII (Jun 1967), 299-306.

————. "A Conjecture Concerning the Writing of 'Arthur Gordon Pym,'" *Studies in Short Fiction* IV (Fall 1966), 83-85.

Ridgely, J. V. and Iola S. Haverstick. "Chartless Voyage: The Many Narratives of Arthur Gordon Pym," *Texas Studies in Literature and Language* VIII (Spring 1966), 63-80.

Tarbox, Raymond. "Blank Hallucinations in the Fiction of Poe and Hemingway," *American Imago* XXIV (Winter 1967), 312-343.

GENERAL

Bandy, W. T. "Baudelaire et Edgar Poe: Vue Retrospective," *Revue de Littérature Comparée* 41 (Apr-Jun 1967), 180-194.

Cox, James M. "Edgar Poe: Style as Pose," *Virginia Quarterly Review* 44 (Winter 1968), 67-89.

DuBois, Arthur E. "Poe and *Lolita,*" *CEA Critic* XXVI (Mar 1964), 1, 7.

Hubbell, Jay B. "Edgar Allan Poe and the South," *South and Southwest: Literary Essays and Reminiscences*, 100-122.

POE, EDGAR ALLEN, Continued

————. "Poe and the Southern Literary Tradition," *Texas Studies in Literature and Language* II (Summer 1960), 151-171.

Kronegger, M. E. "The Theory of Unity and Effect in the Works of E. A. Poe and James Joyce," *Revue de Littérature Comparée* 40 (Apr-Jun 1966), 226-234.

Sprout, Monique. "The Influence of Poe on Jules Verne," *Revue de Littérature Comparée* 41 (Jan-Mar 1967), 125-131.

BIBLIOGRAPHY

Dameron, J. Lasley. *Edgar Allan Poe: A Checklist of Criticism, 1942-1960*.

POOLE, ERNEST

THE HARBOR

Hart, John E. "Heroism Through Social Awareness: Ernest Poole's *The Harbor*," *Critique* IX (No 3, 1967), 84-94.

PORTER, KATHERINE ANNE

SHIP OF FOOLS

Alexander, Jean. "Katherine Anne Porter's Ship in the Jungle," *Twentieth Century Literature* XI (Jan 1966), 179-188.

Auchincloss, Louis. *Pioneers & Caretakers*, 145-151.

Curley, Daniel. "Katherine Anne Porter: The Larger Plan," *Kenyon Review* XXV (Autumn 1963), 671-695.

Hartley, Lodwick. "Dark Voyagers," *University Review* XXX (Dec 1963), 84-94.

Heilman, Robert. "*Ship of Fools:* Notes on Style," *Four Quarters* XII (Nov 1962), 46-55.

Hendrick, George. "Hart Crane Aboard *The Ship of Fools:* Some Speculations," *Twentieth Century Literature* IX (Apr 1963), 3-9.

————. *Katherine Anne Porter*, 118-128.

Hertz, Robert N. "Sebastian Brant and Porter's Ship of Fools," *Midwest Quarterly* VI (Summer 1965), 389-401.

Hoffman, Frederick J. *The Art of Southern Fiction*, 47-50.

Janeway, Elizabeth. "For Katherine Anne Porter 'Ship of Fools' was a Lively Twenty-Two Year Voyage," *New York Times Book Review* 67 (Apr 1, 1962), 4-5.

Joselyn, Sister M. "On the Making of *Ship of Fools*," *South Dakota Review* 1 (May 1964), 46-52.

Kauffmann, Stanley. "Katherine Anne Porter's Crowning Work," *New Republic* 146 (Apr 2, 1962), 23-25.

Lieberman, M. M. "The Responsibility of the Novelist: the Critical Reception of *Ship of Fools*," *Criticism* VIII (Fall 1966), 377-388.

————. "The Short Story as Chapter in *Ship of Fools*," *Criticism* X (Winter 1968), 65-71.

Marsden, Malcolm M. "Love as Threat in Katherine Anne Porter's Fiction," *Twentieth Century Literature* 13 (Apr 1967), 29-38.

Miller, Paul W. "Katherine Porter's *Ship of Fools*: A Masterpiece Manqué," *University Review* XXXII (Dec 1965), 151-157.

Mooney, Harry John, Jr. *The Fiction and Criticism of Katherine Anne Porter*, 55-62.

Nance, William L. *Katherine Anne Porter & the Art of Rejection*, 156-207.

Rubin, Louis D., Jr. " 'We Get Along Together Just Fine . . .' " *Four Quarters* XII (Mar 1963), 30-31.

Ruoff, James. "Katherine Anne Porter Comes to Kansas," *Midwest Quarterly* IV (Summer 1963), 305-314.

Ruoff, James and Del Smith. "Katherine Anne Porter on *Ship Of Fools*," *College English* XXIV (Feb 1963), 396-397.

Ryan, Marjorie. "Katherine Anne Porter: *Ship of Fools* and the Short Stories," *Bucknell Review* XII (Mar 1964), 51-63.

Solotaroff, Theodore. "*Ship of Fools* and the Critics," *Commentary* XXXIV (Oct 1962), 277-286.

Walcutt, Charles Child. "A Sargasso of the Sinister: Katherine Anne Porter's *Ship of Fools*," *Man's Changing Mask: Modes and Methods of Characterization in Fiction*, 145-158.

Wescott, Glenway. "Katherine Anne Porter: The Making of a Novel," *Atlantice Monthly* CCIX (Apr 1962), 43-49.

GENERAL

Auchincloss, Louis. "Katherine Anne Porter," *Pioneers & Caretakers*, 136-151.

Core, George. "The Best Residuum of Truth," *Georgia Review* XX (Fall 1960), 278-291.

Cruttwell, Patrick. "Swift, Miss Porter, and the 'Dialect of the Tribe,' " *Shenandoah* XVII (Spring 1966), 27-38.

Hendrick, George. *Katherine Anne Porter.*

Johnson, James William. "Another Look at Katherine Anne Porter," *Virginia Quarterly Review* XXXVI (Autumn 1960), 598-613.

Joselyn, Sister M., O.S.B. "Animal Imagery in Katherine Anne Porter's Fiction," *Myth and Symbol: Critical Approaches and Applications,* 101-115.

Lopez, Hank. "A Country and Some People I Love," *Harper's Magazine* CCXXXI (Sept 1965), 58-68.

Mooney, Harry John, Jr. *The Fiction and Criticism of Katherine Anne Porter.*

Nance, William L. *Katherine Anne Porter & the Art of Rejection.*

Thompson, Barbara. "An Interview with Katherine Anne Porter: The Art of Fiction XXIX," *Paris Review* VIII No. 29 (Winter-Spring 1963), 86-114.

West, Ray B., Jr. *Katherine Anne Porter.*

————. "Katherine Anne Porter and Historic Memory," *South: Modern Southern Literature in its Cultural Setting,* 301-313.

BIBLIOGRAPHY

Henderick, George. *Katherine Anne Porter,* 161-171.

Nance, William L. *Katherine Anne Porter & the Art of Rejection,* 251-253.

POWERS, J. F.

MORTE D'URBAN

Collignon, Joseph P. "Powers' *Morte D'Urban:* A Layman's Indictment," *Renascence* XVI (Fall 1963), 20-21, 51-52.

Hagopian, John. "Irony and Involution in J. F. Powers' *Morte D'Urban,*" *Contemporary Literature* IX (Spring 1968), 152-171.

————. *J. F. Powers,* 123-151.

Hynes, Joseph. "Father Urban's Renewal: J. F. Powers' Difficult Precision," *Modern Language Quarterly* XXIX (Dec 1968), 450-466.

Poss, Stanley. "J. F. Powers: The Gin of Irony," *Twentieth Century Literature* 14 (Jul 1968), 65-74.

Twombly, Robert G. "Hubris, Health, and Holiness: The Despair of J. F. Powers," *Seven Contemporary Authors,* 143-162.

GENERAL

Degnan, James P. "J. F. Powers: Comic Satirist," *Colorado Quarterly* XVI (Spring 1968), 325-333.

Hagopian, John V. *J. F. Powers.*

POWERS, J. F., Continued

McCarthy, Colman. "J. F. Powers at Smith," *Critic* XXV (Oct-Nov 1966), 50-57.
McDonald, Donald. "Interview with J. F. Powers," *Critic* XIX (Oct-Nov 1960), 20-21, 88-90.
BIBLIOGRAPHY
Hagopian, John V. *J. F. Powers,* 165-168.

PRICE, REYNOLDS

GENERAL
Hoffman, Frederick J. *The Art of Southern Fiction,* 137-143.
Kaufman, Wallace. "A Conversation With Reynolds Price," *Shenandoah* XVII (Spring 1966), 3-25.
Meras, Phyllis. "Talk with Reynolds Price," *New York Times Book Review* 71 (Mar 27, 1966), 44.
Price, Reynolds. "A Question of Influence," *New York Times Book Review* 71 (May 29, 1966), 2, 12.

PROKOSCH, FREDERIC

AGE OF THUNDER
Squires, Radcliffe. *Frederic Prokosch,* 91-96.
THE ASIATICS
Squires, Radcliffe. *Frederick Prokosch,* 48-53.
THE IDOLS OF THE CAVE
Squires, Radcliffe. *Frederick Prokosch,* 96-101.
NINE DAYS TO MUKALLA
Squires, Radcliffe. *Frederick Prokosch,* 61-69.
THE SEVEN SISTERS
Squires, Radcliffe. *Frederick Prokosch,* 120-130.
THE SEVEN WHO FLED
Squires, Radcliffe. *Frederick Prokosch,* 106-120.
THE SKIES OF EUROPE
Squires, Radcliffe. *Frederick Prokosch,* 70-79.
STORM AND ECHO
Squires, Radcliffe. *Frederick Prokosch,* 54-61.
GENERAL
Squires, Radcliffe. *Frederic Prokosch.*

PROKOSCH, FREDERIC, Continued

BIBLIOGRAPHY

Squires, Radcliffe. *Frederick Prokosch*, 151-152.

PURDY, JAMES

EUSTACE CHISHOLM AND THE WORKS

French, Warren. *Seasons of Promise*, 19-26.

Morris, Robert K. "James Purdy and the Works," *Nation* 205 (Oct 9, 1967), 342-344.

MALCOLM

Finkelstein, Sidney. *Existentialism and Alienation in American Literature*, 248-249.

Herr, Paul. "The Small, Sad World of James Purdy," *Chicago Review* XIV (Autumn-Winter 1960), 19-25.

Ishag, Saada. "The American Romance-Parody: A Study of Purdy's *Malcolm* and Heller's *Catch-22*," *The American Novel: Two Studies*, 42-51.

Lorch, Thomas M. "Purdy's *Malcolm:* A Unique Vision of Radical Emptiness," *Wisconsin Studies in Contemporary Literature* VI (Summer 1965), 204-213.

Scharzschild, Bettina. "The Forsaken: An Interpretive Essay on James Purdy's *Malcolm*," *Texas Quarterly* X (Spring 1967) 170-177.

THE NEPHEW

Finkelstein, Sidney. *Existentialism and Alienation in American Literature*, 249-252.

GENERAL

Cott, Jonathan. "The Damaged Cosmos," *On Contemporary Literature*, 498-505.

French, Warren. "The Quaking World of James Purdy," *Essays in Modern American Literature*, 112-122.

Malin, Irving. *New American Gothic*, 44-49, 75-78, 103-107, 151-155.

Pomeranz, Regina. "The Hell of Not Loving: Purdy's Modern Tragedy," *Renascence* XVI (Spring 1964), 149-153.

Schott, Webster. "James Purdy: American Dreams," *Nation* 198 (Mar 23, 1964), 300-302.

Weales, Gerald. "No Face and No Exit: The Fiction of James Purdy and J. P. Donleavy," *Contemporary American Novelists*, 143-149.

PYNCHEON, THOMAS

THE CRYING OF LOT 49

Sklar, Robert. "The New Novel, USA: Thomas Pyncheon," *Nation* 205 (Sept 25, 1967), 277-280.

V.

Hausdorff, Don. "Thomas Pyncheon's Multiple Absurdities, *Wisconsin Studies in Contemporary Literature* 7 (Autumn 1966), 258-269.

Hyman, Stanley Edgar. "The Goddess and the Schlemihl," *On Contemporary Literature,* 506-510.

Sklar, Robert. "The New Novel, USA: Thomas Pyncheon," *Nation* 205 (Sept 25, 1967), 277-280.

GENERAL

Young, James Dean. "The Enigma Variations of Thomas Pyncheon," *Critique: Studies in Modern Fiction* X (No 1, 1968), 69-77.

RAND, AYN

THE FOUNTAINHEAD

Ephron, Nora. "A Strange Kind of Simplicity," *New York Times Book Review* 73 (May 5, 1968), 8, 42.

RAWLINGS, MARJORIE KINNAN

CROSS CREEK

Bigelow, Gordon E. *Frontier Eden: The Literary Career of Marjorie Kinnan Rawlings,* 39-41, 138-144.

THE YEARLING

Bigelow, Gordon E. *Frontier Eden: The Literary Career of Marjorie Kinnan Rawlings,* 135-137, 150-155.

GENERAL

Bigelow, Gordon E. *Frontier Eden: The Literary Career of Marjorie Kinnan Rawlings.*

————. "Marjorie Kinnan Rawlings' Wilderness," *Sewanee Review* LXXIII (Spring 1965), 299-310.

BIBLIOGRAPHY

Bigelow, Gordon E. *Frontier Eden: The Literary Career of Marjorie Kinnan Rawlings,* i-vii.

RECHY, JOHN

THE CITY OF NIGHT
Hoffman, Stanton. "The Cities of Night: John Rechy's *City of Night* and the American Literature of Homosexuality," *Chicago Review* 2, 3 (1964), 195-213.

REECE, BYRON HERBERT

GENERAL
Griffith, E. V. "Byron Herbert Reece: A Personal Memoir with Letters," *Georgia Review* XIX (Summer 1965), 131-168.

REID, MAYNE

GENERAL
Meyer, Roy W. "The Western Fiction of Mayne Reid," *Western American Literature* III (Summer 1968), 115-132.

RHODES, EUGENE MANLOVE

GENERAL
Fife, Jim L. "Two Views of The American West," *Western American Literature* 1 (Spring 1966), 34-43.
Hutchinson, W. H. "I Pay for What I Break," *Western American Literature* 1 (Summer 1966), 91-96.

RICHTER, CONRAD

THE GRANDFATHERS
Gaston, Edwin W., Jr. *Conrad Richter,* 131-137.
THE LIGHT IN THE FOREST
Gaston, Edwin W., Jr. *Conrad Richter,* 125-131.
LaHood, Marvin J. "*The Light in the Forest:* History as Fiction," *English Journal* LV (Mar 1966), 298-304.
THE SEA OF GRASS
Barnes, Robert J. *Conrad Richter,* 16-25.
Gaston, Edwin W., Jr. *Conrad Richter,* 74-84.
A SIMPLE HONORABLE MAN
Gaston, Edwin W., Jr. *Conrad Richter,* 145-151.
TACEY CROMWELL

RICHTER, CONRAD, Continued

Barnes, Robert J. *Conrad Richter*, 25-30.
Gaston, Edwin W., Jr. *Conrad Richter*, 84-89.
THE TOWN
Gaston, Edwin W., Jr. *Conrad Richter*, 107-116.
THE TREES
Gaston, Edwin W., Jr. *Conrad Richter*, 96-103.
THE WATERS OF KRONOS
Gaston, Edwin W., Jr. *Conrad Richter*, 139-145.
GENERAL
Barnes, Robert J. *Conrad Richter*.
Gaston, Edwin W., Jr. *Conrad Richter*.
LaHood, Marvin J. "Richter's Early America," *University Review* XXX (Jun 1964), 311-316.
BIBLIOGRAPHY
Barnes, Robert J. *Conrad Richter*, 43-44.
Gaston, Edwin W., Jr. *Conrad Richter*, 167-170.

ROBERTS, ELIZABETH MADOX

BLACK IS MY TRUE LOVE'S HAIR
McDowell, Frederick P. W. *Elizabeth Madox Roberts*, 74-84.
Rovit, Earl H *Herald to Chaos: The Novels of Elizabeth Madox Roberts*, 116-128.
A BURIED TREASURE
McDowell, Frederick P. W. *Elizabeth Madox Roberts*, 63-74.
Rovit, Earl H. *Herald to Chaos: The Novels of Elizabeth Madox Roberts*, 99-116.
THE GREAT MEADOW
Rovit, Earl H. *Herald to Chaos: The Novels of Elizabeth Madox Roberts,* 48-66.
HE SENT FORTH A RAVEN
McDowell, Frederick P. W. *Elizabeth Madox Roberts*, 128-150.
Rovit, Earl H. *Herald to Chaos: The Novels of Elizabeth Madox Roberts*, 66-88.
JINGLING IN THE WIND
Rovit, Earl H. *Herald to Chaos: The Novels of Elizabeth Madox Roberts*, 89-99.
MY HEART AND MY FLESH
McDowell, Frederick P. W. *Elizabeth Madox Roberts*, 107-127.

ROBERTS, ELIZABETH MADOX, Continued

Rovit, Earl H. *Herald to Chaos: The Novels of Elizabeth Madox Roberts,* 26-47.

THE TIME OF MAN

Auchincloss, Louis. *Pioneers & Caretakers,* 124-128.

McDowell, Frederick P. W. *Elizabeth Madox Roberts,* 37-62.

Rovit, Earl H. *Herald to Chaos: The Novels of Elizabeth Madox Roberts,* 9-25.

GENERAL

Auchincloss, Louis. "Elizabeth Madox Roberts," *Pioneers & Caretakers,* 123-135.

McDowell, Frederick P. W. *Elizabeth Madox Roberts.*

Rovit, Earl H. *Herald to Chaos: The Novels of Elizabeth Madox Roberts,* 1-8, 129-162.

Warren, Robert Penn. "Life is from Within," *Saturday Review* 46 (March 2, 1963), 20-21, 38.

BIBLIOGRAPHY

McDowell, Frederick P. W. *Elizabeth Madox Roberts,* 169-172.

Rovit, Earl H. *Herald to Chaos: The Novels of Elizabeth Madox Roberts,* 165-169.

ROBERTS, KENNETH

GENERAL

Cary, Richard. "Inside Kenneth Roberts," *Colby Library Quarterly* VI (Sept 1962), 130-132.

————. "Roberts and Lorimer: The First Decade," *Colby Library Quarterly* VI (Sept 1962), 106-129.

Gibbs, A. Hamilton. "Letter to a Friend," *Colby Library Quarterly* VI (Sept 1962), 83-89.

West, Herbert Faulkner. "The Work of Kenneth Roberts," *Colby Library Quarterly* VI (Sept 1962), 89-99.

BIBLIOGRAPHY

Ellis, Marjorie Mosser. "Supplementary Bibliography of Kenneth Roberts," *Colby Library Quarterly* VI (Sept 1962), 99-105.

Stemple, Ruth. "Kenneth Roberts: A Supplementary Check-List," *Bulletin of Bibliography* XXII (Sept-Dec 1959), 228-230.

RÖLVAAG, O. E.

GIANTS IN THE EARTH

Fox, Maynard. "The Bearded Face Set Toward the Sun," *Ball State Teachers College Forum* I (Winter 1960-61), 62-64.

GENERAL

Gvale, Gudrun Hovde. *O. E. Rölvaag: nordmann og amerikanar.*

BIBLIOGRAPHY

Gvale, Gudrun Hovde. *O. E. Rölvaag: nordmann og amerikanar,* 413-419.

ROTH, HENRY

CALL IT SLEEP

Fiedler, Leslie A. "Henry Roth's Neglected Masterpiece," *Commentary* XXX (Aug 1960), 102-107.

Freedman, William. "Henry Roth and the Redemptive Imagination," *The Thirties: Fiction, Poetry, Drama,* 107-114.

Geismar, Maxwell. Introduction, *Call It Sleep* (Paterson, N.J., 1960).

Knowles, A. Sidney, Jr. "The Fiction of Henry Roth," *Modern Fiction Studies* XI (Winter 1965-1966), 393-404.

Ledbetter, Kenneth. "Henry Roth's *Call It Sleep:* The Revival of a Proletarian Novel," *Twentieth Century Literature* XII (Oct 1966), 123-130.

Mortara, Elèna "L'arte di Henry Roth," *Studi Americani* 12 (1966), 231-257.

Ribalow, Harold U. "Henry Roth and His Novel *Call It Sleep,*" *Wisconsin Studies in Contemporary Literature* 3 (Fall 1962), 5-14.

ROTH, PHILIP

LETTING GO

Detweiler, Robert. *Four Spiritual Crises in Mid-Century American Fiction,* 25-35.

Hyman, Stanley Edgar. "A Novelist of Great Promise," *On Contemporary Literature,* 532-536.

WHEN SHE WAS GOOD

Gilman, Richard. " 'Let's Lynch Lucy,' " *New Republic* 156 (Jun 24, 1967), 19-21.

ROTH, PHILIP, Continued

GENERAL

Alter, Robert. "When He Is Bad," *Commentary* XLIV (Nov 1967), 86-87.

Hyman, Stanley Edgar. "A Novelist of Great Promise," *On Contemporary Literature*, 532-536.

Landis, Joseph C. "The Sadness of Philip Roth: An Interim Report," *Massachusetts Review* III (Winter 1962), 259-268.

ROYSTON, SAMUEL WATSON

THE ENEMY CONQUERED: OR, LOVE TRIUMPHANT

Cardwell, Guy A. "Mark Twain's Failures in Comedy and *The Enemy Conquered*," *Georgia Review* XIII (Winter 1959), 424-436.

RYLEE, ROBERT

THE RING AND THE CROSS

Blotner, Joseph. *The Modern American Political Novel*, 257-260.

SALINGER, J. D.

THE CATCHER IN THE RYE

Baumbach, Jonathan. "The Saint as a Young Man: *The Catcher in the Rye* by J. D. Salinger," *The Landscape of Nightmare: Studies in the Contemporary American Novel*, 55-67.

————. "The Saint as a Young Man: A Reappraisal of *The Catcher in the Rye*," *Modern Language Quarterly* XXV (Dec 1964), 461-472.

Bowden, Edwin T. *The Dungeon of the Heart: Human Isolation and the American Novel*, 54-65.

Bungert, Hans. "J. D. Salingers *The Catcher in the Rye*: Isolation und Kommunikationsversuche des Jungendlichen," *Neueren Sprachen* (May 1960), 208-217.

————. "Salinger's *The Catcher in the Rye*: The Isolated Youth and His Struggle to Communicate," *Studies in J. D. Salinger*, 177-185.

Burack, Boris. "Holden the Courageous," *CEA Critic* XXVII (May 1965), 1.

SALINGER, J. D., Continued

Cagle, Charles. *"The Catcher in the Rye* Revisited," *Midwest Quarterly* IV (Summer 1963), 343-351.

Chester, Alfred. "Salinger: How To Love Without Love," *Commentary* XXXV (Jun 1963), 467-474.

Chugunov, Konstantin. "Soviet Critics on J. D. Salinger's Novel, *The Catcher in the Rye,*" *Studies in J. D. Salinger,* 186-189.

Cohen, Hubert I. " 'A Woeful Agony Which Forced Me to Begin My Tale': *The Catcher in the Rye,*" *Modern Fiction Studies* XII (Autumn 1966), 355-366.

Corbett, Edward P. J. "Raise High the Barriers, Censors," *J. D. Salinger and the Critics,* 54-59.

————. "Raise High the Barriers, Censors," *Studies in J. D. Salinger,* 134-141.

Costello, Donald P. "The Language of *The Catcher in the Rye,*" *American Speech* XXXIV (Oct 1959), 172-181.

————. "The Language of *The Catcher in the Rye,*" *Salinger: A Critical and Personal Portrait,* 266-276.

————. "From 'The Language of *The Catcher in the Rye,*' " *J. D. Salinger and the Critics,* 45-53.

————. "Salinger and 'Honest Iago,' " *Renascence* XVI (Summer 1964), 171-174.

Creeger, George R. "Treacherous Desertion: Salinger's *The Catcher in the Rye,*" *J. D. Salinger and the Critics,* 98-104.

D'Avanzo, Mario L. "Gatsby and Holden Caulfield," *Fitzgerald Newsletter* 38 (Summer 1967), 4-6.

Davis, Tom. "J. D. Salinger: 'Some Crazy Cliff' Indeed," *Western Humanities Review* XIV (Winter 1960), 97-99.

Ely, Sister M. Amanda, O. P. "The Adult Image in Three Novels of Adolescent Life," *English Journal* LVI (Nov 1967), 1127-1131.

Finkelstein, Sidney. *Existentialism and Alienation in American Literature,* 219-224.

Fogel, Amy. "Where the Ducks Go: *The Catcher in the Rye,*" *Ball State Teachers College Forum* III (Spring 1962), 75-79.

Foran, Donald J., S. J. "A Doubletake on Holden Caulfield," *English Journal* LVII (Oct 1968), 977-979.

French, Warren. "Holden's Fall," *Modern Fiction Studies* X (Winter 1964-65), 389.

————. *J. D. Salinger,* 102-129.

Galloway, David D. *The Absurd Hero in American Fiction,* 140-146.

Gutwillig, Robert. "Everybody's Caught 'The Catcher in the Rye,'" *New York Times Book Review* 66 (Part II, Paperback Book Section, Jan 15, 1961), 38-39.

————. "Everybody's Caught *The Catcher in the Rye,*" *Studies in J. D. Salinger,* 1-39.

Hainsworth, J. D. "Maturity in J. D. Salinger's 'The Catcher in the Rye,'" *English Studies* XLVIII (Oct 1967), 426-431.

Harper, Howard M., Jr. *Desperate Faith,* 66-71.

Howell, John M. "Salinger in the Waste Land," *Modern Fiction Studies* XII (Autumn 1966), 367-375.

Kinney, Arthur F. "J. D. Salinger and the Search for Love," *Texas Studies in Literature and Language* V (Spring 1963), 111-126.

Laser, Marvin and Norman Fruman. "Not Suitable for Temple City," *Studies in J. D. Salinger,* 124-129.

Light, James F. "Salinger's *The Catcher in the Rye,*" *Explicator* XVIII (Jun 1960), No. 59.

Malin, Irving. "The Gothic Family," *Psychoanalysis and American Fiction,* 264-266.

————. *New American Gothic,* 61-63, 87-88, 117-119.

Marcus, Fred H. "*The Catcher in the Rye:* A Live Circuit," *English Journal* LII (Jan 1963), 1-8.

Margolis, John D. "Salinger's *The Catcher in the Rye,*" *Explicator* XXII (Nov 1963), No. 23.

McNamara, Eugene. "Holden as Novelist," *English Journal* LIV (Mar 1965), 166-170.

Miller, James E., Jr. *J. D. Salinger,* 8-19.

Miller, James E. and Arthur Heiserman. "J. D. Salinger: Some Crazy Cliff," *Quests Surd and Absurd: Essays in American Literature,* 31-40.

Moore, Everett T. "Catcher and Mice," *Studies in J. D. Salinger,* 130-134.

Moore, Robert P. "The World of Holden," *English Journal* LIV (Mar 1965), 159-165.

O'Hara, J. D. "No Catcher in the Rye," *The Modern American Novel: Essays in Criticism,* 211-220.

————. "No Catcher in the Rye," *Modern Fiction Studies* IX (Winter 1963-64), 370-376.

Oldsey, Bernard S. "The Movies in the Rye," *J. D. Salinger and the Critics,* 68-75.

SALINGER, J. D., Continued

Parker, Christopher. "Why the Hell Not Smash All the Windows?" *Salinger: A Critical and Personal Portrait*, 254-258.

Peavy, Charles D. "Holden's Courage Again," *CEA Critic* XXVIII (Oct 1965), 1, 6, 9.

Reiman, Donald H. "Salinger's *The Catcher in the Rye*," *Explicator* XXI (Mar 1963), No. 58.

Salinger's Catcher in the Rye: Clamor vs. Criticism.

Seng, Peter J. "The Fallen Idol: The Immature World of Holden Caulfield," *J. D. Salinger and the Critics*, 60-68.

Slabey, Robert M. "*The Catcher in the Rye*: Christian Theme and Symbol," *CLA Journal* VI (Mar 1963), 170-183.

Stone, Edward. "Salinger's Carrousel," *Modern Fiction Studies* XIII (Winter 1967-68), 520-523.

Strauch, Carl F. "Kings in the Back Row: Meaning Through Structure: A Reading of Salinger's *The Catcher in the Rye*," *J. D. Salinger and the Critics*, 76-98.

————. "Kings in the Back Row: Meaning Through Structure: A Reading of Salinger's *The Catcher in the Rye*," *Studies in J. D. Salinger*, 143-171.

————. "Kings in the Back Row: Meaning Through Structure: A Reading of Salinger's *The Catcher in the Rye*," *Wisconsin Studies in Contemporary Literature* 2 (Winter 1961), 5-30.

Tamaya, M. "Salinger: *The Catcher in the Rye*," *Literary Half-Yearly* VII (Jul 1966), 49-60.

Tirumalai, Candadai K. "Salinger's *The Catcher in the Rye*," *Explicator* XXII (Mar 1964), No. 56.

Travis, Mildred K. "Salinger's *The Catcher in the Rye*," *Explicator* XXI (Dec 1962), No. 36.

Trowbridge, Clinton W. "Hamlet and Holden," *English Journal* 57 (Jan 1968), 26-29.

————. "The Symbolic Structure of *The Catcher in the Rye*," *Sewanee Review* LXXIV (Summer 1966), 681-693.

Vanderbilt, Kermit. "Symbolic Resolution in *The Catcher in the Rye*: The Cap, the Carrousel, and the American West," *Western Humanities Review* XVII (Summer 1963), 271-277.

Walcutt, Charles Child. "Anatomy of Alienation: J. D. Salinger's *The Catcher in the Rye*," *Man's Changing Mask: Modes and Methods of Characterization in Fiction*, 317-325.

SALINGER, J. D., Continued

GENERAL

Amoruso, Vito. "La Visione E Il Caos: Il Decadentismo Di Salinger," *Studi Americani* X (1964), 317-342.

Barr, Donald. "Ah, Buddy: Salinger," *The Creative Present*, 27-62.

Baskett, Sam S. "The Splendid Squalid World of J. D. Salinger," *Wisconsin Studies in Contemporary Literature* 4 (Winter 1963), 48-62.

Blotner, Joseph L. "Salinger Now: An Appraisal," *Wisconsin Studies in Contemporary Literature* 4 (Winter 1963), 100-108.

Fink, Guido. "Salinger, o la magia del nome proprio," *Studi Americani* 12 (1966), 259-276.

Finkelstein, Sidney. *Existentialism and Alienation in American Literature*, 224-234.

French, Warren. *J. D. Salinger*.

Galloway, David D. "The Love Ethic," *The Absurd Hero in American Fiction*, 140-169.

Glazier, Lyle. "The Glass Family Saga: Argument and Epiphany," *College English* XXVII (Dec 1965), 248-251.

Goldstein, Bernice and Sanford. "Zen and Salinger," *Modern Fiction Studies* XII (Autumn 1966), 313-324.

Green, Martin. "The Image-Maker," *Salinger: A Critical and Personal Portrait*, 247-253.

————. *Re-Appraisals: Some Commonsense Readings of American Literature*, 197-229.

Hamilton, Kenneth. *J. D. Salinger: A Critical Essay*.

————. "J. D. Salinger's Happy Family," *Queen's Quarterly* LXXI (Summer, 1964), 176-187.

Harper, Howard M., Jr. "J. D. Salinger—Through the Glasses Darkly," *Desperate Faith*, 65-95.

Hassan, Ihab. "Almost the Voice of Silence: The Later Novelettes of J. D. Salinger," *Wisconsin Studies in Contemporary Literature* 4 (Winter 1963), 5-20.

————. "From *Radical Innocence: Studies in the Contemporary American Novel*," *J. D. Salinger and the Critics*, 115-120.

————. "J. D. Salinger: Rare Quixotic Gesture," *Studies in J. D. Salinger*, 57-68.

————. *Radical Innocence: Studies in the Contemporary American Novel*, 259-289.

SALINGER, J. D., Continued

Hayes, Ann L. "J. D. Salinger: A Reputation and a Promise," *Lectures on Modern Novelists*, 15-24.

Kazin, Alfred. "J. D. Salinger: 'Everybody's Favorite,' " *Atlantic Monthly* CCVIII (Aug 1961), 27-31.

————. "J. D. Salinger: Everybody's Favorite," *J. D. Salinger and the Critics*, 158-166.

Kim, Chong-Un. "The Novels of J. D. Salinger," *English Language and Literature* 8 (Jun 1960), 107-119.

Larner, Jeremy. "Salinger's Audience: An Explanation," *Partisan Review* XXIX (Fall 1962), 594-598.

Leitch, David. "The Salinger Myth," *Salinger: A Critical and Personal Portrait*, 69-77.

Lorch, Thomas M. "J. D. Salinger: the Artist, the Audience, and the Popular Arts," *South Dakota Review* 5 (Winter 1967-68), 3-13.

McCarthy, Mary. "J. D. Salinger's Closed Circuit," *Harper's* 225 (Oct 1962), 46-48.

Miller, James E., Jr. *J. D. Salinger*.

Mizener, Arthur. "The American Hero as Poet: Seymour Glass," *The Sense of Life in the Modern Novel*, 227-246.

Nathan, Monique. "J. D. Salinger Et Le Rêve Américain," *Critique* XVIII (Apr 1962), 299-305.

Noland, Richard W. "The Novel of Personal Formula: J. D. Salinger," *University Review* XXXIII (Oct 1966), 19-24.

Rees, Richard. "The Salinger Situation," *Contemporary American Novelists*, 95-105.

Russell, John. "Salinger's Feat," *Modern Fiction Studies* XII (Autumn 1966), 299-311.

Sethom, Mohamed. "L'Univers Verbal de J. D. Salinger," *Études Anglaises* XXI (Jan-Mar 1968), 57-64.

Skow, John. "Sonny: An Introduction," *Salinger: A Critical and Personal Portrait*, 3-21.

Skow, John and others. "Sonny: An Introduction," *J. D. Salinger and the Critics*, 1-7.

Strauch, Carl F. "Salinger: The Romantic Background," *Wisconsin Studies in Contemporary Literature* 4 (Winter 1963), 31-40.

Swados, Harvey. "Must Writers Be Characters?" *Studies in J. D. Salinger*, 119-121.

Walzer, Michael. "In Place of a Hero," *J. D. Salinger and the Critics*, 129-137.

SALINGER, J. D., Continued

Wiegand, William. "The Knighthood of J. D. Salinger," *Salinger: A Critical and Personal Portrait,* 116-122.

―――. "Salinger and Kierkegaard," *Minnesota Review* V (May-July 1965), 137-156.

BIBLIOGRAPHY

Beebe, Maurice and Jennifer Sperry. "Criticism of J. D. Salinger: A Selected Checklist," *Modern Fiction Studies* XII (Autumn 1966), 377-390.

Fiene, Donald M. "J. D. Salinger: A Bibliography," *Wisconsin Studies in Contemporary Literature* 4 (Winter 1963), 109-149.

French, Warren, *J. D. Salinger,* 179-186.

Galloway, David D. *The Absurd Hero in American Fiction,* 226-251.

J. D. Salinger and the Critics, 172-179.

Miller, James E., Jr. *J. D. Salinger,* 46-48.

SANDBURG, CARL

REMEMBRANCE ROCK

Crowder, Richard. *Carl Sandburg,* 140-150.

SANDOZ, MARI

GENERAL

Lowe, David. "A Meeting with Mari Sandoz," *Prairie Schooner* XLII (Spring 1968), 21-26.

SANTAYANA, GEORGE

THE LAST PURITAN

Ballowe, James C. "*The Last Puritan* and the Failure in American Culture," *American Quarterly* XVIII (Summer 1966), 123-135.

Marshall, William H. "An Expanding Theme in *The Last Puritan,*" *Personalist* XLV (Winter 1964), 27-40.

Warren, Austin. *The New England Conscience,* 202-207.

Wermuth, Paul C. "Santayana and Emerson," *Emerson Society Quarterly* 31 (II Quarter 1963), 36-40.

GENERAL

Porte, Joel. "Santayana at the 'Gas House,'" *New England Quarterly* XXXV (Sept 1962), 337-346.

SAROYAN, WILLIAM

THE LAUGHING MATTER
Floan, Howard R. *William Saroyan*, 138-143.
GENERAL
Angoff, Charles. *The Tone of the Twenties and Other Essays*, 203-208.
Floan, Howard R. *William Saroyan.*
Saroyan, William. "Why Does a Writer Write?" *Saturday Review* XLIV (Feb 25, 1961) , 24, 46.
Singer, Felix. "Saroyan at 57: The Daring Young Man After the Fall," *Trace* 60 (Spring 1966) , 2-5.
BIBLIOGRAPHY
Kherdian, David. *A Bibliography of William Saroyan, 1934-1964.*

SCHMITT, GLADYS

GENERAL
Fuller, Edmund. "Gladys Schmitt 'Jacob and the Angel,' " *American Scholar* XXX (Summer 1961) , 411-417.
Schmitt, Gladys. "Is Fiction's Future in the Past?" *New York Times Book Review* 67 (Apr 22, 1962) , 1, 26.

SCOTT, EVELYN

GENERAL.
Welker, Robert L. "Liebstod with a Southern Accent," *Reality and Myth: Essays in American Literature in Memory of Richmond Croom Beatty*, 179-211.

SEAGER, ALLAN

EQUINOX
Bloom, Robert. "Allan Seager: Some Versions of Disengagement," *Critique* V (Winter 1962-1963) , 4-26.
THE INHERITANCE
Bloom, Robert. "Allan Seager: Some Versions of Disengagement," *Critique* V (Winter 1962-1963) , 4-26.
GENERAL
Hanna, Allan. "The Muse of History: Allan Seager and the Criticism of Culture," *Critique* V (Winter 1962-1963) , 37-61.
Kenner, Hugh. "The Insider," *Critique* II (Winter 1959) 3-15.

309

SEAGER, ALLEN, Continued

Lid, R. W. "The Innocent Eye," *Critique* V (Winter 1962-1963), 62-74.
Webster, Harvey Curtis. "Allan Seager as Social Novelist," *Critique* V (Winter 1962-1963), 27-36.
BIBLIOGRAPHY
Hanna, Allan. "An Allan Seager Bibliography," *Critique* V (Winter 1962-1963), 75-90.

SHAW, IRWIN

GENERAL
Eisinger, Chester E. *Fiction of the Forties,* 106-113.
Startt, William. "Irwin Shaw: An Extended Talent," *Midwest Quarterly* II (Summer 1961), 325-337.

SHELDON, CHARLES M.

IN HIS STEPS
Holman, C. Hugh. Introduction, *Ten Nights in a Bar Room,* and *In His Steps* (New York, 1966).

SHULMAN, MAX

GENERAL
Nash, Russell W. "Max Shulman and the Changing Image of Suburbia," *Midcontinent American Studies Journal* IV (Spring 1963), 27-38.

SIMMS, WILLIAM GILMORE

BEAUCHAMPE; OR, THE KENTUCKY TRAGEDY
Gates, W. B. "William Gilmore Simms and *The Kentucky Tragedy*," *American Literature* XXXII (May 1960), 158-166.
CONFESSION; OR, THE BLIND HEART
Bush, Lewis M. "Werther on the Alabama Frontier: A Reinterpretation of Simms' *Confession,*" *Mississippi Quarterly* XXI (Spring 1968), 119-130.
EUTAH
Ridgely, J. V. *William Gilmore Simms,* 107-118.

SIMMS, WILLIAM GILMORE, Continued

THE FORAYERS

Ridgely, J. V. *William Gilmore Simms*, 107-118.

PADDY McGANN

Bush, Robert. "*Paddy McGann,* William Gilmore Simm's Devil Story," *Bulletin of the New York Public Library* LXIX (Mar 1965), 197-204.

WOODCRAFT

Beatty, Richmond C. Introduction, *Woodcraft, or Hawks About the Dovecote: A Story of the South at the Close of the Revolution* (New York, 1961).

Cecil, L. Moffitt, "Simms's Porgy as National Hero," *American Literature* XXXVI (Jan 1965), 475-484.

Ridgely, J. V. *William Gilmore Simms*, 97-104.

————. "*Woodcraft:* Simms's First Answer to *Uncle Tom's Cabin,*" *American Literature* XXXI (Jan 1960), 421-433.

THE YEMASSEE

Cecil, L. Moffitt. "Symbolic Pattern in *The Yemassee,*" *American Literature* XXXV (Jan 1964), 510-514.

Holman, C. Hugh. Introduction, *The Yemassee: A Romance of Carolina* (Boston, 1961).

Ridgely, Joseph V. Introduction, *The Yemassee* (New York, 1964).

GENERAL

Fiedler, Leslie A. *Love and Death in the American Novel,* 219-222.

Guilds, John C. "William Gilmore Simms and the *Southern Literary Gazette,*" *Studies in Bibliography* XXI (1968), 59-92.

Herington, Hugh W. *Cavalier of Old South Carolina: William Gilmore Simms's Captain Porgy,* 3-74.

Holman, C. Hugh. "William Gilmore Simms and the 'American Renaissance,'" *Mississippi Quarterly* XV (Summer 1962), 126-137.

Meriwether, James B. "The Proposed Edition of William Gilmore Simms," *Mississippi Quarterly* XV (Summer 1962), 100-112.

Ridgely, J. V. *William Gilmore Simms.*

Wimsatt, Mary Ann. "Simms and Irving," *Mississippi Quarterly* XX (Winter 1966-1967), 25-37.

BIBLIOGRAPHY

Ridgely, J. V. *William Gilmore Simms,* 138-141.

SINCLAIR, UPTON

BOSTON

Blotner, Joseph. *The Modern American Political Novel*, 286-290.

THE JUNGLE

Downs, Robert B. Afterword, *The Jungle* (New York, 1960) .

Swados, Harvey. "The World of Upton Sinclair," *Atlantic Monthly* CCVIII (Dec 1961) , 96-102.

OIL!

Blotner, Joseph. *The Modern American Political Novel*, 113-115.

GENERAL

Allatt, Edward. "Jack London and Upton Sinclair," *Jack London Newsletter* 1 (Jan-Jun 1968) , 22-27.

Gotesman, Ronald. "Upton Sinclair and the Sinclair Archives," *Manuscripts* XVII (Fall 1965) , 11-20.

Putt, S. Gorley. "World Without End: Upton Sinclair and Lanny Budd," *Scholars of the Heart: Essays in Criticism,* 87-109.

Sinclair, Upton. "Mr. Upton-Sinclair-Lewis," *Harper's* CCXXII (Mar 1961) , 48.

————. *My Lifetime in Letters.*

Springer, Anne M. *The American Novel in Germany: A Study of the Critical Reception of Eight American Novelists Between the Two World Wars,* 39-45.

BIBLIOGRAPHY

Price, Lawrence Marsden. *The Reception of United States Literature in Germany,* 223-224.

SKINNER, B. F.

WALDEN TWO

Stilwell, Robert L. "Literature and Utopia: B. F. Skinner's *Walden Two,*" *Western Humanities Review* XVIII (Autumn 1964) , 331-341.

SMITH, LILLIAN

STRANGE FRUIT

Marcus, Fred H. "*Cry, the Beloved Country* and *Strange Fruit:* Exploring Man's Inhumanity to Man," *English Journal* LI (Dec 1962) , 609-616.

SONTAG, SUSAN

DEATH KIT

Koch, Stephen. "Sontag: Shaking the Tree of Death," *Nation* 205 (Oct 2, 1967), 310-311.

Solotaroff, Theodore. "Death in Life," *Commentary* XLIV (Nov 1967), 87-89.

GENERAL

Ellmann, Mary. "The Sensational Susan Sontag," *Atlantic Monthly* CCXVIII (Sept 1966), 59-63.

Heilbrun, Carolyn G. "Speaking of Susan Sontag," *New York Times Book Review* 72 (Aug 27, 1967), 2, 30.

SORENSEN, VIRGINIA

THE PROPER GODS

Robinson, Cecil. *With the Ears of Strangers: The Mexican in American Literature,* 224-227.

SOUTHERN, TERRY

THE MAGIC CHRISTIAN

Scholes, Robert. *The Fabulators,* 61-66.

GENERAL

Algren, Nelson. "The Donkeyman by Twilight," *Nation* 198 (May 18, 1964), 509-512.

SPENCER, ELIZABETH

GENERAL

Burger, Nash K. "Elizabeth Spencer's Three Mississippi Novels," *South Atlantic Quarterly* LXIII (Summer 1964), 351-362.

STAFFORD, JEAN

THE MOUNTAIN LION

Burns, Stuart L. "Counterpoint in Jean Stafford's *The Mountain Lion,*" *Critique* IX (No 2, 1966), 20-32.

GENERAL

Auchincloss, Louis. "Jean Stafford," *Pioneers & Caretakers,* 152-160.

Eisinger, Chester E. *Fiction of the Forties,* 294-307.

Vickery, Olga W. "Jean Stafford and the Ironic Vision," *South Atlantic Quarterly* LXI (Autumn 1962) , 484-491.

―――――. "The Novels of Jean Stafford," *Critique* V (Spring-Summer, 1962) , 14-26.

STEIN, GERTRUDE

THE MAKING OF AMERICANS

Baldanza, Frank. "Faulkner and Stein: A Study in Stylistic Intransigence," *Georgia Review* XIII (Fall 1959) , 274-286.

Bridgman, Richard. *The Colloquial Style in America,* 182-188.

Hoffman, Michael J. *The Development of Abstractionism in the Writings of Gertrude Stein,* 97-142.

THINGS AS THEY ARE

Bridgman, Richard. *The Colloquial Style in America,* 167-174.

Hoffman, Michael J. *The Development of Abstractionism in the Writings of Gertrude Stein,* 31-61.

THREE LIVES

Bridgman, Richard. *The Colloquial Style in America,* 174-182.

Hoffman, Michael J. *The Development of Abstractionism in the Writings of Gertrude Stein,* 62-96.

GENERAL

Berthoff, Warner. *The Ferment of Realism: American Literature, 1884-1919,* 247-253.

Bridgman, Richard. "Gertrude Stein," *The Colloquial Style in America,* 165-192.

de Morinni, Clara More. "Miss Stein and the Ladies," *New Republic* 157 (Nov 11, 1967) , 17-19.

Dupee, F. W. "Gertrude Stein," *Commentary* XXXIII (Jun 1962) , 519-523.

Hoffman, Frederick J. *Gertrude Stein.*

―――――. "Gertrude Stein in the Psychology Laboratory," *American Quarterly* XVII (Spring 1965) , 127-132.

―――――. "Gertrude Stein and William James," *Personalist* XLVII (Spring 1966) , 226-233.

―――――. "Gertrude Stein's 'Portraits,' " *Twentieth Century Literature* XI (Oct 1965) , 115-122.

Schorer, Mark. "Some Relationships: Gertrude Stein, Sherwood An-

STEIN, GERTRUDE, Continued

derson, F. Scott Fitzgerald, and Ernest Hemingway," *The World We Imagine: Selected Essays*, 299-382.

Shaw, Barnett. "Encounter with Gertrude Stein, Paris, 1944," *Texas Quarterly* IX (Autumn 1966), 21-23.

Stewart, Allegra. *Gertrude Stein and the Present.*

Tanner, Tony. "Gertrude Stein and the Complete Actual Present," *The Reign of Wonder: Naivety and Reality in American Literature*, 187-204.

Toklas, Alice B. *What is Remembered.*

Wright, George T. "Gertrude Stein and Her Ethic of Self-Containment," *Tennessee Studies in Literature* VIII (1963), 17-23.

BIBLIOGRAPHY

Hoffman, Michael J. *The Development of Abstractionism in the Writings of Gertrude Stein*, 217-224.

STEINBECK, JOHN

CANNERY ROW

Alexander, Stanley. "*Cannery Row:* Steinbeck's Pastoral Poem," *Western American Literature* II (Winter 1968), 281-295.

Fontenrose, Joseph. *John Steinbeck*, 101-108.

French, Warren. *John Steinbeck*, 120-136.

CUP OF GOLD

French, Warren. *John Steinbeck*, 31-38.

EAST OF EDEN

Fontenrose, Joseph. *John Steinbeck*, 118-127.

Watt, F. W. *John Steinbeck*, 93-99.

THE GRAPES OF WRATH

Beck, Warren. "On John Steinbeck," *Talks With Authors*, 56-72.

Bowden, Edwin T. *The Dungeon of the Heart: Human Isolation and the American Novel*, 138-148.

Cannon, Gerard. "The Pauline Apostleship of Tom Joad," *College English* XXIV (Dec 1962), 222-224.

A Casebook on the Grapes of Wrath.

Chametzky, Jules. "The Ambivalent Endings of *The Grapes of Wrath*," *Modern Fiction Studies* XI (Spring 1965), 34-44.

A Companion to The Grapes of Wrath.

Crockett, H. Kelly. "The Bible and *The Grapes of Wrath*," *College English* XXIV (Dec 1962), 193-199.

STEINBECK, JOHN, Continued

Dougherty, Charles T. "The Christ-Figure in *The Grapes of Wrath*," *College English* XXIV (Dec 1962), 224-226.

Fontenrose, Joseph. *John Steinbeck*, 67-83.

French, Warren. *John Steinbeck*, 95-112.

————. *The Social Novel at the End of an Era*, 42-86, 157-170.

Hayashi, Tetsumaro T. "Women and the Principle of Continuity in *The Grapes of Wrath*," *Visva-Bharati Quarterly* 31 (No 2, 1965-1966), 201-206.

Hunter, J. P. "Steinbeck's Wine of Affirmation in *The Grapes of Wrath*," *Essays in Modern American Literature*, 76-89.

McCarthy, Paul. "House and Shelter as Symbol in *The Grapes of Wrath*," *South Dakota Review* 5 (Winter 1967-68), 48-67.

Slade, Leonard A., Jr. "The Use of Biblical Allusions in *The Grapes of Wrath*," *CLA Journal* XI (Mar 1968), 241-247.

Watt, F. W. *John Steinbeck*, 63-75.

IN DUBIOUS BATTLE

Fontenrose, Joseph. *John Steinbeck*, 42-53.

French, Warren. *John Steinbeck*, 62-71.

Hartt, Julian N. *The Lost Image of Man*, 74-79.

Levant, Howard. "The Unity of *In Dubious Battle:* Violence and Dehumanization," *Modern Fiction Studies* XI (Spring 1965), 21-33.

THE MOON IS DOWN

French, Warren. *John Steinbeck*, 113-119.

OF MICE AND MEN

Fontenrose, Joseph. *John Steinbeck*, 53-59.

French, Warren G. "The First Theatrical Production of Steinbeck's *Of Mice and Men*," *American Literature* XXXVI (Jan 1965), 525-527.

————. *John Steinbeck*, 72-79.

Ganapathy, R. "Steinbeck's *Of Mice and Men:* A Study in Lyricism Through Primitivism," *Literary Criterion* V (Winter 1962), 101-104.

THE PASTURES OF HEAVEN

French, Warren. *John Steinbeck*, 39-46.

THE PEARL

Bartel, Roland. "Proportioning in Fiction: *The Pearl* and *Silas Marner*," *English Journal* LVI (Apr 1967), 542-546.

Karsten, Ernest E., Jr. "Thematic Structure in *The Pearl*," *English Journal* LIV (Jan 1965), 1-7.

STEINBECK, JOHN, Continued

Morris, Harry. *"The Pearl:* Realism and Allegory," *English Journal* LII (Oct 1963), 487-495.

Scoville, Samuel. "The *Weltanschauung* of Steinbeck and Hemingway: An Analysis of Themes," *English Journal* LVI (Jan 1967), 60-63, 66.

SWEET THURSDAY

Metzger, Charles R. "Steinbeck's Version of the Pastoral," *Modern Fiction Studies* VI (Summer 1960), 115-124.

TO A GOD UNKNOWN

Fontenrose, Joseph. *John Steinbeck,* 13-19.

TORTILLA FLAT

Alexander, Stanley. "The Conflict of Form in *Tortilla Flat,"* *American Literature* 40 (Mar 1968), 58-66.

Fontenrose, Joseph. *John Steinbeck,* 30-41.

French, Warren. *John Steinbeck,* 53-61.

Kinney, Arthur. "The Arthurian Cycle in *Tortilla Flat,"* *Modern Fiction Studies* XI (Spring 1965), 11-20.

THE WINTER OF OUR DISCONTENT

French, Warren. "Steinbeck's Winter Tale," *Modern Fiction Studies* XI (Spring 1965), 66-74.

Gerstenberger, Donna. "Steinbeck's American Waste Land," *Modern Fiction Studies* XI (Spring 1965), 59-65.

GENERAL

Achar, K.R.H. "John Steinbeck—Writer with a Social Purpose," *Journal of the Karnatak University* XI (1967), 36-47.

Bode, Elroy. "The World on Its Own Terms: A Brief for Steinbeck, Miller and Simenon," *Southwest Review* LIII (Autumn 1968), 406-416.

Brown, Daniel R. " 'A Monolith of Logic Against Waves of Nonsense,' " *Renascence* XVI (Fall 1963), 48-51.

————. "The Natural Man in John Steinbeck's Non-Teleological Tales," *Ball State University Forum* VII (Spring 1966), 47-52.

Covici, Pascal, Jr. "John Steinbeck and the Language of Awareness," *The Thirties: Fiction, Poetry, Drama,* 47-54.

Dulsey, Bernard. "John Steinbeck and Jorge Icaza," *American Book Collector* XVIII (Jun 1968), 15-17.

Fontenrose, Joseph. *John Steinbeck.*

French, Warren. *John Steinbeck.*

STEINBECK, JOHN, Continued

―――. "John Steinbeck," *American Winners of the Nobel Literary Prize,* 193-223.

Johnson, Curtis L. "Steinbeck: A Suggestion for Research," *Modern Fiction Studies* XI (Spring 1965) , 75-78.

Lewis, R. W. B. "The Fitful Daemon," *Modern American Fiction: Essays in Criticism,* 265-277.

―――. "John Steinbeck: The Fitful Daemon," *The Young Rebel in American Literature,* 121-144.

Lisca, Peter. "Steinbeck's Image of Man and His Decline as a Writer," *Modern Fiction Studies* XI (Spring 1965) , 3-10.

Madison, Charles A. "Covici: Steinbeck's Editor, Collaborator and Conscience," *Saturday Review* 49 (Jun 25, 1966) , 15-16.

Mizener, Arthur. "Does a Moral Vision of the Thirties Deserve a Nobel Prize?" *New York Times Book Review* 67 (Dec 9, 1962) , 4, 43-45.

Nelson, Harland S. "Steinbeck's Politics Then and Now," *Antioch Review* XXVII (Spring 1967) , 118-133.

Nossen, Evon. "The Beast-Man Theme in the Work of John Steinbeck," *Ball State University Forum* VII (Spring 1966) , 52-64.

Price, Lawrence Marsden. *The Reception of United States Literature in Germany,* 158-160.

Rahn, Walter. *Die Funktionen der kalifornischen Landschaft im epischen Fruhwerk John Steinbecks.*

Roane, Margaret C. "John Steinbeck as a Spokesman for the Mentally Retarded," *Wisconsin Studies in Contemporary Literature* V (Summer 1964) , 127-132.

Tuttleton, James W. "Steinbeck in Russia: The Rhetoric of Praise and Blame," *Modern Fiction Studies* XI (Spring 1965) , 79-89.

Watt, F. W. *John Steinbeck.*

Woodress, James. "John Steinbeck: Hostage to Fortune," *South Atlantic Quarterly* LXIII (Summer 1964) , 385-397.

BIBLIOGRAPHY

A Companion to The Grapes of Wrath.

Beebe, Maurice and Jackson R. Bryer. "Criticism of John Steinbeck: A Selected Checklist," *Modern Fiction Studies* XI (Spring 1965) , 90-103.

Fontenrose, Joseph. *John Steinbeck,* 142-144.

French, Warren. *John Steinbeck,* 175-181.

Hayashi, Tetsumaro. *John Steinbeck: A Concise Bibliography, 1930-1965.*

STEINBECK, JOHN, Continued

Price, Lawrence Marsden. *The Reception of United States Literature in Germany,* 224.

Rahn, Walter. *Die Funktionen der kalifornischen Landschaft im epischen Fruhwerk John Steinbecks,* 194-197.

Steele, Joan. "John Steinbeck: A Checklist of Biographical, Critical, and Bibliographical Material," *Bulletin of Bibliography* XXIV (May-Aug 1965) , 149-152, 162-163.

Watt, F. W. *John Steinbeck,* 115-117.

STEPHENS, ANN SOPHIA

MALAESKA: THE INDIAN WIFE OF THE WHITE HUNTER

Stern, Madeleine B. "The First Beadle Dime Novel and Its Author," *American Book Collector* XIV (Oct 1963) , 27.

STERN, RICHARD G.

GENERAL

Raeder, Robert L. "An Interview with Richard G. Stern," *Chicago Review* XVIII 3, 4 (1966) , 170-175.

STEVENS, JAMES

MATTOCK

Cooperman, Stanley. *World War I and the American Novel,* 145-148.

STEWART, GEORGE R.

GENERAL

Backus, Joseph M., interviewer. "George R. Stewart on Names of His Characters," *Names* 9 (Mar 1961) , 53-57.

STOCKTON, FRANK RICHARD

BIBLIOGRAPHY

Virginia University Library. *The Barrett Library: Frank Richard Stockton: A Checklist of Printed and Manuscript Works.*

GENERAL

Gerhardt, Mia I. " 'Homicide West': Some Observations on the Nero Wolfe Stories of Rex Stout," *English Studies* XLIX (Apr 1968), 107-127.

STOWE, HARRIET BEECHER

DRED

Davis, Richard Beale. "Mrs. Stowe's Characters-in-Situations and a Southern Literary Tradition," *Essays on American Literature in Honor of Jay Hubbell,* 108-125.

OLDTOWN FOLKS

May, Henry F. Introduction, *Oldtown Folks* (Cambridge, 1966).

UNCLE TOM'S CABIN

Adams, John R. *Harriet Beecher Stowe,* 46-61.

Brooks, Van Wyck. Introduction, *Uncle Tom's Cabin* (London, 1961).

Davis, Richard Beale. "Mrs. Stowe's Characters-in-Situations and a Southern Literary Tradition," *Essays on American Literature in Honor of Jay Hubbell,* 108-125.

Duvall, Severn. "*Uncle Tom's Cabin:* The Sinister Side of the Patriarchy," *New England Quarterly* XXXVI (Mar 1963), 3-22.

Eriksson, Paul S. Introduction, *The Annotated Uncle Tom's Cabin* (New York, 1964).

Fiedler, Leslie A. *Love and Death in the American Novel,* 260-267.

Hamblen, Abigail Ann. "Uncle Tom and 'Nigger Jim': A Study in Contrast and Similarities," *Mark Twain Journal* XI (Fall 1961), 13-17.

Hayne, Barrie. "Yankee in the Patriarch: T. B. Thorpe's Reply to *Uncle Tom's Cabin,*" *American Quarterly* XX (Summer 1968), 180-195.

Johnston, Johanna. *Runaway to Heaven: The Story of Harriet Beecher Stowe,* 254-272.

Kaplan, Sidney. "Uncle Tom's Cabin: The Sinister Side of the Patriarchy," *Images of the Negro in American Literature,* 163-180.

Lynn, Kenneth S. Introduction, *Uncle Tom's Cabin; or Life Among the Lowly* (Cambridge, 1962).

Nye, Russel B. Introduction, *Uncle Tom's Cabin* (New York, 1963).

Oliver, Egbert S. "The Little Cabin of Uncle Tom," *College English* XXVI (Feb 1965), 355-361.

STOWE, HARRIET BEECHER, Continued

Price, Lawrence Marsden. *The Reception of United States Literature in Germany*, 99-102.

Reed, Kenneth T. "*Uncle Tom's Cabin* and the Heavenly City," *CLA Journal* XII (Dec 1968), 150-154.

Rossi, Joseph. "*Uncle Tom's Cabin* and Protestantism in Italy," *American Quarterly* XI (Fall 1959), 416-424.

Strout, Cushing. "*Uncle Tom's Cabin* and the Portent of Millennium," *Yale Review* LVII (Spring 1968), 375-385.

Van Doren, Philip. Introduction, *The Annotated Uncle Tom's Cabin* (New York, 1964).

Woodress, James. "*Uncle Tom's Cabin* in Italy," *Essays on American Literature in Honor of Jay Hubbell*, 126-140.

GENERAL

Adams, John R. *Harriet Beecher Stowe.*

Johnston, Johanna. *Runaway to Heaven: The Story of Harriet Beecher Stowe.*

Lombard, Charles M. "Harriet Beecher Stowe's Attitude Towards French Romanticism," *CLA Journal* XI (Mar 1968), 236-240.

Wagenknecht, Edward. *Harriet Beecher Stowe: The Known and the Unknown.*

BIBLIOGRAPHY

Adams, John R. *Harriet Beecher Stowe*, 159-167.

Wagenknecht, Edward. *Harriet Beecher Stowe: The Known and the Unknown*, 253-258.

STRAIGHT, MICHAEL

GENERAL

Milton, John. "Interview: Michael Straight," *South Dakota Review* 6 (Winter 1968-69), 3-13.

STUART, JESSE

BEYOND DARK HILLS

Blair, Everetta Love. *Jesse Stuart: His Life and Works*, 132-137, 151-156.

DAUGHTER OF THE LEGEND

Pennington, Lee. *The Dark Hills of Jesse Stuart*, 115-130.

STUART, JESSE, Continued

FORETASTE OF GLORY
Pennington, Lee. *The Dark Hills of Jesse Stuart,* 87-94.
THE GOOD SPIRIT OF LAUREL RIDGE
Blair, Everetta Love. *Jesse Stuart: His Life and Works,* 174-182.
Pennington, Lee. *The Dark Hills of Jesse Stuart,* 105-111.
HIE TO THE HUNTERS
Pennington, Lee. *The Dark Hills of Jesse Stuart,* 97-102.
MR. GALLION'S SCHOOL
Pennington, Lee. *The Dark Hills of Jesse Stuart,* 133-145.
TAPS FOR PRIVATE TUSSIE
Blair, Everetta Love. *Jesse Stuart: His Life and Works,* 163-169.
Pennington, Lee. *The Dark Hills of Jesse Stuart,* 61-73.
TREES OF HEAVEN
Blair, Everetta Love. *Jesse Stuart: His Life and Works,* 158-163.
Pennington, Lee. *The Dark Hills of Jesse Stuart,* 41-57.
Westerfield, Hargis. "A Reading of Jesse Stuart's *Trees of Heaven,*"
    Ball State University Forum VII (Spring 1966) , 13-14.
GENERAL
Blair, Everetta Love. *Jesse Stuart: His Life and Works.*
Clarke, Mary Washington. *Jesse Stuart's Kentucky.*
Leavall, Frank H. "Desiderata in Jesse Stuart Studies," *American
    Book Collector* XVI (Feb 1966) , 11-13.
Stuart, Jesse. "My Land Has a Voice," *Arizona Quarterly* XXI (Au-
    tumn 1965) , 197-211.
Woodbridge, Hensley C. *Jesse Stuart: A Bibliography with Essays.*
BIBLIOGRAPHY
Blair, Everetta Love. *Jesse Stuart: His Life and Works,* 267-279.
Clarke, Mary Washington. *Jesse Stuart's Kentucky,* 223-232.
Pennington, Lee. *The Dark Hills of Jesse Stuart,* 161-166.
Woodbridge, Hensley C. *Jesse Stuart: A Bibliography with Essays.*
————. "Jesse Stuart: A Critical Bibliography," *American Book Col-
    lector* XVI (Feb 1966) , 11-13.

STYRON, WILLIAM

THE CONFESSIONS OF NAT TURNER
Friedman, Melvin J. *"The Confessions of Nat Turner:* The Con-
    vergence of 'Nonfiction Novel' and 'Meditation of History,' " *Jour-
    nal of Popular Culture* I (Fall 1967) , 166-175.

STYRON, WILLIAM, Continued

Gilman, Richard. "Nat Turner Revisited," *New Republic* 158 (Apr 27, 1968) 23-32.

Hamilton, Charles V. " 'Nat Turner' Reconsidered: The Fiction and the Reality," *Saturday Review* 51 (Jun 22, 1968) , 22-23.

Hicks, Granville. "Race Riot: 1831," *Saturday Review* 50 (Oct 7, 1967) , 29-30.

O'Connell, Shaun. "Styron's Nat Turner," *Nation* 205 (Oct 16, 1967) , 373-374.

Rubin, Louis D., Jr. "William Styron and Human Bondage: *The Confessions of Nat Turner*," *Hollins Critic* IV (Dec 1967) , 1-12.

Thelwell, Mike. "Mr. William Styron and the Reverend Turner," *Massachusetts Review* IX (Winter 1968) , 7-29.

William Styron's Nat Turner: Ten Black Writers Respond.

Woodward, C. Vann. "Confessions of a Rebel: 1831," *New Republic* 157 (Oct 7, 1967) , 25-28.

LIE DOWN IN DARKNESS

Baumbach, Jonathan. "Paradise Lost: *Lie Down in Darkness* by William Styron," *The Landscape of Nightmare: Studies in the Contemporary American Novel,* 123-137.

Finkelstein, Sidney. *Existentialism and Alienation in American Literature,* 215-216.

Galloway, David D. *The Absurd Hero in American Fiction,* 53-61.

Hassan, Ihab. "Encounter with Necessity," *On Contemporary Literature,* 597-606.

————. *Radical Innocence: Studies in the Contemporary American Novel,* 124-133.

Hoffman, Frederick J. *The Art of Southern Fiction,* 148-154.

Rubin, Louis D., Jr. "William Styron: Notes on a Southern Writer in Our Time," *The Faraway Country: Writers of the Modern South,* 189-212.

Stevenson, David L. "Styron and the Fiction of the Fifties," *Critique* III (Summer 1960) , 47-58.

THE LONG MARCH

Brandriff, Welles T. "The Role of Order and Disorder in *The Long March*," *English Journal* LVI (Jan 1967) , 54-59.

Finkelstein, Sidney. *Existentialism and Alienation in American Literature,* 216-218.

Hays, Peter L. "The Nature of Rebellion in *The Long March*," *Critique* VIII (Winter 1965-1966) , 70-74.

McNamara, Eugene. "William Styron's *Long March:* Absurdity and Authority," *Western Humanities Review* XV (Spring 1961), 267-272.

Nigro, August. *"The Long March:* The Expansive Hero in a Closed World," *Critique* IX (No 3, 1967), 103-112.

Walcutt, Charles Child. "Idea Marching on One Leg: William Styron's *The Long March," Man's Changing Mask: Modes and Methods of Characterization in Fiction,* 251-256.

SET THIS HOUSE ON FIRE

Detweiler, Robert. *Four Spiritual Crises in Mid-Century American Fiction,* 6-13.

Finkelstein, Sidney. *Existentialism and Alienation in American Literature,* 218-219.

Foster, Richard. "An Orgy of Commerce: William Styron's *Set This House On Fire," Critique* III (Summer 1960), 59-70.

Galloway, David D. *The Absurd Hero in American Fiction,* 65-81.

Hoffman, Frederick J. *The Art of Southern Fiction,* 154-161.

Lawson, Lewis. "Cass Kinsolving: Kierkegaardian Man of Despair," *Wisconsin Studies in Contemporary Literature* 3 (Fall 1962), 54-66.

Moore, L. Hugh. "Robert Penn Warren, William Styron, and the Use of Greek Myth," *Critique* VIII (Winter 1965-1966), 75-87.

Robb, Kenneth A. "William Styron's Don Juan," *Critique* VIII (Winter 1965-1966), 34-46.

Rubin, Louis D., Jr. "William Styron: Notes on a Southern Writer in Our Time," *The Faraway Country: Writers of the Modern South,* 212-229.

Stevenson, David L. "Styron and the Fiction of the Fifties," *Critique* III (Summer 1960), 47-58.

Urang, Gunnar. "The Broader Vision: William Styron's *Set This House on Fire," Critique* VIII (Winter 1965-1966), 47-69.

GENERAL

Baumbach, Jonathan. "Paradise Lost: The Novels of William Styron," *South Atlantic Quarterly* LXIII (Spring 1964), 207-217.

Bryant, Jerry H. "The Hopeful Stoicism of William Styron," *South Atlantic Quarterly* LXII (Autumn 1963), 539-550.

Davis, Robert Gorham. "The American Individualist Tradition: Bellow and Styron," *The Creative Present,* 130-141.

————. "Styron and the Students," *Critique* III (Summer 1960), 37-46.

STYRON, WILLIAM, Continued

Fenton, Charles A. "William Styron and the Age of the Slob," *South Atlantic Quarterly* LIX (Autumn 1960) , 469-476.

Galloway, David D. "The Absurd Man as Tragic Hero: The Novels of William Styron," *Texas Studies in Literature and Language* VI (Winter 1965) , 512-534.

————. "The Absurd Man as Tragic Hero," *The Absurd Hero in American Fiction,* 50-81.

Gossett, Louise Y. "The Cost of Freedom," *Violence in Recent Southern Fiction,* 117-131.

Hoffman, Frederick J. "William Styron: The Metaphysical Hurt," *The Art of Southern Fiction,* 144-161.

Klotz, Marvin. "The Triumph Over Time: Narrative Form in William Faulkner and William Styron," *Mississippi Quarterly* XVII (Winter 1963-64) , 9-20.

Méras, Phyllis. "Phyllis Méras interviews William Styron," *Saturday Review* 50 (Oct 7, 1967) , 30.

Mudrick, Marvin. "Mailer and Styron: Guests of the Establishment," *Hudson Review* XVII (Autumn 1964) , 346-366.

O'Connell, Shaun. "Expense of Spirit: The Vision of William Styron," *Critique* VIII (Winter 1965-1966) , 20-33.

O'Connor, William Van. "John Updike and William Styron," *Contemporary American Novelists,* 214-221.

Plimpton, George. "William Styron: A Shared Ordeal," *New York Times Book Review* 72 (Oct 8, 1967) , 2, 30, 32, 34.

BIBLIOGRAPHY

Galloway, David D. *The Absurd Hero in American Fiction,* 200-210.

Schneider, Harold W. "Two Bibliographies: Saul Bellow—William Styron," *Critique* III (Summer 1960) , 71-91.

SULLIVAN, WALTER

THE LONG, LONG LOVE
Hoffman, Frederick J. *The Art of Southern Fiction,* 109-112.

SWADOS, HARVEY

OUT WENT THE CANDLE
Hassan, Ihab. *Radical Innocence: Studies in the Contemporary American Novel,* 134-140.

SWADOS, HARVEY, Continued

GENERAL

Feinstein, Herbert, interviewer. "Contemporary American Fiction: Harvey Swados and Leslie Fiedler," *Wisconsin Studies in Contemporary Literature* 2 (Winter 1961), 79-98.

Shapiro, Charles. "Harvey Swados: Private Stories and Public Fiction," *Contemporary American Novelists*, 182-192.

SYLVESTER, HARRY

GENERAL

Blotner, Joseph. *The Modern American Political Novel*, 48-50.

TARKINGTON, BOOTH

THE GENTLEMAN FROM INDIANA

Woodress, James. "Popular Taste in 1899: Booth Tarkington's First Novel," *Essays in American and English Literature Presented to Bruce Robert McElderry, Jr.*, 108-121.

PENROD

Seelye, John D. "That Marvelous Boy—Penrod Once Again," *Virginia Quarterly Review* XXXVII (Autumn 1961), 591-604.

GENERAL

Backus, Joseph M. " 'I Never Done a Burgess!': Three Unpublished Letters from Booth Tarkington Touched Off by His Use of a Name," *Names* 12 (Sept-Dec 1964), 137-153.

Van Nostrand, Albert. *The Denatured Novel*, 98-104.

Wilson, William Edward. "The Titan and the Gentleman," *Antioch Review* XXIII (Spring 1963), 25-34.

TATE, ALLEN

THE FATHERS

Bishop, Ferman. *Allen Tate*, 107-123.

Hemphill, George. *Allen Tate*, 23-30.

Kane, Patricia. "An Irrepressible Conflict: Allen Tate's *The Fathers*," *Critique* X (No 2, 1968), 9-16.

Kermode, Frank. "Old Orders Changing," *Encounter* XV (Aug 1960), 72-76.

TATE, ALLEN, Continued

Meiners, R. K. *The Last Alternatives: A Study of the Works of Allen Tate,* 81-96.

Mizener, Arthur. Introduction, *The Fathers* (Denver, Colorado, 1960) .

————. "*The Fathers,*" *Sewanee Review* LXVIII (Autumn 1959), 604-613.

————. "The Realistic Novel as Symbol," *The Sense of Life in the Modern Novel,* 267-287.

O'Dea, Richard J. "*The Fathers,* A Revaluation," *Twentieth Century Literature* XII (Jul 1966) , 87-95.

Sanders, Frederick K. "Theme and Structure in *The Fathers,*" *Arlington Quarterly* I (Winter 1967-1968) , 244-256.

Tibbetts, A. M. "Allen Tate's *The Fathers:* The Fatal Attraction of Evil," *Tennessee Studies in Literature* XII (1967) , 155-163.

GENERAL

"Homage to Allen Tate: Essays, Notes and Verses in Honor of his Sixtieth Birthday," by R. P. Blackmur, Malcolm Cowley, Donald Davidson, T. S. Eliot, Francis Fergusson, Anthony Hecht, Robert Lowell, Andrew Lytle, Jacques & Raissa Maritain, Arthur Mizener, Howard Nemerov, Katherine Anne Porter, John Crowe Ransom, Sir Herbert Read, Mark Van Doren, Eliseo Vivas, John Hall Wheelock, Reed Whittemore. *Sewanee Review* LXVII (Autumn 1959) , 528-631.

Millgate, Michael. "An Interview with Allen Tate," *Shenandoah* XII (Spring 1961) , 27-34.

BIBLIOGRAPHY

Bishop, Ferman. *Allen Tate,* 161-165.

Hemphill, George. *Allen Tate,* 46-48.

Meiners, R. K. *The Last Alternatives: A Study of the Works of Allen Tate,* 207-214.

Thorp, Willard. "Allen Tate: A Checklist," *Critique: Studies in Modern Fiction* X (No 2, 1968) , 17-34; James Korges, "Allen Tate: A Checklist Continued," 35-52.

TAYLOR, BAYARD

GENERAL

Krumpelmann, John T. *Bayard Taylor and German Letters.*

BIBLIOGRAPHY

Krumpelmann, John T. *Bayard Taylor and German Letters,* 223-234.

TAYLOR, PETER

A WOMAN OF MEANS

Smith, James Penny. "Narration and Theme in Taylor's *A Woman of Means*," *Critique* IX (No 3, 1967), 19-30.

BIBLIOGRAPHY

Smith, James Penny. "A Peter Taylor Checklist," *Critique* IX (No 3, 1967), 31-36.

THOMPSON, JIM

THE KILLER INSIDE ME

Cassill, R. V. "*The Killer Inside Me*: Fear, Purgation, and the Sophoclean Light," *Tough Guy Writers of the Thirties*, 230-238.

THORPE, THOMAS B.

THE MASTER'S HOUSE

Hayne, Barrie. "Yankee in the Patriarchy: T. B. Thorpe's Reply to *Uncle Tom's Cabin*," *American Quarterly* XX (Summer 1968), 180-195.

TOURGEE, ALBION WINEGAR

BRICKS WITHOUT STRAW

Gross, Theodore L. *Albion W. Tourgée*, 96-102.

A FOOL'S ERRAND BY ONE OF THE FOOLS

Gross, Theodore L. *Albion W. Tourgée*, 60-86.

Olsen, Otto H. *Carpetbagger's Crusade: The Life of Albion Winegar Tourgée*, 223-234.

A ROYAL GENTLEMAN

Gross, Theodore L. *Albion W. Tourgée*, 36-48.

GENERAL

Gross, Theodore L. "Albion W. Tourgée: 'Reporter of the Reconstruction,'" *Mississippi Quarterly* XVI (Summer 1963), 111-127.

————. *Albion W. Tourgée*.

Olsen, Otto H. *Carpetbagger's Crusade: The Life of Albion Winegar Tourgée*.

GENERAL

Gross, Theodore L. *Albion W. Tourgée*, 168-173.

Keller, Dean H. "A Checklist of the Writing of Albion W. Tourgée (1838-1905)," *Studies in Bibliography* XVIII (1965), 269-279.

TOURGEE, ALBION WINEGAR, Continued

Olsen, Otto H. *Carpetbagger's Crusade: The Life of Albion Winegar Tourgée,* 355-382.

TRAVEN, B.

GENERAL
Jannach, Hubert. "The B. Traven Mystery," *Books Abroad* XXXV (Winter 1961), 28-29.

Miller, Charles. "B. Traven, American Author," *Texas Quarterly* VI (Winter 1963), 162-168.

————. "B. Traven in the Americas," *Texas Quarterly* VI (Winter 1963), 208-211.

————. "B. Traven, Pure Proletarian Writer," *Proletarian Writers of the Thirties,* 114-133.

TRILLING, LIONEL

THE MIDDLE OF THE JOURNEY
Blotner, Joseph. *The Modern American Political Novel,* 315-320.

Kubal, David L. "Trilling's *The Middle of the Journey:* An American Dialectic," *Bucknell Review* XIV (Mar 1966), 60-73.

Milne, Gordon. *The American Political Novel,* 139-149.

TRUMBO, DALTON

JOHNNY GOT HIS GUN
Kriegel, Leonard. "Dalton Trumbo's *Johnny Got His Gun,*" *Proletarian Writers of the Thirties,* 106-113.

GENERAL
French, Warren. *The Social Novel at the End of an Era,* 125-142.

TWAIN, MARK

THE AMERICAN CLAIMANT
Grimm, Clyde L. "*The American Claimant:* Reclamation of a Farce," *American Quarterly* XIX (Spring 1967), 86-103.

A CONNECTICUT YANKEE IN KING ARTHUR'S COURT
Allen, Gerald. "Mark Twain's Yankee," *New England Quarterly* XXXIX (Dec 1966), 435-446.

Baetzhold, Howard G. " 'The Autobiography of Sir Robert Smith of Camelot': Mark Twain's Original Plan for *A Connecticut Yankee*," *American Literature* XXXII (Jan 1961) , 456-461.

―――――. "The Course of Composition of *A Connecticut Yankee:* A Reinterpretation," *American Literature* XXXIII (May 1961) , 195-214.

Bertolotti, D. S., Jr. "Mark Twain Revisits the Tailor," *Mark Twain Journal* XIII (Summer 1967) , 18-19.

Chae, Dong-Bae. "*A Connecticut Yankee in King Arthur's Court*," *English Language and Literature* 20 (Winter 1966) , 86-103. (In Korean) .

Covici, Pascal. *Mark Twain's Humor: Image of the World*, 91-109.

Cox, James M. "*A Connecticut Yankee* in *King Arthur's Court:* The Machinery of Self-Preservation," *Mark Twain: A Collection of Critical Essays*, 117-129.

―――――. "A Connecticut Yankee in King Arthur's Court: The Machinery of Self-Preservation," *Yale Review* L (Autumn 1960) , 89-102.

―――――. *Mark Twain: The Fate of Humor*, 198-221.

Foster, Edward F. "*A Connecticut Yankee* Anticipated: Max Adeler's *Fortunate Island*," *Ball State University Forum* IX (Autumn 1968) , 73-76.

Gibson, William M. Introduction, *A Connecticut Yankee in King Arthur's Court* (New York, 1960) .

Guttmann, Allen. "Mark Twain's *Connecticut Yankee:* Affirmation of the Vernacular Tradition?" *New England Quarterly* XXXIII (Jun 1960) , 232-237.

Hill, Hamlin. "Barnum, Bridgeport and *The Connecticut Yankee*," *American Quarterly* XVI (Winter 1964) , 615-616.

Holmes, Charles S. "*A Connecticut Yankee in King Arthur's Court:* Mark Twain's Fable of Uncertainty," *South Atlantic Quarterly* LXI (Autumn 1962) , 462-472.

Hough, Robert L. "Twain's Double-Dating in *A Connecticut Yankee*," *Notes and Queries* N.S. 15 (Nov 1968) , 424-425.

Jones, Joseph. "Mark Twain's *Connecticut Yankee* and Australian Nationalism," *American Literature* 40 (May 1968) , 227-231.

Martin, Jay. *Harvests of Change. American Literature 1865-1914*, 178-181.

Maynard, Reid. "Mark Twain's Ambivalent Yankee," *Mark Twain Journal* XIV (Winter 1968-69) , 1-5.

McKee, John DeWitt, "*A Connecticut Yankee* as a Revolutionary Document," *Mark Twain Journal* XI (Summer 1960) , 18-20, 24.

————. "Three Uses of the Arming Scene," *Mark Twain Journal* XII (Summer 1965) , 18-19, 21.

Neider, Charles. Introduction, *A Connecticut Yankee in King Arthur's Court* (New York, 1960) .

————. *Mark Twain*, 20-29.

Salomon, Roger B. *Twain and the Image of History,* 100-127, 146-151.

Smith, Henry Nash. *Mark Twain's Fable of Progress: Political and Economic Ideas in "A Connecticut Yankee."*

Spengemann, William C. "The Yankee Pirate," *Mark Twain and the Backwoods Angel,* 84-104.

Stone, Albert E., Jr. *The Innocent Eye: Childhood in Mark Twain's Imagination,* 165-173.

Wiggins, Robert A. *Mark Twain: Jackleg Novelist,* 77-82.

Williams, James D. "Revision and Intention in Mark Twain's *A Connecticut Yankee,*" *American Literature* XXXVI (Nov 1964) , 288-297.

————. "The Use of History in Mark Twain's *A Connecticut Yankee,*" *PMLA* LXXX (Mar 1965) , 102-110.

THE GILDED AGE

Church, Richard and C. D. Warner. Introduction, *The Gilded Age* (London, 1967) .

French, Bryant Morey. *Mark Twain and The Gilded Age.*

————. "Mark Twain, Laura D. Fair and the New York Criminal Courts," *American Quarterly* XVI (Winter 1964) , 545-561.

Hill, Hamlin. "Escol Sellers from Uncharted Space: A Footnote to *The Gilded Age,*" *American Literature* XXXIV (Mar 1962) , 107-113.

————. "Toward a Critical Text of *The Gilded Age,*" *Papers of the Bibliographical Society of America* LIX (Apr-Jun 1965) , 142-149.

Kaplan, Justin D. Introduction, *The Gilded Age* (New York, 1964) .

Milne, Gordon. *The American Political Novel,* 40-45.

Neider, Charles. Introduction, *The Adventures of Colonel Sellers, Being Mark Twain's Share of The Gilded Age, A Novel Which He Wrote With Charles Dudley Warner* (New York, 1965) .

Poli, Bernard. *Mark Twain: Écrivain de l'ouest,* 195-217.

Smith, Henry Nashe. "The Morals of Power, Business Enterprise as a

Theme in Mid-Nineteenth Century American Fiction," *Essays on American Literature in Honor of Jay Hubbell,* 98-107.

Spengemann, William C. "The Fallen Woman and the Bad Boy," *Mark Twain and the Backwoods Angel,* 31-47.

Wiggins, Robert A. *Mark Twain: Jackleg Novelist,* 33-41.

HUCKLEBERRY FINN, THE ADVENTURES OF

Ashmead, John. "A Possible Hannibal Source for Mark Twain's Dauphin," *American Literature* XXXIV (Mar 1962), 105-107.

Bailey, Roger B. "Twain's *The Adventures of Huckleberry Finn,* Chapters 1 and 2," *Explicator* XXVI (Sept 1967), No. 2.

Baker, Carlos. "Two Rivers: Mark Twain and Hemingway," *Mark Twain Journal* XI (Summer 1962), 2.

Banta, Martha. "Escape and Entry in *Huckleberry Finn,*" *Modern Fiction Studies* XIV (Spring 1968), 79-91.

Barnes, Daniel R. "Twain's *The Adventures of Huckleberry Finn,* Chapter I," *Explicator* XXIII (Apr 1965), No. 62.

"The Bear and Huckleberry Finn: Heroic Quests for Moral Liberation," *Mark Twain Journal* XII (Spring 1963), 12-13, 21.

Beidler, Peter G. "The Raft Episode in *Huckleberry Finn,*" *Modern Fiction Studies* XIV (Spring 1968), 11-20.

Benardete, Jane Johnson. "Huckleberry Finn and the Nature of Fiction," *Massachusetts Review* IX (Spring 1968), 209-226.

Blair, Walter. *Mark Twain and Huck Finn.*

————. "So Noble . . . and So Beautiful a Book," *Twentieth Century Interpretations of The Adventures of Huckleberry Finn,* 61-70.

Boggan, J. R. "That Slap, Huck, Did It Hurt?" *English Language Notes* I (Mar 1964), 212-215.

Bowden, Edwin T. *The Dungeon of the Heart: Human Isolation and the American Novel,* 30-42.

Bridgman, Richard. *The Colloquial Style in America,* 106-130.

Brown, Clarence A. "*Huckleberry Finn:* A Study in Structure and Point of View," *Mark Twain Journal* XII (Spring 1964), 10-15, 5.

Browne, Ray B. "Huck's Final Triumph," *Ball State Teachers College Forum* VI (Winter 1965), 3-12.

————. "Huck's Final Triumph," *Critical Approaches to American Literature: Volume II, Walt Whitman to William Faulkner,* 97-109.

Callan, Richard J. "The Burden of Innocence in Melville and Twain," *Renascence* XVII (Summer 1965), 191-194.

Cambon, Glauco. "What Maisie and Huck Knew," *Studi Americani* VI (1960), 203-220.

Carstensen, Broder. *"The Adventures of Huckleberry Finn:* Die Problematik Des Schlusses," *Neueren Sprachen* (Dec 1961), 541-551.

Casey, Daniel J. "Universality in *'Huckleberry Finn':* A Comparison of Twain and Kivi," *Mark Twain Journal* XIV (Winter 1967-68), 13-18.

Clerc, Charles. "Sunrise on the River: 'The Whole World' of Huckleberry Finn," *Modern Fiction Studies* XIV (Spring 1968), 67-78.

Covici, Pascal. *Mark Twain's Humor: Image of the World,* 65-91.

Cox, James M. *Mark Twain: The Fate of Humor,* 156-184.

————. "Southwestern Vernacular," *Twentieth Century Interpretations of The Adventures of Huckleberry Finn,* 82-94.

Crowe, Charles. "Mark Twain's *Huckleberry Finn* and the American Journey," *Archiv fuer das Studium der Neueren Sprachen und Literaturen* 199 (Aug 1962), 145-158.

Cummings, Sherwood. "What's in *Huckleberry Finn?"* *English Journal* L (Jan 1961), 1-8.

Doyno, Victor A. "Over Twain's Shoulder: The Composition and Structure of *Huckleberry Finn,"* *Modern Fiction Studies* XIV (Spring 1968), 3-9.

Dyson, A. E. "Huckleberry Finn and the Whole Truth," *Critical Quarterly* 9 (Spring 1961), 29-40.

Eby, Cecil D., Jr. "Mark Twain's 'Plug' and 'Chaw': An Anecdotal Parallel," *Mark Twain Journal* XI (Summer 1960), 11, 25.

Elliott, George P. Afterword, *The Adventures of Huckleberry Finn* (New York, 1960).

Ellison, Ralph. "Twentieth-Century Fiction and the Black Mask of Humanity," *Images of the Negro in American Literature,* 119-123.

Ensor, Allison. "The Contributions of Charles Webster and Albert Bigelow Paine to *Huckleberry Finn,"* *American Literature* 40 (May 1968), 222-227.

————. "The 'Opposition Line' to the King and the Duke in Huckleberry Finn," *Mark Twain Journal* XIV (Winter 1968-69), 6-7.

————. "Twain's *The Adventures of Huckleberry Finn,* Chapter 37," *Explicator* XXVI (Nov 1967), No. 20.

Fiedler, Leslie A. *Love and Death in the American Novel,* 553-591.

Flory, Claude R. "Huck, Sam and the Small-Pox," *Mark Twain Journal* XII (Winter 1964-65), 1-2, 8.

Fox, Maynard. "Two Primitives: Huck Finn and Tom Outland," *Western American Literature* 1 (Spring 1966), 26-33.

Ganzel, Dewey. "Samuel Clemens and Captain Marryat," *Anglia* 80 (Heft 4, 1962), 405-416.

Gargano, James W. "Disguises in *Huckleberry Finn,*" *University of Kansas City Review* XXVI (Mar 1960), 175-178.

Gerstenberger, Donna. "Huckleberry Finn and the World's Illusions," *Western Humanities Review* XIV (Autumn 1960), 401-406.

Gibb, Carson. "The Best Authorities," *College English* XXII (Dec 1960), 178-183.

――――. "The Best Authorities," *Huck Finn and his Critics,* 429-437.

Graves, Wallace. "Mark Twain's 'Burning Shame,'" *Nineteenth-Century Fiction* XXIII (Jun 1968), 93-98.

Gross, Seymour L. "Sherwood Anderson's Debt to *Huckleberry Finn,*" *Mark Twain Journal* XI (Summer 1960), 3-5, 24.

Hamblen, Abigail Ann. "The Best-Known Teenager: Huck Finn," *Mark Twain Journal* XIII (Winter 1966-67), 15-19.

――――. "Uncle Tom and 'Nigger Jim': A Study in Contrast and Similarities," *Mark Twain Journal* XI (Fall 1961), 13-17.

Hansen, Chadwick. "The Character of Jim and the Ending of *Huckleberry Finn,*" *Massachusetts Review* V (Autumn 1963), 45-66.

Hart, John E. "Heroes and Houses: The Progress of Huck Finn," *Modern Fiction Studies* XIV (Spring 1968), 39-46.

Hill, Hamlin. Introduction, *Adventures of Huckleberry Finn* (San Francisco 1962).

Hill, Hamlin and Walter Blair. Introduction, *The Art of Huckleberry Finn: Text; Sources; Criticisms.* (San Francisco, 1962).

Hill, John S. "Huck Finn's Reaffirmation of Rejection," *Mark Twain Journal* XIII (Summer 1967), 16-17.

Hoffman, Daniel G. "Black Magic―and White," *A Casebook on Mark Twain's Wound,* 311-334.

――――. *Form and Fable in American Fiction,* 317-350.

――――. "From 'Black Magic- and White- in *Huckleberry Finn,*'" *Mark Twain: A Collection of Critical Essays,* 101-111.

――――. "Jim's Magic: Black or White?" *American Literature* XXXII (Mar 1960), 47-54.

Howell, Elmo. "Uncle Silas Phelps: A Note on Mark Twain's Characterization," *Mark Twain Journal* XIV (Summer 1968), 8-12.

Irwin, Robert. "The Failure of *Tom Sawyer* and *Huckleberry Finn* on Film," *Mark Twain Journal* XIII (Summer 1967), 9-11.

John, George. "A Note on the Ending of *Huckleberry Finn*," *The Literary Criterion* VIII (Winter 1967), 56-61.

Karl, Frederick R. "Joseph Conrad and *Huckleberry Finn*," *Mark Twain Journal* XI (Summer 1960), 21-23.

Kaul, A. N. "*Huckleberry Finn:* A Southwestern Statement," *The American Vision: Actual and Ideal Society in Nineteenth Century Fiction,* 280-304.

Kelly, James J. "They're Trying to Kill *Huckleberry Finn*," *Mark Twain Journal* XIII (Winter 1965-66), 13-14.

Kendall, Lyle H., Jr. "The Walter Scott Episode in *Huckleberry Finn*," *Nineteenth-Century Fiction* XVI (Dec 1961), 279-281.

Kraus, W. Keith. " '*Huckleberry Finn*': A Final Irony," *Mark Twain Journal* XIV (Winter 1967-68), 18-19.

Krause, Sydney J. "Huck's First Moral Crisis," *Mississippi Quarterly* XVIII (Spring 1965), 69-73.

————. "Twain and Scott: Experience Versus Adventures," *Modern Philology* LXII (Feb 1965), 227-236.

LaHood, Marvin I. "Huck Finn's Search for Identity," *Mark Twain Journal* XIII (Winter 1966-67), 11-14.

Lane, Lauriat. Introduction, *The Adventures of Huckleberry Finn* (New York, 1965).

Leary, Lewis. "Mark Twain," *Six American Novelists of the Nineteenth Century,* 136-142.

Levy, Leo B. "Society and Conscience in *Huckleberry Finn*," *Nineteenth-Century Fiction* XVIII (Mar 1964), 383-391.

Linneman, William R. "Punch and *Huckleberry Finn*," *English Language Notes* II (Jun 1965), 293-294.

Loomis, C. C., Jr. "Twain's *Huckleberry Finn*," *Explicator* XVIII (Jan 1960), No. 27.

Lowenherz, Robert J. "The Beginning of *Huckleberry Finn*," *American Speech* XXXVIII (Oct 1963), 196-201.

Manierre, William R. "Huck Finn, Empiricist Member of Society," *Modern Fiction Studies* XIV (Spring 1968), 57-66.

————. " 'No Money for to Buy the Outfit': *Huckleberry Finn* Again," *Modern Fiction Studies* X (Winter 1964-65), 341-348.

————. "On Keeping the Raftsmen's Passage in *Huckleberry Finn*," *English Language Notes* VI (Dec 1968), 118-122.

TWAIN, MARK, Continued

————. "Parallel Scenes in *Tom Sawyer* and *Huck Finn*," *CEA Critic* XXX (Nov 1967), 1, 4, 6-7.

Martin, Jay. *Harvests of Change. American Literature 1865-1914*, 190-193.

Marx, Leo. *The Machine in the Garden: Technology and the Pastoral Ideal in America*, 319-340.

Mayberry, George. "*Huckleberry Finn* Enriched," *Nation* 207 (Aug 26, 1968), 154-157.

McAleer, John J. "Noble Innocence in *Huckleberry Finn*," *Ball State Teachers College Forum* III (Winter 1962-63), 9-12.

McIntyre, James P. "Three Practical Jokes: A Key to Huck's Changing Attitude Toward Jim," *Modern Fiction Studies* XIV (Spring 1968), 33-37.

Metzger, Charles R. "*The Adventures of Huckleberry Finn* as Picaresque," *Midwest Quarterly* V (Spring 1964), 249-256.

Michaelson, L. W. "Four Emmeline Grangerfords," *Mark Twain Journal* XI (Fall 1961), 10-11.

Milstead, John. "The Ending of *Huck Finn*," *CEA Critic* XXVI (Apr 1964), 7.

Mizener, Arthur. "Mark Twain: *Huckleberry Finn*," *Twelve Great American Novels*, 34-48.

Moses, W. R. "The Pattern of Evil in *Adventures of Huckleberry Finn*," *Georgia Review* XIII (Summer 1959), 161-166.

Neider, Charles. *Mark Twain*, 14-20.

O'Connor, William Van. *The Grotesque: An American Genre and Other Essays*, 109-118.

Pearce, Roy Harvey. " 'The End. Yours Truly, Huck Finn': Postscript," *Modern Language Quarterly* XXIV (Sept 1963), 253-256.

Peck, Richard E. "A Mark Twain 'Literary Offense,' " *Mark Twain Journal* XIV (Winter 1968-69), 7-9.

Pederson, Lee A. "Negro Speech in the *Adventures of Huckleberry Finn*," *Mark Twain Journal* XIII (Winter 1965-66), 1-4.

Plante, Patricia R. "Mark Twain, Ferber and the Mississippi," *Mark Twain Journal* XIII (Summer 1966), 8-10.

Poirier, Richard. "Huck Finn and the Metaphors of Society," *Twentieth Century Interpretations of The Adventures of Huckleberry Finn*, 95-101.

————. *A World Elsewhere*, 144-207.

Poli, Bernard. *Mark Twain: Écrivain de l'ouest*, 310-345.

Power, William. "Huck Finn's Father," *University of Kansas City Review* XXVIII (Dec 1961), 83-94.

Ridland, J. M. "Huck, Pip, and Plot," *Nineteenth-Century Fiction* XX (Dec 1965), 286-290.

Rogers, Franklin R. *Mark Twain's Burlesque Patterns,* 127-151.

Rollins, Ronald G. *"Huckleberry Finn* and Christy Mahon: The Playboy of the Western World," *Mark Twain Journal* XIII (Summer 1966), 16-19.

Rossky, William. *"The Reivers* and *Huckleberry Finn:* Faulkner and Twain," *Huntington Library Quarterly* XXVIII (Aug 1965), 373-387.

Rulon, Curt M. "Geographical Delimitation of the Dialect Areas in *The Adventures of Huckleberry Finn,"* *Mark Twain Journal* XIV (Winter 1967-68), 9-12.

Salomon, Roger B. *Twain and the Image of History,* 159-166.

Scanlon, Lawrence E. " 'They're After Us' Again," *Mark Twain Journal* XIII (Summer 1966), 20-21.

————. "Unheroic Huck," *East-West Review* II (Winter 1965-66), 99-114.

Schonhorn, Manuel. "Mark Twain's Jim: Solomon on the Mississippi," *Mark Twain Journal* XIV (Winter 1968-69), 9-11.

Sioui, Tak. *Huckleberry Finn: More Molecules.*

Smith, Henry Nash. "Mark Twain: *The Adventures of Huckleberry Finn,"* *The American Novel from James Fenimore Cooper to William Faulkner,* 61-72.

————. *Mark Twain: The Development of a Writer,* 113-137.

————. "A Sound Heart and a Deformed Conscience," *Mark Twain: A Collection of Critical Essays,* 83-100.

————. "A Sound Heart and a Deformed Conscience," *Twentieth Century Interpretations of The Adventures of Huckleberry Finn,* 71-81.

Solomon, Eric. *"Huckleberry Finn* Once More," *College English* XXII (Dec 1960), 172-178.

————. "Huck Finn Once More," *Huck Finn and his Critics,* 420-428.

Spacks, Barry B. "The Thematic Function of the 'Rescue' in *Huckleberry Finn,"* *Mark Twain Journal* XI (Summer 1959), 8-9.

Spengemann, William C. "The Backwoods Angel," *Mark Twain and the Backwoods Angel,* 61-83.

Stegner, Wallace. Introduction, *The Adventures of Huckleberry Finn* (New York, 1960).

Stephens, George D. *"Huckleberry Finn* as a Journey," *Mark Twain Journal* XIII (Summer 1966), 11-15.

Stone, Albert E., Jr. *The Innocent Eye: Childhood in Mark Twain's Imagination*, 126-158.

Tanner, Tony. *The Reign of Wonder: Naivety and Reality in American Literature*, 255-286.

Tatham, Campbell. " 'Dismal and Lonesome': A New Look at *Huckleberry Finn*," *Modern Fiction Studies* XIV (Spring 1968), 47-55.

Taylor, Nancy Dew. "The River of Faulkner and Mark Twain," *Mississippi Quarterly* XVI (Fall 1963), 191-199.

Tuttleton, James W. "Twain's Use of Theatrical Tradition in the Old Southwest," *CLA Journal* VIII (Dec 1964), 190-197.

Vales, Robert L. "Thief and Theft in *Huckleberry Finn*," *American Literature* XXXVII (Jan 1966), 420-429.

Walcutt, Charles Child. "Freedom Afloat—and Adrift: Mark Twain's *The Adventures of Huckleberry Finn*," *Man's Changing Mask: Modes and Methods of Characterization in Fiction*, 131-144.

Warner, Deane M. "Huck and Holden," *CEA Critic* XXVII (Mar 1965), 4a-4b.

Werge, Thomas. "Huck, Jim and Forty Dollars," *Mark Twain Journal* XIII (Winter 1965-66), 15-16.

Wermuth, Paul C. "Santayana and *Huckleberry Finn*," *New England Quarterly* XXXVI (Mar 1963), 79-82.

West, Ray B., Jr. "Mark Twain's Idyl of Frontier America," *The Writer in the Room: Selected Essays*, 96-101.

White, William. "Teaching Huck Finn in Korea," *Mark Twain Journal* XIII (Winter 1965-66), 5-7.

Wiggins, Robert A. *Mark Twain: Jackleg Novelist*, 55-71.

Woodward, Robert H. "Teaching *Huckleberry Finn* to Foreign Students," *Mark Twain Journal* XIII (Winter 1966-67), 5-7.

Wyatt, Bryant N. *"Huckleberry Finn* and the Art of Ernest Hemingway," *Mark Twain Journal* XIII (Summer 1967), 1-8.

Yates, Norris W. "The 'Counter-Conversion' of *Huckleberry Finn*," *American Literature* XXXII (Mar 1960), 1-10.

JOAN OF ARC

Spengemann, William C. "The Saint," *Mark Twain and the Backwoods Angel*, 105-119.

TWAIN, MARK, Continued

Stone, Albert E., Jr. *The Innocent Eye: Childhood in Mark Twain's Imagination,* 202-227.

THE MYSTERIOUS STRANGER

Anderson, David D. "Melville and Mark Twain in Rebellion," *Mark Twain Journal* XI (Fall 1961), 8-9.

Covici, Pascal. *Mark Twain's Humor: Image of the World,* 227-236.

Cox, James M. *Mark Twain: The Fate of Humor,* 266-284.

Eby, E. H. "Mark Twain's Testament," *Modern Language Quarterly* XXIII (Sept 1962), 254-262.

Klotz, Marvin. "Goethe and Mark Twain," *Notes and Queries* N.S. 7 (Apr 1960), 150-151.

Knox, George. *"The Mysterious Stranger:* Mark Twain's Last Laugh?" *Mark Twain Journal* XI (Summer 1959), 11-12.

Lalli, Biancamaria Tedeschini. "Il Piccolo Satana Di Mark Twain," *Studi Americani* XI (1965), 163-180.

Parsons, Coleman O. "The Background of *The Mysterious Stranger,"* *American Literature* XXXII (Mar 1960), 55-74.

Salomon, Roger B. *Twain and the Image of History,* 200-210.

Spengemann, William C. "The Angel," *Mark Twain and the Backwoods Angel,* 120-134.

Stone, Albert E., Jr. *The Innocent Eye: Childhood in Mark Twain's Imagination,* 241-250.

Tuckey, John S. *Mark Twain and Little Satan: The Writing of The Mysterious Stranger.*

Wiggins, Robert A. *Mark Twain: Jackleg Novelist,* 114-123.

THE PRINCE AND THE PAUPER

Blair, Walter. *Mark Twain and Huck Finn,* 188-197.

Cox, James M. *Mark Twain: The Fate of Humor,* 149-155.

Gale, Robert L. "The Prince and the Pauper and King Lear," *Mark Twain Journal* XII (Spring 1963), 14-17.

Rogers, Franklin R. *Mark Twain's Burlesque Patterns,* 113-127.

Salomon, Roger B. "Mark Twain and Victorian Nostalgia," *Patterns of Commitment in American Literature,* 85-88.

————. *Twain and the Image of History,* 146-156.

Spengemann, William C. "The Cub, The Changeling and The Recruit," *Mark Twain and the Backwoods Angel,* 48-60.

Stone, Albert E., Jr. *The Innocent Eye: Childhood in Mark Twain's Imagination,* 91-125.

Wiggins, Robert A. *Mark Twain: Jackleg Novelist,* 72-77.

PUDD'NHEAD WILSON

Butcher, Philip. "Mark Twain Sells Roxy Down the River," *CLA Journal* VIII (Mar 1965), 225-233.

Chapin, Henry B. "Twain's *Pudd'nhead Wilson*," *Explicator* XXI (Apr 1963), No. 61.

Cox, James M. *Mark Twain: The Fate of Humor*, 225-246.

———. "Pudd'nhead Wilson: The End of Mark Twain's American Dream," *Images of the Negro in American Literature*, 181-193.

Fiedler, Leslie A. *Love and Death in the American Novel*, 385-392.

Freimarck, John. "*Pudd'nhead Wilson*: A Tale of Blood and Brotherhood," *University Review* XXXIV (Jun 1968), 303-306.

Jefferies, William B. "The Montesquiou Murder Case: A Possible Source for Some Incidents in *Pudd'nhead Wilson*," *American Literature* XXXI (Jan 1960), 488-490.

Leary, Lewis. "Mark Twain," *Six American Novelists of the Nineteenth Century*, 144-147.

Leiter, Louis H. "Dawson's Landing: Thematic Cityscape in Twain's *Pudd'nhead Wilson*," *Mark Twain Journal* XIII (Winter 1965-66), 8-11.

Mann, Carolyn. "Innocence in Pudd'nhead Wilson," *Mark Twain Journal* XIV (Winter 1968-69), 18-20.

McKeithan, Daniel Morley. *The Morgan Manuscript of Mark Twain's Pudd'nhead Wilson*.

Miller, Jim Wayne. "*Pudd'nhead Wilson's* Calendar," *Mark Twain Journal* XIII (Winter 1966-67), 8-10.

Rose, Marilyn Gaddis. "*Pudd'nhead Wilson*: A Contemporary Parable," *Mark Twain Journal* XIII (Summer 1966), 5-7.

Schell, Edgar T. " 'Pears' and 'Is' in Pudd'nhead Wilson," *Mark Twain Journal* XII (Winter 1964-65), 12-15.

Smith, Henry Nash. *Mark Twain: The Development of a Writer*, 171-184.

———. "*Pudd'nhead Wilson* and After," *Massachusetts Review* III (Winter 1962), 233-253.

Wiggins, Robert A. "*Pudd'nhead Wilson*: 'A Literary Caesarean Operation,' " *College English* XXV (Dec 1963), 182-186.

SIMON WHEELER, DETECTIVE

Rogers, Franklin R. Introduction, *Simon Wheeler, Detective* (New York, 1963).

TWAIN, MARK, Continued

TOM SAWYER, THE ADVENTURES OF

Bercovitch, Sacvan. "Huckleberry Bumppo: A Comparison of 'Tom Sawyer' and 'The Pioneers,'" *Mark Twain Journal* XIV (Summer 1968), 1-4.

Blair, Walter. Introduction, *The Adventures of Tom Sawyer* (New York, 1962).

————. *Mark Twain and Huck Finn,* 50-70, 71-76.

————. "Tom Sawyer," *Mark Twain: A Collection of Critical Essays,* 64-82.

Bratcher, James T. "Twain's *Tom Sawyer,*" *Explicator* XXII (Jan 1964), No. 40.

Covici, Pascal. *Mark Twain's Humor: Image of the World,* 78-80.

Cox, James M. *Mark Twain: The Fate of Humor,* 127-149.

Dillingham, William B. "Setting and Theme in Tom Sawyer," *Mark Twain Journal* XII (Spring 1964), 6-8.

Halverson, John. "Patristic Exegesis: A Medieval *Tom Sawyer,*" *College English* XXVII (Oct 1965), 50-55.

Hill, Hamlin L. "The Composition and the Structure of *Tom Sawyer,*" *American Literature* XXXII (Jan 1961), 379-392.

Hoffman, Daniel G. *Form and Fable in American Fiction,* 321-330.

Irwin, Robert. "The Failure of *Tom Sawyer* and *Huckleberry Finn* on Film," *Mark Twain Journal* XIII (Summer 1967), 9-11.

Manierre, William R. "Parallel Scenes in *Tom Sawyer* and *Huck Finn,*" *CEA Critic* XXX (Nov 1967), 1, 4, 6-7.

Poli, Bernard. *Mark Twain: Écrivain de l'ouest,* 231-256.

Rubin, Louis D., Jr. "*Tom Sawyer* and the Use of Novels," *The Curious Death of the Novel: Essays in American Literature,* 88-99.

San Juan, Pastora. "A Source for *Tom Sawyer,*" *American Literature* XXXVIII (Mar 1966), 101-102.

Smith, Henry Nash. *Mark Twain: The Development of a Writer,* 81-91.

Spengemann, William C. "The Fallen Woman and The Bad Boy," *Mark Twain and the Backwoods Angel,* 31-47.

Stone, Albert E., Jr. *The Innocent Eye: Childhood in Mark Twain's Imagination,* 58-90.

Welland, Dennis. "A Note on Some Early Reviews of *Tom Sawyer,*" *Journal of American Studies* I (Apr 1967), 99-103.

Wiggins, Robert A. *Mark Twain: Jackleg Novelist,* 42-54.

TOM SAWYER ABROAD

Matthews, Jack. "Mark Twain, 'Cartographer,'" *ETC.* XXIII (Dec 1966), 479-484.

Stone, Albert E., Jr. *The Innocent Eye: Childhood in Mark Twain's Imagination,* 180-188.

GENERAL

Allen, Charles. "Mark Twain and Conscience," *Psychoanalysis and American Fiction,* 131-141.

Anderson, Frederick, William M. Gibson, and Henry Nash Smith, (eds.). *Selected Mark Twain-Howells Letters.*

Babcock, C. Merton. "Mark Twain and the Freedom to Tell a Lie," *Texas Quarterly* V (Autumn 1962), 155-160.

————. "Mark Twain, Mencken and 'The Higher Goofyism,'" *American Quarterly* XVI (Winter 1964), 587-594.

————. "Mark Twain's Map of Paris," *Texas Quarterly* VII (Autumn 1964), 92-97.

————. "Mark Twain's Seven Lively Sins," *Texas Quarterly* VI (Autumn 1963), 92-97.

Baylen, Joseph O. "Mark Twain, W. T. Stead and 'The Tell-Tale Hands,'" *American Quarterly* XVI (Winter 1964), 606-612.

Bergmann, Frank. "Mark Twain and the Literary Misfortunes of John William De Forest," *Jahrbuch für Amerikastudien* 13 (1968), 249-252.

Berthoff, Warner. *The Ferment of Realism: American Literature, 1884-1919,* 61-76.

Blues, Thomas. "The Strategy of Compromise in Mark Twain's 'Boy Books,'" *Modern Fiction Studies* XIV (Spring 1968), 21-31.

Bridgman, Richard. "Henry James and Mark Twain," *The Colloquial Style in America,* 78-130.

Budd, Louis J. *Mark Twain: Social Philosopher.*

Burgess, Anthony. "Mark Twain and James Joyce," *Mark Twain Journal* XIII (Winter 1966-67), 1-2.

Cady, Edwin H. "Howells and Twain: The World in Midwestern Eyes," *Ball State Teachers College Forum* III (Winter 1962-63), 3-8.

Cambon, Glauco. "Mark Twain and Charlie Chaplin as Heroes of Popular Culture," *Minnesota Review* III (Fall 1962), 77-82.

Camp, James E. and X. J. Kennedy. *Mark Twain's Frontier: A Textbook of Primary Materials.*

Cardwell, Guy A. "Mark Twain's Failures in Comedy and *The Enemy Conquered," Discussions of Mark Twain,* 104-112.

————. "Mark Twain's Failures in Comedy and *The Enemy Conquered," Georgia Review* XIII (Winter 1959), 424-436.

Chaput, Donald. "Mark Twain: Copied Originality," *Mark Twain Journal* XII (Summer 1965), 20-21.

Clark, William G. "Mark Twain's Visual and Aural Descriptions," *Mark Twain Journal* XII (Summer 1965), 1-9, 16.

Covici, Pascal, Jr. "Dear Master Wattie: The Mark Twain-David Watt Bowser Letters," *Southwest Review* XLV (Spring 1960), 105-121.

————. *Mark Twain's Humor: Image of the World.*

Cox, James M. *Mark Twain: The Fate of Humor.*

————. "The Muse of Samuel Clemens," *Massachusetts Review* V (Autumn 1963), 127-141.

————. "Walt Whitman, Mark Twain, and the Civil War," *Sewanee Review* LXIX (Spring 1961), 185-204.

Coyle, William. "Never the Twain," *CEA Critic* XXVI (Nov 1963), 1, 3.

Cummings, Sherwood. "Mark Twain and the Sirens of Progress," *Midcontinent American Studies Journal* I (Fall 1960), 17-24.

————. "Mark Twain's Acceptance of Science," *Centennial Review* VI (Spring 1962), 245-261.

Dahl, Curtis. "Mark Twain and the Moving Panoramas," *American Quarterly* XIII (Spring 1961), 20-32.

Day, A. Grove, (ed.). *Mark Twain's Letters from Hawaii.*

Dennis, Larry R. "Mark Twain and the Dark Angel," *Midwest Quarterly* VIII (Winter 1967), 181-197.

Duckett, Margaret. *Mark Twain and Bret Harte.*

Duffy, Myrtle M. "Twain in Howells' *A Modern Instance," American Quarterly* XVI (Winter 1964), 612-614.

Dunne, Finley Peter. "Mr. Dooley's Friends: Teddy Roosevelt and Mark Twain," *Atlantic Monthly* CCXII (Sept 1963), 77-99.

Durocher, Aurele A. "Mark Twain and the Roman Catholic Church," *Midcontinent American Studies Journal* I (Fall 1960), 32-43.

Ellis, Helen E. "Mark Twain: The Influence of Europe," *Mark Twain Journal* XIV (Winter 1968-69), 12-18.

Falk, Robert. *The Victorian Mode in American Fiction: 1865-1885,* 157-166.

Fatout, Paul. *Mark Twain in Virginia City.*

Feinstein, Herbert. "Two Pair of Gloves: Mark Twain and Henry James," *American Imago* XVII (Winter 1960), 349-387.

Fiedler, Leslie A. "The Blackness of Darkness: The Negro and the Development of American Gothic," *Images of the Negro in American Literature,* 91-99.

——. "Faust in the Eden of Childhood," *A Casebook on Mark Twain's Wound,* 277-300.

——. *Love and Death in the American Novel,* 267-271, 277-279, 437-440.

——. *The Return of the Vanishing American,* 81-83, 122-127.

Fifield, William. "Joyce's Brother, Lawrence's Wife, Wolfe's Mother, Twain's Daughter," *Texas Quarterly* X (Spring 1967), 69-87.

Friedrich, Gerhard. "Erosions of Values in Twain's Humor," *CEA Critic* XXII (Sept 1960), 1, 7, 8.

Ganzel, Dewey. *Mark Twain Abroad.*

——. "Samuel Clemens and John Camden Hotten," *Library* XX (Sept 1965), 230-242.

Gerber, John C. "Mark Twain's Use of the Comic Pose," *PMLA* LXXVII (Jun 1962), 297-304.

——. "Mark Twain's Search for Identity," *Essays in American and English Literature Presented to Bruce Robert McElderry, Jr.,* 27-47.

——. "1962: John C. Gerber," *Mark Twain: Selected Criticism,* 271-285.

Gowda, H. H. Anniah. "Mark Twain in India," *Literary Half-Yearly* VII (Jul 1966), 17-23.

Grant, Douglas. *Purpose and Place,* 112-117.

Green, Martin. *Re-Appraisals: Some Commonsense Readings in American Literature,* 113-126, 129-143.

Hamblen, Abigail Ann. "The American Scene: Dickens and Mark Twain," *Mark Twain Journal* XII (Winter 1964-65), 9-11, 16.

Harnsberger, Caroline. *Mark Twain, Family Man.*

——. *Mark Twain's Views on Religion.*

Havard, William C. "Mark Twain and the Political Ambivalence of Southwestern Humor," *Mississippi Quarterly* XVII (Spring 1964), 95-106.

Herzl, Theodor. "Mark Twain and the British Ladies," *Commentary* XXVIII (Sept 1959), 243-245.

TWAIN, MARK, Continued

Hill, Hamlin. "Mark Twain: Audience and Artistry," *American Quarterly* XV (Spring 1963), 25-40.

──────. "Mark Twain's Book Sales, 1869-1879," *Bulletin of the New York Public Library* LXV (Jun 1961), 371-389.

──────. "Mark Twain's 'Brace of Brief Lectures on Science,' " *New England Quarterly* XXXIV (Jun 1961), 228-239.

──────. *Mark Twain and Elisha Bliss.*

──────. "Mark Twain's Quarrels with Elisha Bliss," *American Literature* XXXIII (Jan 1962), 442-456.

──────, (ed.). *Mark Twain's Letters to his Publishers.*

──────. "1963: Hamlin Hill," *Mark Twain: Selected Criticism,* 286-302.

Howell, Elmo. "Mark Twain, William Faulkner and the First Families of Virginia," *Mark Twain Journal* XII (Summer 1966), 1-3, 19.

──────. "Uncle John Quarles' Watermelon Patch," *Midwest Quarterly* IX (Apr 1968), 271-284.

Hunter, Jim. "Mark Twain and the Boy-Book in 19th-Century America," *College English* XXIV (Mar 1963), 430-438.

Jones, Howard Mumford. "The Pessimism of Mark Twain," *Belief and Disbelief in American Literature,* 94-115.

Kahn, Sholom J. "Mark Twain's Final Phase," *Studi Americani* XI (1965), 143-162.

Kamei, Shunsuke. "Mark Twain in Japan," *Mark Twain Journal* XII (Spring 1963), 10-11, 20.

Kanellakou, Chris. "Mark Twain and the Chinese," *Mark Twain Journal* XII (Spring 1963), 7-9, 20.

Kaplan, Justin. *Mark Twain: A Profile.*

──────. *Mr. Clemens and Mark Twain.*

Klotz, Marvin. "Mark Twain and Socratic Dialogue," *Mark Twain Journal* XI (Summer 1959), 1-3.

Krause, Sydney J. "Cooper's Literary Offences: Mark Twain in Wonderland," *New England Quarterly* XXXVIII (Sept 1965), 291-311.

Laing, Nita. "The Later Satire of Mark Twain," *Midwest Quarterly* II (Autumn 1960), 35-48.

Lakin, R. D. "Mark Twain and the Cold War," *Midwest Quarterly* II (Winter 1961), 159-167.

Leary, Lewis. *Mark Twain.*

──────. "Mark Twain," *Six American Novelists of the Nineteenth Century,* 118-154.

TWAIN, MARK, Continued

————. (ed.) . *Mark Twain's Letters to Mary*.

————. "Standing with Reluctant Feet," *A Casebook on Mark Twain's Wound*, 3-32.

Lee, Robert Edson. *From West to East*, 82-111.

Long, E. Hudson. "Twain's Ordeal in Retrospect," *Southwest Review* XLVIII (Autumn 1963) , 338-348.

Macdonald, Dwight. "Mark Twain: An Unsentimental Journey," *Discussions of Mark Twain*, 116-130.

Malin, Irving. "Mark Twain: The Boy as Artist," *Literature and Psychology* XI (Summer 1961) , 78-84.

Martin, Jay. "Mark Twain: The Dream of Drift and the Dream of Delight," *Harvests of Change. American Literature 1865-1914*, 165-201.

Marx, Leo. *The Machine in the Garden: Technology and the Pastoral Ideal in America*, 319-340.

Maxwell, D. E. S. "Twain as Satirist," *American Fiction: The Intellectual Background*, 192-236.

McDermott, John Francis. "Mark Twain and the Bible," *Papers on Language and Literature* IV (Spring 1968) , 195-198.

Mills, Barriss. "Old Times on the Mississippi as an Initiation Story," *College English* XXV (Jan 1964) , 283-289.

Monteiro, George. "A Note on the Mark Twain-Whitelaw Reid Relationship," *Emerson Society Quarterly* 19 (II Quarter 1960) , 20-21.

————. "Publication of Mark Twain in Canada," *American Notes & Queries* I (Oct 1962) , 20.

Morgan, H. Wayne. "Mark Twain: The Optimist as Pessimist," *American Writers in Rebellion*, 1-36.

Myers, Margaret. "Mark Twain and Melville," *Mark Twain Journal* XIV (Summer 1968) , 5-8.

Narain, S. K. "Mark Twain: A Consideration of His Realism," *Literary Criterion* V (Winter 1962) , 66-71.

Noble, David W. *The Eternal Adam and the New World Garden*, 51-67.

Parsons, Coleman O. "Mark Twain in Australia," *Antioch Review* XXI (Winter 1961) , 455-468.

Pearson, Norman Holmes. "New Resources for American Studies II: The Mark Twain Memorial in Hartford, Connecticut," *Midcontinent American Studies Journal* I (Fall 1960) , 11-16.

Poli, Bernard. *Mark Twain: Écrivain de l'ouest*.

Price, Lawrence Marsden. *The Reception of United States Literature in Germany*, 111-117.

Ratner, Marc L. "Two Letters of Mark Twain," *Mark Twain Journal* XII (Spring 1964) , 9, 17.

Reid, John T. *Indian Influences in American Literature and Thought*, 74-76.

Rodnon, Stewart. "Mark Twain's Get-Rich-Quick Schemes: A Balance Sheet," *Mark Twain Journal* XII (Winter 1964-65) , 3-5.

Rogers, Franklin R. Introduction, *Mark Twain's Satires and Burlesques* (Berkley, 1967) .

————. *Mark Twain's Burlesque Patterns.*

Roper, Gordon. "Mark Twain and His Canadian Publishers," *American Book Collector* X (Jun 1960) , 13-30.

Ryan, Pat M., Jr. "Mark Twain: Frontier Theatre Critic," *Arizona Quarterly* XVI (Autumn 1960) , 197-209.

Salomon, Roger B. "Mark Twain and Victorian Nostalgia," *Patterns of Commitment in American Literature*, 73-91.

————. "Realism as Disinheritance: Twain, Howells and James," *American Quarterly* XVI (Winter 1964) , 531-544.

————. *Twain and the Image of History.*

Salsbury, Edith C., (ed.) . *Susy and Mark Twain: Family Dialogues.*

Schlesinger, Arthur, Jr. "Mark Twain or the Ambiguities," *Atlantic Monthly* CCXVIII (Aug 1966) , 61-64.

Scott, Arthur L. "Letters from Mark Twain to William Walter Phelps, 1891-1893," *Huntington Library Quarterly* XXVII (Aug 1964) , 375-381.

————. "Mark Twain Today," *Midcontinent American Studies Journal* I (Fall 1960) , 2-10.

Scott, Winfield Townley. "Hannibal and the Bones of Art: In Mark Twain's Pastures," *New Mexico Quarterly* XXX (Winter 1960-61) , 338-346.

Smith, Bradford. "Mark Twain and the Mystery of Identity," *College English* XXIV (Mar 1963) , 425-430.

Spengemann, William C. "The Backwoodsman and the Pilgrim: The Genesis of the Innocent Hero," *Mark Twain and the Backwoods Angel*, 1-14.

Stone, Albert E., Jr. *The Innocent Eye: Childhood in Mark Twain's Imagination.*

Stone, Edward. *Voices of Despair*, 63-68, 109-113, 168-171.

Strong, Leah A. *Joseph Hopkins Twitchell, Mark Twain's Friend and Pastor.*

Tanner, Tony. "The Literary Children of James and Clemens," *Nineteenth-Century Fiction* XVI (Dec 1961), 205-218.

————. "The Lost America—The Despair of Henry Adams and Mark Twain," *Mark Twain: A Collection of Critical Essays,* 159-174.

————. "Mark Twain and Wattie Bowser," *Mark Twain Journal* XII (Spring 1963), 1-6.

————. *The Reign of Wonder: Naivety and Reality in American Literature,* 97-254.

————. "Samuel Clemens and the Progress of a Stylistic Rebel," *British Association for American Studies* 3 (Dec 1961), 31-42.

Vagts, Alfred. "Mark Twain at the Courts of the Emperors," *Jahrbuch Für Amerikastudien* 9 (1964), 149-151.

Vandersee, Charles. "The Mutual Awareness of Mark Twain and Henry Adams," *English Language Notes* V (Jun 1968), 285-292.

Vitelli, J. R. "The Innocence of Mark Twain," *Bucknell Review* IX (Dec 1960), 187-198.

Wagenknecht, Edward. "Literature and Love," *A Casebook on Mark Twain's Wound,* 301-310.

Wager, Willis. *American Literature: A World View,* 131-139.

Webb, Howard W., Jr. "Mark Twain and Ring Lardner," *Mark Twain Journal* XI (Summer 1960), 13-15.

West, Ray B., Jr. "Mark Twain's Idyl of Frontier America," *The Writer in the Room: Selected Essays,* 83-101.

Wiggins, Robert A. *Mark Twain: Jackleg Novelist,* 3-32.

Ziff, Larzer. "Literary Absenteeism," *The American 1890s: Life and Times of a Lost Generation,* 66-72.

BIBLIOGRAPHY

Beebe, Maurice and John Feaster. "Criticism of Mark Twain: A Selected Checklist," *Modern Fiction Studies* XIV (Spring 1968), 93-139.

Blair, Walter. *Mark Twain and Huck Finn,* 423-427.

A Casebook on Mark Twain's Wound, 337-346.

Duckett, Margaret. *Mark Twain and Bret Harte,* 345-353.

Mathews, J. Chesley. "Bibliographical Supplement: A Selective Checklist, 1955-1962," *Eight American Authors: A Review of Research and Criticism,* 451-458.

TWAIN, MARK, Continued

Meine, Franklin J. "Some Notes on the First Editions of 'Huck Finn,'" *American Book Collector* X (Jun 1960), 31-34.

Morgan, W. Wayne. *American Writers in Rebellion*, 203-204.

Poli, Bernard. *Mark Twain: Écrivain de l'ouest*, 475-490.

Price, Lawrence Marsden. *The Reception of United States Literature in Germany*, 204-206.

Rogers, Franklin R. *Mark Twain's Burlesque Patterns*, 179-183.

Six American Novelists of the Nineteenth Century, 237-240.

TYLER, ROYALL

THE ALGERINE CAPTIVE

Tanselle, G. Thomas. "Early American Fiction in England: The Case of *The Algerine Captive*," *Papers of the Bibliographical Society of America* LIX (Oct-Dec 1965) 367-384.

Tanselle, G. Thomas. *Royall Tyler*.

UPDIKE, JOHN

THE CENTAUR

Alley, Alvin D. "*The Centaur:* Transcendental Imagination and Metaphoric Death," *English Journal* LVI (Oct 1967), 982-985.

Finkelstein, Sidney. *Existentialism and Alienation in American Literature*, 246-247.

Galloway, David D. *The Absurd Hero in American Fiction*, 40-49.

Hamilton, Alice and Kenneth. *John Updike: A Critical Essay*, 31-39.

Harper, Howard M., Jr. *Desperate Faith*, 173-182.

Walcutt, Charles Child. "The Centripetal Action: John Updike's *The Centaur* and *Rabbitt, Run*," *Man's Changing Mask: Modes and Methods of Characterization in Fiction*, 326-330.

COUPLES

Hicks, Granville. "God Has Gone, Sex is Left," *Saturday Review* 51 (Apr 6, 1968), 21-22.

Thompson, John. "Updike's *Couples*," *Commentary* 45 (May 1968), 70-73.

Yglesias, Jose. "Coupling and Uncoupling," *Nation* 206 (May 13, 1968), 637-638.

ON THE FARM

Hamilton, Alice and Kenneth. *John Updike: A Critical Essay*, 40-46.

Harper, Howard M., Jr. *Desperate Faith,* 182-186.

THE POORHOUSE FAIR

Galloway, David D. *The Absurd Hero in American Fiction,* 21-27.

Hamilton, Alice and Kenneth. *John Updike: A Critical Essay,* 13-22.

RABBIT, RUN

Alley, Alvin D. and Hugh Agee. "Existential Heroes: Frank Alpine and Rabbit Angstrom," *Ball State University Forum* IX (Winter 1968), 3-5.

Brenner, Gerry. "*Rabbit, Run:* John Updike's Criticism of the 'Return to Nature,' " *Twentieth Century Literature* XII (Apr 1966), 3-14.

Detweiler, Robert. *Four Spiritual Crises in Mid-Century American Fiction,* 14-24.

Finkelstein, Sidney. *Existentialism and Alienation in American Literature,* 244-246.

Galloway, David D. *The Absurd Hero in American Fiction,* 27-40.

Hamilton, Alice and Kenneth. *John Updike: A Critical Essay,* 31-36.

Harper, Howard M., Jr. *Desperate Faith,* 165-173.

Hertzel, Leo J. "Rabbit in the Great North Woods," *University Review* XXXIII (Dec 1966), 143-147.

Standley, Fred L. "Rabbit, Run: An Image of Life," *Midwest Quarterly* VIII (Summer 1967), 371-386.

Stubbs, John C. "The Search for Perfection in *Rabbit, Run,*" *Critique* X (No 2, 1968), 94-101.

Walcutt, Charles Child. "The Centripetal Action: John Updike's *The Centaur* and *Rabbit, Run,*" *Man's Changing Mask: Modes and Methods of Characterization in Fiction,* 330-336.

GENERAL

De Logu, Pietro. "La Narrativa Di John Updike," *Studi Americani* X (1964), 343-368.

Galloway, David D. "The Absurd Man as Saint," *The Absurd Hero in American Fiction,* 21-50.

————. "The Absurd Man as Saint: The Novels of John Updike," *Modern Fiction Studies* X (Summer 1964), 111-127.

Hamilton, Alice and Kenneth. *John Updike: A Critical Essay.*

Harper, Howard M., Jr. "John Updike—the Intrinsic problem of Human Existence," *Desperate Faith,* 162-190.

Hicks, Granville. "Generations of the Fifties: Malamud, Gold, and Updike," *The Creative Present,* 232-237.

Mizener, Arthur. "The American Hero as High-School Boy: Peter

UPDIKE, JOHN, Continued

Caldwell," *The Sense of Life in the Modern Novel,* 247-266.

Muradian, Thaddeus. "The World of Updike," *English Journal* LIV (Oct 1965) , 577-584.

Nichols, Lewis. "Talk With John Updike," *New York Times Book Review* 73 (Apr 7, 1968) , 34-35.

O'Connor, William Van. "John Updike and William Styron," *Contemporary American Novelists,* 207-214.

Rupp, Richard H. "John Updike: Style in Search of a Center," *Sewanee Review* LXXV (Autumn 1967) , 693-709.

Samuels, Charles Thomas. "The Art of Fiction XLIII: John Updike," *Paris Review* 12 (Winter 1968) , 85-117.

Tate, Sister M. Judith, O. S. B. "John Updike of Rabbits and Centaurs," *Critic* XXII (Feb-Mar 1964) , 44-51.

Updike, John. "Writers I Have Met," *New York Times Book Review* 73 (Aug 11, 1968) , 2, 23.

Ward, J. A. "John Updike's Fiction," *Critique* V (Spring-Summer, 1962) , 27-40.

Wyatt, Bryant N. "John Updike: The Psychological Novel in Search of Structure," *Twentieth Century Literature* XIII (Jul 1967) , 89-96.

Yates, Norris W. "The Doubt and Faith of John Updike," *College English* XXVI (Mar 1965) , 469-474.

BIBLIOGRAPHY

Galloway, David D. *The Absurd Hero in American Fiction,* 183-200.

Hamilton, Alice and Kenneth. *John Updike: A Critical Essay,* 47-48.

VAN DINE, S. S., pseud.
(Wright, W. H.)

GENERAL

O'Brien, Frances Blazer. "Faulkner and Wright, Alias S. S. Van Dine," *Mississippi Quarterly* XIV (Spring 1961) , 101-107.

Schier, Donald. "Recollections of Philo Vance: A Digression," *Carleton Miscellany* IV (Spring 1963) , 109-115.

VAN VECHTEN, CARL

BLIND BOW-BOY

Lueders, Edward. *Carl Van Vechten,* 72-78.

VAN VECHTEN, CARL, Continued

GENERAL

Lueders, Edward. *Carl Van Vechten.*

BIBLIOGRAPHY

Jonas, Klaus W. "Additions to the Bibliography of Carl Van Vechten," *Papers of the Bibliographical Society of America* 55 (Jan-Mar 1961), 42-45.

Lueders, Edward. *Carl Van Vechten,* 148-152.

VIDAL, GORE

JULIAN

Vidal, Gore. "Vidal to Vidal: On Misusing the Past," *Harper's* CCXXXI (Oct 1965), 162-164.

GENERAL

Vidal, Gore. "Making and Remaking," *New York Times Book Review* 70 (Nov 14, 1965), 2, 82.

VONNEGUT, KURT, JR.

CAT'S CRADLE

Scholes, Robert. *The Fabulators,* 42-44, 47-51.

MOTHER'S NIGHT

Scholes, Robert. *The Fabulators,* 51-55.

GENERAL

Bryan, C. D. B. "Kurt Vonnegut on Target," *New Republic* 155 (Oct 8, 1966), 21-26.

Pagetti, Carlo. "Kurt Vonnegut, tra fantascienza e utopia," *Studi Americani* 12 (1966), 301-322.

Scholes, Robert. " 'Mithridates, he died old': Black Humor and Kurt Vonnegut, Jr.," *Hollins Critic* III (Oct 1966), 1-12.

WAGONER, DAVID

GENERAL

Schafer, William J. "David Wagoner's Fiction: In the Mills of Satan," *Critique* IX (No 1, 1966), 71-89.

WALLACE, HORACE BINNEY

GENERAL

Hatvary, George Egon. "Horace Binney Wallace: A Study in Self-Destruction," *Princeton University Library Chronicle* XXV (Winter 1964), 137-149.

WALLANT, EDWARD LEWIS

THE CHILDREN AT THE GATE

Rubin, Louis D., Jr. "The Experience of Difference," *The Curious Death of the Novel: Essays in American Literature*, 268-271.

THE PAWNBROKER

Baumbach, Jonathan. "The Illusion of Indifference: *The Pawnbroker* by Edward Lewis Wallant," *The Landscape of Nightmare: Studies in the Contemporary American Novel*, 138-151.

GENERAL

Lorch, Thomas M. "The Novels of Edward Lewis Wallant," *Chicago Review* XIX (No 2, 1967), 78-91.

Schulz, M. F. "Wallant and Friedman: The Glory and the Agony of Love," *Critique* X (No 3, 1968), 31-47.

WARNER, CHARLES DUDLEY

THE GILDED AGE

Church, Richard. Introduction, *The Gilded Age* (London, 1967).

Kaplan, Justin D. Introduction, *The Gilded Age* (New York, 1964).

See also Mark Twain, *The Gilded Age*.

WARNER, REX

THE WILD GOOSE CHASE

Hawkes, John. "Symposium: Fiction Today; Notes on the *Wild Goose Chase*," *Massachusetts Review* III (Summer 1962), 784-788.

WARREN, ROBERT PENN

ALL THE KING'S MEN

Baumbach, Jonathan. "The Metaphysics of Demagoguery: *All the Kings Men* by Robert Penn Warren," *The Landscape of Nightmare: Studies in the Contemporary American Novel*, 16-34.

WARREN, ROBERT PENN, Continued

Casper, Leonard. *Robert Penn Warren: The Dark and Bloody Ground,* 107-116.

Clements, A. L. "Theme and Reality in *At Heaven's Gate* and *All the King's Men,*" *Criticism* V (Winter 1963) , 27-44.

Longley, John Lewis, Jr. " 'At Heaven's Gate': The Major Themes," *Modern Fiction Studies* VI (Spring 1960) , 13-24.

————. "Self-Knowledge, the Pearl of Pus, and the Seventh Circle: The Major Themes in *At Heaven's Gate,*" *Robert Penn Warren: A Collection of Critical Essays,* 60-74.

Poenicke, Klaus. *Robert Penn Warren: Kunstwerk und Kritische Theorie,* 59-77.

BAND OF ANGELS

Bohner, Charles H. *Robert Penn Warren,* 127-135.

Casper, Leonard. "Miscegenation as Symbol: *Band of Angels,*" *Robert Penn Warren: A Collection of Critical Essays,* 140-158.

————. *Robert Penn Warren: The Dark and Bloody Ground,* 148-162.

Poenicke, Klaus. *Robert Penn Warren: Kunstwerk und Kritische Theorie,* 120-130.

THE CAVE

Bohner, Charles H. *Robert Penn Warren,* 146-153.

Casper, Leonard. "Journey to the Interior: 'The Cave,' " *Modern Fiction Studies* VI (Spring 1960) , 65-72.

Davison, Richard Allan. "Robert Penn Warren's 'Dialectical Configuration' and *The Cave,*" *CLA Journal* X (Jun 1967) , 349-357.

Glazier, Lyle. "Reconstructed Platonism: Robert Penn Warren's *The Cave,*" *Litera* VII (1960) , 16-26.

Justus, James H. "The Uses of Gesture in Warren's *The Cave,*" *Modern Language Quarterly* XXVI (Sept 1965) , 448-461.

FLOOD

Longley, John Lewis, Jr. "When All is Said and Done: Warren's *Flood,*" *Robert Penn Warren: A Collection of Critical Essays,* 169-177.

Shepherd, Allen. "Character and Theme in R. P. Warren's *Flood,*" *Critique* IX (No 3, 1967) , 95-102.

Wain, John. "After the Deluge, What?" *New Republic* 150 (May 16, 1964) , 23-25.

NIGHT RIDER

Bohner, Charles H. *Robert Penn Warren,* 61-70.

WARREN, ROBERT PENN, Continued

GENERAL

Bohner, Charles H. *Robert Penn Warren.*

Carter, Everett. "The 'Little Myth' of Robert Penn Warren," *Modern Fiction Studies* VI (Spring 1960), 3-12.

Casper, Leonard. *Robert Penn Warren: The Dark and Bloody Ground.*

Clark, Marden J. "Religious Implications in the Novels of Robert Penn Warren," *Brigham Young University Studies* IV (Autumn 1961), 67-79.

Davis, Joe. "Robert Penn Warren and the Journey to the West," *Modern Fiction Studies* VI (Spring 1960), 73-82.

Eisinger, Chester E. *Fiction of the Forties,* 198-229.

Fiedler, Leslie A. *Love and Death in the American Novel,* 392-394.

Gossett, Louise Y. "Violence and the Integrity of the Self," *Violence in Recent Southern Fiction,* 52-75.

Gross, Seymour L. "Robert Penn Warren," *Critic* XVIII (Oct-Nov 1959), 11-13, 82.

Hardy, John Edward. "Robert Penn Warren's Double-Hero," *Virginia Quarterly Review* XXXVI (Autumn 1960), 583-597.

Havard, William C. "The Burden of the Literary Mind: Some Meditations on Robert Penn Warren as Historian," *Robert Penn Warren: A Collection of Critical Essays,* 187-194.

———. "The Burden of the Literary Mind: Some Meditations on Robert Penn Warren as Historian," *South Atlantic Quarterly* LXII (Autumn 1963), 516-531.

Hoffman, Frederick J. *The Art of Southern Fiction,* 31-36.

Jones, Madison. "The Novels of Robert Penn Warren," *South Atlantic Quarterly* LXII (Autumn 1963), 488-498.

Justus, James H. "The Mariner and Robert Penn Warren," *Texas Studies in Literature and Language* VIII (Spring 1966), 117-128.

Moore, John Rees. "Robert Penn Warren: You Must Go Home Again," *Southern Review* IV (Spring 1968), 320-332.

Moore, L. Hugh, Jr. "Robert Penn Warren and the Terror of Answered Prayer," *Mississippi Quarterly* XXI (Winter 1967-68), 29-36.

Noble, David W. *The Eternal Adam and the New World Garden,* 177-186.

Poenicke, Klaus. *Robert Penn Warren: Kunstwerk und Kritische Theorie.*

Stewart, John L. *The Burden of Time: The Fugitives and Agrarians,* 427-542.

WARREN, ROBERT PENN, Continued

Stone, Edward. *Voices of Despair,* 202-205.

Strandberg, Victor. "Warren's Osmosis," *Criticism* X (Winter 1968), 23-40.

Symons, Julian. "Fables for Our Time," *Critical Observations,* 119-125.

West, Paul. *Robert Penn Warren.*

White, Ellington. "Robert Penn Warren," *South: Modern Southern Literature in its Cultural Setting,* 198-209.

BIBLIOGRAPHY

Beebe, Maurice and Erin Marcus. "Criticism of Robert Penn Warren: A Selected Checklist," *Modern Fiction Studies* VI (Spring 1960), 83-88.

Bohner, Charles H. *Robert Penn Warren,* 166-168.

Casper, Leonard. *Robert Penn Warren: The Dark and Bloody Ground,* 191-208.

Huff, Mary Nance. *Robert Penn Warren: A Bibliography.*

Poenicke, Klaus. *Robert Penn Warren: Kunstwerk und Kritische Theorie,* 156-160.

Robert Penn Warren: A Collection of Critical Essays, 247-257.

West, Paul. *Robert Penn Warren,* 46-48.

WASSON, GEORGE S.

Eby, Cecil D., Jr. "Americanisms in the Down-East Fiction of George S. Wasson," *American Speech* XXXVII (Dec 1962), 249-254.

WATERS, FRANK

GENERAL

Huntress, Diana. "The Man Who Resurrected the Deer," *South Dakota Review* 6 (Winter 1968-69), 69-71.

Lyon, Thomas J. "An Ignored Meaning of the West," *Western American Literature* III (Spring 1968), 51-59.

Pilkington, William T. "Character and Landscape: Frank Waters' Colorado Trilogy," *Western American Literature* II (Fall 1967), 183-193.

BIBLIOGRAPHY

Waters, Frank. "Bibliography of the Works of Frank Waters," *South Dakota Review* 4 (Summer 1964), 77-78.

DELTA WEDDING

Hardy, John Edward. "*Delta Wedding:* Region and Symbol," *Man in the Modern Novel,* 175-193.

Hoffman, Frederick J. *The Art of Southern Fiction,* 59-63.

Vande Kieft, Ruth M. *Eudora Welty,* 93-110.

THE PONDER HEART

Appel, Alfred, Jr. *A Season of Dreams: The Fiction of Eudora Welty,* 51-60.

Holland, Robert B. "Dialogue as a Reflection of Place in *The Ponder Heart,*" *American Literature* (Nov 1963), 352-358.

GENERAL

Appel, Alfred, Jr. *A Season of Dreams: The Fiction of Eudora Welty.*

Daniel, Robert W. "Eudora Welty: The Sense of Place," *South: Modern Southern Literature in Its Cultural Setting,* 276-286.

Eisinger, Chester E. *Fiction of the Forties,* 258-283.

Felheim, Marvin. "Eudora Welty and Carson McCullers," *Contemporary American Novelists,* 41-48.

Gossett, Louise Y. "Violence as Revelation," *Violence in Recent Southern Fiction,* 98-117.

Hardy, John Edward. "The Achievement of Eudora Welty," *Southern Humanities Review* II (Summer 1968), 269-278.

————. "Eudora Welty's Negroes," *Images of the Negro in American Literature,* 221-232.

Hoffman, Frederick J. *The Art of Southern Fiction,* 51-65.

Jones, Alun R. "The World of Love: The Fiction of Eudora Welty," *The Creative Present,* 175-192.

Opitz, Kurt. "Eudora Welty: The Order of a Captive Soul," *Critique* VII (Winter 1964-1965), 79-91.

Vande Kieft, Ruth M. *Eudora Welty.*

Welty, Eudora. "Must the Novelist Crusade?" *Atlantic Monthly* CCXVI (Oct 1965), 104-108.

————. "Words into Fiction," *Southern Review* I (Jul 1965), 543-553.

BIBLIOGRAPHY

Appel, Alfred, Jr. *A Season of Dreams: The Fiction of Eudora Welty,* 265-267.

Jordan, Leona. "Eudora Welty: Selected Criticism," *Bulletin of Bibliography* XXIII (Jan-Apr 1960), 14-15.

McDonald, W. U., Jr. "Eudora Welty Manuscripts: An Annotated

Finding List," *Bulletin of Bibliography* XXIV (Sept-Dec 1963), 44-46.

Vande Kieft, Ruth M. *Eudora Welty,* 195-199.

WESCOTT, GLENWAY

APARTMENT IN ATHENS
Rueckert, William H. *Glenway Wescott,* 116-121.
THE APPLE OF THE EYE
Rueckert, William H. *Glenway Wescott,* 39-45.
THE GRANDMOTHERS
Rueckert, William H. *Glenway Wescott,* 47-56.
THE PILGRIM HAWK
Gallos, Stephen. "An Analysis of Wescott's *The Pilgrim Hawk,*" *Critique* VIII (Winter 1965-1966), 13-19.
Rueckert, William H. *Glenway Wescott,* 108-114.
GENERAL
Kahn, Sy. "Glenway Wescott: The Artist at Work," *Papers on English Language and Literature* I (Summer 1965), 250-258.
Kane, Patricia. "Glenway Wescott's Odyssey," *Critique* VIII (Winter 1965-1966), 5-12.
Rueckert, William H. *Glenway Wescott.*
BIBLIOGRAPHY
Rueckert, William H. *Glenway Wescott,* 165-171.

WEST, NATHANAEL

A COOL MILLION
Blotner, Joseph. *The Modern American Political Novel,* 244-247.
Comerchero, Victor. *Nathanael West: The Ironic Prophet,* 103-119.
Edenbaum, Robert I. "A Surfeit of Shoddy: Nathanael West's *A Cool Million,*" *Southern Humanities Review* II (Fall 1968), 427-439.
Galloway, David D. "A Picaresque Apprenticeship: Nathanael West's *The Dream Life of Balso Snell* and *A Cool Million,*" *Wisconsin Studies in Contemporary Literature* V (Summer 1964), 118-126.
Light, James F. *Nathanael West: An Interpretative Study,* 117-129.
Reid, Randall. *The Fiction of Nathanael West: No Redeemer, No Promised Land,* 106-115.

THE DAY OF THE LOCUST

Comerchero, Victor. *Nathanael West: The Ironic Prophet*, 120-151.

Fiedler, Leslie A. *The Return of the Vanishing American*, 147-149.

Light, James F. *Nathanael West: An Interpretative Study*, 155-181.

————. "Nathanael West and the Ravaging Locust," *American Quarterly* XII (Spring 1960) , 44-54.

Phillips, Robert S. "Fitzgerald and *The Day of the Locust*," *Fitzgerald Newsletter* 15 (Fall 1961) , 2-3.

Reid, Randall. *The Fiction of Nathanael West: No Redeemer, No Promised Land*, 116-157.

Widmer, Kingsley. "The Sweet Savage Prophecies of Nathanael West," *The Thirties: Fiction, Poetry, Drama*, 103-106.

THE DREAM LIFE OF BALSO SNELL

Comerchero, Victor. *Nathanael West: The Ironic Prophet*, 51-71.

Galloway, David D. "A Picaresque Apprenticeship: Nathanael West's *The Dream Life of Balso Snell* and *A Cool Million*," *Wisconsin Studies in Contemporary Literature* V (Summer 1964), 110-118.

Light, James F. *Nathanael West: An Interpretative Study*, 40-60.

Reid, Randall. *The Fiction of Nathanael West: No Redeemer, No Promised Land*, 13-40.

Tibbetts, A.M. "Nathanael West's *The Dream Life of Balso Snell*," *Studies in Short Fiction* II (Winter 1965), 105-112.

White, William. "Nathanael West's 'Balso Snell' in Cloth," *Papers of the Bibliographical Society of America* LX (Oct-Dec 1966) , 474-476.

MISS LONELYHEARTS

Abrahams, Roger. "Androgynes Bound: Nathanael West's *Miss Lonelyhearts*," *Seven Contemporary Authors*, 51-72.

Andreach, Robert J. "Nathanael West's *Miss Lonelyhearts:* Between the Dead Pan and the Unborn Christ," *Modern Fiction Studies* XII (Summer 1966) , 251-260.

Bush, C. W. "This Stupendous Fabric: the Metaphysics of Order in Melville's *Pierre* and Nathanael West's *Miss Lonelyhearts*," *Journal of American Studies* I (Oct 1967) , 269-274.

Comerchero, Victor. *Nathanael West: The Ironic Prophet*, 72-102.

Daniel, Carter A. "West's Revisions of *Miss Lonelyhearts*," *Studies in Bibliography* XVI (1963) , 232-243.

Edenbaum, Robert I. "To Kill God and Build a Church: Nathanael West's *Miss Lonelyhearts*," *CEA Critic* XXIX (Jun 1967) , 5-7, 11.

Light, James F. *Nathanael West: An Interpretative Study,* 74-101.

Lorch, Thomas M. "West's *Miss Lonelyhearts:* Skepticism Mitigated?" *Renascence* XVIII (Winter 1966), 99-109.

Reid, Randall. *The Fiction of Nathanael West: No Redeemer, No Promised Land,* 41-105.

Richardson, Robert D., Jr. *"Miss Lonelyhearts,"* *University Review* XXXIII (Dec 1966) 151-157.

Smith, Marcus. "Religious Experience in Miss Lonelyhearts," *Contemporary Literature* IX (Spring 1968), 172-188.

Volpe, Edmond L. "The Waste Land of Nathanael West," *Renascence* XIII (Winter 1961), 69-77, 112.

Widmer, Kingsley. "The Sweet Savage Prophecies of Nathanael West," *The Thirties: Fiction, Poetry, Drama,* 99-102.

GENERAL

Aaron, Daniel. "Late Thoughts on Nathanael West," *Massachusetts Review* VI (Winter-Spring 1965), 307-317.

Comerchero, Victor. *Nathanael West: The Ironic Prophet,* 1-50.

Fiedler, Leslie A. *Love and Death in the American Novel,* 316-318, 461-467.

Galloway, David D. "Nathanael West's Dream Dump," *Critique* VI (Winter 1963-1964), 46-64.

Herbst, Josephine. "Nathanael West," *Kenyon Review* XXIII (Autumn 1961), 611-630.

Hyman, Stanley Edgar. "Nathanael West," *Seven Modern American Novelists: An Introduction,* 226-264.

Kraus, W. Keith. "An Uncited Nathanael West Story," *American Notes & Queries* V (Jun 1967), 163-164; reply by William White, VI (Jan 1968), 72-73.

Light, James F. *Nathanael West: An Interpretative Study.*

Lokke, V. L. "A Side Glance at Medusa: Hollywood, the Literature Boys, and Nathanael West," *Southwest Review* XLVI (Winter 1961), 35-45.

Ratner, Marc L. " 'Anywhere Out of This World': Baudelaire and Nathanael West," *American Literature* XXXI (Jan 1960), 456-463.

Solberg, S. E. "The Novels of Nathanael West: A Sargasso of the Imagination," *English Language and Literature* 14 (Jun 1963-Oct 1963), 125-146.

Symons, Julian. "The Case of Nathanael West," *Critical Occasions,* 99-105.

WEST, NATHANAEL, Continued

Tibbetts, A. M. "The Strange Half-World of Nathanael West," *Prairie Schooner* XXXIV (Spring 1960), 8-14.

White, William. "Ernest Hemingway and Nathanael West: How Well Known Is Your Collector's 'Item?'" *American Book Collector* XIV (May 1964), 29.

————. "Some Uncollected Authors XXXII: Nathanael West, 1903?-1940," *Book Collector* XI (Summer 1962), 206-210.

————. "Unpublished Faulkner: Reply to a Nathanael West Questionnaire," *American Book Collector* XVII (Sept 1966), 27.

Widmer, Kingsley. "The Sweet Savage Prophecies of Nathanael West," *The Thirties: Fiction, Poetry, Drama,* 97-106.

BIBLIOGRAPHY

Reid, Randall. *The Fiction of Nathanael West: No Redeemer, No Promised Land,* 165-169.

WHARTON, EDITH

THE AGE OF INNOCENCE

Auchincloss, Louis. Introduction, *The Age of Innocence* (New York, 1962).

Kellogg, Grace. *The Two Lives of Edith Wharton: The Woman and Her Work,* 224-232.

Lamar, Lillie B. "Edith Wharton's Foreknowledge in *The Age of Innocence,*" *Texas Studies in Literature and Language* VIII (Fall 1966), 385-389.

Mizener, Arthur. "Edith Wharton: *The Age of Innocence,*" *Twelve Great American Novels,* 68-86.

Rothwell, Kenneth S. "From Society to Babbittry: Lewis' Debt to Edith Wharton," *Midcontinent American Studies Journal* I (Spring 1960), 32-37.

ETHAN FROME

Brennan, Joseph X. "*Ethan Frome:* Structure and Metaphor," *Modern Fiction Studies* VII (Winter 1961-62), 347-356.

Kellogg, Grace. *The Two Lives of Edith Wharton: The Woman and Her Work,* 159-174.

THE GODS ARRIVE

Tuttleton, James W. "Edith Wharton: Form and the Epistemology of Artistic Creation," *Criticism* X (Fall 1968), 334-351.

THE HOUSE OF MIRTH

Auchincloss, Louis. *Pioneers & Caretakers,* 25-29.

Bristol, Marie. "Life Among the Ungentle Genteel: Edith Wharton's *The House of Mirth* Revisited," *Western Humanities Review* XVI (Autumn 1962), 371-374.

Friman, Anne. "Determinism and Point of View in *The House of Mirth,*" *Papers on Language and Literature* II (Spring 1966), 175-178.

Hierth, Harrison E. "The Class Novel," *CEA Critic* XXVII (Dec 1964), 1, 3-4.

Howe, Irving. Introduction, *The House of Mirth* (New York, 1962).

————. "A Reading of *The House of Mirth,*" *Edith Wharton: A Collection of Critical Essays,* 119-129.

Kellogg, Grace. *The Two Lives of Edith Wharton: The Woman and Her Work,* 106-114.

Lewis, R. W. B. *Trials of the Word,* 129-147.

Poirier, Richard. "Edith Wharton: *The House of Mirth,*" *The American Novel from James Fenimore Cooper to William Faulkner,* 117-132.

————. *A World Elsewhere,* 215-235.

Trilling, Diana. "*The House of Mirth* Revisited," *American Scholar* XXXII (Winter 1962-63), 113-128.

————. "*The House of Mirth* Revisited," *Edith Wharton: A Collection of Critical Essays,* 103-118.

HUDSON RIVER BRACKETED

Tuttleton, James W. "Edith Wharton: Form and the Epistemology of Artistic Creation," *Criticism* X (Fall 1968), 334-351.

THE REEF

Auchincloss, Louis. Introduction, *The Reef* (New York, 1965).

GENERAL

Anderson, Hilton. "Edith Wharton and the Vulgar American," *Southern Quarterly* VII (Oct 1968), 17-22.

Auchincloss, Louis. "Edith Wharton," *Pioneers & Caretakers,* 20-55.

————. "Edith Wharton," *Seven Modern American Novelists: An Introduction,* 11-45.

————. Introduction, *The Edith Wharton Reader* (New York, 1965).

Baxter, Annette K. "Caste and Class: Howells' Boston and Wharton's New York," *Midwest Quarterly* IV (Summer 1963), 353-361.

Buchan, Alexander M. "Edith Wharton and 'The Elusive Bright-

Winged Thing,' " *New England Quarterly* XXXVII (Sept 1964), 343-362.

Buitenhuis, Peter. "Edith Wharton and the First World War," *American Quarterly* XVIII (Fall 1966), 493-505.

Coard, Robert L. "Names in the Fiction of Edith Wharton," *Names* 13 (Mar 1965), 1-10.

Coolidge, Olivia. *Edith Wharton: 1862-1937.*

Hamblen, Abigail Ann. "Edith Wharton in New England," *New England Quarterly* XXXVIII (Jun 1965), 239-244.

Howe, Irving. "The Achievement of Edith Wharton," *Encounter* XIX (Jul 1962), 45-52.

————. "Edith Wharton: Convention and the Demands of Modernism," *A World More Attractive: A View of Modern Literature and Politics,* 41-58.

————. "Introduction: The Achievement of Edith Wharton," *Edith Wharton: A Collection of Critical Essays,* 1-18.

Kellogg, Grace. *The Two Lives of Edith Wharton: The Woman and Her Work.*

Lawson, Richard H. "Herman Sudermann and Edith Wharton," *Revue de Littérature Comparée* 41 (Jan-Mar 1967), 125-131.

————. "The Influence of Gottfried Keller on Edith Wharton," *Revue de Littérature Comparée* 42 (Jul-Sept 1968), 366-379.

Martin, Jay. *Harvests of Change. American Literature 1865-1911,* 263-277.

Maxwell, D. E. S. "Edith Wharton and the Realists," *American Fiction: The Intellectual Background,* 236-264.

Miller, James E., Jr. "Wharton and Cather: The Quest for Culture," *Quests Surd and Absurd: Essays in American Literature,* 76-86, 90-92.

Millgate, Michael. *American Social Fiction: James to Cozzens,* 54-66.

Morgan, H. Wayne. "Edith Wharton: The Novelist of Manners," *Writers in Transition: Seven Americans,* 23-41.

Plante, Patricia. "Edith Wharton and the Invading Goths," *Midcontinent American Studies Journal* V (Fall 1964), 18-23.

Rubin, Larry. "Aspects of Naturalism in Four Novels of Edith Wharton," *Twentieth Century Literature* II (Jan 1957), 182-192.

Sanna, Vittoria. "I Romanzi Di Edith Wharton E La Narrativa Jamesiana," *Studi Americani* X (1964), 229-291.

Thorp, Willard. *American Writing in the Twentieth Century,* 19-24.

WHARTON, EDITH, Continued

Tuttleton, James W. "Edith Wharton, High Priestess of Reason," *Personalist* XLVII (Summer 1966), 382-398.
———. "Fiction as the House of Fame," *Midcontinent American Studies Journal* 7 (Spring 1966), 25-36.
———. "Leisure, Wealth and Luxury: Edith Wharton's Old New York," *Midwest Quarterly* VII (Summer 1966), 337-352.
——— "The President and the Lady: Edith Wharton and Theodore Roosevelt," *Bulletin of the New York Public Library* LXIX (Jan 1965), 49-57.

BIBLIOGRAPHY

Brenni, Vito Joseph. *Edith Wharton: A Bibliography*.
Bruccoli, Matthew J. "Hidden Printings in Edith Wharton's *The Children*," *Studies in Bibliography* XV (1962), 269-273.
Kellogg, Grace. *The Two Lives of Edith Wharton: The Woman and Her Work*, 325-327.

WHEELER, EDWARD L.

DEADWOOD DICK ON DECK

Durham, Philip. Introduction, *Seth Jones* and *Deadwood Dick on Deck* (New York, 1966).

WHITLOCK, BRAND

THE HAPPY AVERAGE
Anderson, David D. *Brand Whitlock*, 36-43.
J. HARDIN & SON
Anderson, David D. *Brand Whitlock*, 98-109.
THE THIRTEENTH DISTRICT
Anderson, David D. *Brand Whitlock*, 27-33.
THE TURN OF THE BALANCE
Anderson, David D. *Brand Whitlock*, 50-60.
GENERAL
Anderson, David D. *Brand Whitlock*.
BIBLIOGRAPHY
Anderson, David D. *Brand Whitlock*, 149-153.
Thorburn, Neil. "Brand Whitlock (1869-1934)," *American Literary Realism* 3 (Summer 1968), 30-35.

WIGGIN, KATE

GENERAL

Erisman, Fred. "Transcendentalism for American Youth: The Children's Books of Kate Douglas Wiggin," *New England Quarterly* XLI (Jun 1968), 238-247.

WILDER, THORNTON

THE BRIDGE OF SAN LUIS REY

Burbank, Rex. *Thornton Wilder*, 44-56.

Goldstein, Malcolm. *The Art of Thornton Wilder*, 49-62.

Papajewski, Helmut. *Thornton Wilder*, 23-39.

THE CABALA

Burbank, Rex. *Thornton Wilder*, 35-44.

Goldstein, Malcolm. *The Art of Thornton Wilder*, 34-48.

THE EIGHTH DAY

French, Warren. *Season of Promise*, 7-14.

Kauffmann, Stanley. "Thornton Wilder," *New Republic* 156 (Apr 8, 1967), 26, 45-46.

HEAVEN'S MY DESTINATION

Burbank, Rex. *Thornton Wilder*, 72-81.

Goldstein, Malcolm. *The Art of Thornton Wilder*, 82-94.

THE IDES OF MARCH

Burbank, Rex. *Thornton Wilder*, 112-122.

Goldstein, Malcolm. *The Art of Thornton Wilder*, 131-145.

Papajewski, Helmut. *Thornton Wilder*, 60-83.

THE WOMAN OF ANDROS

Goldstein, Malcolm. *The Art of Thornton Wilder*, 63-71.

Papajewski, Helmut. *Thornton Wilder*, 40-50.

GENERAL

Edgell, David P. "Thornton Wilder Revisited," *Cairo Studies in English* (1960), 47-59.

Firebaugh, Joseph J. "Farce and the Heavenly Destination," *Four Quarters* XVI (May 1967), 10-17.

Gold, Michael. "Wilder: Prophet of the Genteel Christ," Frederick J. Hoffman, ed., *Perspectives on Modern Literature*, 175-180.

Goldstone, Richard H. "The Wilder 'Image,'" *Four Quarters* XVI (May 1967), 1-7.

Grebenier, Bernard. *Thornton Wilder*.

WILDER, THORNTON, Continued

Haberman, Donald. "The Americanization of Thornton Wilder," *Four Quarters* XVI (May 1967), 18-27.

Kosok, Heinz. "Thornton Wilder," *Jahrbuch Für Amerikastudien* 9 (1964), 196-227.

Modic, John. "The Eclectic Mr. Wilder," *Ball State Teachers College Forum* I (Winter 1960-61), 55-61.

Popper, Hermine I. "The Universe of Thornton Wilder," *Harper's Magazine* CCXXX (Jun 1965), 72-81.

Viebrock, Helmut. "Thornton Wilders Hauptmotiv," *Neueren Sprachen* (Aug 1961), 349-363.

BIBLIOGRAPHY

Burbank, Rex. *Thornton, Wilder,* 150-153.

Bryer, Jackson R. "Thornton Wilder and the Reviewers," *Papers of the Bibliographical Society of America* 58 (Jan-Mar 1964), 35-49.

Edelstein, Jerome M. *A Bibliographical Checklist of the Writings of Thornton Wilder.*

Goldstein, Malcolm. *The Art of Thornton Wilder,* 171-176.

Kosok, Heinz. "Thornton Wilder: Bibliography of Criticism," *Twentieth Century Literature* IX (Jul 1963), 93-100.

WILLIAMS, BEN AMES

GENERAL

Cary, Richard. "Ben Ames Williams and Robert H. Davis: The Seedling in the Sun," *Colby Library Quarterly* VI (Sept 1963), 302-325.

Williams, Florence Talpey. "About Ben Ames Williams," *Colby Library Quarterly* VI (Sept 1963), 263-277.

Yokelson, Joseph B. "Ben Ames Williams: Pastoral Moralist," *Colby Library Quarterly* VI (Sept 1963), 278-293.

BIBLIOGRAPHY

Cary, Richard. "Ben Ames Williams in Books," *Colby Library Quarterly* VI (Sept 1963), 293-302.

WILLIAMS, TENNESSEE

THE ROMAN SPRING OF MRS. STONE

Falk, Signi Lenea. *Tennessee Williams,* 144-149.

WILLIAMS, WILLIAM CARLOS

WHITE MULE
Guimond, James. *The Art of William Carlos Williams*, 106-125.
GENERAL
Brinnin, John Malcolm. *William Carlos Williams.*
BIBLIOGRAPHY
Guimond, James. *The Art of William Carlos Williams*, 245-252.

WILLIAMS, WIRT

ADA DALLAS
Blotner, Joseph. *The Modern American Political Novel*, 180-185.

WILSON, EDMUND

I THOUGHT OF DAISY
Paul, Sherman. *Edmund Wilson: A Study of Literary Vocation in Our Time*, 53-77.
MEMOIRS OF HECATE COUNTY
Paul, Sherman. *Edmund Wilson: A Study of Literary Vocation in Our Time*, 146-165.
GENERAL
Berthoff, Warner. *Edmund Wilson.*
BIBLIOGRAPHY
Berthoff, Warner. *Edmund Wilson*, 46-47.

WINTHROP, THEODORE

JOHN BRENT
Bergmann, Frank. "A Note on Two Nineteenth-Century German Editions of Theodore Winthrop's *John Brent*," *Bulletin of the New York Public Library* LXXII (Dec 1968), 656-658.
BIBLIOGRAPHY
Colby, Elbridge. "More Facts about the Publishing of Theodore Winthrop's Novels," *Bulletin of the New York Public Library* LXIX (May 1965), 314-316.

WOLFE, BERNARD

GENERAL

Galloway, David. "An Erratic Geography: The Novels of Bernard Wolfe," *Critique* VII (Spring 1964), 75-86.

WOLFE, THOMAS

THE HILLS BEYOND

Field, Leslie A. *"The Hills Beyond: A Folk Novel of America," Thomas Wolfe: Three Decades of Criticism,* 241-252.

LOOK HOMEWARD, ANGEL

Bowden, Edwin T. *The Dungeon of the Heart: Human Isolation and the American Novel,* 66-73.

Carlile, Robert Emerson. "Musical Analogues in Thomas Wolfe's *Look Homeward, Angel," Modern Fiction Studies* XIV (Summer 1968), 215-223.

Eichelberger, Clayton L. "Eliza Gant as Negative Symbol in *Look Homeward, Angel," Arlington Quarterly* I (Winter 1967-1968), 269-278.

Gardner, Thomas. "The Form of *Look Homeward, Angel," Archiv für das Studium der Neueren Sprachen und Literaturen* 202:3 (1966), 189-193.

Hawthorne, Mark D. "Thomas Wolfe's Use of the Poetic Fragment," *Modern Fiction Studies* XI (Autumn 1965), 234-244.

Hill, John S. "Eugene Gant and the Ghost of Ben," *Modern Fiction Studies* XI (Autumn 1965), 245-249.

Kennedy, Richard S. *The Window of Memory: The Literary Career of Thomas Wolfe,* 124-146, 146-161.

————. "Wolfe's *Look Homeward, Angel* as a Novel of Development," *Thomas Wolfe: Three Decades of Criticism,* 195-203.

McElderry, B. R., Jr. *Thomas Wolfe,* 45-66.

Moser, Thomas C. "Thomas Wolfe: *Look Homeward, Angel," The American Novel from James Fenimore Cooper to William Faulkner,* 206-218.

Reaver, J. Russell and Robert I. Strozier. "Thomas Wolfe and Death," *The Modern American Novel: Essays in Criticism,* 79-89.

Rubin, Louis D., Jr. "Thomas Wolfe: Time and the South," *The Faraway Country: Writers of the Modern South,* 73-82.

Skipp, Francis E. "The Edition of *Look Homeward, Angel," Papers of the Bibliographical Society of America* 57 (Jan-Mar 1963), 1-13.

OF TIME AND THE RIVER

Kennedy, Richard S. *The Window of Memory: The Literary Career of Thomas Wolfe,* 199-209, 259-273.

McElderry, B. R., Jr. *Thomas Wolfe,* 67-87.

Reeves, Paschal. "Wolfe's *Of Time and the River,*" *Explicator* XXVI (Oct 1967), No. 18.

THE WEB AND THE ROCK

Chase, Richard. Introduction, *The Web and The Rock* (New York, 1960).

Kennedy, Richard S. *The Window of Memory: The Literary Career of Thomas Wolfe,* 388-402.

McElderry, B. R., Jr. *Thomas Wolfe,* 90-98.

Reeves, Paschal. "Esther Jack as Muse," *Thomas Wolfe: Three Decades of Criticism,* 221-227.

YOU CAN'T GO HOME AGAIN

Clements, Clyde C., Jr. "Symbolic Patterns in *You Can't Go Home Again,*" *Modern Fiction Studies* XI (Autumn 1965), 286-296.

_____. "Symbolic Patterns in *You Can't Go Home Again,*" *Thomas Wolfe: Three Decades of Criticism,* 229-240.

Kennedy, Richard S. The Window of Memory: *The Literary Career of Thomas Wolfe,* 299-391, 403-411.

McElderry, B. R., Jr. *Thomas Wolfe,* 98-103.

GENERAL

Angoff, Charles. *The Tone of the Twenties and Other Essays,* 84-92.

Appel, Benjamin. "Elizabeth Nowell and Thomas Wolfe," *Carleton Miscellany* VIII (Winter 1967), 70-77.

Austin, Neal F. *A Biography of Thomas Wolfe.*

Beja, Morris. "Why You Can't Go Home Again: Thomas Wolfe and 'The Escapes of Time and Memory,'" *Modern Fiction Studies* XI (Autumn 1965), 297-314.

Bell, Alladine. "T. Wolfe of 10 Montague Terrace," *Antioch Review* XX (Fall 1960), 377-390.

Boyle, Thomas E. "Thomas Wolfe: Theme Through Imagery," *Modern Fiction Studies* XI (Autumn 1965), 259-268.

Burger, Nash K. "A Story to Tell: Agee, Wolfe, Faulkner," *South Atlantic Quarterly* LXIII (Winter 1964), 32-43.

Čapek, Abe. "The Development of Thomas Wolfe in the Light of His Letters," *Zeitschrift Für Anglistik und Amerikanistik* X (Heft 2, 1962), 162-178.

Chittick, V. L. O. "Tom Wolfe's Farthest West," *Southwest Review* XLVIII (Spring 1963), 93-110.

Church, Margaret. "Thomas Wolfe: Dark Time," *Thomas Wolfe: Three Decades of Criticism,* 85-103.

Eaton, Clement. "Student Days with Thomas Wolfe," *Georgia Review* XVII (Summer 1963), 146-155.

Fifield, William. "Joyce's Brother, Lawrence's Wife, Wolfe's Mother, Twain's Daughter," *Texas Quarterly* X (Spring 1967), 69-87.

Fisher, Vardis, "Thomas Wolfe as I Knew Him," *Thomas Wolfe as I Knew Him and Other Essays,* 24-41.

————. "Thomas Wolfe and Maxwell Perkins," *Thomas Wolfe as I Knew Him and Other Essays,* 42-55.

Fuchs, Konrad. "Thomas Wolfe, der suchende Realist," *Neueren Sprachen* (Mar 1963), 110-117.

Giaccari, Ada. "Struttura E Stile Nell'Opera Di Thomas Wolfe," *Studi Americani* IX (1964), 287-352.

Gossett, Louise Y. *Violence in Recent Southern Fiction,* 5-16.

Helmcke, Hans. "Die 'Thomas-Wolfe-Renaissance' in den Vereinigten Staaten," *Jahrbuch Für Amerikastudien* 9 (1964), 181-195.

Hilfer, Anthony Channell. "Wolfe's Altamont: The Mimesis of Being," *Georgia Review* XVIII (Winter 1964), 451-456.

Holman, C. Hugh. " 'The Dark, Ruined Helen of His Blood': Thomas Wolfe and the South," *South: Modern Southern Literature in its Cultural Setting,* 177-197.

————. "The Dark, Ruined Helen of His Blood: Thomas Wolfe and the South," *Thomas Wolfe: Three Decades of Criticism,* 17-36.

————. "Europe as Catalyst for Thomas Wolfe," *Essays in American and English Literature Presented to Bruce Robert McElderry, Jr.,* 122-137.

————. Introduction, *The Short Novels of Thomas Wolfe* (New York, 1961).

————. Introduction, *The Thomas Wolfe Reader* (New York, 1962).

————. *Thomas Wolfe.*

————. "Thomas Wolfe and the Stigma of Autobiography," *Virginia Quarterly Review* XL (Autumn 1964), 614-625.

————. "Thomas Wolfe," *Seven Modern American Novelists: An Introduction,* 189-225.

————. *Three Modes of Modern Southern Fiction,* 49-71.

Holman, C. Hugh and Sue Fields Ross, (eds.). *Letters of Thomas Wolfe to his Mother.*

Johnson, Pamela. *The Art of Thomas Wolfe.*

Kennedy, Richard S. "Thomas Wolfe and the American Experience," *Modern Fiction Studies* XI (Autumn 1965), 219-233.

————. *The Window of Memory: The Literary Career of Thomas Wolfe.*

————. "Wolfe's *Look Homeward, Angel* as a Novel of Development," *South Atlantic Quarterly* LXIII (Spring 1964), 218-226.

Lanzinger, Klaus. *Die Epik im Amerikanischen Roman: Eine Studie zu James F. Cooper, Herman Melville, Frank Norris und Thomas Wolfe.*

————. "Die Reise im Zug als Vorwurf und Sinnbild bei Thomas Wolfe," *Neueren Sprachen* (Jul 1962), 293-307.

McElderry, B. R., Jr. *Thomas Wolfe.*

Morgan, H. Wayne. "Thomas Wolfe: The Web of Memory," *Writers in Transition: Seven Americans,* 127-152.

Muller, Herbert Joseph. *Thomas Wolfe, in Selbstzeugnissen und Bilddokumenten.*

Nowell, Elizabeth. *Thomas Wolfe: A Biography.*

Price, Lawrence Marsden. *The Reception of United States Literature in Germany,* 150-152.

Raynolds, Robert. *Thomas Wolfe: Memoir of a Friendship.*

Reaver, J. Russell and Robert I. Strozier. "Thomas Wolfe and Death," *Georgia Review* XVI (Fall 1962), 330-350.

————. "Thomas Wolfe and Death," *Thomas Wolfe: Three Decades of Criticism,* 37-58.

Reeves, Paschal. "Thomas Wolfe: Notes of Three Characters," *Modern Fiction Studies* XI (Autumn 1965), 275-285.

————. "Thomas Wolfe on Publishers: Reaction to Rejection," *South Atlantic Quarterly* LXIV (Summer 1965), 385-389.

————. "Thomas Wolfe's 'Old Catawba,'" *Names* 11 (Dec 1963), 254-256.

Rubin, Larry. "Thomas Wolfe and the Lost Paradise," *Modern Fiction Studies* XI (Autumn 1965), 250-258.

Rubin, Louis D., Jr. "Thomas Wolfe: Time and the South," *The Faraway Country: Writers of the Modern South,* 72-104.

————. "Thomas Wolfe: Time and the South," *Thomas Wolfe: Three Decades of Criticism,* 59-83.

WOLFE, THOMAS, Continued

McElderry, B. R., Jr. *Thomas Wolfe*, 184-196.

Muller, Herbert Joseph. *Thomas Wolfe, in Selbstzeugnissen und Bilddokumenten*, 169-176.

Price, Lawrence Marsden. *The Reception of United States Literature in Germany*, 225-226.

WOLFERT, IRA

TUCKER'S PEOPLE

Eisinger, Chester E. "Character and Self in Fiction on the Left," *Proletarian Writers of the Thirties*, 177-182.

WOOD, SARAH SAYWARD BARRELL KEATING

GENERAL

Fife, Hilda M. "Madam Wood's 'Recollections,'" *Colby Library Quarterly* VII (Sept 1965), 89-115.

WOOLSON, CONSTANCE FENIMORE

ANNE

Moore, Rayburn S. *Constance Fenimore Woolson*, 81-87.

EAST ANGELS

Moore, Rayburn S. *Constance Fenimore Woolson*, 93-100.

FOR THE MAJOR

Moore, Rayburn S. *Constance Fenimore Woolson*, 87-93.

HORACE CHASE

Moore, Rayburn S. *Constance Fenimore Woolson*, 109-116.

JUPITER LIGHTS

Moore, Rayburn S. *Constance Fenimore Woolson*, 100-108.

GENERAL

Moore, Rayburn S. *Constance Fenimore Woolson*.

White, Robert L. "Cultural Ambivalence in Constance Fenimore Woolson's Italian Tales," *Tennessee Studies in Literature* XII (1967), 121-129.

BIBLIOGRAPHY

Moore, Rayburn S. *Constance Fenimore Woolson*, 163-165.

————. "Constance Fenimore Woolson (1840-1894)," *American Literary Realism* 3 (Summer 1968), 36-38.

WOUK, HERMAN

THE CAINE MUTINY

Stuckey, W. J. *The Pulitzer Prize Novels: A Critical Backward Look,* 158-164.

Whipple, William. "Justice: The Phantom of the Literary Trial," *Ball State Teachers College Forum* II (Winter 1961-62), 33-38.

MARJORIE MORNINGSTAR

Fiedler, Leslie A. *Love and Death in the American Novel,* 248-253.

WRIGHT, HAROLD BELL

THE EYES OF THE WORLD

Randall, Dale B. J. "The 'Seer' and 'Seen' Themes in *Gatsby* and Some of Their Parallels in Eliot and Wright," *Twentieth Century Literature* X (Jul 1964), 51-63.

WRIGHT, RICHARD

ISLAND OF HALLUCINATION

Webb, Constance. *Richard Wright,* 369-374.

NATIVE SON

Baldwin, James. "Many Thousands Gone: Richard Wright's *Native Son,*" *Images of the Negro in American Literature,* 233-248.

Bayliss, John F. "*Native Son:* Protest or Psychological Study?" *Negro American Literature Forum* 1 (Fall 1967), 5-6.

Britt, David. "*Native Son:* Watershed of Negro Protest Literature," *Negro American Literature Forum* 1 (Fall 1967), 4-5.

French, Warren. *The Social Novel at the End of an Era,* 171-180.

Green, Gerald. "Back to Bigger," *Kenyon Review* XXVIII (Sept 1966), 521-539.

Margolies, Edward. *Native Sons: A Critical Study of Twentieth-Century Negro American Authors,* 71-86.

Reilly, John. Afterword, *Native Son* (New York, 1966).

Webb, Constance. "Native Son," *Richard Wright,* 167-175.

THE OUTSIDER

Webb, Constance. *Richard Wright,* 306-313.

Widmer, Kingsley. "The Existential Darkness: Richard Wright's *The Outsider,*" *Wisconsin Studies in Contemporary Literature* 1 (Fall 1960), 13-21.

WRIGHT, RICHARD, Continued

SAVAGE HOLIDAY
Webb, Constance. *Richard Wright*, 314-317.

GENERAL
Algren, Nelson. "Remembering Richard Wright," *Nation* 192 (Jan 28, 1961), 85-86.

Baldwin, James. "Richard Wright," *Encounter* XVI (Apr 1961), 58-60.

Bone, Robert. *The Negro Novel in America*, 140-152.

Charney, Maurice. "James Baldwin's Quarrel with Richard Wright," *American Quarterly* XV (Spring 1963), 65-75.

Fuller, Hoyt. "On the Death of Richard Wright," *Southwest Review* XLVI (Autumn 1961), vi-vii, 334-337.

Hand, Clifford. "The Struggle to Create Life in the Fiction of Richard Wright," *The Thirties: Fiction, Poetry, Drama*, 81-87.

Hill, Herbert. "Reflections on Richard Wright: A Symposium on an Exiled Native Son," *Anger and Beyond: The Negro Writer in the United States*, 196-212.

Howe, Irving. "Black Boys and Native Sons," *A World More Attractive: A View of Modern Literature and Politics*, 100-105.

————. "Richard Wright: A Word of Farewell," *New Republic* 144 (Feb 13, 1961), 17-18.

Littlejohn, David. *Black on White, A Critical Survey of Writings by American Negroes*, 102-110.

Margolies, Edward. *Native Sons: A Critical Study of Twentieth-Century Negro American Authors*, 65-71.

Webb, Constance. *Richard Wright*.

BIBLIOGRAPHY
Bryer, Jackson R. "Richard Wright (1908-1960): A Selected Checklist of Criticism," *Wisconsin Studies in Contemporary Literature* 1 (Fall 1960), 22-33.

Fabre, Michel and Edward Margolies. "Richard Wright (1908-1960): A Bibliography," *Bulletin of Bibliography* XXIV (Jan-Apr 1965), 131-133, 137.

Webb, Constance. *Richard Wright*, 423-429.

WRIGHT, W. H.

(*see* S. S. Van Dine, pseud.)

WYLIE, ELINOR

GENERAL

Angoff, Charles. "Recollections of Elinor Wylie, Thomas Mann, Joseph Hergesheimer, James Stevens, Logan Clendening," *Literary Review* X (Winter 1966-67), 169-179.

Wright, Celeste Turner. "Elinor Wylie: The Glass Chimaera and the Minotaur," *Twentieth Century Literature* XII (Apr 1966) 15-26.

YERBY, FRANK

GENERAL

Turner, Darwin T. "Frank Yerby as Debunker," *Massachusetts Review* IX (Summer 1968), 569-577.

Yerby, Frank. "How and Why I Write the Costume Novel," *Harper's* CCXIX (Oct 1959), 145-150.

YOUNG, MARGUERITE

MISS MacINTOSH, MY DARLING

Byatt, A. S. "The Obsession with Amorphous Mankind," *Encounter* XXVII (Sept 1966), 63-69.

GENERAL STUDIES

NINETEENTH CENTURY

Adams, Richard P. "Southern Literature in the 1890s," *Mississippi Quarterly* XXI (Fall 1968), 277-281.

Arrington, Leonard J. and Jon Haupt. "Intolerable Zion: The Image of Mormonism in Nineteenth Century American Literature," *Western Humanities Review* XXII (Summer 1968), 243-260.

Boewe, Charles. "Romanticism Bracketed," *Emerson Society Quarterly* 35 (II Quarter 1964), 7-10.

Boggs, W. Arthur. "*Looking Backward* at the Utopian Novel, 1888-1900," *Bulletin of the New York Public Library* LXIV (Jun 1960), 329-336.

Carroll, Martin C., Jr. "Watersheds of American Literature," *Literary Criterion* V (Winter 1962), 6-21.

Cracroft, Richard H. "The American West of Karl May," *American Quarterly* XIX (Summer 1967), 249-258.

Crawford, Bartholow V. "The Civil War and American Literature," *Emerson Society Quarterly* 44 (III Quarter 1966), 91-94.

Duggan, Francis X. "Doctrine and the Writers of the American Renaissance," *Emerson Society Quarterly* 39 (II Quarter 1965), 45-51.

Duncan, Robert W. "The London *Literary Gazette* and American Writers," *Papers on English Language and Literature* I (Spring 1965), 153-166.

Eisinger, Chester E. "The American Renaissance: The Era and Its Greatest Writers," *The American Renaissance, the History of an Era: Essays and Interpretations*, 5-21.

Falk, Robert. "The Search for Reality: Writers and Their Literature," *The Gilded Age: A Reappraisal*, 196-220.

———. *The Victorian Mode in American Fiction: 1865-1885*.

Friedrich, Gerhard. "The Teaching of Early American Literature," *English Journal* XLIX (Sept 1960), 387-394.

Gross, John J. "Religion and Community in the American Renaissance," *Emerson Society Quarterly* 44 (III Quarter 1966), 59-64.

Gross, Theodore L. "The South in the Literature of Reconstruction," *Mississippi Quarterly* XIV (Spring 1961), 68-78.

Hoffman, Daniel G. *Form and Fable in American Fiction*.

Kaul, A. N. "Nineteenth-Century Fiction: Themes and Patterns," *The*

American Vision: Actual and Ideal Society in Nineteenth Century Fiction, 45-83.

————. "Social Reality and the Form of American Fiction," *The American Vision: Actual and Ideal Society in Nineteenth Century Fiction*, 305-324.

Lawrence, D. H. *The Symbolic Meaning: The Uncollected Versions of Studies in Classic American Literature*.

Linneman, William R. "Satires of American Realism, 1880-1900," *American Literature* XXXIV (Mar 1962), 80-93.

Mathews, J. Chesley. "The Interest in Dante Shown by Nineteenth-Century American Men of Letters," *Studi Americani* XI (1965), 77-104.

Miller, James E., Jr. "Uncharted Interiors: The American Romantics Revisited," *Emerson Society Quarterly* 35 (II Quarter 1964), 34-39.

Parks, Edd Winfield. "The Intent of the Ante-Bellum Southern Humorists," *Mississippi Quarterly* XIII (Fall 1960), 163-168.

Pizer, Donald. "Late Nineteenth-Century American Realism: An Essay in Definition," *Nineteenth-Century Fiction* XVI (Dec 1961), 263-269.

————. "Nineteenth-Century American Naturalism: An Essay in Definition," *Bucknell Review* XIII (Dec 1965), 1-18.

————. *Realism and Naturalism in Nineteenth-Century American Literature*.

Plumstead, A. W. "Puritanism and Nineteenth Century American Literature," *Queen's Quarterly* LXX (Summer 1963), 209-222.

Raleigh, John Henry. "The Novel and the City: England and America in the Nineteenth Century," *Victorian Studies* XI (Mar 1968), 291-328.

Santangelo, G. A. "Towards a Definition of American Victorianism," *Dalhousie Review* XLV (Autumn 1965), 256-267.

Schwartz, Arthur. "The American Romantics: An Analysis," *Emerson Society Quarterly* 35 (II Quarter 1964), 39-44.

Six American Novelists of the Nineteenth Century.

Smith, Henry Nash. "The Morals of Power, Business Enterprise as a Theme in Mid-Nineteenth Century Fiction," *Essays on American Literature in Honor of Jay Hubbell*, 90-107.

Staehelin-Wackernagel, Adelheid. *The Puritan Settler in the American Novel before the Civil War*.

Suderman, Elmer F. "Criticisms of the Protestant Church in the American Novel: 1870-1900," *Midcontinent American Studies Journal* V (Spring 1964), 17-23.

————. "Skepticism and Doubt in Late Nineteenth Century American Novels," *Ball State University Forum* VIII (Winter 1967), 66-72.

Wilson, Edmund. *Patriotic Gore: Studies in the Literature of the American Civil War.*

Wright, Nathalia. "The Influence of Their Travels on the Writers of the American Renaissance," *Emerson Society Quarterly* 42 (I Quarter 1966), 12-17.

Zanger, Jules. "The 'Tragic Octoroon' in Pre-Civil War Fiction," *American Quarterly* XVIII (Spring 1966), 63-70.

Ziff, Larzer. *The American 1890s: Life and Times of a Lost Generation.*

————. "The Other Lost Generation," *Saturday Review* 48 (Mar 20, 1965), 15-18.

TWENTIETH CENTURY

Aaron, Daniel. "The American Left: Some Ruins and Monuments," *University of Denver Quarterly* I (Summer 1966), 5-23.

————. "A Decade of Convictions: the Appeal of Communism in the 1930's," *Massachusetts Review* II (Summer 1961), 736-747.

————. "The Thirties: Now and Then," *American Scholar* XXXV (Summer 1966), 490-494.

————. "The Treachery of Recollection: The Inner and the Outer History," *Carleton Miscellany* VI (Summer 1965), 3-19.

————. *Writers on the Left: Episodes in American Literary Communism.*

Aldridge, John W. "The Novel and the Critic," *New York Times Book Review* 71 (Mar 6, 1966), 2, 59.

————. "The Price of Being Taken Seriously," *New York Times Book Review* 69 (Sept 6, 1964), 1, 21.

————. "The War Writers Ten Years Later," *Contemporary American Novelists,* 32-40.

————. "What Became of Our Postwar Hopes?" *New York Times Book Review* 67 (Jul 29, 1962), 1, 24.

The American Negro Writer and His Roots: Selected Papers from the First Conference of Negro Writers, March, 1959.

Angoff, Allan. "Protest in American Literature Since the End of World War II," *CLA Journal* V (Sept 1961), 31-40.

Angoff, Charles. "The Mystique of *The Smart Set*," *Literary Review* XI (Autumn 1967), 49-60.

————. "The Tone of the Twenties," *Literary Review* IV (Autumn 1960), 5-15.

Auchincloss, Louis. "The Novel as a Forum," *New York Times Book Review* 70 (Oct 24, 1965), 2.

Baker, Carlos. "On Campus, It's the Generation of the Mixed Book Bag," *New York Times Book Review* 67 (Part II, Jan 14, 1962), 3, 36.

Barksdale, Richard K. "Alienation and the Anti-Hero in Recent American Fiction," *CLA Journal* X (Sept 1966), 1-10.

Baumbach, Jonathan. *The Landscape of Nightmare: Studies in the Contemporary American Novel.*

Bendiner, Robert. "The Thirties: When Culture Came to Main Street," *Saturday Review* 50 (Apr 1, 1961), 19-21.

Berthoff, Warner. "Renaissance: 1912 and After," *The Ferment of Realism: American Literature, 1884-1919,* 287-298.

Bier, Jesse. "Recent American Literature: The Great Debate," *Bucknell Review* XIV (May 1966), 98-105.

Blotner, Joseph. *The Modern American Political Novel.*

Bonosky, Phillip. "The Background to American Progressive Literature," *Zeitschrift Für Anglistik und Amerikanistik* IX (Heft 3, 1961), 253-260.

Boyer, Paul S. "Boston Book Censorship in the Twenties," *American Quarterly* XV (Spring 1963), 3-24.

Bradbury, John M. *Renaissance in the South: A Critical History of the Literature of the South.*

Breyer, Bernard R. "Diagnosis of Violence in Recent Southern Fiction," *Mississippi Quarterly* XIV (Spring 1961), 59-67.

Brown, Deming. *Soviet Attitudes Toward American Writing.*

Brumm, Ursula. "Die Kritik des American Way of Life im Roman der Gegenwart," *Jahrbuch Für Amerikastudien* 9 (1964), 23-35.

Brüning, Eberhard. "The Spanish Civil War (1936-1939) and the American Novel," *Zeitschrift Für Anglistik und Amerikanistik* XI (Heft 1, 1963), 42-55.

Brustein, Robert. "Who's Killing the Novel?" *New Republic* 153 (Oct 23, 1965), 22-24.

Bryant, Jerry H. "The Last of the Social Protest Writers," *Arizona Quarterly* XIX (Autumn 1963), 315-325.

Buckeye, Robert. "The Anatomy of the Psychic Novel," *Critique* IX (No 2, 1967), 33-45.

Bullins, Ed. "The Polished Protest: Aesthetics and the Black Writer," *Contact* IV (Jul 1963), 67-68.

Burgess, Anthony. "The Postwar American Novel: A View from the Periphery," *American Scholar* XXXV (Winter 1965-66), 150-156.

Butcher, Philip. "The Younger Novelists and the Urban Negro," *CLA Journal* IV (Mar 1961), 196-203.

Butler, Frank A. "On the Beat Nature of Beat," *American Scholar* XXX (Winter 1960-61), 79-92.

Cooperman, Stanley. *World War I and the American Novel.*

Cowley, Malcolm. "1944: The Generation That Wasn't Lost," *College English* XXII (Nov 1960), 93-98.

————. "The 1930s Were an Age of Faith," *New York Times Book Review* 69 (Dec 13, 1964), 4-5, 14-17.

————. "The Unsettled Literary Future of the U. S.," *Saturday Review* 45 (Jun 9, 1962), 15-17, 61.

Cowley, Malcolm and W. M. Fruhock, Irving Howe, Stanley Edgar Hyman, Alfred Kazin, Arthur Mizener. Symposium: "Who's To Take the Place of Hemingway and Faulkner?" *New York Times Book Review* 67 (Oct 7, 1962), 4, 26.

The Creative Present.

Davidson, W. L., Jr. "H. L. Mencken, *The Smart Set,* and the Expatriate Movement," *William and Mary Review* 2 (Spring 1964), 71-83.

De Mott, Benjamin. "How to Write a College Novel," *Hudson Review* XV (Summer 1962), 243-252.

Dempsey, David. "Writers of the First World War Marched on a Road From Glory," *New York Times Book Review* 69 (Aug 2, 1964), 5, 12.

Detweiler, Robert. *Four Spiritual Crises in Mid-Century American Fiction,* 1-5.

Diggins, John P. "The American Writer, Fascism and the Liberation of Italy," *American Quarterly* XVIII (Winter 1966), 599-614.

Edel, Leon. *The Modern Psychological Novel,* revised edition.

Editors. "Anathematizing the Asylum," *Times Literary Supplement* 64 (Nov 25, 1965), 1053-1054.

————. "New Light on the Invisible," *Times Literary Supplement* 64 (Nov 25, 1965), 1046-1049.

————. "Writers in the Public Eye," *Times Literary Supplement* 64 (Nov 25, 1965), 1042-1043.

Eisinger, Chester E. *Fiction of the Forties.*

Elliott, George P. "Destroyers, Defilers, and Confusers of Men," *Atlantic Monthly* 222 (Dec 1968), 74-80.

————. "Writers on Campus," *New York Times Book Review* 70 (Dec 26, 1965) , 2.

Emanuel, James A. "The Invisible Men of American Literature," *Books Abroad* XXXVII (Autumn 1963) , 391-394.

Englemann, Ruth. "A Note on the American Fiction Market," *Literary Half-Yearly* VII (Jul 1966) , 68-71.

Feinstein, Herbert. "Contemporary American Fiction: Harvey Swados and Leslie Fiedler," *Wisconsin Studies in Contemporary Literature* 2 (Winter 1961) , 79-98.

Fenton, Charles A. "A Literary Fracture of World War I," *American Quarterly* XII (Summer 1960) , 119-132.

Fiedler, Leslie A. "The New Mutants," *Partisan Review* XXXII (Fall 1965) , 505-525.

————. *Waiting for the End.*

————. "The War Against the Academy," *Wisconsin Studies in Contemporary Literature* 5 (Winter-Spring 1964) , 5-17.

Finkelstein, Sidney. *Existentialism and Alienation in American Literature.*

Fisher, Vardis. "The Western Writer and the Eastern Establishment," *Western American Literature* 1 (Winter 1967) , 244-259.

Flanner, Janet, moderator. "Then and Now," *Paris Review* IX (No 33 1965) , 158-170. Comments by James Jones, William Gardner Smith, and others.

Fleming, Thomas. "The Novelist as Journalist," *New York Times Book Review* 73 (Jul 21, 1968) , 2, 34.

Ford, Jesse Hill. "To a Young Southern Writer," *Southern Review* IV (Spring 1968) , 291-298.

Freedman, William. "American Jewish Fiction: So What's the Big Deal?" *Chicago Review* XIX (No 1, 1966) , 90-107.

French, Michael R. "The American Novel in the Sixties," *Midwest Quarterly* IX (Jul 1968) , 365-379.

French, Warren. *Season of Promise,* 1-7, 37-43.

————. *The Social Novel at the End of an Era.*

Frohock, W. M. *Strangers to This Ground: Cultural Diversity in Contemporary American Writing.*

Fuller, Edmund. "The National Book Awards: A Dissenting Opinion," *Critic* XX (Feb-Mar 1962) , 37-40.

Fuller, Hoyt W. "Contemporary Negro Fiction," *Southwest Review* L (Autumn 1965) , 321-335.

Galinsky, Hans. "Exchange—Literature and Culture; Understanding

Twentieth Century America Through Its Literature: A German View," *Midcontinent American Studies Journal* 8 (Fall 1967), 58-69; Warren G. French, "But Bear in Mind: A Reaction to Galinsky's Essay," 69-71.

Galloway, David D. *The Absurd Hero in American Fiction.*

————. "Clown and Saint: The Hero in Current American Fiction," *Critique* VII (Spring-Summer 1965), 46-65.

Gardner, Erle Stanley. "Getting Away With Murder," *Atlantic Monthly* CCXV (Jan 1965), 72-75.

Geismar, Maxwell. "Society and the Novel," *A Time of Harvest: American Literature, 1910-1960,* 33-41.

Gessner, Robert. "The Film: A Source of New Vitality to the Novel," *New York Times Book Review* 65 (Aug 7, 1965), 4, 20-21.

Gibson, Walker. *Tough, Sweet and Stuffy: An Essay on Modern American Prose Styles.*

Gill, Richard. "The Imagination of Disaster," *Saturday Review* 47 (Sept 5, 1964), 10-13, 47.

Glicksberg, Charles I. "A Jewish American Literature?" *Southwest Review* LIII (Spring 1968), 196-205.

————. "The Literature of the Angry Young Men," *Colorado Quarterly* VIII (Spring 1960), 293-303.

————. "The Lost Self in Modern Literature," *Personalist* XLIII (Autumn 1962), 527-538.

————. "The Rage of Repudiation: Polemic of the Beats," *Southwest Review* XLV (Autumn 1960), 338-344.

————. "Sex in Contemporary Literature," IX (Winter 1961), 277-287.

Gold, Herbert. "Where the Action Is," *New York Times Book Review* 72 (Feb 19, 1967), 1, 50-52.

Graelle, L. L. "An Interview with Malcolm Cowley," *Dalhousie Review* 44 (Autumn 1964), 290-298.

Greenberg, Alvin. "The Death of the Psyche: A Way to the Self in the Contemporary Novel," *Criticism* VIII (Winter 1966), 1-18.

Guttmann, Allen. "The Conversions of the Jews," *Wisconsin Studies in Contemporary Literature* VI (Summer 1965), 161-176.

Hackett, Alice P. "Do You Remember?: Popular Books 1924-1964," *Saturday Review* 47 (Aug 29, 1964), 109-125.

Hall, Donald. "Writers on the Campus," *Atlantic Monthly* CCXVII (Mar 1966), 87-90.

Hall, James. *The Lunatic Giant in the Drawing Room.*

Halprin, Lee S. "American Liberalism, Literature, and World War II," *Minnesota Review* III (Winter 1963), 179-191.

Handy, William J. *Kant and the Southern New Critics.*

Harris, Henry. "The Symbol of Frontier in the Social Allegory of the 'Thirties," *Zeitschrift Für Anglistik und Amerikanistik* XIV (Heft 2, 1966), 127-140.

Harris, Mark. "An Author Must Do More Than Run for Local Office," *New York Times Book Review* 66 (Jan 15, 1961), 4.

Harris, Wendell V. "Style and the Twentieth-Century Novel," *Western Humanities Review* XVIII (Spring 1964), 127-140.

Hassan, Ihab. "The Avant-Garde: Which Way is Forward?" *Nation* 193 (Nov 18, 1961), 396-399.

————. "The Character of Post-War Fiction in America," *English Journal* LI (Jan 1962), 1-8.

————. "The Character of Post-War Fiction in America," *On Contemporary Literature,* 36-47.

————. "The Dial and Recent American Fiction," *CEA Critic* XXIX (Oct 1966), 1, 3.

————. "The Dismemberment of Orpheus: Notes on Form and Antiform in Contemporary Literature," *Learners and Discerners: A Newer Criticism,* 156-165.

————. "Laughter in the Dark: The New Voice in American Fiction," *American Scholar* XXXIII (Autumn 1964), 636-640.

————. "The Literature of Silence: From Henry Miller to Beckett and Burroughs," *Encounter* XXVIII (Jan 1967), 74-82.

————. "The Novel of Outrage: A Minority Voice in Postwar American Fiction," *American Scholar* XXXIV (Spring 1965), 239-253.

————. "The Pattern of Fictional Experience," *Modern American Fiction: Essays in Criticism,* 315-337.

————. *Radical Innocence: Studies in the Contemporary American Novel.*

————. "Symposium: Fiction Today; the Existential Novel," *Massachusetts Review* III (Summer 1962), 795-797.

Henkin, William A., Jr. "A Garden of Forked Paths: Literary Directions in Review," *Tri-Quarterly* 10 (Fall 1967), 220-232.

Hertzel, Leo J. "Rabbit in the Great North Woods," *University Review* XXXIII (Dec 1966), 143-147.

Hicks, Granville. "Signatures to the Significance of the Self," *Saturday Review* 47 (Aug 29, 1964), 67-72.

Hill, Hamlin. "Black Humor: Its Cause and Cure," *Colorado Quarterly* XVII (Summer 1968), 57-64.

──────. "Modern American Humor: The Janus Laugh," *College English* XXV (Dec 1963), 170-176.

Hoffman, Frederick J. "Appendix One: Marginal Societies and the Contemporary American Novel," *The Modern Novel in America*, 225-255.

──────. *The Art of Southern Fiction*.

──────. "Dogmatic Innocence: Self-Assertion in Modern American Literature," *Texas Quarterly* VI (Summer 1963), 152-162.

──────. *The Mortal No: Death and the Modern Imagination*.

──────. "The Temper of the Twenties," *Minnesota Review* I (Fall 1960), 36-45.

──────. *The Twenties: American Writing in the Postwar Decade*, revised edition.

Holman, C. Hugh. "The Novel in the South," *A Time of Harvest: American Literature, 1910-1960*, 83-94.

──────. *Three Modes of Modern Southern Fiction*.

Holmes, John Clellon. *Nothing More to Declare*.

Howe, Irving. "In Search of a Moral Style," *New Republic* 145 (Sept 25, 1961), 21-27.

──────. "Mass Society and Post-Modern Fiction," *A World More Attractive: A View of Modern Literature and Politics*, 77-97.

Hughes, D. J. "Symposium: Fiction Today; Character in Contemporary Fiction," *Massachusetts Review* III (Summer 1962), 788-795.

Ihde, Horst. "Black Writer's Burden: Bemerkungen zu John Oliver Killens," *Zeitschrift für Anglistik und Amerikanistik* 16 (1968), 117-137.

Jones, LeRoi. "Philistinism and the Negro Writer," *Anger and Beyond*, 51-61.

Josephson, Matthew. *Life Among the Surrealists: A Memoir*.

Kaminsky, Alice R. "The American Jew in the Academic Novel," *Midwest Quarterly* III (Summer 1962), 305-318.

Karanikas, Alexander. *Tillers of a Myth: Southern Agrarians as Social and Literary Critics*.

Karolides, Nicholas J. *The Pioneer in the American Novel, 1900-1950*.

Kazin, Alfred. "The Alone Generation: A Comment on the Fiction of the 'Fifties," *Harper's* CCXIX (Oct 1959), 127-131.

──────. "The Alone Generation: A Comment on the Fiction of the Fifties," *Writing in America*, 14-26.

————. "The Bitter 30's from a Personal History," *Atlantic Monthly* CCIX (May 1962), 82-99.

————. "The Jew as Modern Writer," *Commentary* 41 (Apr 1966), 37-41.

————. "Psychoanalysis and Literary Culture Today," *Partisan Review* XXVI (Winter 1959), 45-55.

Kelly, R. Gordon. "Ideology in Some Modern Science Fiction Novels," *Journal of Popular Culture* II (Fall 1968), 211-227.

Kennedy, James G. "More General than Fiction: The Uses of History in the Criticism of Modern Novels," *College English* XXVIII (Nov 1966), 150-163.

Klein, Marcus. *After Alienation: American Novels in Mid-Century.*

Knickerbocker, Conrad. "Humor With a Mortal Sting," *New York Times Book Review* 69 (Sept 27, 1964), 3, 60.

Knopf, Alfred A. "Publishing's Last 50 Years: A Balance Sheet," *Saturday Review* 47 (Nov 21, 1964), 21-23, 53-54; (Nov 28, 1964), 17, 69-70.

————. "Publishing Then and Now: 1912-1964," *Bulletin of the New York Public Library* LXVIII (Nov 1964), 555-573.

Kort, Wesley. "Recent Fiction and its Religious Implications," *Comparative Literature Studies* III (No 2, 1966), 223-234.

Krishnamurthi, M. G. "The Distaff Faulknerians," *Literary Criterion* VIII (Winter 1967), 69-78.

Kronenberger, Louis. "Gambler in Publishing: Horace Liveright," *Atlantic Monthly* CCXV (Jan 1965), 94-104.

————. "The Thirties: Frayed Collars and Large Visions," *Atlantic Monthly* CCXVII (Jan 1966), 79-81.

Kruse, Horst Hermann. "Die Romane der 'Flaming Youth': Ein Beitrag zur Interpretation des a amerikanischen Romans von 1920 bis 1930," Beihefte zum *Jahrbuch für Amerikastudien* 7 (1962), 1-144.

Krutch, Joseph Wood. "Must Writers Hate the Universe?" *Saturday Review* 50 (May 6, 1967), 19-21, 47.

Lalli, Biancamaria Tedeschini. "Letteratura e Sperimentalismo Linguistico," *Studi Americani* VII (1961), 429-442.

Landess, Thomas H. "The Present Course of Southern Fiction: *Everynegro* and Other Alternatives," *Arlington Quarterly* I (Winter 1967-1968), 61-85.

Lawson, Lewis A. "Portrait of a Culture in Crisis: Modern Southern Literature," *Texas Quarterly* X (Spring 1967), 143-155.

Leer, Norman. "Three American Novels and Contemporary Society: A Search for Commitment," *Wisconsin Studies in Contemporary Literature* 3 (Fall 1962), 61-86.

Levin, Harry. "The Unbanning of the Books," *Atlantic Monthly* CCXVII (Feb 1966), 77-81.

————. "What Was Modernism?" *Massachusetts Review* I (Summer 1960), 609-630.

Lewis, R. W. B. "Literary Possibilities of the Next Decade," *Trends in Modern Society*, 17-191.

————. "Recent Fiction: Picaro and Pilgrim," *A Time of Harvest: American Literature, 1910-1960*, 144-153.

L'Hereux, John. "On the Eighth Day: The Death of God in Contemporary American Literature," *Critic* XXIV (Jun-Jul 1966), 46-55.

A Library of Literary Criticism: Modern American Literature.

Link, Franz H. "Tendenzen in der Amerikanischen Literaturgeschichtsschreibung der letzten zwanzig Jahre," *Jahrbuch Für Amerikastudien* 6 (1961), 48-58.

Lottman, Herbert. "'The Action Is Everywhere The Black Man Goes,'" *New York Times Book Review* 73 (Apr 21, 1968), 6-7, 48-49.

Loukides, Paul. "New Directions in the Novel: Some Notes on the Novel of the Absurd," *CEA Critic* XXX (Jan 1968), 8, 13.

Ludwig, Jack. *Recent American Novelists.*

Macauley, Robie. "The Writer as Independent Spirit: The Pre-empted Domain," *Saturday Review* 49 (June 1, 1966), 20-21.

MacShane, Frank. "The Transatlantic Review," *Dalhousie Review* 41 (Autumn 1961), 303-313.

Mailer, Norman. "Some Children of the Goddess," *Contemporary American Novelists*, 3-31.

Malamud, Bernard. "Theme, Content and the 'New Novel,'" *New York Times Book Review* 72 (Mar 26, 1967), 2, 29.

Malin, Irving. *New American Gothic.*

Margolies, Edward. *Native Sons: A Critical Study of Twentieth-Century Negro American Authors.*

Maxwell, D. E. S. "Modern American Fiction and Its Inheritance," *American Fiction: The Intellectual Background*, 265-287.

May, James Boyer. "The Novel: Where Is It?" *Trace* 61 (Summer 1966), 125-129, 236-239.

McConnell, Virginia. "Alan Swallow and Western Writers," *South Dakota Review* 5 (Summer 1967), 88-97.

McDonnell, Thomas. "The Emergence of the Negro in Literature," *Critic* XX (Dec 1961-Jan 1962), 31-34.

McNamara, Eugene. "The Post-Mortem American Novel," *Queen's Quarterly* LXIX (Summer 1962), 265-275.

McTaggart, Dr. "The Beat Generation," *English Language and Literature* 9 (Dec 1960), 156-162.

Meeker, Richard K. "The Youngest Generation of Southern Fiction Writers," *Southern Writers: Appraisals in Our Time,* 162-191.

Meyer, Roy W. *The Middle Western Farm Novel in the Twentieth Century.*

Milton, John R. *"The American West:* A Challenge to the Literary Imagination," *Western American Literature* 1 (Winter 1967), 267-284.

————. "The Novel in the American West," *South Dakota Review* 2 (Autumn 1964), 56-76.

Mizener, Arthur. "The 'Lost Generation,'" *A Time of Harvest: American Literature, 1910-1960,* 73-82.

Mohl, Gertrud. *Die Aufnahme amerikanischer Literatur in der deutschsprachigen Schweiz wahrend der Jahre 1945-1950.*

Montgomery, Marion. "Bells for John Stewart's Burden: A Sermon upon the Desirable Death of the 'New Provincialism' Here Typified," *Georgia Review* XX (Summer 1966), 145-181.

Morrissette, Bruce. "Narrative 'You' in Contemporary Literature," *Comparative Literature Studies* II (No 1, 1965), 1-24.

Mudrick, Marvin. "Who Killed Herzog? or, Three American Novelists," *University of Denver Quarterly* I (Spring 1966), 61-97.

Munson, Gorham. "A Comedy of Exiles," *Literary Review* XII (Fall 1968), 41-75.

Muste, J. M. *Say That We Saw Spain Die: The Literary Consequences of the Spanish War.*

New, William H. "The Island and the Madman: Recurrent Imagery in the Major Novelists of the Fifties," *Arizona Quarterly* XXII (Winter 1966), 328-337.

Newman, Charles. "Beyond Omniscience: Notes Toward a Future for the Novel," *Tri-Quarterly* 10 (Fall 1967), 37-52.

"The 1930's, a Symposium," by Dorothy Allen, Russell Ames, Benjamin Appel, James T. Farrell, B. A. Botkin, Edwin Georgrichard Bruell, Jack Conroy, Malcolm Cowley, David Cornel DeJong, August Derleth, Paul 'Doc' Evans, Ben Hagglund, David Ignatow, Calvin C. Hernton, Ruth Lechlitner, John Rood, Robert Traver, Peter Brand,

Wayne Carver, Nelson Algren, Robert Tracy. *Carleton Miscellany* VI (Winter 1965), 6-113.

O'Connor, William Van. "The Writer and the University," *Texas Quarterly* III (Summer 1960), 51-63.

Ong, Walter J., S.J. "Synchronic Present: The Academic Future of Modern Literature in America," *Approaches to the Study of Twentieth Century Literature,* 55-78.

Parkinson, Thomas. "After the Beat Generation," *Colorado Quarterly* XVII (Summer 1968), 45-56.

Pearce, Richard. "The Walker: Modern American Hero," *Massachusetts Review* V (Summer 1964), 761-764.

Peterson, Levi S. "The Primitive and the Civilized in Western Fiction," *Western American Literature* 1 (Fall 1966), 197-207.

Phillips, William. "Notes on the New Style," *Nation* 201 [One Hundredth Anniversary Issue] (Sept 20, 1965), 232-236.

————. "Writing about Sex," *Partisan Review* XXXIV (Fall 1967), 552-563.

Pilkington, William T. "Aspects of the Western Comic Novel," *Western American Literature* 1 (Fall 1966), 209-217.

Piper, Henry Dan. "Modern American Classics," *Saturday Review* 45 (Feb 17, 1962), 20.

Placido, Beniamino. "La Critica Americana Contemporanea," *Studi Americani* VIII (1962), 293-357.

Prescott, Orville. "What's Happening to Fiction?" *Saturday Review* 49 (Nov 26, 1966), 21-22.

Proletarian Writers of the Thirties.

Pugh, David. "Reading the Proletarians—Thirty Years Later," *The Thirties: Fiction, Poetry, Drama,* 89-95.

Redding, Saunders. "The Negro Writer and American Literature," *Anger and Beyond: The Negro Writer in the United States,* 1-19.

————. "The Problems of the Negro Writer," *Massachusetts Review* VI (Autumn-Winter 1964-65), 57-70.

Reeves, Paschal. "From Halley's Comet to Prohibition," *Mississippi Quarterly* XXI (Fall 1968), 285-290.

Rubin, Louis D., Jr. "The Curious Death of the Novel: What to Do about Tired Literary Critics," *Kenyon Review* XXVIII (Jun 1966), 305-325.

————. *The Faraway Country: Writers of the Modern South.*

————. "The Literature of a Changing South," *The Deep South in Transformation,* 147-175.

Sandra, Sister Mary, S. S. A. "The Priest-Hero in Modern Fiction," *Personalist* XLVI (Autumn 1965), 527-542.

Schickel, Richard. "The Old Critics and the New Novel," *Wisconsin Studies in Contemporary Literature* 5 (Winter-Spring 1964), 26-36.

Scholes, Robert E. "For Nonrealistic Fiction," *New York Times Book Review* 72 (Oct 22, 1967), 2.

————. "The Modern American Novel and the Mason-Dixon Line," *Georgia Review* XIV (Summer 1960), 193-204.

Schulberg, Budd. "The Writer and Hollywood," *Harper's* CCXIX (Oct 1959), 132-137.

Schulz, Max F. "Pop, Op, and Black Humor: The Aesthetics of Anxiety," *College English* 30 (Dec 1968), 230-241.

Scott, James F. "Beat Literature and the American Teen Cult," *American Quarterly* XIV (Summer 1962), 150-160.

Scott, Nathan A. *The Broken Center: Studies in the Theological Horizon of Modern Literature,* 212-231.

Smith, Chard Powers. "Perkins and the Elect," *Antioch Review* XXII (Spring 1962), 85-102.

Sonnichsen, C. L. "The New Style Western," *South Dakota Review* 4 (Summer 1964), 22-28.

Sonnonfeld, Albert. "Twentieth Century Gothic: Reflections on the Catholic Novel," *Southern Review* I (Apr 1965), 388-405.

South: Modern Southern Literature in its Cultural Setting.

Southern, Terry. "Dark Laughter in the Towers," *Nation* 190 (Apr 23, 1960), 348-350.

Spender, Stephen. "The Literary Mood of the 1930's," *Tri-Quarterly* 1 (Fall 1964), 15-24.

Spevack, Marvin. "Young Voices on the American Literary Scene: The Beat Generation," *Geist einer Freien Gesellschaft: Festschrift zu Ehren von Senator James William Fulbright aus Anlass des zehnjahrigen Bestehens des deutschen Fulbright-Programms,* 313-330.

Spilka, Mark. "The Necessary Stylist: A New Critical Revision," *Modern Fiction Studies* VI (Winter 1960-61), 283-297.

Springer, Anne M. "Die Jungsten: John Dos Passos, Ernest Hemingway, William Faulkner, Thomas Wolfe," *The American Novel in Germany: A Study of the Critical Reception of Eight American Novelists Between the Two World Wars,* 75-95.

Stanford, Derek. "Violence in the Modern Novel," *Critic* XXII (Aug-Sept 1963), 32-36.

Stanford, Raney. "The Return of Trickster: When a Not-a-hero is a Hero," *Journal of Popular Culture* I (Winter 1967), 228-242.

Straumann, Heinrich. *American Literature in the Twentieth Century*, revised edition.

Stuckey, W. J. *The Pulitzer Prize Novels: A Critical Backward Look.*

Sühnel, Rudolf. "The Marxist Trend in Literary Criticism in the USA in the Thirties," *Jahrbuch für Amerikastudien* 7 (1962), 53-66.

Sullivan, Walter. "In Time of the Breaking of Nations: The Decline of Southern Fiction," *Southern Review* IV (Spring 1968), 299-305.

Sutton, Walter. *Modern American Criticism.*

Swados, Harvey. Introduction, *The American Writer and the Great Depression* (New York, 1966).

————. "The Coming Revolution in Literature," *Saturday Review* 48 (Aug 21, 1965), 14-17.

————. "The Writer in Contemporary American Society," *Anger and Beyond: The Negro Writer in the United States*, 62-75.

Swallow, Alan. "The Mavericks," *Critique* II (Winter 1959), 74-92.

Talks With Authors.

Tate, Allen. "Random Thoughts on the 1920's," *Minnesota Review* I (Fall 1960), 46-56.

————. "A Southern Mode of the Imagination Circa 1918 to the Present," *Carleton Miscellany* I (Winter 1960), 9-23.

The Thirties: Fiction, Poetry, Drama, 233-237.

Thompson, John. "Fantasy & Circumstance," *Commentary* 45 (Apr 1968), 71-74.

Thorp, Willard. *American Writing in the Twentieth Century.*

————. "The Newest American Fiction," *Literary Criterion* V (Winter 1961), 94-107.

————. "Suggs and Sut in Modern Dress: The Latest Chapter in Southern Humor," *Mississippi Quarterly* XIII (Fall 1960), 169-175.

A Time of Harvest: American Literature 1910-1960.

Tischler, Nancy M. "The Negro in Modern Southern Fiction: Stereotype to Archetype," *Negro American Literature Forum* 2 (Spring 1968), 3-6.

Tough Guy Writers of the Thirties.

Trachtenberg, Stanley. "The Hero in Stasis," *Critique* VII (Winter 1964-1965), 5-17.

Trilling, Diana. "The Image of Women in Contemporary Literature," *The Woman in America*, 52-71.

Turner, Darwin T. "The Negro Novel in America: In Rebuttal," *CLA Journal* X (Dec 1966), 121-134.

———. "The Negro Novelist and the South," *Southern Humanities Review* 1 (Spring 1967), 21-29.

———. "Southern Fiction, 1900-1910," *Mississippi Quarterly* XXI (Fall 1968), 281-285.

Ulanov, Barry. "The Novel," *The Two Worlds of American Art: The Private and The Popular,* 209-283.

Van Benschoten, Virginia. "Changes in Best Sellers Since World War I," *Journal of Popular Culture* I (Spring 1968), 379-388.

Vincent, C. J. "Dilemma in Modern Literature," *Queen's Quarterly* LXIX (Autumn 1962), 428-441.

Vonnegut, Kurt, Jr. "Science Fiction," *New York Times Book Review* 70 (Sept 5, 1965), 2.

Wagner, Geoffrey. "The Non-Fiction Novel," *Critic* XVIII (Apr-May 1960), 19-20, 86-88.

Wakefield, Dan. "The Personal Voice and the Impersonal Eye," *Atlantic Monthly* CCXVII (Jun 1966), 86-90.

Waldmeir, Joseph. "Quest Without Faith," *Nation* 193 (Nov 18, 1961), 390-396.

Weaver, Richard M. "Realism and the Local Color Interlude," *Georgia Review* XXII (Fall 1968), 301-305.

Weimer, David R. *The City as Metaphor.*

West, Thomas Reed. *Flesh of Steel: Literature and the Machine in American Culture.*

Whittington, Curtis, Jr. "The 'Burden' of Narration: Democratic Perspectives and First Person Point of View in the American Novel," *Southern Humanities Review* II (Spring 1968), 236-245.

Widmer, Kingsley. "The American Road: The Contemporary Novel," *University of Kansas City Review* XXVI (Jun 1960), 309-317.

———. "The Literary Rebel," *Centennial Review* VI (Spring 1962), 182-201.

Williams, John. "The 'Western': Definition of the Myth," *Nation* 193 (Nov 18, 1961), 401-406.

Williams, John A. "The Literary Ghetto," *Saturday Review* 46 (Apr 20, 1963), 21, 40.

GENERAL

Angoff, Charles. "Reflections Upon Aspects of American Literature," *Literary Review* X (Autumn 1966), 5-17.

————. "Van Wyck Brooks and Our Critical Tradition," *Literary Review* VII (Autumn 1963), 27-35.

Askew, Melvin W. "The Pseudonymic American Hero," *Bucknell Review* X (Mar 1962), 224-231.

Asselineau, Roger. "The French Stream in American Literature," *Yearbook of Comparative and General Literature* 17 (1968), 29-39.

Auoruso, Vito. "Cecchi, Vittorini, Pavese e La Letteratura Americana," *Studi Americani* VI (1960), 9-71.

Balakian, Nona. "The Prophetic Vogue of the Anti-heroine," *Southwest Review* XLVII (Spring 1962), 134-141.

Barzun, Jacques. "Meditations on the Literature of Spying," *American Scholar* XXXIV (Spring 1965), 167-178.

Beardsley, Monroe C. "The New Criticism Revisited: An Affirmative View," *Four Quarters* XIII (Jan 1964), 11-19.

Beja, Morris. "It Must Be Important: Negroes in Contemporary American Fiction," *Antioch Review* XXIV (Fall 1964), 323-336.

Bellow, Saul. "The Writer as Moralist," *Atlantic Monthly* CCXI (Mar 1963), 58-62.

Berthoff, Warner. "American Realism: A Grammar of Motives," *The Ferment of Realism: American Literature, 1884-1919,* 1-47.

————. "Humorists and Moralists: The Heirs of Howells and James," *The Ferment of Realism: American Literature, 1884-1919,* 126-147.

Bettersworth, John K. "The Humor of the Old Southwest: Yesterday and Today," *Mississippi Quarterly* XVII (Spring 1964), 87-94.

Bignami, Marialuisa. "La Letteratura Americana in Italia," *Studi Americani* X (1964), 443-495.

Bigsby, C. W. E. "Two Types of Violence," *University Review* XXXII (Dec 1965), 129-136.

Bloom, Robert. "Past Indefinite: The Sherman-Mencken Debate on an American Tradition," *Western Humanities Review* XV (Winter 1961), 73-81.

Bluestone, George. "The Changing Cowboy: From Dime Novel to Dollar Film," *Western Humanities Review* XIV (Summer 1960), 331-337.

Boatright, Mody C. "The Beginnings of Cowboy Fiction," *Southwest Review* LI (Winter 1966), 11-28.

Bone, Robert. *The Negro Novel in America.*

Booth, Wayne. "The Use of Criticism in the Teaching of Literature," *College English* XXVII (Oct 1965), 1-13; see also: Frederick J.

Hoffman, "The Use of Criticism in the Teaching of Literature: A Reply," *College English* XXVII (Oct 1965), 13-17.

Bosworth, Allan R. "The Golden Age of Pulps," *Atlantic Monthly* CCVIII (Jul 1961), 57-60.

Bowden, Edwin T. *The Dungeon of the Heart: Human Isolation and the American Novel.*

Bower, Warren. "The Writer as Independent Spirit; Locus: Washington Square," *Saturday Review* 49 (June 4, 1966), 23-24.

Brace, Gerald Warner. "The Essential Novel," *Texas Quarterly* VIII (Spring 1965), 28-38.

Brady, Charles A. "From Broceliande to the Forest Primeval: The New-World Quest of the Chevalier Chateaubriand," *Emerson Society Quarterly* 42 (I Quarter 1966), 17-31.

Bridgman, Richard. *The Colloquial Style in America.*

Brooks, A. Russell. "The Comic Spirit and the Negro's New Look," *CLA Journal* VI (Sept 1962), 35-43.

Brooks, Cleanth. "Southern Literature: The Wellsprings of Its Vitality," *Georgia Review* XVI (Fall 1962), 238-253.

Brophy, Brigid. "Detective Fiction: A Modern Myth of Violence?" *Hudson Review* XVIII (Spring 1965), 11-30.

Brown, Sterling A. "A Century of Negro Portraiture in American Literature," *Massachusetts Review* VII (Winter 1966), 73-96.

Brumm, Ursula. *Die Religiose Typologie in Amerikanischen Denken.*

Buchen, Irving H. "Jewish-American Writers as a Literary Group," *Renascence* XIX (Spring 1967), 142-150.

Budd, Louis J. "The Forgotten Decades of Southern Writing, 1890-1920: Introduction," *Mississippi Quarterly* XXI (Fall 1968), 275-277.

Burt, Nathaniel. "Outpost of Sensibility: or The Literary Tradition of the Town of Princeton from Annis Stockton to John O'Hara," *Princeton University Library Chronicle* XXVIII (Spring 1967), 156-170.

Bush, Alfred L. "Literary Landmarks of Princeton," *Princeton University Library Chronicle* XXIX (Autumn 1967), 1-88.

Carpenter, Frederic I. "Fiction and the American College," *American Quarterly* XII (Winter 1960), 443-456.

Casey, Bill. "Nurse Novels," *Southwest Review* XLIX (Autumn 1964), 332-341.

Chamber, John. "The Cult of Science Fiction," *Dalhousie Review* XL (Spring 1960), 78-86.

Chametzky, Jules. "Notes on the Assimilation of the American-Jewish Writer: Abraham Cahan to Saul Bellow," *Jahrbuch Für Amerikastudien* 9 (1964), 173-180.

Chapman, Abraham. "The Harlem Renaissance in Literary History," *CLA Journal* XI (Sept 1967), 38-58.

Chase, Richard. "Leslie Fiedler and American Culture," *Chicago Review* XIV (Autumn-Winter 1960), 8-18.

Clark, Edward. "Images of the Negro in the American Novel," *Jahrbuch Für Amerikastudien* 5 (1960), 175-184.

Clough, Wilson O. "The Cult of the Bad Man of the West," *Texas Quarterly* V (Autumn 1962), 11-20.

————. *The Necessary Earth: Nature and Solitude in American Literature.*

Coffin, Tristram P. "Harden E. Taliaferro and the Use of Folklore by American Literary Figures," *South Atlantic Quarterly* LXIV (Spring 1965), 241-246.

Colvert, James B. "Views of Southern Character in some Northern Novels," *Mississippi Quarterly* (Spring 1965), 59-68.

Cowley, Malcolm. "American Myths, Old and New," *Saturday Review* 45 (Sept 1, 1962), 6-8, 47.

Curley, Thomas F. "Catholic Novels and American Culture," *Commentary* XXXVI (Jul 1963), 34-42.

Davis, Richard Beale. "American Literature in the World Today," *Tennessee Studies in Literature* VIII (1963), 119-139.

Deal, Borden. "The Function of the Artist: Creativity and the Collective Unconscious," *Southwest Review* LI (Summer 1966), 239-253.

De Mott, Benjamin. "Jewish Writers in America," *Commentary* XXXI (Feb 1961), 127-134.

The Dilemma of the Southern Writer.

Duggan, Francis X. "Paul Elmer More and the New England Tradition," *American Literature* XXXIV (Jan 1963), 542-561.

Durham, Frank. "Not According to the Book: Materialism and the American Novel," *Georgia Review* XX (Spring 1966), 90-98.

Durham, Philip. "The Cowboy and the Myth Makers," *Journal of Popular Culture* I (Summer 1967), 58-62.

Eby, Cecil D., Jr. " 'The Real War' and the Books," *Southwest Review* XLVII (Summer 1962), 259-264.

Edel, Leon. "Henry James and *The Nation*," *Nation* 201 [One Hundredth Anniversary Issue] (Sept 20, 1965), 237-240.

Elliott, George P. "Against Pornography," *Harper's* CCXXX (Mar 1965) , 51-60.

———. "A Defense of Fiction," *Hudson Review* XVI (Spring 1963) , 9-48.

———. "The Novelist as Meddler," *Virginia Quarterly Review* LX (Winter 1964) , 96-113.

Engel, Bernard F. "Bawdry and Purpose in the Novel," *Midwest Quarterly* IV (Autumn 1962) , 23-31.

Escarpit, Robert. "The Teaching of English Literature: Hemingway, Shakespeare & Co.," *Times Literary Supplement* 67 (Sept 12, 1968) , 965-966.

Essays on Determinism in American Literature.

Feibleman, James K. "Literary New Orleans Between World Wars," *Southern Review* I (Jul 1965) , 702-719.

Fenton, Charles. "The Lost Years of Twentieth-Century American Literature," *South Atlantic Quarterly* LIX (Summer 1960) , 332-338.

———. "A Note on American Expatriation," *Western Humanities Review* XIV (Summer 1960) , 323-329.

Feuerlicht, Ignace. "Christ Figures in Literature," *Personalist* XLVIII (Autumn 1967) , 461-472.

Fiedler, Leslie A. "An American Abroad," *Partisan Review* XXXIII (Winter 1966) , 77-91.

———. *Love and Death in the American Novel.*

———. "Master of Dreams," *Partisan Review* XXXIV (Summer 1967) , 339-356.

———. "My First Gothic Novel," *Novel* I (Fall 1967) , 9-11.

———. "The Novel and America," *Partisan Review* XXVII (Winter 1960) , 41-61.

———. *The Return of the Vanishing American.*

Figg, Robert M., III. "Naturalism as a Literary Form," *Georgia Review* XVIII (Fall 1964) , 308-316.

Flanagan, John T. "A Half-Century of Middlewestern Fiction," *Critique* II (Winter 1959) , 16-34.

———. "The Impact of Folklore on American Literature," *Jahrbuch für Amerikastudien* 7 (1962) , 67-76.

Fleischmann, Wolfgang Bernard. "The Contemporary 'Jewish Novel' in America," *Jahrbuch für Amerikastudien* 12 (1967) , 159-166.

Folsom, James K. *The American Western Novel.*

Foster, Richard. "Frankly, I Like Criticism," *Antioch Review* XXII (Fall 1962) , 273-283.

Frankel, Max. "My Spy Can Lick Your Spy," *Atlantic Monthly* CCXVII (Apr 1966), 103-108.

French, Warren. "West as Myth: Status Report and Call for Action," *Western American Literature* 1 (Spring 1966), 55-58.

Frohock, W. M. "The Idea of the Picaresque," *Yearbook of Comparative and General Literature* 16 (1967), 43-52.

Furness, Edna L. "Image of the Schoolteacher in Western Literature," *Arizona Quarterly* XVIII (Winter 1962), 346-357.

Fussell, Edwin. *Frontier: American Literature and the American West.*

Gaston, Edwin W., Jr. *The Early Novel of the Southwest.*

Glicksberg, Charles I. "The Ironic Vision in Modern Literature," *Arizona Quarterly* XXII (Winter 1966), 293-311.

———. "The Numinous in Fiction," *Arizona Quarterly* XV (Winter 1959), 305-313.

Gohdes, Clarence. "The Earliest Description of 'Western' Fiction?" *American Literature* XXXVII (Mar 1965), 70-71.

Goldberg, M. A. "Chronology, Character and the Human Condition: A Reappraisal of the Modern Novel," *Criticism* V (Winter 1963), 1-12.

Gorlier, Claudio. "Il Pellegrinaggio Del Buon Ribelle," *Studi Americani* X (1964), 135-179.

Graber, Ralph S. "Baseball in American Fiction," *English Journal* LVI (Nov 1967), 1107-1114.

Grant, Douglas. *Purpose and Place,* 1-6.

The Great Experiment in American Literature.

Green, Claud B. "The Rise and Fall Of Local Color in Southern Literature," *Mississippi Quarterly* XVIII (Winter 1964-1965), 1-6.

Green, Martin. *Re-Appraisals: Some Commonsense Readings in American Literature,* 1-33, 231-247.

Griffin, John Howard. "Current Trends in Censorship," *Southwest Review* XLVII (Summer 1962), 193-200.

Gross, Harvey. "History as Metaphysical Pathos: Modern Literature and the Idea of History," *University of Denver Quarterly* I (Autumn 1966), 1-22.

Gross, Theodore L. "Our Mutual Estate: The Literature of the American Negro," *Antioch Review* XXVIII (Fall 1968), 293-303.

Guttmann, Allen. "Jewish Radicals, Jewish Writers," *American Scholar* XXXII (Autumn 1963), 563-575.

Hague, John. "American Character in American Literature: An

Acceptance of Experience," *Essays in Modern American Literature*, 1-13.

Hale, Nancy. "Can Writers Ignore Critics?" *Saturday Review* 51 (Mar 23, 1968), 22-24, 60-61.

Handy, William. "Toward a Formalist Criticism of Fiction," *Texas Studies in Literature and Language* III (Spring 1961), 81-88.

Harris, Wendell V. "Of Time and the Novel," *Bucknell Review* XVI (Mar 1968), 114-129.

Hasley, Louis. "American Literature of the Westward Movement," *College English* XXVI (Nov 1964), 154-156.

————. "The Interpretation of Beliefs in Literature," *CLA Journal* V (Dec 1961), 95-105.

Hassan, Ihab H. "Love in the Modern American Novel: Expense of Spirit and Waste of Shame," *Western Humanities Review* XIV (Spring 1960), 149-161.

Heald, William F. "The Appeal of Southern Literature," *Mississippi Quarterly* XVII (Fall 1964), 208-218.

Hertzel, Leo J. "What About Writers in the North?" *South Dakota Review* 5 (Spring 1967), 3-19.

Hillegas, Mark R. "Dystopian Science Fiction: New Index to the Human Situation," *New Mexico Quarterly* XXXI (Autumn 1961), 238-249.

Himes, Chester. "Dilemma of the Negro Novelist in the US," *Beyond the Angry Black*, 52-58.

Hoffman, Frederick J. Introduction, *Marginal Manners: The Variants of Bohemia* (Evanston, Illinois, 1962), 1-13.

————. *Perspectives in Modern Literature*.

Hoffman, Stanton. "The Cities of Night: John Rechy's *City of Night* and the American Literature of Homosexuality," *Chicago Review* 2, 3 (1964), 195-213.

Holman, C. Hugh. "Of Everything the Unexplained and Irresponsible Specimen: Notes on How to Read American Realism," *Georgia Review* XVIII (Fall 1964), 316-324.

————. "The Southerner as American Writer," *The Southerner as American*, 180-199.

Howard, Leon. *Literature and the American Tradition*.

Howe, Irving. "Anarchy and Authority in American Literature," *University of Denver Quarterly* II (Summer 1967), 5-30.

————. "Mass Society and Post-Modern Fiction," *Partisan Review* XXVI (Summer 1959), 421-436.

————. "The Quest for Moral Style," *A World More Attractive: A View of Modern Literature and Politics*, 59-76.

Hubbell, Jay B. *South and Southwest: Literary Essays and Reminiscences.*

————. *Southern Life in Fiction.*

Hutchins, John K. "California Literature; Penmen of the Golden West: Heritage of the Frontier," *Saturday Review* 50 (Sept 23, 1967), 34-35, 97-98.

Hynes, Samuel. "The New Criticism Revisited: A Revisionist View," *Four Quarters* XIII (Jan 1964), 19-26.

The Idea of an American Novel.

Images of the Negro in American Literature.

Interpretations of American Literature.

Jackson, Blyden. "The Negro's Image of the Universe as Reflected in His Fiction," *CLA Journal* IV (Sept 1960), 22-31.

Jacobson, Dan. "The American Novel and English Studies in South Africa: A Suggestion," *English Studies in Africa* 4 (Mar 1961), 58-62.

Jones, Archie H. "Cops, Robbers, Heroes and Anti-Heroines: The American Need to Create," *Journal of Popular Culture* I (Fall 1967), 114-127.

Jones, Howard Mumford. *Belief and Disbelief in American Literature.*

————. *Jeffersonians and the American Novel.*

Justus, James. "Beyond Gothicism. *Wuthering Heights* and an American Tradition," *Tennessee Studies in Literature* V (1960), 25-33.

Karl, Frederick R. "Picaresque and the American Experience," *Yale Review* LVII (Winter 1968), 196-212.

Kauffmann, Stanley. "Greatness as a Literary Standard," *Harper's* CCXXXI (Nov 1965), 151-156.

Kazin, Alfred. "The First and the Last: New England in the Novelist's Imagination," *Saturday Review* 46 (Feb 2, 1963), 12-15, 45.

————. "The Literary Mind," *Nation* 201 [One Hundredth Anniversary Issue] (Sept 20, 1965), 203-206.

————. "The Scholar Cornered: A Procession of Children," *American Scholar* XXXIII (Spring 1964), 171-183.

————. "The Useful Critic," *Atlantic Monthly* CCXVI (Dec 1965), 73-80.

Kern, Jean B. "American Satire, the Elusive Muse," *Western Humanities Review* XIV (Spring 1960), 201-208.

Killinger, John. "The Death of God in American Literature," *Southern Humanities Review* II (Spring 1968), 149-171.

Koch, Stephen. "Premature Speculations on the Perpetual Renaissance," *Tri-quarterly* 10 (Fall 1967), 4-19.

Krause, Herbert. "Myth and Reality on the High Plains," *South Dakota Review* I (Dec 1963), 3-20.

Lavender, David. "The Petrified West and the Writer," *American Scholar* 37 (Spring 1968), 293-306.

Lawson, Lewis A. "The Rogue in the Gray Flannel Suit," *College English* XXII (Jan 1961), 249-252.

Leary, Lewis. "Bibliographical and Textual Studies and American Literary History," *Texas Quarterly* III (Summer 1960), 160-166.

Lee, Robert Edson. *From West to East.*

Leithead, Edward J. "Legendary Heroes and the Dime Novel," *American Book Collector* XVIII (Mar 1968), 22-27.

————. "The Outlaws Rode Hard in Dime Novel Days," *American Book Collector* XIX (Dec 1968), 13-19.

LeRoy, Gaylord C. "American Innocence Reconsidered," *Massachusetts Review* IV (Summer 1963), 623-646.

Levant, Howard. "Aspiraling We Should Go," *Midcontinent American Studies Journal* IV (Fall 1963), 4-20.

Levin, Harry. "Symbolism and Fiction," *Learners and Discerners: A Newer Criticism,* 1-27.

Levine, Paul. "The American Novel Begins," *American Scholar* XXXV (Winter 1965-66), 134-148.

Lewis, R. W. B. "American Letters: A Projection," *Yale Review* LI (Winter 1962), 211-226.

Liptzin, Sol. *The Jew in American Literature.*

Littlejohn, David. *Black on White: A Critical Survey of Writings by American Negroes.*

Lupo, Cesira. "Eugenio Montale E La Letteratura Americana," *Studi Americani* IX (1964), 467-488.

Macauley, Robie. " 'Let Me Tell You About The Rich. . . ,' " *Kenyon Review* XXVII (Autumn 1965), 645-671.

————. "A Local Habitation and a Name," *Texas Quarterly* VII (Summer 1964), 29-40.

Macdonald, Dwight. "Masscult and Midcult," *Partisan Review* XXVIII (Spring 1960), 203-233; Part II, (Fall 1960), 589-631.

Maclachlan, John M. "Southern Humor as a Vehicle of Social Evaluation," *Mississippi Quarterly* XIII (Fall 1960), 157-162.

Madison, Charles A. "Writers and Publishers," *American Scholar* XXXV (Summer 1966), 531-541.

Male, Roy R. "The Story of the Mysterious Stranger in American Fiction," *Criticism* III (Fall 1961), 281-294.

Manfred, Frederick and Frank Waters, Walter Van Tilburg Clark, Vardis Fisher, Harvey Fergusson, Forrester Blake, Paul Horgan, Michael Straight. "Symposium: The Western Novel," *South Dakota Review* 2 (Autumn 1964), 3-36.

Marcus, Steven. "The Novel Again," *Partisan Review* XXIX (Spring 1962), 171-195.

Martin, Jay. *Harvests of Change. American Literature 1865-1914.*

Martin, Terence J. *The Instructed Vision: Scottish Common Sense Philosophy and the Origins of American Fiction.*

Marx, Leo. *The Machine in the Garden: Technology and the Pastoral Ideal in America.*

————. "Two Kingdoms of Force," *Massachusetts Review* I (Fall 1959), 62-95.

————. "The Vernacular Tradition in American Literature," *Studies in American Culture: Dominant Ideas and Images,* 109-122.

McAleer, John J. "Biblical Symbols in American Literature: A Utilitarian Design," *English Studies* XLVI (Aug 1965), 310-322.

————. "Fictional New England: Empire in Dissolution," *Four Quarters* XIV (Mar 1965), 23-29.

————. "Transcendentalism and the Improper Bostonian," *Emerson Society Quarterly* 39 (II Quarter 1965), 73-78.

McCarthy, Mary. "Characters in Fiction," *Partisan Review* XXVIII (Mar-Apr 1961), 171-191.

McCormick, John O. "Notes on a Comparative American Literary History," *Comparative Literature Studies* V (Jun 1968), 167-179.

McDonald, Walter R. "Coincidence in the Novel: A Necessary Technique," *College English* 29 (Feb 1968), 373-388.

McIntyre, John P., S.J. "The Modes of Disillusionment: Irony in Modern Fiction," *Renascence* XVII (Winter 1964), 70-76, 96.

Meixner, John A. "The Uses of Biography in Criticism," *College English* XXVIII (Nov 1966), 108-113.

Melchiori, Giorgio. "The English Novelist and the American Tradition," *Sewanee Review* LXVIII (Summer 1960), 502-515.

Meyer, Roy W. "Naturalism in American Farm Fiction," *Midcontinent American Studies Journal* II (Spring 1961), 27-37.

Michaelson, L. W. "Science Fiction, Censorship, and Pie-in-the-Sky," *Western Humanities Review* XIII (Autumn 1959), 409-413.

Miller, James E. *Quests Surd and Absurd: Essays in American Literature.*

Miller, Perry. *The Life of the Mind in America from the Revolution to the Civil War.*

Millgate, Michael. *American Social Fiction: James to Cozzens.*

Milne, Gordon. *The American Political Novel.*

Milton, John R. "The American Novel: The Search for Home, Tradition, and Identity," *Western Humanities Review* XVI (Spring 1962), 169-180.

————. "The Western Novel: Sources and Forms," *Chicago Review* XVI (Summer 1963), 74-100.

Mizener, Arthur. *The Sense of Life in the Modern Novel.*

Moers, Ellen. "The Angry Young Women," *Harper's* 227 (Dec 1963), 88-95.

Molz, Kathleen. "The Public Custody of the High Pornography," *American Scholar* XXXVI (Winter 1966-67), 93-103.

Montgomery, Marion. "Fiction's Use of History," *Georgia Review* XVII (Spring 1963), 44-50.

————. "The Sense of Violation: Notes toward a Definition of 'Southern' Fiction," *Georgia Review* XIX (Fall 1965), 278-287.

Moore, Geoffrey. *American Literature and the American Imagination.*

Morgan, H. Wayne. *American Writers in Rebellion.*

Mudrick, Marvin. "Character and Event in Fiction," *Yale Review* L (Winter 1961), 202-218.

Mulder, William. "Dream and Disenchantment in American Literature," *Literary Criterion* V (Winter 1962), 179-189.

Munro, David A. "A Case? for 'Semi-Fiction,'" *Trace* 48 (Spring 1963), 17-19.

Narasimshaiah, C. D. "Traditional Values in American Literature," *Literary Criterion* VIII (Summer 1968), 1-12.

Nichols, Charles H. "Color, Conscience and Crucifixion: A Study of Racial Attitudes in American Literature and Criticism," *Jahrbuch Für Amerikastudien* 6 (1961), 37-47.

Nikoljukin, A. N. "Die amerikanische Romantik und unsere Epoche," *Zeitschrift für Anglistik und Amerikanistik* 15:4 (1967), 347-374.

Noble, David W. *The Eternal Adam and the New World Garden.*

Nolte, William. "Criticism with Vine Leaves," *Texas Studies in Liter-*

ature and Language III (Spring 1961), 16-39.

————. "Mencken on Prose Fiction," *Texas Quarterly* VII (Autumn 1964), 139-153.

O'Connor, William Van. *The Grotesque and Other Essays.*

————. "Parody as Criticism," *College English* XXV (Jan 1964), 241-248.

Olan, Levi A. "The Voice of the Lonesome: Alienation from Huck Finn to Holden Caulfield," *Southwest Review* XLVIII (Spring 1963), 143-150.

Oliver, Egbert S. "The Orient and American Literature," *Studies in American Literature: Whitman, Emerson, Melville, and Others,* 166-173.

Orel, Harold. "The American Detective-Hero," *Journal of Popular Culture* II (Winter 1968), 395-403.

Patterns of Commitment in American Literature.

Paul Elmer More's Shelburne Essays on American Literature.

Paul, Leslie. "The Writer and the Human Condition," *Kenyon Review* XXIX (Jan 1967), 21-38.

Pearce, Roy Harvey. "Literature, History and Humanism: An Americanist's Dilemma," *College English* XXIV (Feb 1963), 364-372.

Pearson, Norman Holmes. "The American Writer and the Feeling for Community," *English Studies* XLIII (Oct 1962), 403-412.

Poirier, Richard. "The Politics of Self-Parody," *Partisan Review* XXXV (Summer 1968), 339-353.

————. *A World Elsewhere: The Place of Style in American Literature,* 3-92.

Poli, Bernard. "The Hero in France and in America," *Journal of American Studies* II (Oct 1968), 225-238.

Price, Lawrence Marsden. *The Reception of United States Literature in Germany.*

Psychoanalysis and American Fiction.

Quinn, Sister M. Bernetta, O.S.F. "A New Approach to Early American Literature," *College English* XXV (Jan 1964), 267-273.

Raleigh, John Henry. *Time, Place, and Idea, Essays on the Novel.*

The Reinterpretation of American Literature.

Rexroth, Kenneth. "California Literature; Penman of the Golden West: Renaissance by the Bay," *Saturday Review* 50 (Sept 23, 1967), 35-36.

Riley, Anthony W. "Notes on Thomas Mann and English and American Literature," *Comparative Literature* XVII (Winter 1965), 57-72.

Robinson, Cecil. *With the Ears of Strangers: The Mexican in American Literature.*

Rosenberg, Marvin. "The Mind of the Critic," *American Scholar* XXXI (Autumn 1962), 551-563.

Roth, Philip. "Writing American Fiction," *Commentary* XXXI (Mar 1961), 223-233.

Rovit, Earl H. "The Ambiguous Modern Novel," *Yale Review* XLIX (Spring 1960), 413-424.

————. "Fathers and Sons in American Fiction," *Yale Review* LIII (Winter 1964), 248-257.

————. "The Revolving Bookstand: Books About Books," *American Scholar* XXXV (Summer 1966), 542-558.

Rubenstein, Gilbert M. "The Businessman in Literature," *American Book Collector* XVII (May 1967), 26-29.

Rubin, Louis D., Jr. *The Curious Death of the Novel: Essays in American Literature.*

————. "The Image of An Army: The Civil War in Southern Fiction," *Southern Writers: Appraisals in Our Time,* 50-70.

————. "Notes on the Literary Scene: Their Own Language," *Harper's* CCXXX (Apr 1965), 173-175.

————. "The Self Recaptured," *Kenyon Review* XXV (Summer 1963), 393-415.

————. "The South and the Faraway Country," *Virginia Quarterly Review* XXXVIII (Summer 1962), 444-459.

————. "Three Modes of American Fiction: A Symposium, Introduction," *Georgia Review* XVIII (Fall 1964), 298-300.

Rudolph, Earle Leighton. "The Frontier in American Literature," *Jahrbuch für Amerikastudien* 7 (1962), 77-91.

Sanford, Charles L. *The Quest for Paradise: Europe and the American Moral Imagination.*

San Juan, Epifanio, Jr. "Spatial Orientation in American Romanticism," *East-West Review* II (Spring-Summer 1965), 33-55.

Saum, Lewis O. "The Fur Trader and the Noble Savage," *American Quarterly* XV (Winter 1963), 554-571.

————. "The Success Theme in Great Plains Realism," *American Quarterly* XVIII (Winter 1966), 579-598.

Schneider, Robert W. *Five Novelists of the Progressive Era.*

Scott, Nathan A., Jr. "Judgment Marked by a Cellar: The American Negro Writer and the Dialectic of Despair," *University of Denver Quarterly* II (Summer 1967), 5-35.

Seelye, John D. "The American Tramp: A Version of the Picaresque," *American Quarterly* XV (Winter 1963), 535-553.

Seward, William W., Jr. *Contrasts in Modern Writers: Some Aspects of British and American Fiction Since Mid-Century.*

Shapiro, Stephen A. "The Ambivalent Animal: Man in the Contemporary British and American Novel," *Centennial Review* XII (Winter 1968), 1-22.

Sikes, Herschel M. "William Howard Gardiner and the American Historical Novel," *Bulletin of the New York Public Library* LXVI (May 1962), 290-296.

Simons, Rev. John W. "The Catholic and the Novel," *Four Quarters* IX (Nov 1959), 15-20.

Simonson, Harold P. "The Closed Frontier and American Tragedy," *Texas Quarterly* XI (Spring 1968), 56-59.

Simpson, Lewis P. "The City and the Symbolism of Literary Community in the United States," *Texas Quarterly* III (Autumn 1960), 97-111.

————. "The Humor of the Old Southwest," *Mississippi Quarterly* XVII (Spring 1964), 63-66.

Slosson, Preston. "Dictatorship in Modern Fiction," *Midwest Quarterly* I (Summer 1960), 333-341.

Smith, David E. "The English Pilgrimage of Man: Metamorphosis of a Theme in American Literature," *Ball State University Forum* VII (Spring 1966), 65-72.

Spencer, Benjamin T. "Nationality During the Interregnum (1892-1912)," *American Literature* XXXII (Jan 1961), 434-445.

Spiller, Robert E. "English, Anglo-Irish, and American Literature," *Books Abroad* XLI (Winter 1967), 30-36.

Stanton, Robert. "The Plot-Tone Conflict: A New Key to the Novel," *College English* 29 (May 1968), 602-607.

Stegner, Wallace. "Born a Square: The Westerners' Dilemma," *Atlantic Monthly* CCXIII (Jan 1964), 46-50.

Stewart, Randall. "Human Nature and the American Dream," *Ball State University Forum* VII (Spring 1966), 3-5.

————. *Regionalism and Beyond: Essays of Randall Stewart.*

Stone, Edward. *Voices of Despair.*

Straight, Michael. "Truth and Formula for the Western Novel," *South Dakota Review* 2 (Autumn 1964), 88-93.

Strandberg, Victor. "The Crisis of Belief in Modern Literature," *English Journal* LIII (Oct 1964), 475-483.

Suderman, Elmer F. "The Social-Gospel Novelists' Criticisms of American Society," *Midcontinent American Studies Journal* 7 (Spring 1966), 45-59.

Sullivan, Walter. "The Decline of Regionalism in Southern Fiction," *Georgia Review* XVIII (Fall 1964), 300-308.

Susman, Warren I. "A Second Country: The Expatriate Image," *Texas Studies in Literature and Language* III (Summer 1961), 171-183.

Swallow, Alan. "American Publishing and the American Writer," *Chicago Review* XIV (Autumn-Winter 1960), 82-98.

Symons, Julian. *Critical Occasions* (London, England, 1966).

"Symposium on the Teaching of Creative Writing," responses by John F. Kennedy, Don Wolfe, Theodore Morrison, Bernard Wirth, Walter Havighurst, Karl Shapiro, Malcolm Cowley, Nolan Miller, Earle G. Eley, John Fandel. *Four Quarters* X (Nov 1960), 8-17.

"Symposium on the Teaching of Creative Writing," responses by Anthony West, Ray Bradbury, John Knowles, Nathaniel Benchley, Sean O'Faolain, Jean Stafford, Allan Seager, John O'Hara, Sister Madeleva, Katherine Anne Porter, James A. Michener, Frank O'Connor, Paul Bowles, Flannery O'Connor, John Ciardi, Art Buchwald, Frank Bookhouser, Brother Antoninus. *Four Quarters* X (Jan 1961), 10-22.

"Symposium on the Teaching of Creative Writing," responses by John Ashmead, Jr., Frederick Eckman, George Shuster, Edward Lyons, Mark Schorer, Carl F. Hartman, Sam Hynes, Andrew Lytle, John Cogley, George Herman, Mervin R. Lowe, Mary McGrory, Ralph J. Salisbury, Richard Sullivan, Stringfellow Barr, Caroline Gordon, Grant H. Redford, Richard A. Bodtke, Leon Edel. *Four Quarters* X (Mar 1961), 19-32.

Tanner, Tony. *The Reign of Wonder: Naivety and Reality in American Literature.*

Thorp, Willard. "The Writer as Pariah in the Old South," *Southern Writers: Appraisals in Our Time,* 3-18.

Todd, Edgely W. "A Note on 'The Mountain Man as Literary Hero,' " *Western American Literature* 1 (Fall 1966), 219-221.

Trachtenberg, Stanley. "American Dreams, American Realities," *Antioch Review* XXVIII (Fall 1968), 277-292.

Traschen, Isadore. "Modern Literature and Science," *College English* XXV (Jan 1964), 248-255.

Van Nostrand, Albert. *The Denatured Novel.*

Wagenknecht, Edward. "The Hog Butcher to the World Was Home to Many Writers," *New York Times Book Review* 69 (Feb 23, 1964), 4.

Wager, Willis. *American Literature: A World View.*

Waggoner, Hyatt H. " 'Point of View' in American Literary Scholarship and Criticism," *Comparative Literature Studies* II (No 4, 1965), 293-302.

Wainstein, Lia. "La Letterature Americana In Russia," *Studi Americani* XI (1965), 447-462.

Walker, Don D. "The Mountain Man as Literary Hero," *Western American Literature* 1 (Spring 1966), 15-26.

————. "Wister, Roosevelt and James: A Note on the Western," *American Quarterly* XII (Fall 1960), 358-366.

Ward, Robert J. "Europe in American Historical Romances, 1890-1910," *Midcontinent American Studies Journal* 8 (Spring 1967), 90-97.

Warren, Austin. *The New England Conscience.*

Warren, Robert Penn and William Styron, Robert Coles and Theodore Solotaroff. "Violence in Literature," panel discussion, *American Scholar* 37 (Summer 1968), 482-496.

Weaver, Richard M. "The American as a Regenerate Being," *Southern Review* IV (Summer 1968), 633-646.

Weems, John Edward and J. Frank Dobie, Joseph M. Dawson, Frank H. Wardlaw, Lon Tinkle, Ernest Campbell Mossner, Frank E. Vandiver, Paul E. Boller. "Talking Back to Censors," *Southwest Review* XLVII (Summer 1962), 201-219.

Wegelin, Christof. "The Rise of the International Novel," *PMLA* LXXVI (Jun 1962), 305-310.

Welty, Eudora. "Must the Novelist Crusade?" *Atlantic Monthly* CCXVI (Oct 1965), 104-108.

West, Ray B., Jr. *The Writer in the Room: Selected Essays.*

Westbrook, Max. "Conservative, Liberal, and Western: Three Modes of American Realism," *South Dakota Review* 4 (Summer 1966), 3-19.

————. "The Practical Spirit: Sacrality and the American West," *Western American Literature* III (Fall 1968), 193-205.

Williams, Raymond. "Realism and the Contemporary Novel," *Partisan Review* XXVI (Spring 1959), 200-213.

Winner, Anthony. "Adjustment, Tragic Humanism and Italy," *Studi Americani* VII (1961), 311-361.

Witham, W. Tasker. *The Adolescent in the American Novel: 1920-1960.*

Wright, Morris. "The Lunatic, the Lover, and the Poet," *Kenyon Review* XXVII (Autumn 1965), 727-737.

Wright, Nathalia. *American Novelists in Italy: The Discoverers: Allston to James.*

Yates, Norris W. "What Makes the Modern American Novel Modern?" *Jahrbuch Für Amerikastudien* 11 (1966), 59-68.

Yerby, Frank. "How and Why I write the Costume Novel," *Writing in America,* 125-138.

Young, Philip. "The Assumptions of Literature," *College English* XXIV (Feb 1963), 352-357.

Zimmerman, Michael. "Literary Revivalism in America: Some Notes Toward a Hypothesis," *American Quarterly* XIX (Spring 1967), 71-85.

Zimpel, Lloyd. "The Damnation Is Real: Aspects of the New Anti-Hero," *University Review* XXXII (Dec 1965), 91-100.

BIBLIOGRAPHY

Adler, Sidney. "The Image of the Jew in the American Novel: A Selected Checklist," *Bulletin of Bibliography* XXIII (Sept-Dec 1962), 211-213.

The American Writer and the Great Depression, xxxvii-xli.

Berthoff, Warner. "Selected Bibliography," *The Ferment of Realism: American Literature, 1884-1919,* 299-310.

Blotner, Joseph. *The Modern American Political Novel,* 370-389.

Boger, Lorise C. *The Southern Mountaineer in Literature: An Annotated Bibliography.*

Bone, Robert. *The Negro Novel in America,* 255-270.

Clough, Wilson O. *The Necessary Earth: Nature and Solitude in American Literature,* 213-218.

Cooperman, Stanley. *World War I and the American Novel,* 243-251.

Critical Approaches to American Literature: Volume II, Walt Whitman to William Faulkner, 331-332.

Editor and Staff. "Annual Bibliography of Studies in Western American Literature," *Western American Literature* I (Winter 1967), 323-329.

————. "Annual Bibliography of Studies in Western American Literature," *Western American Literature* II (Winter 1968), 315-325.

Editors. "Selected Bibliography of Materials Relating to the Western American Novel," *South Dakota Review* 2 (Autumn 1964), 101-108.

————. "Selected Bibliography of Materials Relating to the Western American Novel," *South Dakota Review* 4 (Summer 1966), 79-80.

Feied, Frederick. *No Pie in the Sky: The Hobo as American Cultural Hero in the Works of Jack London, John Dos Passos, and Jack Kerouac,* 93-95.

Folsom, James K. *The American Western Novel,* 213-220.

Gaston, Edwin W., Jr. *The Early Novel of the Southwest,* 292-302.

Gross, Seymour L. "The Negro in American Literature: A Checklist of Criticism and Scholarship," *Images of the Negro in American Literature,* 289-315.

Hall, James. *The Lunatic Giant in the Drawing Room,* 227-236.

Hoffman, Frederick J. *The Modern Novel in America,* 257-266.

Holman, C. Hugh. *The American Novel Through Henry James.*

————. *Three Modes of Modern Southern Fiction,* 87-92.

Hubbell, Jay B. *Southern Life in Fiction,* 97-99.

Karanikas, Alexander. "Selected Bibliography," *Tillers of a Myth: Southern Agrarians as Social and Literary Critics,* 227-242.

Kaul, A. N. *The American Vision: Actual and Ideal Society in Nineteenth Century Fiction,* 325-334.

Liptzin, Sol. *The Jew in American Literature,* 235-246.

Margolies, Edward. *Native Sons: A Critical Study of Twentieth-Century Negro American Authors,* 201-202.

Mathews, J. Chesley. "Bibliographical Supplement: A Selective Checklist, 1955-1962," *Eight American Authors: A Review of Research and Criticism,* 119-121.

Meyer, Roy W. *The Middle Western Farm Novel in the Twentieth Century,* 243-252.

Milne, Gordon. *The American Political Novel,* 186-199.

Price, Lawrence Marsden. *The Reception of United States Literature in Germany,* 191-204, 211-214.

Robinson, Cecil. *With the Ears of Strangers: The Mexican in American Literature,* 325-330.

See, Carolyn. "The Hollywood Novel: A Partial Bibliography," *Bulletin of Bibliography* XXIV (Jan-Apr 1966), 208-216.

Seven Modern American Novelists: An Introduction, 265-279.

Springer, Anne M. *The American Novel in Germany: A Study of the Critical Reception of Eight American Novelists Between the Two World Wars,* 99-112.

Staehelin-Wackernagel, Adelheid. *The Puritan Settler in the American Novel before the Civil War,* 155-157.

411

Suderman, Elmer F. "A Bibliography of Social-Gospel Novels," *Midcontinent American Studies Journal* 7 (Spring 1966), 59-60.

The Thirties: Fiction, Poetry, Drama, 233-237.

Thorp, Willard. *American Writing in the Twentieth Century*, 325-332.

Whicher, Stephen E. "Swedish Knowledge of American Literature, 1920-1952: A Supplementary Bibliography," *Journal of English and Germanic Philology* LVIII (Oct 1959), 666-671.

Wright, Lyle H. *American Fiction, 1876-1900: A Contribution Toward a Bibliography.*

BIBLIOGRAPHY

Note: *Books which are collections of essays by different authors are indexed by the title of the volume. Titles should be checked in any case in which an entry cannot be found under the name of the author.*

Aaron, Daniel. *Writers on the Left: Episodes in American Literary Communism.* New York: Harcourt, Brace & World, 1961.

The Achievement of Sherwood Anderson: Essays in Criticism. Edited by Ray Lewis White. Chapel Hill: University of North Carolina Press, 1966.

Adams, John R. *Harriet Beecher Stowe.* Twayne's United States Authors Series, no. 42. New York: Twayne Publishers, 1963.

Adams, Richard P. *Faulkner: Myth and Motion.* Princeton, N.J.: Princeton University Press, 1968.

The Added Dimension: The Art and Mind of Flannery O'Connor. Edited by Melvin J. Friedman and Lewis A. Lawson. New York: Fordham University Press, 1966.

Aderman, Ralph M., (ed.). *The Letters of James Kirke Paulding.* Madison: University of Wisconsin Press, 1962.

Aguilar, Esperanza. *Yoknapatawpha, Propiedad de William Faulkner.* Santiago, Chile: Editorial Universitaria, 1964.

The Ambassadors: An Authoritative Text; The Author on the Novel; Criticism. Edited by S. P. Rosenbaum. A Norton Critical Edition. New York: W. W. Norton, 1964.

The American Negro Writer and His Roots: Selected Papers from the First Conference of Negro Writers, March, 1959. New York: American Society of African Culture, 1960.

The American Novel from James Fenimore Cooper to William Faulkner. Edited by Wallace Stegner. New York and London: Basic Books, 1965.

The American Renaissance, the History of an Era: Essays and Interpretations. Edited by George Hendrick. Die Neuren Sprachen, Beiheft 9. Frankfurt, West Germany: Diesterweg, 1961.

American Winners of the Nobel Literary Prize. Edited by Warren G. French and Walter E. Kidd. Norman: University of Oklahoma Press, 1968.

The American Writer and the Great Depression. The American Heritage Series. Edited by Harvey Swados. New York: Bobbs-Merrill, 1966.

Anderson, David D. *Brand Whitlock*. Twayne's United States Authors Series, no. 129. New York: Twayne Publishers, 1968.

————. *Louis Bromfield*. Twayne's United States Authors Series, no. 55. New York: Twayne Publishers, 1964.

————. *Sherwood Anderson: An Introduction and Interpretation*. New York: Barnes & Noble, 1967.

Anderson, Frederick, William M. Gibson, and Henry Nash Smith, (eds.). *Selected Mark Twain-Howells Letters*. Cambridge, Mass.: Harvard University Press, 1967.

Anger and Beyond: The Negro Writer in the United States. New York: Harper and Row, 1966.

Angoff, Charles. *The Tone of the Twenties and Other Essays*. South Brunswick and New York: A. S. Barnes; London: Thomas Yoseloff, 1966.

Appel, Alfred, Jr. *A Season of Dreams: The Fiction of Eudora Welty*. Baton Rouge: Louisiana State University Press, 1965.

Approaches to the Study of Twentieth Century Literature. Edited by Hazard Adams and others. East Lansing: Michigan State University Press, 1961.

Approaches to the Twentieth-Century Novel. Edited by John Unterecker. New York: Thomas Y. Crowell, 1965.

Arnold, Lloyd R. *High on the Wild with Hemingway*. Caldwell, Ida.: The Caxton Printers, 1968.

Aronowitz, Ernest. *Hemingway: The Life and Death of a Man*. New York: Lancer Books, 1961.

Arvin, Newton. *The American Pantheon*. Edited by Daniel Aaron and Sylvan Schendler. New York: Delacorte Press, 1966.

————. *Longfellow: His Life and Work*. Boston and Toronto: Little, Brown, 1962.

Astre, Georges-Albert. *Ernest Hemingway in Selbstzeugnissen und Bilddokumenten*. Hamburg, Germany: Rowohlt, 1961.

Auchincloss, Louis. *Ellen Glasgow*. University of Minnesota Pamphlets on American Writers, no. 33. Minneapolis: University of Minnesota Press, 1964.

————. *Pioneers & Caretakers*. Minneapolis: University of Minnesota Press, 1961.

Austin, James C. *Petroleum V. Nasby (David Ross Locke)*. Twayne's United States Authors Series, no. 89. New York: Twayne Publishers, 1965.

Austin, Neal F. *A Biography of Thomas Wolfe*. Austin, Tex.: Roger Beacham, 1968.

Backman, Melvin. *Faulkner: The Major Years: A Critical Study*. Bloomington: Indiana University Press, 1966.

Baden, Hans Jurgen. *Literatur und Selbstmord: Cesare Pavese, Klaus Mann, Ernest Hemingway*. Stuttgart, Germany: Ernst Klett Verlag, 1965.

Baer, Helene G. *The Heart is Like Heaven: The Life of Lydia Maria Child*. Philadelphia: University of Pennsylvania Press, 1964.

Baker, Sheridan. *Ernest Hemingway: An Introduction and Interpretation*. New York: Barnes & Noble, 1967.

Barnes, Robert J. *Conrad Richter*. Austin, Tex.: Steck-Vaughn, 1968.

Baumbach, Jonathan. *The Landscape of Nightmare: Studies in the Contemporary American Novel*. New York: New York University Press, 1965.

Baxter, Annette Kar. *Henry Miller: Expatriate*. Pittsburgh, Penn.: University of Pittsburgh Press, 1961.

Bayley, John. *The Characters of Love: A Study in The Literature of Personality*. New York: Basic Books, 1960.

Beard, James Franklin, (ed.). *The Letters and Journals of James Fenimore Cooper*. 6 vols. Cambridge, Mass.: Harvard University Press, 1960-68.

Beck, Warren. *Man in Motion: Faulkner's Trilogy*. Madison: The University of Wisconsin Press, 1961.

Bell, Millicent. *Edith Wharton and Henry James: The Story of Their Friendship*. New York: George Braziller, 1965.

————. *Hawthorne's View of the Artist*. New York: State University of New York, 1962.

Bennett, George N. *William Dean Howells: The Development of a Novelist*. Norman: University of Oklahoma Press, 1959.

Benson, Frederick R. *Writers in Arms: The Literary Impact of the Spanish Civil War*. New York: New York University Press, 1967.

Bentz, Hans W. *Ernest Hemingway in Ubersetzungen*. Frankfurt, Germany: Hans W. Bentz Verlag, 1963.

Bernstein, John. *Pacifism and Rebellion in the Writings of Herman Melville*. The Hague, The Netherlands: Mouton, 1964.

Berthoff, Warner. *Edmund Wilson*. University of Minnesota Pamphlets on American Writers, no. 67. Minneapolis: University of Minnesota Press, 1968.

415

————. *The Example of Melville.* Princeton, N.J.: Princeton University Press, 1962.

————. *The Ferment of Realism: American Literature, 1884-1919.* New York: Macmillan, 1965.

Beyond the Angry Black. Edited by John A. Williams. New York: Cooper Square Publishers, 1966.

Bibliographical Committee of the Melville Society. *Melville Bibliography, 1952-1957.* Providence: Providence, Rhode Island Public Library, 1959.

Bigelow, Gordon E. *Frontier Eden: The Literary Career of Marjorie Kinnan Rawlings.* Gainesville: University of Florida Press, 1966.

Bishop, Ferman. *Allen Tate.* Twayne's United States Authors Series, no. 124. New York: Twayne Publishers, 1967.

Blackall, Jean Frantz. *Jamesian Ambiguity and The Sacred Fount.* Ithaca, N.Y.: Cornell University Press, 1965.

Blackmur, R. P. *A Primer of Ignorance.* New York: Harcourt, Brace & World, 1967.

Blair, Everetta Love. *Jesse Stuart: His Life and Works.* Columbia: University of South Carolina Press, 1967.

Blair, Walter. *Mark Twain and Huck Finn.* Berkeley and Los Angeles: University of California Press, 1960.

Bloom, Edward A. and Lillian D. *Willa Cather's Gift of Sympathy.* Carbondale: Southern Illinois University Press, 1962.

Blotner, Joseph. *The Modern American Political Novel.* Austin: University of Texas Press, 1966.

————. *William Faulkner's Library—A Catalogue.* Charlottesville: University Press of Virginia, 1964.

Boger, Lorise C. *The Southern Mountaineer in Literature: An Annotated Bibliography.* Morgantown: West Virginia University Library, 1964.

Bohner, Charles H. *John Pendleton Kennedy.* Baltimore: Johns Hopkins Press, 1961.

————. *Robert Penn Warren.* Twayne's United States Authors Series, no. 69. New York: Twayne Publishers, 1964.

Bone, Robert. *The Negro Novel in America,* revised edition. New Haven and London: Yale University Press, 1965.

Bottorff, William K. *James Lane Allen.* Twayne's United States Authors Series, no. 56. New York: Twayne Publishers, 1964.

Bowden, Edwin T. *The Dungeon of the Heart: Human Isolation and the American Novel.* New York: Macmillan, 1961.

Bowen, Merlin. *The Long Encounter: Self and Experience in the Writings of Herman Melville.* Chicago, Ill.: University of Chicago Press, 1960.

Bowman, Sylvia E. *Edward Bellamy Abroad.* New York: Twayne Publishers, 1962.

Bradbury, John M. *Renaissance in the South: A Critical History of the Literature, 1920-1960.* Chapel Hill: University of North Carolina Press, 1963.

Branch, Edgar M. *James T. Farrell.* University of Minnesota Pamphlets on American Writers, no. 29. Minneapolis: University of Minnesota Press, 1963.

Brantley, John D. *The Fiction of John Dos Passos.* Paris: Mouton, 1968.

Brasil, Assis. *Faulkner e a Técnica do romance: Ensaio.* Rio de Janeiro: Lectura, 1964.

Brenni, Vito Joseph. *Edith Wharton: A Bibliography.* Morgantown: West Virginia University Library, 1966.

Briand, Paul L., Jr. *In Search of Paradise: The Nordhoff-Hall Story.* New York: Duell, Sloan & Pearce, 1966.

Bridgman, Richard. *The Colloquial Style in America.* New York: Oxford University Press, 1966.

Brinnin, John Malcolm. *William Carlos Williams.* University of Minnesota Pamphlets on American Writers, no. 24. Minneapolis: University of Minnesota Press, 1963.

Brodtkorb, Paul, Jr. *Ishmael's White World: A Phenomenological Reading of Moby Dick.* New Haven, Conn.: Yale University Press, 1965.

Brooks, Cleanth. *The Hidden God.* New Haven, Conn., and London: Yale University Press, 1963.

—————. *William Faulkner: The Yoknapatawpha County.* New Haven, Conn.: Yale University Press, 1963.

Brown, Deming. *Soviet Attitudes Toward American Writing.* Princeton, N.J.: Princeton University Press, 1962.

Brown, John. *Hemingway.* Paris: Gallimard, 1961.

Bruccoli, Mathew J. *The Composition of Tender is the Night: A Study of the Manuscripts.* Pittsburgh, Penn.: University of Pittsburgh Press, 1963.

—————. *Raymond Chandler: A Checklist.* Kent, Ohio: Kent State University Press, 1968.

Brumm, Ursula. *Die Religiose Typologie in Amerikanischen Denken.*

Leiden: E. J. Brill, 1963.

Bryer, Jackson R. *The Critical Reputation of F. Scott Fitzgerald. A Bibliographical Study.* Hamden, Conn.: Archon Books, 1967.

Brylowski, Walter. *Faulkner's Olympian Laugh: Myth in the Novels.* Detroit, Mich.: Wayne State University Press, 1968.

Budd, Louis J. *Mark Twain: Social Philosopher.* Bloomington: Indiana University Press, 1962.

Burbank, Rex. *Sherwood Anderson.* Twayne's United States Authors Series, no. 65. New York: Twayne Publishers, 1964.

————. *Thornton Wilder.* Twayne's United States Authors Series, no. 5. New York: Twayne Publishers, 1961.

Busch, Frieder. *Erzahler-, Figuren- und Leserperspektive in Henry James Roman The Ambassadors.* Munchen, Germany: Max Hueber, 1967.

Butcher, Philip. *George W. Cable.* Twayne's United States Authors Series, no. 24. New York: Twayne Publishers, 1962.

Cady, Edwin H. *Stephen Crane.* Twayne's United States Authors Series, no. 23. New York: Twayne Publishers, 1962.

Calder-Marshall, Arthur. *Lone Wolf: The Story of Jack London.* New York: Duell, Sloan and Pearce, 1961.

Callaghan, Morley. *That Summer in Paris.* New York: Coward-McCann, 1963.

Cameron, Kenneth Walter. *Hawthorne Among his Contemporaries: A Harvest of Estimates, Insights, and Anecdotes from the Victorian Literary World and an Index.* Hartford, Conn.: Transcendental Books, 1968.

————. *Hawthorne Index to Themes, Motifs, Topics.* Hartford, Conn.: Transcendental Books, 1968.

Camp, James E. and X. J. Kennedy. *Mark Twain's Frontier: A Textbook of Primary Materials.* New York: Holt, Rinehart and Winston, 1963.

Cargill, Oscar. *The Novels of Henry James.* New York: Macmillan, 1961.

Carrington, George C., Jr. *The Immense Complex Drama: The World and Art of the Howells Novel.* Columbus: Ohio State University Press, 1966.

Carson, Edward Russell. *The Fiction of John O'Hara.* Pittsburgh, Penn.: University of Pittsburgh Press, 1961.

Carter, Paul J. *Waldo Frank.* Twayne's United States Authors Series, no. 125. New York: Twayne Publishers, 1967.

Cary, Richard. *Mary N. Murfree.* Twayne's United States Authors Series, no. 121. New York: Twayne Publishers, 1967.

————. *Sarah Orne Jewett.* Twayne's United States Authors Series, no. 19. New York: Twayne Publishers, 1962.

A Casebook on The Grapes of Wrath. Edited by Agnes McNeill Donohue. New York: Thomas Y. Crowell, 1968.

A Casebook on the Hawthorne Question. Edited by Agnes McNeill Donohue. New York: Thomas Y. Crowell, 1962.

A Casebook on Mark Twain's Wound. Edited by Lewis Leary. New York: Thomas Y. Crowell, 1962.

Casper, Leonard. *Robert Penn Warren: The Dark and Bloody Ground.* Seattle: University of Washington Press, 1960.

Charters, Ann. *A Bibliography of Works of Jack Kerouac (Jean Louis Lebris de Kerouac), 1939-1967.* New York: Phoenix Book Shop, 1967.

Clair, John A. *The Ironic Dimension in the Fiction of Henry James.* Pittsburg, Penn.: Duquesne University Press, 1965.

Clark, Mary Washington. *Jesse Stuart's Kentucky.* New York: McGraw-Hill, 1968.

Clayton, John J. *Saul Bellow: In Defense of Man.* Bloomington: Indiana University Press, 1968.

Clough, Wilson O. *The Necessary Earth: Nature and Solitude in American Literature.* Austin: University of Texas Press, 1964.

Colum, Padraic and Margaret Freeman Cabell, (eds.). *Between Friends: Letters of James Branch Cabell and Others.* New York: Harcourt, Brace, and World, 1962.

Comerchero, Victor. *Nathanael West: The Ironic Prophet.* Seattle and London: University of Washington Press, 1964.

A Companion to The Grapes of Wrath. Edited by Warren French. New York: Viking, 1963.

Contemporary American Novelists. Edited by Harry T. Moore. Carbondale: Southern Illinois University Press, 1964.

Coolidge, Olivia. *Edith Wharton, 1862-1937.* New York: Charles Scribner and Sons, 1965.

Cooperman, Stanley. *World War I and the American Novel.* Baltimore, Md.: Johns Hopkins Press, 1967.

Covici, Pascal. *Mark Twain's Humor: Image of the World.* Dallas, Tex.: Southern Methodist University Press, 1962.

Cowley, Malcolm. *The Faulkner-Cowley File: Letters and Memories, 1944-1962.* New York: Viking, 1966.

Cox, James M. *Mark Twain: The Fate of Humor*. Princeton, N.J.: Princeton University Press, 1966.

Coyle, Lee. *George Ade*. Twayne's United States Authors Series no. 63. New York: Twayne, 1964.

Cranfill, Thomas Mabry and Robert Lanier Clark, Jr. *An Anatomy of The Turn of the Screw*. Austin: University of Texas Press, 1965.

The Creative Present. Edited by Nona Balakian and Charles Simmons. Garden City, N.Y.: Doubleday, 1963.

Crews, Frederick C. *The Sins of the Fathers: Hawthorne's Psychological Themes*. New York: Oxford University Press, 1966.

Critical Approaches to American Literature: Volume I, Roger Williams to Herman Melville. Edited by Ray B. Browne & Martin Light. New York: Thomas Y. Crowell, 1965.

Critical Approaches to American Literature: Volume II, Walt Whitman to William Faulkner. Edited by Ray B. Browne & Martin Light. New York: Thomas Y. Crowell, 1965.

The Critical Heritage. Edited by Roger Gard. New York: Barnes and Noble, 1968.

Cross, K. G. W. *Scott Fitzgerald*. New York: Barnes and Noble, 1966.

Crowder, Richard. *Carl Sandburg*. Twayne's United States Authors Series, no. 47. New York: Twayne, 1964.

Dahl, Curtis. *Robert Montgomery Bird*. Twayne's United States Authors Series, no. 31. New York: Twayne Publishers, 1963.

Dameron, J. Lasley. *Edgar Allan Poe: A Checklist of Criticism, 1942-1960*. Charlottesville: Bibliographical Society of The University of Virginia, 1966.

Davis, Joe Lee. *James Branch Cabell*. Twayne's United States Authors Series, no. 21. New York: Twayne Publishers, 1962.

Davis, Merrell R. and William H. Gilman. *The Letters of Herman Melville*. New Haven, Conn.: Yale University Press, 1960.

Davis, Robert G. *John Dos Passos*. University of Minnesota Pamphlets on American Writers, no. 20. Minneapolis: University of Minnesota Press, 1962.

Day, A. Grove. *James A. Michener*. Twayne's United States Authors Series, no. 60. New York: Twayne Publishers, 1964.

————, (ed.). *Mark Twain's Letters from Hawaii*. New York: Appleton-Century, 1966.

The Deep South in Transformation. Edited by Robert B. Highsaw. University: University of Alabama Press, 1964.

Dekker, George. *James Fenimore Cooper: The American Scott.* New York: Barnes & Noble, 1967.

Denny, Ruel. *Conrad Aiken.* University of Minnesota Pamphlets on American Writers, no. 38. Minneapolis: University of Minnesota Press, 1964.

Derleth, August. *Three Literary Men: A Memoir of Sinclair Lewis, Sherwood Anderson, Edgar Lee Masters.* New York: Candlelight Press, 1963.

Detweiler, Robert. *Four Spiritual Crises in Mid-Century American Fiction.* Gainesville: University of Florida Press, 1963.

Dick, Kenneth C. *Henry Miller: Colossus of One.* The Netherlands: Alberts and Sittard, 1967.

The Dilemma of the Southern Writer. Institute of Southern Culture Lectures. Edited by Richard K. Meeker. Farmville, Va.: Longwood College, 1961.

Dillistone, F. W. *The Novelist and the Passion Story.* London: Collins, 1960.

Discovery of a Genius: William Dean Howells and Henry James. Compiled and edited by Albert Mordell. New York: Twayne Publishers, 1961.

Discussions of Henry James. Edited by Naomi Lebowitz. Boston, Mass.: D. C. Heath, 1962.

Discussions of Mark Twain. Edited by Guy Cardwell. Boston, Mass.: D. C. Heath, 1963.

Discussions of Moby-Dick. Edited by Milton R. Stern. Boston, Mass.: D. C. Heath, 1960.

Dooley, D. J. *The Art of Sinclair Lewis.* Lincoln: University of Nebraska Press, 1967.

Dornbusch, C. E. *Charles King: American Army Novelist. A Bibliography from the Collection of the National Library of Australia, Canberra.* Cornwallville, N.Y.: Hope Farm Press, 1963.

Doughty, Howard. *Francis Parkman.* New York: Macmillan, 1962.

Doyle, Paul A. *Pearl S. Buck.* Twayne's United States Authors Series, no. 85. New York: Twayne Publishers, 1965.

Drake, Robert. *Flannery O'Connor: A Critical Essay.* Grand Rapids, Michigan: William B. Eerdmans, 1966.

Dryden, Edgar A. *Melville's Thematics of Form: The Great Art of Telling the Truth.* Baltimore, Md.: Johns Hopkins Press, 1968.

Duckett, Margaret. *Mark Twain and Bret Harte.* Norman: University of Oklahoma Press, 1964.

Dupee, F. W. *Henry James,* revised edition. New York: Dell, 1964.

Durham, Frank M. *DuBose Heyward's Use of Folklore in His Negro Fiction.* The Citadel Monograph Series, no. 2. Charleston, S.C.: Citadel Press, 1961.

Durham, Philip. *Down These Mean Streets a Man Must Go: Raymond Chandler's Knight.* Chapel Hill: University of North Carolina Press, 1963.

Eble, Kenneth. *F. Scott Fitzgerald.* Twayne's United States Authors Series, no. 36. New York: Twayne Publishers, 1963.

Eckman, Fern Marja. *The Furious Passage of James Baldwin.* New York: M. Evans, 1966.

Edel, Leon. *Henry James:* Vol. 1, *1843-1870: The Untried Years;* Vol. 2, *1870-1881: The Conquest of London;* Vol. 3, *1882-1895: The Middle Years.* Philadelphia: J. B. Lippincott, 1953, 1962.

————. *Henry James.* University of Minnesota Pamphlets on American Writers, no. 4. Minneapolis: University of Minnesota Press, 1960.

————. *The Modern Psychological Novel,* revised edition. New York: Grosset and Dunlap, 1964.

————. *Willa Cather: The Paradox of Success.* Washington: Reference Department, Library of Congress, 1960.

Edelstein, Jerome M. *A Bibliographical Checklist of the Writings of Thornton Wilder.* New Haven, Conn.: Yale University Library, 1959.

Edener, Wilfried. *Die Religionskritik in den Romanen von Sinclair Lewis. Jahrbuch für Amerikastudien,* no. 10 Heidelberg: Carl Winter, 1963.

Edith Wharton: A Collection of Critical Essays. Edited by Irving Howe. Englewood Cliffs, N. J.: Prentice-Hall, 1962.

Edstrom, Kjell. *George Washington Cable: A Study of His Early Life and Work.* New York: Haskell House, 1966.

Edward Dahlberg: American Ishmael of Letters. Edited by Harold Billings. Austin, Tex.: Roger Beacham, 1968.

Egri, Péter. *Hemingway.* Budapest: Gondolat, 1967.

Eight American Authors: A Review of Research and Criticism. Edited by Jay B. Hubbell and others. New York: W. W. Norton, 1963.

Eisinger, Chester E. *Fiction of the Forties.* Chicago, Ill.: University of Chicago Press, 1963.

Elliott, Fannie Mae and others. *The Barrett Library: Richard Harding*

Davis: A Checklist of Printed and Manuscript Works. Charlottesville: University of Virginia Press, 1963.

Ernest Hemingway: Critiques of Four Major Novels. Edited by Carlos Baker. New York: Charles Scribner's Sons, 1962.

Essays and Studies in Language and Literature, Duquesne Studies, Philological Series, no. 5. Edited by Herbert H. Petit. Pittsburgh, Penn.: Duquesne University Press, 1964.

Essays in American and English Literature Presented to Bruce Robert McElderry, Jr. Edited by Max F. Schultz, William D. Templeman, and Charles R. Metzger. Athens: Ohio University Press, 1967.

Essays in Literary History. Edited by Rudolf Kirk and C. F. Main. New Brunswick, N.J.: Rutgers University Press, 1960.

Essays in Modern American Literature. Edited by Richard E. Langford. DeLand, Fla.: Stetson University Press, 1963.

Essays on American Literature in Honor of Jay Hubbell. Edited by Clarence Gohdes. Durham, N.C.: Duke University Press, 1967.

Essays on Determinism in American Literature. Kent Studies in English, no. 1. Edited by Sydney J. Krause. Kent, Ohio: Kent State University Press, 1964.

Evans, Oliver. *Anaïs Nin.* Carbondale: Southern Illinois University Press, 1968.

————. *The Ballard of Carson McCullers: A Biography.* New York: Coward-McCann, 1965. Published by Peter Owen in England under the title, *Carson McCullers: Her Life and Work.*

Explorations of Literature. Edited by Rima Drell Reck. Louisiana State University Studies: Humanities Series, no. 18. Baton Rouge: Louisiana State University Press, 1966.

F. Scott Fitzgerald: A Collection of Critical Essays. Edited by Arthur Mizener. Englewood Cliffs, N. J.: Prentice-Hall, 1963.

Fairbanks, Henry George. *The Lasting Loneliness of Nathaniel Hawthorne.* Albany, N.Y.: Magi Books, 1965.

Falk, Robert. *The Victorian Mode in American Fiction: 1865-1885.* East Lansing: Michigan State University Press, 1964.

Falk, Signi Lenea. *Tennessee Williams.* Twayne's United States Authors Series, no. 10. New York: Twayne Publishers, 1961.

Fant, Joseph L., III, and Robert Ashley. *Faulkner at West Point.* New York: Random House, 1964.

Farr, Finis. *Margaret Mitchell of Atlanta.* New York: Morrow, 1965.

Fatout, Paul. *Mark Twain in Virginia City.* Bloomington: Indiana University Press, 1964.

Faulkner: A Collection of Critical Essays. Edited by Robert Penn Warren. Englewood Cliffs, N.J.: Prentice-Hall, 1966.

Feied, Frederick. *No Pie in the Sky: The Hobo as American Cultural Hero in the Works of Jack London, John Dos Passos, and Jack Kerouac.* New York: Citadel Press, 1964.

Fiedler, Leslie A. *Love and Death in the American Novel.* New York: Criterion Books, 1960.

————. *The Return of the Vanishing American.* New York: Stein and Day, 1968.

————. *Waiting for the End.* New York: Stein and Day, 1964.

Field, Andrew. *Nabokov: His Life in Art.* Boston, Mass. and Toronto: Little, Brown, 1967.

Finkelstein, Dorothee M. *Melville's Orienda.* New Haven, Conn.: Yale University Press, 1961.

Finkelstein, Sidney. *Existentialism and Alienation in American Literature.* New York: International Publishers, 1965.

Fisher, Vardis. *Thomas Wolfe As I Knew Him and Other Essays.* Denver, Colo.: Alan Swallow, 1963.

Floan, Howard R. *William Saroyan.* Twayne's United States Authors Series, no. 100. New York: Twayne Publishers, 1966.

Flora, Joseph M. *Vardis Fisher.* Twayne's United States Authors Series, no. 76. New York: Twayne Publishers, 1965.

Fogle, Richard Harter. *Hawthorne's Fiction: The Light & the Dark,* revised edition. Norman: University of Oklahoma Press, 1964.

————. *Melville's Shorter Tales.* Norman: University of Oklahoma Press, 1960.

Folsom, James K. *The American Western Novel.* New Haven, Conn.: College and University Press, 1966.

————. *Man's Accidents and God's Purposes: Multiplicity in Hawthorne's Fiction.* New Haven, Conn.: College and University Press, 1963.

————. *Timothy Flint.* Twayne's United States Authors Series, no. 83. New York: Twayne Publishers, 1965.

Foner, Philip S. *Jack London: American Rebel,* revised edition. New York: Citadel Press, 1964.

Fontenrose, Joseph. *John Steinbeck.* New York: Barnes & Noble, 1963.

Ford, Margaret Patricia and Suzanne Kincaid. *Who's Who in Faulkner.* Baton Rouge: Louisiana State University Press, 1963.

Ford, Thomas W. *A. B. Guthrie, Jr.* Southwest Writers Series, no. 15. Austin, Tex.: Steck-Vaughn Company, 1968.

Foster, Richard. *Norman Mailer*. University of Minnesota Pamphlets on American Writers, no. 73. Minneapolis: University of Minnesota Press, 1968.

Frank, Max. *Die Farb—und Lichtsymbolik im Prosawerk Herman Melvilles*. Beihefte zum *Jahrbuch für Amerikastudien,* no. 19. Heidelberg, Germany: Carl Winter, 1967.

Franklin, H. Bruce. *The Wake of the Gods: Melville's Mythology.* Stanford, Cal.: Stanford University Press, 1963.

French, Bryant Morey. *Mark Twain and The Gilded Age*. Dallas, Tex.: Southern Methodist University Press, 1965.

French, Warren. *Frank Norris*. Twayne's United States Authors Series, no. 25. New York: Twayne Publishers, 1962.

———. *J. D. Salinger*. Twayne's United States Authors Series, no. 40. New York: Twayne Publishers, 1963.

———. *John Steinbeck*. Twayne's United States Authors Series, no. 2. New York: Twayne Publishers, 1961.

———. *Season of Promise*. Columbia: University of Missouri Press, 1968.

———. *The Social Novel at the End of an Era*. Carbondale: Southern Illinois University Press, 1966.

Frohock, W. M. *Frank Norris*. University of Minnesota Pamphlets on American Writers, no. 68. Minneapolis: University of Minnesota Press, 1968.

———. *Strangers to This Ground: Cultural Diversity in Contemporary American Writing*. Dallas, Tex.: Southern Methodist University Press, 1961.

Fussell, Edwin. *Frontier: American Literature and the American West*. Princeton, N.J.: Princeton University Press, 1965.

Gale, Robert L. *The Caught Image: Figurative Language in the Fiction of Henry James*. Chapel Hill: University of North Carolina Press, 1964.

———. *Plots and Characters in the Fiction of Henry James*. Hamden, Conn.: Archon Books, 1965.

Galloway, David D. *The Absurd Hero in American Fiction*. Austin and London: University of Texas Press, 1966.

———. *Henry James: The Portrait of a Lady*. London: Edward Arnold, 1967.

Ganzel, Dewey. *Mark Twain Abroad*. Chicago: University of Chicago Press, 1968.

Gardner, Ralph D. *Horatio Alger, or The American Hero Era*. Mendota, Ill.: Wayside Press, 1964.

Gaston, Edwin W., Jr. *Conrad Richter*. Twayne's United States Authors Series, no. 81. New York: Twayne Publishers, 1965.

————. *The Early Novel of the Southwest*. Albuquerque: The University of New Mexico Press, 1961.

Geismar, Maxwell. *Henry James and the Jacobites*. Boston, Mass.: Houghton Mifflin, 1963.

Geist einer freien Gesellschaft: Festschrift zu Ehren von Senator James William Fulbright aus Anlass des zehnjahrigen Bestehens des deutschen Fulbright-Programms. Heidelberg, Germany: Quelle and Meyer, 1962.

Geld, Ellen Bromfield. *The Heritage: A Daughter's Memories of Louis Bromfield*. New York: Harper & Brothers, 1962.

Gerber, Philip L. *Theodore Dreiser*. Twayne's United States Authors Series no. 52. New York: Twayne Publishers, 1964.

Giannone, Richard. *Music in Willa Cather's Fiction*. Lincoln: University of Nebraska Press, 1968.

Gibson, Donald B. *The Fiction of Stephen Crane*. Carbondale and Edwardsville: Southern Illinois University Press; London and Amsterdam: Feffer & Simons, 1968.

Gibson, Walker. *Tough, Sweet and Stuffy: An Essay on Modern American Prose Styles*. Bloomington: Indiana University Press, 1966.

Gibson, William M. *William D. Howells*. University of Minnesota Pamphlets on American Writers, no. 63. Minneapolis: University of Minnesota Press, 1967.

The Gilded Age; A Reappraisal. Edited by H. Wayne Morgan. Syracuse, N. Y.: Syracuse University Press, 1963.

Gilkes, Lillian. *Cora Crane: A Biography of Mrs. Stephen Crane*. Bloomington: Indiana University Press, 1960.

Gold, Joseph. *William Faulkner: A Study in Humanism: From Metaphor to Discourse*. Norman: University of Oklahoma Press, 1966.

Goldhurst, William. *F. Scott Fitzgerald and His Contemporaries*. Cleveland, Ohio: World, 1963.

Goldman, Sherli E. *Mary McCarthy: A Bibliography*. New York: Harcourt, Brace and World, 1968.

Goldstein, Malcolm. *The Art of Thornton Wilder*. Lincoln: University of Nebraska Press, 1965.

Gordon, William A. *The Mind and Art of Henry Miller*. Baton Rouge: Louisiana State University Press, 1967.

————. *Writer and Critic: A Correspondence with Henry Miller*. Baton Rouge: Louisiana State University Press, 1968.

Gossett, Louise Y. *Violence in Recent Southern Fiction*. Durham, N.C.: Duke University Press, 1965.

Graham, Sheilah. *College of One*. New York: Viking, 1966.

Grant, Douglas. *Purpose and Place: Essays on American Writers*. New York: St. Martin's, 1965.

The Great Experiment in American Literature. Edited by Carl Bode. New York: Frederich Praeger, 1961.

Grebenier, Bernard. *Thornton Wilder*. University of Minnesota Pamphlets on American Writers, no. 34. Minneapolis: University of Minnesota Press, 1964.

Grebstein, Sheldon Norman. *John O'Hara*. Twayne's United States Authors Series, no. 103. New York: Twayne Publishers, 1966.

————. *Sinclair Lewis*. Twayne's United States Authors Series, no. 14. New York: Twayne Publishers, 1962.

Green, Martin. *Re-Appraisals: Some Commonsense Readings in American Literature*. New York: W. A. Norton, 1963.

Gross, John J. *John P. Marquand*. Twayne's United States Authors Series, no. 33. New York: Twayne Publishers, 1963.

Gross, Theodore L. *Albion W. Tourgée*. Twayne's United States Authors Series, no. 39. New York: Twayne Publishers, 1963.

————. *Thomas Nelson Page*. Twayne's United States Authors Series, no. 111. New York: Twayne Publishers, 1967.

Grumbach, Doris. *The Company She Kept*. New York: Coward-McCann, 1967.

Guetti, James. *The Limits of Metaphor: A Study of Melville, Conrad, and Faulkner*. Ithaca, N.Y.: Cornell University Press, 1967.

Guimond, James. *The Art of William Carlos Williams*. Urbana: University of Illinois Press, 1968.

Gurko, Leo. *Ernest Hemingway and the Pursuit of Heroism*. New York: Thomas Y. Crowell, 1968.

Gvale, Gudrun Hovde. *O. E. Rölvaag: nordmann og amerikanar*. Oslo, Norway: Scandinavian University Books, 1962.

Haan, Jacques den. *Milleriana*. Amsterdam: Uitgeverij de Bezige Bij., 1963.

Hagopian, John V. *J. F. Powers*. Twayne's United States Authors Series, no. 130. New York: Twayne Publishers, 1968.

Hagopian, John V. and Martin Dolch. *Insight I: Analyses of American Literature*. Frankfurt, Germany: Hirschgraben-Verlag, 1964.

Hahn, Emily. *Romantic Rebels: An Informal History of Bohemianism in America*. Boston, Mass.: Houghton Mifflin; Cambridge, Mass.: Riverside, 1967.

Hall, James. *The Lunatic Giant in the Drawing Room*. Bloomington and London: Indiana University Press, 1968.

Hamblen, Abigail Ann. *The New England Art of Mary E. Wilkins Freeman*. Amherst, Mass.: Green Knight, 1966.

Hamilton, Alice and Kenneth. *John Updike: A Critical Essay*. Contemporary Writers in Christian Perspective. Grand Rapids, Mich.: W. B. Eerdmans, 1967.

Hamilton, Kenneth. *J. D. Salinger: A Critical Essay*. Grand Rapids, Mich.: William B. Eerdmans, 1967.

Handy, William J. *Kant and the Southern New Critics*. Austin: University of Texas Press, 1963.

Hanneman, Audre. *Ernest Hemingway: A Comprehensive Bibliography*. Princeton, N.J.: Princeton University Press, 1967.

Hardwick, Elizabeth. *A View of My Own: Essays in Literature and Society*. New York: Farrar, Straus and Cudahy, 1962.

Harnsberger, Caroline. *Mark Twain, Family Man*. New York: Citadel, 1960.

—————. *Mark Twain's Views on Religion*. Evanston, Ill.: Schori Press, 1961.

Harper, Howard M., Jr. *Desperate Faith*. Chapel Hill: University of North Carolina Press, 1967.

Hartt, Julian. *The Lost Image of Man*. Baton Rouge: Louisiana State University Press, 1963.

Harwell, R. B. *Hawthorne and Longfellow: A Guide to an Exhibit*. Brunswick, Me.: Bowdoin College Library, 1966.

Hasler, Jorg. *Switzerland in the Life and Work of Henry James*. The Cooper Monographs on English and American Language and Literature, no. 10. Bern, Switzerland: A. Francke, 1966.

Hassan, Ihab. *The Literature of Silence: Henry Miller and Samuel Beckett*. Studies in Language and Literature. New York: Alfred A. Knopf, 1967.

—————. *Radical Innocence: Studies in the Contemporary American Novel*. New York: Harper and Row, 1961.

Hawthorne: A Collection of Critical Essays. Edited by A. N. Kaul. Englewood Cliffs, N.J.: Prentice-Hall, 1966.

Hawthorne's Centenary Essays. Edited by Roy Harvey Pearce. Columbus: Ohio State University Press, 1964.

Hayashi, Tetsumaro. *John Steinbeck: A Concise Bibliography,* 1930-1965. Metuchen, N.J.: Scarecrow, 1967.

Heimer, Jackson W. *The Lesson of New England: Henry James and His Native Region.* Ball State Monograph no. 9. Publications in English, no. 5. Muncie, Ind.: Ball State University, 1967.

Hemingway: A Collection of Critical Essays. Edited by Robert P. Weeks. Englewood Cliffs, N.J.: Prentice-Hall, 1962.

Hemingway: Collection Génies et Réalités. Edited by Georges-Albert Astre and others. Paris: Hachette, 1966.

Hemingway and his Critics: An International Anthology. Edited by Carlos Baker. New York: Hill and Wang, 1961.

Hemingway, Leicester. *My Brother, Ernest Hemingway.* Cleveland, Ohio, and New York: World, 1962.

Hemphill, George. *Allen Tate.* University of Minnesota Pamphlets on American Writers, no. 39. Minneapolis: University of Minnesota Press, 1964.

Hendrick, George. *Katherine Anne Porter.* Twayne's United States Authors Series, no. 90. New York: Twayne Publishers, 1965.

Henry James: Modern Judgements. Edited by Tony Tanner. London: Macmillan, 1968.

Henry Miller and the Critics. Edited by George Wickes. Carbondale: Southern Illinois University Press, 1963.

Henry Miller—Between Heaven and Hell: A Symposium. Edited by Emil White. Big Sur, Cal.: Emil White, 1961.

Henry Miller on Writing. Edited by Thomas H. Moore. New York: New Directions, 1964.

Henson, Clyde E. *Joseph Kirkland.* Twayne's United States Authors Series, no. 13. New York: Twayne Publishers, 1962.

Hetherington, Hugh W. *Cavalier of Old South Carolina: William Gilmore Simms's Captain Porgy.* Chapel Hill: University of North Carolina Press, 1966.

Hicks, Granville. *James Gould Cozzens.* University of Minnesota Pamphlets on American Writers, no. 58. Minneapolis: University of Minnesota Press, 1966.

Hill, Hamlin Lewis. *Mark Twain and Elisha Bliss.* Columbia: University of Missouri Press, 1964.

————, (ed.). *Mark Twain's Letters to his Publishers.* Berkeley: University of California Press, 1967.

Hillway, Tyrus. *Herman Melville.* Twayne's United States Authors Series, no. 37. New York: Twayne Publishers, 1963.

Hindus, Milton. *F. Scott Fitzgerald: An Introduction and Interpretation*. New York: Holt, Rinehart and Winston, 1968.

Hochfield, George. *Henry Adams: An Introduction and Interpretation*. New York: Barnes and Noble, 1962.

Hoeltje, Hubert H. *Inward Sky: The Mind and Heart of Nathaniel Hawthorne*. Durham, N.C.: Duke University Press, 1962.

Hoffman, Daniel G. *Form and Fable in American Fiction*. New York: Oxford University Press, 1961.

Hoffman, Frederick J. *The Art of Southern Fiction*. Carbondale: Southern Illinois University Press, 1967.

————. *Conrad Aiken*. Twayne's United States Authors Series, no. 17. New York: Twayne Publishers, 1962.

————. *Gertrude Stein*. University of Minnesota Pamphlets on American Writers, no. 10. Minneapolis: University of Minnesota Press, 1961.

————. *The Great Gatsby: A Study*. New York: Charles Scribner's Sons, 1962.

————. *The Imagination's New Beginning: Theology and Modern Literature*. Notre Dame, Ind.: University of Notre Dame Press, 1967.

————. *The Modern Novel in America*, revised edition. Chicago, Ill.: Henry Regnery, 1963.

————. *The Mortal No: Death and The Modern Imagination*. Princeton, N.J.: Princeton University Press, 1964.

————. *Perspectives in Modern Literature*. Evanston, Ill.: Row, Peterson, 1962.

————. *The Twenties: American Writing in the Postwar Decade*, revised edition. New York: Macmillan, 1962.

————. *William Faulkner*. Twayne's United States Authors Series, no. 1. New York: Twayne Publishers, 1961.

Hoffman, Michael J. *The Development of Abstractionism in the Writings of Gertrude Stein*. Philadelphia: University of Pennsylvania Press, 1965.

Holder, Alan. *Three Voyagers in Search of Europe: A Study of Henry James, Ezra Pound, and T. S. Eliot*. Philadelphia: University of Pennsylvania Press, 1966.

Holder-Barell, Alexander. *The Development of Imagery and Its Functional Significance in Henry James's Novels*. Cooper Monographs on English and American Language and Literature, no. 3. Bern, Switzerland: A. Francke, 1959.

430

Holland, Laurence Bedwell. *The Expense of Vision: Essays on the Craft of Henry James.* Princeton, N.J.: Princeton University Press, 1964.

Holloway, Jean. *Hamlin Garland: A Biography.* Austin: University of Texas Press, 1960.

Holman, C. Hugh. *The American Novel Through Henry James.* Goldentree Bibliographies. New York: Appleton-Century-Crofts, 1966.

————. *Thomas Wolfe.* University of Minnesota Pamphlets on American Writers, no. 6. Minneapolis: University of Minnesota Press, 1960.

————. *Three Modes of Modern Southern Fiction.* Mercer University Lamar Memorial Lectures, no. 9. Athens: University of Georgia Press, 1966.

Holman, C. Hugh and Sue Fields Ross, (eds.) *Letters of Thomas Wolfe to his Mother.* Chapel Hill: University of North Carolina Press, 1968.

Holmes, Edward M. *Faulkner's Twice-Told Tales; His Re-Use of His Material.* The Hague, 'The Netherlands: Mouton, 1966.

Holmes, John Clellon. *Nothing More to Declare.* New York: E. P. Dutton, 1967.

Hotchner, A. E. *Papa Hemingway: A Personal Memoir.* New York: Random House, 1966.

Hough, Robert L. *The Quiet Rebel: William Dean Howells as Social Commentator.* Lincoln: University of Nebraska Press, 1959.

House, Kay Seymour. *Cooper's Americans.* Columbus: Ohio State University Press, 1965.

Hovey, Richard B. *Hemingway: The Inward Terrain.* Seattle and London: University of Washington Press, 1968.

Howard, Leon. *Literature and the American Tradition.* New York: Doubleday, 1960.

————. *Wright Morris.* University of Minnesota Pamphlets on American Writers, no. 69. Minneapolis: University of Minnesota Press, 1968.

Howe, Irving. *William Faulkner: A Critical Study,* revised edition. New York: Random House, 1962.

————. *A World More Attractive: A View of Modern Literature and Politics.* New York: Horizon, 1963.

Howells: A Century of Criticism. Edited by Kenneth E. Eble. Dallas, Tex.: Southern Methodist University Press, 1962.

Hubbell, Jay B. *South and Southwest: Literary Essays and Reminiscences.* Durham, N.C.: Duke University Press, 1965.

————. *Southern Life in Fiction.* Athens: University of Georgia Press, 1960.

Huck Finn and his Critics. Edited by Richard Lettis and others. New York: Macmillan, 1962.

Huff, Mary Nance. *Robert Penn Warren: A Bibliography.* New York: D. Lewis, 1968.

Humphreys, A. R. *Melville.* London: Oliver and Boyd, 1962.

Hunt, John W. *William Faulkner: Art in Theological Tension.* Syracuse, N.Y.: Syracuse University Press, 1965.

Hyman, Stanley Edgar. *Flannery O'Connor.* University of Minnesota Pamphlets on American Writers, no. 54. Minneapolis: University of Minnesota Press, 1966.

The Idea of an American Novel. Edited by Louis D. Rubin and J. R. Moore. New York: Thomas Y. Crowell, 1961.

Images of the Negro in American Literature. Edited by Seymour L. Gross and John Edward Hardy. Chicago, Ill.: University of Chicago Press, 1966.

Interpretations of American Literature. Edited by Charles Feidelson, Jr., and Paul Brodtkorb, Jr. New York: Oxford University Press, 1959.

Isabelle, Julanne. *Hemingway's Religious Experience.* New York: Vantage, 1964.

Ishag, Saada. *The American Novel: Two Studies.* Emporia State Research Studies. Emporia: Kansas State Teachers College, 1965.

Isle, Walter. *Experiments in Form: Henry James's Novels, 1896-1901.* Cambridge, Mass.: Harvard University Press, 1968.

J. D. Salinger and the Critics. Edited by William F. Belcher and James W. Lee. Belmont, Cal.: Wadsworth, 1962.

Jacobson, Richard J. *Hawthorne's Conception of the Creative Process.* Cambridge, Mass.: Harvard University Press, 1965.

James's Daisy Miller: The Story, the Play, the Critics. Edited by William T. Stafford. New York: Charles Scribner, 1963.

Jefferson, D. W. *Henry James.* New York: Grove Press, 1960.

————. *Henry James and the Modern Reader.* New York: St. Martin's Press, 1964.

Johnson, Elmer. *Of Time and Thomas Wolfe: A Bibliography with a Character Index of His Works.* New York: Scarecrow Press, 1959.

Johnston, Johanna. *Runaway to Heaven: The Story of Harriet Beecher Stowe.* New York: Doubleday & Company, 1963.

Johnson, Pamela Hansford. *The Art of Thomas Wolfe*. New York: Charles Scribner and Sons, 1963.

Jones, B. A. *A Checklist of Hawthorne Criticism, 1951-1966*. Hartford, Conn.: Transcendental Books, 1967.

Jones, Howard Mumford. *Belief and Disbelief in American Literature*. Chicago, Ill.: University of Chicago Press, 1967.

————. *Jeffersonianism and the American Novel*. New York: Teacher's College Press, 1967.

Joost, Nicholas. *Ernest Hemingway and the Little Magazines: The Paris Years*. Barre, Mass.: Barre Publishers, 1968.

Josephson, Matthew. *Life Among the Surrealists: A Memoir*. New York: Holt, Rinehart and Winston, 1962.

Kaplan, Justin. *Mark Twain, A Profile*. New York: Hill and Wang, 1967.

————. *Mr. Clemens and Mark Twain: A Biography*. New York: Simon and Schuster, 1966.

Karanikas, Alexander. *Tillers of a Myth: Southern Agrarians as Social and Literary Critics*. Madison: University of Wisconsin Press, 1966.

Karolides, Nicholas J. *The Pioneer in the American Novel, 1900-1950*. Norman: University of Oklahoma Press, 1967.

Kaul, A. N. *The American Vision: Actual and Ideal Society in Nineteenth-Century Fiction*. New Haven, Conn.: Yale University Press, 1963.

Kelley, Cornelia Pulsifer. *The Early Development of Henry James*, revised edition. Urbana: University of Illinois Press, 1965.

Kellog, George. *Vardis Fisher: A Bibliography*. Moscow: University of Idaho Library, 1961.

Kellogg, Grace. *The Two Lives of Edith Wharton: The Woman and Her Work*. New York: Appleton-Century, 1965.

Kelly, W. W. *Ellen Glasgow, A Bibliography*. Charlottesville: University Press of Virginia, 1964.

Kennard, Nina H. *Lafcadio Hearn*. Port Washington, N.Y.: Kennikat Press, 1967.

Kennedy, Richard S. *The Window of Memory: The Literary Career of Thomas Wolfe*. Chapel Hill: University of North Carolina Press, 1962.

Keynes, Geoffrey. *Henry James in Cambridge*. Cambridge, England: H. Heffer and Sons, 1967.

Kherdian, David. *A Bibliography of William Saroyan, 1934-1964*. San Francisco: Roger Beacham, 1965.

Kiley, Jed. *Hemingway: An Old Friend Remembers.* New York: Hawthorn Books, 1965.

Kimball, Arthur. *Rational Fictions: A Study of Charles Brockden Brown.* McMinnville, Ore.: Linfield Research Institute, 1968.

Kirk, Clara Marburg. *W. D. Howells and Art in his Time.* New Brunswick, N.J.: Rutgers University Press, 1965.

————. *W. D. Howells, Traveler from Altruria, 1889-1894.* New Brunswick, N.J.: Rutgers University Press, 1962.

Kirk, Clara M. and Rudolph, (eds.). *Letters from an Altrurian Traveler.* New York: Hill and Wang, 1961.

————. *William Dean Howells.* Twayne's United States Authors Series, no. 16. New York: Twayne Publishers, 1962.

Kirk, Robert W. *Faulkner's People: A Complete Guide and Index to Characters in the Fiction of William Faulkner.* Berkeley: University of California Press, 1963.

Klein, Marcus. *After Alienation: American Novels in Mid-Century.* Cleveland, Ohio, and New York: World, 1964.

Kosok, Heinz. *Die Bedeutung der Gothic Novel für das Erzahlwerk Herman Melvilles.* Britannica et Americana, vol. 12. Hamburg, Germany: Cram, de Gruyter, 1963.

Krook, Dorothea. *The Ordeal of Consciousness in Henry James.* Cambridge, Mass.: Cambridge University Press, 1962.

Krumpelmann, John T. *Bayard Taylor and German Letters.* Britannica et Americana, vol. 4. Hamburg, Germany: Cram, de Gruyter, 1959.

Krzyzanowski, Jerzy R. *Ernest Hemingway.* Warsaw: Wiedza Powszechna, 1963.

Langford, Gerald, (ed.). *Ingenue Among the Lions: The Letters of Emily Clark to Joseph Hergesheimer.* Austin: University of Texas Press, 1965.

Lanzinger, Klaus. *Die Epik im Amerikanischen Roman: Eine Studie zu James F. Cooper, Herman Melville, Frank Norris und Thomas Wolfe.* Studien zur Sprache und Literatur Amerikas, no. 1. Frankfurt, Germany: Moritz Diesterweg, 1965.

————. *Primitivismus und Naturalismus im Prosaschaffen Herman Melvilles.* Innsbruck, Austria: Universitätsverlag Wagner, 1959.

Lawrence, D. H. *The Symbolic Meaning: The Uncollected Versions of Studies in Classic American Literature.* Edited by Armin Arnold. Great Britain: Centaur Press, 1962.

Lawrence, Don H. *Robert Nathan, A Bibliography*. New Haven, Conn.: Yale University Library, 1960.

Learners and Discerners: A Newer Criticism. Edited by Robert T. Scholes. Charlottesville: University Press of Virginia, 1964.

Leary, Lewis. *Mark Twain*. University of Minnesota Pamphlets on American Writers, no. 5. Minneapolis: University of Minnesota Press, 1960.

————, (ed.). *Mark Twain's Letters to Mary*. New York: Columbia University Press, 1961.

Leatherstocking and the Critics. Edited by Warren S. Walker. Chicago, Ill.: Scott, Foresman, 1965.

Lebowitz, Naomi. *The Imagination of Loving: Henry James's Legacy to the Novel*. Detroit, Mich.: Wayne State University Press, 1965.

Lectures on Modern Novelists. Edited by Arthur T. Broes. Carnegie Series in English, no. 7. Pittsburgh, Penn.: Department of English, Carnegie Institute of Technology, 1963.

Lee, James W. *William Humphrey*. Southwest Writers Series, no. 7. Austin, Tex.: Steck-Vaughn, 1967.

Lee, Robert Edson. *From West to East*. Urbana and London: University of Illinois Press, 1966.

Lehan, Richard D. *F. Scott Fitzgerald and the Craft of Fiction*. Carbondale: Southern Illinois University Press, 1966.

Letters from Jack London, Containing an Unpublished Correspondence Between London and Sinclair Lewis. Edited by King Hendricks and Irving Shepard. New York: Odyssey Press, 1965.

Levin, David. *In Defense of Historical Literature*. New York: Hill and Wang, 1967.

Lewis, R. W. B. *Trials of the Word*. New Haven, Conn.: Yale University Press, 1965.

Lewis, Robert W., Jr. *Hemingway on Love*. Austin: University of Texas Press, 1965.

Leyburn, Ellen Douglass. *Strange Alloy: The Relation of Comedy to Tragedy in the Fiction of Henry James*. Chapel Hill: University of North Carolina Press, 1968.

A Library of Literary Criticism: Modern American Literature. Edited by Dorothy Nyren. New York: Ungar, 1964.

Lieberman, H. *The Man and His Perfidy*. New York: Bloch Publishing, 1964.

Light, James F. *John William De Forest*. Twayne's United States Authors Series, no. 82. New York: Twayne Publishers, 1965.

435

—————. *Nathanael West: An Interpretative Study*. Evanston, Ill.: Northwestern University Press, 1961.

Lion in the Garden: Interviews with William Faulkner. Edited by James B. Meriwether and Michael Millgate. New York: Random House, 1968.

Liptzin, Sol. *The Jew in American Literature*. New York: Bloch Publishing, 1966.

The Literary Criticism of Frank Norris. Edited by Donald Pizer. Austin: University of Texas Press, 1964.

The Literary Reputation of Hemingway in Europe. Edited by Roger Asselineau. New York: New York University Press, 1965.

Literature and Society: Nineteen Essays by Germaine Brée and others. Edited by Bernice Slote. Lincoln: University of Nebraska Press, 1964.

Littlejohn, David. *Black on White, A Critical Survey of Writings by American Negroes*. New York: Grossman Publishers, 1966.

Longley, John Lewis, Jr. *The Tragic Mask: A Study of Faulkner's Heroes*. Chapel Hill: University of North Carolina Press, 1963.

Lowery, Bruce. *Marcel Proust et Henry James: Une confrontation*. Paris: Librairie Plon, 1964.

Ludwig, Jack. *Recent American Novelists*. Minneapolis: University of Minnesota Press, 1964.

Lueders, Edward. *Carl Van Vechten*. Twayne's United States Authors Series, no. 74. New York: Twayne Publishers, 1965.

Lyday, Jo W. *Mary Austin: The Southwest Works*. Southwest Writers Series, no. 16. Austin, Tex.: Steck-Vaughn, 1968.

Machlin, Milton. *The Private Hell of Hemingway*. New York: Paperback Library, 1962.

Madden, David. *Wright Morris*. Twayne's United States Authors Series, no. 71. New York: Twayne Publishers, 1964.

Malin, Irving. *New American Gothic*. Carbondale: Southern Illinois University Press, 1962.

Manley, Seon. *Nathaniel Hawthorne: Captain of the Imagination*. New York: Vanguard Press, 1968.

Marder, Daniel. *Hugh Henry Brackenridge*. Twayne's United States Authors Series, no. 114. New York: Twayne Publishers, 1967.

Margolies, Edward. *Native Sons: A Critical Study of Twentieth-Century Negro American Authors*. Philadelphia and New York: J. B. Lippincott, 1968.

Mark Twain: A Collection of Critical Essays. Edited by Henry Nash Smith. Englewood Cliffs, N.J.: Prentice-Hall, 1963.

Mark Twain: Selected Criticism. Edited by Arthur L. Scott, revised edition. Dallas, Tex.: Southern Methodist University Press, 1967.

Marks, Robert. *James's Later Novels: An Interpretation.* New York: William-Frederick Press, 1960.

Martin, Carter W. *The True Country: Themes in the Fiction of Flannery O'Connor.* Nashville, Tenn.: Vanderbilt University Press, 1968.

Martin, Jay. *Conrad Aiken: A Life of His Art.* Princeton, N.J.: Princeton University Press, 1962.

————. *Harvests of Change. American Literature 1865-1914,* Englewood Cliffs, N.J.: Prentice-Hall, 1967.

Martin, Ronald E. *The Fiction of Joseph Hergesheimer.* Philadelphia: University of Pennsylvania Press, 1965.

Martin, Terence. *The Instructed Vision: Scottish Common Sense Philosophy and the Origins of American Fiction.* Bloomington: University of Indiana Press, 1961.

————. *Nathaniel Hawthorne.* Twayne's United States Authors Series, no. 75. New York: Twayne Publishers, 1965.

Marx, Leo. *The Machine in the Garden: Technology and the Pastoral Ideal in America.* New York: Oxford University Press, 1964.

Maxwell, D. E. S. *American Fiction: The Intellectual Background.* New York: Columbia University Press, 1963.

————. *Cozzens.* Edinburgh and London: Oliver and Boyd, 1964.

————. *Herman Melville.* The Profiles in Literature Series. London: Routledge & Kegan Paul; New York: Humanities Press, 1968.

Mayoux, Jean-Jacques. *Melville.* London: Evergreen Books, 1960.

McAleer, John J. *Theodore Dreiser: An Introduction and Interpretation.* New York: Holt, Rinehart and Winston, 1968.

McDowell, Frederick P. W. *Caroline Gordon.* University of Minnesota Pamphlets on American Writers, no. 59. Minneapolis: University of Minnesota Press, 1966.

————. *Elizabeth Madox Roberts.* Twayne's United States Authors Series, no. 38. New York: Twayne Publishers, 1963.

————. *Ellen Glasgow and the Ironic Art of Fiction.* Madison: University of Wisconsin Press, 1960.

McElderry, Bruce R., Jr. *Henry James.* Twayne's United States Authors Series, no. 79. New York: Twayne Publishers, 1965.

————. *Thomas Wolfe.* Twayne's United States Authors Series, no. 50. New York: Twayne Publishers, 1964.

McKeithan, Daniel Morley. *The Morgan Manuscript of Mark Twain's Pudd'nhead Wilson.* Essays and Studies on American Language and

Literature, no. 12. Cambridge, Mass.: Harvard University Press, 1961.

McKenzie, Barbara. *Mary McCarthy*. Twayne's United States Authors Series, no. 108. New York: Twayne Publishers, 1966.

McMurray, William. *The Literary Realism of William Dean Howells*. Carbondale and Edwardsville: Southern Illinois University Press; London and Amsterdam: Feffer & Simons, 1967.

Meiners, R. K. *The Last Alternatives: A Study of the Works of Allen Tate*. Denver, Colo.: Alan Swallow, 1963.

Meltzer, Milton. *Tongue of Flame: The Life of Lydia Maria Child*. New York: Thomas Y. Crowell, 1965.

Melville: A Collection of Critical Essays. Edited by Richard Chase. Englewood Cliffs, N.J.: Prentice-Hall, 1962.

Meriwether, James B., (ed.). *Essays, Speeches and Public Letters by William Faulkner*. New York: Random House, 1965.

_____. *The Literary Career of William Faulkner: A Bibliographical Study*. Princeton, N.J.: Princeton University Library, 1961.

Meyer, Roy W. *The Middle Western Farm Novel in the Twentieth Century*. Lincoln: University of Nebraska Press, 1965.

Miller, James E., Jr. *F. Scott Fitzgerald: His Art and His Technique*. New York: New York University Press, 1964.

_____. *J. D. Salinger*. University of Minnesota Pamphlets on American Writers, no. 51. Minneapolis: University of Minnesota Press, 1965.

_____. *Quests Surd and Absurd: Essays in American Literature*. Chicago and London: University of Chicago Press, 1967.

_____. *A Reader's Guide to Herman Melville*. New York: Noonday Press, 1962.

Miller, Perry. *The Life of the Mind in America from the Revolution to the Civil War*. New York: Harcourt, Brace and World, 1965.

Millgate, Michael. *The Achievement of William Faulkner*. London: Constable, 1966.

_____. *American Social Fiction: James to Cozzens.* New York: Barnes and Noble, 1964.

Milne, Gordon. *The American Political Novel*. Norman: University of Oklahoma Press, 1966.

Mizener, Arthur. *The Sense of Life in the Modern Novel*. Boston, Mass.: Houghton Mifflin, 1964.

_____. *Twelve Great American Novels*. New York: New American Library, 1967.

Moby Dick: An Authoritative Text; Reviews and Letters by Melville; Analogues and Sources; Criticism. Edited by Harrison Hayford and Hershel Parker. A Norton Critical Edition. New York: W. W. Norton, 1967.

Modern American Fiction: Essays in Criticism. Edited by A. Walton Litz. New York: Oxford University Press, 1963.

The Modern American Novel: Essays in Criticism. Edited by Max Westbrook. New York: Random House, 1966.

Mohl, Gertrud. *Die Aufnahme amerikanischer Literatur in der deutschsprachigen Schweiz wahrend der Jahre 1945-1950.* Zurich, Switzerland: Juris, 1961.

Monteiro, George. *Henry James and John Hay: The Record of a Friendship.* Providence, R.I.: Brown University Press, 1965.

Montgomery, Constance Cappel. *Hemingway in Michigan.* New York: Fleet Publishing, 1966.

Mooney, Harry John, Jr. *The Fiction and Criticism of Katherine Anne Porter,* revised edition. Pittsburgh, Penn.: University of Pittsburgh Press, 1962.

————. *James Gould Cozzens: Novelist of Intellect.* Pittsburgh, Penn.: University of Pittsburgh Press, 1963.

Moore, Geoffrey. *American Literature and the American Imagination.* Hull, England: University of Hull Publications, 1964.

Moore, Rayburn S. *Constance Fenimore Woolson.* Twayne's United States Authors Series, no. 34. New York: Twayne Publishers, 1963.

Moore, Thomas H. *Bibliography of Henry Miller.* Minneapolis, Minn.: Henry Miller Literary Society, 1961.

Morgan, H. Wayne. *American Writers in Rebellion.* New York: Hill and Wang, 1965.

————. *Writers in Transition: Seven Americans.* New York: Hill and Wang, 1963.

Moss, Leonard. *Arthur Miller.* Twayne's United States Authors Series, no. 115. New York: Twayne Publishing, 1967.

Muller, Herbert Joseph. *Thomas Wolfe, in Selbstzeugnissen und Bilddokumenten.* Hamburg, Germany: Rowohlt, 1962.

Mumford, Lewis. *Herman Melville: A Study of His Life and Vision,* revised edition. New York: Harcourt, Brace & World, 1962.

Muste, J. M. *Say That We Saw Spain Die: The Literary Consequences of the Spanish War.* Seattle: University of Washington Press, 1966.

Myth and Symbol: Critical Approaches and Applications. Edited by Bernice Slote. A Selection of Papers Delivered at the Joint Meeting of the Midwest Modern Language Association and the Central Renaissance Conference, 1962. Lincoln: University of Nebraska Press, 1963.

Nabokov: The Man and his Work. Edited by L. S. Dembo. Madison, Milwaukee and London: University of Wisconsin Press, 1967.

Nance, William L. *Katherine Anne Porter & the Art of Rejection.* Chapel Hill: University of North Carolina Press, 1963.

Nathan, Monique. *Faulkner par luimeme.* Paris: Editions du Seuil, 1963.

Neider, Charles. *Mark Twain.* New York: Horizon Press, 1967.

Nevius, Blake. *Robert Herrick: The Development of a Novelist.* Berkeley and Los Angeles: University of California Press, 1962.

Nilon, Charles H. *Faulkner and the Negro.* New York: Citadel Press, 1965.

Noble, David W. *The Eternal Adam and the New World Garden.* New York: George Braziller, 1968.

Normand, Jean. *Nathaniel Hawthorne: Esquisse d'une Analyse de la Création Artistique.* Paris: Presses Universitaires de France, 1964.

Nowell, Elizabeth. *Thomas Wolfe: A Biography.* New York: Doubleday & Company, 1960.

O'Connor, Evangeline M. J. *An Analytical Index to the Works of Nathaniel Hawthorne with a Sketch of his Life.* Boston: Houghton, Mifflin, 1882. Authorized reprint by Ann Arbor: University Microfilms, 1964.

O'Connor, Richard. *Bret Harte: A Biography.* Boston and Toronto: Little, Brown, 1966.

————. *Jack London: A Biography.* Boston and Toronto: Little, Brown, 1964.

O'Connor, William Van. *The Grotesque and Other Essays.* Carbondale: Southern Illinois University Press, 1962.

————. *William Faulkner.* University of Minnesota Pamphlets on American Writers, no. 3, revised edition. Minneapolis: University of Minnesota Press, 1964.

O'Donnell, Thomas F. and Hoyt C. Franchere. *Harold Frederic.* Twayne's United States Authors Series, no. 3. New York: Twayne Publishers, 1961.

Ohlin, Peter H. *Agee.* New York: Ivan Obolensky, 1966.

Oliver, Egbert S. *Studies in American Literature: Whitman, Emerson, Melville and Others.* Ram Nagar, New Delhi, India: Eurasia Publishing House, n.d.

Olsen, Otto H. *Carpetbagger's Crusade: The Life of Albion Winegar Tourgée.* Baltimore, Md.: Johns Hopkins Press, 1965.

Omarr, Sydney. *Henry Miller: His World of Urania.* London: Villiers Publications, 1960.

On Contemporary Literature. Edited by Richard Kostelanetz. New York: Avon Books, 1964.

Opdahl, Keith Michael. *The Novels of Saul Bellow: An Introduction.* University Park and London: Pennsylvania State University Press, 1967.

Papajewski, Helmut. *Thornton Wilder.* Bonn, Germany: Athenaum Verlag, 1961.

Parent, Monique. *Ellen Glasgow: Romancière.* Paris: A. G. Nizet, 1962.

Patterns of Commitment in American Literature. Edited by Marston LaFrance. Toronto, Canada: University of Toronto Press, 1967.

Paul Elmer More's Shelburne Essays on American Literature. Edited by Daniel Aaron. New York: Harcourt, Brace & World, 1963.

Paul, Sherman. *Edmund Wilson: A Study of Literary Vocation in Our Time.* Urbana: University of Illinois Press, 1965.

Pearce, T. M. *Mary Hunter Austin.* Twayne's United States Authors Series, no. 92. New York: Twayne Publishers, 1965.

Pennington, Lee. *The Dark Hills of Jesse Stuart.* Cincinnati, Ohio: Harvest Press, 1967.

Perles, Alfred. *My Friend Henry Miller.* New York: Belmont Books, 1962.

Perosa, Sergio. *The Art of F. Scott Fitzgerald.* Ann Arbor: University of Michigan Press, 1965.

Perspectives on James's The Portrait of a Lady: A Collection of Critical Essays. Edited by William T. Stafford. New York: New York University Press, 1967.

Phelps, Robert (ed.). *The Letters of James Agee to Father Flye.* New York: George Braziller, 1962.

Philbrick, Thomas. *James Fenimore Cooper and the Development of American Sea Fiction.* Cambridge, Mass.: Harvard University Press, 1961.

Pilkington, John, Jr. *Francis Marion Crawford.* Twayne's United States Author Series, no 67. New York: Twayne Publishers, 1964.

Piper, Henry Dan. *F. Scott Fitzgerald: A Critical Portrait.* New York: Holt, Rinehart and Winston, 1965.

Pizer, Donald, (ed.). *Hamlin Garland's Diaries*. San Marino, Cal.: Huntington Library, 1968.

————. *The Novels of Frank Norris*. Bloomington and London: Indiana University Press, 1966.

————. *Realism and Naturalism in Nineteenth-Century American Literature*. Carbondale and Edwardsville: Southern Illinois University Press, 1966.

Poe: A Collection of Critical Essays. Edited by Robert Regan. Englewood Cliffs, N.J.: Prentice-Hall, 1967.

Poenicke, Klaus. *Robert Penn Warren: Kunstwerk und Kritische Theorie*. Beihefte zum *Jahrbuch für Amerikastudien,* no. 4. Heidelberg: Carl Winter, 1959.

Poirier, Richard. *The Comic Sense of Henry James: A Study of the Early Novels*. New York: Oxford University Press, 1960.

————. *A World Elsewhere: The Place of Style in American Literature*. New York: Oxford University Press, 1966.

Poli, Bernard. *Mark Twain: Ecrivain de l'ouest*. Paris: Presses Universitaires de France, 1965.

Porter, Bernard H. *What Henry Miller Said and Why It Is Important*. Pasadena, Cal.: D. Turrell, 1964.

Price, Lawrence Marsden. *The Reception of United States Literature in Germany*. University of North Carolina Studies in Comparative Literature, no. 39. Chapel Hill: University of North Carolina Press, 1966.

Proffer, Carl R. *Keys to Lolita*. Bloomington: Indiana University Press, 1968.

Proletarian Writers of the Thirties. Edited by David Madden. Carbondale and Edwardsville: Southern Illinois University Press; London and Amsterdam: Feffer & Simons, 1968.

Psychoanalysis and American Fiction. Edited by Irving Malin. New York: E. P. Dutton and Company, 1965.

Putt, S. Gorley. *Henry James: A Reader's Guide*. Ithaca, N.Y.: Cornell University Press, 1966.

————. *Scholars of the Heart: Essays in Criticism*. London: Faber and Faber, 1962.

Rahn, Walter. *Die Funktionen der kalifornischen Landschaft im epischen Fruhwerk John Steinbecks*. Munchen, Germany: Max Hueber, 1962.

Raleigh, John Henry. *Time, Place, and Idea, Essays on the Novel*. Carbondale: Southern Illinois University Press, 1968.

Randall, John H., III. *The Landscape and the Looking Glass: Willa Cather's Search for Value.* Boston: Houghton Mifflin Company; Cambridge, Mass.: Riverside Press, 1960.

Randel, William. *Edward Eggleston.* Twayne's United States Authors Series, no. 45. New York: Twayne Publishers, 1963.

Ravitz, Abe C. *David Graham Phillips.* Twayne's United States Authors Series, no. 96. New York: Twayne Publishers, 1966.

Raynolds, Robert. *Thomas Wolfe: Memoir of a Friendship.* Austin & London: University of Texas Press, 1964.

Reality and Myth: Essays in American Literature in Memory of Richmond Croom Beatty. Edited by William E. Walker and Robert L. Welker. Nashville, Tenn.: Vanderbilt University Press, 1964.

The Recognition of Herman Melville: Selected Criticism Since 1846. Edited by Hershel Parker. Ann Arbor: University of Michigan Press, 1967.

The Red Badge of Courage: An Annotated Text; Backgrounds and Sources; Essays in Criticism. Edited by Sculley Bradley and others. A Norton Critical Edition. New York: W. W. Norton, 1962.

Reid, John T. *Indian Influences in American Literature and Thought.* New Delhi, India: Indian Council for Cultural Relations, 1965.

Reid, Randall. *The Fiction of Nathanael West: No Redeemer, No Promised Land.* Chicago, Ill., and London: University of Chicago Press, 1967.

The Reinterpretation of American Literature. Edited by Norman Foerster. New York: Russell and Russell 1959

Renken, Maxine. *A Bibliography of Henry Miller.* Denver, Colo.: A. Swallow, 1962.

Richardson, Kenneth E. *Force and Faith in the Novels of William Faulkner.* Studies in American Literature, Vol. VII. The Hague, The Netherlands: Mouton, 1967.

Richman, Sidney. *Bernard Malamud.* Twayne's United States Authors Series, no. 109. New York: Twayne Publishers, 1966.

Ridgely, J. V. *John Pendleton Kennedy.* Twayne's United States Authors Series, no. 102. New York: Twayne Publishers, 1966.

————. *William Gilmore Simms.* Twayne's United States Authors Series, no. 28. New York: Twayne Publishers, 1962.

Riley, Esta Lou. *Henry Miller: An Informal Bibliography, 1924-1960.* Fort Hays: Fort Hays Kansas State College, 1961.

Ringe, Donald A. *Charles Brockden Brown.* Twayne's United States Authors Series, no. 98. Twayne Publishers, 1966.

————. *James Fenimore Cooper*. Twayne's United States Authors Series, no. 11. New York: Twayne Publishers, 1962.

Robert Penn Warren: A Collection of Critical Essays. Edited by John Lewis Longley, Jr. New York: New York University Press, 1965.

Robert Penn Warren's All the King's Men: A Critical Handbook. Edited by Maurice Beebe and Leslie A. Fields. Belmont, Cal.: Wadsworth, 1966.

Robinson, Cecil. *With the Ears of Strangers: The Mexican in American Literature*. Tucson: University of Arizona Press, 1963.

Rogers, Franklin R. *Mark Twain's Burlesque Patterns*. Dallas, Tex.: Southern Methodist University Press, 1960.

Ross, Lillian. *Portrait of Hemingway*. New York: Simon and Schuster, 1961.

Rouse, Blair. *Ellen Glasgow*. Twayne's United States Authors Series, no. 26. New York: Twayne Publishers, 1962.

Rovit, Earl. *Ernest Hemingway*. Twayne's United States Authors Series, no. 41. New York: Twayne Publishers, 1963.

————. *Herald to Chaos: The Novels of Elizabeth Madox Roberts*. Lexington: University of Kentucky Press, 1960.

————. *Saul Bellow*. University of Minnesota Pamphlets on American Writers, no. 65. Minneapolis: University of Minnesota Press, 1967.

Rubin, Louis D., Jr. *The Curious Death of the Novel: Essays in American Literature*. Baton Rouge: Louisiana State University Press, 1967.

————. *The Faraway Country: Writers of the Modern South*. Seattle: University of Washington Press, 1963.

Rueckert, William H. *Glenway Wescott*. Twayne's United States Authors Series, no. 87. New York: Twayne Publishers, 1965.

Runyan, Harry. *A Faulkner Glossary*. New York: Citadel Press, 1964.

Salinger: A Critical and Personal Portrait. Edited by Henry Anatole Grunwald. New York: Harper & Brothers, 1962.

Salinger's Catcher in the Rye: Clamor vs. Criticism. Edited by Harold Simonson. Boston, Mass.: D. C. Heath, 1963.

Salomon, Roger B. *Twain and the Image of History*. New Haven, Conn.: Yale University Press, 1961.

Salsbury, Edith C., (ed.). *Susy and Mark Twain; Family Dialogues*. New York: Harper and Row, 1965.

Samuels, Charles E. *Thomas Bailey Aldrich*. Twayne's United States Authors Series, no. 94. New York: Twayne Publishers, 1965.

444

Samuels, Ernest. *Henry Adams: The Major Phase.* Cambridge, Mass.: Harvard University Press, 1964.

Sanders, David. *John Hersey.* Twayne's United States Authors Series, no. 112. New York: Twayne Publishers, 1967.

Sanderson, Stewart. *Ernest Hemingway.* New York: Grove Press, 1961.

Sanford, Charles L. *The Quest for Paradise: Europe and the American Moral Imagination.* Urbana: University of Illinois Press, 1961.

Sanford, Marcellene H. *At the Hemingways.* Boston, Mass.: Little, Brown, 1962.

Santas, Joan Foster. *Ellen Glasgow's American Dream.* Charlottesville: University Press of Virginia, 1965.

Saul Bellow and his Critics. Edited by Irving Malin. New York: New York University Press; London: University of London Press, 1967.

The Scarlet Letter: An Annotated Text; Backgrounds and Sources; Essays in Criticism. Edited by Sculley Bradley and others. A Norton Critical Edition. New York: W. W. Norton, 1961.

Schmiele, Walter. *Henry Miller in Selbstzeugnissen und Bilddokumenten.* Hamburg, Germany: Rowohlt Taschenbuch Verlag, 1961.

Schneider, Robert W. *Five Novelists of the Progressive Era.* New York: Columbia University Press, 1965.

Scholes, Robert. *The Fabulators.* New York: Oxford University Press, 1967.

Schorer, Mark. *Sinclair Lewis.* University of Minnesota Pamphlets on American Writers, no. 27. Minneapolis: University of Minnesota Press, 1963.

————. *Sinclair Lewis: An American Life.* New York: McGraw-Hill, 1961.

————. *The World We Imagine: Selected Essays.* New York: Farrar, Straus and Giroux, 1968.

Schwab, Arnold T. *James Gibbons Huneker: Critic of the Seven Arts.* Stanford, Cal.: Stanford University Press, 1963.

Scott, Nathan A. *The Broken Center: Studies in the Theological Horizon of Modern Literature.* New Haven, Conn., and London: Yale University Press, 1966.

————. *Ernest Hemingway: A Critical Essay.* Grand Rapids, Mich.: William B. Eerdmans, 1966.

Sears, Sallie. *The Negative Imagination: Form and Perspective in the Novels of Henry James.* Ithaca, N.Y.: Cornell University Press, 1968.

Seib, Kenneth. *James Agee: Promise and Fulfillment. Critical Essays in Modern Literature.* Pittsburgh, Penn.: University of Pittsburgh Press, 1968.

Seven Contemporary Authors. Edited by Thomas B. Whitbread. Austin: University of Texas Press, 1966.

Seven Modern American Novelists: An Introduction. Edited by William Van O'Connor. Minneapolis: University of Minnesota Press, 1959.

Seward, William W., Jr. *Contrasts in Modern Writers: Some Aspects of British and American Fiction Since Mid-Century.* New York: Frederick Fell, 1963.

Shain, Charles E. *F. Scott Fitzgerald.* University of Minnesota Pamphlets on American Writers, no. 15. Minneapolis: University of Minnesota Press, 1961.

Shapiro, Charles. *Theodore Dreiser.* Carbondale: Southern Illinois University Press, 1962.

Shapiro, Samuel. *Richard Henry Dana, Jr.* East Lansing: Michigan State University Press, 1961.

Sharp, Sister M. Corona, O.S.U. *The Confidante in Henry James: Evolution and Moral Value of a Fictive Character.* Notre Dame, Ind.: University of Notre Dame Press, 1963.

Sheean, Vincent. *Dorothy and Red.* Boston: Houghton Mifflin, 1963.

Sheehy, Eugene P. and Kenneth A. Lohf. *Sherwood Anderson: A Bibliography.* Los Gatos, Cal.: Talisman Press, 1960.

Simonson Harold P. *Zona Gale.* Twayne's United States Authors Series, no. 18. New York: Twayne Publishers, 1962.

Sinclair Lewis: A Collection of Critical Essays. Edited by Mark Schorer. Englewood Cliffs, N. J.: Prentice-Hall, 1962.

Sinclair, Upton. *My Lifetime in Letters.* Columbia: University of Missouri Press, 1960.

Singer, Kurt. *Hemingway: Life and Death of a Giant.* Los Angeles, Cal.: Holloway House Publishing, 1961.

Sioui, Tak. *Huckleberry Finn: More Molecules.* Privately printed, 1962.

Six American Novelists of the Nineteenth Century: An Introduction. Edited by Richard Foster. Minneapolis: University of Minnesota Press, 1968.

Six Contemporary Novels: Six Introductory Essays in Modern Fiction. Edited by William O. S. Sutherland. Austin: University of Texas Department of English, 1962.

Sklar, Robert. *F. Scott Fitzgerald: The Last Laocoon.* New York: Oxford University Press, 1967.

Slatoff, Walter J. *Quest for Failure: A Study of William Faulkner.* Ithaca, N.Y.: Cornell University Press, 1960.

Sleeth, Irene L. *William Faulkner: A Bibliography of Criticism.* Swallow Pamphlets, no. 13. Denver, Colo.: A. Swallow, 1962.

Slote, Bernice. *The Kingdom of Art: Willa Cather's First Principles and Critical Statements.* Lincoln: University of Nebraska Press, 1966.

Small, Miriam Rossiter. *Oliver Wendell Holmes.* Twayne's United States Authors Series, no. 29. New York: Twayne Publishers, 1962.

Smart, George K. *Religious Elements in Faulkner's Early Novels: A Selective Concordance.* Coral Gables, Fla.: University of Miami Press, 1965.

Smetana, Josette. *La Philosophie de l'Action Chez Hemingway et Saint-Exupery.* Paris: La Marjolaine, 1965.

Smith, Henry Nash. *Mark Twain: The Development of a Writer.* Cambridge, Mass.: Harvard University Press, 1962.

———. *Mark Twain's Fable of Progress: Political and Economic Ideas in a "A Connecticut Yankee."* New Brunswick, N.J.: Rutgers University Press, 1964.

——— and William M. Gibson, editors. *Mark Twain-Howells Letters.* Cambridge, Mass.: Harvard University Press, 1960.

Solomon, Eric. *Stephen Crane: From Parody to Realism.* Cambridge, Mass.: Harvard University Press, 1966.

———. *Stephen Crane in England: A Portrait of the Artist.* Columbus: Ohio State University Press, 1964.

South: Modern Southern Literature in Its Cultural Setting. Edited by Louis D. Rubin, Jr. and Robert D. Jacobs. Garden City, N.Y.: Doubleday, 1961.

Southern Writers: Appraisals in Our Time. Edited by R. C. Simonini, Jr. Charlottesville: University Press of Virginia, 1964.

The Southerner as American. Edited by Charles G. Sellers, Jr. Chapel Hill: University of North Carolina Press, 1960.

Spengemann, William C. *Mark Twain and The Backwoods Angel.* Kent Studies in English, no. 4. Kent, Ohio: Kent State University Press, 1966.

Spiller, Robert E. *James Fenimore Cooper.* University of Minnesota Pamphlets on American Writers, no. 48. Minneapolis: University of Minnesota Press, 1965.

Spivey, Ted R. *Religious Themes in Two Modern Novelists.* School of Arts and Sciences Research Papers, no. 12. Atlanta: Georgia State College, 1965.

Springer, Anne M. *The American Novel in Germany: A Study of the Critical Reception of Eight American Novelists Between the Two World Wars*. Hamburg, Germany: Cram, de Gruyter, 1960.

Squires, Radcliffe. *Frederic Prokosch*. Twayne's United States Authors Series, no. 61. New York: Twayne Publishers, 1964.

Staehelin-Wackernagel, Adelheid. *The Puritan Settler in the American Novel Before The Civil War*. The Cooper Monographs on English and American Language and Literature, no. 7., Bern, Switzerland: A. Francke Verlag, 1961.

Stallman, Robert W. *The Houses that James Built and Other Literary Studies*. East Lansing: Michigan State University Press, 1961.

————. *Stephen Crane: A Biography*. New York: George Braziller, 1968.

Stanonik, Janez. *Moby Dick, The Myth and Symbol: A Study in Folklore and Literature*. Ljubljana, Yugoslavia: Ljubljana University Press, 1962.

Stegner, Page. *Escape into Aesthetics: The Art of Vladimir Nabokov*. New York: Dial Press, 1966.

Stephen Crane: A Collection of Critical Essays. Edited by Maurice Bassan. Englewood Cliffs, N. J.: Prentice-Hall, 1967.

Stephen Crane's Maggie: Text and Context. Edited by Maurice Bassan. Belmont, Cal.: Wadsworth, 1966.

Stevenson, Elizabeth. *Lafcadio Hearn*. New York: Macmillan, 1961.

Stewart, Allegra. *Gertrude Stein and the Present*. Cambridge, Mass.: Harvard University Press, 1967.

Stewart, John L. *The Burden of Time: The Fugitives and Agrarians*. Princeton, N. J.: Princeton University Press, 1965.

Stewart, Randall. *Regionalism and Beyond: Essays of Randall Stewart*. Nashville, Tenn.: Vanderbilt University Press, 1968.

Stock, Irvin. *Mary McCarthy*. University of Minnesota Pamphlets on American Writers, no. 72. Minneapolis: University of Minnesota Press, 1968.

Stone, Albert E., Jr. *The Innocent Eye: Childhood in Mark Twain's Imagination*. New Haven, Conn.: Yale University Press, 1961.

Stone, Edward. *The Battle and the Books: Some Aspects of Henry James*. Athens: Ohio University Press, 1964.

————. *Voices of Despair*. Athens: Ohio University Press, 1966.

Straumann, Heinrich. *American Literature in the Twentieth Century*, revised edition. New York: Harper and Row, 1965.

Stresau, Hermann. *Ernest Hemingway*. The Hague, The Netherlands: Kruseman, 1961.

Strong, Leah A. *Joseph Hopkins Twitchell, Mark Twain's Friend and Pastor*. Athens: University of Georgia Press, 1966.

Stuckey, W. J. *The Pulitzer Prize Novels: A Critical Backward Look*. Norman: University of Oklahoma Press, 1966.

Studies in American Culture: Dominant Ideas and Images. Edited by Joseph J. Kwiat and Mary C. Turpie. Minneapolis: University of Minnesota Press, 1960.

Studies in American Literature. Edited by Waldo McNeir and Leo B. Levy. Baton Rouge: Louisiana State University Press, 1960.

Studies in J. D. Salinger. Edited by Marvin Laser and Norman Fruman. New York: Odyssey Press, 1963.

Sutton, Walter. *Modern American Criticism*. Englewood Cliffs, N.J.: Prentice Hall, 1963.

Sutton, William A. *Exit to Elsinore*. Ball State Monograph Number Seven. Muncie, Ind.: Ball State University, 1967.

Swanberg, W. A. *Dreiser*. New York: Charles Scribner's Sons, 1965.

Swiggart, Peter. *The Art of Faulkner's Novels*. Austin: University of Texas Press, 1962.

Talks With Authors. Edited by Charles F. Madden. Carbondale: Southern Illinois University Press, 1968.

Tanner, Tony. *The Reign of Wonder: Naivety and Reality in American Literature*. New York: Harper and Row, 1965.

————. *Saul Bellow*. Edinburgh and London: Oliver and Boyd, 1965.

Tanselle, G. Thomas. *Royall Tyler*. Cambridge: Harvard University Press, 1967.

Tarrant, Desmond. *James Branch Cabell: The Dream and the Reality*. Norman: University of Oklahoma Press, 1967.

Taylor, J. Golden. *Hawthorne's Ambivalence Toward Puritanism*. Monograph Series, no. 12. Logan: Utah State University Press, 1965.

Tebbel, John. *From Rags to Riches: Horatio Alger, Jr., and the American Dream*. New York: Macmillan, 1963.

Tharpe, Jac. *Nathaniel Hawthorne: Identity and Knowledge*. Carbondale and Edwardsville: Southern Illinois University Press; London and Amsterdam: Feffer & Simons, 1967.

The Thirties: Fiction, Poetry, Drama. Edited by Warren French. Deland, Fla.: Everett Edwards, 1967.

Thomas Wolfe: Three Decades of Criticism. Edited by Leslie A. Field.

New York: New York University Press; London: University of London Press, 1968.

Thompson, Lawrance. *William Faulkner: An Introduction and Interpretation*. New York: Barnes and Noble, 1963.

Thorp, Willard. *American Writing in the Twentieth Century*. Cambridge, Mass.: Harvard University Press, 1960.

Tilley, W. H. *The Background of the Princess Casamassima*. University of Florida Monographs, Humanities no. 5. Gainesville: University of Florida Press, 1960.

A Time of Harvest: American Literature 1910-1960. Edited by Robert E. Spiller. New York: Hill and Wang, 1962.

Titus, Warren I. *Winston Churchill*. Twayne's United States Authors Series, no. 43. Twayne Publishers, 1963.

Tjader, Marguerite. *Theodore Dreiser: A New Dimension*. Norwalk, Conn.: Silvermine Publishers, 1965.

Toklas, Alice B. *What is Remembered*. New York: Holt, Rinehart and Winston, 1963.

Tough Guy Writers of the Thirties. Edited by David Madden. Carbondale and Edwardsville: Southern Illinois University Press; London and Amsterdam: Feffer & Simons, 1968.

Tradition and Tolerance in Nineteenth Century Fiction: Critical Essays on Some English and American Novels. Edited by David Howard and others. New York: Barnes and Noble, 1967.

Trends in Modern Society. Edited by Clarence Morris. Philadelphia: University of Pennsylvania Press, 1962.

Tuck, Dorothy. *Crowell's Handbook of Faulkner*. New York: Thomas Y. Crowell, 1964.

Tuckey, John S. *Mark Twain and Little Satan: The Writing of The Mysterious Stranger*. West Lafayette, Indiana: Purdue University Studies, 1963.

Turnbull, Andrew, (ed.). *The Letters of F. Scott Fitzgerald*. New York: Scribners, 1963.

―――, (ed.). *Scott Fitzgerald: Letters to His Daughter*. New York: Scribners, 1965.

―――. *Scott Fitzgerald*. London: Bodley Head, 1962.

―――. *Thomas Wolfe*. New York: Scribner's, 1967.

Turner, Arlin. *George W. Cable: A Biography*. Durham, N.C.: Duke University Press, 1956.

―――. *Mark Twain and George W. Cable: The Record of a Literary Friendship*. East Lansing: Michigan State University Press, 1960.

————. *Nathaniel Hawthorne: An Introduction and Interpretation.* New York: Barnes & Noble, 1961.

The Twenties: Poetry and Prose. Edited by Richard E. Langford and William E. Taylor. Deland, Fla.: Everett Edwards Press, 1966.

Twentieth Century Interpretations of The Adventures of Huckleberry Finn. Edited by Claude M. Simpson. Englewood Cliffs, N. J.: Prentice-Hall, 1968.

Twentieth Century Interpretations of Arrowsmith. Edited by Robert J. Griffin. Englewood Cliffs, N. J.: Prentice-Hall, 1968.

Twentieth Century Interpretations of the Great Gatsby: A Collection of Critical Essays. Edited by Ernest H. Lockridge. Englewood Cliffs, N.J.: Prentice-Hall, 1968.

Twentieth Century Interpretations of The Old Man and the Sea. Edited by Katharine T. Jobes. Englewood Cliffs, N.J.: Prentice-Hall, 1968.

Twentieth Century Interpretations of The Portrait of a Lady: A Collection of Critical Essays. Edited by Peter Buitenhuis. Englewood Cliffs, N.J.: Prentice-Hall, 1968.

Twentieth Century Interpretations of The Scarlet Letter: A Collection of Critical Essays. Englewood Cliffs, N. J.: Prentice-Hall, 1968.

Twentieth Century Interpretations of The Sound and the Fury: A Collection of Critical Essays. Englewood Cliffs, N. J.: Prentice-Hall, 1968.

Ulanov, Barry. *The Two Worlds of American Art: The Private and The Popular.* New York: Macmillan, 1965.

University of Southern California Library. *Hamlin Garland, A Bibliography.* Los Angeles: University of Southern California Library, 1963.

Van Ghent, Dorothy. *Willa Cather.* University of Minnesota Pamphlets on American Writers, no. 36. Minneapolis: University of Minnesota Press, 1964.

Van Nostrand, Albert. *The Denatured Novel.* Indianapolis, Ind.: Bobbs-Merrill, 1960.

————. *Everyman His Own Poet.* New York: McGraw-Hill, 1968.

Vande Kieft, Ruth M. *Eudora Welty.* Twayne's United States Authors Series, no. 15. New York: Twayne Publishers, 1962.

Vanderbilt, Kermit. *The Achievement of William Dean Howells: A Reinterpretation.* Princeton, N.J.: Princeton University Press, 1968.

Varieties of Literary Experience: Eighteen Essays in World Literature.

Edited by Stanley Burnshaw. New York: New York University Press, 1962.

Vickery, Olga W. *The Novels of William Faulkner: A Critical Interpretation,* revised edition. Baton Rouge: Louisiana State University Press, 1964.

Virginia University Library. *The Barrett Library: Frank Richard Stocktons: A Checklist of Printed and Manuscript Works.* Charlottesville: University of Virginia Press, 1963.

Virginia University Library. *The Barrett Library: Oliver Wendell Holmes.* Charlottesville: University of Virginia Press, 1960.

Voigt, Walter. *Die Bildersprache Thomas Wolfe: Mit Besonderer Berucksichtigung der Metaphorik des Amerikanischen Englisch.* Munchen, Germany: Max Hueber, 1960.

Wagenknecht, Edward. *Harriet Beecher Stowe: The Known and the Unknown.* New York: Oxford University Press, 1965.

————. *Nathaniel Hawthorne: Man and Writer.* New York: Oxford University Press, 1961.

Wager, Willis. *American Literature: A World View.* New York: New York University Press, 1968.

Waggoner, Hyatt H. *Hawthorne: A Critical Study,* revised edition. Cambridge, Mass.: Harvard University Press, 1963.

Walcutt, Charles Child. *Jack London.* University of Minnesota Pamphlets on American Writers, no. 57. Minneapolis: University of Minnesota Press, 1966.

————. *Man's Changing Mask: Modes and Methods of Characterization in Fiction.* Minneapolis: University of Minnesota Press, 1966.

Walker, Franklin. *Jack London and the Klondike: The Genesis of an American Writer.* San Marino, Cal.: Huntington Library, 1966.

Walker, Warren S. *James Fenimore Cooper: An Introduction and Interpretation.* New York: Barnes and Noble, 1962.

The War of the Critics over William Dean Howells. Edited by Edwin H. Cady and David L. Frazier. Elmsford, N.Y.: Row, Peterson, 1962.

Ward, J. A. *The Imagination of Disaster: Evil in the Fiction of Henry James.* Lincoln: University of Nebraska Press, 1961.

————. *The Search for Form: Studies in the Structure of James's Fiction.* Chapel Hill: University of North Carolina Press, 1967.

Warren, Austin. *The New England Conscience.* Ann Arbor: University of Michigan Press, 1966.

Watt, F. W. *John Steinbeck.* New York: Grove Press, 1962.

Webb, Constance. *Richard Wright.* New York: G. P. Putnam's Sons, 1968.

Webb, James W. and A. Wigfall Green. *William Faulkner of Oxford.* Baton Rouge: Louisiana State University Press, 1965.

Weber, Brom. *Sherwood Anderson.* University of Minnesota Pamphlets on American Writers, no. 43. Minneapolis: University of Minnesota Press, 1964.

Weimer, David R. *The City as Metaphor.* New York: Random House, 1966.

Wells, Arvin R. *Jesting Moses: A Study in Cabellian Comedy.* Gainesville: University of Florida Press, 1962.

West, Paul. *Robert Penn Warren.* University of Minnesota Pamphlets, no. 44. Minneapolis: University of Minnesota Press, 1964.

West, Ray B., Jr. *Katherine Anne Porter.* University of Minnesota Pamphlets on American Writers, no. 28. Minneapolis: University of Minnesota Press, 1963.

————. *The Writer in the Room: Selected Essays.* East Lansing: Michigan State University Press, 1968.

West, Thomas Reed. *Flesh of Steel: Literature and the Machine in American Culture.* Nashville, Tenn.: Vanderbilt University Press, 1967.

Westbrook, Perry D. *Mary Ellen Chase.* Twayne's United States Authors Series, no. 86. New York: Twayne Publishers, 1965.

————. *Mary Wilkins Freeman.* Twayne's United States Authors Series, no. 122. New York: Twayne Publishers, 1967.

Wheaton, Mabel, with LeGette Blythe. *Thomas Wolfe and his Family.* New York: Doubleday, 1961.

Wickes, George. *Henry Miller.* University of Minnesota Pamphlets on American Writers, no. 56. Minneapolis: University of Minnesota Press, 1966.

————. *Lawrence Durrell and Henry Miller: A Private Correspondence.* New York: E. P. Dutton, 1963.

Widmer, Kingsley. *Henry Miller.* Twayne's United States Authors Series, no. 44. New York: Twayne Publishers, 1963.

Wiesenfarth, Joseph, F.S.C. *Henry James and the Dramatic Analogy: A Study of the Major Novels of the Middle Period.* New York: Fordham University Press, 1963.

Wiggins, Robert A. *Mark Twain: Jackleg Novelist.* Seattle: University of Washington Press, 1964.

Willa Cather and her Critics. Edited by James Schroeter. Ithaca, N.Y.: Cornell University Press, 1967.

William Faulkner: Three Decades of Criticism. Edited by Frederick J. Hoffman and Olga W. Vickery. East Lansing: Michigan State University Press, 1960.

William Styron's Nat Turner: Ten Black Writers Respond. Edited by John Henrik Clarke. Boston: Beacon Press, 1968.

Williams, Cecil B. *Henry Wadsworth Longfellow.* Twayne's United States Authors Series, no. 68. New York: Twayne Publishers, 1964.

Wilson, Edmund. *Patriotic Gore: Studies in the Literature of the American Civil War.* New York: Oxford University Press, 1962.

Winesburg, Ohio: A Critical Commentary. New York: American R. D. M., 1963.

Winesburg, Ohio: Text and Criticism. Edited by John H. Ferres. The Viking Critical Library. New York: Viking Press, 1966.

Witham, W. Tasker. *The Adolescent in the American Novel: 1920-1960.* New York: Frederick Ungar, 1964.

The Woman in America. Edited by Robert Jay Lifton. Boston: Houghton Mifflin, 1965.

Wood, Richard C. *Collector's Quest: The Correspondence of Henry Miller and J. Rives Childs,* 1947-1965. Charlottesville: University Press of Virginia, 1968.

Woodbridge, Hensley C. *Jesse Stuart: A Bibliography.* Harrogate, Tenn.: Lincoln Memorial University Press, 1960.

————, John London and George Tweney. *Jack London: A Bibliography.* Georgetown, Calif.: Talisman Press, 1966.

Woodworth, Stanley D. *William Faulkner en France (1931-1952).* Paris: M. J. Minard, 1959.

The World of Thomas Wolfe. Edited by C. Hugh Holman. A Scribner Research Anthology. New York: Charles Scribner's Sons, 1962.

Wrenn, John H. *John Dos Passos.* Twayne's United States Authors Series, no. 9. New York: Twayne Publishers, 1961.

Wright, Lyle H. *American Fiction, 1876-1900: A Contribution Toward a Bibliography.* San Marino, Cal.: Huntington Library, 1966.

Wright, Nathalia. *American Novelists in Italy: The Discoverers: Allston to James.* Philadelphia: University of Pennsylvania Press, 1965.

Wright, Walter F. *The Madness of Art: A Study of Henry James.* Lincoln: University of Nebraska Press, 1962.

Writing in America. Edited by John Fischer and Robert B. Silvers. New Brunswick, N.J.: Rutgers University Press, 1960.

Young, Philip. *Ernest Hemingway: A Reconsideration,* revised edition. University Park and London: Pennsylvania State University Press, 1966.

The Young Rebel in American Literature. Edited by Carl Bode. New York: Frederick A. Praeger, 1960.

Yu, Beongcheon. *An Ape of Gods: The Art and Thought of Lafcadio Hearn.* Detroit, Mich.: Wayne State University Press, 1964.

Ziff, Larzer. *The American 1890s: Life and Times of a Lost Generation.* New York: Viking Press, 1966.

Zimmer, Dieter E. *Vladimir Nabokov, Bibliographie des Gesamtwerks.* Hamberg, Germany: Reinbek, 1964.

PERIODICALS

American Book Collector
American Imago
American Literary Realism 1870-1910
American Literature
American Notes and Queries
American Quarterly
American Scholar
American Speech
Anglia
Antioch Review
Approach
Archiv fuer das Studium der Neueren Sprachen und Literaturen
Arizona Quarterly
The Arlington Quarterly
Atlantic Monthly
Ball State University Forum (*formerly:* Ball State Teachers College Forum)
Book Collector
Books Abroad
Books at Brown
Brigham Young University Studies
British Association for American Studies Bulletin (*new series*)
Bucknell Review

Bulletin of Bibliography
Bulletin of the New York Public Library
CLA Journal
Cairo Studies in English
Carleton Miscellany
CEA Critic
Centennial Review
Chicago Review
Claremont Quarterly
The Colby Library Quarterly
College English
Colorado Quarterly
Commentary
Comparative Literature
Comparative Literature Studies
Contact
Contemporary Literature (*formerly* Wisconsin Studies in Contemporary Literature)
The Critic
Critical Quarterly
Criticism
Critique (*Paris*)
Critique: Studies in Modern Fiction
The Dalhousie Review
The East-West Review
ELH: A Journal of English Literary History
Emerson Society Quarterly
Encounter
English
English Institute Essays
English Journal
The English Language and Literature
English Language Notes
English Studies
English Studies in Africa
Etc.
Études Anglaises
Evergreen Review
Explicator
Fitzgerald Newsletter

Four Quarters
Genre (Chicago Circle)
Georgia Review
Harper's Magazine
Harvard Library Bulletin
The Hollins Critic
Hudson Review
Huntington Library Quarterly
The Indian Journal of English Studies
Jack London Newsletter
Jahrbuch für Amerikastudien
Journal of American Folklore
Journal of American Studies
Journal of English and Germanic Philology
Journal of History of Ideas
Journal of the Karnatak University
Journal of Popular Culture
Kenyon Review
The Library
Library Chronicle of the University of Texas
Litera
Literature and Psychology
The Literary Criterion
The Literary Half-Yearly
Literary Review
Manuscripts
Mark Twain Journal
The Massachusetts Review
Midcontinent American Studies Journal
Midwest Quarterly
Minnesota Review
Mississippi Quarterly
Modern Fiction Studies
Modern Language Quarterly
Modern Language Review
Modern Philology
Names
The Nation
Negro American Literature Forum
Die Neueren Sprachen

New American Review
New England Quarterly
New Mexico Quarterly
New Republic
New York Times Book Review
Nineteenth-Century Fiction
Notes & Queries
Novel: A Forum on Fiction
The Papers of the Bibliographical Society of America
Papers on Language and Literature (*formerly:* Papers on English Language & Literature)
Paris Review
Partisan Review
Personalist
Philological Quarterly
Princeton University Library Chronicle
Psychoanalytic Review
Prairie Schooner
PMLA
Queen's Quarterly
Renaissance & Modern Studies
Renascence
Revue de Litterature Comparée
Rutgers University Library Journal
Saturday Review
Sewanee Review
Shenandoah
South Atlantic Quarterly
South Dakota Review
Southern Humanities Review
The Southern Literary Journal
Southern Quarterly
Southern Review
Southwest Review
Studi Americani
Studies in Bibliography
Studies in the Literary Imagination
Studies in Philology
Studies in Romanticism (*formerly:* Boston University Studies in English)

Studies in Short Fiction
Tennessee Studies in Literature
Texas Quarterly
Texas Studies in Literature and Language
Times Literary Supplement
Trace
Tri-Quarterly
Tulane Studies in English
Twentieth Century Literature
The University of Denver Quarterly
University Review (formerly: University of Kansas City Review)
University of Toronto Quarterly
Victorian Studies
Virginia Quarterly Review
Visva-Bharati Quarterly
Western American Literature
Western Humanities Review
The William and Mary Review
Yale Review
Yearbook of Comparative and General Literature
Zeitschrift für Anglistik und Amerikanistik